Martin Luther King, Jr.
The FBI File

Also by Michael Friedly

Malcolm X: The Assassination

Also by David Gallen

Malcolm X: The FBI File with Clayborne Carson
Malcolm A to X
Malcolm X: As They Knew Him
Remembering Malcolm with Benjamin Karim and Peter Skutches
Thurgood Marshall: Justice for All with Roger Goldman

Martin Luther King, Jr.
The FBI File

Michael Friedly with David Gallen

Carroll & Graf Publishers, Inc.
New York

First Carroll & Graf edition 1993

Carroll & Graf Publishers, Inc.
260 Fifth Avenue
New York, NY 10001

Library of Congress Cataloging-in-Publication Data

Friedly, Michael.
    Martin Luther King, Jr. : the FBI file / Michael Friedly ; edited
by David Gallen.—1st Carroll & Graf ed.
        p.   cm.
    Includes index.
    ISBN 0-88184-940-5 : $27.00—ISBN 0-88184-992-8 (pbk.) : $14.95
    1. King, Martin Luther, Jr., 1929–1968. 2. United States.
Federal Bureau of Investigation. 3. Hoover, J. Edgar (John Edgar),
1895–1972. I. Gallen, David. II. Title.
E185.97.K5G35   1993
323'.092—dc20   93-8503
                                                                CIP

Manufactured in the United States of America

Acknowledgments

I wish to thank the following people for their generous editorial advice:

Sheryl Spain, Amy Whitcomb, Clayborne Carson, Shelly Leanne, Sofía Martínez, and David Blumenthal.

I would also like to thank the following people for their support in the process:

Hazim Ansari, Amy Arends, Heidi Ballard, Raphe Beck, Vanita Bhargava, Colette Cann, Jesse Castro, Alan Chan, Jane Chang, Rebekah Chow, Meena Deo, Allison Dillon, Benjamin Evans, Sylvia Fan, Melissa Feinberg, Anne Fleming, Gail Griffin, Laura Langlie, Patrick Lin, Lisa and Eric Loh, Shaista Malik, Sunderarajan Sunderesan Mohan and his parents, Lindsey Pedersen, Rob Robinson, Rohit Singla, Chuck Sparnecht, Jack Wang, May Woo and Jennifer Yeh. My friends at the Martin Luther King, Jr., Papers Project, the Stanford University Office of Government Relations and the Office of Public Affairs have also been extremely supportive and understanding during the writing process.

—Michael Friedly

Contents

Martin Luther King, Jr.
The FBI File

I

Martin Luther King, Jr., and the FBI

I reckon now God is the only refuge we have because there wasn't nobody there from the Justice Department, nobody there to say nuthin'—just the Negro out by theirself.

—Activist Fanny Lou Hamer, on the failure of the federal government to protect civil-rights workers after a 1963 beating by police in Winona, Mississippi.[1]

1

The American Dilemma

Americans have always thought of themselves as a unified people. The longevity of the American political system and the common investment in the capitalist view of economics are often cited as evidence that despite petty differences, Americans are united in their beliefs and their vision of the future. Observers of American society have commented on the unity since the founding of the Republic. "You can not spill a drop of American blood without spilling the blood of the whole world," Herman Melville observed. "On this Western Hemisphere all tribes and people are forming into one federated whole."[2] A Frenchman who emigrated to the American colonies before the Revolutionary War was awed by the diversity of the immigrants in the New World and by their desire to shed their former allegiances and assimilate into American society. "From this promiscuous breed, that race called Americans have arisen."[3] But this common lore of American unity is an overgeneralization that obscures the reality of the individuals and groups that combine to create the United States. In truth, America has always been a divided nation. Despite the rhetoric of unity and the shared belief in the American melting pot, the United States has throughout its history been a patchwork of different nationalities, races, and ethnicities, bonded only through the mutual acceptance of the fundamental ideals embodied in the American Constitution. Although Americans commonly

13

believe in the concepts of democracy, liberty, and equality, there is little unanimity in the application of these abstract ideals.

The rift in American society has been particularly acute in the racial arena. The United States has always been a nation of whites, dominant in number and in their control of the political and economic systems on which the nation has been based. One of the primary responsibilities of the government throughout American history has been to protect the interests of the white citizens that are its main constituency. African Americans have traditionally found themselves banned from the circles of American power and have only quite recently been able to exert a significant amount of political pressure. Full citizenship was only granted to African Americans after the Civil War, and the open discrimination by the American government and society prohibited many blacks from using that citizenship until the 1960s. Economically, politically, and socially, African Americans have been shunted outside the mainstream, forcing them to maintain their own segregated communities.

Traditionally African Americans have been marginalized from power, excluded from the governmental bodies that determine policies for all Americans. The federal government constitutes the political system in which Americans have invested their faith in democracy. But as the implementer of American democracy, the government's relationship with African Americans has always been tenuous, since it tailors its treatment of blacks to the political ramifications of its actions. During the Civil War, political considerations forced the government to adopt the liberation of slaves as a major justification for its war against the South. After Reconstruction, the government again ignored the plight of African Americans until favorable treatment became politically acceptable after World War II. The government, although based on the principles of freedom and equality, has generally refused to recognize the legitimate aspirations of its black constituents. Institutions such as the Federal Bureau of Investigation have even been openly hostile to the needs of black citizens and to their demands for greater political power.

One of the fundamental reasons for the continuation of the American racial divide is the failure of the United States to live up to what sociologist Gunnar Myrdal labeled "the American Creed." Americans—black and white—share a common trait, the belief in the ideals of freedom and democracy, but they have been unable to create institutions that adequately reflect their stated goals. "Americans of all national origins, classes, regions, creeds, and colors," Myrdal instructs, "have something in common: a social *ethos,* a political creed. It is

difficult to avoid the judgment that this 'American Creed' is the cement
in the structure of this great and disparate nation.''[4] Even most African
Americans accept the American rhetoric of democracy and liberty, although it is blacks who have the most reasons to doubt the legitimacy
of the American ideal. The acceptance of the principles of the Constitution and the Declaration of Independence are nearly universal for
Americans, regardless of race or political beliefs; the implementation
of these accepted ideals is where Americans diverge.

American institutions, according to Myrdal, have never accurately
represented the ideals embodied in the Constitution, largely because
Americans espouse conflicting values. While Americans profess their
beliefs in freedom, equality and liberty, they simultaneously demonstrate the exclusionary traits of racism and elitism. The egalitarian
American Creed has produced not a truly representative democracy but
rather a political and economic system of patriarchy and rigid racial
hierarchy. ''Nearly all of us Americans will admit that our government
contains imperfections and anachronisms,'' one writer explained a half
century ago. ''We who have been born and brought up under the evils
of gang rule, graft, political incompetence, inadequate representation,
and some of the other weaknesses of democracy, American plan, have
developed mental callouses and are no longer sensitive to them.''[5]

Americans have failed to translate their fundamental beliefs into a
pragmatic system of government, and African Americans have borne
the brunt of this failure. As Martin Luther King, Jr., queried shortly
before his death, ''Why is the issue of equality still so far from solution
in America, a nation that professes itself to be democratic, inventive,
hospitable to new ideas, rich, productive and awesomely powerful? The
problem is so tenacious because, despite its virtues and attributes,
America is deeply racist and its democracy is flawed both economically
and socially.''[6] The failure of institutions to achieve the ideals of the
American creed have created in the American psyche a cognitive disso-
nance—an ''American Dilemma,'' in Myrdal's words—that forces
Americans to choose between pragmatic exclusivity and unattainable
egalitarianism. According to Myrdal, these ''inconsistent attitudes are
blended into none too logical a scheme which, in turn, may be quite
inconsistent with the wider personal, moral, religious, and civic sentiments and ideas of the Americans.''[7] ''Throughout American history,
political institutions have reflected these values but have always fallen
short of realizing them in a satisfactory manner,'' political scientist
Samuel P. Huntington said of the American Dilemma. ''. . . Being

human, Americans have never been able to live up to their ideas; being Americans, they have been unable to abandon them."[8]

The American civil rights movement of the 1950s and 1960s was an emphatic attempt to relieve the American Dilemma by restoring democracy to American institutions. It was an attempt "to eliminate or reduce the gap between ideals and institutions by moralistic efforts to reform their institutions and practices so as to make them conform to the ideals of the American Creed."[9] The movement attempted to inject new meaning into the stale phrases of American liberty and democracy and to alter the institutions that had failed to serve African Americans. It was an effort to create a democracy in which all sectors of society would be represented and an economy in which all sectors could benefit. The African-American freedom struggle of the 1960s was one of the clearest demonstrations of American democracy in the history of the United States. In response to a continuing betrayal of the principles upon which America had been founded, African Americans and their supporters rose up in huge numbers to demand that democracy be applied uniformly to all Americans. The early movement was based almost entirely on the issue of segregation—seeking to break down racial barriers and increase open communication between the races. The movement labored to renew the political system by extending the franchise to those African Americans who had been forcibly denied the vote. Activists also attacked the American economic system in an attempt to redistribute the wealth that had eternally been cloistered among the few. Despite the enormous transformation, the movement was overwhelmingly nonviolent, using legal means to secure legal rights. The civil rights struggle was a truly democratic movement, embodying the very concepts that Americans had always preached but rarely practiced.

The Reverend Martin Luther King, Jr., is in many ways a symbol of the American Creed, a representation of the challenge against the undemocratic institutions in the United States. It was he who was primarily responsible for turning the nascent anger of African Americans into direct action against the system that produced it. King fought for the return to the American ideal and for the extension of true democracy to the disenfranchised. His efforts to rid the nation of a racial caste system were intended to be a first step in the realization of American rhetoric stated in the Constitution, which, according to King, "says that each individual has certain basic rights that are neither conferred by nor derived from the state. . . . Very seldom if ever in the history of the world has a sociopolitical document expressed in such profoundly eloquent and unequivocal language the dignity and the worth of human personality.''[10] His various voting-rights campaigns throughout the South sought to broaden the political spectrum to include the African-American voices that had been silenced throughout American history. The American Creed, to Martin Luther King, was an American dream. ''We are simply seeking to bring into full realization the American dream—a dream yet unfulfilled,'' King orated.

> A dream of equality of opportunity, of privilege and property widely distributed; a dream of a land where men no longer argue that the color of a man's skin determines the content of his character; the dream of a land where every man will respect the dignity and worth of human personality—this is the dream. When it is realized, the jangling discords of our nation will be transformed into a beautiful symphony of brotherhood, and men everywhere will know that America is truly the land of the free and the home of the brave.[11]

If Martin Luther King is the symbol of the American Creed, then J. Edgar Hoover may be symbolic of the institutions that failed to live up to the American ideals. Although he preached the rhetoric of liberty as fervently as any American, Hoover institutionalized concepts of total-itarianism rather than democracy in his Federal Bureau of Investigation. During his almost fifty years as head of the FBI, Hoover carefully expanded his power and increased his independence from those who were supposed to control him. Hoover built a personal empire, impervi-ous to the political pressures that often threatened to dethrone him. By the time the civil rights movement began to challenge the American establishment, Hoover was reaching the zenith of his power. His control over his empire was absolute; he used his dictatorial power arbitrarily and without oversight. Hoover created an empire in his own image, employing his own prejudices and preferences. The FBI became virtu-ally a religious cult, with Hoover playing the part of the prophet dis-pensing justice among his followers. His powers extended far beyond those who worked for him in the Bureau. With the information he copiously gathered and selectively dispensed, Hoover influenced gov-ernment policy to meet his own predilections and effectively lobbied the Congress and the Executive branch of government. He disrupted leftist movements in the United States for over fifty years and used the specter of communism as a weapon against those who sought to change the status quo. Hoover exercised his powers secretly, covering his acts with a demonstration of public relations that convinced the American public that J. Edgar Hoover was the personification of the American ideal of justice and equality of opportunity.

Indeed, Hoover genuinely believed in many of the same ideals that King professed. "In all the civilized world there is no story which compares with America's effort to become free and to incorporate freedom in our institutions," Hoover wrote in 1958. "I am sure that most Americans believe that our light of freedom is a shining light. As Americans we should stand up, speak of it, and let the world see this light."[12] But Hoover, while publicly paying lip service to the American ideal, privately waged war on civil liberties and civil rights, thereby making a mockery of the principles upon which the United States had been founded. Hoover sought to prevent democratic rights from spreading to African Americans, while justifying his actions as necessary for the continuation of American democracy. He used the full powers of the Federal Bureau of Investigation for that purpose and often exceeded the Bureau's jurisdiction and authority. Hoover was a vivid embodiment of the perpetual conflict between the ideals of freedom and liberty and the governmental institutions that sought to restrict the application of the American Creed.

The philosophical enmity between J. Edgar Hoover and Martin Luther King, Jr., inevitably translated into a political and personal struggle between the two. It started earnestly enough when the Bureau began to question the communist affiliations of two of King's aides. Over the six years of the animosity—from early 1962 until King's death in 1968—the FBI attempted to reduce communist infiltration into King's Southern Christian Leadership Conference. But when King questioned the effectiveness of the Bureau's civil rights efforts and the misdirected attempt to hunt communists, the thin-skinned Director made the conflict personal. Hoover assumed a new objective in the face of King's criticism: the utter denigration of Martin Luther King, Jr., and his removal from the leadership of the civil rights movement. Throughout the six-year battle, Hoover hated King intensely, and King returned the sentiment with a mixture of pity and scorn.

The animosity between Martin Luther King, Jr., and J. Edgar Hoover is a clear illustration of Myrdal's American Dilemma, in which the United States is forced to contend with conflicting ideals and institutions. Out of democratic ideals sprang a totalitarian institution that worked to silence the plaintive voice of American freedom. The conflicting beliefs held by Americans created a governmental body—the Federal Bureau of Investigation—that actively campaigned to reduce the civil liberties of certain Americans. Martin Luther King, Jr., in particular, was targeted by the undemocratic tendencies of the Federal Bureau of Investigation, and as a consequence his ability to fight for racial justice was seriously diminished. The totalitarianism of the FBI and the failure of the federal government to adequately respond to the need for civil rights embittered King and his allies. "The shocking fact is that while the government moves sluggishly, and in patchwork fashion, to achieve equal rights for all citizens, in the daily conduct of its own massive economic and social activities it participates directly and indirectly in the denial of these rights," King said in 1961. "We must face the tragic fact that the federal government is the nation's highest investor in segregation."[13]

America is incomparably less endangered by its own Communists than by the hysterical hunt for the few Communists there are here.

—Albert Einstein, in a letter to Norman Thomas in 1954

2

Hunting for Communists

Reverend Martin Luther King, Jr., had been in the public spotlight for six years before the FBI began to take an active interest in the southern minister. He first captured the national spotlight in 1956, when he led the black residents of Montgomery, Alabama, on a successful boycott of the city buses. The African-American residents of the original Confederate capitol for years tolerated a never-ending series of abuses at the hands of city bus drivers. When seamstress Rosa Parks finally refused to give up her bus seat for a white patron in December 1955, Montgomery was ready for a boycott, and the young minister Martin Luther King, Jr., was surprisingly thrust into the leadership. His brilliant oration and the success of the year-long boycott gave King and his fellow civil rights workers a national audience, and brought the South to the verge of a major civil rights struggle.

King spent the next several years solidifying the foundations of the emerging civil rights movement. Along with other southern ministers, he founded the Southern Christian Leadership Conference in 1957 as a vehicle for change, giving the movement the spiritual base that it needed. King made a journey to India in 1959 to fully explore the intricacies of nonviolent resistance that Gandhi had used against the British and that the Montgomery boycotters had successfully adapted to the civil rights movement. His efforts to woo the Eisenhower administration into a greater involvement in civil rights were largely unsuccessful, despite the President's uncharacteristic support of school desegregation in Little Rock, Arkansas. In 1960, the civil rights struggle was reinvigorated by the spontaneous outbreak of student sit-ins at lunch counters around the South. King remained in the spotlight for his support of the sit-ins and his assistance in founding the Student Nonviolent Coordinating Committee (SNCC). The southern preacher got his first taste of influence in national politics from behind bars, as presidential candidate John Kennedy and his brother Robert interceded to convince a Georgia judge to release King, thereby collecting African-American votes from across the country. The FBI, however, took little note.

The Bureau never developed a keen interest in Martin Luther King as he attempted to build a southern movement. The FBI followed King from afar, collecting random information from newspaper clippings and other sources. Much of the biographical data that the FBI initially collected came from his entry in the name-dropping encyclopedia, *Who's Who in America.* A seventy-one-page report dated September 28, 1960, outlined all available information on King; however, the report contained mostly synopses of newspaper articles about the civil rights leader. Although the Bureau had little original information, King's SCLC was nevertheless considered a key target for communist infiltration. The Bureau tracked any influence that communists had in the organization. When King was stabbed during a book signing in New York City in 1958, the FBI took note when Benjamin Davis, an open member of the Communist Party, donated blood for him. The use of King's name in support of the Committee to Secure Justice for Morton Sobell, who was convicted in the 1953 espionage trial with Julius and Ethel Rosenberg, also initially inspired the concern of the FBI. The Bureau regarded the Committee as a communist front organization and worried that King was being used for the ''subversive'' goals of the group. The FBI also noted that King's name had appeared on a petition urging clemency for Carl Braden, who had been imprisoned for contempt of Congress when he refused to testify before the House Un-American Activities Committee.

Despite King's contacts with supposed communists, the Bureau was well aware that King was neither a communist nor affiliated with the Communist Party. *Stride Toward Freedom,* King's book on the Montgomery bus boycott, clearly outlined his attitude toward communism when it was published in 1958. King rejected the materialistic, rather than spiritual, approach of communism and stated that ''communism, avowedly secularistic and materialistic, has no place for God. This I could not accept, for as a Christian I believe that there is a creative personal power in this universe who is the ground and essence of all reality—a power that cannot be explained in materialistic terms.''[14] Despite his stated anticommunism, the Bureau continued to worry that King was being influenced by communists to support their objectives. According to the Bureau, King's stand against communism meant little if he continued to support the causes for which communists were fighting. One FBI memorandum asserted that "though nothing has come to the Bureau's attention to indicate that Reverend Martin Luther King is a Communist Party member, he has been linked with numerous leftist and communist front organizations and is currently active in racial and segregation matters.''[15]

The Bureau first began to take serious note of the young minister when King mentioned the FBI in an article that he wrote for *The Nation* magazine on February 4, 1961. King argued that federal law-enforcement agencies, including the Bureau, should be used to combat southern violations of civil rights and contended that the lack of African Americans in the FBI contributed to its unwillingness to investigate civil rights violations. "We can easily see how an end to discriminatory practices in Federal agencies would have tremendous value in changing attitudes and behavior patterns. If, for instance, the law-enforcement personnel in the FBI were integrated, many persons who now defy Federal law might come under restraints from which they are presently free.''[16] Despite the criticism of the Bureau, the FBI did not attempt to dispute King's charges, in part because their information on King remained limited. In a memo summarizing King's article, the FBI stated that "Martin Luther King, Jr., is well known for his activities in behalf of the National Association for the Advancement of Colored People," which indicates that the writer did not fully understand the difference between the NAACP and King's SCLC. The memo concludes with the recommendation that "although King is in error in his comments relating to the FBI, it is believed inadvisable to call his hand on this matter as he obviously would only welcome any controversy or resulting publicity that might ensue.''[17] The Director, in his familiar handwriting, scribbled, "I concur," at the bottom of the page. Hoover's interest was nevertheless growing. A May 22, 1961, memo responding to the Director's request for information on King and others stated that "King has not been investigated by the FBI." Hoover underlined the sentence and scrawled, "Why not?"[18]

But it was not until the next year that the FBI began to actively investigate King and his alleged communist connections. Six years after

King became a public figure, the Bureau finally found what it was looking for: an alleged direct tie between Martin Luther King, Jr., and the Communist Party, USA. The Bureau discovered that Stanley David Levison, a supposed member of the Communist Party, was an advisor to the civil rights leader. Six years passed before the Bureau discovered how close the relationship between Levison and King was, testimony to the lack of attention that the FBI had afforded King. The two had first met during the Montgomery bus boycott in 1956 when Levison, a New York lawyer, offered his services in support of the racial struggle. The FBI's failure to notice the budding relationship led the Bureau to believe that the link between King and Levison was secret, but this was never the case. They had worked together openly for six years, often conversing over the telephone and in person on various civil rights matters. Their business relationship had developed into a strong friendship, and King valued the New York lawyer's advice.

Levison provided valuable services, primarily as a fund-raiser through a New York group that funneled money to the southern civil rights movement. In addition, Levison contributed his skills as a lawyer and provided free legal advice to the Montgomery movement's successful court battle against the bus company. Although he was not the movement's main lawyer, Levison's services ingratiated him to King, who came to rely on Levison's political judgment. Once the bus boycott ended, Levison set to work securing a publisher for a book by King on the Montgomery movement. Levison offered invaluable criticism of King's manuscript and even drafted sections of the book. The finished product, published in 1958 under the title *Stride Toward Freedom,* was heavily influenced by Levison, who had urged King to discuss voting rights and to downplay King's own role in the movement to avoid sounding too vain.[19] Levison also helped prepare King's income tax returns and furnished important legal advice in 1960 when King was arrested in Alabama on trumped-up charges of perjury on his tax returns; with Levison's assistance, King was found innocent, even before an all-white jury.

The extent of the Levison-King relationship first became evident to the Bureau in January 1962. Charges against Levison had originally been made in the 1950s by a Bureau source inside the Communist Party, and the Bureau had then launched an investigation of him. The New York lawyer left the Party in 1954 (or went underground, as the Bureau insisted), and joined King two years later. According to Bureau sources, Levison had worked with the financial aspects of the CPUSA, managing the monies that the Party received from the Soviet Union and from the various businesses that it controlled. According to the

Bureau, his involvement apparently lasted two years before he discontinued his work with the Party, although the reason for the split is unclear. After 1955, the Bureau no longer considered Levison to be an active Party member and even attempted to recruit him in 1960 to reactivate his membership and spy on the Party for the Bureau. Levison declined the offer.

The Bureau quickly disseminated the information of an alleged linkage between King and the Communist Party. Letters containing the allegations against Levison were sent in early 1962 to Attorney General Robert F. Kennedy, Assistant to the President Kenneth O'Donnell, and Vice President Lyndon B. Johnson. Although evidence suggested that Levison was no longer involved in Party activities, this was not an impediment to the Bureau's contentions. Hoover argued that Levison had dropped his public membership but was still controlled by Communist Party leaders. The Bureau maintained that Levison remained a "secret" Party member, and was thereby an even greater threat to the civil rights movement. Bureau agents wasted no time in installing a wiretap on Levison's office phone in March 1962 and followed with a tap on his home phone in November. Attorney General Robert Kennedy authorized both wiretaps, but the Bureau moved beyond its legal authority and planted a hidden microphone in Levison's office in March 1962. Kennedy was not informed of the Bureau's deed.

Attorney General Kennedy moved into action when he heard of the King-Levison connection. Assuming that King was unaware of Levison's Communist Party past, Kennedy asked his aide John Seigenthaler to warn King of the possible threat. Seigenthaler talked to King during the civil rights leader's next visit to the Justice Department in Washington. Pulling King aside after a meeting with the Attorney General and other civil rights leaders, Seigenthaler warned King of a high-ranking communist in the SCLC, but refused to name Levison. "King listened quietly, looking Seigenthaler directly in the eye. He gave no indication of familiarity with the subject. He thanked Seigenthaler for his interest, and said that he didn't question the motives of people who sought to assist him, and that absent some clear evidence, he took people at face value."[20] The President's civil rights advisor, Harris Wofford, reluctantly warned King of Levison's alleged communist connections soon after Seigenthaler's talk with King. According to Wofford, King seemed "depressed and dumbfounded when I talked to him about Levison; he could not believe it, and said he had far more reason to trust Levison than to trust Hoover."[21] King refused to act against the man who had been his friend and advisor for the past six years.

The Second Subversive

Stanley Levison, however, was not the only King advisor who had ties to the American Communist Party, according to the Bureau. Before the discovery of Levison's ties, the Bureau had noted the presence of Hunter Pitts "Jack" O'Dell in the New York office of the SCLC. Almost a year before the FBI stumbled across the relationship between King and Levison, a special agent of the Bureau anonymously called the New York office and spoke with O'Dell, who the Bureau believed to be a communist. Feigning interest in donating money to the SCLC, the agent solicited information on the difference between the SCLC; the Committee to Defend Martin Luther King, Jr., which was established to raise money for King's defense against the tax evasion charges; and the Committee to Aid the Southern Freedom Struggle. O'Dell's response was that for all practical purposes, the three organizations were identical, and a check made out to any of them would be directed to the SCLC. Later that year, on October 27, the Bureau watched O'Dell enter the New York SCLC office and made another pretense phone call, this time to determine O'Dell's role in the organization. O'Dell responded that he was the administrator of the New York office.[22] The Bureau was concerned about O'Dell's presence, but the concern assumed an immediacy only after the FBI discovered Levison's ties. With both O'Dell and Levison in the movement, the Bureau felt justified in raising the red flag of communist infiltration.

The basis of the Bureau's concern over Jack O'Dell's status within the SCLC stemmed from his involvement with the Communist Party during the 1950s. O'Dell did not deny his past affiliations, but insisted that his Party involvement had ended before he began working for the SCLC. Because of his Communist Party connections, O'Dell was expelled in 1950 from the CIO National Maritime Union, ostensibly for working against the federal government by circulating petitions urging the end of the Cold War. O'Dell had made several appearances before the House Un-American Activities Committee and the Senate Internal Security Subcommittee, where he refused to answer questions concerning his alleged membership in the Communist Party. He first testified before the Senate subcommittee on April 12, 1956, and pleaded the Fifth Amendment in response to questions about his Party activities. In March 1957, O'Dell was arrested in New Orleans for participating in a subversive organization, advocating the overthrow of the American government, and failing to register with the state of Louisiana as a communist.[23] He was pulled before a House committee on July 30,

1958, where he was called a "dedicated zealot of the Communist movement," and was again called on February 3, 1960.[24] Both times he refused to answer questions, although in 1960 a fellow Party member, Albert Gaillard, testified that he had known O'Dell to be a member and had been sent on a Party assignment by O'Dell.[25]

Clearly, O'Dell had a checkered past when he began working for Martin Luther King and the SCLC in 1960. But he proved to be an effective organizer and a valuable addition to the SCLC staff, and Martin Luther King was reluctant to let him leave the movement when he faced charges of being a communist. The FBI had initially followed O'Dell's career in the SCLC from a distance. His name appeared in a number of FBI memoranda that summarized available information on King before 1962. Even though the Bureau knew O'Dell's communist past and his involvement in the New York SCLC office, his connection to Dr. King was only one of a series of troubling signs. It was not until the discovery of Stanley Levison's personal relationship with King that the Bureau decided that their fears of communist infiltration of the SCLC had been realized.

It appears strange, at first, that the Bureau would become so concerned over Levison's presence in the civil rights struggle when it had already known that Jack O'Dell, a known communist, was de facto head of the New York SCLC office. But Stanley Levison was different from O'Dell in several key ways. First, Levison had a much stronger relationship with Dr. King. He had worked with King for six years when the FBI discovered their friendship and had been consulted on many of the key decisions that the SCLC had made in the intervening years. Levison was a political strategist whose opinions were well respected by King, whereas O'Dell's influence was far less pronounced. Secondly, the Bureau believed Levison had a far greater status within the ranks of the Communist Party and was therefore a greater threat. The Bureau alleged that Levison had knowledge of the CPUSA's entire financial network, including the funds donated annually by the Soviet Union. Levison was rumored to be personally acquainted with American Communist leaders, such as Gus Hall and Lem Harris. Whereas O'Dell never reached the higher Party ranks, the Bureau believed Levison to be a key Party leader.* Levison, the Bureau concluded, was the direct link between King and the leadership of the Communist Party.

---

*The Bureau, however, later claimed that O'Dell had been admitted to the central committee of the Communist Party, although there is no evidence to substantiate that charge.

A third reason for the Bureau's belief that Levison represented a greater threat than O'Dell was that Levison's affiliation with the Communist Party was not as readily apparent as Jack O'Dell's. According to the FBI, Levison was being disingenuous in misrepresenting his ties to the Communist Party. By not openly admitting membership, Levison demonstrated the subversive nature of his connection. The FBI assumed that Levison's lack of forthrightness indicated he was on a secret mission overseen by the Party leadership. His apparent withdrawal from the Party in 1954 led the Bureau to believe not that he had split from the Party ranks but that he had gone underground in the expectation of infiltrating and exploiting the nascent civil rights movement. This logic presented the New York lawyer with an impossible situation, and Levison faced a decisive choice. He could either admit membership in the CPUSA, even if his admission was false, in which case he would have been persecuted by the Bureau. Or he could have denied membership, which he continued to do, yet still suffer the wrath of the FBI's paranoia.

Levison's continual failure to disclose his former Party membership to King was most likely because the Bureau's accusations against him were substantially inaccurate. Although Levison did have ties with a number of Communist Party members, there is no indication that he ever actually joined the Party. The Bureau's evidence against Levison consisted of the testimony of a high-level member of the CPUSA that revealed Levison's associations with Party members.[26] But association is not proof of membership or of personal belief—although the Bureau refused to recognize this distinction. In 1963, after listening to his wiretaps for over a year, the New York Bureau office reluctantly concluded that "Levison is not now under CP discipline in the civil rights field." But the Bureau qualified its assertion with the statement that "there has been no indication, however, that Mr. Levison has not continued his ideological adherence to communism"—an allegiance that the Bureau had never originally proved.[27] Levison continually denied ever being a member of the Party, even long after King was assassinated and the interest in Levison dissipated. "I was neither an international agent nor even a domestic party member," he later told historian Arthur Schlesinger, Jr. But Levison insisted that he could not have actively combated the charges of communist influence. "At that time Hoover's credibility was unchallenged: it would have diverted the movement at a critical stage to take on so difficult a civil liberties battle."[28]

Conspiracy

The Bureau discovered proof of what they regarded as a communist conspiracy in the SCLC in June 1962, when Levison recommended O'Dell for the position of administrative assistant to King. The Bureau learned of the recommendation from a conversation between O'Dell and Levison that was picked up on an FBI phone tap. J. Edgar Hoover summarized the conversation in a memo to Attorney General Robert Kennedy dated June 21, 1962, in which he falsely attributed the information to "a confidential source, who has furnished reliable information in the past."* According to Hoover, Levison told O'Dell that "King said he was thinking of getting another administrative assistant. Levison stated that in the past, Levison had not considered it wise for O'Dell to take on such a position but he is the only one who could do the job and should be considered for it. Levison stated that as long as O'Dell did not have the title of Executive Director, there would not be 'as much lightning flashing around him.'" According to Hoover, King responded positively to the idea, adding that "no matter what a man was, if he could stand up now and say he is not connected [to the Communist Party], then as far as I'm concerned, he is eligible to work for me."[29] Upon Levison's recommendation, O'Dell began working for King in both Atlanta, where King had his headquarters, and Albany, Georgia, where King was involved in an ill-fated civil rights campaign to desegregate bus stations and other public facilities.

The FBI accelerated its investigation of Levison and O'Dell when it discovered Levison's recommendation. The Bureau began collecting old newspaper articles that reported O'Dell's arrests and various appearances before congressional anticommunist committees, and it found SCLC advertisements with O'Dell's name on them to add to its files. The ads were further proof, the Bureau assumed, of O'Dell's influence in the SCLC. The FBI carefully followed the progress of the Albany campaign during the summer of 1962 and kept alert for further examples of communist infiltration. The Bureau discovered what it considered to be another potential subversive in the civil rights movement: Clarence Jones, a New York City lawyer who was often in contact with both King and Levison. Jones was the executive director of the Gandhi Society for Human Rights, a fund-raising organ of the SCLC of which

---

*This was a common phrase used by the Bureau to hide the original sources of information, in this case electronic surveillance.

King was honorary president. According to a September 12, 1962, Bureau teletype to the Director, "Jones was identified as a leader in the Labor Youth League in late '53 or early '54 and had denounced the State Dept. ban on travel behind iron curtain in May '52."[30] Such paltry information was all the Bureau needed to make the accusation of communist influence.

On October 23, 1962, both the New York and Atlanta offices were instructed to begin a full COMINFIL (communist infiltration) investigation of the SCLC. The FBI did not wait for the results of its investigation before it began to attack King for his supposed communist connections. In a Bureau memorandum dated September 28, 1962, the New York special agent in charge (SAC) proposed that the FBI anonymously leak information on O'Dell's Communist Party background to various newspapers that had previously reported on O'Dell before he began to work for the SCLC. The SAC wrote that "it is suggested that a notation be made, 'Isn't Jack H. O'Dell identical with O'Dell, the Communist leader in the South you wrote about? . . .' It is believed that such an exposure would cause other Negro organizations such as the Negro American Labor Council (NALC) to clean out anyone who possibly could cause embarrassment because of Communist affiliation or background."[31] The *Long Island Star-Journal,* among other newspapers, carried the story on October 26, using information directly from FBI files. The stories announced that a high-level member of the Communist Party had infiltrated the New York office of King's Southern Christian Leadership Conference.

King almost immediately announced the resignation of Jack O'Dell from the SCLC but told the press that he was not aware of O'Dell's Party background and said that O'Dell denied being a communist. His resignation was offered, however, "in order to avoid embarrassment to SCLC. . . . We have offered it pending further inquiry and clarification."[32] King also refuted a number of the statements made in the articles in an attempt to downplay O'Dell's role in the SCLC. According to King's press release:

It is totally inaccurate and false that Mr. O'Dell is Southeastern director of the Southern Christian Leadership Conference. Not only has he never been director but was never considered for the position. Mr. O'Dell has functioned purely as a technician with 90 per cent of his work taking place in the North where he resides, and involving the mechanization of our mailing procedures.[33]

Although King was less than forthright about the extent of O'Dell's involvement in the civil rights movement, O'Dell's presence did not indicate the communist conspiracy that the Bureau had led the various newspapers to believe. King went on in his press release to denounce communism as a "crippling totalitarianism" that was not welcome in the SCLC. He pointed out that "it is also a firm policy that no person of known Communist affiliation can serve on [SCLC's] staff, executive board or its membership at large."[34]

The Bureau, however, through the use of selected leaks to newspapers of derogatory information against O'Dell, had apparently succeeded in lessening the influence of a "subversive" in the civil rights movement. O'Dell had been temporarily sidelined solely by the Bureau's intervention. The actions against King began with this attempt to reduce communist infiltration of the SCLC by attacking those surrounding him who allegedly had communist affiliations. But the focus of the attacks became increasingly personal, and the FBI's actions soon took on a different goal: the destruction of Martin Luther King, Jr., as a force in the civil rights movement.

Measured concern over Dr. King's connections with supposed subversives turned to heated anger when he challenged the FBI over its behavior during the Albany campaign. King commented on the Bureau to reporters after a speech at the Riverside Church in New York before three thousand people. During the interview in the church's robing room, King stated:

> One of the great problems we face with the FBI in the South is that the agents are white Southerners who have been influenced by the mores of the community. To maintain their status, they have to be friendly with the local police and people who are promoting segregation. Every time I saw FBI men in Albany, they were with the local police force.... If an FBI man agrees with segregation, he can't honestly and objectively investigate.

King went on to say that the government should assign northern agents to the South "who are at least in agreement with the law of the land."[35]

King's attack on the Bureau was a reflection of the attitudes of both civil rights workers and African Americans in general. The role of the FBI had been a long-simmering issue in the civil rights movement. Resentment over the Bureau's failure to protect civil rights workers had been building in recent years, as stories of FBI indifference to the beating of southern blacks proliferated. The Bureau, citing its role as an investigatory rather than a prosecutorial organization, even stood by and took notes as integrated bus riders were viciously beaten by southern racists during the 1961 Freedom Rides. Indeed, the beating of Justice Department representative John Seigenthaler during the Freedom Rides did nothing to spur the Bureau into action. The FBI's glaring indifference to violations of civil rights laws, combined with its extensive cooperation with local police that had often been the source of such violations, increased the animosity between southern blacks and the federal government. Howard Zinn, a professor at Spelman College, quoted a young African American during an interview with the newspaper *The Worker* as telling him that FBI agents are "a bunch of racists." Zinn commented that "whether true or not, this is the feeling of many Negroes who have had contact with the FBI and, even if distorted, it is a general reflection of the efficacy of the FBI's role in the area of civil rights."[36]

King's statements against the Bureau were not technically correct, and the FBI went to great lengths to assert its innocence. The Bureau refuted King's statement that southern-based agents were raised in the South by claiming that 70 percent of agents in the South originated in the North, and that four of five of the Albany, Georgia, agents were northerners. The FBI failed to report that the fifth agent, a southerner, was a known racist who set the tone of that particular FBI field office.[37] Although the statistics could be used to prove the opposite, the substance of King's assertion was certainly correct. Although many of the agents were from the North, the FBI certainly sympathized with local police forces, even in cases in which those police actively combated the civil rights movement through legal and extralegal means. The Bureau's alliance with the police, which began during the FBI's glory days of battling gangsters, was extended to civil rights matters, and the Bureau was often reluctant to investigate police officers who were accused of brutality.

In the face of criticism, J. Edgar Hoover had a habit not of fixing the object of criticism but attacking the source, and he did not break his habit when King castigated the Bureau in 1962. Rather than attempting to deal with the FBI's apparent lack of civil rights activity, the Director instead assailed Martin Luther King. First, J. Edgar Hoover dispatched FBI Assistant Director Cartha DeLoach to give the press the Bureau's side of the controversy. DeLoach fed the media data on the birthplaces of FBI agents in the South and insisted that "FBI agents carry out their investigative responsibilities irrespective of their state of origin.'' He also tried to dispel the notion that the Bureau had been ineffective in dealing with civil rights crimes. ''Perhaps Dr. King has had a lapse of memory in recalling that last August and September, five Negro churches were burned in Georgia and firearms were discharged into several homes. . . . The FBI instituted extensive investigations which led to the prompt solution'' of one of the church bombings. DeLoach then took direct aim at King. ''The other statements by Dr. King reveal a total ignorance not only of the true character of FBI Director J. Edgar Hoover, but also of the FBI record in protecting civil rights.''[38]

Hoover asked Cartha DeLoach to meet with King personally to give him the FBI's version of their efforts to enforce civil rights laws. DeLoach phoned King's Atlanta office on November 27, 1962, and spoke to King's secretary, who told DeLoach that King was working on the manuscript for a book (*Why We Can't Wait*, which was published in 1963) and could not be disturbed. DeLoach then asked the Atlanta SAC to schedule an interview with King as soon as possible. The agent called King's office and left a message, after being informed that King did not have the time for an interview because of his busy schedule, but that King would call when he found a convenient time. Apparently King never found a convenient time and never called back. This was not unusual. King's hectic schedule of traveling around the country often did not allow him time for routine matters such as returning phone calls. Although King's associates knew his tendency not to call back, the FBI interpreted it as a deliberate attempt to avoid them. ''It would appear obvious that Rev. King does not desire to be told the true facts,'' DeLoach concluded in a memo written on January 15, 1963, that was distributed within the Bureau. But DeLoach went far beyond this conclusion, and attributed King's failure to return the phone calls as sinister behavior that was encouraged by the ''subversives'' that were abundant within the SCLC. King ''has obviously used deceit, lies and treachery as propaganda to further his own causes. . . .''

The record concerning Rev. King's allegations has been covered. Interviews with the publishers of the newspapers who carried Rev. King's lies have been conducted and they have been set straight. I see no further need to contacting Rev. King inasmuch as he obviously does not desire to be given the truth. The fact that he is a vicious liar is amply demonstrated in the fact that he constantly associates

with and takes instructions from Stanley Levison who is a hidden
member of the Communist Party in New York.[34]

King had inadvertently triggered a war with the FBI.

Electronic Surveillance

One crucial weapon that the Bureau employed in the emerging battle
with King was electronic surveillance. The Bureau often used wiretaps
and recording devices to intercept valuable information on its investigative targets, and it had first initiated electronic surveillance on Levison
soon after the discovery of his relationship with King. FBI agents broke
into Levison's office in the early morning of March 16, 1962, and
implanted a hidden microphone to pick up office conversations. The
agents then followed with a phone tap several days later, installed with
the help of a source in the telephone company. The microphones were
intended to establish definitive evidence of Levison's Communist Party
connections. The Bureau was certain that Levison was providing King
with instructions from his communist bosses; overhearing and recording
the bosses giving the instructions would provide proof. The surveillance
of Levison, however, provided the Bureau with no such proof. No information was ever found of Levison's supposed Communist Party ties, but
the wiretaps provided important information on the political activities of
King and the SCLC. Since King often consulted Levison on political
decisions, the wiretap provided an ideal opportunity to detect King's
future actions and Levison's role in the decision-making process within
the SCLC. When an opening appeared in the Supreme Court in 1962,
King sought Levison's advice on whether he should recommend Appeals Court Judge William Hastie, an African American, as a potential
replacement. The Bureau intercepted this information and passed it on
to the Attorney General, along with information developed by the Bureau that Hastie had been "connected with ten organizations which
have been . . . cited as communist fronts."* An additional wiretap for

*King FBI File. Memorandum from the Director, FBI, to The Attorney General. April
2, 1962, section 1. Ironically, the Kennedy administration wanted to nominate an African American to the Court, but rejected Judge Hastie because they felt his credentials
were too conservative, not radical as Hoover portrayed them. According to Arthur
Schlesinger, Jr., Robert Kennedy solicited Supreme Court Chief Justice Earl Warren's
opinion on Hastie. "He's not a liberal," Warren replied, "and he'd be opposed to all
the measures that we are interested in, and he would just be completely unsatisfactory."
(Schlesinger, p. 405.)

Levison's home telephone was approved by the Attorney General in late 1962.

The surveillance of King continued as the SCLC began a major civil rights campaign in Birmingham, Alabama. The FBI took careful note of Levison's aid in drafting an article that King wrote for *The Nation* magazine in early 1963, and Hoover forwarded information to the Attorney General and the White House that Jack O'Dell continued to advise King, despite earlier public statements that O'Dell had resigned from the SCLC. The Bureau also forwarded information on the development of plans for a major march on Washington to be tentatively scheduled for August, 1963. During the summer of 1963, Robert Kennedy became increasingly concerned that King's relationship with supposed communists would be exposed in the press. As their sensitivity to racial injustice grew, the President and Attorney General allied themselves with King and the civil rights movement. Any rumors of communist infiltration of the movement would threaten not only King but also the passage of civil rights legislation that the President had finally introduced in the summer of 1963.

In January 1963, Robert Kennedy sent Burke Marshall once again to warn Dr. King of the impending threat. Despite the sincerity of Marshall's effort, King refused to remove O'Dell or Levison from the SCLC without more evidence of communist infiltration than Marshall could provide. Marshall could only offer the undocumented assertion that both men were secret members of the Communist Party, since J. Edgar Hoover would not release any other information for fear of exposing his source in the Party. King was well aware of O'Dell's communist affiliations, so Marshall's arguments against him did not fall on deaf ears. But King believed O'Dell to be sincere when he said that all communist activities were in the past and King was unwilling to fire him on the basis of the Bureau's assertions that he remained part of the Party leadership. King remained adamant in his defense of Stanley Levison, who assured King that the charges against him were groundless.

Marshall again warned him of the danger to the movement on June 22, 1963, when King traveled to Washington for a scheduled meeting between civil rights leaders and the President to discuss the Civil Rights Bill and the upcoming March on Washington. Marshall spoke with King on the instructions of both the Attorney General and the President, and he found a more receptive audience than he had in their previous meetings. According to Marshall, King agreed that his relationship with

Levison could jeopardize the progress of civil rights, and "stated that the connection would be ended."[40]

In order to ensure that King would follow through on his promise, the President pulled him aside after their meeting later in the day. Kennedy walked King out into the Rose Garden and told him of the danger to the passage of the civil rights bill if Levison's ties to him were discovered. "I assume you know you're under very close surveillance," Kennedy told King, warning him that he should not discuss important issues over the phone to Levison.[41] Kennedy specifically mentioned both Levison and O'Dell. "They're communists," he said. "You've got to get rid of them." Kennedy then went on to warn King that if the opponents of the civil rights bill got the information about Levison, the bill would not be passed and the Kennedy administration would be embarrassed. "If they shoot you down, they'll shoot us down too—so we're asking you to be careful."[42] But King seemed less agreeable in his meeting with the President than he had appeared earlier in the day with Marshall. He told Kennedy that he would have to prove the charges against Levison, and the President assured him that Marshall would furnish the proof to Andrew Young.

King did not wait for evidence against O'Dell before he wrote to inform him that his earlier temporary resignation would be permanent. "In these critical times we cannot afford to risk any such impressions" of communist infiltration.[43] Meanwhile, Andrew Young met with Burke Marshall in New Orleans, but Marshall still could not provide the proof that the FBI supposedly had to demonstrate that Levison was a Soviet spy. According to Young, "Burke never said anything about any evidence he had. . . . He always quoted what the Bureau said it had. I didn't feel this was conclusive. They were all scared to death of the Bureau; they really were."[44] King still demurred, refusing to disassociate with Levison based on unproven allegations. Levison, however, finally took action and agreed to remove himself from the movement in order to free King from charges of communist influence. He cut off all visible ties with King to save the movement from the FBI's persecution.

Dr. King continued to come under fire for his alleged ties to communists during the summer of 1963 when Congress held hearings on the administration's Civil Rights Bill. In response to charges from Alabama Governor George Wallace that King was a communist sympathizer, and questions from prominent senators on whether Wallace's charges were true, President Kennedy spoke out at a press conference on July 17, 1963. "We have no evidence that any of the leaders of the civil rights movement in the United States are Communists. We have no evidence that the demonstrations are Communist-inspired. There may be occasions when a Communist takes part in a demonstration. We can't prevent that. But I think it is a convenient scapegoat to suggest that all of the difficulties are Communist and that if the Communist movement would only disappear that we would end this.''[45] The Attorney General responded a week later in a written statement to two senators, stating:

> Based on all available evidence from the FBI and other sources, we have no evidence that any of the top leaders of the major civil rights groups are Communists, or Communist controlled. This is true as to Martin Luther King, Jr., about whom particular accusations were made, as well as other leaders. It is natural and inevitable that Communists have made efforts to infiltrate the civil rights groups and to exploit the current racial situation. In view of the real injustices that exist and the resentment against them, these efforts have been remarkably unsuccessful.[46]

But the Bureau did not ease its surveillance of Martin Luther King as evidence arose that he had curtailed his contact with both O'Dell and Levison. To the contrary, the idea of installing a wiretap on Martin Luther King's home telephone was debated by the Attorney General during July 1963, although it remains unclear whether that idea originated with Robert Kennedy or J. Edgar Hoover. In any case, Kennedy finally decided that installing a wiretap would produce little information, since King traveled constantly, and would be a serious embarrassment if it were discovered that the Bureau had electronic surveillance on King. Kennedy did, however, approve a wiretap on Clarence Jones, the New York attorney and advisor to King who was alleged to have been a former member of the Labor Youth League. This wiretap proved to be especially beneficial to the Bureau, when they discovered that the break between Levison and King had been largely superficial. Although direct contacts had stopped, King still sought Levison's advice through Clarence Jones, who passed messages between the two men.

Wiretapping King

The pressure to place wiretaps on Martin Luther King's telephone had been increasing on the Attorney General as the civil rights arena bustled with activity. The need for more intelligence information on the upcoming March on Washington and the need for more information to combat congressional charges that King was a communist increased the incentive for Robert Kennedy to authorize electronic surveillance on King. Plans for the March on Washington proceeded through the summer of 1963, and the Kennedy administration made every effort to ensure that the march would remain a positive demonstration of support for the President rather than a protest of the administration's inaction. Assistant Attorney General John Douglas worked full time on the March for five weeks during the summer and helped prevent the event from becoming a negative attack on the government that would have lost congressional votes for the President's civil rights legislation. The FBI also noted that the Communist Party USA had publicly endorsed the March and instructed its members to participate. The FBI's wiretaps on Stanley Levison's telephones provided some basic information on the plans of the March leaders, but the desperate need for more inside information only reinforced the pressure to tap King's telephones.

J. Edgar Hoover also turned up the pressure on Robert Kennedy to approve wiretaps. At the end of July 1963, Hoover sent the Attorney General a report entitled "Martin Luther King, Jr.: Affiliation with the Communist Movement." The report contained various allegations against King and Levison, including the third-hand report that King had once said, "I am a Marxist." On October 15, the Bureau distributed another report with allegations against King, this time titled "Communism and the Negro Movement—A Current Analysis." FBI Assistant to the Director Alan Belmont warned his superiors at the Bureau that the report "can be regarded as a personal attack on Martin Luther King. There is no doubt it will have a heavy impact on the Attorney General ... particularly in view of his past associations with King, and the fact that we are disseminating this outside the Department. He may resent this."[47] Hoover waved away the warning, arguing that "we must do our duty."[48] The Attorney General was indeed outraged when he read the report, particularly when he was told that it had also been given to the secretaries of state and defense, as well as to various agencies in the intelligence community. According to Kennedy, the report was "very, very unfair" and contained derogatory information concerning Levison, but no information "which indicated that he didn't want to have anything to do with the Communists."[49] Kennedy ordered the report recalled, and Hoover reluctantly agreed.* But the Bureau continued its

---

*Hoover rereleased the report the next year, however, after Robert Kennedy left the Justice Department to run for the U.S. Senate seat from New York.

assault on the civil rights leader. In the wake of the successful March and the almost universal praise for Reverend King's "I Have a Dream" speech on the steps of the Lincoln Memorial, FBI Assistant Director William Sullivan attacked the oration as a "demagogic speech" that proved that King was "the most dangerous and effective Negro leader in the country."[50] When King was named *Time* magazine's Man of the Year at the end of 1963, Hoover remarked that "they had to dig deep in the garbage to come up with this one."[51]

The civil rights legislation introduced by the President on June 19, 1963, further increased the pressure on Robert Kennedy to approve the use of wiretaps on King. As expected, the legislation elicited fierce opposition from Southern senators and representatives. Although the bill initially fared well in the House of Representatives, the Senate Judiciary Committee, which was dominated by southerners, blocked the legislation. Their arguments against it were numerous. Southern Senators contended variously that it was a violation of state's rights, that discrimination in the South was exaggerated and did not need outside intervention, and, as Senator Sam Ervin said, that the bill was "as drastic and indefensible a proposal as has ever been submitted to this Congress."[52] These arguments were nothing new, and the Kennedy administration was largely prepared for them. However, the assertion that the civil rights movement was infiltrated by communists particularly rankled the Attorney General. Senator James Eastland of Mississippi, taking his cue from information leaked to him from the FBI, accused King of being advised by communists and of having communist sympathies himself.

The charge of communist infiltration was not original, but it was a powerful instrument in the hands of segregationists intent on derailing civil rights legislation by any possible means. Moderate Democrats and Republicans who might otherwise vote for the bill could easily be swayed by anticommunist rhetoric. Robert Kennedy was particularly sensitive to this charge, in part because he had not yet resolved for himself whether it was true. He had publicly aligned himself and the Kennedy administration with Martin Luther King, and the allegations against Levison damaged not only King but the Kennedys as well. As the debate heated on Capitol Hill, Robert Kennedy came under increasing pressure to determine the truth of the accusations. According to Burke Marshall, the charges against King "were grave and serious, and the inquiries from the Senate and from the public, both to the President and to the Attorney General, as well as the Bureau, had to be answered and they had to be answered fully."[53] Also, the Attorney General feared

the intervention of the FBI Director into the political process if he did
not consent to Hoover's demands. "He felt that if he did not [approve
the wiretaps], Hoover would move to impede or block the passage of
the Civil Rights Bill," Kennedy's former press secretary said.[54] On
October 7, 1963, when the FBI again proposed the installation of a
wiretap "on King at his current address or at any future address to
which he may move," the Attorney General reluctantly agreed, with
the stipulation that the taps be reevaluated after thirty days. But in
November, just when the wiretaps were scheduled for reevaluation,
President John F. Kennedy was murdered in Dallas.

The Bureau wasted little time in installing the wiretaps. The SCLC's
New York office came under electronic surveillance on October 24,
1963, and King's home and Atlanta office were added two weeks later.
The Bureau broadly interpreted their authorization to tap Dr. King and
quickly moved beyond the intent of the Attorney General. After personally reauthorizing the wiretaps for an additional three months, J. Edgar
Hoover instructed his agents to begin planting microphones in the hotel
rooms in which King stayed on his trips outside Atlanta. On at least
fifteen occasions over the next two years, the FBI bugged King's hotel
rooms, beginning with the Willard Hotel in Washington, D.C., on January 5, 1964, and then continuing through King's trips to Milwaukee,
Honolulu, Los Angeles, and other cities. The Willard microphone was
installed, according to a Bureau memorandum, as a result of the "intelligence *and counterintelligence* possibilities which through coverage of
Dr. King's activities might develop."[55] The Willard bug was a boon
for the FBI, but not for the reasons they suspected.

Rather than developing information that King was taking advice from
communists, the Bureau instead recorded "a lively party involving
King, several SCLC colleagues, and two black women who worked at
the Philadelphia Naval Yard."[56] It was the first time that Bureau agents
had peered into King's private life, and they were delighted by the
extramarital affair that they discovered. The FBI recorded nineteen reels
of tape from the party, and the tapes were quickly transcribed. William
Sullivan described the contents of the tapes in a memorandum to the
Director a week later, with the recommendation that the information be
forwarded to the White House. According to Sullivan, the White House
should be informed "inasmuch as Dr. King is seeking an appointment
with President Johnson."[57] Hoover asked Cartha Deloach to bring the
news to Walter Jenkins, who had replaced the Kennedy favorite Courtney Evans as the Bureau liaison to the White House. According to
DeLoach, "Jenkins was of the opinion that the FBI could perform a

good service to the country if this matter could somehow be confidentially given to members of the press. I told him the Director had this in mind, however, he also believed we should obtain additional information prior to discussing it with certain friends."*

The Bureau continued trying to find the details of Dr. King's extramarital affairs. Three weeks after the first microphone was installed in the Willard, the Bureau bugged Milwaukee's Shroeder Hotel, where King was staying. The Milwaukee SAC, however, argued against the bug, telling William Sullivan that stringent police protection for King most likely would preclude any activity on King's part. "I don't share the conjecture," Hoover scrawled on Sullivan's memo recommending the removal of the bug. "King is a 'tom cat' with degenerate sexual urges."[58] The bug remained, but recorded nothing of interest to the Bureau. Yet the FBI was undaunted and installed a microphone the next month in the Hilton Hawaiian Village Hotel during King's vacation in Honolulu. The justification for the microphones had changed since their original use in Washington. No longer did the Bureau claim to be investigating the connection between King and members of the Communist Party. Rather, the Honolulu bug was installed, the Bureau stated, to record "the [private] activities of Dr. King and his associates" so that he could be "completely discredited."[59] (William Sullivan even suggested replacing King as the most visible civil rights leader with a more moderate African American whose attitudes were more suitable to the Bureau.)

The discovery of the weakness in King's private life gave the Bureau another major weapon to use against him. J. Edgar Hoover, who had often used allegations of sexual deviance—meaning any sexual act of which Hoover disapproved—against enemies in the past, now seized the opportunity to use the tactic against King. Hoover had expended enormous amounts of the Bureau's resources in tracking down allegations of homosexuality, infidelity, or excessive sexual appetites in a wide range of public figures. The Director turned his personal fascination into a bureaucratic weapon. King's sex life offended Hoover both because King was a married man who had broken his vow of fidelity, and because ministers were required to be above such carnal urges. Hoover was not alone in his belief that King had committed an outra-

---

*King FBI File. Memorandum from Cartha DeLoach to J. Edgar Hoover, 1/14/64. Jenkins, however, later disputed DeLoach's contention that he had suggested giving the material to the press.

geous moral offense, and the publicity around such an offense would
be certain to stigmatize him. As one FBI agent reported, "we are continuing to follow closely King's activities and giving consideration to
every possibility for future similar coverage that will add to our record
on King so that in the end he might be discredited and thus be removed
from his position of great stature in the Negro community."[60]

The Bureau continued to follow King as he returned from Hawaii
through Los Angeles, where the Bureau found more evidence of his
adultery. During a party one evening at the Hyatt House Motel in Los
Angeles, the Bureau recorded several jokes of a sexual nature told by
King, one of which involved former First Lady Jacqueline Kennedy
and her dead husband. J. Edgar Hoover immediately passed the information both to Walter Jenkins at the White House and to Attorney General
Robert Kennedy, since Kennedy was considering inviting King to a
memorial for his brother. This information will "remove all doubt from
the Attorney General's mind as to the type of person King is. It will
probably also eliminate King from any participation" in the planned
memorial.[61] Hoover also passed information gained from wiretaps and
microphones to the White House when King visited Los Angeles to
speak to the Republican National Convention in July 1964. The Bureau
wiretapped King's hotel phone during his trip the next month to the
Democratic National Convention in Atlantic City, and all useful political
information was automatically sent to the White House. President Lyndon B. Johnson, pleased at the information that he was receiving from
the FBI, asked no questions about where the information came from,
thereby indirectly encouraging the Bureau to continue its microphone
surveillance.

Martin Luther King, meanwhile, sought to combat the growing FBI-
inspired impression that the civil rights struggle was heavily infiltrated
by communists. "It is time for this question [of communist infiltration]
to be buried all over the nation," King said in a press conference on
May 10, 1964. "Communism is based on a denial of human freedom."
"It's tough enough being black without being black and red at the same
time," James Farmer chimed in at the news conference.[62] At a rally
before twenty-five hundred people in Jackson, Mississippi, on July 23,
King said he was "sick and tired of people saying this movement has
been infiltrated by communists and communist sympathizers.... There
are as many communists in this freedom movement as there are eskimos
in Florida."[63]

During 1964, the FBI stepped up its pace of spreading opprobrious
information against Martin Luther King. In March, when the Bureau

was informed that King might receive an honorary degree from Marquette University in Milwaukee, Bureau agents were dispatched to brief a university official on the FBI's derogatory information about him. "It is shocking indeed that the possibility exists that King may receive an Honorary Degree from the same institution which honored the Director with such a degree in 1950," one Bureau official wrote.[64] Similar attempts were made to discourage Springfield College from awarding King a degree the next month. The FBI even tried to prevent the Pope from granting him an audience during King's visit to Europe in September 1964. "It would be shocking indeed for such an unscrupulous character as King to receive an audience with the Pope," one agent reported. "It ought to be nipped in the bud."[65] The Bureau dispatched the assistant SAC of the New York office to brief Catholic official Francis Cardinal Spellman on King's personal life, but the attempt to discredit King failed, since he met with the Pope on schedule the next month.

The Bureau also attempted to dilute the glory of Martin Luther King's Nobel Peace Prize, which was announced on October 14, 1964. The Bureau briefed numerous American government officials who would play a part in King's receipt of the prize, giving them information on his private life and supposed connection with communists. The Bureau disseminated information to the American ambassadors to Norway, Sweden, England, and Denmark. According to the Bureau, "the Ambassadors might consider entertaining King while he is in Europe to receive the Nobel Peace Prize," so the FBI sought to "forestall such action by the Ambassadors."[66] American representatives to the United Nations Ralph Bunche and Adlai Stevenson were also briefed, as were various politicians, including Vice President Hubert Humphrey and New York Governor Nelson Rockefeller, both of whom were potential participants in the congratulatory ceremonies for King when he returned from Europe.[67]

The Bureau also sought to undercut congressional support for King and the civil rights movement. In his annual appearance before the House Appropriations Committee in April 1964, Hoover explained that communists had infiltrated the movement and were in a position to influence large numbers of people. Dr. King sent out an immediate response to Hoover's comments, which were reported in the press the next day. "It is very unfortunate," King said

> that Mr. J. Edgar Hoover, in his claims of alleged communist infiltration in the civil rights movement, has allowed himself to aid and abet the salacious claims of southern racists and the extreme right-wing elements. . . . It is difficult to accept the word of the FBI on

communist infiltration in the civil rights movement, when they have been so completely ineffectual in resolving the continued mayhem and brutality inflicted upon the Negro in the deep south. It would be encouraging to us if Mr. Hoover and the FBI would be as diligent in apprehending those responsible for bombing churches and killing little children as they are in seeking out alleged communist infiltration in the civil rights movement.[68]

"The Most Notorious Liar"

The personal animosity between J. Edgar Hoover and Martin Luther King, Jr., went public during a press conference in November 1964. It was a rare appearance for Hoover, who generally avoided contacts with the media, but on this occasion he invited eighteen female reporters to his office for coffee. In line with his habit of talking incessantly, the press conference went on for three hours, while Hoover extemporized on a wide range of subjects. He outlined what he considered to be his evenhanded approach to the southern struggle for racial equality by attacking both sides of the conflict. In Mississippi, he noted, "in the swamp country, the only inhabitants seem to be rattlesnakes, water moccasins, and redneck sheriffs." But in explaining the failure of the FBI to intercede on behalf of the civil rights activists, Hoover explained that the Bureau "can't wet nurse everybody who goes down to try to reform or re-educate the Negro population of the South."[69]

It was his comments on King, however, that made the headlines the next day. Hoover launched into a criticism of Dr. King, who had not been forgiven for his 1962 comments concerning the southern bias of the Bureau. Off the record, he called King "one of the lowest characters in the country." But the most quotable comments on King were made for the record. "I asked [for a meeting] with Dr. King, but he would not make the appointment, so I have characterized him as the most notorious liar in the country."[70] In an effort to head off a public-relations disaster, Cartha DeLoach, who attended the press conference, slipped Hoover a note in which he asked that the Director clarify that this comment was off the record, but Hoover ignored DeLoach's plea. DeLoach sent two more notes to Hoover, who finally in a fit of anger declared loudly to DeLoach, "I will not." Then turning back to the reporters, he said, "DeLoach is trying to tell me to take that off the record, but I will not."[71]

The press reaction was immediate, and editorial pages denounced either King or Hoover, depending on the political orientation and geographic location of the newspaper. *The Herald* from Albany, Georgia, wrote an editorial entitled "The Demagogue King" on November 19, which reflected on the year that King had been having. "On the one hand, he received the Nobel Peace Prize after fomenting the greatest upheaval in this country since the Boston Tea Party. On the other, he earned the dubious distinction of being labeled 'the most notorious liar in the country' by no less an authority than the chief investigative officer of the United States government. Quite evidently, somebody is wrong about the man. Could it be the Nobel Peace Prize Committee, which sits from afar to view men and events? Or could it be J. Edgar Hoover, director of the Federal Bureau of Investigation, whose knowledge of individuals and their activities in the United States is unsurpassed by that of any other single citizen in the nation?"[72]

The news of Hoover's intemperate attack interrupted a much-needed vacation for King in the Bahamas. As King deliberated his response to Hoover, his advisor Harry Wachtel penned a sample statement that King could issue, in which he referred to the necessity of Hoover's retirement from the Bureau. "The distemper of Mr. Hoover," Wachtel wrote, "does, however, establish one thing clearly to the American people and that is that he has outlived his usefulness as the head of the FBI or as a public servant. I am confident that this public display of distemper will not go unnoticed by the President." Wachtel discussed the possible response with King's aide Bayard Rustin on the day after Hoover's comments, and Rustin approved of the draft with a few modifications. The FBI monitored this conversation, as indicated in a November 19 memo to William Sullivan.

The memo made note of Rustin's past communist affiliations. It also commented that "Harry Wachtel is not known to have been a Communist Party member; however, there are indications he may also have been associated with the communist movement in the 1940's and we presently are conducting [an] investigation to determine this." Based on the assumed communist affiliations of Rustin and Wachtel, the memo goes on to indicate that

> The significant thing involved here is not that these individuals have jumped quickly to King's defense, but rather that they are seizing the opportunity, in line with a long-held communist objective, to launch a campaign to oust the Director as head of the FBI. The important thing at this point is to follow this matter closely to deter-

mine the degree to which King follows their advice in regard to issuing the statement prepared by Wachtel for we will then have further evidence of the extent to which King is being used by communist sympathizers in support of communist objectives.[73]

King did not use Wachtel's sample response as his official statement to the press, but he did indicate his agreement with the "communist objective" that Hoover should step down as FBI Director. King's office in Atlanta sent a telegram to Hoover on the morning of November 19, and also submitted copies to the press. "I was appalled and surprised," he wrote,

at your reported statement maligning my integrity. What motivated such an irresponsible accusation is a mystery to me. I have sincerely questioned the effectiveness of the Federal Bureau of Investigation in racial incidents, particularly where bombings and brutalities against Negroes are at issue, but I have never attributed this merely to the presence of Southerners in the FBI. This is a part of the broader question of federal involvement in the protection of Negroes in the South and the seeming inability to gain convictions in even the most heinous crimes perpetuated against civil rights workers. It remains a fact that not a single arrest was made in Albany, Georgia, during the many brutalities against Negroes. Neither has a single arrest been made in connection with the tragic murder of the four children in Birmingham, nor in the case of the three murdered civil rights workers in Mississippi. Moreover, FBI agents inevitably work with local law enforcement officers in car thefts, bank robberies, and other interstate violations. This makes it difficult for them to function effectively in cases where the rights and safety of Negro citizens are being threatened by these same law enforcement officers. I will be happy to discuss this question with you at length in the near future. Although your statement said that you have attempted to meet with me I have sought in vain for any record of such a request. I have always made myself available to all FBI agents of the Atlanta office and encouraged our staff and affiliates to cooperate with them in spite of the fact that many of our people have suspicions and distrust of the FBI as a result of the slow pace of justice in the South.[74]

King also made a brief public statement to the press in which he more directly attacked the FBI Director. "I cannot conceive of Mr.

Hoover making a statement like this without being under extreme pressure. He has apparently faltered under the awesome burden, complexities, and responsibilities of his office. Therefore, I cannot engage in a public debate with him. I have nothing but sympathy for this man who has served his country so well.'' King also told his Atlanta secretary in a phone call monitored by the FBI that the Director was "too old and broken down" to continue in his position.[75] The official response from Hoover's supposed superiors in Washington was silence. Acting Attorney General Nicholas Katzenbach, in a press conference in Miami, told reporters that he would not "add or detract" from Hoover's statement against King. He did, however, indicate his confidence in the Director and his desire that Hoover remain in his position at the FBI. President Johnson had even less to say in response to the conflict. At a meeting with several civil rights leaders, Roy Wilkins of the NAACP told the President that they were in substantial agreement with King in his charges against Hoover. The President, however, "gave no comment and no opinion," Wilkins later reported.[76]

President Johnson attempted to stay in the background of the controversy, avoiding criticizing either his powerful FBI Director or his powerful civil rights ally. When asked in a press conference about the conflict, Johnson artfully avoided the question, arguing that both men had simply exercised their "freedom of speech." In an ambiguous response, he added that Hoover "has been diligent and rather effective, and I would hope that in the months ahead we would have further evidence of the outstanding capacity of his people, and that this would not degenerate into a battle of personalities."[77] Reporters were split in their interpretation of the answer, some contending that it represented unadulterated praise for the Director, while others saw it as a warning to the Director to increase his involvement in civil rights. According to one reporter, "correspondents at President Johnson's news conferences have learned that his footwork in avoiding a direct answer to a troublesome question is similar to that of a championship boxer ducking a punch."[78] Johnson was unequivocal, however, in his effort to squelch rumors that he planned to replace Hoover as FBI Director.

The Meeting

"I do not plan to engage in public debate with Mr. Hoover," King announced at a press conference at Stamford, Connecticut, on November 30, "and I think the time has come for all this controversy to end and for all of us to get on with the larger job of civil rights and law enforcement. On the basis of this, I request a conference with Mr. Hoover to talk about this whole problem of law enforcement in the South."[79] King and his aides had finally decided that a face-to-face meeting would prevent the Hoover controversy "from becoming the principal focus of the [civil rights] struggle."[80] The summit meeting between King and Hoover was arranged for the next day, December 1, through a mutual friend to King and Cartha DeLoach. King arrived at FBI headquarters in Washington for his three-thirty meeting with the Director, flanked by his aides Ralph Abernathy, Andrew Young, and SCLC Washington representative Walter Fauntroy.

Abernathy began the meeting with some conciliatory words and then turned to King for more detailed remarks. According to DeLoach's record of the conversation, King lavished praise on the Director, stating that "some Negroes had told him that the FBI had been ineffective, however, he was inclined to discount such criticism. Reverend King asked that the Director please understand that any criticism of the Director and the FBI which had been attributed to King was either a misquote or an outright misrepresentation. . . . Reverend King stated he has never made any personal attack upon Mr. Hoover."* When King concluded his brief remarks, the Director launched into a fifty-five-minute monologue, lauding the efforts of the Bureau in solving civil-rights crimes and attacking the communist influence in the civil rights movement. King and Abernathy made only rare comments, splicing them in between Hoover's ranting. The hour-long meeting having concluded without substantive dialogue, the King party got up and politely left the Director's office. King read a prepared statement to the assembled members of the media, calling it an "amicable meeting" to clear up the misunderstandings between the FBI and the SCLC. "I think it is important that we forget the confusions of the past and get on with the tasks which the President, the Supreme Court, and Congress have outlined," he said.[81]

Reactions to the meeting varied. Cartha DeLoach said later that "I fully expected it to be a confrontation. However, to the contrary, it was more or less of a love feast with Mr. Hoover telling Dr. King that Dr. King is a symbol of leadership for 12 million Negroes and should be

---

*King FBI File. Memorandum from Cartha DeLoach to John Mohr, December 2, 1964. Andrew Young later disagreed with DeLoach's recollection of the meeting, stating that King's praise for Hoover was far more reserved than DeLoach indicated.

careful about his associations and about his personal conduct.''[82] Andrew Young, however, later called it ''a completely non-functional
meeting'' because of the lack of dialogue and the failure to resolve the
issues that had precipitated the difficulties between King and Hoover.[83]
But there was, Young agreed, ''not even an attitude of hostility. In fact
Hoover was very disarming in that he congratulated Dr. King for having
won the Nobel Prize, and as far as we are concerned, this was not the
same man that called Martin a notorious liar. We attributed it to the
fact of his age and the kinds of possible fluctuations that are possible
with people under pressure in advanced years.''[84] Tensions between the
SCLC and the FBI dissipated somewhat after the meeting, and observers
generally regarded the summit as a success. According to Young, the
FBI soon arrested suspects in the triple murder of civil rights workers
in Philadelphia, Mississippi. ''So in a sense we were reassured that the
FBI was doing its law enforcement job, and we hoped the personal
tensions, as far as Dr. King was concerned, were over and done.''[85]

But the public controversy between King and Hoover escalated privately, as the Bureau initiated the cruelest counterintelligence program
that they had yet used against King. After returning from Oslo, where
the civil rights leader accepted the Nobel Peace Prize, King's wife
Coretta discovered a package that had been mailed anonymously by the
Bureau thirty-four days before Christmas and ten days before the summit meeting with Hoover. The package contained an unsigned letter
along with a recording of some excerpts of the Bureau's surveillance
on King. The tape included the unmistakable sounds of King's voice
making lewd sexual jokes and additional recordings of sexual activity
in which King presumably had been a participant. The ungrammatical
letter warned King that the tape was about to be made public.

King, look into your heart. You know you are a complete fraud and
a great liability to all of us Negroes. White people in this country
have enough frauds of their own but I am sure they don't have one
at this time that is anywhere near your equal. You are no clergyman
and you know it. I repeat you are a colossal fraud and an evil, vicious
one at that. . . . The American public, the church organizations that
have been helping—Protestant, Catholic and Jews will know you for
what you are—an evil, abnormal beast. So will others who have
backed you. You are done. King, there is only one thing for you to
do. You have just 34 days in which to do (this exact number has been
selected for a specific reason, it has definite practical significant). You

are done. There is but one way out for you. You better take it before your filthy, abnormal self is bared to the nation.[86]

The meaning of the threat was unclear. The recipients of the tape interpreted a far more sinister implication than was apparently intended by the Bureau. FBI Assistant Director William Sullivan told congressional investigators a decade later that the Bureau simply sought to embarrass King publicly and force him to resign his position in the SCLC. But King and his aides saw a different message. According to Andrew Young, "I think the most disturbing thing to Martin was that he felt somebody was trying to get him to commit suicide."[87] King and his aides interpreted the note as a directive to King to kill himself before Christmas Day or the tape would be made public. Although many historians have described this event as an explicit attempt to force King to kill himself, it is more likely that Sullivan was correct in his belief that "the FBI's goal was simply to convince Dr. King to resign from the SCLC, not to kill himself."[88]

The revelations in the tape would almost certainly ruin King, since the lewd jokes and the sexual acts would be seen as unbecoming a married minister. The public disclosure of King's private life had been a concern of civil rights leaders for years, since his dalliances with other women were not a well-kept secret. The revelations would have a detrimental effect not only on King and his family, but also on the SCLC and the entire civil rights movement.

The source of the tape was never in doubt. Only the Federal Bureau of Investigation would have the resources to place surveillance devices in King's hotel rooms. Andrew Young and other King aides knew immediately upon hearing the tape that J. Edgar Hoover was responsible. "Because it was a tape of a meeting in Washington and the postmark was from Florida, we assumed nobody had the capacity to do that other than the Federal Bureau of Investigation."[89] "They are out to break me," King reported to a friend. "They are out to get me, harass me, break my spirit," he told another.[90] King was increasingly distraught over the Bureau's attempts to malign him and was almost overcome by the constant pressures in his life. FBI agents, who were aware of these pressures, tried to compound them. As King was trying to rest in Atlanta and recover from the stress caused by the FBI's anonymous package, agents called the fire department and sent fire trucks to King's address to unnerve him.[91]

But despite the high level of tension at the end of 1964, the next two years were relatively quiescent in the relationship between King and the FBI. Although the tensions remained, they did not boil over publicly again before King's death. The Bureau, at the behest of J. Edgar Hoover, continued to disseminate derogatory information concerning King, but the FBI's actions demonstrated a calculated approach to discrediting King rather than the raw emotional approach of the previous years. The Bureau sought to remove King from the civil rights movement simply by collecting and spreading embarrassing information about him. Efforts such as the anonymous package would not be repeated in the three years before his death, and the emotional pressure on King from the FBI reached its peak at the end of 1964 and lessened thereafter. The Bureau also decreased the level of electronic surveillance on King in 1965, most likely in response to Missouri Senator Edward Long's call for congressional investigations into the FBI's practices of wiretapping and bugging. Ironically, the threatened investigation was being encouraged by President Johnson, although he had little concern over the excess of the Bureau. Instead, Johnson quietly pushed for the hearings in order to discredit Robert Kennedy, than Johnson's main Democratic opponent, for his role in approving wiretapping as Attorney General. "He is out to get Bobby," presidential aide Bill Moyers reported.[92] The FBI Director also became far more reluctant to use electronic surveillance in his final years, apparently in fear of being caught installing illegal microphones.

Discrediting King

The Bureau spread allegations against King to three primary groups: government officials, the media, and private citizens who sought to aid King. The Bureau continued to supply members of Congress with reproachful information about King, including details from both his alleged ties with communists and his private life. In August 1965, DeLoach briefed House Speaker John McCormack on the details of King's private life at the Speaker's request. DeLoach later reported that McCormack "now recognized the gravity of the situation and that something obviously must be done about it."[93] The Bureau also briefed the governor of a state that had considered sponsoring a Martin Luther King Day; members of the Internal Revenue Service who had invited King to be a guest lecturer; and the commandant of the Marine Corps, who was interested in the budding ties between King and peace protesters.[94]

The press had always been a favorite target for the Bureau and had been used successfully against King earlier in the 1960s with the Jack O'Dell stories. Friendly media people were cultivated by FBI personnel and would be rewarded with selective leaks of information from FBI files. Ralph McGill of the *Atlanta Constitution* was a frequent recipient of the Bureau's information about King, and McGill went out of his way to remain in the Bureau's favor. According to William Sullivan, McGill helped the Bureau contact Atlanta bankers who were providing funds for a congratulatory banquet in early 1965 after King won the Nobel Peace Prize. According to the FBI, McGill initially succeeded in convincing the bankers to withdraw from the banquet.*

The Bureau, however, was remarkably unsuccessful in convincing reporters to print the derogatory information concerning King. Most refused to print the potentially libelous material. FBI agents even played surveillance tapes of King to reporters, allowing them to peer into his private life. But they still refused. According to former *Atlanta Constitution* editor Eugene Patterson,

> Agents of the Atlanta FBI bureau visited us in our offices and alleged they had proof of Dr. King's involvement in extra-marital affairs. . . . When I tried to explain we did not publish a peephole journal, and told the agent a person's private life is not news, he hotly criticized *The Constitution* for supporting Dr. King's public leadership and binding its readers to his private 'immorality'. . . . [We] were astonished and outraged that our friends in the FBI Atlanta bureau had been assigned, obviously by Hoover, to such a dirty business as character assassination, and by these sleazy means.[95]

The Bureau, however, was undeterred and continued in its attempts to influence the media against King. In one case, the Bureau approached *Washington Post* reporter Ben Bradlee and offered him information on King's private life. Bradlee refused, and word of the Bureau's offer found its way back to the Justice Department. Nicholas Katzenbach, Robert Kennedy's replacement as attorney general, was shocked when he learned of the Bureau's actions. On a scheduled visit to the Presi-

---

*The Atlanta bankers, however, were threatened by Haitian bankers with whom they were concluding a lucrative deal that the deal would be off if support for the banquet was not assured. According to William Sullivan, the Atlanta bankers "got cold feet and decided to go ahead with financing King's party." (King FBI File. Memorandum from William Sullivan to Alan Belmont, 1/21/65).

dent's ranch in Texas, Katzenbach told Johnson of the Bureau's obvious breach of impartiality. The President, rather than being upset with the FBI's attempt to discredit King, became upset only with the public manner in which it had been done. When he returned to Washington, he instructed his aide Bill Moyers to inform the FBI that Bradlee had been talking about the episode and that he could not be trusted. The President did not, however, tell the Bureau to stop leaking information on King, only that it should be careful to whom it was leaked. Johnson, always thinking of politics first, apparently thought only of the damage that would be done to his political enemy Robert Kennedy if his ally King were discredited. The damage to King and the civil rights movement was apparently only peripheral in his mind.

The Bureau also sought to curry the favor of those in the private sector and turn them against King. When the FBI learned that the Ford Foundation was preparing a grant for King and the Southern Christian Leadership Conference, the Bureau asked a former FBI agent who was then the vice president of Ford Motors to intervene with the foundation director, McGeorge Bundy. Bundy, however, refused to speak to the former agent about King, insisting that he would not accept second-hand rumors as fact. J. Edgar Hoover did not try to influence Bundy any further, arguing that "we would get no where with Bundy."[96] The Bureau also briefed various religious leaders who associated with King under the assumption that they would be morally offended by King's actions. The head of the American Church in Paris was told of King's private life and of his alleged communist connections, as was the Archbishop of the Diocese in Chicago, John Cardinal Cody, who had recently declared his support for King's civil rights movement. It is not known, however, whether these briefings or others had any effect on Martin Luther King, although the FBI reported that Cardinal Cody indicated he would "do everything possible to neutralize King's effect."*

The FBI stepped back into high gear in 1967, as Dr. King's awareness of—and opposition to—the war in Vietnam intensified. Although he had made various statements about his moral opposition to the war, he had been steadily pressured not to speak out too vehemently against the war. His active involvement in the anti-Vietnam movement would have deleterious effects on the civil-rights movement, King's aides ad-

---

*Cardinal Cody later denied that he had agreed to oppose Reverend King, insisting that the report was "absolutely untrue." Gruenberg, Robert. "FBI's Try to Use Cody Against Dr. King Told." *Chicago Daily News,* June 10, 1976.

vised him. First, it would take attention away from civil rights and force King to spend less time crusading for civil rights and more time denouncing the war. Second, opposition to Vietnam would place King in direct conflict with President Johnson, who had been very responsive to the need for civil rights gains and who had been instrumental in the passage of the 1964 Civil Rights Act and the 1965 Voting Rights Act. But Vietnam was Lyndon Johnson's personal war. Whereas President Kennedy had sought to defuse the crisis through a negotiated settlement, President Johnson sought to escalate it through military engagement. King's vocal opposition to the Vietnam War would almost certainly eliminate any opportunity for further cooperation with the President or additional congressional legislation on civil rights.

There was little debate in Martin Luther King's mind over the morality of the war. He was a pacifist by nature and objected to the headlong plunge into military conflict without first seriously attempting a negotiated peace. King also quickly realized that he could not stay silent about an issue that weighed so heavily on his conscience. He was, after all, a recipient of the Nobel Peace Prize, and his views on Vietnam could not be easily dismissed. "I'm not going to sit by and see the war escalate without saying something about it," he said in 1965. "It is worthless to talk about integrating if there is no world to integrate in. The war in Vietnam must be stopped."[97] But King refrained from making the war a major issue in his speeches. The few statements he did make about it elicited almost universal condemnation, since in the mid-1960s the war remained popular with the American public and in Congress.

The Federal Bureau of Investigation carefully tracked King's development in the peace movement and reported his anti-Vietnam comments to the White House. President Johnson was keenly interested in those who opposed his policies in Vietnam and asked the Bureau to follow dissenters, such as Martin Luther King, who could affect public opinion about the war. The increasing violence in Vietnam—and the increasing dissent at home—finally forced King to make public his views about Vietnam. He gave up the middle ground that he had been treading on April 4, 1967, exactly a year before he was killed. In a major speech at the Riverside Church in New York under the sponsorship of the Clergy and Laymen Concerned about Vietnam, King attacked both the immorality of the war and the American government for conducting it. It was a passionate and eloquent speech, full of moral conviction and personal anguish. He told the three thousand listeners that he was making a "passionate plea to my beloved country" to end the war. He talked of the promises that were made to the American people by the Johnson Administration that there would be a War on Poverty rather than a war on the people of Vietnam. "We have been repeatedly faced with the cruel irony of watching Negro and white boys on TV screens as they kill and die together for a nation that has been unable to seat them together in the same schools. So we watch them in brutal solidarity burning the huts of a poor village, but we realize that they would never live on the same block in Detroit. I could not be silent in the face of such cruel manipulation."[98] He told the audience that he could not attack violence in urban America without condemning "the greatest purveyor of violence in the world today—my own government."[99]

Transcripts of the speech were sent to the White House by the Bureau, and the President was predictably angered by King's statements. The speech ended the lull in the relationship between King and the FBI, and the Bureau eagerly began collecting information on King's political associations and statements concerning Vietnam. The speech at the Riverside Church, the FBI reported, demonstrated that King "has been influenced by communist advisers." The Bureau augmented that statement with the justification that King's speech was "a direct parallel of the communist position on Vietnam."[100] The 1963 report that was distributed by the Bureau and recalled by Robert Kennedy was revised to include more recent material and redistributed. Copies were sent to the Attorney General, the White House, the secretaries of defense and state, the commandant of the Marine Corps, and the director of the Secret Service. The report was revised again the next year and distributed shortly before King's death.

The Bureau continued its pattern of spreading information about King, as it collected political information on him and sent it to the White House, briefed members of the press and government agencies about his alleged communist connections and supposed moral depravity, and brainstormed for methods of reducing his effectiveness in the civil rights field and the anti-Vietnam protest movement. At the end of 1967, the FBI formally initiated the counterintelligence program (COINTEL-PRO) against "black nationalist hate groups," and King's SCLC was included along with organizations such as the Nation of Islam and the Revolutionary Action Movement. In March 1968, the Bureau outlined the goals of the COINTELPRO, which included the need to

prevent the rise of a "Messiah" who could unify and electrify the militant black nationalist movement. Malcolm X might have been such a "messiah;" he is the martyr of the movement today. Martin

Luther King, Stokely Carmichael, and Elijah Muhammad all aspire to this position. Elijah Muhammad is less of a threat because of his age. King could be a real contender for this position should he abandon his supposed "obedience" to "white, liberal doctrines" (nonviolence) and embrace black nationalism.[101]

Martin Luther King was murdered in Memphis, Tennessee, on April 4, 1968, one month after this memo was written. According to one FBI agent, "the Director didn't exactly light any candles after King was killed."[102] The Bureau worked dutifully to capture King's killer and finally aided in tracking him down in London two months later. But the FBI continued to dabble in politics even after King's death. Rather than immediately announcing the capture of King's assailant, the Bureau cynically waited to announce the development until the funeral of Robert Kennedy—a Hoover enemy—was underway, in order to take attention away from the second slain Kennedy brother. The FBI did not suspend its campaign against King even after his death. The next year, as Congress considered instituting a national holiday on King's birthday, the Bureau agreed to brief select members of Congress on King's "true" nature. The rationale was that Congress would not vote for such a memorial if "they realize King was a scoundrel." Cartha DeLoach noted that the briefing "is a delicate matter—but can be handled very cautiously." "I agree," the Director added. "It must be handled *very* cautiously."[103] A year after Martin Luther King's death, the Atlanta Bureau office proposed to headquarters a plan to begin an operation against King's widow, Coretta Scott King. The plan was to serve "in the event the bureau (FBI) is inclined to entertain counter-intelligence action against [her] and-or the continuous projection of the public image" of Dr. King. In a rare display of restraint, J. Edgar Hoover rejected the idea, simply stating that "the bureau does not desire counterintelligence action against Coretta King at this time."[104]

With the passing of J. Edgar Hoover, I am reminded that almighty God conducts the ultimate surveillance.

—SCLC Director Ralph Abernathy on the death of the Bureau Director on May 2, 1972.

3

Politics and Prejudice

The saga of Martin Luther King, Jr., and the FBI is one of the clearest examples of the corruption of the American intelligence community in the postwar era. Never subject to the oversight of government investigators, the Federal Bureau of Investigation conducted a war against an American citizen for over six years. The FBI was in essence a mercenary army, dedicated to fulfilling the desires of a single man, J. Edgar Hoover. The extent of his control over the Bureau can hardly be exaggerated. It was a dictatorship in which dissenters were continually disciplined and dismissed so that Hoover could retain hegemonic control. The persecution of Martin Luther King was Hoover's own private war, driven by his intense abhorrence of the southern preacher and by his own unquestioned grip on the reigns of power at the FBI. The animosity between the Bureau and Martin Luther King was the result of two connected factors: Hoover's personal hatred of King and the inability of anyone inside or outside the FBI to temper it.

The motivation behind the FBI's fascination with Martin Luther King is at first far from obvious. King sought to work in conjunction with the federal government rather than against it and did not present a direct danger to the government. Indeed, King was a moderate among civil rights leaders, with Roy Wilkins of the NAACP on his right and John Lewis and Stokely Carmichael of the Student Nonviolent Coordinating

Committee on his left. The FBI, and the federal government in general, certainly had an interest in controlling radical tendencies within the movement that could incite violence. But the desire to control radical and violent tendencies was not the motivation behind the FBI's harassment of King. The civil rights movement presented far more radical leaders whose challenges to the government were far more dangerous than King's.

The various leaders of SNCC fell into this category. When SNCC began as an offshoot of King's Southern Christian Leadership Conference in the wake of the 1960 student sit-ins, it presented no immediate threat from the government's perspective. But the students soon began to outgrow the paternalistic attitude of the SCLC and showed an independence of thought and action that was far more hostile to the government than was SCLC. Beginning with John Lewis' unforgiving speech at the 1963 March on Washington that was moderated under pressure, the leaders of SNCC displayed an attitude that directly challenged the federal government. With the rise of Stokely Carmichael and his slogan of "Black Power," SNCC adopted an even more militant attitude. But the FBI's choice of a target in the civil rights movement apparently had little to do with the level of radicalism.

Malcolm X also afforded the FBI a far more attractive target than King. Although he was not a part of the southern civil rights struggle— and often attacked the southern-based movement—the FBI considered the New York Muslim leader a racial agitator who endangered the nation's security. Malcolm X's earnest belief that whites were a race of devils who would be overcome by the darker races in an eventual war of Armageddon was in marked contrast to King's nonviolent approach and his exhortations to love one's enemies. But despite Malcolm X's belligerent, and sometimes violent, pronouncements against whites, his FBI files do not indicate the type of obsession that the FBI had with Dr. King. Although the FBI was certainly concerned about the increasing audience that Malcolm X was gaining through the early 1960s, it did little to try to disturb his activities. The FBI did attempt to heighten the animosity in the already failing relationship between Malcolm X and his spiritual leader, Elijah Muhammad, but it did not demonstrate the contempt that it held for King. In part, this is the result of the FBI's knowledge that despite Malcolm X's violent speeches, he was unlikely to carry out violent acts. But the relative lack of attention to Malcolm X was the result of the FBI's unique fascination with King.

Historians, in an attempt to analyze the relationship between King and the FBI, have devised a number of theories that attempt to explain the fundamental causes of the animosity. Most of these theories are based on the assumption that there was a single incident or attitude that sparked and drove the conflict, whether it was King's criticism of the FBI in 1962, or the general conservative attitude of the FBI and its failure to recognize the need for a civil rights movement. But the true causes of the animosity cannot be dissected as easily as most historians believe. Rather than finding its root in a single source, the struggle between Hoover and King is a complicated matter that was influenced by a number of factors, including the upbringing of both men, their demeanor, politics, attitudes, and even their self-images. All of these factors fed upon one another and forced an inevitable conclusion.

Conflict in Personalities

The dramatic differences in personality between J. Edgar Hoover and Martin Luther King, Jr., inflamed the political animosity between the two. They had little in common, born and bred in separate generations and across the southern racial partition that prevented cross-cultural understanding. Their common southern heritage was a divisive factor rather than an attribute that they shared in common. Racial segregation in the South was based upon a rigid system in which blacks and whites became foreigners to each other. The division was particularly devastating in terms of the inability of whites to understand the African Americans who had been in the South for four hundred years. Whereas blacks were often forced to learn the customs and histories of European Americans, whites were not required to know anything about the descendants of their former slaves.

J. Edgar Hoover was the product of the white South, raised in Washington, D.C., which retained its strong southern heritage in 1895 when Hoover was born. Washington was a segregated city, displaying all the visible signs of racism that told African Americans where they could sit, drink, and eat. Although Hoover was not a rabid racist, as were many of his southern contemporaries, his experience in the white South certainly tempered any sympathy that he may have had toward African Americans. The only contact he had with nonwhites was through the various servants that his family employed to clean their house and cook their meals. His experience as a child served not to open his mind to the differences of other cultures and peoples, but instead sheltered him from the outside. Hoover almost never left Washington before he became Director of the Bureau of Intelligence in 1924, and he did not attempt to broaden his perspective. Never in his life did he leave the United States, except for a brief drive across the Mexican border in 1939. Hoover displayed a natural intelligence, but turned down a scholarship at the University of Virginia in favor of night school at George Washington University so that he could remain "at home under the watchful eye of his mother."[105] Hoover grew in a period in which racism was respectable, when the racist movie *Birth of a Nation* glorified the Ku Klux Klan in its fight against miscegenation, and when prominent African Americans such as heavyweight champion Jack Johnson were being prosecuted by the Justice Department for spoiling the "virtue of womanhood" by escorting a woman—a white woman—across state lines.[106]

Hoover had, in short, an insulated development, in which issues of civil rights or unequal treatment of African Americans were never discussed. With regard to racial issues, Hoover merely accepted the cultural biases of the society in which he was raised. The racism that he displayed in his later years was the result of this acceptance. His belief in the natural inferiority of the black race was never questioned in his early years and was not even considered abnormal until the civil rights struggle exploded in the 1950s. The Bureau of Investigation that Hoover inherited in 1924 when he was still a young man did nothing to counter his racial insensitivity; the Bureau itself was plagued by the same attitude. In 1910, in response to an increase in the number of lynchings of blacks in the South, the Justice Department, in which the Bureau of Investigation had recently been created, claimed "no authority . . . to protect citizens of African descent in the enjoyment of civil rights generally."[107] When Hoover took over the Bureau more than a decade later, he saw no reason to alter the policy.

In fact, Hoover demonstrated his agreement with it. He did not try to hide the motivation behind his decision to seek a method of prosecuting Marcus Garvey, an outspoken black nationalist who had as many as a million American followers. Hoover attacked Garvey for his "defiantly assertive" notions of "the Negro's fitness for self-government," as well as for his promotion of "sex equality."[108] Hoover finally succeeded in prosecuting Garvey for mail fraud, for which he was found guilty and eventually deported. When civil rights first became a major issue to the government during the Eisenhower administration, Hoover fought against those, including Attorney General Herbert Brownell, who advocated that Eisenhower take a strong stance in favor of civil rights. The Attorney General sought congressional legislation that would create a civil rights commission and allow the Justice Department to support

voting rights through civil suits. Hoover objected to the proposed legislation and made his opposition clear in a Cabinet meeting that he was
invited to address in 1956. He told Eisenhower's Cabinet that the South
was fearful of such legislation because of "the specter of racial intermarriages," a concept that he also abhorred.[109] He argued that the communist threat was far more important than the desire for civil rights,
and that communists had made great progress in infiltrating civil rights
organizations such as the NAACP. "Delicate situations are aggravated
by some overzealous but ill-advised leaders of the NAACP and by the
Communist Party, which seeks to use incidents to further the so-called
class struggle."[110] He also mistakenly told the meeting that the vehemently anti-white Nation of Islam was involved in the fight for civil
rights, although the Muslims were actually opposed to integration and
the struggle for civil rights. And according to one historian, "in discussing 'the alleged lynching' of Emmett Till, the director worried more
about a 'pressure campaign on government officials' than a brutal, racist
murder."[111] But despite the racism in his arguments, it was Hoover's
position that finally held the day, as Eisenhower decided not to take a
stand on civil rights.

Hoover's clearest demonstration of his own racism was his refusal
to admit blacks or other nonwhites into the ranks of FBI agents. In
addition to possessing a college degree in either law or accounting,
potential FBI agents also had to pass the test of color. One FBI agent
first noticed this policy during his required three-month stay at the
Bureau training school. "As I took a closer look at my classmates, I
started to notice a certain sameness about the fifty of us. Although we
came from every part of the country and from every type of background,
there were no Jews, blacks, or Hispanics in the class. I was later to
learn that this was Hoover's policy."[112] Hoover's mission in the FBI
was to assemble the most efficient and hardworking group of agents
possible and to set them loose against the rampant crime in America.
It was a natural assumption for him that the most efficient, hardworking
people would of course be white men. "I won't appoint a man to the
FBI because his uncle is a powerful senator," Hoover reasoned. "And
I won't appoint a Negro just because he is a Negro. There are Negroes
now in the FBI and they got their jobs like everyone else—by careful
examination of their qualifications, the same examination that any other
applicant receives. There has been no case of a Negro who was qualified
being turned down. I do not intend at this time or at any time to bring
into the FBI any man, regardless of his race or creed, if he does not
measure up to the FBI's standards."[113] One of Hoover's standards, how-

ever, was that his agents be white. "For good reason we were referred to as the 'Lily White' FBI," William Sullivan wrote to Hoover in a forceful letter upon his ouster from the Bureau.

> We should have hired Negro agents and clerks many years ago but you absolutely refused. Years ago you told me yourself you were opposed to it adamantly, and the remark was attributed to you: 'There will never be a Negro Special Agent as long as I am Director of the FBI.' This is not only prejudice of the worst kind it is also poor leadership and impractical.[114]

Hoover's vow to keep African Americans from becoming special agents of the FBI was largely successful, despite the token number of blacks that Hoover claimed to be agents. The Bureau actually had four or five black agents before the 1960s, when Attorney General Robert Kennedy forced Hoover to increase the diversity of his staff. But the black special agents carried only the title, and not the responsibility of true agents. One black FBI agent, James Crawford, served as Hoover's chauffeur in Washington, and two other black chauffeurs with the token title of special agent served Hoover in other cities. Another African-American agent, Sam Noisette, actually served as Hoover's doorman, ushering guests into Hoover's office and handing towels to the perspiring Director. Hoover often used these black employees to demonstrate that the Bureau was an integrated agency, but he failed to mention the second-class treatment of the black agents. In fact, the only reason that the black employees were called special agents was in order to exempt them from the draft during World War II. All of them passed the FBI Academy, but on a segregated course that was designed to keep them away from the white cadets. But Hoover kept up the public-relations front, convincing many outsiders of the supposedly progressive attitude of the Bureau toward African Americans. One ironically complimentary article in *Ebony* magazine wrote of the cordial relations between Hoover and Sam Noisette, explaining that "the relationship between the two men virtually sets the race relations pattern for the huge agency."[115]

Hoover's demonstrable racism was not merely a personal predilection; it was also a major factor in the development of Hoover's attitudes toward the civil rights movement and Martin Luther King. King and his fellow civil rights leaders saw the movement as a moral crusade against the injustices of a racist society. It was, they believed, a divine call for an alteration of the social structure and for the elimination of the evils of segregation. But Hoover failed to see the morality of the struggle for civil rights, in large part because of his inability—and unwillingness—to relate to the plight of Southern blacks. The civil rights movement to Hoover was not a battle between good and evil. Instead, it was a political brawl in which neither side held the moral high ground. The proper approach to such a partisan fight, Hoover believed, was neutrality and noninvolvement. He demonstrated this attitude in his testimony before the House Appropriations Committee in 1956. "In civil rights cases," Hoover explained, "the Bureau is in a situation that if it obtains facts which result in prosecution it is unpopular and if it doesn't obtain facts, it is unpopular. Our sole purpose is to do our job objectively."[116] William Sullivan states it more bluntly:

> We never enforced the civil rights law, because Hoover was opposed to the whole civil rights program. Bobby Kennedy came in and started putting the pressure on it, and then we had to change our ways, but for years we completely ignored the violation of civil rights on the part of Southern law enforcement. . . . Hoover wasn't in favor of civil rights.[117]

Martin Luther King was the natural target of Hoover's racism and his suspicion of the civil rights movement. As the most prominent and vocal of the civil rights leaders, King was often viewed—incorrectly— as the impetus of the movement. Hoover and other opponents of the movement naturally gravitated toward the position that King was a personification of the struggle for civil rights. Although King did not control most of the activities conducted under the rubric of the movement, and although he was reviled by many who fought for the betterment of the American Negro, Hoover attacked King as a method of destroying the entire movement. Since King was not the unquestioned leader of the movement, it is unlikely that Hoover would have been able to succeed, although he certainly would have damaged the freedom struggle by discrediting King. But the movement was caused not by King but by the racial intolerance and oppression that pervaded American society, and without ameliorating the root causes of the civil rights movement, the desire for equality would not be eliminated. Hoover failed to recognize this distinction in his battle against Martin Luther King.

Hoover had other reasons for his disapproval of the civil rights movement—and Martin Luther King—than his innate racism. His FBI was a natural ally of the very forces in the South that were enforcing the Jim Crow laws that separated black from white. The Bureau began cultivating contacts with local law enforcement across the country since long before World War II, when the Bureau was in its heyday of battling famed gangsters. Cooperation between the Bureau and local police was vital in the outcome of the FBI's investigation into crimes such as auto theft or kidnapping. The FBI worked closely with local law enforcement in almost all cases, except those in which Hoover disliked an individual sheriff or police chief, as was the case in Los Angeles.

The alliance between police and the FBI was a critical factor in the success of the Bureau, but it soon became a burden when the civil rights movement erupted. Southern policemen were responsible for some of the most brutal beatings of civil rights workers, and often passed intelligence to organizations such as the Ku Klux Klan that would punish local blacks for their involvement in the movement. Although the FBI had occasionally investigated isolated cases of police brutality, it was reluctant to initiate a case in the South for fear of losing police contacts throughout the southern states. The Bureau was thereby paralyzed. Unwilling to investigate its southern friends, the FBI continued the relationship with local law enforcement, despite its role in escalating violence against the movement. Evidence suggests that the FBI even cooperated with local police in combating the movement, at one time passing critical information during the 1961 Freedom Rides to hostile police.

It was this cooperation with police that initially sparked King's criticism of the Bureau in 1962, as he argued that "every time I saw FBI men in Albany [Georgia], they were with the local police force." The cooperation with police embittered many blacks—including King—against the Bureau and inspired a great deal of criticism. But rather than breaking his contacts with local police, Hoover responded instead by attempting to break King. According to William Sullivan, Hoover refused to investigate local police because "if you went after the sheriffs and if you went after the other men, then they wouldn't cooperate with you on bank robberies, on stolen automobiles, they wouldn't cooperate with you on all the other crimes that the FBI handled, and so you'd be left without support from the whole Southern police force."[118]

The animosity between J. Edgar Hoover and Martin Luther King, Jr., focused attention on the larger question of the FBI's role in the civil rights movement. The Bureau clearly trod a fine line, hoping to satisfy both its allies in southern police departments and the African Americans often brutalized by those same police. The main issue was whether the

Bureau would provide protection for civil rights workers, as the Secret Service protected the President and other government leaders. Calls for protection for southern activists began in 1961, as the Freedom Rides were met with vicious violence from southern segregationists. FBI agents who were present watched the brutality and refused to intervene on behalf of the defenseless Freedom Riders. Gary Rowe, an FBI infiltrator of the Ku Klux Klan, participated in the Freedom Ride beatings, and he observed FBI agents at the scene "taking movies of the beatings."[119] Hoover continued to argue, successfully, that the FBI was an investigative agency, and had no business protecting civil rights workers. The thought of protecting racial agitators was clearly distasteful to him, and that legalistic argument was Hoover's best weapon in fighting the pressures from the civil rights movement.

President Kennedy and his Attorney General, however, felt a moral urgency to protect African American activists. "They deserve the protection of the United States Government, the protection of the state, the protection of local communities," the President said, "and we shall do everything we possibly can to make sure that protection is assured and if it requires extra legislation and extra force, we shall do that."[120] The problem was far more intractable than the President realized, however. Under the federal system, local police officers had primary responsibility for law enforcement, and federal law had no provision to compensate for the failure of local officers to protect its citizens. "We do not have a national police force," Burke Marshall exclaimed, "and *cannot* provide protection in a physical sense for everyone who is disliked because of the exercise of his constitutional rights."[121] Robert Kennedy and his aides at the Justice Department recognized the inability of the government to provide protection to civil rights workers within existing legislation and the inability of the administration to pass new civil rights legislation through a hostile Congress. As Burke Marshall said in a speech in 1961, "there is no substitute under the federal system for the failure of local law enforcement responsibility. There is simply a vacuum, which can be filled only rarely, with extraordinary difficulty, at monumental expense, and in a totally unsatisfactory fashion."[122]

Hoover's supporters across the country endorsed his refusal to protect civil rights workers. John Chamberlain, editorializing in the *Red Bank Register* in New Jersey, wrote about the conflict between African-American demands and federal responsibilities soon after Hoover attacked King as "the most notorious liar" in 1964:

J. Edgar Hoover did have good reason for getting hot under the collar. When Dr. Martin Luther King said that not a single arrest had been made in Albany, Georgia, during a period in which the Negroes were complaining of brutalities, he inferentially pointed an insinuating finger at the FBI. But, as Mr. Hoover has had to explain over and over again, his organization is purely an investigative one.... Dr. King is understandably vexed because the wheels of justice grind slowly. He doesn't like it that FBI agents work with local officers on criminal cases. This, he has said, makes it difficult in the South for the FBI to function effectively where Negroes are threatened. But the FBI is not a national police force, and it has necessarily to co-operate with local officers. J. Edgar Hoover is understandably vexed when the FBI is condemned for doing the best it can within the limits of its authority. The basic question is, do we want a national police force with power to function on its own even in the limited field of civil rights? . . . A central police power can all too easily become an engine of tyranny.[123]

Chamberlain correctly asserted that a national police force would upset the federalist balance that the Constitution had established, a fact that the Kennedy administration, too, fully recognized. But the Bureau had a far broader ability to involve itself in the protection of civil rights workers than it claimed. Clearly, the agency could not provide around-the-clock protection to King or other leaders. But it did have some latitude in dealing with criminal activities that it witnessed. FBI agents were more than simply investigators. They were also fully equipped law enforcement officials who, in the 1930s, had been granted the power of arrest and the right to carry firearms. FBI agents would have been within their powers to intervene in brutalities such as the beatings of Freedom Riders, rather than just standing on the sidelines and taking notes. But the agents were under strict orders from the Director not to intervene. The selective intervention of the Bureau would not have confronted the government with a constitutional issue of federal powers. It would, however, have forced a confrontation between J. Edgar Hoover and Robert Kennedy, who would have had to force the Director to do his duty.

Sexual Politics

Race and racial politics were not the only issues that divided J. Edgar Hoover and Martin Luther King, Jr. Their conflicting attitudes toward sexuality played a prominent role in the relationship between the two, with Hoover continually attacking King for his extramarital escapades. The men were on the opposite sides of the sexual spectrum. Where Hoover was seemingly asexual and presumably had little firsthand sexual experience, King was fully aware of his sexuality and exercised it beyond his marriage.

Continually plagued by the interminable problems of the civil rights struggle, King sometimes gained temporary relief from the enormous pressures on him by telling jokes of a sexual nature before his closest aides and by occasionally engaging in extramarital sex. He was away from home—and his wife—much of his adult life, so he had innumerable opportunities to engage in extramarital affairs. He spent most of his time traveling to various southern cities in support of the movement, then flying north for fund-raising purposes. King used his loneliness as a justification for his behavior. As King told one friend, "I'm away from home twenty-five to twenty-seven days a month. . . . Fucking is a form of anxiety reduction."[124]

Sex did not free King from the tensions from which he hoped to escape. His conscience nagged at him, reminding him that his public life was in dramatic contrast to his personal behavior. His guilt intensified not only because he knew that his adultery contradicted his religious pronouncements, but also because his sexuality threatened to become an issue in the expanding civil rights movement. King realized his own weakness and understood that the proliferation of rumors concerning his sexual escapades could develop into a danger to the movement. The FBI's discovery of his sex life magnified the dangers and confirmed the rumors for those who sought to attack him. Ralph Abernathy argued that "I was worried that with the materials being circulated by the FBI as an incentive, some of the more hostile members of the press might be tempted" to write stories on King's sex life.[125] While King publicly decried promiscuity as sin, he privately realized his own hypocrisy. According to Abernathy, King "understood and believed in the biblical prohibition against sex outside of marriage. It was just that he had a particularly difficult time with that temptation."[126]

Hoover was far less open in issues of sexuality and left his associates—as well as historians—guessing as to even his basic sexual orientation. Although Hoover virulently sought to minimize them, rumors of his homosexuality were rife throughout the FBI, largely because of the unusually close relationship between Hoover and Assistant Director Clyde Tolson and the lifelong lack of any women in Hoover's personal life. But it is Hoover's attitude toward sexuality, and not his sexual orientation, that is significant in his relationship to Martin Luther King. Hoover was, in many respects, puritanical in his opposition to the type of behavior that King repeatedly displayed. He objected to the open display of sexuality and professed to be offended by what he regarded as the abnormal use of sex. The Director was keenly interested in the sexual activities of those in the public spotlight, and he instructed his agents to go to great lengths in order to determine their sexual deviances. Deviance was interpreted broadly by Hoover. Homosexuality, sexual excess, miscegenation, and sex with the wrong people (e.g., communists) were all used by Hoover in order to defame or blackmail those around him. Hoover kept extensive files on politicians, entertainers, athletes, and others, and their sexual behavior was a major piece of intelligence that Hoover collected.

Hoover did not hesitate to use sexual behavior against those who offended him. Navy intelligence officer John F. Kennedy was one of Hoover's early targets, as the FBI monitored the young Kennedy at the beginning of World War II with Inga Arvad, an alleged Nazi spy. Although John Kennedy was still unknown, his father, Joseph Kennedy, had long served in the Roosevelt administration and had earlier been falsely accused of having Nazi sympathies. Hoover reported John Kennedy's activities to the President, as well as to the Office of Naval Intelligence. As a result of the silent scandal, Kennedy was transferred from his post in Washington, D.C., to the Pacific theater, where he demonstrated his courage when the Japanese sank his PT boat. His status as war hero led directly to a successful political career in Congress and the presidency. According to Hoover biographer Curt Gentry, "if Hoover felt in any way responsible for Kennedy's rise, he never bragged about it."[127] But Hoover held his knowledge of Kennedy's sex life over the President's head. In one meeting, he warned Kennedy that one woman with whom he had been having an affair had ties to the Mafia. Although Hoover's visit was ostensibly to warn the President of a possible political problem, the real reason was clear. Hoover wanted Kennedy to know that he was being watched. It was a subtle form of blackmail that Hoover used constantly and successfully.

Martin Luther King was an easy target for Hoover's sexual blackmail. Hoover claimed to be offended by King's sexual life, but the issue was not raised until well after Hoover had initially indicated his disdain for

King. Communist infiltration had been Hoover's main motivation for detesting King, and King's sexual behavior only added to the hatred. Also, as King historian David Garrow observes, Hoover was more of a voyeur than a puritan.[128] He took a certain pleasure out of looking into the private lives of others, and as much as he claimed to be offended by it, he was actually pleased when he found more information to use as blackmail. William Sullivan relates a story in his memoirs in which the FBI discovered photographs of African-American activist Angela Davis having sex. The photos, which were widely circulated within the FBI, did not reach Hoover's desk. When Hoover was told of the pictures, he was outraged that he had not seen them, and he upbraided his associates for failing to bring them to his attention. According to Sullivan, the agent who kept them from Hoover "received a scorching letter of censure. He was unable to get the promotion that was due him for six months."[129] Hoover was not offended by King's behavior as much as he was delighted that he had a new weapon to use in his crusade. The Director did not detest King merely because of his extramarital activities; he viewed those activities as a useful tool that could be used to discredit King.

Hoover had a number of other characteristics, including his inability to accept criticism, that made it almost inevitable that his relationship with King would be one of animosity rather than amity. By the time King became a factor in national politics, Hoover had been the Director of the Bureau for over thirty-five years. He spent much of that time creating the image of the FBI as a unified collection of dedicated crime fighters making the country safe for ordinary citizens. It was an ambitious, successful attempt to remold the Bureau's corrupt reputation, and Hoover was intolerant of any criticism of his efforts. He viewed it as personal criticism of J. Edgar Hoover. He would not tolerate such negativity from his own staff, and he was particularly averse to public criticism. He did everything he could to minimize dissent within the Bureau, firing those who refused to accept his idealization of the FBI, and he simultaneously sought to crush external criticism. According to one of Hoover's Washington friends,

> If ever you wrote an article that was critical of the FBI, [Hoover] answered you. He came right back. He answered anybody in the world. I'm not sure I approve. I've always gone on the theory that people will forget it in two weeks. But he would get incensed, call them scavengers, garbage collectors, all that stuff.[130]

King had inadvertently committed a serious offense against Hoover in 1962 when he suggested to the press that the Bureau was biased in its approach to civil rights cases. He had publicly questioned the effectiveness of the nation's most powerful law-enforcement officer and even dared to suggest methods by which Hoover and the FBI could improve. King did not initially recognize Hoover's aversion to criticism, and he accidentally started a war with the Director. King invited open discussion and criticism within the SCLC and did not understand that such discussion was not welcome in the FBI. Hoover had created an aura of infallibility, and King's criticism of the Bureau could only undermine Hoover's image. As William Sullivan told the Director in a farewell critique of the Bureau in 1971:

> Our effort (though you may deny it) to create the impression in the mind of the American people that we are infallible, perfect and sort of superhuman has over the years done us far more harm than good. Why can't we take a cold, factual, sensible position and set forth where necessary what we have done that is right and good, and also set forth our mistakes when we make them and what was wrong with our action? We would be respected far more. Often we have gone into long-winded explanations as to why we were not wrong when actually we were. Truth needs no lengthy explanation. We have wasted much time and money arguing and defending ourselves when a brief, simple statement of error would have paid us richer dividends. Let us get away from infallibility and present ourselves as ordinary human beings trying to do the best job possible but not always succeeding.[131]

As expected, Hoover was infuriated by Sullivan's critique.

Organizational Sources of Conflict

Personality conflicts between Martin Luther King and J. Edgar Hoover can provide a partial explanation for the extent of the animosity between them, but it cannot answer the fundamental question of how the Bureau was allowed to conduct its vicious campaign against King and the rest of the civil rights struggle. The Bureau had a number of organizational peculiarities that allowed Hoover to conduct his war against King and other civil rights leaders without fear of censure from above. Hoover and his Federal Bureau of Investigation operated in a vacuum of responsibility, in which there was no oversight of the Bureau by either Hoover's nominal superiors in the Executive branch or by the Congress that authorized the Bureau's expenditures. Hoover's independence from oversight was a historical accident, in which a career bureaucrat slowly accumulated powers and built his reputation in such a way that supervision was soon regarded as unnecessary.

When Hoover was named acting director of the Bureau of Intelligence in 1924, he was kept on a short leash by Attorney General Harlan Fiske Stone, whose goal was to reshape the corrupt Bureau into an efficient instrument for gathering intelligence. Hoover agreed with Stone's assessment of the Bureau as "lawless, maintaining many activities which were without any authority in federal statutes, and engaging in many practices which were brutal and tyrannical in the extreme."[132] The new Director set out to correct the excesses of the Bureau's past, firing incompetent political appointees and replacing them with qualified special agents. Stone realized the dangerous potential of an organization such as the Bureau, and ensured that Hoover would prevent the Bureau from conducting political investigations. According to Attorney General Stone,

> The Bureau of Investigation is not concerned with political or other opinions of individuals. It is concerned only with their conduct and then only with such conduct as is forbidden by the laws of the United States. When a police system passes beyond these limits, it is dangerous to the proper administration of justice and to human liberty, which it should be our first concern to cherish.[133]

The Bureau of Investigation thrived under Hoover despite the tight leash and channeled its energies into fighting interstate criminal activity that could not be successfully prosecuted in local jurisdictions. Its success in this area, particularly in its celebrated battles with gangsters such as John Dillinger and Ma Karpis, enormously increased the prestige of the Bureau, as well as its independence from the Attorney General and Congress. The power of the Bureau began to increase dramatically after Hoover had finished his first of almost five decades at its head. With the ominous rise of the Nazi movement in Europe, and the potential for a second world war, the Bureau began an extensive intelligence program, under the orders of President Franklin D. Roosevelt, to uncover evidence of subversion of the national security of the United States. Its initial foray into domestic counterintelligence was largely undefined and unsupervised. Given little guidance from the "vague and conflicting" instructions to investigate subversives, Hoover began his quest to expose those individuals and groups that dissented from the American government, and thereby "the foundation was laid for excessive intelligence gathering about Americans."[134]

At the direction of the President, Congress was kept uninformed about the new domestic intelligence initiative and showed little interest in investigating the powers of the FBI once it learned of the Bureau's new role. With the spread of fascism in Europe, the Bureau investigated alleged Nazi sympathizers in the United States, and the outbreak of World War II increased Hoover's latitude in dealing with potential subversives. Hoover's FBI focused on the apparent infiltration of mainstream organizations by Nazi operatives, and anti-American or antigovernment activities were immediately viewed as pro-Nazi sentiments. President Roosevelt gave "vague and conflicting executive orders" to the Bureau to investigate any "matters involving actually or potentially any espionage, counterespionage, or sabotage."[135] In a further extension of its power, the FBI was asked to investigate the political enemies of the President as the White House forwarded hundreds of negative telegrams it received. According to the 1976 report of the Congressional Select Committee to Study Governmental Operations with respect to Intelligence Activities, "a domestic intelligence program without clearly defined boundaries almost invited such action" as the partisan investigation of political enemies.

The end of World War II and the rise of the Soviet Union as the primary strategic enemy of the United States brought new responsibilities to the FBI. The investigation of communist infiltration had been an interest of J. Edgar Hoover's since his active participation in the 1920 Palmer raids, in which thousands of aliens were rounded up and deported by the government for their "subversive" views. The investigation of domestic communism was a natural extension of the previous investigations of the Nazi influence in the United States and further increased the powers of the FBI. As during World War II, the investigation of various leftist organizations was justified by tagging them as potential targets for infiltration.

As Hoover gained power, he eased the Bureau away from the various attorneys general under whom he served. He worked hard to consolidate his power and attempted where possible to report directly to the president or to no one at all. Usually it was the latter, as he often gave his superiors no indication of the activities of the Bureau, failing to tell them of the Bureau's use of illegal bugging and wiretapping in counterespionage cases. Few attorneys general dared to challenge the Director or try to control the activities of the Bureau. One of the challengers was the brash Bobby Kennedy, who refused to allow Hoover to continue his dictatorial rule over his unsupervised kingdom. Kennedy constantly sought to pressure Hoover, pushing him to get more involved in civil rights and organized-crime cases and to hire more blacks into the Bureau. Hoover instinctively fought back, but had little choice but to relent as long as the Attorney General's brother was the President. Kennedy even had the Justice Department install a direct phone line between his office and Hoover's, so that the Director could be reached instantly by the Attorney General without having to go through his secretary, who was known to all Bureau personnel only as Miss Gandy. No previous attorney general had such audacity, and Hoover's hatred of his boss was evident. Hoover resisted Kennedy's pressures, and only reluctantly made token increases in African-American Bureau personnel and took on a few more civil rights cases.

But it was Hoover, as usual, who won in the end. The Director finally got his chance with the death of the President on November 22, 1963. It was Hoover who first told Robert Kennedy that his brother had been murdered. Kennedy was later asked if Hoover was excited when he reported the news of the assassination. "No, not a bit. No, nor upset ... not quite as excited as if he was reporting the fact that he had found a Communist on the faculty of Howard University."[136] With Lyndon B. Johnson's accession to the presidency, it became easier to parry Robert Kennedy's pressures on the Bureau. Since Johnson was a friend of Hoover's—and a political enemy of Robert Kennedy's—Hoover held all the cards. When Kennedy first used the direct line between his office and Hoover's after the death of the President, the Director just let the phone ring. According to one special agent, "Mr. Hoover didn't answer it, so everyone tried to ignore it. When it finally stopped, Mr. Hoover said, 'Put that damn thing back on Miss Gandy's desk where it belongs.' "[137] Hoover refused to speak to the Attorney General for the several months before Kennedy resigned from the Johnson administration. The independence of the Bureau from the Attorney General had been secured, and Kennedy was unable to stop the FBI from persecuting Martin Luther King.

Hoover also maintained his independence from the succession of presidents for whom he served and did not allow them to interfere with his activities. No president dared to challenge the Director and risk the wrath of his conservative supporters in the Congress and the country. "His strength was with the ultraconservatives, with the Southern and the Northern conservatives, conservatives wherever they were,'' one agent reported.[138] President Kennedy, for example, was elected by a slim margin in 1960 and believed that he did not have the support to replace a figure of the Director's stature. One of Kennedy's first official acts in the wake of his election was the announcement that he would retain J. Edgar Hoover as FBI Director after his inauguration. It was the only choice of the President-elect, but one that he would often regret. Lyndon B. Johnson, despite his friendship with Hoover, sought to replace the Director and had the perfect opportunity when Hoover turned seventy, the mandatory retirement age for government employees. His plans were stalled, however, when Ben Bradlee, the D.C. bureau chief for the *Washington Post,* reported in a story for *Newsweek* that the search for Hoover's replacement was under way. The backlash from Hoover's conservative supporters was immediate, and Johnson was forced to back off and announce that Hoover's retirement would be waived indefinitely. After the public announcement, Johnson turned to his aide Bill Moyers and angrily intoned, ''You call up Ben Bradlee and tell him, 'Fuck you.' ''[139]

Bureaucratic Domination

Hoover's unquestioned dominance over the FBI bureaucracy was another major factor in his relationship with Martin Luther King. The Director's power within the agency was virtually unlimited, and his word was law. The gradual increase in independence from external oversight mirrored his increase of power within agency. His control over the agency was cemented in the early years of the Roosevelt administration, when the Bureau was threatened with the extension of civil-service requirements to most government departments. Hoover fought hard to exempt the Bureau from Roosevelt's executive order, arguing that the ability of agents, rather than their seniority, should determine promotions. He also told the president that ''he would resign before being forced to accept Communists and other undesirables'' into the Bureau.[140] Hoover's arguments were in line with his hard work to transform the Bureau into an efficient machine with the most dedicated workers in government. His eventual success in retaining the FBI's exemption from civil-service requirements was another important step in consolidating his power over his agents. According to Hoover biographer Curt Gentry, Hoover's success meant that he could hire or fire, promote or demote, anyone he chose, without having to justify his actions or have them subject to review. Few others, no matter how high in government, had such unlimited power. J. Edgar Hoover would retain *and use* it until the day he died.[141]

Hoover ruled the Bureau with an arbitrary and tyrannical hand. Agents in Washington lived in fear of his wrath, trying desperately to stay in favor by showering him with presents, talking incessantly about his favorite subjects, and most important, staying out of his way. Former agents told continuous stories of being reprimanded for the smallest of infractions, from being a single pound overweight to reading a newspaper while on duty. One agent described the "atmosphere of anxiety and fear that pervaded the halls and offices of the FBI."[142] Disagreeing with Hoover was perhaps the most egregious offense that an agent could commit, and agents were forced to accept Hoover's view of the world above their own. If Hoover believed that Martin Luther King was an immoral hypocrite, then all agents would be required to accept that view and recite it as if it were their own.

One of the best examples of Hoover's dictatorial control over the beliefs of FBI agents was his attitude toward the Mafia. Organized crime in America had been steadily gaining power since the 1930s. Fresh from successful battles against gangsters such as John Dillinger, the Bureau was the natural police agency to battle the national crime syndicate, which crossed numerous state borders and local police jurisdictions. The FBI, however, refused to engage in fighting the Mafia for a single reason: the refusal of J. Edgar Hoover to admit that national organized crime even existed. Hoover continually maintained that the Mafia was a figment of police officers' imaginations and that all crime was local rather than organized in a national network. As he once said, "no single individual or coalition of racketeers dominates organized crime across the nation." And since Hoover refused to admit that the Mafia existed, it officially did not exist to the Bureau. The Bureau was paralyzed, unable to combat the growing influence of organized crime because of the stubbornness of the Director and his refusal to accept alternate views. Only in 1957, when a policeman stumbled upon a meeting of crime figures across the country in Apalachin, New York, was J. Edgar Hoover forced to reluctantly revise his view. And only when Robert Kennedy, whose first priority was fighting organized crime, became Attorney General was Hoover forced to take a tough stand against the Mafia.

The same mechanism was at work in the battle against Martin Luther King and the movement for civil rights. Although many agents may have disagreed with Hoover's treatment of Dr. King, it was rare to hear a dissenting voice in the FBI. Hoover's iron hand squashed any dissent and prevented the type of open exchange vital to policy formulation. The policy toward Martin Luther King resulted from the personal predilections of the Director rather than from enlightened debate over various options. Once the policy was established, it could not be rescinded, and agents worked diligently to subvert the ambitions of their target.

The case of William Sullivan provides the best insight into this phenomenon at the Bureau. Sullivan was a hardworking bureaucrat who rose through the ranks of the Federal Bureau of Investigation, eventually becoming the assistant director in charge of the Domestic Intelligence Division. In that capacity, Sullivan oversaw the investigation of King and others in the civil rights movement. When Sullivan joined the Bureau at the beginning of World War II, he quickly learned of the Bureau's "stress on blind obedience and rigid discipline."[143] In one of his first assignments, Sullivan was matched with an experienced agent, Charlie Winstead, who told him how to survive in the Bureau.

"Never initiate a meeting with Hoover for any reason," Charlie once told me, because if the director was less than impressed for any reason, "your career would end on that very day. If Hoover ever calls you in," he went on, "dress like a dandy, carry a notebook, and write in it furiously whenever Hoover opens his mouth. You can throw the notes away afterward if you like. And flatter him," Charlie added, "everyone at headquarters knows Hoover is an egomaniac, and they all flatter him constantly. If you don't you'll be noticed."[144]

These were lessons that Sullivan took to heart, and he quickly moved up through the organization after he was permanently assigned to headquarters in Washington. Although Sullivan displayed an independent streak, he spent over two decades on his job before he began to dispute some of Hoover's sometimes irrational positions. He would eventually pay dearly for his disrespect. In 1971, Sullivan had a heated argument with Hoover over the Director's failure to accept dissent within the Bureau, among other issues. "The next morning I couldn't get into my office," Sullivan reported. "The locks had been changed. My name had been removed from the door. After thirty years in the FBI, I was out."[145]

Sullivan first displayed his independence in 1963 as a result of Hoover's hatred of Martin Luther King and paranoia about communist influence in the civil rights movement. On August 23, 1963, Sullivan presented the Director with a sixty-seven-page report on behalf of the Domestic Intelligence Division. The report concluded that the Communist Party, USA, had been completely ineffectual in its efforts to infiltrate the racial struggle. "Despite tremendous sums of money and time spent by the Communist Party, USA, on the American Negro during the past 44 years, the Party had failed to reach its goal with the Negroes," the report concluded. "There has been an obvious failure of the Communist Party of the United States to appreciably infiltrate, influence, or control large numbers of American Negroes in this country."[146]

The report ran counter to the official position of the Bureau and directly contradicted the beliefs and statements of the Director himself. The Bureau's entire approach to the civil rights movement and Martin Luther King was predicated upon the assumption that communists were actively infiltrating the movement and directing the course of the struggle. Hoover had continually stated his position that Martin Luther King was being directed by communists and that many civil rights activities were inspired by communists. To accept Sullivan's contention that the movement was largely free of communists would be tantamount to an admission that the Director had been wrong. This, clearly, was unacceptable. Although Sullivan and his staff had merely intended to present the truth as they saw it, they had invoked the wrath of the Director. Sullivan knew the dangers of contradicting J. Edgar Hoover, but he was determined to "state the facts just as they are" and "then let the storm break."[147]

The storm broke when the report was returned, replete with condescending comments in the Director's handwriting. "This memo reminds me vividly of those I received when Castro took over Cuba. You contended then that Castro and his cohorts were not communists and not influenced by communists. Time alone proved you wrong."[148] Sullivan knew that his career was in jeopardy, along with those of his entire staff in Domestic Intelligence. "This set me at odds with Hoover," Sullivan later reported. "A few months went by before he would speak to me. Everything was conducted by exchange of written communications. It was evident that we had to change our ways or we would all be out on the street."[149] According to Sullivan,

The men and I discussed how to get out of trouble. To be in trouble with Mr. Hoover was a serious matter. These men were trying to buy homes, [and had] mortgages on homes, children in school. They lived in fear of getting transferred, losing money on their homes, as they usually did. . . . They wanted another memorandum written to get us out of this trouble we were in. I said I would write the memorandum this time. The onus always falls on the person who writes a memorandum.

Sullivan and his staff revised their original report one week later. The revision contained all the necessary apologies.

The Director is correct. We were completely wrong about believing the evidence was not sufficient to determine some years ago that Fidel Castro was not a communist or under communist influence. On investigating and writing about communism and the American Negro, we had better remember this and profit by the lesson it should teach us.

The report went on to attack Martin Luther King, which Sullivan realized would ingratiate him to Hoover.

In the light of King's powerful and demagogic speech yesterday (at the March on Washington) he stands head and shoulders over all other Negro leaders put together when it comes to influencing great masses of Negroes. We must mark him now, if we have not done so before, as the most dangerous Negro of the future in this nation from the standpoint of communism, the Negro and national security.[150]

But Hoover did not let Sullivan and his staff off the hook so easily, telling Sullivan that he "can't understand how you can so agilely switch your thinking and evaluation."[151] Sullivan was forced to make one last apology and proposed an intensification of the counterintelligence against Martin Luther King before Hoover finally relented. It was in this manner that Hoover exerted complete control over the Federal Bureau of Investigation. Hoover's orders could not be questioned, nor could the wisdom behind them be examined. The personal prejudices and predilections of the Director automatically became the official policy of the FBI. J. Edgar Hoover demanded, and received, a loyalty from his agents that was unparalleled anywhere in government. Lifetime FBI bureaucrats cowered in fear of him, always afraid of being uprooted by a sudden transfer or dismissal. More than one agent was disciplined for asking Hoover how his "vacation" was; although Hoover spent several weeks in both California and Florida every year, he falsely insisted that his relaxation was Bureau business, not vacation. The arbitrariness of the disciplinary actions led one agent to conclude that Hoover employed a blindfolded chimpanzee named Fate who would throw a dart with an agent's name on it at a map of the United States, thereby determining where an agent would be transferred.[152] If agents particularly rankled the Director, they would be dismissed "with prejudice," a phrase that Hoover coined that guaranteed the agent would never work in government again.

J. Edgar Hoover created a system at the FBI that guaranteed he would only hear the opinions of those agents who agreed with him, while constructive dissent died an early death. "While the late J. Edgar Hoover was directing agents of his Federal Bureau of Investigation to smear and ruin private citizens he didn't like," one reporter later editorialized, "he was being deluded within his own headquarters, we now learn, by deceitful reports from assistants who apparently told the director what he wanted to hear. Not only was Hoover dangerously misusing the federal police powers, he was being fed false and obsequious information on which to base his reprehensible acts."[153] The agents themselves who acted as yes-men to the Director can only be partially faulted; it is Hoover himself who refused to allow his colleagues to question or contradict him.

Agents were not allowed to question the morality of the actions that they were asked to undertake. The only factor agents were supposed to consider was whether the action was sanctioned by the Director. According to one former agent, "there was only one man who could make the decisions in the FBI and although we were able to keep some matters from him, if he was on to something, if he was up on a case, there was nothing we could do. All the well-meaning people in the bureau did exactly what he told them, for if they didn't, they'd be pounding the pavements."[154] According to William Sullivan's testimony to a Congressional committee:

> Everybody in the Division went right along with Hoover's policy. I do not recall anybody ever raising a question. . . . Never once did I hear anybody, including myself, raise the question, is this course of action which we have agreed upon lawful, is it legal, is it ethical or moral? We never gave any thought to this realm of reasoning, because we were just naturally pragmatists. The one

thing we were concerned about will this course of action work, will it get us what we want, will we reach the objective that we desire to reach?[155]

Those who rose through the Bureau ranks without being shot down by Hoover generally shared his attitudes and political orientation, leaving no room for dissent or disagreement. Hoover was a lifelong conservative, both socially and politically. He would have preferred to see Nixon beat Kennedy in the election of 1960, and he abhorred the "sexual revolution" in the 1960s. In most bureaucracies, the opinions of the leader have a certain weight, but not the binding, overriding importance of Hoover's. His conservatism permeated the Bureau to the extent that virtually every investigation it conducted reflected his political orientation.

This institutional conservatism was fueled by a number of factors. First, the organization itself, whose image was one of fighting for law and order over the immoral forces of crime, attracted conservative agents. Their orientation was reinforced by an environment in which liberal opinions were never allowed to flourish, and in which only conservatives could be promoted into the top ranks. There were some exceptions, most notably William Sullivan, a lifetime Democrat. But even Sullivan could not display the political opinions that he professed to hold. "I personally believed that Martin Luther King, Jr., could be the leader his people needed," Sullivan wrote in his 1979 autobiography. "I was one hundred percent for King at that time because I saw him rising as an effective and badly needed leader for the black people in their desire for civil rights."[156] But even Sullivan, who claimed that he supported King, was forced to adopt the political opinion that King was being duped by communists.

The dictatorial manner in which Hoover led the Bureau is a critical factor in the persecution of Martin Luther King, Jr. Some historians have tried to place much of the blame for the FBI's treatment of King on individuals within the ranks of the Bureau, such as William Sullivan. But it was Hoover that set the tone for the rest of the FBI and made the policies that agents had to follow. Hoover was encouraged by doting employees such as Sullivan and DeLoach, who would try to stay in favor by suggesting even more extreme tactics to use against King than even Hoover had contemplated. But Hoover created an organization that made this behavior inevitable. The Director surrounded himself with yes-men who sought only to advance in the Bureau and avoid his wrath; one proven method of demonstrating loyalty to Hoover was to virulently attack Martin Luther King, regardless of personal belief. Former Attorney General Ramsey Clark said that the Bureau had suffered from "the excessive domination of a single person, J. Edgar Hoover."[157]

The root cause of the excesses [of the American intelligence community] has been failure to apply the wisdom of the constitutional system of checks and balances to intelligence activities. Our experience as a nation has taught us that we must place our trust in laws, and not solely in men.

—Final Report, Senate Select Committee to Study Governmental Operations with respect to Intelligence Activities.[158]

4

Hoover, King, and the Cold War

Although the struggle between the FBI and the SCLC was in many ways a battle between two individuals, it must be seen and analyzed in the larger context of the Cold War. The conflict between Martin Luther King and J. Edgar Hoover was exacerbated—and to some extent precipitated—by the Cold War mentality that had struck the United States. The communist menace presented by the Soviet Union and its allies was not seen as merely an external threat to the United States. Rather, it became a domestic concern that motivated many of the internal decisions of the American government during the forty years following World War II. For the first time since the founding of the republic, Americans saw themselves as an integral part of an international community and developed a preoccupation with events beyond the borders of the United States. This new preoccupation—and paranoia—was the result of America's economic and military domination over its European allies and enemies, coupled with the realization that only with sustained American interest in the reconstruction of Europe could a stable peace be maintained. The Soviet Challenge to American hegemony embittered the relationship between the two new world superpowers and forced an internal American reappraisal of the extent of American power; both foreign and domestic policies were re-analyzed in the context of the Cold War. The African-American freedom struggle was shaped in part by the American fascination with foreign affairs.

The onset of the Cold War was an important impetus for the civil rights struggle, but it also restrained the movement from realizing its full potential. While civil rights activists hailed the new appreciation of American democracy that accompanied the Cold War and tried to apply it to all sectors of American society, others such as J. Edgar Hoover attacked the movement's efforts as unnecessary in the more important battle against the Soviet Union. Many—including Hoover—even saw the movement as a victory for communist forces, as the law and order of southern communities was transformed to direct confrontation between civil rights workers and southern segregationists. Hoover viewed the increasing disorder in American society not as a developmental stage in the extension of democracy but instead as proof of the far-reaching influence of American communists.

The Cold War provided an impetus for Martin Luther King and the civil rights movement in two important ways. First, it helped frame the moral and intellectual arguments that inspired the movement. The Cold War sharpened the normative conflict that had been ever present in American society between the rhetoric of democracy and its actual application. The grand vision of the architects of American foreign policy was that democracy would triumph over nonrepresentative government, that totalitarianism would inevitably succumb to the will of the people. But the increasing rhetoric of the infallibility of the American form of democracy emphasized the startling contrast between the American ideal and reality in the racial arena. The state of racial relations in the United States was a shining example of the failure of the American dream. The international challenge from the Soviet Union inspired a renewed realization of the American paradox that had not been acknowledged since the Civil War. The obvious conflict between America's ideals and its realities convinced many liberals that civil rights should be a domestic priority. The struggle for civil rights was an effort to match America's actions to its words, in large part inspired by the determination that if America was to be portrayed as the greatest democracy in the world, then it should begin to act like it.

The stark contradiction between American democratic rhetoric and the brutal treatment of the descendants of slaves was reemphasized in the war against the Nazis during World War II and the subsequent struggle with the Soviet Union. The United States government continually attacked the Nazis for their racially biased policies against Jews and others, and for the inhumane treatment of its non-Aryan citizens. But it was an inherently hypocritical argument; America had little moral advantage in the area of racial bias. The United States, however, confronted with a war against a totalitarian government, used the issue of race in its defense of the ideals of democracy and equality. "Fascism and nazism are based on a racial superiority dogma," one scholar wrote, ". . . and they came to power by means of racial persecution and oppression. In fighting fascism and nazism, America had to stand before the whole world in favor of racial tolerance and cooperation of racial equality."[159] The United States, in the global public-relations war, attacked the German government for its racially biased policies, and stressed that racial intolerance was incompatible with a democratic government. Ralph Bunche attacked the hypocrisy of the American position, arguing that "there should be no illusions about the nature of this struggle [against the Nazis]. . . . The fight now is not to save democracy, for that which does not exist cannot be saved. But the fight is to maintain those conditions under which people may continue to strive for realization of the democratic ideals. This is the inexorable logic of the nation's position as dictated by the world antidemocratic revolution and Hitler's projected new world order."[160]

The new rhetoric of racial equality inspired many African Americans to demand the rights that the American government insisted that German Jews should retain. Sociologist Gunnar Myrdal explained the effect of this rhetoric on African Americans:

> Their caste system being what it is in America, Negroes would, indeed, not be ordinary human beings if such dissatisfaction and bitterness were not their reaction to all the morale talk about democracy, the four freedoms, the American way of life, all the violent denunciations of Nazi race hatred and the lack of freedom under totalitarian rule. . . . The only thing Negroes ask for is to be accepted as Americans. . . . Negroes are standing only for the democratic principles, to defend which America is waging war. They are dissatisfied because these principles are ignored in America itself. . . . They can, with new reason, point to the inconsistency between American ideals and practices.[161]

A member of the American Communist Party also equated the fight for civil rights with the war against Germany. "The struggle for the rights of the Negro people is an inseparable part of the struggle against fascism and reaction, for democracy and equality; it is an inseparable part of the international people's front to defeat and destroy Hitler's fascism."[162] The return of black American soldiers after World War II also increased the call for an extension of civil rights. African-American soldiers had been sent overseas to battle the oppressive governments in Germany and Japan during the war, and many blacks were ready to apply the same lessons in the fight against the oppressive governments of Mississippi and Alabama. Rev. Ralph Abernathy, King's loyal lieutenant, was only one of thousands of African Americans to return from the war with a greater sense of racial justice and a greater willingness to fight for the ideal of American democracy.

The assertion of the American democratic way continued unabated as the United States found itself in a battle with another, more powerful, totalitarian regime after World War II. The United States used the same verbal weapons against the Soviet Union that it had used against Nazi Germany. It was, according to American pronouncements, another fight against an antidemocratic state that had no respect for individual equality and civil liberties. The United States castigated the Soviet Union for its treatment of its Jewish citizens, although America had few responses to Soviet countercharges of abuses against the American Negro. While the United States sought to counter Soviet moves on a global scale, many Americans also sought to open a second front against communist influence at home, in part by removing any totalitarian strains of American politics. The favorable decision in the 1954 *Brown v. Board of Education* case that outlawed school segregation was often hailed as a defeat of the Soviet Union through the extension of domestic freedoms. "This is a great day for the Negro," Adam Clayton Powell exclaimed. "This is democracy's finest hour. This is Communism's greatest defeat."[163] As Martin Luther King preached in a commencement address in 1961,

> Ever since the Founding Fathers of our nation dreamed this noble dream, America has been something of a schizophrenic personality, tragically divided against herself. On the one hand we have proudly professed the principles of democracy, and on the other hand we have sadly practiced the very antithesis of those principles. Indeed slavery and segregation have been strange paradoxes in a nation founded on the principle that all men are created equal. . . . But the shape of the world today does not permit the luxury of an anemic democracy. The price America must pay for the continued exploitation of the Negro and other minority groups is the price of its own destruction. The hour is late; the clock of destiny is ticking out. . . . Now, more than ever before, America is challenged to bring her noble dream into reality, and those who are working to implement the American dream are the true saviors of democracy.[164]

International Pressure

The Cold War added momentum to the civil rights movement in another important manner. While African Americans absorbed the rhetoric of the American concept of equality, U.S. government officials came under increasing pressure from the world community to alter racist practices in the United States. The racial caste system in the United States became an international issue almost immediately after World War II concluded. Newspapers around the world began to report on the wave of violence that had greeted returning black soldiers. Black GIs came home to the U.S. expecting to find an appreciation for their fight against fascism; instead they found a white backlash against the confidence and the independence that they had gained in the military. The plight of African Americans deteriorated as returning white soldiers reclaimed their domestic jobs from blacks who had filled them during the war. Lynchings again became common in a broader effort to reduce African Americans to their prewar status. Nations that now looked to the United States for leadership were shocked by the obvious contrast between American rhetoric and the brutal violence against its black citizens.

Increasing the international pressure on the United States, the USSR publicized examples of American racial bigotry and spread the notion that America was the land of racial bigotry rather than equal opportunity. The campaign was part of an effort to convince Third World nations that the United States sought to continue the racist, colonialist practices used by its European allies. The United States found itself in a global public-relations war with the Soviet Union, and realized that it could not win on the racial front. The decolonization of Asia and Africa gave a new immediacy to the need for a solution to the racial crisis in America, as the emerging nations were often forced to choose between the United States and the Soviet Union as their primary ally. John F. Kennedy, in particular, realized the importance of Africa in the global struggle of the superpowers, and he sought to mend racial relations in the United States as a means of convincing African nations to forsake Soviet aid. A further incentive for the government to resolve racial issues was offered by Malcolm X, who twice traveled to Africa in 1964 to paint a more accurate picture of the plight of African Americans than American propaganda had indicated.

The effect of the American government's fight against communism on domestic programs cannot be ignored. According to Albert Gore, Jr., in his book *Earth in the Balance,* anticommunism was the "central organizing principle'' for American society in the postwar world. It was this concept that unified the country and served as a justification for the internal improvement of the United States. ''Opposition to communism was the principle underlying almost all of the geo-political strategies and social policies designed by the West after World War II,'' Gore writes.

> ... When we built the interstate highway system, the Defense Interstate Highway Bill authorized the money, and the legislation was approved by a majority partly because it would serve our overriding objective, the defeat of communism. When the Soviet Union demonstrated its technological prowess by sending Sputnik into orbit in 1957, the United States implemented its first federal aid-to-education policy—not because the president and a majority in Congress finally recognized the importance of improving education for its own sake, but because of the new importance of training scientists and engineers in service of our struggle with the communist system. . . . Virtually every policy and program was analyzed and either supported or rejected primarily according to whether it served our basic organizing principle.[165]

The same rationale was at work in the pursuit of civil rights. The federal government realized that action on civil rights was necessary to improve the image of American democracy among Third World nations. According to Myrdal, the American racial conflict in America had

> acquired tremendous international implications, and this is another and decisive reason why the white North is prevented from compromising with the white South regarding the Negro. The situation is actually such that any and all concessions to Negro rights in this phase of the history of the world will repay the nation many times, while any and all injustices inflicted upon him will be extremely costly. . . . The main international implication is . . . that America, for its international prestige, power, and future security, needs to demonstrate to the world that American Negroes can be satisfactorily integrated into its democracy.[166]

The federal government was well aware of this fact. ''The existence of discrimination against our minority groups in this country has an adverse effect upon our relations with other countries," Acting Secretary of State Dean Acheson wrote in 1946.

> We are reminded over and over by some foreign newspapers and spokesmen, that our treatment of various minorities leaves much to be desired. . . . We will have better international relations when these reasons for suspicion and resentment [against the United States] have been removed.[167]

Indeed, the 1946 report of President Truman's Commission on Civil Rights concluded that "the United States is not so strong, the final triumph of the democratic ideal not so inevitable that we can ignore what the world thinks of us or our record."[168]

The government's support for the NAACP in the *Brown v. Board of Education* case came in part as a result of this concern for the "international implications" of its actions. In an amicus brief filed with the Court, the Justice Department argued that the *Brown* decision was important because "the United States is trying to prove to the nations of the world, of every nationality, race and color, that a free democracy is the most civilized and most secure form of government yet devised by man."[169] The federal government believed that the extension of civil rights to African Americans could be used successfully in its foreign public relations. Even Richard Nixon argued that civil rights was a sore spot in the American ideal of democracy during the 1960 presidential campaign. In his campaign biography, *The Challenges We Face,* he wrote that "in the world-wide struggle in which we are engaged, racial and religious prejudice is a gun we point at ourselves."[170]

The Kennedy Administration's response to the 1961 Freedom Rides was perhaps indicative of the influence of foreign affairs on domestic government action. The Freedom Rides were sponsored by the Congress on Racial Equality for the purpose of testing a recent Supreme Court case outlawing segregation in interstate travel facilities. Two buses with integrated passengers set out from Washington, D.C., in May 1961, pausing at interstate bus stops to ensure that any signs of segregation were removed. The Freedom Riders were virtually untouched until they reached Anniston, Alabama, where local whites boarded the buses and viciously beat the civil rights workers. The passengers suffered another brutal beating when they later rolled into Birmingham.

The Kennedy administration knew nothing of the rides until the Anniston beating, and regretted finding out about them when they finally did. The melee was an international embarrassment, coming on the eve of the President's trip to Vienna to meet Soviet leader Nikita Khrushchev. The President had only recently been compromised by the Bay of Pigs invasion, and this first meeting between the American and Soviet leaders was viewed as critical to the future relations of the two superpowers. The negative publicity of the Freedom Rides was something the new President desperately wanted to avoid. According to Kennedy historian Arthur Schlesinger, the Attorney General "said that racial troubles would embarrass the President of the United States in his meeting with Khrushchev."* When they realized that nothing could be done to stop the rides, the Kennedy brothers sought to protect the riders to avoid another confrontation so that the embarrassment would end before Kennedy's trip to Vienna. The Attorney General finally sent in six hundred federal marshals in order to keep the peace and worked constantly to force southern law-enforcement agents to carry out their duties. When the crisis had diminished, Robert Kennedy initiated suits against southern police officers accused of interfering with interstate travel and worked with the Interstate Commerce Commission to destroy the last remnants of segregation in interstate transportation. "By the end of 1962," Kennedy aide and biographer Theodore Sorenson wrote, "enforced segregation in interstate transportation . . . had finally ceased to exist."[171] It was an effort by the federal government that was undertaken both because of the moral instincts of the Attorney General and because of the international pressures that would accompany a failure to act. The external competition between the Soviet Union and the United States forced the President and the Attorney General to adopt an internal policy that they would not likely have adopted as quickly or forcefully. The movement for civil rights thereby indirectly benefited from the international battle between America and the USSR.

The Specter of Communist Infiltration

But the Cold War had an even more powerful negative effect on the civil rights movement. The movement, as well as other domestic priorities, suffered both because of the external preoccupation with the machi-

---

*Schlesinger, p. 321. Ralph Abernathy responded to the prospect of Kennedy's embarrassment with expected cynicism: "Doesn't the Attorney General know that we've been embarrassed all our lives?"

nations of the Soviet Union, which precluded concentrated effort on domestic issues, and because of the internal paranoia of communist infiltration that pitted one American against another. The focus on communist influence in domestic organizations was the major factor that damaged King's credibility and brought King and the FBI into a confrontational posture. Leftist groups, including civil rights organizations, were particularly traumatized by the charges, valid or not, of communist infiltration. Those leaders who actively opposed the status quo in the United States were easy targets of the communist slur. According to Professor Manning Marable, "the impact of the Cold War, the anti-communist purges, and near-totalitarian social environment, had a devastating effect upon the cause of blacks' civil rights and civil liberties. . . . The paranoid mood of anticommunist America made it difficult for any other reasonable reform movement to exist."[172] This "sterile legacy of anti-communism" affected movements from the civil rights struggle to the nuclear-test-ban movement of the late 1950s.[173]

Much of the controversy surrounding the FBI's initial animosity toward Dr. King focused on the issue of communist influence in the African-American civil rights struggle. To Hoover, King's unwillingness to remove suspected communists within the ranks of the SCLC only added evidence to the claim that King himself was a communist sympathizer. The pressures on King to remove Levison and O'Dell consumed enormous amounts of his time, energy, and political resources, thereby diminishing his power to fight for civil rights. This paranoia surrounding domestic communism in the United States framed the struggle for civil rights, preventing it from reaching its full potential as a reformist movement.

Martin Luther King was not the only African-American leader who had been damaged by charges of communist affiliations. W.E.B. DuBois, the original founder of the NAACP, was a brilliant, elderly man with a distinguished life behind him when the United States and the Soviet Union ended World War II and embarked upon the Cold War. Originally suspicious of the communist movement, DuBois gradually drifted leftward as his cynicism about American racial relations grew. He made several extensive trips through the Soviet Union, learning on his journeys that the Soviets had a great deal to teach Americans about racial toleration. He stayed aloof, however, from the American Communist Party but nevertheless remained under the careful surveillance of the federal government. In 1951, he was arrested by the Truman administration for acting as an agent of a foreign country for his advocacy of peace talks with North Korea in the midst of the Korean War. Later that year, at the age of eighty-three, DuBois was acquitted of the charges. Ten years later, DuBois finally took the step that he had avoided for so long and joined the Communist Party, adding that "I have been long and slow in coming to this conclusion, but at last my mind is settled."[174] The FBI, in an effort to diminish DuBois' substantial influence in Africa, passed derogatory information to the U.S. Information Agency to be used in broadcasts across the continent.*

Paul Robeson—the black athlete, actor, and singer—had a far greater dedication to the communist ideal and the Marxist experiment in the Soviet Union. He had also traveled extensively through the Soviet Union and often expounded upon the success of communism in overcoming racial differences. Robeson sought to overcome the American racial divide through the acceptance of socialism as a political model. Although he was permitted to articulate his vision before World War II, his productive acting career plummeted with the onset of the Cold War, as producers refused to associate with a known communist. Robeson was continually denounced by the American government and labeled as a "Black Stalin among Negroes" by the House Un-American Activities Committee.[175] The government's allegations against Robeson that he was a Soviet agent effectively ended his career and destroyed his credibility as a leader for civil rights. The federal government had a well-established legacy of persecuting suspected communists in the civil rights arena when Martin Luther King and Stanley Levison ran headlong into J. Edgar Hoover in 1962.

The pressures on the civil rights movement to assert an anticommunist stance affected the struggle from both within and without. The American government sought to root out any communist influence in the civil rights arena by endlessly investigating possible examples of infiltration and persecuting those who were found to have a communist taint. Congress was particularly virulent in its attempts to destroy the potential of undue communist influence. Beginning with the tirades of Senator Joseph McCarthy in the 1950s, Congress consistently proved to be more vocal in its opposition to domestic communism than were the various administrations that occupied the White House when the civil rights movement was in progress. For half a decade during the

---

*Martin Luther King, surprisingly, castigated DuBois publicly for the decision to join the CPUSA. "There can be no doubt," he said, "that if the problem of racial discrimination is not solved in the not too distant future, some Negroes, out of frustration, discontent, and despair, will turn to some other ideology." Branch, p. 563.

1950s, Joe McCarthy used his heavyhanded tactics to intimidate his political enemies and used a broad brush to smear the communist charge across a multitude of leftist and centrist organizations. "He walked, then, with a heavy tread over large parts of the Constitution of the United States," wrote McCarthy biographer Richard Rovere, "and he cloaked his own gross figure in the sovereignty it asserts and the powers it distributes. He usurped executive and judicial authority whenever the fancy struck him. It stuck him often."[176] Although he was not as vociferous as Senator McCarthy, J. Edgar Hoover held the same fervent belief that the communist menace was the nation's paramount domestic concern and that the civil liberties of individuals could be sacrificed in order to strike a blow against communist infiltration. Both Hoover and McCarthy cast a terrifying shadow over leftist groups and hindered the development of legitimate noncommunist organizations that could conceivably be the target of communist infiltration.

But the organizations that were the primary targets of anticommunist smear tactics were often not free from culpability. Indeed, many civil rights organizations eagerly participated in the search for domestic communists and fought to keep communists out of their ranks. In part, this can be explained by the drastic consequences of allowing communists into the civil rights movement. But many civil rights leaders shared in the paranoia of anticommunism and fervently believed that the sole motivation of American communists was the overthrow of the United States government. The NAACP, for example, prohibited communists from joining its organization and occasionally even purged its membership to rid itself of hidden Marxists. The SCLC was no different, as Martin Luther King indicated in his public response to the Jack O'Dell media attention. It is "a firm policy that no person of known Communist affiliation can serve on [SCLC's] staff, executive board or its membership at large," King told the press.[177] According to one civil rights historian, "the black middle class's almost complete capitulation to anti-communism . . . made the Negroes unwitting accomplices of a Cold War domestic policy which was, directly, both racist and politically reactionary."[178]

In a certain sense, the charge of communist infiltration of the civil rights movement was a weapon more than a legitimate concern. Segregationists, searching for a club to use in their battle to preserve the white race, cast about and seized upon communist infiltration as a primary mode of attack. James Eastland, a virulent segregationist and powerful southern senator, invoked the threat of communism not necessarily because that was the primary threat of the movement, but because it was the most convenient method of attacking civil rights organizations. Eastland's primary concern was the continuation of segregation, and he would have opposed integration even if it could be demonstrated that communists opposed it too.

But the issue of communist infiltration was far more than a method of attacking the civil rights movement. The specter of domestic communism had a powerful effect in influencing many moderate whites with limited knowledge of the issues in the struggle for civil rights. FBI files are replete with letters from ordinary citizens, asking for information on whether King actually was a communist. Although many of these correspondents were sympathetic to the plight of African Americans, they expressed concern that the rumors of communism were indeed true. The confirmation of such rumors, which the FBI refused to provide because of the supposedly strict confidentiality of their files, would have turned many potential civil rights activists into fence-sitters, and those already astride the fence might well have become the opposition.

One fundamental assumption made by the Bureau during the Cold War was that communism was not a local phenomenon. Domestic communism was seen as inextricably linked to the international conspiracy led by the Soviet Union. Communists, as well as other American leftists, were seen as obeying the commands of the Soviet Union above those of the United States. J. Edgar Hoover successfully argued that Stanley Levison—and by implication, Martin Luther King—were loyal servants of the Soviet Union. In the eyes of the Bureau, ideology determined loyalty, and governmental purges against communists were justifiable, since communists were incapable of loyally serving the United States. As Roy Cohn stated, "the domestic Communist movement is part of the international Communist movement, so you never view a local Communist movement as local because none of them are local. Their strength or their weakness depends upon the strength or weakness of the international movement of which directly or indirectly, loosely or tightly, they might be a part."[179] J. Edgar Hoover also subscribed to the theory that American communists were by their nature disloyal to the United States and inherently beholden to the Soviet Union. In his 1969 book *On Communism*, he emphasized several basic points. "Communism means primarily a threat from the Soviet Union and its satellites (as well as Red China and other Communist nations)," he wrote. "The Communist Party, U.S.A., the largest communist group in the country, has remained obediently loyal to Moscow. A person cannot be a communist and a loyal American at the same time."[180]

Another similar argument made by Hoover and other rabid anticommunists was that the level of communist infiltration into mainstream organizations was virtually irrelevant. A lower level of infiltration did not necessarily lessen the threat. Even the presence of a single communist operative in the entire civil rights movement would have necessitated urgent action against that person. This notion was supported by Hoover's continual assertion that it was only a tiny number of Bolsheviks who engineered the communist revolution in Russia. According to Hoover, in his book *Masters of Deceit,* "when the Communist Party was at its peak in the United States it was stronger in numbers than the Soviet Party was at the time it seized power in Russia."[181]

The implication, of course, was that a similar revolution was possible in the United States with only a small number of dedicated communists. The notion of a communist overthrow of the United States was a fanciful product of Hoover's imagination, but it had a powerful and chilling effect on American leftist movements. This paranoia over the abilities of small numbers of communists heightened the opposition to the civil rights movement and took away a convincing argument that the movement used to deflate charges of communist infiltration. The Communist Party, USA, made almost no progress in converting American blacks to their cause, in part because the goals of American Communist Party members and African Americans were only superficially intertwined. Even William Sullivan agreed that the civil rights movement was relatively free of communists. In a 1970 speech to United Press International editors, Sullivan was asked whether communists were responsible for the racial unrest across the country. Although he realized that if he answered truthfully, he would inspire the anger of the Director, Sullivan decided to take the chance. He answered the question honestly, arguing that communists had nothing to do with the racial struggle and that the Communist Party was not as influential as it had been in the past.[182] But when Dr. King and other civil rights leaders pointed to this lack of conversion of blacks to communism, Hoover countered with his assertion that the level of communist infiltration was not important. According to Hoover, a single communist could taint an entire movement.

King's argument that the Communist Party had made few inroads into African-American communities was a sound assertion, although the failure of the Communist Party was not for a lack of effort or a lack of dedication to the cause of civil rights. According to Congressman Adam Clayton Powell, "there is no group in America, including the Christian Church, that practices racial brotherhood one-tenth as much as the Communist Party."[183] But despite their public advocacy of African-

American equality in such cases as the indictment of the Scottsboro boys in 1931 for allegedly raping two white women, communists could not achieve a credible foothold in the struggle for civil rights. Whereas communists analyzed social reform from a class perspective, African Americans knew that their class was a function of their race, as economic opportunities were closed to them in America as a result of the color of their skin. While communists sought economic equality, the civil rights movement initially sought racial equality. Religion was another major cause of differences between African Americans and communists. Broadly speaking, American blacks in the southern states were a religious people, using spirituality to remind them of the salvation that would come to them in the next world despite the hardships in their present lives. Communism could provide no such spiritual replacement for the black church, and this damaged its ability to recruit blacks. Although their tactics may have coincided, communists and African Americans had different goals.

Both J. Edgar Hoover and Martin Luther King were strongly anticommunist, although for somewhat different reasons. Both had studied the concepts of Marxism earlier in their lives and had concluded that communism was an unworkable philosophy with potentially dangerous implications for the United States. But King had a far deeper understanding of the motivations of those who held a fervent belief in communism and those who had become disillusioned with communism. To King, communism was a legitimate system of belief that was an option—albeit undesirable—among those searching for a philosophical grounding. Many of the same beliefs that led to the support of communism also led to the support of leftist movements such as the civil rights movement: racial equality, the need for economic redistribution of wealth, and the failure of capitalism to provide social justice.

The threat of communist infiltration of the SCLC and other civil rights organizations was a genuine concern for King. He realized the goals of the Party differed from most of those in the movement, and communist infiltration would steer the movement away from its emphasis on racial justice. But despite his concerns, King was not willing to conduct purges of the movement in which noncommunists would almost certainly be caught up in the anticommunist net. Proof of communist affiliation would spur King into action, but such proof was almost impossible to attain.

Hoover required no such proof. He fervently believed that the taint of communist activity was sufficient to place the communist label on an individual. Jack O'Dell's invocation of the Fifth Amendment in response to congressional inquiries about his communist affiliation was sufficient to prove to Hoover that O'Dell was a communist, and therefore subversive and dangerous. King, however, realized that the invocation of the Fifth Amendment did not necessarily prove guilt. Presented with only fragmentary evidence of communist activity, King stalled and initially allowed O'Dell and Levison to remain as advisors. King lacked the unregulated fear of communists that Hoover demonstrated and refused to act against his friends.

Foreign Preoccupation

The paranoia about communist infiltration of the freedom struggle was not the only insidious effect of the Cold War in African-American politics. The primary focus of the American government during the 1950s and 1960s was international. Rather than concentrating on the pressing domestic problems that had beset the United States, Eisenhower, Kennedy, and Johnson instead tended to look to the struggle between America and the Soviet Union as the primary threat to the American way of life. Domestic initiatives—including the civil rights movement—often suffered from the lack of attention. The upsurge in agitation for civil rights coincided with a difficult period in American foreign relations. The Cold War was at its peak, and the failure of American leaders to respond to the demand of civil rights activists represented their preoccupation with what they saw as the far more pressing problem presented by the Soviet Union and its allies.

The Eisenhower administration was concentrating on a number of foreign crises when the Supreme Court invalidated school segregation and when a young minister named Martin Luther King, Jr., led a movement in Montgomery, Alabama, to desegregate city buses. Eisenhower was a foreign-policy president. He had gained his experience in the American military, where he concentrated on the external military threats to the United States, and he showed little interest in domestic issues. When Eisenhower's Attorney General pressured the President to engage himself in civil rights, the former general resisted, unwilling to commit to a firm position. Although he showed little ingenuity in his handling of domestic issues, he was active on the world scene. Involved in crises in Taiwan, Lebanon and elsewhere in the Middle East, Eisenhower sought to secure the position of the United States in world affairs and combat the communist menace. In 1956, as Martin Luther King led a boycott in Alabama, Eisenhower found himself in a crisis at the

Suez Canal that threatened to escalate into a superpower conflagration. Relations with the Soviet Union were severely strained by the downing of an American U2 spy plane over Russia in 1960. Given the tenuous state of Soviet-American relations, Eisenhower had little time to devote to domestic affairs such as civil rights, even if he had demonstrated the inclination.

When elected President in 1960, John Fitzgerald Kennedy intended to follow in his predecessor's footsteps and become a foreign-policy president. As his special counsel, Theodore Sorenson, later wrote, "although he came to know and understand . . . the problems of poor housing and unemployment he had never experienced as a Kennedy, [the President's] chief interests were in foreign policy."[184] His training and interests were focused on foreign affairs, a predilection demonstrated in his inaugural address. The eloquent speech barely mentioned domestic issues, instead expounding upon the constant threat to the nation from the Soviet Union and the need for the United States to be willing to "pay any price, bear any burden, meet any hardship, support any friend, oppose any foe to assure the survival and the success of liberty."[185] Kennedy articulated a vision of America that focused outward, toward the possibility of establishing absolute peace among nations. He asked that both sides of the superpower confrontation "begin anew the quest for peace . . . remembering on both sides that civility is not a sign of weakness, and sincerity is always subject to proof."[186] Kennedy's sole reference to domestic affairs came in passing, and was shrouded in the context of foreign affairs. "Let the word go forth from this time and place, to friend and foe alike, that the torch has been passed to a new generation of Americans, born in this century, tempered by war, disciplined by a hard and bitter peace, proud of our ancient heritage, and unwilling to witness or permit the slow undoing of those human rights to which this nation has always been committed, and to which we are committed today at home and around the world."[187]

President Kennedy was almost immediately beset by a number of international crises that pitted the United States against the Soviet Union and its allies. The fallout from the 1959 Cuban revolution was continuing to rain down on Washington when Kennedy assumed the reigns of power two years later. The new President was immediately confronted with two unpalatable choices with regard to Cuba: allow Castro to secure his power and establish a Marxist government, or use military force to oust him and restore the Batista regime. Kennedy reluctantly opted for the latter, acquiescing to the CIA-led invasion at the Bay of Pigs. It was a mistake that Kennedy would eternally regret. The disastrous invasion transformed Cuba from a worrisome regional issue into a global preoccupation that brought the United States and the Soviet Union into direct conflict. The Cuban problem diverted the attention of virtually the entire American government from domestic issues at a critical moment, just as Freedom Riders began to invade the South. The Kennedy administration at first attempted to intervene against the civil rights movement and stop the Freedom Rides because of the negative publicity that it would have caused before the 1961 superpower summit between Kennedy and Khrushchev. "Tell them to call it off," the President instructed his civil rights advisor, Harris Wofford. "Stop them." But Wofford responded plainly, "I don't think anybody's going to stop them right now." When the Kennedy administration finally decided to work actively to support the Freedom Riders, the Cuban dilemma still loomed in the foreground. The Attorney General was called upon to oversee a critical, time-consuming study of the failed Bay of Pigs invasion and was forced to divert his attention from his work on civil-rights issues to foreign-policy matters. He temporarily ceded his responsibilities at the Department of Justice during the critical month of May 1961, just as the violence against Freedom Riders had reached its peak. "After spending the day on the Bay of Pigs, Kennedy generally worked in his office on racial justice and other matters till late at night."[188] Because of an international escalation in the Cold War, Robert Kennedy could not focus his energy on the civil rights movement at precisely the time when his undivided attention was critically needed.

The pattern of sacrificing domestic concerns such as civil rights to the necessities of the Cold War continued through the Kennedy administration and reached a new peak during Lyndon B. Johnson's stewardship. Johnson launched an enormous domestic initiative under the rubric of his Great Society program, designed to feed the poor, teach the uneducated, and free the oppressed. It was the largest domestic initiative since the New Deal, with billions of dollars budgeted for new programs. But, according to Johnson aide Joseph Califano, "Lyndon Johnson was riding two horses at the same time," the Great Society and the escalating war in Vietnam.[189] Johnson's liberal critics argued that "the Great Society programs must not be gutted because of the war in Vietnam," and the President assured the nation that both the domestic and the international goals could be met without sacrifice.[190] "I believe that we can continue the Great Society while we fight in Vietnam," the President told the nation in his 1965 inaugural address. "But if there are some who do not believe this, then, in the name of justice, let them call for the contribution of those who live in the fullness of our blessing, rather than try to strip it from the hands of those that are most in need."[191]

But Johnson's predictions of domestic and foreign success were overly optimistic, and the military conflict in Southeast Asia consumed an increasing share of the funds that were scheduled to go to domestic programs. "There were experiments, hopes, new beginnings," Martin Luther King noted of Johnson's Great Society in his first major anti-Vietnam speech:

> Then came the build-up in Vietnam and I watched the program broken and eviscerated as if it were some idle political plaything of a society gone mad on war, and I knew that America would never invest the necessary funds or energies in rehabilitation of its poor so long as adventures like Vietnam continued to draw men and skills and money like some demoniacal destructive suction tube.[192]

Johnson also quickly lost interest in the civil rights movement as his time was increasingly monopolized by the war. His working relationship with Martin Luther King evaporated overnight as King began to criticize the war effort, and Johnson effectively ended his pursuit of civil rights.

The schizophrenic Cold War had a dual effect on the civil rights movement, at the same time both encouraging its progress and impeding its development. It was the negative effects of the Cold War that proved in the end to be the more powerful, as J. Edgar Hoover's McCarthyist attacks against the struggle for civil rights outweighed the leverage that foreign affairs provided African Americans over government officials. The civil rights movement, an ambitious attempt to force the United States to live up to its own promises of freedom, paid a heavy price for its efforts. The conflict between Hoover and Martin Luther King was the result not just of the personal animosities that sparked the controversy, but also by the contextual framework of the Cold War.

Free from the burdens of congressional or executive oversight, and charged with sweeping responsibilities to keep America safe from communism, the intelligence community thrived during the Cold War. "The founding fathers foresaw excess as the inevitable consequence of granting any part of government unchecked power," the Select Committee to Study Governmental Operations with respect to Intelligence Activities reported in 1976. "This has been demonstrated in the intelligence field where, too often, constitutional principles were subordinated to a pragmatic course of permitting desired ends to dictate and justify improper means." This lack of oversight allowed J. Edgar Hoover to conduct the business of the FBI according to his own prejudices and preferences. Martin Luther King, who inadvertently offended the Director, became a major target of Hoover's wrath. It was, according to historian Arthur Schlesinger, Jr., "a weird crusade" in which "the Bureau on Hoover's orders stalked Martin Luther King much as allied psychological warfare had stalked Nazi *Gauleiter* during the Second World War."[193] Former Attorney General Robert Jackson summed up the danger that unregulated prosecutors such as J. Edgar Hoover could inflict on targets such as Martin Luther King:

The most dangerous power of the prosecutor: that he will pick people that he thinks he should get, rather than pick cases that need to be prosecuted. With the law books filled with a great assortment of crimes, a prosecutor stands a fair chance of pinning at least a technical violation of some act on the part of almost anyone. . . . It is this realm—in which the prosecutor picks some person he dislikes or desires to be embarrassed, or selects some group of unpopular persons and then looks for an offense, that the greatest danger of abuse of prosecuting power lies.[194]

Notes

1. O'Reilly, Kenneth. *"Racial Matters."* New York: The Free Press, 1989, p. 3.
2. Quoted in Schlesinger, Arthur, Jr. *The Disuniting of America.* New York: Whittle Direct Books, 1991, p. 6.
3. Ibid, p. 1.
4. Myrdal, Gunnar. *An American Dilemma.* New York: Harper & Brothers Publishers, 1944, p. 3.
5. Donald Young, quoted in Myrdal, p. 21.
6. Washington, James M., ed. *A Testament of Hope.* San Francisco: Harper Collins Publishers, 1986, p. 314.
7. Myrdal, p. xiv.
8. Huntington, Samuel P. "American Ideals versus American Institutions," in Ikenberry, G. John, ed. *American Foreign Policy.* Boston: Scott, Foresman and Company, 1989, p. 223.
9. Huntington, pp. 223–24.
10. King, quoted in Washington, p. 208.
11. King, quoted in Washington, p. 105.
12. Hoover, J. Edgar. *Masters of Deceit,* New York: Henry Holt and Company, 1958, p. 334.
13. King, Martin Luther. "Equality Now." *The Nation.* February 4, 1961.
14. King, Martin Luther, Jr. *Stride Toward Freedom.* San Francisco: Harper & Row Publishers, 1958, p. 92.
15. King FBI File. Letter from J.E. Hoover, November 15, 1961. section, 1 p. 2.
16. King FBI File. Memorandum from N. P. Callahan to the Director, May 3, 1961, section 1.
17. King FBI File. Memorandum from M. A. Jones to Mr. DeLoach, February 7, 1961, section 1.
18. Ibid.
19. Much of the biographical information on Levison comes from David Garrow's *The FBI and Martin Luther King, Jr.* New York: Penguin Books, 1981, pp. 26–27.
20. Garrow, p. 44.
21. Wofford, Harris. *Of Kennedys and Kings.* Pittsburg: University of Pittsburgh Press, 1992, p. 216.
22. King FBI File. April 13, 1962 report on Martin Luther King, Jr., section 1, p. 16.
23. "O'Dell Charged in Baton Rouge." *The Times-Picayune,* New Orleans, Louisiana. March 28, 1957, p. 6.
24. Mullen, Perry. "Witness Tries to Discuss Race Issue in Red Probe." *The Times-Picayune,* New Orleans, Louisiana. July 31, 1958.

25. King FBI File, section 2.
26. For more information on the source of the Bureau's allegations against Levison, see Garrow, chapter 1.
27. Final Report of the Senate Select Committee to Study Governmental Operations with Respect to Intelligence Activities. Book 6, p. 170 Hereafter referred to as the Church Committee report.
28. Schlesinger, Arthur Jr. *Robert Kennedy and his Times.* New York: Ballantine Books, 1978, p. 388.
29. King FBI File. Memo from J. Edgar Hoover to Robert Kennedy. June 21, 1962, section 2.
30. King FBI File. Teletype from SAC, New York to Director, FBI. September 12, 1962, section 2, p. 2.
31. King FBI File. Memorandum from SAC, New York to Director, FBI. September 28, 1962, volume II.
32. "O'Dell Resigns Place in SCLC." *The Times-Picayune.* November 2, 1962.
33. Ibid.
34. Ibid.
35. "Rev. King Blasts Dixie FBI Agents." *The New York Courier.* December 1, 1962.
36. "The Southern Mobsters and Their Federal Friends." *The Worker.* December 2, 1962.
37. Garrow, p. 56.
38. FBI Aide Hits Claim Agents Side With Dixie." *The Chicago Defender.* December 6, 1962.
39. King FBI File. Memorandum from Cartha DeLoach to John Mohr, January 15, 1963.
40. King FBI File. Memorandum from Burke Marshall to J. Edgar Hoover, 9/12/63.
41. Testimony of Andrew Young to the Church Committee, 2/19/76, p. 40. Quoted in Church Committee report, Book III, p. 97.
42. Schlesinger, p. 384.
43. Ibid., p. 384.
44. Ibid.
45. Church Committee report. Book III, p. 99.
46. Ibid., p. 100.
47. King FBI File. Note from Alan Belmont to Clyde Tolson, 10/17/63.
48. Ibid.
49. Schlesinger, p. 389.
50. King FBI File. Memo from William Sullivan to Alan Belmont, 8/30/63, p. 1.
51. King FBI File. J. Edgar Hoover note on UPI press release announcing King's honor. December 29, 1963.
52. Schlesinger, p. 394.

53. Testimony to the Church Committee, Book III, p. 117.
54. Guthman, Edwin O., in testimony to the Church Committee. Book III, p. 92.
55. King FBI File. Memorandum from William Sullivan to Alan Belmont, 1/6/64. Italics added.
56. Garrow, p. 105.
57. King FBI File. Memorandum from William Sullivan to Alan Belmont, 1/13/64.
58. King FBI File. Memorandum from Sullivan to Alan Belmont, 1/27/64.
59. King FBI File. Memorandum from Frederick Baumgardner to William Sullivan, 1/28/64.
60. King FBI File. Memorandum from Frederick Baumgardner to William Sullivan, 7/15/64.
61. King FBI File. Memorandum from Frederick Baumgardner to William Sullivan, 3/4/64.
62. King FBI File. Press release from United Press International. June 2, 1964.
63. King FBI File. Press release from United Press International. August 5, 1964.
64. King FBI File. Memorandum from Frederick Baumgardner to William Sullivan, 3/4/64.
65. King FBI File. Memorandum from Frederick Baumgardner to William Sullivan, 8/31/64.
66. King FBI File. Memorandum from Frederick Baumgardner to William Sullivan, 11/30/64.
67. Church Committee report, Book III, pp. 143–44.
68. Church Committee report, Book III, p. 155.
69. Gentry, Curt. *J. Edgar Hoover: The Man and The Secrets.* New York: Plume, 1992, p. 573.
70. Shelton, Elizabeth. "Hoover in Blast at Police Corruption Opens Fire on Some Other Targets." *Washington Post.* November 19, 1964, p. A1.
71. Ungar, Sanford. *FBI.* Boston: Little, Brown and Company, 1976, p. 295.
72. "The Demagogue King," in *The Albany Herald.* November 19, 1964.
73. King FBI File. Baumgardner to Sullivan, 11/19/64, section 19.
74. King FBI File. Telegram from King to Hoover, 11/19/64, section 20.
75. King FBI File. "Organization of the Current Attack Against the FBI by Martin Luther King." 12/1/64, section 21, p. 10.
76. Lewis, Anthony. "Negro Leaders Support Dr. King." *New York Times.* November 20, 1964, p. 18.
77. Eaton, William. "President Wards Off Trouble With the Answer That Isn't." *The Washington Post and Times Herald.* December 17, 1964, p. A50.
78. Ibid.

79. King FBI File. United Press International press release. December 1, 1964.
80. Church Committee report. Book III, p. 163.
81. King FBI File. United Press International press release. December 1, 1964.
82. Testimony to the Church Committee. Book III, p. 166.
83. Garrow, p. 130.
84. Testimony to the Church Committee. Book III, p. 167.
85. Ibid.
86. Garrow, p. 126.
87. Church Committee report. Book III, p. 159.
88. Ibid, p. 161.
89. Ibid, p. 159.
90. Garrow, p. 134.
91. Ibid.
92. Schlesinger, p. 818.
93. King FBI File. Memorandum from Cartha DeLoach to John Mohr, 8/14/65.
94. Church Committee report. Book III.
95. Patterson, Eugene. "Sweet Lies Soothe Hoover." *The Atlanta Constitution,* Mar 31, 1976, p. 5A.
96. King FBI File. Handwritten comments on memorandum from Cartha De-Loach to Clyde Tolson, 10/26/66.
97. Oates, Stephen B. *Let the Trumpet Sound.* Mentor Books, New York, 1982. p. 365.
98. Washington, ed. p. 233.
99. Oates, p. 418.
100. King FBI File. Memorandum from Charles Brennan to William Sullivan, 4/10/87.
101. King FBI File. Memorandum from J. Edgar Hoover to all special agents in charge, 3/4/68.
102. Turner, William V. *Hoover's FBI.* New York: Thunder's Mouth Press, 1993, p. 99.
103. King FBI File. Memorandum from Milton Jones to Thomas Bishop, 3/18/69.
104. Gruenberg, Robert. "FBI's try to use Cody against Dr. King told," *Chicago Daily News,* June 10, 1976.
105. Genry, p. 67.
106. The quotation is from J. Edgar Hoover, as quoted in O'Reilly, p. 147.
107. O'Reilly, p. 9.
108. O'Reilly, p. 14.
109. O'Reilly, p. 41.
110. Ibid.
111. Ibid.

112. Sullivan, p. 16.
113. Hoover quoted in de Toledano, p. 264.
114. Sullivan, p. 268.
115. Gentry, p. 280.
116. Hoover quoted in de Toledano, p. 265.
117. Sullivan quoted in Ovid Demaris, p. 209.
118. Sullivan, quoted in Demaris, p. 209.
119. Wofford, p. 152.
120. Wofford, p. 160.
121. Ibid.
122. Ibid.
123. Chamberlain, John. "J. Edgar Hoover and Dr. King." *Red Bank (NJ) Register.* December 3, 1964.
124. *Bearing the Cross,* p. 375.
125. Abernathy, Ralph. *And the Walls Came Tumbling Down.* New York: Harper and Row, 1989, p. 474.
126. Ibid., p. 471.
127. Gentry, p. 469.
128. Garrow, chapter 4.
129. Sullivan, p. 140.
130. George E. Allen quoted in Demaris, p. 11.
131. Sullivan, p. 274.
132. Letter from Harlan Fiske Stone to Jack Alexander, September 21, 1937. Quoted in Mason, Alpheus T. *Harlan Fiske Stone.* New York: Viking, 1956, p. 149.
133. Stone in *New York Times,* May 5, 1924. Quoted in Church Committee report. Book II, p. 23.
134. Ibid., p. 24.
135. Church Committee report. Book II, p. 26. Confidential Memorandum from the President to Bureau Heads, 6/26/39.
136. Schlesinger, p. 656.
137. Schott, p. 204.
138. Sullivan in Demaris, pp. 209–210.
139. Bernstein, Carl, and Robert Woodward. *All the President's Men.* New York: Simon and Schuster, 1974, p. 289.
140. Gentry, p. 156.
141. Ibid.
142. Schott, Joseph. *No Left Turns.* New York: Praeger Publishers, 1975, p. 27.
143. Sullivan, William. *The Bureau.* New York: W.W. Norton & Company, 1979, p. 21.
144. Ibid., p. 33.
145. Ibid., p. 14.

146. Memorandum from Frederick Baumgardner to William Sullivan, August 23, 1963.
147. Church Committee report. Book III, p. 106.
148. Ibid.
149. Church Committee report. Book III, p. 107.
150. Memo from William Sullivan to Alan Belmont, August 30, 1963.
151. Ibid.
152. Schott, p. 20.
153. Patterson, Eugene. "Sweet Lies Soothe Hoover," *The Atlanta Constitution.* May 31, 1976, p. 5A.
154. Sullivan, p. 136.
155. Church Committee report. Book III, p. 135.
156. Sullivan, p. 135.
157. Clark, Ramsey. *Crime in America.* Quoted in Demaris, p. 214.
158. Church Committee report. Book II, p. iii.
159. Myrdal, p. 1004.
160. Bunche, Ralph. "The Negro in the Political Life of the United States." *Journal of Negro Education.* July, 1941, p. 583.
161. Myrdal, p. 1007.
162. Quoted in Dudziak, Mary L. "Desegregation as a Cold War Imperative." *The Stanford Law Review.* Volume 41:61, November 1988.
163. Lomax, Louis E. *The Negro Revolt.* New York: Harper & Brothers, 1962, p. 74.
164. Commencement address at Lincoln University in Pennsylvania, June 6, 1961. Quoted in Washington, pp. 208–209.
165. Gore, Albert, Jr. *Earth in the Balance.* Boston: Houghton Mifflin Company, 1992, pp. 271–72.
166. Myrdal, pp. 1015–16.
167. Acheson quoted in Dudziak, p. 101.
168. Quoted in King, Martin Luther. "Equality Now," *The Nation.* February 4, 1961.
169. Dudziak, p. 65.
170. Richard Nixon quoted in Burk, Robert Fredrick, *The Eisenhower Administration and Black Civil Rights.* Knoxville: University of Tennessee Press, 1984, p. 257. Nixon later backed off his apparent endorsement of civil rights.
171. Sorenson, Theodore. *Kennedy.* New York: Harper & Row, 1988, p. 478.
172. Marable, Manning. *Race, Reform, and Rebellion.* London: Macmillan Press, 1984, p. 18.
173. Ibid.
174. Branch, Taylor. *Parting the Waters.* New York: Simon & Schuster, 1988, p. 563.
175. Marable, p. 28.

176. Rovere, Richard. *Senator Joe McCarthy.* New York: Harper & Row, 1959, p. 5.
177. "O'Dell Resigns Place in SCLC." *The Times-Picayune.* November 2, 1962.
178. Marable, p. 33.
179. Demaris, p. 161.
180. Hoover, J. Edgar. *On Communism.* New York: Random House, 1969, p. 53.
181. Hoover, J. Edgar. *Masters of Deceit.* New York: Henry Holt and Company, 1958, p. 5.
182. Ungar, p. 306. Gentry, pp. 659–60.
183. Adam Clayton Powell, quoted in Marable, p. 22.
184. Sorenson, p. 17.
185. Ibid., p. 246.
186. Ibid.
187. Ibid., p. 245.
188. Schlesinger, p. 480.
189. Califano, Joseph Jr. *The Triumph and Tragedy of Lyndon Johnson.* New York: Simon and Schuster, 1991, p. 120.
190. Ibid., p. 112.
191. Ibid., p. 119.
192. Oates, p. 418.
193. Schlesinger, p. 390.
194. Jackson, quoted in Schlesinger, p. 304.

II

The FBI File on
Martin Luther King, Jr.

Editor's note. *The Federal Bureau of Investigation amassed thousands of pages of paperwork in its surveillance file on Martin Luther King, Jr. The file on America's foremost civil-rights leader was opened in 1958 and was still active in 1975, seven years after King's assassination on April 4, 1968. It contains more than a hundred sections that record in detail King's activities and the Bureau's predilections. While the file has been necessarily extensively edited for the purposes of this book, the substantial extracts that remain clearly delineate FBI procedures (and prejudices) in this case as well as the fiber of the Bureau's investigation of Martin Luther King.*

Deletions throughout the text are indicated by ellipses. Many of the deletions within the documents themselves were made by the FBI in accordance with exemptions allowed under the Freedom of Information Act. Subsection b2 of Title 5, United States Code, Section 552, permits the withholding of information "related solely to the internal personnel rules and practices of any agency," while subsection b7 permits the deletion of references that might "constitute an unwarranted invasion of personal privacy" or that might "disclose the identity of a confidential source, including a State, local, or foreign agency or authority or any private institution which furnished information on a confidential basis. . . ."

Because many of the entries in the file have been transcribed by Bureau typists from tapes or shorthand, typographical errors and stylistic inconsistencies are numerous; so are misspellings, especially of proper names. Transpositions, dropped or appended letters, mispunctuation, or faulty agreement can distract a reader; any errors or inconsistencies apparently made in the process of transcription have therefore been corrected, as has the Bureau's often careless grammar. These corrections, however, as well as the occasional addition of a bracketed word or two to clarify phrasing, in no way alter the meaning or intent of the Bureau's text.

To lend clarity to the course of the FBI investigation of King, the documents selected from the file have been placed in chronological order by the date on which they were written. Many of the documents in the file in fact appear out of chronological sequence, particularly after March 1968, so that the section numbers, as they stand in this edition, are not always consecutive. Nor is every section of the file represented.

Finally, following the documents for each year from 1962 to 1969 are excerpts from the electronic surveillance file that was illegally maintained by the Bureau on King throughout that seven-year period.

1958–1962

1958–1962

[Section 1]

Report: Background of Subject

Noveber 3, 1958– March 10, 1960	Report: Activities of Subject
April 18, 1960	Memorandum: Welte to Rosen
October 16, 1960– May 12, 1961	Report: Activities of Subject
May 22, 1961	Report
July 14, 1961	Report
December 17, 1961	Memorandum: McGowan to Rosen
December 28, 1961	Memorandum: El Paso to Director
April 13, 1962	Letter: Director to Vice President
April 13, 1962	Memorandum: Director to Attorney General
April 13, 1962	Airtel: New York to Director
April 18, 1962	Memorandum: New York
April 18, 1962	Airtel: New York to Director
April 20, 1962	Letter: Director to Special Assistant to President
April 20, 1962	Memorandum: Atlanta Identification Record of Subject

[Section 2]

June 12, 1962	Memorandum: New York
June 25, 1962	Memorandum: Director to Attorney General
July 25, 1962	Memorandum: Rosen to Belmont
August 6, 1962	Memorandum: New York
August 11, 1962	Memorandum: Director to Attorney General
September 10, 1962	Teletype: New York to Director
November 15, 1962	Memorandum: New York
November 20, 1962	Memorandum: New Orleans to Director
December 7, 1962	Letter: Director to Special Assistant to President

[Section 1]

The biographical details that follow are attached to a report dated April 25, 1962, in Section 1 of the FBI file on Martin Luther King, Jr.

The 1961 edition of *Who's Who in America* furnishes the following background information concerning subject:

MARTIN LUTHER KING, JR., clergyman, born Atlanta on January 15, 1929, to MARTIN KING and ALBERTA WILLIAMS. Received A.B. Morehouse College, 1948 LHD, 1957; B.D. Crozer Theological seminary, 1951; Ph.D. J. Louis Crozer Fellow Boston University, 1955, D.D. 1959; D.D. Chicago Theological Seminary, 1957; LL.D. Howard University, 1957, Morgan State College, 1958; L.H.D. Central State College, 1958; Special Student, University of Pennsylvania, Department of Philosophy, Harvard. Married CORETTA SCOTT, June 17, 1953; children—YOLANDA DENISE, and MARTIN LUTHER III. Pastor of Dexter Avenue Baptist Church, Montgomery, Alabama; President of Southern Christian Leadership Conference (SCLC); Vice President of National Sunday School and Baptist Training Union, Congress of National Baptist Convention, Inc.; President of Montgomery Improvement Association; recipient of Pearl Plafkner Award for Scholastics, Crozer Theological Seminary, Chester, Pennsylvania, 1951; selected one of ten outstanding personalities of 1956 by *Time* magazine, 1957. Member of National Association for the Advancement of Colored People (NAACP), Alpha Pi Alpha, Sigma Pi Phi, Elk, Author of *Stride Toward Freedom*, 1958, and contributor of articles to popular and religious periodicals. Home—309 South Jackson Street; Office—454 Dexter Avenue, Montgomery, Alabama.

The *Atlanta Daily World* newspaper on December 1, 1959, carried an article entitled "Dr. King Resigns to Take Post in Atlanta." This article stated that subject had resigned as Pastor of the Dexter Avenue Baptist Church in Montgomery, Alabama, and had accepted the post of co-pastor of the Ebenezer Baptist Church in Atlanta, Georgia, with his father. The article stated that he had been pastor of the Dexter Avenue Church since 1954 and that he would come to Atlanta on February 1, 1960. The article reported that he had founded and headed the Montgomery Improvement Association which organized the successful protest that ended bus segregation in Montgomery, Alabama. The subject was also described as President of the SCLC.

The May 23, 1961, issue of the *New York Herald Tribune* carried an article entitled "Dr. King Maps Alabama Strategy." This article stated that the SCLC was an outgrowth of the Montgomery bus boycott of 1955 to 1956 in which the subject, then pastor of the Dexter Avenue Baptist Church in Montgomery, sprung into national prominence as a leader of Negroes seeking to end segregation by using such tactics as sit-in movements and freedom rides.

Selected references to the activities of the subject as reported in the news media and by FBI informants for the period from November 1958 to March 1960 follow.

. . . claimed he learned that Rev. Martin Luther King, Jr., would leave Montgomery at 8:15 P.M. on **11/3/58** for Mobile. Also that King would travel alone in his automobile. . . . implied that this would have been a good chance to kill or at least to do bodily harm to King. . . . said he would try to find out when King planned to return to Montgomery.

. . . a Temple meeting held at MTI [Muslim Temple of Islam] No. 2, 5335 south Greenwood Ave., Chicago, Ill. Elijah Muhammad, national leader of MTI, spoke on civil rights, stating that Rev. Martin Luther King's intentions were good but that he, King, should be fighting for independence in the form of a separate state.

. . . a Temple meeting . . . stated that King was seeking to become more closely associated with the white man instead of trying to improve his black brother. . . . said King's ways were wrong and if 10,000 of the so-called Negroes got together, they would be able to demand more from this Government and become more economically independent.

. . . furnished the Birmingham Office an unsigned copy of a statement made on **12/8/58** . . . by the unidentified informant . . . This statement, which was quoted verbatim in reference, contained information regarding the collection of money to have some Negroes killed and noted that a list of ten names picked out of the air included Martin Luther King of Ala. It was also noted that the news that King was going to be killed had gotten out all over the country and the plans were stopped.

. . . reported that judging from remarks made by members . . . the Ku Klux Klan, . . . they were constantly looking for an opportunity to harm Rev. Martin Luther King, Jr.

... WSFA-TV Television Station, Montgomery, while discussing the apparent sabotage of the station on that date when Harry Belafonte, well-known Negro singer, was scheduled to have a featured spot on a program, pointed out that a very similar act was done about one year before when King was scheduled to be interviewed by Martin Agronsky, ...

The **March 1960** issue of "The Packinghouse Worker," the official publication of the United Packinghouse Workers of America (UPWA) (100–35658) published an article entitled "Alabama Hits Rev. M. L. King: Lasley Joins Defense Group." This article revealed that UPWA Vice-President Russell R. Lasley had joined a committee to defend Rev. Martin Luther King against perjury charges brought against him by Ala. authorities.

The state of Ala. had accused King, who addressed UPWA's 1957 National Wage Policy conference, of failing to declare $45,000 income in 1958. The committee stated that the state created the $45,000 figure by adding King's personal income to expenses incurred in his leadership in the civil rights movement. The committee planned to raise $200,000 to defend King and to aid the SCLC in a drive to register Negro voters.

King headed the SCLC and was the leader of the successful Montgomery, Ala. bus boycott.

In a public statement the committee declared "the Dixiecrats have unleashed this evil and groundless attack on his honesty, hoping to remove Dr. King from the scene and to restore themselves as the unchallenged, tyrannical masters of the life and destiny of the Negro in the South."

The **3/10/60** issue of the "Evening Star" published an article entitled "Halt Reign of Terror! King Asks President," which concerned a telegram sent to President Eisenhower by Martin Luther King, Jr., president of the SCLC, at Atlanta. King requested the President to end a reign of terror in Montgomery, Ala., by instructing the AG "to take immediate action in your name" to restore law and order. King declared that Gestapo-like methods were being used to intimidate Negroes in Montgomery.

This article also revealed that King led a successful boycott to integrate Montgomery's city buses before he moved to Atlanta.

UNITED STATES
Memorandum

TO: Mr. Rosen   DATE: 4/18/60

FROM: W. B. Welte

SUBJECT: DR. MARTIN LUTHER KING JR.
           TELEVISION APPEARANCE
           "MEET THE PRESS," 4/17/60

On 4/17/60 Dr. King appeared on the television show "Meet the Press." He made no specific mention of the FBI and he spoke of the racial situation in general. Among some of the comments made by Dr. King are these: When questioned as to whether the Negroes were breaking the law by engaging in "sit-ins" at lunch counters, he stated the law of the land called for integration; therefore, in breaking local laws "we are affirming the law of the land." When this question was pursued in regard to the ends justifying the means, he stated there are moral laws and whenever man-made law is in conflict with moral law, we should protest and when local law is in conflict with federal law, we should also protest. King expressed the opinion that the Executive Branch of the Government should afford the Negroes more protection and he stated that he was disappointed in the Civil Rights Bill as it pertained to schools and voter registration. He felt the president should do more in the area of executive orders and moral persuasion.

When questioned as to whether he would not be on safer ground by engaging in "sit-ins" in schools rather than at lunch counters, he stated it sometimes is necessary to dramatize an issue and therefore lunch counters were selected because it also had an economic effect.

King criticized former President Harry Truman for expressing the opinion that if anyone entered a store which he ran to engage in a demonstration, "I would throw him out." King said this statement "serves to aid and abet violent forces in the South," and he could not reconcile this with Harry Truman's strong pro-civil-rights record as a President.

The foregoing is submitted for your information.

The following selected references to the activities of Martin Luther King, Jr., cover the period of time from October 1960 to May 1961.

The *Atlanta Daily World* newspaper on **October 16, 1960**, carried an article entitled "Sit-inners Meet at Morehouse College and Clark in 3-Day Conference." The article reported that the subject, who was one of the speakers, urged the students to accept the philosophy of non-violence not only "as a technique but as a way of life." KING also stated that non-violence rejects the method of Communism.

. . . Reidsville, Ga., advised that Martin Luther King was received at the prison on **10/26/60** to serve a four-month sentence on a traffic violation for which he was on probation. . . . stated he had been informed that there was to be a hearing on this matter in Atlanta, Ga., on **10/27/60** and after the hearing a motorcade was to proceed to the prison.

An article in the **10/28/60** edition of the "Savannah Evening Press," Savannah, Ga., indicated that King had been released from Reidsville Prison and had returned to Atlanta.

. . . advised . . . telephoned the Chicago Branch of the NAACP to inform them that on **10/30/60** a nationwide demonstration was to be held in protest of the arrest of Rev. Martin King in Atlanta. . . . stated that all members of the NAACP were to be advised and urged to participate.

. . . advised on **11/3/60** that the White House was to be picketed on election day. One of the individuals heading the picketing was reportedly named King. . . . believed that the King mentioned could possibly be Martin Luther King, Southern Negro leader.

A press release dated **11/6/60** from the "Washington Capital News Service" revealed that Dr. Martin Luther King, Jr., praised senator John F. Kennedy for his stand on the civil rights issue. King's statement was the closest he had come in an outright endorsement of Kennedy for President.

King criticized the Republican position on their civil rights issue because there was too much disagreement and double talk from the Republican Party.

The **12/2/60** issue of the "Mobile Press" reported that the "New York Times" had requested a new trial of the $500,000 libel suit brought by Montgomery, Ala., Police Commissioner L. B. Sullivan. A State Court Jury on 11/3/60 awarded Sullivan the full amount. Sullivan had claimed he was libeled by an advertisement in the 3/29/60 issue of the "New York Times" which solicited funds for the defense of Martin Luther King. The ad dealt in part with police handling of Negro student demonstrations in Montgomery during the spring of 1960.

. . . advised that the active African Nationalist groups in the NYC area referred to men like Martin Luther King as "tools of the white man" and as "Uncle Toms."

Atlanta Journal newspaper of **February 23, 1961,** carried an article entitled "Highlanders and Dr. King Join Forces." This article stated that the Atlanta SCLC, headed by the Rev. MARTIN LUTHER KING, JR., and Tennessee controversial Highlander Folk School have joined forces to train Negro leaders for the southern civil rights struggle. The article said that the Highlander Folk School located in Tennessee Cumberland Mountains had been involved in the past in several political controversies. It had been staunchly defended by Mr. FRANKLIN D. ROOSEVELT, among others, but in 1960 a Tennessee State Court revoked its charter after a legislative investigation charged that Communists had lectured there.

On **May 12, 1961,** inquiry in the neighborhood of 584 Alfred Street, NW, determined that Rev. WYATT TEE WALKER resided at that address.

An article appearing in the *Atlanta Journal* newspaper, issue of April 30, 1961, identifies WALKER as the newly-appointed Executive Secretary of the SCLC, having offices in Atlanta, Georgia. This article quoted Rev. WALKER as advising that his activities with this appeal are as an individual and not as an SCLC official.

. . . that some people in Washington, D. C., area had received letters with the return address of 584 Alfred Road, NW, Atlanta 18, Georgia. These letters enclosed a petition for clemency addressed to the Honorable JOHN F. KENNEDY, President of the United States. The petitions requested presidential clemency for CARL BRADEN to "reaffirm the position of the federal Government supporting peaceful and orderly integration in the South." The letters enclosing the petitions were signed by several persons, one of whom was MARTIN LUTHER KING, Atlanta Georgia, as well as WYATT TEE WALKER, Atlanta.

Atlanta Journal newspaper, issue of May 2, 1961, contained an article captioned "King Sees McCarthyism in 2 U.S. Contempt Sentences." This article stated that subject said the one-year jail sentences given CARL BRADEN and FRANK WILKINSON [of the National Committee to Abolish the Un-American Activities Committee (NCAUAC)] are evidences that "McCarthyism" is on the rise again. According to the article, the subject stated he had no doubt they are being punished, particularly MR. BRADEN, for his integration activities. Subject went on to say he was not upholding Communism in any way, but it was felt the HUAC should not be used to thwart integration.

This article went on to state that BRADEN and WILKINSON would

serve one-year jail sentences for contempt of Congress because they
refused to tell the Committee in a 1958 Atlanta hearing whether they
have ever been Communists.

RE: CARL BRADEN

Mrs. ALBERTA AHEARN, 2311 Payne Street, Louisville, Kentucky,
a self-admitted former member of the CP, Louisville, in testifying on
December 11, and 13, 1954, in Jefferson County, Kentucky, Criminal
Court, in a state sedition prosecution against CARL BRADEN, identified CARL BRADEN and his wife, ANNE BRADEN, as having been
known to her members of the CP Louisville, from January 1951, to
shortly prior to the time of her testimony.

The *Courier-Journal*, Louisville, Kentucky, a newspaper of general
circulation, on February 3, 1959, reported that CARL BRADEN had
been sentenced to one year in prison on a charge of contempt of Congress on February 2, 1959, in Atlanta, Georgia. The story noted that
he had been convicted under this charge on January 21, 1959, and that
the charge arose from his refusal to answer questions before the House
Committee on Un-American Activities (HCUA).

The *Louisville Times*, Louisville, Kentucky, a newspaper of general
circulation, on February 27, 1961, reported that the United States Supreme Court had, on that date, affirmed the contempt of Congress conviction of BRADEN.

The *Courier-Journal*, on May 2, 1961, reported that CARL BRADEN
had surrendered to the United States Marshal at Atlanta, Georgia, on
May 1, 1961, to begin serving a one-year prison sentence for contempt
of Congress.

The *Courier-Journal*, Louisville, Kentucky, on February 2, 1962, reported that CARL BRADEN had been released from Federal Prison
Camp at Allenwood, Pennsylvania, on February 1, 1962. BRADEN
indicated that he would return to his home, Louisville, Kentucky.

The December 1961, issue of the Southern Patriot which, according
to its masthead, is published by the Southern Conference Education
Fund, Inc. (SCEF), identifies CARL BRADEN and his wife, ANNE
BRADEN as field secretaries and editors. The address of the editorial
offices of this publication is given as 4403 Virginia Avenue, Louisville
11, Kentucky, which is the home address of the BRADENs.

May 22, 1961

MARTIN LUTHER KING, JR.

Martin Luther King, Jr., clergyman and integrationist, was born on January 15, 1929, at Atlanta, Georgia. King has not been investigated by the FBI.

King has been widely publicized since he led a bus boycott by Negroes in Montgomery, Alabama, as President of the Montgomery Improvement Association, Montgomery, Alabama. He has remained nationally prominent in integration efforts particularly with regard to the so-called "sit-in demonstrations" and his association with the National Association for the Advancement of Colored People and the Congress of Racial Equality.

In 1960 he left Montgomery, Alabama, to become joint pastor with his father of the Ebenezer Baptist Church, Atlanta, Georgia. As a result of his above activities, King has been arrested on numerous occasions charged with misdemeanors and has claimed he was the victim of police brutality. Many of King's speeches have stressed nonviolent action in integration efforts.

Bureau files reveal the following information concerning King.

In January 1957, it was reported that King was honorary chairman of "Enroll for Freedom" campaign to provide economic relief for victims of racist terror in the South sponsored by the Young Socialist League.

In 1957 and 1958 the Bureau was advised that efforts were being made to obtain funds for the purpose of assassinating leaders in integration efforts in the South, including King.

In September 1958, King was stabbed by a female in Harlem, New York, and subsequent thereto directed a letter to Benjamin Davis, Jr., Communist Party official, thanking Davis for the donation of blood made when King was a patient in a New York hospital recuperating from the above attack.

In August 1960, it was reported King's secretary advised the Committee to Secure Justice for Morton Sobell (cited by the House Committee on Un-American Activities as a Communist front succeeding the National Committee to Secure Justice in the Rosenberg Case) that King would be happy to lend his support for obtaining freedom for Morton Sobell.

The February 4, 1961, issue of "The Nation" magazine published an article by King making a plea for faster integration of the races by indicating much could be done by the present administration through Executive Order. In this regard, King stated, "if, for instance, the law enforcement personnel in the FBI were integrated, many persons who now defy federal law might come under restraints from which they are presently free . . ."

The Bureau has been advised that on May 21, 1961, Martin Luther King was in attendance at the church of Reverend Ralph D. Abernathy in Montgomery, Alabama, along with other integration leaders. Reportedly, a large mob had gathered outside this church.

A Bureau memorandum dated **July 14, 1961** revealed that a national meeting of the Knights of the Ku Klux Klan (KKKK) was held jointly with the Dixie Klans in Anniston, Alabama, on July 8, 1961. At this meeting Earl George and James Venable, both of Atlanta, Georgia, and the leaders of the US/KKKK were speakers. Venable during his speech advocated the killing of Martin Luther King. George stated "King has to go and we might as well make up our minds to get him killed even if someone has to go to prison."

UNITED STATES GOVERNMENT
Memorandum

TO: Mr. Rosen   DATE: December 17, 1961

FROM: C. L. McGowan

SUBJECT: RACIAL SITUATION
          ALBANY, GEORGIA
          RACIAL MATTERS

A limited investigation has been requested in this matter into the arrest and detention of Dr. Martin Luther King.

At 12:50 P.M. Departmental Attorney Murphy contacted the Bureau, at about the same time Mr. Barrett contacted supervisor Lavin, and at 1:17 P.M. Mr. Marshall called your office, all with regard to the same matter. Mr. Marshall advised that Governor Rockefeller had called the Attorney General and expressed concern about the arrest and safety of Dr. Martin Luther King. The Attorney General asked Mr. Marshall to determine if "we" were doing all that we should be doing to make sure that "he was safe."

Mr. Marshall had been informed that Dr. King had been transferred to the Jail at Americus, Georgia. The Department attorneys and Mr. Marshall asked that we determine why Dr. King was taken to Americus, the nature of the charges against him, if he had been afforded a hearing, and generally, the situation surrounding his confinement at Americus, including a description of the jail. Americus police authorities were to be contacted to determine if they had knowledge of any threats to Dr. King and what precautions they had taken in his regard. Mr. Marshall also asked to be advised of any information we had received from any contacts or sources indicating any potential violence or harm to Dr. King. Both Mr. Murphy and Mr. Marshall wanted to be telephonically furnished results at home this date. (Marshall, OL 2-3562; Murphy, WH 6-2786).

ACTION:

The Department's request was forwarded to Atlanta Supervisor . . . at 1:30 with instructions to advise the Bureau immediately of the results and follow with a summary teletype this date. . . . said Negro leaders had scheduled a press conference at 2:00 P.M. in Atlanta and would advise of any pertinent developments.

UNITED STATES GOVERNMENT
Memorandum

TO: DIRECTOR, FBI   DATE: 12-28-61

FROM: SAC, EL PASO (62-0) (RUC)

SUBJECT: MARTIN LUTHER KING, JR.
              MISCELLANEOUS—INFORMATION CONCERNING

The following is being submitted for the information of the Bureau and Atlanta since the person furnishing the information, . . . El Paso, Texas, stated that he had been considering writing a letter directly to the Bureau regarding the following information. He stated, that if the information were passed on to the Bureau, it would not be necessary for him to write.

On December 21, 1961, . . . furnished the following information orally to Special Agent. . . .

. . . would like to see "a case made" indicating that MARTIN LUTHER KING, Jr., of Albany, Georgia, was a card carrying Communist. . . . was of the opinion that MARTIN LUTHER KING, JR., was a card-carrying Communist. His opinion was based on reading newspapers and talking with people who have been in Alabama and Georgia.

Considerable effort was made to attempt to get more specific information from ... without success.

At times during the conversation, ... did not appear to be entirely rational.

El Paso indices regarding ... are negative.

Honorable Lyndon B. Johnson   April 13, 1962
The Vice President
Washington 25, D.C.

My dear Mr. Vice President:

A source who has furnished reliable information in the past advised on April 10, 1962, that Martin Luther King, Jr., prominent southern Negro leader, in discussing his recent trip to Washington, D.C., with Stanley David Levison stated that he, King, had visited you and the Attorney General.

I thought you would be interested in knowing that King is a close associate of Levison and Hunter Pitts O'Dell.

This information has been furnished to the Attorney General.

                                        Sincerely yours,
                                        J. Edgar Hoover

The Attorney General   April 13, 1962

Director, FBI

MARTIN LUTHER KING, JR.
SECURITY MATTER-C

A confidential source that has furnished reliable information in the past advised on April 11, 1962, that Stanley David Levison had recently told Hunter Pitts O'Dell he was writing a speech for Martin Luther King, Jr. According to Levison, King will deliver the speech at the convention of the United Packing House Workers of America, American Federation of Labor-Congress of Industrial Organizations, in May 1962, and the effectiveness of the speech may determine the amount of money the union will give King.

Another source who has furnished reliable information in the past advised on April 10, 1962, that King had recently informed Levison

that he had had a successful trip to Washington, D.C., where he raised
$3,000 and had visited you and the Vice-President. King agreed to have
one Harry Wachtel visit him at his Atlanta home during the latter part of
this month. According to Levison, Wachtel could be of great assistance
in obtaining funds for King. Wachtel is possibly identical with Harry H.
Wachtel, a New York City attorney and variety store executive.

In addition, the informant learned that Levison and King discussed
arrangements for a concert to be held in Atlanta in June to raise funds.
According to the source, Harry Belafonte would be one of the performers at the concert.

This informant also stated that King was extremely pleased when informed by Levison of the reaction of an official of the National Association for the Advancement of Colored People to the trip by King's wife to
Geneva since it indicates that Negroes are also interested in other issues
besides civil rights. King was extremely pleased to hear this reaction.

                              FBI

                                             Date: 4/13/62

AIRTEL

To: DIRECTOR, FBI (100-3-75)

From: SAC, NEW YORK (100-80640)

Subject: CPUSA
           NEGRO QUESTION
           IS-C
           (00: NY)

... advised on 4/10/62, that STANLEY LEVISON in conversation with
HUNTER PITTS O'DELL discussed a "March on Washington." Infor-
mant stated that no date for this march was mentioned; however, LE-
VISON stated that it should be a "midnight prayer service at Lincoln
Memorial."

LEVISON stated that this type of mass meeting should attract two
or three thousand people and would be of "news quality."

Atlanta and Washington Field are requested to attempt to ascertain,
through their established sources, the date of the march referred to above
and the name of the organization under which it will be sponsored.

Any further information in this respect furnished by NY sources will
be forwarded to the Bureau.

UNITED STATES DEPARTMENT OF JUSTICE

FEDERAL BUREAU OF INVESTIGATION

New York, New York
April 18, 1962

Re: Martin Luther King
Security Matter-C

A confidential source, who has furnished reliable information in the past, advised on April 16, 1962, that Stanley Levison discussed plans for an organization to be formed on behalf of Martin Luther King.

According to Levison, this organization, which he referred to as the Gandhi Society for Human Rights, will hold a luncheon in Washington, D.C. on May 17, 1962. This luncheon will be attended by approximately twenty people who will be invited because of their prominence in various fields of industry and government.

Among those being considered, according to Levison, are President John F. Kennedy; Attorney General Robert Kennedy; Senator Clifford Case, New Jersey; Senator Eugene McCarthy, Wisconsin; and former Attorney General William P. Rogers, Minnesota.

A second confidential source, who has furnished reliable information in the past, advised on April 17, 1962, that this luncheon may possibly be held at the Sheraton Park Hotel in Washington, D. C.

FBI

Date: 4/18/62

AIRTEL

To: DIRECTOR, FBI (100-106670)
                (100-392452)

From: SAC, NEW YORK (100–136585)

Subject: MARTIN LUTHER KING

           STANLEY LEVISON
           SM-C

... advised on 4/18/62 that STANLEY LEVISON plans to leave NYC on either Thursday evening (4/19/62) or Friday morning (4/20/62) and fly to Atlanta, Georgia, where he will confer with MARTIN LU-THER KING.

Atlanta is requested to alert established sources to the fact that LEV-ISON will be in the area for any information they may be able to furnish regarding his activities while there.

April 20, 1962

Honorable P. Kenneth O'Donnell
Special Assistant to the President
The White House
Washington, D. C.

My dear Mr. O'Donnell:

On February 14, 1962, I furnished you information concerning Martin Luther King, Jr. I thought you would be interested in additional information concerning the influence of Stanley David Levison, a secret member of the Communist Party, on King.

A confidence source who has furnished reliable information in the past advised on April 16, 1962, that he had learned that Levison is forming in King's name an organization to be known as the Gandhi Society for Human Rights. Levison contemplates sending invitations signed by King to approximately twenty prominent people to attend a luncheon on May 17, 1962, in Washington, D.C. A public announcement will be made at that time of the formation of the organization. The President and the Attorney General are among those being considered to be invited to the luncheon. Senator Clifford Case, Senator Eugene McCarthy and former Attorney General William P. Rogers may also be invited to the luncheon.

The informant said that he is under the impression that Theodore Kheel, arbitrator for the New York City Transit Authority; Harry Belafonte, well-known singer; and A. Philip Randolph, prominent labor leader, are involved in the formation of the organization.

This information is being furnished to the Attorney General.

This information has been classified "Secret" because of the sensitive nature of our sources.

Sincerely yours,

J. EDGAR HOOVER

UNITED STATES DEPARTMENT OF JUSTICE

FEDERAL BUREAU OF INVESTIGATION

Atlanta, Georgia
April 20, 1962

MARCH ON WASHINGTON
MAY 1962

... advised that he has heard rumors there would be a demonstration in Washington, D.C., on May 17, 1962, to commemorate the Supreme Court school decision of 1954. He stated that in addition to commemorating this decision, there would be a protest concerning racial segregation along other lines, such as employment.

... said that he knew of no plans by the Student Non-Violent Coordinating Committee in connection with this demonstration but he believes that if it does take place, it will be handled mainly by the Non-Violent Action Group (NAG) which has members mainly on the campus of Howard University, Washington, D.C. He said the office is located at 1332 Belmont Street, NW, Washington, D.C. and the chairman of NAG is William Mahoney of Howard University.

... also stated he has heard of another demonstration allegedly to take place sometime in May 1962 in Washington, D.C. He said this is a peace demonstration, but is also to be interracial in nature. He said that he knows of no plans for SNCC to take part in this demonstration and believes it is being handled mainly by the Committee on Non-Violent Action (CNVA) located at 158 Grand Street, New York 13, New York. He stated the national chairman of the group is A. J. Muste, who is a longtime, well-known pacifist. ... said that another group allegedly to be involved in this peace demonstration is the Student Peace Union, with headquarters in Chicago, Illinois.

... added that the demonstration is to be a "three-pronged walk" on Washington, D.C. He stated the demonstrators are to start from three different points on foot, one group to walk from Nashville, Tennessee, to Washington, D.C., and this will be an interracial group; the second group from somewhere in New England to Washington, D.C., on foot and the third group from Chicago to Washington, D.C., on foot. He did not know the date these walks are to start and he does not know the dates they are scheduled to arrive in Washington, D.C.

Also included in Section 1 of the FBI file on Martin Luther King, Jr., is the master copy of an Identification Record, which represents data furnished the Bureau by fingerprint contributors. It contains the information that follows.

CONTRIBUTOR OF FINGERPRINTS	NAME AND NUMBER	ARRESTED OR RECEIVED	CHARGE	DISPOSITION
Police Department Montgomery, Alabama	Martin Luther King, Jr. #80161	January 26, 1956	speeding	$10. & cost appealed
Sheriff's Office Montgomery, Alabama	M. L. King #7089	February 22, 1956	violation Title 14, Section 54.1940 Code of Alabama	Nolle Prosequi
Sheriff's Office Montgomery, Alabama	Martin Luther King, Jr. #10281	February 29, 1960	purgery [sic]	Nolle Prosequi
Police Department Atlanta, Georgia	Martin Luther King, Jr. #198979	October 19, 1960	violation Act 497 Georgia Law of 1960 (misdemeanor, refused to leave premises)	3/21/68 Unavailable per contr
State Board of Correction Atlanta, Georgia	Martin Luther King, Jr. #M-97326/39966	October 26, 1960	no driver's license	12 months or $25,000, probation and 4 months revoked
Police Department Birmingham, Alabama	Martin Luther King #118593	April 12, 1963	violation Section 1159 "GCC"	fined $105.00 180 days
SO Birmingham Ala	M. L. King, Jr. #122235			

Residence: 234 Sunset Ave. Atlanta, Ga.

Died 4-4-68 per information received from FBI Memphis, TN date 4-5-68

[Section 2]

UNITED STATES DEPARTMENT OF JUSTICE

FEDERAL BUREAU OF INVESTIGATION

New York, New York
June 12, 1962

Bureau File
100-106670

RE: Martin Luther King
Security Matter-C

A confidential source, who has furnished reliable information in the past, advised on June 11, 1962, that on that date, Martin Luther King visited the office of Stanley Levison, 6 East 39th Street, New York City.

Levison, at this time, told King that he was glad that King had followed his advice in calling off a planned sit-in demonstration in Atlanta, following the plane crash which took the lives of many prominent Atlantans. King agreed it was a good idea, a smart move which undoubtedly achieved better feelings toward his group.

Levison and King discussed future affairs planned by the National Association for the Advancement of Colored People (NAACP). King detailed one in particular which they planned to hold at the Waldorf Hotel, indicating it would be scaled at $25.00 a plate with an expected attendance of 1,000. Levison commented that he thought it was priced too high and thought that 300 would be a more accurate figure for attendance.

Levison and King then discussed a new book authored by the lawyer, Edward Bennett Williams. Levison stated that Williams, in his book, the part concerned with civil rights, develops the same line that he, Levison set out in the "speech." This is apparently a reference to the recent speech prepared for King by Levison. They both agreed that the similarity of development of thought, as contained in Williams' book and the speech, was amazing.

King then mentioned that a group is attempting to make arrangements for him to appear in a television series which would provide a vehicle for the transmission of his philosophy. He said that this group has already talked to sponsors and to the National Broadcasting Company (NBC) and Columbia Broadcasting System (CBS) studios. Levison commented that this possibility should be closely followed.

Following the discussion in the office, Levison accompanied King to the airline terminal, King indicating he was leaving the city that afternoon.

The Attorney General   June 25, 1962

Director, FBI

MARTIN LUTHER KING, JR.
SECURITY MATTER-C

You will recall that I have previously furnished you with information concerning the influence which Stanley David Levison, a secret member of the Communist Party (CP), exerts on King.

According to a confidential source who has furnished reliable information in the past, Levison told Hunter Pitts O'Dell on June 20, 1962, that in a recent conversation with King, King said he was thinking of getting another administrative assistant. When Levison recommended O'Dell for the job, King said he liked the suggestion, adding, ''No matter what a man was, if he could stand up now and say he is not connected, then as far as I am concerned, he is eligible to work for me.'' It is noted that O'Dell was elected under a pseudonym to the National Committee of the CP, USA, at the 17th National Convention of the CP, USA, in December, 1959.

Memorandum

TO: Mr. Belmont   DATE: July 24, 1962

FROM: A. Rosen

SUBJECT: RACIAL SITUATION
                 ALBANY, GEORGIA
                 RACIAL MATTERS

SYNOPSIS

Negro Attorney Donald Hollowell has filed petition with Fifth Circuit Court of Appeals to vacate restraining order issued 7/20/62 by U.S. District Judge J. Robert Elliott. Hearing set for 7/24/62.

Department consulted in view of above as to whether interviews of persons named in restraining order should be interviewed. Department advised us to proceed with interviews.

Negro Attorneys on 7/23/62 attempted to have U.S. District Judge William A. Bootle vacate restraining order. He refused.

Mass meeting of Albany Movement held 7/23/62 with 800 in attendance. Reverend Ralph Abernathy and Slater King were speakers.

Abernathy spoke of [the] beating [of] Mrs. Slater King by officers at Mitchell County Jail when she visited prisoners. Slater King attacked local, state and Federal government.

After meeting a group of Negroes were arrested when they failed to disperse and blocked sidewalk.

Martin Luther King, Jr., offered to leave Albany if Police and City Commission would hear grievances of Albany Movement . . .

Slater King in his speech denounced the municipal, state and Federal government. He is quoted as stating "damnable Federal government has turned their backs on us." Slater King stated he was tired of waiting for his rights and he was ready to fight . . .

Chief of Police Laurie Pritchett, Albany Police department (PD), advised the Reverend Martin Luther King, Jr., and three other leaders of Negro movement conferred with him on 7/23/62 and offered to leave Albany if Pritchett and City Commissioner would agree to hear grievances of Albany Movement. Pritchett declined in view of pending court action. During conversation Martin Luther King asked Dr. Anderson of the Albany Movement, who accompanied King, "Do you think Bobby Kennedy would prosecute me when he calls me at various places throughout the country for advice?"

The petition upon which the restraining order signed by Judge Elliot was based contains in item 19 a remark that defendants had at various times threatened police officers and engaged in acts of violence involving the throwing of rocks, bottles and other objects endangering lives of citizens, police officers and Agents of the Federal Bureau of Investigation (FBI). The information concerning FBI Agents relates to an incident on 7/10/62 when young Negro hoodlums threw rocks and bottles at a marked and an unmarked police car in which two Agents of Albany Resident Agency (RA) were interviewing two police officers of Albany PD concerning up-to-the-minute details on the Albany situation. The "Albany Herald" newspaper on 7/11/62 contained a short reference to the item which mentioned that there was a spot of violence when young Negroes near Shiloh Baptist Church threw a brick and shattered the $100 dome light of a police cruiser. The article reported two FBI Agents were in the patrol car at the time. The article is in error since the Agents were in the unmarked car.

The Albany City Attorney has advised that he does not contemplate requesting any testimony of FBI Agents in the above matter.

On 7/23/62 Martin Luther King complained to Albany RA that Mrs. Slater King visited prisoners at Mitchell County Jail, Camilla, Georgia, was beaten, knocked to ground and kicked by two police officers.

Chief of Police Pritchett had heard of incident and attempted to interview Mrs. King but was refused admission. According to Chief Pritchett, newsmen had already interviewed and photographed Mrs. King.

The above information was furnished to the Civil Rights Division of the Department. The Department requested interview of Mrs. King, any subjects identified by her and readily available witnesses. The extent of injuries should be ascertained and any visible effects photographed.

Agents of Atlanta Office went to King's residence on 7/23/62 to interview Mrs. King. She was under sedation and Agents talked to Slater King. King abused SA . . . stating he was the Agent who interviewed him in December 1961, at the Albany City Jail when he was pushed against the bars. King stated, "the damn Federal government is no damn good. What are you wasting our time for?" He thereafter told Agents to go ahead and interview his wife. King remained present during the interview.

Mrs. King was interviewed and furnished a signed statement in which she alleges she was pushed, kicked, and shoved to the ground, by two unidentified police officers outside Mitchell County Jail. Mrs. King is five and one-half months pregnant. Attending physician, Dr. Jacob L. Shurley appeared before interview was over and advised of bruises on Mrs. King and that unborn fetus appeared to be all right.

Other known witnesses will be interviewed today and attempts to identify and interview subjects.

UNITED STATES DEPARTMENT OF JUSTICE

FEDERAL BUREAU OF INVESTIGATION

New York, New York
August 6, 1962

Re: Martin Luther King
Security Matter-C

A confidential source, who has furnished reliable information in the past, advised on August 3, 1962, that on that date Stanley Levison had a conversation with an unidentified male in Levison's office located at 6 East 39th Street, New York City.

Levison told the unidentified male that Clarence (believed to be Clarence Jones, who is associated with the fund-raising projects on behalf of Martin Luther King and the Southern Christian Leadership Conference) had informed him of a telephone conversation that had taken place between "Bobby" Kennedy and Martin Luther King.

Clarence told Levison that when King was considering violating the Federal Injunction (apparently at Albany, Georgia), he informed Kennedy of this decision and according to Clarence "He could hear Bobby Kennedy fall at the other end of the phone. That's how absolutely shocked he was."

Clarence also informed Levison that Kennedy attempted to talk King out of violating the Injunction and King "began telling him off in real tough terms."

Levison then told the unidentified male that yesterday (August 2, 1962) he had received a copy of a letter from King, from jail, in which King called on Kennedy to arrest the City Council in Albany, Georgia.

The Attorney General   August 11, 1962

Director, FBI

RACIAL SITUATION
ALBANY, GEORGIA
RACIAL MATTERS

Reverend Martin Luther King, Jr., Dr. W. G. Anderson, Reverend Ralph Abernathy, and Slater King were all found guilty in Albany City

Recorders Court on August 10, 1962. Each was sentenced to sixty days and $200 fine with both suspended.

According to ... Albany, Georgia, Police Department, all Negro demonstrators previously arrested have been released on a blanket bond and have been given summons. He estimated sixty persons were released on the night of August 10, 1962, including those in out-of-town jails.

Mr. William M. Kunstler, attorney for the American Civil Liberties Union, New York, New York, on August 10, 1962, presented a petition for a writ of habeus corpus to the Clerk, United States District Court, Albany, asking the release of Elizabeth Porter Wyckkolf, white, of New York City, who was arrested in Albany on July 30, 1962, in a kneel-in at the City Hall along with fifteen Negroes. Wyckkolf is the only one still in custody and is eligible for bond; however, she does not desire to make bond. To date, the court has taken no action on this position.

A mass meeting was held on the night of August 10, 1962, at the Mt. Zion Church with a capacity crowd attending. No incidents were reported.

Officials of the Albany Movement on this afternoon of August 10, 1962, sent a telegram to the Albany City Commission requesting an audience and announced they were withholding further demonstrations pending an audience. The City Commission was to meet at 9:00 A.M. on August 11, 1962.

TELETYPE

TO DIRECTOR 100-106670
FROM SAC, NEW YORK 100-36585
MARTIN LUTHER KING
SECURITY MATTER—Communist

... ADVISED THAT STANLEY LEVISON CONVERSED WITH CLARENCE JONES THIS AFTERNOON WITH RESPECT TO THE CHURCH BURNINGS IN THE SOUTH. JONES AND LEVISON SAID THAT MARTIN LUTHER KING SHOULD NOT BE SILENT WITH REGARD TO THIS MATTER BUT SHOULD SEND SOME SORT OF A HOT WIRE TO "KENNEDY" ALONG THE LINES THAT THE GOVERNMENT CAN NOT CONTROL A SMALL COMMUNITY. THEY STATED THE WIRE SHOULD BE INDIGNANT.

COMPARISON SHOULD BE MADE IN THE TELEGRAM THAT
THE UNITED STATES WORLDWIDE OBLIGATIONS ARE SO
GREAT THAT IT CAN NOT TAKE CARE OF A SMALL COMMU-
NITY. JONES STATED THAT HE WOULD BE TALKING TO KING
BY PHONE THIS EVENING AND WOULD SUGGEST THE IDEA
OF THE TELEGRAM TO HIM.

UNITED STATES DEPARTMENT OF JUSTICE

FEDERAL BUREAU OF INVESTIGATION

New York, New York
November 15, 1962

Bureau 100-106670

Re: Martin Luther King
Internal Security-C

A confidential source, who has furnished reliable information in the
past, advised on November 14, 1962, that on that date, Stanley Levison
had a discussion with "Lottie" Kuntsler [*sic*], wife of New York Attorney William Kuntsler.

Mrs. Kuntsler stated that she had heard that there was a story in a
New Orleans, Louisiana, newspaper to the effect that Jack O'Dell
(Hunter Pitts O'Dell) had resigned from the Southern Christian Leader-
ship Conference (SCLC), an organization which is headed by Martin
Luther King.

Levison advised Mrs. Kuntsler that Jack O'Dell has denied any active
participation in the CP and offered to resign from the SCLC in order
to avoid any embarrassment to the organization. Levison stated that he
believes that Martin Luther King and the SCLC are holding the resignation in abeyance because they first wanted a conference with the paper
carrying the story that O'Dell had been active in the CP. According to
Levison, the Attorney for the SCLC happens to be in New Orleans at
the present time and intends to contact the newspaper regarding the
story.

Mrs. Kuntsler expressed concern over the fact that the O'Dell story
could affect attendance at an affair that is being held in Westchester
County, New York, on December 11, 1962. She stated that this affair,
which will feature Sammy Davis, Jr., and Peter Lawford, is getting help
from the SCLC. She stated that many people would not attend the affair

if they felt there was any connection between the SCLC and the CP. She stated that if the American Legion became aware of the situation, it could have an adverse effect on the attendance at the affair. She asked that Levison discuss the situation with Jack O'Dell and let her know. Levison assured her that he would.

Memorandum

TO: DIRECTOR, FBI (100-358916)   DATE: 11/20/62

FROM: SAC, NEW ORLEANS (100-14516) (RUC)

SUBJECT: HUNTER PITTS O'DELL
           IS-C; ISA-50
           00: New York

Set forth below for the information of the New York and Atlanta Divisions is an article quoted from the daily New Orleans morning newspaper, The Times-Picayune, of November 2, 1962:

"O'DELL RESIGNS PLACE IN SCLC

"Was Never Director, Asserts Rev. King

"Jack H. O'Dell, sometimes known as Hunter Pitts O'Dell, has resigned his position with the Southern Christian Leadership Conference, which is headed by the Rev. Martin Luther King, Jr., Negro integrationist advocate.

"The resignation followed publication by The Times-Picayune on Oct. 26 of O'Dell's connection with the SCLC and of O'Dell's record of invoking the Fifth Amendment when asked if he was Southern district organizer of the Communist party.

"A report of O'Dell's resignation was received by mail Thursday by The Times-Picayune from headquarters of the SCLC in Atlanta. It was contained in a statement in which the Rev. Mr. King denied that he knew of any of O'Dell's activities for the Communist party.

"The statement received from Atlanta follows:

" 'Martin Luther King Jr., today denied knowledge of any previous Communist activities of a former employee, J.H. O'Dell. The Times-Picayune several days ago charged that O'Dell functioned in a top position with SCLC and that he had been active as a Communist organizer prior to 1958.

" 'Dr. King said: ''It is totally inaccurate and false that Mr. O'Dell is Southeastern director of the Southern Christian Leadership Conference. Not only has he never been director but was never considered for the position. Mr. O'Dell has functioned purely as a technician with 90 per cent of his work taking place in the North where he resides, and involving the mechanization of our mailing procedures. He was briefly and temporarily filling in in some areas of voter registration, but ceased functioning there long before this publicity appeared. Furthermore, SCLC is so firmly established as a Christian non-violent movement, that it would be impossible to be influenced in any way by the method or philosophy of communism. SCLC is a movement of Christian non-violent reform. Communism breeds violent revolution. It is also a firm policy that no person of known Communist affiliation can serve on the staff, executive board or its membership at large.

" ' "It is our firm conviction that communism is based on an ethical relativism, a metaphysical materialism, and a crippling totalitarianism, and a denial of human freedom which we could never accept. We adhere to the philosophy of Christian non-violence, realizing that the means we use must be as pure as the end we seek. But included in our tradition is the American concept of fair play.

" ' "We are, therefore, making exacting and fair inquiry. While Mr. O'Dell advises us that he rejects the implications of the charges made against him, in order to avoid embarrassment to SCLC he has tendered his resignation. We have accepted it pending further inquiry and clarification." '

"After attending Xavier university here, O'Dell served for several years in the merchant marine.

"In July 1950, however, he was expelled from the National Maritime Union at Galveston, Tex. The union took exception to his circulation of pro-Soviet peace petitions attacking the United States government.

"On April 12, 1956, identifying himself as Hunter Pitts O'Dell, a New Orleans waiter, he testified before the Senate internal security committee. He invoked the Fifth Amendment and refused to say whether he was a Southern district organizer for the Communist party.

"Robert Morris, counsel for the subcommittee, said information had been received that O'Dell was, in fact, a district organizer for the Communist party in New Orleans; that O'Dell gave 'directives to the professional group' here, and that he operated under three different names—the two others being John Vesey and Ben Jones.

"It was learned that hundreds of documents seized at his residence, 2319 Louisiana Ave., by New Orleans police clearly established his key position in the Communist movement in the South."

December 7, 1962

Honorable P. Kenneth O'Donnell
Special Assistant to the President
The White House
Washington, D. C.

Dear Mr. O'Donnell:

On December 4, 1962, a confidential source who has furnished reliable information in the past advised that on that date Stanley Levison had a discussion with a New York attorney named William Kuntsler [sic]. Kuntsler told Levison that the ticket sales for the affair to be held at the Westchester County Center in White Plains, New York, on December 11, 1962, would increase daily and that the box-office sales on that night should be good. This affair will feature entertainers Sammy Davis, Jr., and Peter Lawford and will benefit the Southern Christian Leadership Conference, of which Martin Luther King, Jr., is the President. Levison remarked to Kuntsler that he should make suggestions to King for King's speech to be made at the affair.

Kuntsler and Levison then discussed the segregation problem in Jackson, Mississippi. Kuntsler said he had been in Jackson four weeks ago and had fired up the Negro community when he spoke in seven different places concerning segregation problems. Kuntsler also said a picket line has been planned which will be composed of white and Negro individuals and will be followed by a massive Christmas boycott.

Kuntsler then told Levison he hopes to have King duplicate the walk made by William Seward on January 1, 1863, from Lafayette Square to the White House with the Emancipation Proclamation. Kuntsler plans for King to make the same walk on January 1, 1963, at which time he will be presented with a check for $35,000 at the White House to be used for the Gandhi Society for Human Rights. This check, according to Kuntsler, will symbolize that now the Negro has become full grown. Kuntsler said he would like to have Carl Sandburg or Robert Frost accompany King on this walk; however, he has already determined that Sandburg has prior commitments. Levison stated he does not like the idea of a check being presented but Kuntsler remarked that he does not believe the President will be at the White House on New Year's Day and said he thinks they can get an okay to walk into the White House.

Stanley David Levison, who recently organized the Gandhi Society for Human Rights in King's name, has been described by an informant who has furnished reliable information in the past as a secret member of the Communist Party.

William M. Kunstler, who may be identical with the William Kuntsler mentioned above, is a member of the firm Kunstler and Kunstler, 511 Fifth Avenue, New York City; has been attorney for the American Civil Liberties Union; and has, in the past, acted as the legal representative of several "freedom riders" in Mississippi.

This matter is being classified "Secret" in view of the sensitive nature of the sources.

Sincerely yours,
J. Edgar Hoover

Excerpts from Electronic Surveillance File 1962

3/26/62

Levison stated that the previous day, Martin Luther King had called Levison regarding King's wife being invited to go to Geneva by the Women's Strike For Peace Convention. King stated Mrs. Cyrus Eaton would be going, and King was concerned that the "Communist Label would be pinned on us." Levison told King that although Eaton is eccentric, neither Eaton nor his wife have ever been called Communists.

3/30/62

Wyatt Tee Walker: . . . One of the matters I'm calling you now, I talked with Martin (Luther King) this morning and as you know Whittaker is resigning and Martin wanted to get an opinion from you and from me as to what might be his strategy in regard to pushing Hastie (phonetic) . . . as to which would be the better of the two ways to do it, to do it publicly and put him right on the spot or to do it through channels, through protocol.

Stan Levison: My tendency is the following; I think it should be public. I think it should be public, not only to put Kennedy on the spot, although it's a value in itself, but because I think Negroes would expect a leader to step forward at a time like this and declare what Negro should be put on the Supreme Court. . . . Another thing I think, if he feels cautious about it, I see no reason why he couldn't call Hastie himself and ask his opinion, he'd have a good judgement about this and I don't think it would be bad to have Martin let him know. But my tendency is for Martin to issue a statement on it and speak of it as a superb opportunity coming at a critical juncture in history and the man is qualified, the moment of history needs it, and . . .

Walker: . . . I think we ought to get a little more insistent with the President. He hasn't had the kind of strong moral leadership in the area of Civil Rights that we have needed and I don't see where we have anything to lose.

Levison: Not on this, I don't even consider this a real strong demand because it's so obvious, you know, he's got so few choices to make, Ribicoff is just a farce, he's no lawyer, he's not Supreme Court material at all, Goldberg has been in Federal areas for a very limited time and he's also not of judicial temperament. But here's a man who has been on the Court of Appeals for years and years now, eminently qualified. This is a case where you just don't have to strain at all to say the man is qualified and he is superior to any of the others, in my opinion, as a judge.

Walker: ... He's wondering, should he say to the President in terms of "Now is the time to name a Negro, and the Negro is Judge William Hastie," or should he say that "Judge William H. Hastie is the man?"

Levison: ... Well, I take the point of view that both Judge William Hastie is the man, if he was purple ...

Walker: For the moment if it were to be a coincidence for him to be a Negro.

Levison: That's right, it makes it of particular importance ... significance, but at this moment where negroes are under-represented in all areas of American life for a man like Hastie, so qualified, to be selected for a post of this eminence. The man fits it and the post fits him.

4/10/62

Stan Levison called Martin Luther King. Stan asked Martin how they treated him in Washington. Martin said he had quite a day, guessed they got something done. Martin got an SCLC unit organized and then spent the afternoon with the Attorney General and the Vice President; then had a mass meeting and raised about $3,000 of which expenses shouldn't be more than $500, so they cleared about $2,500.

4/10/62

"Jack" states that he (Jack) does not think a "mass turnout" can be held in Washington on New Years. Levison states he (Levison) thinks that two or three thousand people at the Lincoln Memorial would make a big impression. He adds that the Women for Peace marched in the rain at the White House and made a big impression. Levison goes on to say that two or three thousand people at the Lincoln Memorial would be "news quality" and "It is so great that I can see a TV camera being sent over there to pick it up." (Continue to talk about a meeting of thousands of people on New Years at Lincoln Memorial in Washington, if it can be worked out.) Levison states it should be a "prayer service" and not a "mass demonstration" at Lincoln Memorial, "a midnight prayer service."

5/18/62

Clarence Jones talked to Martin King this morning and he said to him "You and Stan Levison have a major task." He also told him that he is speaking before the National Press Club in Washington. It will be the first time an American Negro addresses the Press Club in Washington. He is being invited as the National Civil Rights spokesman of America. It will be a minimum of a thirty minute speech. It will take place around the first of June. (Levison is evidently to prepare the speech.)

6/11/62

Martin Luther King visited Stanley Levison, 6 East 39th Street, New York City. Levison told King that he was glad King had followed Levison's advice in calling off a planned sit-in demonstration in Atlanta following the plane crash which took the lives of many prominent Atlantans. Levison and King also discusses future affairs planned by the National Association for the Advancement of Colored People (NAACP). They also discussed the possibility of King appearing in a television series which would provide a vehicle for the transmission of his philosophy.

6/20/62

Stanley Levison conversed with Hunter Pitts O'Dell, a former Communist Party member. Levison stated that in recent conversation with Martin Luther King, King said he was thinking of getting another Administrative Assistant. Levison had not considered it wise for O'Dell to take on such a position in the past, but he is the only one who could do the job and should be considered for it. Levison stated that King liked Levison's suggestion with respect to O'Dell taking this position because King felt that O'Dell must face it sooner or later, stating "That no matter what a man was, if he could stand up now and say he is not connected, then as far as I am concerned, he is eligible to work for me."

8/3/62

Conversation between Stanley Levison and UNMale.
Levison: Meeting called with Wilkins and several other leaders of Civil Rights. This is a bad situation, worse since whole thing started. I have a feeling that for this reason Bobby Kennedy may have let Martin go. Clarence Jones told me I should have heard the way Martin talked to him (Kennedy) on the phone. When Martin was considering violating the Federal Injunction Bobby Kennedy called and Martin told him he was going to violate it, Clarence said he could hear Bobby Kennedy fall at the other end of the phone, that's how absolutely shocked he

was, then he talked persuading Martin and Martin began telling him off in real tough terms "this can't go on, be patient, do something else, we're tired, very tired, I'm tired, we're sick of it." Clarence said he (Martin) talked to him in terms that he was unaccustomed to being talked to. And I think its very possible that at the end of the conjunction (believed speaker meant injunction) the NAACP and the Administration would like to see Martin King kill himself. And the tactic of course is to let him languish in jail and then if it doesn't arouse a lot of support then gradually people will get discouraged and they will win, the city officials will win. . . . The big job now is to put the heat on Washington and not let Kennedy get away with anything, and to get the Court's attention to the struggle down there, it's the way we work. . . . This letter I got from Martin yesterday, from jail, to Kennedy calling on him to arrest the City Council under Federal Statute (71871?) for depriving Negroes of their civil rights. I put in this sentence "ironically this would bring to jail those seeking justice and those denying justice," and I was toying with adding another sentence to it "and then perhaps we could negotiate in jail," but that sounds too vindictive. This is not the time for the Federal Government to be weak. If it is not able to correct this gross miscarriage of justice in Albany, Ga., how can it command respect in the nation?

8/10/61

Toni Hamilton to "Mr. L." (Stanley Levison) at his home.

Toni Hamilton: tells Levison that she doesn't want to spoil his weekend but that "we" got a summons from (phonetic) lawyer "for that apartment on 77th Street" about the rent and that it has to be answered within seven days.

Stan Levison: tells Tony that this cannot spoil his weekend because "they suspended sentence on Martin." Levison calls this a sign of weakness on "their part" because he says "they" had taken the position earlier that Martin King had overreached himself; that they were going to let him rot in jail and that nobody was going to make such a fuss about it. He reminds Tony that "everybody else was afraid to put King in jail" but that "they" weren't. Levison says that "they" discovered that when "they" did they got "such a tornado" that "they" suspended sentence on him and on "all the others." Levison calls this "a real victory." He says one can be darned sure that if the people were not supporting King "they" would have given him the book on "this one." Toni says that's the best news she has heard today.

9/20/62

Toni Hamilton to Mr. L. (Stanley Levison) at SU 7-1430 (tape).

Levison feels better. Toni tells of falling down subway stairs last night, etc. . . . has to go and take x-rays. Levison tells her to go ahead and call him later and let him know what doctor said, etc. . . . Toni asked if Levison had seen Dr. King on TV this morning? Levison said no. Toni said a friend of hers called and told her that King was interviewed by Hugh Downs this morning . . . was very good . . . spoke about why he was in New York, about various situations and about the President. King mentioned that if the case in Mississippi goes through, that the fellow gets in college, that this will be the death toll [*sic*] for everything in the South.

1963

1963

[Section 3]

[Section 4]

[Section 5]

[Section 6]

November 4, 1963   Memorandum: New York
November 18, 1963   Letter to Asst. Deputy Director

[Section 7]

November 22, 1963   Letter
November 24, 1963   Report
December 4, 1963   Memorandum: New York
December 6, 1963   Memorandum: New York

[Section 3]

UNITED STATES GOVERNMENT
Memorandum

TO: Mr. W. C. Sullivan   DATE: January 11, 1963

FROM: Mr. J. F. Bland

SUBJECT: MARTIN LUTHER KING, JR.
           SECURITY MATTER-C

Information has been received indicating Martin Luther King, Jr., had requested Stanley Levison and Clarence Jones to meet with him at Dorchester. This was determined to be the Dorchester Cooperative Center which is located in McIntosh, Georgia, a small Negro rural community south of Savannah, Georgia, which Savannah has advised is a place which the Southern Christian Leadership Conference, which is headed by Martin Luther King, Jr., has used as a training base for the "Albany Movement." During 1962 large groups of Negroes had been reported to hold meetings there on weekends and appeared to be training for marches and mass demonstrations.

This meeting was to be held on January 10 or 11, 1963. New York had set out leads for Atlanta and Savannah to follow Levison's activities while in their areas.

During the morning of January 11, 1963, Inspector Joseph A. Sizoo telephonically advised ASAC Charles Cusick of Savannah to determine if photographic coverage was feasible and whether it was possible to get pictures of King in association with Stanley Levison, Hosea Judson, Clarence Jones, Hunter Pitts O'Dell and any other individuals who can be identified with the Communist Party or CP fronts. Cusick was cautioned to be extremely cautious in order to avoid embarrassment to the Bureau. He was instructed to make no contact with the press without clearance from the Bureau.

The following excerpt reports on the FBI surveillance of King, Levison, O'Dell, and others on the day of January 11, 1963.

. . . advised, . . . that reservations for Delta Flight # 422, leaving Savannah 8:25 A.M., on January 11, 1963, were held by R. D. ABERNATHY to Atlanta; F. SHUTTLEWORTH to Cincinnati, and J. LOWERY to Nashville. These individuals advised that they could be reached through telephone # TU 4-216 at Midway, Georgia. On January 11, 1963, . . . advised that LOWERY, SHUTTLEWORTH, O'DELL, KING, and WALKER held reservations on EASTERN AIR LINES Flight # 166 to Nashville, and SHUTTLEWORTH had reservations to Cincinnati via Flight # 740. . . . stated that O'DELL had a reservation in his name, but later canceled the reservation and changed the name of the reservation to HUNTER. Through the cooperation of . . . it was determined that LEVISON had a reservation on Atlantic Coast Line train #62, "WEST COAST CHAMPION," bedroom D, car A, leaving Savannah at 8:45 P.M. on January 11, 1963, scheduled to arrive New York City, 11:50 A.M., on January 12, 1963.

A photo fisur was instituted at the Savannah railroad terminal, about 7:00 P.M., on January 11, 1963, by SAS . . . with ASAC . . . in charge. About 8:30 P.M., STANLEY LEVISON was observed to enter the Savannah railroad terminal, after shaking hands with a Negro male who was identified as ANDREW YOUNG and YOUNG was observed leaving in a 1962 Ford which had on it 1963 Georgia license 1 J 52875. LEVISON was observed to meet in the depot three women and two men, all of the Negro race. The three Negro women and one Negro man were observed to leave in a late model car bearing 1963 Georgia license 3 J 196; while the other Negro man was observed to leave in a 1956 Dodge bearing 1962 Georgia license. . . . It was determined that f1962 Georgia license. . . . is registered to a . . ., who, through a search of the . . . records, disclosed that he is a Master Sergeant in the United States Air Force and is a Negro male. It is assumed that . . . possibly traded this car for a newer model and that the vehicle was subsequently purchased by the unidentified Negro male.

UNITED STATES GOVERNMENT
Memorandum

TO: MR. MOHR   DATE: January 15, 1963

FROM: C.D. DeLoach

SUBJECT: RACIAL SITUATION, Albany, Ga.
           RACIAL MATTERS (Article by Martin Luther King, Jr.,
           critical of FBI)

Mr. Belmont's memorandum of November 26, 1962, reflected the alternatives in interviewing Rev. Martin Luther King, Jr., who had criticized the work of the FBI in relation to the Albany situation. The Director approved the suggestion that Mr. Sullivan and I handle the interview with Rev. King.

Following approval, I immediately tried to contact Rev. King telephonically on November 27, 1962.

Rev. King does not have a phone at his residence. We then attempted to contact him at his church in Atlanta. His secretary advised, upon being told who was trying to contact him, that Rev. King was "off in another building writing a book." She further stated that Rev. King preferred not to be disturbed and that it would be impossible to talk to him. That same day I called that SAC at Atlanta and instructed him to attempt to contact Rev. King and set up an interview for Mr. Sullivan and me. SAC Atlanta advised the following day, November 28, 1962, that Rev. King had left instructions with his secretary that he did not have time for an interview, that he was moving around the country. The secretary further advised the SAC that Rev. King would call us when he was willing to sit down for an interview. Rev. King has not called since that date.

It would appear obvious that Rev. King does not desire to be told the true facts. He obviously used deceit, lies and treachery as propaganda to further his own causes.

Realizing the above, I recommended, the Director approved, that I talk with Mr. MacKay, publisher of the four Afro-American newspapers. This interview was handled and reported by memorandum. The interview was based on the fact that the Afro-American newspapers had published Rev. King's lies, quoting him exclusively. In talking with Mr. MacKay I carefully went over each allegation by Rev. King and set him straight with respect to these lies. MacKay offered no argument and in the following week's issue of his newspapers quoted us for the record. A letter was also prepared to John H. Sengstacke, Publisher, "Chicago Defender," dated November 29, 1962, (copy attached) setting the record straight. Sengstacke, whom we know most favorably, published the letter putting the lie to Rev. King's allegations.

ACTION:

The record concerning Rev. King's allegations has been covered. Interviews with the publishers of the newspapers who carried Rev. King's lies have been conducted and they have been set straight. I see no further need to contacting Rev. King inasmuch as he obviously does not desire to be given the truth. The fact that he is a vicious liar is amply demonstrated in the fact he constantly associates with and takes instructions from Stanley Levison who is a hidden member of the Communist Party in New York.

The Attorney General   January 30, 1963

Director, FBI

MARTIN LUTHER KING, JR.
SECURITY MATTER-C

On January 28, 1963, a source who has furnished reliable information in the past advised that Stanley Levison was in contact with Bill, believed to be William Kunstler, a New York attorney. According to the source, Kunstler and Levison discussed an affair which had been held recently in Westchester County, New York, as a fund-raising campaign for Reverend Martin Luther King, Jr. They also discussed a proposed rally which was to have been held in Madison Square Garden this coming spring for the same purpose, which rally however has been canceled by Levison.

According to the source, Kunstler mentioned that the Gandhi Society for Human Rights was doing a lot of legal work and the society has a boy it is sponsoring for the University of Mississippi. The Gandhi Society for Human Rights was recently organized by Stanley Levison, who has been described by an informant who has furnished reliable information in the past, as a secret member of the Communist Party.

Kunstler mentioned that the boy's name is Dewey Green, who is seven years younger than James Meredith, who is presently enrolled at the University of Mississippi. Green is single and has three years service in the Navy. He is to walk on the campus of the University of Mississippi at 11:00 A.M. on January 31, 1963, and attempt to register. Kunstler indicated he thought Green would be thrown off the campus and stated he has written and called Assistant Attorney General Burke Marshall for protection for the boy.

Kunstler indicated to Levison that he spoke to James Meredith on January 27, 1963, and Meredith is not sure he is going to quit the University of Mississippi and his grades may be good enough for him to remain. Someone is trying to get Meredith to write a book and this would mean his leaving the University.

Kunstler suggested to Levison that Reverend Mr. King call Meredith concerning his staying at the University of Mississippi and mention that the idea of a book is not a good one.

According to the source, Kunstler indicated that Green had applied once before for admission to the University of Mississippi and had been rejected. The sponsoring of Dewey Green, according to the source, is a combination affair of the Gandhi Society for Human Rights and the American Civil Liberties Union. Green's grades are not particularly good but they are good enough for the University of Mississippi. Green is now attending a Negro vocational college in Mississippi.

Kunstler indicated that Assistant Attorney General Marshall is attempting to talk Kunstler and Bill Higgs out of filing a case against the Attorney General. It is believed that this has reference to the civil action filed in the U.S. District Court, Washington, D.C., on January 2, 1963, captioned "Robert Moses, et al., versus Robert F. Kennedy, Attorney General of the United States, and J. Edgar Hoover, Director of the Federal Bureau of Investigation," which is in the nature of a mandamus proceeding to compel the defendants to perform certain duties owed to the plaintiffs and to the class which they represent in the field of civil rights.

UNITED STATES DEPARTMENT OF JUSTICE

FEDERAL BUREAU OF INVESTIGATION

New York, New York
February 11, 1963

Re: Stanley David Levison
Internal Security-C

A confidential source who has furnished reliable information in the past, advised on February 5, 1963, that Stanley Levison and Martin Luther King, Jr., planned to meet in New York City on February 5, 1963.

According to the first source, Levison was to meet King at King's room at the Sheridan-Atlantic Hotel in the late afternoon of February 5, 1963. Levison was to give King some notes that King could use in preparation for a speech that he was making that evening, at the Essex House Hotel, 160 Central Park South, New York City. According to the source, this speech was to be given at a dinner which was to commence at six thirty that evening.

... advised the following on February 11, 1963: The only dinner affair held at the hotel on February 5, 1963, was a dinner of the American Jewish Congress.

UNITED STATES DEPARTMENT OF JUSTICE

FEDERAL BUREAU OF INVESTIGATION

New York, New York
March 7, 1963

Re: Martin Luther King
Racial Matters

On March 6, 1963, a confidential source that has furnished reliable information in the past, advised that Dr. Martin Luther King, Jr. and Stanley Levison had a lengthy discussion on that date.

According to the first source, King and Levison discussed an article that King is preparing for the magazine, "The Nation." King is trying to finalize this article which he had to delay because of his travelling around the country. King is of the opinion that the article needs to be changed now in the light of President John F. Kennedy's Civil Rights message. King feels that the article which deals with the 1962 program of the Administration in Civil Rights, isn't quite as relevant now as it would have been prior to the President's Civil Rights message.

Levison asked King to bear in mind that what "The Nation" was presenting each year were King's observations about the preceding year so that it would be proper to confine this latest article to observations about 1962. Levison pointed out, however, that it may be too stale to be discussing only 1962 this late in 1963, and that nothing compels King to stick to the formula of only discussing 1962. Levison stated that he would obtain a copy of the President's message and send it to King with "any other points on it," and although this would delay the article even more, it will improve the timeliness of it. King stated that the article does not need an extensive revision, but the message has to be mentioned somewhere.

Levison and King then discussed the President's Civil Rights message. King said he made a statement after the message came out to the effect that "if we can get a significant break-through in voter registration it will mean a great deal ... in the total struggle, but it doesn't go far enough." King referred to the "schizophrenic tendency of the Administration, on one hand it appoints a Thurgood Marshall as a Federal Judge and then appoints judges in the South who are outright segregationists." King stated that "Kennedy has often said to me—that you can't get this through ... There is no point in introducing strong Civil Rights legislation because you can't get it through." King concluded by stating that his contention is that if he (President Kennedy) would get out and really fight [and] crusade for it, it would have a stronger chance of getting through." Levison agreed with King on this observation.

UNITED STATES DEPARTMENT OF JUSTICE

FEDERAL BUREAU OF INVESTIGATION

New York, New York
May 21, 1963

Re: Sit Ins
Birmingham, Alabama
Racial Matters

A confidential source that has furnished reliable information in the past, advised on May 21, 1963, that on that date, Martin Luther King had a lengthy discussion with Stanley Levison.

Levison inquired of King as to the feeling of the Birmingham community of the expulsion of Negro students by the Birmingham Board of Education. King replied that he thought "we" could hold them together. He does not, in his opinion, want to follow an unwise act on the part of the Board of Education, with an unwise act on "our" part. King believes that (Eugene) "Bull" Connor, City Commissioner of Public Safety, is doing this to provoke the Negro community to the point that they will do something to so confuse the situation that it will upset the agreement now in effect. Levison suggested that King issue a statement that he will not be trapped by these tactics. King stated that he made it very clear that this was a temporary move and that it would be unwise to move without looking at the total situation.

Levison told King that he had a discussion with Clarence Jones, Chief Counsel, Gandhi Society of Human Rights, concerning setting up temporary educational facilities for the expelled students and going to the public and to prominent individuals to ask for contributions for this purpose. King thought this was a good idea, but he hoped it would not be necessary as he felt that "we are going to get them back in school."

Levison then suggested that King write a book concerning his experiences in Birmingham. Levison indicated that King had previously discussed writing a paperback book in collaboration with New York Attorney William Kunstler, but Levison feels that Kunstler is attempting to make a joint venture out of the book and this is not fair to King as King should be the only recipient of royalties from the book.

Levison informed King that Negro writer Ossie Davis had told Levison that he would be glad to assist King in a few weeks when he finishes a movie script he is working on. Levison stated Davis would only want a fee for his work, and that the book published simultaneously in clothbound and paperback editions would sell 150,000 to 200,000 copies. Levison stated it would be "a sure fire book." King indicated his approval to Levison's suggestions regarding the book.

waco [*sic*], Texas
May 28, 1963

Mr. J. Edgar Hoover
Federal Bureau of Investigation
Washington, D.C.

Dear Mr. Hoover:

As long as men like you are in key positions of our government I feel fairly safe that the rights of individuals will be protected, but with the growing power of the colored people through the NAACP and the lack of concern of our Supreme Court Judges for the rights of white people as well as the Supreme Court Judges lack of concern for the traditional culture and heritage of the white people whose ancestors founded this nation I find myself dreading to face the future. I think often of a statement made by ex-Pres. Herbert Hoover in one of his birthday speeches. He said this . . . "America's greatest danger is not communism but its fuzzy-minded intellectuals"! I can see these fuzzy-minded intellectuals are gaining control of more key positions in government each year as well as the strong influence of apparent communist controlled agitators. My ancestors for many generations back here in America, England, Wales, etc. are white and in studying the history I find that they are not aggressive [*sic*], but they will not be pushed into anything that is against their principles, honor and best judgment.

Now for the reason for writing this letter. . . . I have been told that Martin Luther King is a communist controlled agitator and is carrying out a communist plan called "operation paralysis," which is designed to destroy our nation internally. If this is so, why can't they [be] exposed by our government and dealt with accordingly? As you can plainly see from the tone of my letter I am confused, my friends are confused and it seems top men in the government are confused.

Again I say as long as you are with us I feel that truth will be protected, and pray that God will prepare not only one man to carry on after you retire but a great army of men with your dedication to truth and justice.

Respectfully yours,
[Signature deleted]

May 31, 1963

Honorable P. Kenneth O'Donnell
Special Assistant to the President
The White House
Washington, D.C.

My dear Mr. O'Donnell:

A source, who has furnished reliable information in the past, has advised that on May 30, 1963, Reverend Martin Luther King, Jr., and Stanley Levison held a discussion concerning a conference which Reverend Mr. King reportedly has requested with the President and the Attorney General.

Levison and Reverend Mr. King agreed that this is a good time for such a conference and Levison stated that no Administration has ever been as worried about the Negro problem as is the present Administration. Levison added that this is based upon the Administration's concern with the problems arising from the Common Market in Europe. Levison expressed the opinion that the prestige of the United States is very important at this time and the inability to control the racial situation makes the Administration's task more difficult. He also said that the President is ready for a different policy if it can bring about the kind of controlled situation that he feels he needs.

Reverend Mr. King and Levison agreed that it was necessary to keep the situation moving so that the President will be forced to look for an alternative. It was stated that the President can then be presented with certain alternatives which will benefit the Administration as the President's fear of violence will be done away with. Levison expressed the thought that the President is ready to make a change and that a conference at this time would be fruitful. He added that if a conference cannot be worked out, then the movement must be enlarged. Reverend Mr. King said he would like to put so much pressure on the President that he will have to sign an Executive Order making segregation unconstitutional.

Levison stated that the method of negotiation used in Birmingham, Alabama, will set the pattern for a series of Southern cities. He explained this method by stating that you come in with a package, come up with demands, discuss them and come out with a victory, and that in doing so you ask for more than you expect to get. He described the goals of the movement as desegregation, jobs and the right to vote. He described the methods of obtaining these goals as being direct action, nonviolence and negotiation.

I advised the Attorney General of the above information and he suggested that the President should see this letter.

Sincerely yours,

J. EDGAR HOOVER

NOTE: This memorandum is being classified "Confidential" because it contains information from a source, the unauthorized disclosure of which would seriously impair the investigation of the Communist Party, USA, and such impairment could have an adverse effect upon the national defense interests of the country.

[Section 4]

UNITED STATES GOVERNMENT
Memorandum

TO: Mr. Belmont   DATE: May 31, 1963

FROM: A. Rosen

SUBJECT: MARTIN LUTHER KING
           RACIAL MATTERS

King and Levison agreed that the situation has to be kept moving so that the President will have to look for an alternative. The President can then be presented with certain alternatives. This will benefit the President, for then his problem, fear for violence, will be done away with. It was Levison's thought that the President is all ready to make a change. A conference now would be fruitful, but if a conference cannot be worked out, then the movement must be enlarged. King stated that he would have to sign an Executive Order making segregation unconstitutional.

Levison said that the method of negotiating used in Birmingham will set the pattern for a whole series of southern cities. That is, you come in with a package, come up with demands, discuss them and come out with a victory. You ask for more than you expect to get. The goals of the movement, according to Levison, are desegregation, jobs and the right to vote. The methods to get them are direct action, nonviolence, and negotiations.

ACTION:
This information is being brought to the attention of the Attorney General and the Honorable P. Kenneth O'Donnell, Special Assistant to the President, by letter presently being prepared under todays [*sic*] date.
I phoned substance of this to A.G.
H.

June 3, 1963

STANLEY DAVID LEVISON

Stanley David Levison was born May 2, 1912, in New York City. He attended public schools in the New York City area and graduated from Far Rockaway High School in June 1930. He attended the University of Michigan from September 1930, to June 1931, and Columbia University for approximately two years during the period 1931 to 1936 but received no degrees. He entered St. John's Law School, New York City, in September 1936, and received a Bachelor of Laws degree in June 1938, and was awarded a Master's degree in law in June 1939. Levison is an attorney and businessman and maintains his office at Six East 39th Street, New York City. Levison has had an interest in a variety of businesses having to do with real estate, manufacturing and servicing of photographic equipment, machine tool manufacturing and various other enterprises. Among past business associates of Levison who have been described as members of the Communist Party by informants who have furnished reliable information in the past are Samuel Harshaur, Halbro Frasier, Roger H. Loewi and Victor Ludwig. Stanley Levison resides at 585 West End Avenue, New York City, with his wife Beatrice. He was classified 4-Y by his draft board and has had no military service.

An informant who has furnished reliable information in the past advised in April 1962, that Levison had been subpoenaed to appear before the Senate Internal Security Subcommittee (SISS) in Washington, D. C., on April 30, 1962. The same informant advised on May 1, 1962, that Levison had stated that he had appeared the previous day before the SISS and the Senator John McClelland had remarked that he, Levison, was the worst witness who had ever appeared before that Committee.

In March 1963, an informant who has furnished reliable information in the past advised that Stanley Levison was a secret member of the Communist Party, USA (CPUSA). The informant also advised in June

1956, that several years previously Stanley Levison and his brother, Roy Bennett, were organizers for the Communist Party in the Rockaway district of New York. Another informant who has furnished reliable information in the past advised in 1954 that Stanley Levison was a member of the CPUSA Committee on Finances and that he was an assistant to Jack King who then functioned as national treasurer of the CPUSA.

CONTACTS OF LEVISON CONCERNING REVEREND MARTIN LUTHER KING, JR., AND CLARENCE JONES

On March 20, 1962, Levison received a call from one of Reverend Mr. King's assistant's [sic], Reverend Wyatt Tee Walker, concerning Judge William Henry Hastie. According to the source, King wanted Levison's opinion as to the strategy he, King, should use in attempting to influence the President to appoint Judge Hastie to the Supreme Court. Levison said that King should publicly advocate the appointment of Judge Hastie since the Negroes would expect a Negro leader to step forth and state which Negro should be appointed to the Supreme Court. (Furnished AG 4/2/62 . . .)

On April 10, 1962, a source advised that Martin Luther King had recently informed Levison that he had had a successful trip to Washington, D.C., where he raised $3,000 and had visited the Attorney General and the Vice President.

Levison and King also discussed arrangements for a concert to be held in Atlanta in June 1962, to raise funds and, according to the source, Harry Belafonte would be one of the performers at the concert. (Furnished AG 4/13/62 . . .)

A source advised on April 11, 1962, that Stanley Levison had recently told Hunter Pitts O'Dell that he was writing a speech for Martin Luther King, Jr. According to Levison, King was to deliver the speech at the convention of the United Packing House Workers of America, American Federation of Labor—Congress of Industrial Organizations, in May 1962, and the effectiveness of the speech might determine the amount of money the union would give King. (Furnished AG 4/13/62 . . .)

On August, 3, 1962, a source advised that Clarence Jones told Levison that when Martin Luther King was considering violating the Federal injunction (apparently at Albany, Georgia), King informed "Kennedy" of this decision. He said "Bobby" Kennedy was absolutely shocked. Jones stated that the Attorney General attempted to talk King out of violating the injunction and that King "Began telling him off in real tough terms." Levison told Jones that on August 2, 1962, he had received a copy of a letter from King from jail in which King called on "Kennedy" to arrest the City Council in Albany, Georgia, under a Federal Statute for depriving Negroes of their civil rights. (Furnished AG 8/8/62 ...)

A source advised on September 10, 1962, that Clarence Jones and Levison were discussing the burning of churches in the South. Both expressed the opinion that Martin Luther King, Jr., should not be silenced in this matter but should send a hot wire to "Kennedy" expressing his indignance at the Government's failure to control one small community. Levison and Jones agreed that the telegram should say something to the effect that the world-wide obligations of the United States are so great that it cannot take care of a small community. (Furnished AG 9/11/62 ...)

A source advised that on December 4, 1962, Stanley Levison had a discussion with William Kunstler, a New York attorney, concerning ticket sales for an affair to be held at the Westchester County Center in White Plains, New York, on December 11, 1962. This affair was to have sponsored entertainers Sammy Davis, Jr., and Peter Lawford and was to benefit the Southern Christian Leadership Conference. Levison remarked to Kunstler that he should make suggestions to King for King's speech to be made at the affair.

Kunstler then told Levison he hoped to have King duplicate the walk made by William Seward on January 1, 1863, from Lafayette Square to the White House with the Emancipation Proclamation. Kunstler planned for King to make the same walk on January 1, 1963, at which time he was to have been presented with a check for $25,000 at the White House to be used for the Gandhi Society for Human Rights. The check, according to Kunstler, would symbolize that now the Negro has become full grown. (Furnished AG & White House 12/7/62 ...)

There is no indication this walk by King ever actually took place.

A source advised that Clarence Jones and Stanley Levison had a discussion in New York City on December 19, 1962.

Jones mentioned that he had recently talked with Martin Luther King, Jr., and King advised him that he had recently been to see President Kennedy and was most impressed with the President's awareness of events in the civil rights field.

Jones stated it was obvious to King that President Kennedy had been well briefed prior to the meeting and he had apparently done considerable reading along this line. Jones told Levison that King had made the statement that the President is so well informed that he cites "your own material to you." Levison asked Jones what specific points the President had cited to King. Jones was unable to answer this question and Levison told Jones that it would be worthwhile for him to call King to find out what specific points the President had made in his conversation with King to determine the Administrator's thinking with respect to the civil rights problem. (Furnished AG & White House 12/27/62 . . .)

On January 4, 1963, a source advised that Clarence Jones was in contact with Levison to inform Levison that King had requested that he and Levison meet King in Dorchester, Georgia, on January 10 or 11, 1963, because "they're going to be having a closeted review of where they are—a critical review." They made arrangements to leave New York on January 9, 1963, to effect this meeting.

This same source advised on January 6, 1963, that Jones again contacted Levison to advise that Hunter Pitts O'Dell was returning from Atlanta to New York City. Levison voiced the opinion that O'Dell should be in on the planned discussions. (Furnished AG 1/10/63 . . .)

It should be noted that Levison met King, Jones, O'Dell and others at the Savannah Airport, Savannah, Georgia, on January 10, 1963.

* * *

A source advised on May 26, 1963, that Clarence Jones had a discussion with Stanley Levison concerning a conference which Jones said he attended on May 24, 1963. Jones informed Levison that he had attended a conference on May 24, 1963, at which Attorney General Kennedy was present. Jones said that the Attorney General was under the sharpest attack that he had seen anyone undergo and that there was nothing that the Attorney General could say. Each time he said something, it merely underlined the deep gulf. Levison commented that the Attorney General really needed it.

Jones agreed with Levison and said that the Attorney General had come there thinking that he knew everything and had not been prepared to change his mind. According to Jones, the Attorney General took the simple approach, stating that the current Administration had done more than anyone else in the area of civil rights. Levison replied, "so he thinks he can get away with that, well he doesn't know what year this is. He doesn't know what Birmingham means." Levison then suggested that in view of the fact that Martin Luther King is going to see the President soon, he should get advice on how to present this matter to the President. It was Jones' opinion that this would not make much difference because the Attorney General is running the civil rights movement.

Jones told Levison that after the meeting, Jones learned that the Attorney General was very critical of Jones because he had been in

Birmingham with King and knew what had been done and should have defended the Attorney General at the conference. Jones continued that the Attorney General did not think that any purpose would be served by President Kennedy leading a Negro into the University of Alabama, and that this provoked some bitter comments from the people attending the conference, including one person who told the Attorney General that the only reason he was in this room was because he was concerned with the 1964 elections. This same individual, according to Jones, described the Attorney General as, "the worst illustration of white arrogant liberalism." Levison said that this was a good description of the Attorney General. (Furnished AG 5/29/63 ... New York teletype, 5/28/63)

A source advised on May 28, 1963, Levison had a conversation with an unknown male, possibly Clarence Jones.

Levison told the unknown male that at the meeting Friday they would have to sit down and really discuss the Attorney General's concern. The unknown male told Levison that the Attorney General was really turned on his heels. Levison then commented that the Attorney General has been able to lick every competitor he has come up against and has made this the passion of his life, but has run into the first force that he can't knock over. The unknown male indicated that a list was handed to the Attorney General of all the judges "Kennedy," probably referring to President Kennedy, appointed and the dates of appointment.

The unknown male indicated that the day after the conference held in New York, the FBI came around to all the people who were there. The unknown male indicated that he expected such action, and Levison commented that the FBI "bit" was really shocking.

It should be noted that with regard to the comment that the FBI came around to all the people who were at the conference with you on May 24, 1963, that this Bureau was not aware of the conference until articles appeared in newspapers and at no time did any Agents from this Bureau make any contact with individuals who were at the meeting. (Furnished AG 5/31/63 ... New York teletype 5/29/63)

On May 30, 1963, King and Levison held a discussion concerning a conference which King reportedly requested with the Attorney General and the President. Levison and King agreed that this is a good time for such a conference and Levison stated that no Administration has ever been as worried about the Negro problem as is the present Administration. Levison added that this is based upon the Administration's concern with the problems arising from the Common Market in Europe. Levison expressed the opinion that the prestige of the United States is very important at this time and that inability to control the racial situation makes the Administration's task more difficult. He also said that the President is ready for a different policy if it can bring about the kind of controlled situation that he feels he needs.

UNITED STATES DEPARTMENT OF JUSTICE

FEDERAL BUREAU OF INVESTIGATION

New York, New York
June 4, 1963

Re: Martin Luther King
Racial Matters

On June 1 and 2, 1963, a Confidential Source, who has furnished reliable information in the past, advised of a discussion of the above dates among Stanley Levison, a New York Attorney; Martin Luther King, leader of the Southern Christian Leadership Conference (SCLC); and Clarence Jones, Acting Executive Director of the Gandhi Society for Human Rights.

King mentioned that Roy Wilkins of the National Association for the Advancement of Colored People (NAACP) had been imprisoned but may now be out on bond. Levison suggested that King send a telegram to the President protesting the incarceration of Wilkins.

King told Levison he had read his, Levison's, memorandum, but did not quite understand what Levison proposed be done now.

Levison explained that it was his thought that "the Birmingham pattern" can be followed in other cities where there are unresolved problems. He noted that in Atlanta, there is no bi-racial committee and the establishment of one could be a first demand. In other cities, it may be desirable to have direct action first "followed by the Birmingham pattern." Levison said that each day should be examined separately.

King commented that he has never seen the Negro community as aroused, as determined, as enthusiastic as at this time. He said that "more than ever before is this national determination and feeling that time is running out." He stated that he thought "we are on the threshold of a significant breakthrough and the greatest weapon is mass demonstration."

King stated "we are at the point where we can mobilize all of this religious indignation into a powerful mass movement."

King suggested that there be a mass march or the impression be given that a mass march of "literally thousands and thousands of people" is going to be organized on Washington. He added "the threat itself may so frighten the President that he would have to do something." He asked Levison "are we ready for that?"

Levison said there were two things which must be considered:

1. There must be unanimity among all groups.

2. Is there more pressure generated on Washington by the series of local situations than by a mass march on Washington?

King said he felt there could be unanimity. He said Roy (Wilkins) would probably not be opposed as "pressure builds from the bottom" and the NAACP would exert such pressure on Wilkins.

With respect to the second point raised by Levison, King pointed out he was not thinking of concentrating on Washington alone, but was thinking of activity in every state. He said there should be a simultaneous protest on the local level "and at the same time a work stoppage would be called for all over America." He stated that the sort of thing he envisaged would have such an impact that "something would have to give." He again asked Levison if Levison thought the time was right for such a move and Levison agreed that "the time is now."

Clarence Jones suggested that King should discuss his proposal with Roy Wilkins and Phil (A. Philip Randolph) before any announcement is made publicly. He felt the timing of such a move is most important.

Levison felt that King was the proper person to make such an announcement and felt that it could be announced when King addresses a scheduled Trade Union meeting and at his commencement address at City College of New York on June 12, 1963. Following this, Levison felt King could discuss it with both Roy Wilkins and "Phil." Levison felt that since it was then publicly announced, Wilkins would have a hard time objecting. King was of the opinion that he should call a special press conference, possibly in Atlanta, and make his announcement. Levison immediately agreed with this proposal and suggested he implement it in his speeches.

King stated that in all probability, he would get a call from Washington, suggesting that since the President is leaving for Europe shortly, it would be embarrassing for him.

Levison commented that because of the President's trip to Europe, he will have to pay attention. He again suggested that a press conference would have a real impact but suggested that "Phil" should be advised beforehand.

King said that such an undertaking would require a real job of mobilization and people would be needed full time.

Levison said the effect of such an announcement will "tip" the President towards Civil Rights legislation and this new legislation "will be a powerful lever."

King suggested that either Levison or Jones see "Phil" and "the two of you work out the statement" along the lines of the new militancy throughout the country.

King felt that such an undertaking would take six to eight weeks to organize.

Levison said that the summer can be a factor as many organizations are on vacation. It was indicated that Clarence Jones had attended a meeting at which the National Council of Churches had expressed an interest in King's "direct action" approach and had specifically mentioned a march on Washington. Levison asked Jones if it would be possible to quote individuals without mentioning names who had attended the aforementioned meeting, as "this is new when White Church leadership is looking for something in the way of direct action." He said this would give it the biggest, broadest front ever as "you can see the effect of Negroes joined by the National Council of Churches and not just the Negro Churches."

When Jones demurred to Levison's proposal, Levison agreed that perhaps it would be inadvisable.

Levison asked King if he would be willing to appear on a television program with James Baldwin, the writer. King was not enthusiastic about the idea because he felt that Baldwin was uninformed regarding his movement. King noted that Baldwin, although considered a spokesman of the Negro people, by the press, is not a civil rights leader.

June 14, 1963

Honorable P. Kenneth O'Donnell
Special Assistant to the President
The White House
Washington, D.C.

Dear Mr. O'Donnell:

There is attached for your information a memorandum prepared by our New York Office setting forth the details of a conversation between

Stanley Levison and Reverend Martin Luther King, Jr., which conversation took place on June 12, 1963.

Levison is more fully identified in the memorandum.

The memorandum sets forth information concerning Levison's and Reverend Mr. King's reaction to the speech of President Kennedy on June 11, 1963, concerning the racial problem in the United States.

Stanley Levison commented to Reverend Mr. King that "we" cannot put the President in the position of being the enemy and that the enemy to be dealt with is the Congress. Reverend Mr. King agreed completely with Levison on this point.

The Attorney General is being furnished a copy of the attached New York memorandum.

Sincerely yours,
J. Edgar Hoover

UNITED STATES DEPARTMENT OF JUSTICE

FEDERAL BUREAU OF INVESTIGATION

New York, New York
June 12, 1963

Re: Martin Luther King
Racial Matters

On June 12, 1963, a confidential source, who has furnished reliable information in the past, advised that Stanley Levison, a New York attorney, had a discussion with Martin Luther King, leader of the Southern Christian Leadership Conference (SCLC) on June 12, 1963.

Stanley Levison informed Martin Luther King that, after he had read President Kennedy's speech of June 11, 1963, his feelings are stronger than ever that the focus of any Washington action should not be directed against the President. King agreed and asked Levison if he had heard the President's speech. King said it was the strongest statement the President has made and "he was really great."

Levison commented that he had not heard the President's speech, but this is what King has been asking the President to do and, therefore, King has to take a positive approach to it, otherwise it would sound as if King was not dealing with changing realities of himself.

They then discussed the proposal that had been made by the National

Council of Churches that a commission of 25 persons be set up which is to get in touch with Martin Luther King for the purpose of assisting King in his fight for racial equality. They agreed that the assistance from the National Council of Churches on the proposed march on Washington would be invaluable, particularly if a white churchman was to lead a demonstration to the Capital in protest of the anticipated filibuster of the Civil Rights legislation, which is to be presented to Congress.

The source further advised on June 10, 1963, that Levison took part in a conference with the Reverend Martin Luther King, Clarence Jones, the Reverend Wyatt Tee Walker and the Reverend Ralph Abernathy, among others. According to the source, the purpose of this conference was to obtain ideas as to how to dramatize the proposed march on Washington. Reverend King stated that the basic purpose of the march on Washington would be to put the pressure on Congress so that the civil rights legislation would be passed. King said that President Kennedy would be able to get off the hook if the legislation was not passed by saying that he attempted to get it through.

It was felt that the National Council of Churches can be utilized in this demonstration and also in the similar demonstrations that will be simultaneously held throughout the rest of the country. Reverend King stated that he had mixed emotions about President Kennedy in that the President should be made to know that "we" are not satisfied with him and what he has done in the field of civil rights. On the other hand, according to King, there are some Negro people that think Kennedy has done a good job in this field.

Those participating in the conference were in agreement that the Washington demonstration should be focused on the Congress rather than the White House. It was felt that the timing of the demonstration should be coincided with the anticipated filibuster of the civil rights legislation. However, Clarence Jones did not agree with this because he felt it would be impossible to properly prepare a demonstration in advance if the demonstration has to wait for the filibustering to begin before it can be put into effect. It was felt that possibly 100,000 people, including children, would be utilized in the Washington demonstration in order for it to be politically impressive and that the demonstrations can possibly start in the balcony of Congress. It was felt that, more than likely, some time in August 1963 would be when the demonstration and the march on Washington would take place.

FBI

Date: 6/20/63

AIRTEL

To: DIRECTOR, FBI (100-166670)

From: SAC, NEW YORK (100-136585)

Subject: MARTIN LUTHER KING
          SM-C
          (00: Atlanta)

ReNYairtel, 6/13/63. b(2) b7(D)

On 6/19/63 ... advised that STANLEY LEVISON had a discussion with his secretary re MARTIN LUTHER KING. LEVISON stated that KING is going to "give up" his planned trip to Europe this summer. According to LEVISON, KING hated to do this because KING really needs a vacation and his wife was looking forward to it. Also, KING had arranged a whole series of engagements abroad including the Baptist World Convention. LEVISON then stated that "KING is so busy with civil rights that we forget that KING is not only a minister but that he was born and bred in it; that it means a lot to him."

Meridian, Mississippi
June 25, 1963

Honorable J. Edgar Hoover, Director
Federal Bureau of Investigation
Washington 25, D.C.

Dear Mr. Hoover:

It has been reported that the Rev. Martin Luther King, Jr., belongs to at least sixty Communist-front organizations, this was reported from the Augusta Georgia Courier by Mr. Karl Prussion. Can this be verified and to what organizations does he refer?

Thanking you, I am

Sincerely yours,
[Signature deleted]

FBI

6/26/63

AIRTEL

TO: SACS, Atlanta Birmingham

FROM: Director, FBI

UNSUBS; KKK THREAT TO BOMB
LOS ANGELES TIMES BUILDING,
LOS ANGELES, CALIFORNIA, AND
THREAT TO LIFE OF PRESIDENT JOHN F. KENNEDY,
MARTIN LUTHER KING AND
JIMM A. HOOD, 6/21/63
BONDING MATTERS

Re Los Angeles teletype to Bureau and Atlanta 6/25/63.

Atlanta promptly upon receipt advise local authorities of the implied threat to *Reverend Martin Luther King, Jr.,* as set forth in referenced teletype.

For the information of Birmingham, on 6/25/63, Lou Davis, The Times-Mirror Company, publishers of the "Los Angeles Times," furnished a letter which is quoted as follows:

"6–21–63. Mr. President John F. Kennedy. a Negger lover. I have a offer on your lafe [*sic*] two five zero zero zero dollars. To depose you. But you have too many guards. Next offer is on Mr. Martin Luther King one zero zero zero zero. Next offer Mr. Jimm A. Hood five zero zero zero. This is my work for money to kill. You know the majority rules minority. You dont [*sic*] give the rights to American Indian. Keep in concentration camps. The niggers have some rights the whites have. Oll [*sic*] we want the Niggers stay away from whites places. If not be too *many killings*. I get my man if takes a year. K. K. K."

"Los Angeles Times. I want you print this copy in your paper [*sic*] I place bomb in your building."

[Section 5]

UNITED STATES DEPARTMENT OF JUSTICE

FEDERAL BUREAU OF INVESTIGATION

New York, New York
August 29, 1963

Re: Martin Luther King
Security Matter-C

A confidential source advised on August 28, 1963, that Stanley Levison in commenting on the March on Washington that day, singled out Martin Luther King as the "Man of the hour" for everybody. Levison stated it was marvelous the way King handled the white and Negro question in his speech, completely repudiating "the nonsense" of Adam (Clayton) Powell and the "Muslims" (Nation of Islam). Levison also said King measures up to his introduction "the moral leader of America." Levison described this as the "mark of a man." Levison characterized King as a "pure guy."

[Section 6]

September 16, 1963

Mr. J. Edgar Hoover, Director
Federal Bureau of Investigation
United States Department of Justice
Washington 25, D.C.

Dear Mr. Hoover:

Recognizing the dangers of Communism, I subscribe on some patriotic publications explaining the Communist menace and also attend any near by meeting of noted speakers on the subject.

I am enclosing a clipping from a newspaper which associates Martin Luther King with communist fronts. A speaker I heard also mentioned that the National Council of Churches Group had pastors who belonged to communist fronts.

It is hard for me to believe that a christian pastor could be a communist and yet this is what so many public speakers and printed publications seem to say.

Attorney General Robert Kennedy has stated that there is no evidence that any of the top leaders of the Civil Rights groups were connected with communism.

The enclosed newspaper article mentions Martin Luther King who I believe is a leader in Civil Rights as a member of communist fronts from a quote.

I do not know if your office can give out any information of this nature, but what I am interested in knowing is if from your records you have any proof of any communist infiltration in any way whatsoever in our churches?

I am writing because I have heard and read so many charges against some of our church leaders. I have never heard of any action against such charges by the church men, such as libel suits.

If it is possible for you to give me any information it would be appreciated.

Thank you.

Sincerely,

UNITED STATES DEPARTMENT OF JUSTICE

FEDERAL BUREAU OF INVESTIGATION

New York, New York
September 24, 1963

Re: James Baldwin
Racial Matters;
Security Matter-C

On September 19, 1963, a confidential source who has furnished reliable information in the past, advised that on that date Clarence Jones (Counsel to Martin Luther King) and James Baldwin (Negro author) held a discussion regarding Baldwin's appearance on the USIA television program in Washington on August 28, 1963. Jones stated that he had requested from USIA a transcript of the entire show and had received this transcript and noted that Baldwin's remarks regarding the Federal Bureau of Investigation (FBI) and Mr. Hoover were not contained therein and therefore Jones assumed that these remarks had been edited out. Baldwin stated that he had witnesses to the statements that he had made on the program. In recalling his statement regarding the FBI, Baldwin stated that the substance of his remarks on this program were "part of the problem in the civil rights movement is J. Edgar Hoover." Jones then stated that he would "like to blow the whistle on this." Jones stated that any legitimate critical opinion of the FBI is apparently "off limits or taboo." Jones further stated that he had composed a letter to the rest of the participants on the USIA show informing them of the deletion made. Jones then stated that he intends to inform the USIA that he knows of the deletion and intends also to bring this information to the attention of the public and the Attorney General. Jones continued that he was going to do this immediately and stated that he would also like to draft a statement and stated "we cannot let this deletion go."

The Attorney General   September 26, 1963

Director, FBI

COMMUNIST PARTY, USA
NEGRO QUESTION
COMMUNIST INFLUENCE IN RACIAL MATTERS
INTERNAL SECURITY-C

A source who has furnished reliable information in the past advised that Stanley David Levison, in discussing the racial situation in Birmingham on September 21 and 22, 1963, praised the appointment of the men selected by President Kennedy to go to Birmingham to study the Birmingham situation, stating that they are military men and Southerners who will understand the situation there.

Levison indicated that Martin Luther King, Jr., is having difficulty in understanding the Birmingham situation because it is basically a police problem. When it was suggested to Levison that he see King and advise him in this respect, Levison replied that "he made a promise and has got to keep it."

Levison and his brother, Roy Bennett, were critical of James Baldwin and his group. They agreed that the condemnation of the presidential commission to study the Birmingham situation and their idea of boycotting Christmas shopping in Birmingham were extremely ridiculous. The opinion was expressed that Baldwin's group was "not too deep intellectually."

James Baldwin, a Negro author, has been prominent in the Student Nonviolent Coordinating Committee, and in 1960 was an active member of the Fair Play for Cuba Committee.

UNITED STATES DEPARTMENT OF JUSTICE

FEDERAL BUREAU OF INVESTIGATION

New York, New York
October 2, 1963

Communist Party, United States of
America (CPUSA)
Negro Question
Communist Influence on Racial Matters
Internal Security-C

On October 1, 1963, a confidential source, who has furnished reliable information in the past, furnished information which indicated that on that date, Stanley Levison held a discussion with Clarence Jones about a book written by Martin Luther King soon to be published.

Jones remarked that King is very much concerned about finishing his book and is particularly concerned about writing an effective chapter concerning Birmingham. Jones stated that King is coming to New York on Saturday at which time he plans to make inquiries on the progress of his book.

Levison remarked that the chapter following the one on Birmingham is very dull and will need a lot of rewriting. He said that King discussed his book with persons in Richmond and the impression is that King's book will be "the book of books" and will be released shortly.

Levison told Jones that he had something to discuss with him and would like to see him that evening. Jones agreed to meet with Levison that evening after dinner.

FBI

10/3/63

AIRTEL

To: DIRECTOR, FBI (100-3-116)

From: SAC, NEW YORK (100-151548)

Subject: CP, USA
          NEGRO QUESTION
          COMMUNIST INFLUENCE IN RACIAL MATTERS
          IS-C

It is to be noted that speech "I Have a Dream" made by Reverend KING, mentioned in LHM, could possibly pertain to a speech made by KING at the recent march on Washington, D.C., held 8/28/63.

The enclosed LHM is being classified "Secret" because of the extreme sensitive nature of . . . The unauthorized disclosure of this source could seriously impair the investigation of subversive matters and thereby endanger the national defense interests of the U.S.

UNITED STATES DEPARTMENT OF JUSTICE

FEDERAL BUREAU OF INVESTIGATION

New York, New York
October 3, 1963

Communist Party, United States of America
Negro Question
Communist Influence in Racial Matters
Internal Security-C

On October 3, 1963, a confidential source, who has furnished reliable information in the past, furnished information which indicated that on that date Clarence Jones was preparing a complaint to be filed on behalf of Martin Luther King.

Reverend King is setting a temporary restraining order against Twentieth Century Fox and Mr. Maestro, Incorporated to prohibit them from selling recordings of King's speech "I Have a Dream," which he recently made in Washington, D.C.

King wants any proceeds received from this recording to go to the United Civil Rights Leadership to be used for the Civil Rights movement.

Source further advised that a person by the name of Clay, not further identified, discussed with Jones a meeting of District 65 Affiliated Retail, Wholesale and Department Store Workers Union to be held on October 23, 1963, at Madison Square Garden, New York. Jones was requested to make arrangements for television coverage of this meeting because the union is to invite Reverend King to make a major civil rights speech during the evening.

Jones agreed, and mentioned that he had a contact at the Columbia Broadcasting Company (CBS).

UNITED STATES DEPARTMENT OF JUSTICE

FEDERAL BUREAU OF INVESTIGATION

New York, New York
November 4, 1963

Communist Party, USA
Negro Question
Communist Influence in Racial Matters
Internal Security-C

On November 2, 1963, a confidential source, who has furnished reliable information in the past, furnished information which indicated that Martin Luther King contacted Clarence Jones on that date. King stated that he would be in Washington, D.C., on November 6, 1963, for an appearance at Howard University. Jones mentioned that he would also be in Washington on that date, and he suggested that they should get together either before or after King's appearance in order to discuss a number of things including a matter pertaining to "our friend."

King indicated to Jones that he (King) would have to go into Danville, Virginia. He said that he really does not want to go at this time, but he said that in order to boost morale he must go in as he had promised. He made the statement that if he loses Danville, he will lose all of Virginia. He advised that he will go to Danville on November 15, 1963, and is considering a new type of operation which he described as "operation dialogue." King said that he plans to have Negroes go in teams to the various business organizations and to the homes of white people in order to talk directly with the people. He indicated that if the people were not receptive to this method, he would resort to direct action by the end of the month.

Jones said that he did not agree with the decision, but he cautioned King about over-extending. King mentioned his concern about going into Danville, because he said that we have not cleared up things in Birmingham.

King mentioned that the press is now asking about the lull in the civil rights movement, and he said that it has been interpreted as a sign of battle weariness and financial problems. King suggested that perhaps the country needs another dramatic push but was not quite sure whether this should take place in the streets or if it should be faced politically. King said that at the present time Goldwater is certainly the front runner for the Republican Party, and he said that he (King) knows that Kennedy "is scared to death because of the civil rights issue." He said that the only salvation is for the Democratic Party to regain losses in the South by gains in the North.

Jones agreed with the foregoing remarks by King. King stated that he could not be partisan, but he mentioned that if they could get enough people registered to vote then the Republicans might be afraid to nominate Goldwater.

Jones mentioned that if the Gandhi [sic] Society gets a tax exempt status, they will be able to contribute large sums for voter registration. Jones said that he has an appointment with the Internal Revenue Service in Washington, D.C., this week to discuss the matter.

Jones stated that he and "our friend" have concluded that "the meaning" of the March on Washington was its unity, not its militancy and that perhaps the other march organizations should be called together again for support of another campaign.

November 18, 1963

Asst. Deputy Director
F.B.I.
Washington 25, D. C.

Dear Sir:
The Dartmouth has received some literature from Governor Wallace supporting that Martin Luther King is a Communist and a member of at least 60 front organizations. The mail source for it is information is

Karl Prussion, who claims to have been an undercover agent for the FBI from 1947 to 1959.

1. Was Prussian such an agent and did he receive such information?

2. What are Martin Luther King's communist affiliations, if any?

3. Is the Highlander Folk School in Monteagle, Tennessee, a front organization?

4. What is Bayard Rustin's status if any, in the Communist movement and the civil rights movement? What communist influence is there if any in the civil rights movement?

Any answers you can give in full or in part would enable *The Dartmouth* to write a more accurate and informative article on the subject and any assistance would be greatly appreciated.

Yours truly,

[Signature deleted]

[Section 7]

SPOKANE WASH.

November 22, 1963

To whom it may concern:

A situation arose in my congregation which has given me some concern. In regards some literature and pronouncements issued by our synodical offices, The American Lutheran Church, Minneapolis, Minn., encouraging positive attitudes and action in the Civil Rights issue. Included have been favorable comments toward Rev. Martin Luther King, Jr.

Certain individuals have taken strong exception to this literature. Having identified Mr. King with Communism they are not transferring this identification also to officials of The American Lutheran Church because of their "endorsement" of Mr. King and the Civil Rights Movement.

Therefore I am requesting as much information as possible concerning Mr. King's activities, past and present, which either definitely associate him with or definitely disassociate him from the Communist Party. I would assume that the Civil Rights cause would be a fertile area for Communist intervention and so could bring Mr. King into frequent, albeit uninvited contacts with Communist interests. However I would hope that there is positive evidence which would clarify Mr. King's relationship with Communism one way or the other.

My purpose in using the information which I request is:

1. If the charges that Mr. King is a Communist are substantiate [sic], then this matter must be called to the attention of the officials of The American Lutheran church. Positive evidence must be supplied so that their future literature and pronouncements may be issued with more digression.

2. If the charges that Mr. King is a Communist are false, then those who are making vehement charges and arousing situations such as occurred in this congregation must be given authoritative evidence which can persuade them to desist.

Requesting your prompt attention to this matter I remain:

Gratefully,

[Signature deleted]

Re: Communist Party,
    United States of America—
    Negro Question
    Communist Influence in
    Racial Matters
    Internal Security-C

The "New York Herald Tribune" of Sunday **November 24, 1963** on page 13, column three, contains an article captioned, "An appreciation of Kennedy: Dr. King and Wilkins on Rights." This article was written in two parts; one written by Martin Luther King and the other by Roy Wilkins, of the National Association for the Advancement of Colored People (NAACP). The article written by King indicated that in a period of change, the nation has lost a leader who was unafraid of change. It said that he (President Kennedy) had the courage to be a friend of civil rights and a stalwart. King said that it is sad commentary on our time that it took a brave man to be a leader for those human necessities. King stated in the article, "The murder of the President, regardless of the precise identity of the assassin, occurred in a context of violence and hatred that has been building up in our nation for the past several years." King mentioned "We have seen children murdered in church, men shot down in ambush in a manner so similar to the assassination of President Kennedy that we must face the fact that we are dealing with a social disease that can be neglected or avoided, as we have done only to our deadly peril." King said the tragic fact must be faced that President Kennedy was the victim of developments that have made violence and hatred a popular pastime in all too many quarters of our nation. It was indicated that many people will ask the question of whether the assassination of President Kennedy will mean an inevitable setback for the cause of civil rights. In answer to this question, King said, "When Abraham Lincoln was assassinated, he was succeeded by a Vice-President of Southern origin" and "his successor had neither the experience nor the passion of Lincoln." King stated in the article that "the reconstruction movement ended and the release from physical slavery was carried through because the forces which had generated that change were too powerful to be turned back." He stated that "later Negroes suffered a setback in being denied full freedom and equality, but different elements were responsible." It was also indicated in the statement that the Negroes will continue their movement for civil rights, and it was stated, "It will not dissolve, because it was not a protest of one man, or one leader, but a genuine movement of millions whose long patience had run out." King stated, "I had several meetings with President Johnson when he served as Vice-President," and King said, "I felt he had a statesman-like grasp of the problem and great political sagacity. I think he will realize that civil rights is not one of several issues, but is the dominant domestic issue."

In closing, King quoted from President Lincoln's Gettysburg Address and used President Kennedy's words that "those who do nothing are inviting shame as well as violence. Those who act boldly are recognizing right as well as reality."

UNITED STATES DEPARTMENT OF JUSTICE

FEDERAL BUREAU OF INVESTIGATION

New York, New York
December 4, 1963

Communist Party, United States of America
Negro Question
Communist Influence in Racial Matters
Internal Security-C

On November 30, 1963, a confidential source, who has furnished reliable information in the past, furnished information which indicated that Clarence Jones contacted Stanley Levison on that date. Levison asked if Martin Luther King had been invited to the White House, and he said that it is very important that King get such an invitation. Levison said that King must not do or say anything which "will compromise his position of non-violence." Levison advised that the (civil rights) movement cannot rely on Roy Wilkins alone, and he said the administration will be hurt in the next election if they do not give King "a play." Levison said that he thinks this is being down on purpose, and that King must react to it. Jones asked if Levison had received a clipping. Levison replied that he had read it, and he said it is terrible inasmuch as it reads as though King was still in contact with Jack. Jones said he would contact King immediately.

Roy Wilkins is Executive Secretary
of the National Association For
Advancement of Colored People

On November 30, 1963, a second confidential source who has furnished reliable information in the past, furnished information which indicated that Clarence Jones contacted Martin Luther King. King advised that he is to meet with the President on Tuesday, December 3, 1963. King advised that a meeting was held last Thursday in which it was discussed that he, King, should have a meeting with the President. King advised that he was hurt because he had not been invited to the funeral, and he stated that "Roy's (Wilkins) ego was hurt because he was not invited." King mentioned that it looks bad to have civil rights leaders meet the President individually instead of in a group because it will look like the movement is disorganized. King said he read the "clippings from the Long Island Express" and said that he "was horrified." Jones suggested that King should meet with the Attorney General in regard to this. Jones said he felt that the timing of the article was on purpose and that this dealt with an issue which could compromise King's position. Jones advised that if King remains silent "implications from this will flow." Jones said that a great deal of thought went into the article and suggested that possibly "it is a trial balloon." King mentioned he thought it was a little early to talk to the Attorney General, but he said that he might talk to him next week. King said if there were any truth in the article why did Louis Martin (Vice Chairman of the Democratic National Committee in Washington, D.C.) confer with him (King). Jones said that other people are also saying things which are reflecting on King's character. King indicated that there are people who have said that he, King, "has pocketed $100,000." Jones said he can not understand the attitude of these people inasmuch as "you (King) have taken the extreme left-wing position on many issues and now they attack you as being a tool of big money." King said that he will meet Jones and Harry Wachtel at the Washington, D.C., Airport to discuss what he will say to the President. King said he is meeting with the President at 11:30 A.M. on December 3, 1963. King indicated he will fly back to New York City with Jones and Wachtel, and he said that he will fly to Washington from Michigan where he is to give a speech on December 2, 1963.

The "Long Island Press" of November 25, 1963, on Page 9, contains an article written by Robert S. Allen and Paul Scott captioned "RFK Faces Two Politically Explosive Decisions Involving Negroes" date-lined Washington. In this article it was stated that Attorney General Robert Kennedy faces two explosive decisions involving important Negro leaders that could have a far-reaching political impact. According to the article, it was stated that as the government's chief prosecutor, Attorney General Kennedy must decide whether to prosecute one of the highest negro state officials in the country for failing to file income tax returns. The Internal Revenue Service, according to the article, has forwarded its recommendations to the Justice Department after a six-month investigation of this tax case.

It was further stated that the Attorney General must soon pass on whether to permit Democratic National Committee officials to work closely with a Negro leader, who is known by the Federal Bureau of Investigation to be linked with a Soviet agent, in a massive drive to register Negro voters throughout the country. According to the article, this case "which involves evidence obtained by tapping telephones, puts the Attorney General on the spot since the Negro leader has been in close contact with both the White House and the Justice Department in the past." It was suggested that if the Attorney General orders a break with this Negro leader, he (the Negro leader) "could throw a monkey-wrench into Democratic plans to register more than one million Negro voters by next year's presidential election."

Continuing, the article stated that "if this close association isn't ended, the new administration faces public disclosures of this individual's RED ties in the midst of the coming congressional debate on civil rights legislation."

Stanley Levison was a secret member of the Communist Party, United States of America.

With respect to the name Jack which was mentioned by Stanley

Levison as a possible contact of King, it is to be noted that Hunter Pitts O'Dell who uses the name Jack O'Dell was formerly administrator of the New York Office of the Southern Christian Leadership Conference (SCLC), and was associated with King in this capacity.

UNITED STATES DEPARTMENT OF JUSTICE

FEDERAL BUREAU OF INVESTIGATION

New York, New York
December 6, 1963

Communist Party, United States of America (CPUSA)
Negro Question
Communist Influence in Racial Matters
Internal Security-C

On December 5, 1963, a confidential source, who has furnished reliable information in the past, furnished information which indicated that Bayard Rustin contacted Martin Luther King on that date. Rustin, explaining why he did not send some documents to King, stated that there was a great deal of conflict and that he did not want to get King involved in it. Rustin said that it was clear to him that Roy's (Wilkins) "objective was to close down the March on Washington" (office) and he said that when he learned that Phil (A. Phil Randolph) was not prepared to put up a fight about it, he (Rustin) did not want King calling Roy. Rustin stated he did not want King to be "pushed out on limb when (James) Farmer and the rest of them were not going to do anything." Rustin indicated that there had been a vote and that "we were supposed to be working on this legislation." In regard to this, Rustin said he had gotten "the stuff" and sent some of it to the Southern Christian Leadership Conference (SCLC). Rustin said, "But by the time it got out Roy then wanted the whole business done under the leadership conference. So I just decided that the better thing to do was just let that rest and not make a fight about it, because it's a fight nobody could win when the other boys were just going to let Roy have his way as they always do."

King, when asked by Rustin if he was going to Kenya, said that he had given up the idea. Rustin indicated that he did not intend to go either.

Rustin informed King that on December 13, 1963, at 8:00 P.M. Senator (Joseph) Clark and "a couple of other intellectuals" are speaking at a conference in New York on Peace, Civil Rights, and Labor. Rustin stated that it is being put on by a "bunch of intellectuals up here under Turn Toward Peace!" Rustin said that they would like to have King speak at this affair. Rustin told him that he would get $500.00 for himself, not for the SCLC, if he would speak. King stated he would have to review his schedule before making a decision. Rustin made arrangements with King to contact him later in the day at the office of Turn Toward Peace.

Rustin said that the affair on December 13, 1963, would be held at the Carnegie Center, "that UN Center." He also stated that they wanted him to speak on the relationship between civil rights and peace or on peace as King sees it. Rustin offered to help King "by jotting down a few things."

Roy Wilkins is Executive Secretary of the National Association for the Advancement of Colored People.

The March on Washington, which took place in Washington, D.C., on August 28, 1963, was a civil rights demonstration.

A. Philip Randolph was the Director of the March on Washington and is a Vice-President of the AFL-CIO.

James Farmer is National Director of the Congress of Racial Equality.

The "New York Herald Tribune" issue of August 14, 1963, page 7, column 1, contains an article captioned "Thurmond Assails a Leader of March."

The article stated that, in answer to charges by Senator Strom Thurmond, Bayard Rustin admitted joining the Young Communist League (YCL) in 1936. Rustin also reportedly stated that he broke completely with the YCL in June 1941, after the Nazi attack on Russia.

The YCL has been designated pursuant to executive Order 10450.

The "Daily Worker" issue of February 25, 1957, page 1, column 1, contained an article which stated that Bayard Rustin, Executive Secretary, War Resisters League was one of eight non-Communist observers at the Communist Party National Convention in 1957.

The "Daily Worker" was an East Coast Communist newspaper which suspended publication on January 13, 1958.

Excerpts from
Electronic Surveillance File
1963

1/31/63

Stanley Levison to Bill Kunstler at "8317." Stan tells Bill that he wasn't able to reach Shad Polier but that he will keep trying. Stan then tells Bill that he just wanted to say, in connection with "getting an initial burst of support for Higgs (phonetic) when this thing develops," that a key figure would be Meredith. . . . Kunstler says that "he tutored him" (Higgs tutored Meredith) and Stan agrees. Stan then remarks that . . . Martin is too removed from "that situation," . . . but that if Meredith is fighting for the white lawyer, who helped him and "who is now being framed," "this would be . . . one hell of a dramatic and attention-compelling event." . . . Kunstler remarks that there's no doubt about it that Higgs' part, both as Meredith's tutor and as the attorney for almost everybody under the sun, mentioning CORE, NAACP, ACLU and Ghandi [sic] (Society), and "thirdly this kind of peculiar microcosm of being the only white lawyer that'll touch these . . . plus just about to get the award . . . the Florin (phonetic) Lasker (phonetic) award" is "so much." Levison agrees but points out that Higgs wasn't technically Meredith's attorney. Kunstler confirms that he wasn't but he says "he helped a great deal" and that "he was there constantly" and that "he's very close to Meredith."

Kunstler then comments that "by the way, it's going to be a rather dramatic moment on the twelfth if Higgs is in jail, or can't get up there" when he is supposed to receive "this award." Levison agrees and Kunstler remarks that "that might be the place for Meredith to take" as he says there will be a lot of people there and that he is sure they would raise $10,000 to $12,000 dollars. Levison says that's right and suggests that if Higgs could ask Meredith to accept the award for him "this" would be "a most dramatic way of putting the thing forward." . . .

Stan Levison to Shad Polier.
Levison: asks if Shad knows of William Higgs (phonetic), the white attorney in Jackson.
Polier: replies that he knows of Higgs and asks, "What about him?"
Levison: "We just got word that the state of Mississippi is set to frame him . . . on a sodomy charge." "Apparently they put a plant in his

182

house as a workman, a young kid, and he has signed a complaint
. . . and he expects to be arrested very shortly." . . . the Civil Liberties
Union is giving Higgs an award on the twelfth and that "they've
been alerted on this and say they'll get behind him." But Levison
says it's something that he thinks Congress ought to think about.
Polier: "Well certainly, but . . . how can they do anything until something happens?"

4/1/63

Bea Levison to Stanley Levison at the office.
Bea said that she wanted to remind Levison to send a check to her
mother.

Clarence to Stan Levison.
. . . Clarence states the big thing that came up with Martin and Fred
Shuttlesworth (phonetic) . . . [was] what is to be if an injunction is
issued out of State Courts of Alabama . . . Clarence says Martin and
Fred had difference of opinion on this, says Martin felt they couldn't
ignore experience of Albany, Ga., said it is consistent with unjust laws
and applications of them regarding how much respect can be accorded
court orders of Segregationist Court as contrasted to orders of Federal
Court, says Martin took the position that this is the time for movement
to break injunctions (State), to violate these injunctions, even without
recourse of appealing dissolution of them to Federal Courts, since law
states you will have to go to State Courts first. Clarence states Fred's
position was that this is most advanced position for movement to take.
Clarence states he had reservations on this stand also. Stan Levison
states that much depends on the movement there, says if people will
stand behind and go along with it he agrees with Martin, . . .

4/13/63

*Stanley Levison called Western Union and dictated the following tele-
gram which he told the operator to sign with the name Beatrice Murkin,
585 West End Ave.:*
To Police Commissioner Connors, Birmingham, Alabama,
"Whether you chose to recognize it or not, you have in custody one
of the world's formost (*sic*) citizens, Dr. Martin L. King. Since you
were responsible for his arrest, the burden of his safety is in your
hands. Our nation would never live down its shame if by some cowardly manouver (*sic*) he was harmed in your jail."
The telegram was charged to Stanley Levison.

4/18/63

Stanley Levison to Alice Loewi at Templeton.

. . . Alice asks Levison how everything is down in "Glochamora" (phonetic—apparently referring to Birmingham or the South in general). Levison replies that he thinks it's going good as he says "they're keeping the thing rolling." Levison adds that with all the pressure on the administration "this Mississippi Commission and the Civil Rights commission" turned out to be a "dirty old bunch of wild eyed revolutionarists." Levison laughs as he tells Alice that this Civil Rights Commission is really "a terribly conservative body" and he indicates that he thinks they're coming out with the proposal that the federal government cut off federal funds from the state of Mississippi goes a hundred miles further than any Negro civil rights organization ever went. Levison calls it a most extraordinary proposal and he says it may be enough to move Kennedy into some effective action. Levison indicates that up to this point Kennedy has not taken effective action. However, he says Kennedy does make the right telephone calls such as to call "Coretta" (phonetic—apparently Mrs. Martin Luther King) and asks her if she needs anything. Levison says he spoke to Coretta the next day and asked her why she didn't ask Kennedy to get her a housekeeper as that's what she needs right now. . . .

4/19/63

Joan Davis to Stan Levison.

. . . Davis then asks Levison what he hears from "Martin." Levison replies that he hears from jail that he is in good spirits and that there is "a very promising outlook that they're going . . . to achieve a settlement and what amounts to a very important victory there." Levison says "there are people working . . . behind the scenes on it." Levison tells Davis that it will be very important because he says Birmingham is "the big fortress;" that most people don't realize it but that Birmingham is the largest segregated city in the world. Davis says she just shudders to think of somebody like that—first of all having been in solitary confinement. Levison agrees and tells Davis that it is medieval solitary confinement as he says that (Martin Luther King) had no mattress and had to sleep on the bed spring until the President called; that it took the President to get him a mattress. Levison adds that King has no light; that when the sun goes down it becomes dark in his cell. Levison confirms that King has no light; that "they" said yesterday that they would see what they could do about putting a light in his cell. Levison explains that "they're trying to break him." They agree that it makes one cringe when one thinks of someone being subjected to such inhuman treatment in this country. Davis then adds that it's even worse than that as she says with the absolute power of "these people" they can hit King on the head right this minute and that there is not a person in the world who can do anything (to stop it). Levison tells Davis that that's the danger and tells her that's why the President called; more for that than anything else; to let "them" know that they had better not pull "that kind of thing." ...

5/3/63

Stanley Levison to Clarence Jones.

... Jones tells Levison that he just got off the phone with "Martin" a little while ago and he says that "Martin" told him that conservatively 500 more people were just arrested and that he thinks that it's more in the neighborhood of about 900. Jones confirms that he means that these people were just arrested today and tells Levison that it is exclusive of the 417 reported in *The Times* this morning. They agree that *The Post* reported more arrests this afternoon but Jones tells Levison that the new element is now police brutality—"The old Birmingham has returned." Jones says that the police used police dogs and fire hoses on the demonstrators, including the small children. Jones says that "Martin" says it's "one of the most ... brutal uses of violent dogs and armed might against non-violent and unarmed people." Jones then tells Levison that he is going to be getting in touch with a number of people but he says that he would like Levison to do one thing definitely sometime within the next hour. Jones then asks if Levison will work on a draft telegram as Jones says he will not have the time for this himself as he says he has about 30 calls to make. Jones confirms that he means a telegram to the President, adding "and to the Attorney General," based upon "the fact that the police dogs have been unleashed again ... and they have turned the fire hoses on."

... Stan said he composed the following telegram: More than 1000 Negroes, predominantly young people, have been jailed in Birmingham in two days. In today's mass jailing totally unprovoked vicious police brutality compounded the violation of our constitutional rights. Peaceful and unarmed, nonviolent demonstrators were set upon by unleashed police dogs and high pressure firing hoses were used in an appalling display of unprovoked violence. The Negro community has firmly declared its adherence to nonviolence, and it has maintained perfect discipline. We are enduring injustice and brutality to attain our simple rights

as citizens. Our national government does not have to endure nor tolerate these evils, it possesses both the power and obligation to act. We
urge your immediate effective intervention to safeguard constitutional
rights from this notorious abuse. We have threatened no one, we will
harm no one, but we will not permit brutality to stop us. Will you
permit this recrudescence of violence in Birmingham to threaten our
lives and deny us our rights?

Jones told Stan that it sounds good.

5/8/63

Stan Levison to [name deleted].

[name deleted] said he guesses that Stan is happy about the truce.
Stan told him the latest news is that Martin Luther King has been
sentenced to six months on a contempt charge. Stan said he would like
[name deleted] to send a telegram, that he has composed to the President, remarking that his own name on it would be unimpressive. Stan
gave the following message to send to the White House: The President
of the United States should settle the Birmingham outrage, which the
President declares is internationally significant, not local people. You
debase yourself by this evasion. Having seen many constructive qualities in you I worked hard for your election. I know you are now losing
more support than you can afford by this amoral neutral posture.

. . . Stan mentioned that there is to be the biggest demonstration
tomorrow—may be trouble.

5/12/63

Call from Stanley Levison to "Naomi."

Stanley told Naomi about the destruction of the home of Martin's
brother and the bombing of the Gaston Motel. . . . Stanley said that the
organizers of violence in Birmingham are the police; it's an official
Klan organization. . . . Stanley suggested to Naomi the sending of a
delegation to Washington, because there is basis for the FBI now to
move in very solidly: the bombings, the fact that the police force used
brutality, and Dick Gregory has given long affidavits on this—he really
was beaten up in jail, lays the basis for the show of some real muscle
on the part of the Justice Department. Stanley continued, they already
announced now, belatedly, they've offered going to do it on a token
basis at which the local segregationist can laugh or do it on a basis
which will put some fear in them. Naomi said do you think we could
get a delegation to get an appointment to see Kennedy? Stanley replied
he did know. Stanley said even if it were not Kennedy, it would be

useful if a delegation went to Washington and said: here's a mayor really without a police force, a police force that's against him, here are merchants with the police force against them and a section of the white community against them—and somebody has to help them. Naomi said, well if we can't see Kennedy, it would be useful if we could see someone of importance in this like Bob Kennedy. Justice Department— Burt Marshall is supposed to be back in Washington. Naomi said we should urge FBI intervention to give the mayor some kind of police force which he can really use to keep quiet. Stanley added, effective FBI, underline effective. Stanley said there is a responsibility of the FBI to investigate police brutality in jail—there were police brutalities in jail—even to King. Stanley said something has to be done to keep the police force from gathering the Klan elements—especially when the governor is standing on the side encouraging them.

Call from Stanley Levison to "Jack" (believed, from the voice, to be Jack O'Dell).

Stan and Jack discussed the bombing of the motel, etc. Stanley said the FBI offered its services. Jack replied, "well that's a waste of time, we know that." Jack added that Birmingham has a history of bombings, and they have never done anything about any of them. Stanley said that in bombings there is a Federal statue. Jack replied, "but they have never used it." Stanley said, "yes I know, but this offers an opportunity for several groups, especially the American Jewish Congress, to send delegations to Washington to demand effective FBI intervention" (underlined word stressed). Jack said that perhaps an alternative would be to send in the marshals, to send in the FBI really to do it.

5/21/63

Martin Luther King to Stanley Levison (Stanley had placed a call to King in Alabama earlier and left a message for King to call him when he returned).

King apologized for calling so late and explained that he had just returned from a mass meeting. (Follows an abbreviated dialogue of a conversation):

Levison: I guess you had a busy day?

King: Very busy.

Levison: How is the community taking these expulsions of black students from Birmingham public schools?

King: I think we'll be able to hold them together pretty well. Naturally they're upset about it. I don't want us to follow an unwise act on the part of the board with a hasty unwise act on our part. (Levison acknowledges). My feeling is that they are determined to upset this agreement some way. They just want to do something.

Levison: That's right.

King: And the Board of Education is controlled by Bull Connor (phonetic). He appoints the superintendent as well as the board. This is something that Bull Connor is doing to provoke the Negro community to the point that we will do something to so confuse the situation that will upset this agreement. And my feeling is that we've got to hold out and not do anything right now . . .

Levison: This is an attack on the kids and following the President's call for educated white southerners to give leadership and these are not just educated white southerners. These are people in charge of education who did this thing. A good many people are going to be strongly moved and we were trying to think of something along the lines of setting up for the expelled students some kind of—if necessary—temporary educational facilities and going to the public and to prominent individuals, to ask for contributions to set it up. In other words, a school aid fund. I would think that there would be a number of foundations that might be able to come into this aspect of the picture. Or an ad in the *Times*. . . .

King: That's a good idea but I really think we're going to get them back in school.

Levison: I do too.

King: You see, the white community is divided on this. It was a mistake on the part of the Board of Education. There were two members who didn't even show up. They barely got a quorum. There were only three there. They had three who voted but two didn't show and one, I understand, resigned because he was against it. And the people with whom we negotiated feel it was a mistake. They feel that this was too drastic, so that I feel that we would have made a mistake today if we had called for a mass walkout tomorrow and renewed demonstrations. We would have put ourselves in a position of moving before we really thought though—we still have the moral offensive you see, and these troopers are here—they want to beat the heads of Negroes as much as possible. They are just waiting—they are standing out there now with their guns. I have never seen anything like it, those guns cocked just like we are some kind of lawless criminals, and if all of these kids are out of school they are going to beat some, and I do not feel right now that we have the violent elements of the Negro community in hand enough to keep a riot from emerging. So

I'm trying to control the situation so that if we get the Supreme Court to rule by Wednesday he will probably be out and then Boutwell will instruct Chief Moore, who doesn't want these state troopers here anyway, to request that they be moved immediately, that the city does not need them. Then if the new administration doesn't act, I think we can mount a great protest which will still keep us in a good light and a good position.

Levison: I think that's sound. You are not letting them trap you into an action that can influence the decision, and that's sound. It may be that there are going to be some people who are going to misunderstand this because they are not aware of the thinking behind it. No one knows—the papers here haven't indicated that Connor appoints this Board. That would spell out so much if it were made clear, and that you're biding your time would be another thing that people could understand. But I think you're right to hold back while you still have the moral offensive. It doesn't weaken you.

5/26/63

Roy Bennett to Stanley Levison.

Bennett asked Levison if he should mail the letter and Levison said yes. Levison said to send him a card at the same time that he mails the letter to Alice Loewi so he, Levison, can study her reaction to the letter. Levison and Bennett talked about the returns on real estate deals. At the close of the conversation Levison said to Bennett to have a good time. Bennett is taking a trip (maybe to Europe) and was supposed to leave today.

Stanley Levison to Clarence Jones.

. . . Levison asked Jones if he had fun on Friday (evidently referring to a conference with the Attorney General). Jones said that the Attorney General had no conception of what the Negro problem was all about . . . that he had come there thinking that he knew everything and had not been prepared to change his mind. He took a very simple approach, that they had done more than anyone else in this area, that there was nothing further that they could do, and so what was everybody complaining about? Levison said "so he thinks that he can get away with that, well he doesn't know what year this is, he doesn't know what Birmingham means. It seems to me that the President is very worried about Birmingham, and that we shouldn't be thrown off by Bobby Kennedy's ignorance." Since Martin is going to see him, he should get advice on how to present the matter to the President. Jones said that he didn't think that it would make much difference because he thought that the President's position would be one that was approved by the Attorney General. That the Attorney General is running the civil rights movement. . . . Jones said that the Attorney General didn't think that any purpose would be served by the President's leading a Negro into the University of Alabama and that this provoked some very bitter comments that one person had told him that the only reason that he was in this room was because he was concerned with the 1964 elections, that he was the "worst illustration of white arrogant liberalism" and that was the way he was to be regarded. Levison said that that was a good description . . .

6/1/63

Conference call to Mr. Stanley Levison. Other parties are Dr. Martin Luther King and Clarence Jones.

. . . King states in his travels, the Negro element is really aroused and there is a feeling of nationalism. King further states that he thinks we are on a breakthrough, and we need a mass protest. King wants to know if we are ready to go on a national level with our protests. . . . They discuss the organizational problems involved in properly arranging for a mass march on Washington, D.C., involving possibly 100,000 people, in conjunction with accompanying demonstrations and action all over the United States and involving all the leading civil rights organizations in it so as to make it really effective in influencing the President to present civil rights legislation, to get him to really push it, and in impressing Congress enough for them to realize that they have to pass it now. They indicate that they don't think that the mass action involved cannot *(sic)* be organized properly to have it take place before August.

6/14/63

Stanley Levison to Frank Montero (phonetic) at Gandhi Society.

Frank says he called Stan the other day but that in the meantime he has gotten the *Saturday Evening Post* article and that Ted Brown was talking about it and said that Stan had seen it. Frank then asks if Stan has caught up with a little bit of the hassle "on this fund that is involved in the NAACP business." Stan replies that he doesn't know about it but that he can anticipate what it is; that "NAA" resents it. Frank confirms that that's right. Both Frank and Stan then indicate that they think that the NAACP was right in this instance. Stan says he had a feeling that it was jumping too fast. Frank agrees and says it was ill

advised. Frank adds that as a matter of fact *The Times* is reacting
against "Martin" unfortunately. Frank then reads to Stan from a Times
story on Jackson, Mississippi, in which *The Times* says that some concern was expressed in Negro circles over an apparent move by the
Reverend Dr. Martin Luther King, Jr., to take a hand in the Jackson
controversy. The story mentions that one of King's associates came to
Jackson that afternoon to inform local Negroes of King's availability.
It also relates that a source close to the NAACP leaders said that they
resented King's announcement of a Medgar Evans fund since such a
fund has already been started by the NAACP. Frank says this has caused
a lot of furor behind the scenes. Stan then says that he would not place
too much weight on the starting of this fund although he says he thinks
it was unwise to do it (by King). But Stan says that the furor that Frank
is talking about has long and very much deeper roots. Stan tells Frank
that the antagonism towards Martin at NAA has been a disgrace now
for a long time; that it has been a disgrace in its "dirt," "filth," and
"dishonesty." Stan tells Frank, who expresses surprise at this, that
Roy Wilkins and every single member of his staff except John Morsell
(phonetic), who he says is "an awful decent guy," have carried on
(against Martin). . . . Stan then tells Frank that "Roy has ripped Phil
Randolph up the back" to Stan; that Roy has done the same with
Martin to Stan; that "Roy unfortunately is a guy who hasn't got what
these other two guys have got and he's damned aware of it." Stan says
that the first time he met Roy he spent nearly an hour telling Stan that
Phil Randolph wasn't responsible for the march on Washington and
that Roy made the flat statement that "Phil Randolph couldn't organize
eleven guys to cross the street;" that Phil doesn't know how to organize
anything and that it was NAA who had the organization while Phil got
all the credit. . . . Stan then tells Frank that Martin insisted on a meeting
with Roy as "people like Ruby Hurley (phonetic) were carrying on
such a dirty campaign, spreading rumors about him—about money and
other things— . . . that he was getting big money from insurance companies— . . . Negro insurance companies and what not—all kinds of slanders— . . . that this was systematically being carried on— . . . and if
Roy didn't put a stop to it, Martin would have to bring it into the
open." Frank comments that the rumors are ridiculous. Stan tells Frank
that above all Martin has bent over backward all the time to maintain
unity but he says that Martin has had to do it while accepting "these
slanders calculated to undermine him." Stan says that one of the worst
offenders is Ruby Hurley and Stan also mentions Kelly Alexander as
another but Stan says that Roy, himself, has been involved in "this"

and that Roy certainly hasn't done enough to put it down. Stan confirms that his own position is wholly on Martin's side in "this hassle" because Stan says he has really seen Martin be "so patient with the amount of garbage that's heaped on him." . . . Stan says he heard a report that was spread around Washington that came to Stan through "A.D.A." that Martin King was getting $1,000,000 a month from Negro insurance companies in Atlanta and that that's why King moved to Atlanta. Frank asks what this has to do with the NAACP and Stan retorts that he will leave Frank to form his own conclusion as to where these rumors came from.

6/19/63

Toni Hamilton to Stanley Levison.

Hamilton: . . .

Levison: . . . "during the day we had a meeting on this proposed march to Washington . . . with Randolph and a number of others and another meeting's to take place with Randolph and Dr. King and Roy Wilkins to try to get Roy Wilkins to go along with it. In the meantime they're working out general plans on it." . . . (continuing yesterday's meeting) "we discussed his trip to Europe" and "he's going to give it up." King hates to because he really needs the vacation and his wife was looking forward to it but even though King said he can go without leaving any gap or anything he's sure to be criticized for it. "They'll say he picked up and left in the middle of all this" . . . "he figures he'll just hold out." . . .

7/24/63

Roy Bennett to Stanley Levison.

Bennett said that he had heard that Levison had been friendly toward the President in the conference call that Levison, Jones, Walker, King, and O'Dell had on the phone. Levison said that was right that he had tried to talk them out of a march on the President and make it on Washington.

8/28/63

Alice Loewi to Stanley Levison.

Sam Levison said that he thought that King was great in his speech at the "March." He said that it has taken a lot of years and a lot of demonstrations to lead up to this one . . . He said that this is the one that was needed to finally say "it" and to show how much muscle there is. Levison said that it was marvelous in Martin's speech, the way he handled the white and negro question completely repudiating this kind of nonsense of Adam Powell and the "Muslims" and everybody else in a way that was so positive that the crowd responded to it as they did to everything else that he, King, said . . . Levison said that he thought that King's introduction was real good; "The Moral Leader of America" and then to measure up to it, that is a "Mark of a Man." Levison said that (*sic*) was no question that King was the "man of the hour" for everybody. Levison said that it is a remarkable thing that he is such a "pure guy," that's what's really marvelous . . . Levison said that he was bowled over by the tribute that Roy Wilkins gave to King. Levison said that Wilkins would not invite King to the 50th anniversary of the NAACP even though he is a founder . . .

9/21/63

Alice Loewi to Stanley Levison.

. . . Levison said that he wasn't satisfied with the President's reaction to Birmingham, nor was he satisfied with Martin's reaction to Birmingham. Levison said that Martin should have made something of the funeral. He, King, should have said "that this murder was committed by every white citizen of the USA" or something like that. . . .

Mrs. Loewi asked if there was going to be a mass meeting tomorrow.

Levison said that Bayard was organizing it and . . . that Bayard is a "Shrieker." To him everything is simple. He would scream at the "Whitehouse" to send troops in and that would be the answer to him.

Mrs. Loewi asked, "What was the answer?"

Levison said the answer was that the police force, it has to be completely reorganized. Levison said that an agency becomes strong and entrenched and you can't do anything about it. Levison said that she, Mrs. Loewi, had heard of the "FBI" (*sic*).

Mrs. Loewi said yes she had.

Levison said that there is an example of an agency becoming so entrenched that even if the "President" wanted to get rid of it he couldn't. Levison said that this is what is true about Birmingham police. He said that the Birmingham police are tied in with all kinds of rackets that exist in an industrial city and that they are undoubtedly completely infiltrated by the "Klan." . . .

11/22/63

Alice Loewi to Stanley Levison.

Levison said that he was shocked and that this was no accident in the south. He said the same thing happened to Evers. Levison said, look what happened to Stevenson when he was down there recently. Levison said that they let these people go wild down there and shoot anyone who is in the say. Levison said that Johnson may be good as he met with King about one and a half years ago and King was impressed with Johnson. King said that he thought Johnson was a real statesman. Levison also said that he thought that Johnson could win in the next Presidential election. Levison said that this was no act of a crazy person, that it was a political action.

1964

1964

[Section 8]

January 8, 1964	Memorandum: Baumgardner to Sullivan
January 10, 1964	Airtel: Director to Charlotte/Atlanta/New York
January 13, 1964	Memorandum: Richmond
January 16, 1964	Memorandum: Sullivan to Belmont
January 24, 1964	Memorandum: Charlotte
January 27, 1964	Teletype: Milwaukee to Director
February 5, 1964	Memorandum: Director to Tolson, et al.

[Section 9]

February 5, 1964	Informal Memo to Mr. Mohr
February 10, 1964	Memorandum: New York
February 10, 1964	Memorandum: New York
February 11, 1964	Memorandum: New York
February 29, 1964	Memorandum: Houston
March 3, 1964	Memorandum: Director to Attorney General
March 4, 1964	Memorandum: Baumgardner to Sullivan

[Section 10]

March 7, 1964	Newspaper article
March 20, 1964	Memorandum: Baumgardner to Sullivan

[Section 11]

April 8, 1964	Memorandum: DeLoach to Mohr
April 17, 1964	Memorandum: Cincinnati
April 24, 1964	Radiogram: San Francisco to Director
May 11, 1964	Memorandum: Baumgardner to Sullivan
May 11, 1964	Memorandum: Jones to DeLoach

[Section 12]

May 15, 1964	Airtel: Cincinnati to Director
May 15, 1964	Memorandum: Cincinnati
June 9, 1964	Memorandum; New Haven
June 9, 1964	Teletype: Director to Atlanta/Jacksonville
June 10, 1964	Letter: Director to Special Assistant to President
June 11, 1964	Airtel: Director to Jacksonville/Atlanta
June 11, 1964	Memorandum: San Diego
June 16, 1964	Memorandum: New York
June 26, 1964	Memorandum: New York

[Section 13]

| July 7, 1964 | Memorandum: New York |

[Section 14]

July 5, 1964	Report
July 28, 1964	Memorandum: New York
July 30, 1964	Memorandum: New York
August 3, 1964	Memorandum: New York

[Section 15]

August 13, 1964	Memorandum: Baumgardner to Sullivan
August 14, 1964	Memorandum: New York
August 17, 1964	Memorandum: Philadelphia
August 25, 1964	Memorandum: New York

[Section 17]

| October 16, 1964 | Memorandum: New York |
| November 2, 1964 | Memorandum: Baumgardner to Sullivan |

[Section 18]

| November 19, 1964 | Memorandum: Jones to DeLoach |

[Section 19]

[Section 20]

[Section 21]

[Section 8]

To: Mr. W. C. Sullivan   January 8, 1964

From: Mr. F. J. Baumgardner

COMMUNIST PARTY, USA
NEGRO QUESTION
COMMUNIST INFLUENCE IN RACIAL MATTERS
INTERNAL SECURITY—COMMUNIST

Memorandum from W. C. Sullivan to A. H. Belmont 12/24/64 summarized the results of a conference held at the seat of Government 12/23/63 between Bureau officials and supervisors and field representatives designed to explore how best to carry on our investigation of captioned matter to produce the desired results without embarrassment to the Bureau. We completely analyzed avenues of approach aimed at neutralizing Martin Luther King, Jr., as an effective Negro leader. One of the avenues explored was that concerning any facets of the financial operations of King and the organizations through which he operates which investigation might reveal either violations of the law or other potentials for discrediting King or otherwise neutralizing his effectiveness.

Bufiles contain two items of particular significance. A Washington Capital News Service release dated 10/22/63 reveals that King's integration organization had an income of more than $735,000 during the past fiscal year and spent only about half of it. It is stated that in a report of the financial status of the Southern Christian Leadership Conference (SCLC), of which King is President, King disclosed that the organization had a balance of $351,992.20 left 8/31/63 at the end of the fiscal year from a total income of $735,534.03. Another such news release dated 11/4/63 revealed that Representative George Andrews (D-Ala.) asked the Internal Revenue Service (IRS) to investigate the tax status of the SCLC. Andrews is quoted as saying, "Thousands and thousands of dollars are collected and spent each year by so-called civil rights organizations and many people are beginning to suspect they could be a front for a full-grown racket."

It is noted that King's operations revolve principally around the SCLC. However, fund-raising operations on his part are further augmented by the activities of the Gandhi Society for Human Rights, which commenced operations in 1962.

FBI

January 10, 1964

AIRTEL

To: SACS, Charlotte (157-260)
           Atlanta (100-6530)
           New York (100-151548)

From: Director, FBI (100-3-116)

COMMUNIST PARTY, USA
NEGRO QUESTION
COMMUNIST INFLUENCE IN RACIAL MATTERS
INTERNAL SECURITY-C

ReAllet to the Bureau, copies to Charlotte and New York, 12/31/63 which revealed plans for a retreat which Martin Luther King, Jr., and his associates in the Southern Christian Leadership Conference planned to have on property owned by the Episcopal Church near Asheville, North Carolina. The original plan was for this retreat to take place 1/6–8/64 and also to be invited were some people in the current Negro movement possibly not directly a part of the Southern Christian Leadership Conference.

ReCEairtel to the Bureau, copies to Atlanta and New York, 1/7/64 which disclosed the results of a discreet inquiry made which determined that the site of the retreat would likely be the In-The-Oaks Episcopal Center, Black Mountain, North Carolina. Charlotte requested advice as to what coverage of the retreat was desired and that no open investigation would be conducted unless requested by Atlanta, New York, or the Bureau.

For the information of Charlotte, subsequent information developed revealed that the retreat is now scheduled to take place the latter part of January 1964.

Because of the extremely discreet nature of the Bureau's inquiry to date concerning Martin Luther King, Jr., and because the retreat may involve the legitimate activities of the Southern Christian Leadership Conference, no coverage whatsoever of the retreat itself is desired. Of course, if any of the receiving offices should receive information, particularly through sensitive sources available to Atlanta and New York, concerning activities taking place at the retreat, the Bureau and interested offices should be advised.

UNITED STATES DEPARTMENT OF JUSTICE

FEDERAL BUREAU OF INVESTIGATION

Richmond, Virginia
January 13, 1964

Re: Reverend Martin Luther King

On January 8, 1964, a confidential source who is familiar with most aspects of the racial situation in Lynchburg, Virginia, furnished the following information:

About two years ago, Reverend Martin Luther King came to Lynchburg, Virginia, at the invitation of the Lynchburg Chapter of the Southern Christian Leadership Conference, at which time he addressed a very large audience on various integration activities.

During the meeting a collection was taken up from the audience. After the meeting, Reverend King and some of his associates who came to Lynchburg with him from his headquarters gathered up all the money in sacks and placed the money in the trunk of their car, taking it with them when they left Lynchburg.

At no time was any accounting made of the money that was collected and to this date, it is not known how much money was collected or what disposition was made of it, except that it was taken by the Reverend King and his associates.

The source expressed great admiration for Reverend King in his integration activities and expressed the opinion that Reverend King is a "good Christian."

The source then stated that "when all the integration activity is over, Reverend King will not be a pure man."

The source declined to elaborate further on this comment, except to state that failure to account properly for money collected as outlined above was not correct and to indicate that it was possible that Reverend King was in a position to keep all or any part of the money collected in Lynchburg for his own personal use.

To: Mr. A. H. Belmont   1/16/64

From: Mr. W. C. Sullivan

COMMUNIST PARTY, USA
NEGRO QUESTION
COMMUNIST INFLUENCE IN RACIAL MATTERS
INTERNAL SECURITY-C

Yesterday afternoon (1/15/64) I talked on the telephone with our Atlanta Office and at that time spoke with SA . . . who is working on the Martin Luther King case. . . . advised me that he is a very close personal friend of. . . . Realizing what a scoundrel King is . . . began to think about possible ways and means of exposing King which would be of benefit to the Bureau. While talking to . . . on other matters, . . . theorized with . . . about men of questionable character in public life and did . . . think they should be exposed. . . . took a strong stand on the matter and said it would be a public service if some people were exposed. Of course, no reference at all was made to King by . . . said that knowing . . . personally and getting his views indirectly on this general subject matter leads . . . to believe that if any time in the future the Bureau would want to utilize . . . and his . . . it could be done very securely.

I thanked . . . for his interest in this matter and told him that this type of thing would be handled out of the Bureau headquarters and that if we thought this particular person could be utilized he would be advised but to take no action until that time.

ACTION:
For the record.

UNITED STATES DEPARTMENT OF JUSTICE

FEDERAL BUREAU OF INVESTIGATION

Copy to: 1-USA, Asheville, N.C.

Office: CHARLOTTE

Report of: SA . . .

Date: 1/24/64

Field Office File No.: Charlotte 149-83   Bureau File No.:

Title: UNKNOWN SUBJECT;
                  Anonymous Telephone Call concerning
                  Reverend MARTIN LUTHER KING, JR.,
                  Asheville, North Carolina, January 22, 1964

Character: DESTRUCTION OF AIRCRAFT

Synopsis:

Anonymous telephone call received approximately 8:10 P.M., 1/22/64, at United Airlines, Asheville, N.C., Airport. Female alleged to be telephone operator in Birmingham, Alabama, asked for Rev. MARTIN LUTHER KING. KING would not take the call but call taken by his assistant, WYATT TEE WALKER. WALKER advised person on other end of line, thought to be white female, guessed to be 38–44 years of age, stated "You had better get that S.O.B. out of Asheville, North Carolina. I hope there is a bomb on the plane." WALKER stated the caller then hung up. Piedmont Airlines Flight 45 scheduled to depart Asheville, N. C., 8:31 P.M., 1/22/64, searched by local authorities and airline officials. No bomb found and plane departed for Atlanta, Ga., 11:17 P. M., 1/22/64, with KING and staff members and other passengers. FAA and ICG notified. USA, Asheville, N. C., advised did not think facts constituted Federal violation.

DETAILS:

AT ASHEVILLE, NORTH CAROLINA

This investigation was predicated upon information telephonically furnished by . . . , Buncombe County Sheriff's Office, Asheville, North Carolina, at 8:30 P.M., January 22, 1964.

. . . , Buncombe County Sheriff's Office, Asheville, North Carolina, stated that he had received a call from one of the deputies from that office from the Asheville Airport where Reverend MARTIN LUTHER KING, JR., and members of his staff were scheduled to depart on Piedmont Airlines Flight 45 at 8:31 P.M. that same day. He stated that according to his deputy at the airport, one of Reverend KING's assistants accepted a long-distance telephone call, allegedly from Birmingham, Alabama, and that the unidentified person calling said something about a bomb on the plane. He stated that the plane was being held for a search by his men and that the details regarding the telephone call could be obtained from Reverend KING's chief assistant, name unknown, who was standing by at the Asheville Airport.

. . . stated that he had received a call from a female caller on January 21, 1964, who refused to give her identity and who said something about they better get MARTIN LUTHER KING out of Black Mountain before somebody kills him, and then hung up. He stated that between 6:45 and 7:00 P.M. on January 22, 1964, he received two calls from a female, thought to be the same person who called the day before, and wanted to know where KING and his party were staying and that the second time she called she wanted to know what flight he was supposed to leave Asheville, North Carolina, on. He stated that he thought the woman sounded as if she were drunk and that he did not attempt to give her any information. He stated that the female did not identify herself.

. . . United Airlines, Asheville Airport, Asheville, North Carolina, advised that at about 8:10 P.M., January 22, 1964, a telephone call came to the United Airlines telephone and that the female calling stated that she was the long-distance operator from Birmingham, Alabama, and asked if he could page Reverend MARTIN LUTHER KING, JR. . . . stated that he saw Reverend KING and members of his staff standing nearby and told KING he had a long-distance telephone call from Birmingham, Alabama. He stated that Reverend KING would not accept the call but asked his assistant, WYATT TEE WALKER, to take the call. . . . stated that WALKER asked him, . . . to find out the identity of the person calling. . . . stated that when he told the operator that Reverend KING wold not accept the call unless he knew the identity of the person calling that the operator paused momentarily and then stated that the party on the other end did not desire to give his identity. . . . stated that he thought he heard a male muffled voice in the background. . . . stated that the operator then told him that the party would not give his identity but would speak to Reverend KING's assistant.

. . . stated that at first he was convinced that it was actually the long-distance operator because the female voice was clear like that of an operator, but that when he could not hear her talking to the party on the other end and when he heard a muffled male voice, he became suspicious that it was probably a local call and perhaps was not a long-distance operator talking with him. He stated that he then turned the phone over to Reverend KING's assistant.

FBI WASH DC

FBI MILWAUK
4-22PM URGENT1-27-64TJC
TO DIRECTOR
FROM MILWAUKEE (157-122) 2P

VISIT OF RECEREND [sic] MARTIN LUTHER KING TO MIL-
WAUKEE, WISCONSIN, JANUARY TWENTY SEVEN, NINETEEN
SIXTY FOUR. RACIAL MATTERS; CPUSA-NEGRO QUESTION-
COMMUNIST INFLUENCE IN RACIAL MATTERS, IS-C.

REV. KING IS SCHEDULED TO SPEAK AT A PUBLIC RALLY
IN THE MILWAUKEE AUDITORIUM DURING THE EVENING OF
JANUARY TWENTY SEVEN, SIXTY FOUR, AT EIGHT P.M. THE
SPEECH WILL BE PRECEDED BY A RECEPTION ATTEND BY AP-
PROXIMATELY SEVENTY FIVE MINISTERS AND STEERING
COMMITTEE OF SPONSORING ORGANIZATIONS. THIS COM-
MENCES AT SIX THIRTY P.M. ALSO IN THE AUDITORIUM.

AT ONE THIRTY P.M. THIS DATE MI PD ADVISED OF RE-
CEIPT OF THE FOLLOWING INFORMATION FROM ... CITY
DESK,/MILWAUKEE JOURNAL/AT ELEVEN TWENTY FIVE A.M.
THIS DATE ... TELEPHONE OPERATOR,/MILWAUKEE JOUR-
NAL/RECEIVED A CALL FROM A MALE VOICE WHICH SHE IS
UNABLE TO DESCRIBE BEYOND THE FACT THAT IT WAS
CALM AND MIDDLE AGED STATING, "THERE IS GOING TO BE
A BOMB PLANTED IN THE ARENA TONIGHT." THE CALLER
THEN HUNG UP.

MILWAUKEE PD, WHICH IS PROVIDING GUARD SERVICE
FOR KING WHILE IN MILWAUKEE, THOROUGHLY CHECK THE
AUDITORIUM IMMEDIATELY, WILL RECHECK IT PRIOR TO
THE MEETING THIS P.M. AND WILL HAVE DETECTIVES STA-
TIONED ABOUT THE PREMISES TO CHECK ANY SUSPICIOUS
PERSONS.

NOTE, THE CALLER REFERRED TO THE ARENA WHEREAS
THE RALLY AND RECEPTION ARE TO BE HELD IN THE AUDI-
TORIUM. THESE ARE ADJOINING BUILDINGS UNDER ONE
ROOF.

MILITARY INTELLIGENCE HAS BEEN ADVISED LOCALLY.
LETTERHEAD MEMO FOLLOWS.

9:51 A.M.   **February 5, 1964**

MEMORANDUM FOR MR. TOLSON
                          MR. BELMONT
                          MR. ROSEN
                          MR. SULLIVAN
                          MR. DE LOACH
                          MR. EVANS

The Attorney General called and stated he had heard that there has been some discussion about a report on Martin Luther King before the Rooney Committee and also some discussion about the Department of Justice wanted to recall that report and he, the Attorney General, wanted to recall our conversation about it because someone got the impression he, the Attorney General, requested it be recalled. I told the Attorney General that the only discussion before the Rooney Committee was off the record; that there was inquiry off the record as to the association of Martin Luther King with the Communist movement and I reviewed the information that we had developed in the monograph and said copies of the monograph had been delivered to the Secretary of Defense, the Secretary of State, and the White House, and that it was later recalled because it was feared it might leak out. I stated one of the members of the committee, a Republican, made the statement that he thought it ought to be exposed and Chairman Rooney said he thought information of that kind should be kept in the back of the head rather than come out as public information. I stated I made the remark that that was the intention in recalling the document. The Attorney General stated he understands that they are saying he had requested it be withdrawn. I stated it was nothing of the kind; that in other words he, the Attorney General, and I had talked about it several times and he had questioned the wisdom of its distribution and I indicated I would have the copies withdrawn and I did. The Attorney General stated he did not want to have the idea that he had requested it. I stated both of us had feared a leak might get out from the Departments which had copies of the monograph; and if it happened during a sensitive time of negotiations going on with the Negro leaders, it would have caused a ruckus insofar as King was concerned.

The Attorney General said another thing he was calling about is that Mr. DeLoach said to Ed Guthman that the Attorney General should be concerned about the letter written about King and speaking on behalf of the FBI, if they were he, the Attorney General, they would be concerned. The Attorney General stated he did not know what is going on with this thing, that he just knew the letter was cleared with the FBI before it was sent. I stated I did not know what the letter is, that I would check on it because that is a new development I had not heard about. The Attorney General stated that just last weekend he heard that there was apparently some conspiracy on the part of President Kennedy and himself in connection with this; that he did not mind it coming out, but he wanted the facts. I stated there was no discussion on the record at all, it was all off the record and as I had stated, there was one member who thought this information about King ought to be exposed and Rooney spoke up that it is better at times to have matters of this kind in the back of the head rather than have it leak out or be disseminated, and I stated that was the intention of recalling the document. The Attorney General stated he remembered the conversation we had had. I stated in regard to this matter of some letter that DeLoach mentioned, I did not know what that is about and I would talk to DeLoach about it and check on it.

10:00 A.M.

I called the Attorney General and advised him I spoke to DeLoach about it and he emphatically denies he made any such statement to Guthman, press is getting information regarding Martin Luther King which concerned him. DeLoach says his remark was it also concerned us because it imperils any sources of information we might have. I continued that there was a reporter in Atlanta who, I believe, arrived in Washington yesterday and who is doing an article for the Saturday Evening Post exposing King; that while he was in Atlanta he made the statement down there concerning O'Dell's connection with the Communist Party and was concerned about Levison writing King's speeches and he was then coming on to Washington to see the Department people here to supplement this or get any additional information he could. I stated that gives us great concern because of the fact what Levison does, [sic] that is a highly confidential matter from one of our informants who is associated with Levison. I stated there has been a leak somewhere concerning that particular thing, but at no time was any reference made concerning the fact that he, the Attorney General, should be concerned about any letter he wrote.

[Section 9]

Informal Memo to: February 5, 1964
   MR. MOHR:

DR. MARTIN LUTHER KING, JR.
INFORMATION CONCERNING

The Atlanta Division has received information indicating that a reporter by the name of Cleghorn, who writes for the Atlanta Journal and
also is a free-lancer for the Saturday Evening Post, is doing an article
for the Saturday Evening Post on Dr. Martin Luther King. A memorandum, from Mr. Sullivan to Mr. Belmont dated February 4, 1964, reflected this fact inasmuch as the Atlanta Division had written in to tip
off the Bureau that Cleghorn might be in contact with FBI Headquarters.
Cleghorn apparently has information concerning King's association not
only with Hunter Pitts O'Dell but additionally with Stanley Levison.

Guthman came over to see me February 4, 1964, at 4 P.M. He stated
that he had been tipped off by Schanke (phonetic) of the Saturday
Evening Post that Cleghorn was preparing an article on Dr. Martin
Luther King and that the article would expose King's connections with
the Communist Party. Guthman stated he was quite concerned inasmuch
as it appeared there had been a leak from the FBI in connection with
this matter. He told me that the Attorney General had been most hopeful
that there would be no "leaks" concerning King. Guthman quickly
added that he actually did have communistic connections. . . . In a very
apologetic tone of voice, Guthman added that the Attorney General's
record concerning King was perfectly clean and that no exposure of
King could have any reaction whatsoever against the Attorney General.

I told Guthman he had raised several points that should be straightened out. I mentioned that there had been no leaks from the FBI concerning Dr. Martin Luther King, however, Congressmen had made
speeches concerning King's background and there had been a number
of articles in newspapers. I mentioned that the Attorney General's connections with King were none of our business, however, I could understand why Guthman might be somewhat perturbed inasmuch as the
Attorney General had made public statements before the Congress
which indicated King had no communistic connections.

Guthman stated that he wanted to repeat once again that an exposure
of King would not hurt the Attorney General in any way. He stated

his only interest, and the Attorney General's only interest, in keeping information concerning King out of the newspapers, was because both he and the Attorney General felt that FBI sources might be unduly exposed. I made no comment to this, however, certainly did not believe Guthman.

Guthman told me he had no proof whatsoever that the FBI had furnished information to the newspapers concerning King. He stated that obviously the Department had not leaked any information inasmuch as only four individuals in the Department, the Attorney General, Katzenbach, Assistant Attorney General Miller and Guthman, were the only ones who knew of King's connections with Stanley Levinson [sic]. I told Guthman that Burke Marshall undoubtedly knew of such connections inasmuch as I believe he had talked to King. Guthman admitted this was true.

From the tone of Guthman's entire remarks, it would appear he had two thoughts in mind without actually stating such thoughts. These thoughts were (1) that the Attorney General is most anxious that information concerning King not be released; and (2) that the Attorney General's connections with King, and his defensive statements concerning King to the Congress in Civil Rights hearings, could certainly injure the Attorney General's political chances for the future.

I made it a point to tell Guthman before he left that the Department was, of course, very close to the Saturday Evening Post, particularly in view of the deliberate leaks of information to the Saturday Evening Post on the Cassini and Valachi matters. I told Guthman that if the Saturday Evening Post had obtained information concerning King, it would appear that they might have received such information from the same sources where they had gotten their previous facts. Guthman reacted to this quite anxiously and stated all this may be true, however, under no circumstances would they give any publication the facts concerning King. In a very hurt tone of voice, he told me once again the Attorney General was not worried about what an exposure of King could do to him. He stated he and the Attorney General are only trying to protect FBI sources of information.

Following my conversation with the Director at approximately 10 A.M. this morning, after the Director had talked with the Attorney General, I called Guthman and told him he apparently had misquoted my conversation with him of last night. I asked Guthman if he had told the Attorney General, in quoting me, that I had been "quite concerned about a letter the Attorney General had written in which he defended Martin Luther King." I told Guthman I had not mentioned any letter in my conversation with him. Guthman replied that the Attorney General had gotten all mixed up in his conversation with the Director. Guthman admitted I made no reference to any letter. He also admitted I had not indicated that I was "quite concerned" in referring to the Attorney General. Guthman explained the basis of the Attorney General's call to the Director by stating that he and Burke Marshall had gone over to see the Attorney General and while in his office had mentioned the information which apparently has been accumulated by the Atlanta, Georgia, reporter. In explaining to the Attorney General, Guthman stated he told the Attorney General he had discussed this matter with me last night and that from the tone of my remarks, Guthman understood that (1) any exposure of King might possibly jeopardize FBI sources; and (2) any exposure of King might react publicly against the Attorney General inasmuch as the Attorney General had defended King before the Congress. I told Guthman my remarks to him had not meant to imply any potential embarrassment whatsoever to the Attorney General and that I had brought the Attorney General's name into the conversation only because of the many newspaper articles which had been written quoting the Attorney General and his defense of King. Guthman stated that the Attorney General was very fond of me, and that he and the Attorney General, though they would not be around much longer, felt their relations with my office had been of the closest nature. He stated the Attorney General did not under any circumstances believe that my remarks had implied possible potential embarrassment but the Attorney General had called the Director merely to keep the record straight.

Guthman referred once again to the so-called "letter" the Attorney General had written concerning King. He admitted once again this matter did not come up in our conversation last night. He stated there had been a letter, however, as a result of the Attorney General's appearance before the Magnuson Committee in the Senate. This occurred at the time of the Attorney General's appearance concerning Civil Rights legislation. Senator Monroney had questioned the Attorney General as to King's communistic connections, according to Guthman. The Attorney General promised to write Senator Monroney a letter. Guthman stated that such a letter had been prepared and had been couched in a very careful language. He mentioned that the letter had been cleared by Assistant Director Evans and had then been delivered to Senator Monroney. He stated that following delivery of this letter, either Katzenbach, or Burke Marshall, along with Mr. Evans, had orally briefed Senators Russell and Monroney regarding communistic connections.

No record was located in Bureau files to indicate that the Attorney General or anyone in the Department contacted us regarding what information should be supplied to the Senators and Congressman relative to King. Mr. Evans has declared that he most certainly did not clear any letter written to the Senators or the Congressman on this topic.

UNITED STATES DEPARTMENT OF JUSTICE

FEDERAL BUREAU OF INVESTIGATION

New York, New York
February 10, 1964

Re: Communist Party, United States of America
Negro Question
Communist Influence in Racial Matters
Internal Security-C

On February 6, 1964, a confidential source, who has furnished reliable information in the past, furnished information which indicated that Martin Luther King contacted Bayard Rustin on that date. King congratulated Rustin on the boycott and said that it was the greatest "fizzle" he had ever seen. In response to King's question about having another boycott, Rustin said that he hoped there would not be another one, and he said that he thought they had to work on the Board (of Education) behind the scenes. King remarked that he read in the newspaper about (February) the 25th, and Rustin replied, "Well, we have to work on this thing."

King said that he was to go on television for an interview and would need some information. King inquired as to exactly what (Rev. Milton A.) Galamison really wants. Rustin replied that this is one of the weaknesses which will have to be worked out, and he advised King to stay away from that question. He stated that "they" (Citywide Committee for Integrated Schools) want to see the Princeton Plan adopted and a plan to fight for integration and improvement in the quality of education. King asked what the Princeton Plan was. Rustin told him that it was a plan to make the first three grades in a Negro school available to everyone and to make the next three grades in a white school available to everyone. Rustin remarked that it is impossible to deal with the Princeton Plan in the hard rock ghetto because it would mean busing all the Negroes out and the whites in over a long distance. Rustin indicated that the main criticism of the plan which came from the Board of Education is that it affects only 20 to 25 segregated elementary and junior high schools. Rustin said that they did not take into consideration the building of 25 segregated schools which would move it back to the starting point. Rustin said they would have to stop the building of new schools in ghettos. He stated they wanted the new schools built where they can be integrated. Rustin said the Negro leadership is not only interested in integration but also in bettering the educational system and the schools themselves. Rustin indicated that when there are new and better schools, parents will not care about the bus transportation, and he pointed out that wealthy people have been transporting their students by bus to private schools for years. Rustin stated that they point out that ''busing'' is only transportation and not segregation. King asked how they get around the question that ''busing'' is more of a burden on the people, and Rustin replied that he tells people that they will be willing to bus their children for a better education. King said that one of the things which he points out is that one cannot use residential segregation as an excuse to perpetuate de facto segregation at the expense of better education. King suggested that they meet tomorrow (February 7, 1964) at 12:30 P.M. at the Park Sheraton Hotel, 7th Avenue and 55th Street, New York City. King indicated that he wanted Clarence Jones also to come to the meeting on February 7, 1964.

With respect to the foregoing information, the boycott of New York City Public Schools took place on February 3, 1964. It was a demonstration to protest the alleged racial imbalance in the New York City Public Schools. Reverend Milton A. Galamison is chairman of the Citywide Committee for Integrated Schools.

UNITED STATES DEPARTMENT OF JUSTICE

FEDERAL BUREAU OF INVESTIGATION

New York, New York
February 10, 1964

Re: Communist Party,
    United States of America
    Negro Question
    Communist Influence in
    Racial Matters
    Internal Security-C

    Boycott Demonstration at
    New York City Public Schools
    Racial Matters

On February 7, 1964, a confidential source, who has furnished reliable information in the past, advised that Bayard Rustin was contacted by Milton Galamison, who stated there was a 13 branch National Association For the Advancement of Colored People (NAACP) meeting last night (February 6, 1964). Galamison said there were two themes to the whole meeting:

1. "to do me in" and 2. get some kind of plan to give the Board of Education. Rustin said it was very important to know exactly what happened. Galamison said he got the report from someone who was not at the meeting. Galamison said "Roy (Wilkins) is out to kill me man and do the whole movement in." Rustin asked how firm the Harlem Parent's (Committee) (HPC) is and Galamison said the HPC hates the NAACP. Rustin said "they've got to be got to." Galamison said "if they hurt us I'm going to blow them sky high. I'm tired of protecting them." Rustin said play it soft and talk to someone who was there.

Galamison contacted Rustin again later in the morning and described the previous night's meeting as a "lynch Galamison meeting" which lasted three hours. Galamison said his defenders were few and outvoiced. No one was proposed to take Galamison's place. Rustin queried what would they (NAACP) tell the public about Galamison going; call the boycott (February 3, 1964) a failure? Galamison said that apparently the basis for their action is they dislike his making "unilateral decisions" and that stuff.

Rustin said they (NAACP) have two problems:

1. they have no one equally strong or equally important to take over and 2. what do they tell the public.

Galamison said he has the Brooklyn ministers with him and if he can keep the HPC, he will be all right in Manhattan. Rustin suggested Galamison talk to the HPC.

During the conversation, Galamison said the HPC hates the NAACP and vice-versa and he, Galamison, keeps the HPC off the NAACP's back at every meeting.

Rustin was also contacted on February 7, 1964, by an unmale [unidentified male] who said the HPC will hold a meeting that evening at which they will accuse Rustin of being a "Red." Rustin laughed and indicated he would be talking to (Martin Luther) King at approximately 12:15 P.M., that date.

UNITED STATES DEPARTMENT OF JUSTICE

FEDERAL BUREAU OF INVESTIGATION

New York, New York
February 11, 1964

Re: Communist Party, United States
of America—Negro Question
Communist Influence in Racial Matters
Internal Security-C

Boycott Demonstration
New York City Public Schools
Racial Matters

On February 8, 1964, a confidential source, who has furnished reliable information in the past, furnished information which indicated that a woman named June (phonetic) contacted Bayard Rustin on that date. June stated that an article appearing in the "Post" indicated that the civil rights leaders are divided, and Rustin replied that the papers are just confusing the issue. They mentioned Milton (Reverend Milton A. Galamison, who is chairman of the Citywide Committee for Integrated

Schools), and Rustin stated if he (Galamison) should be ousted, Galamison would go out on his own and take the whole issue to the public personally.

On February 8, 1964, the same source furnished information which indicated that Tom Kahn contacted Rustin on that date. Rustin mentioned that he had been up for half the night with "the Negroes who have been fighting over the situation" (the movement to oust Galamison). Rustin mentioned an article appearing in "The New York Times" in which "they realize there is a fight going on but they don't know what the fight is about." According to Rustin, "the real fight is about Galamison and the fact that they want to replace Galamison with me as their leader." Continuing, Rustin said, "I can't do that because he has been in this movement for ten years and although he has made some mistakes you can't change horses in the middle of the stream without affecting the whole community, and I don't want to get into that because on the 15th of March, I am taking a new job with (Martin Luther) King as his man in the north." Kahn suggested that Rustin keep out of it. Rustin replied that he cannot stay out of it because if he does "they will elevate me and I have got to let Galamison know through discussions that I am not playing that game with those people."

Kahn asked Rustin if he took the job with King, would he drop the Student Nonviolent Coordinating Committee (SNCC), and Rustin replied that he does not intend to drop anything.

On February 8, 1964, the same source furnished information which indicated that Bayard Rustin contacted Velma (phonetic) on that date. Rustin pointed out to her that the Congress of Racial Equality (CORE), the National Association for the Advancement of Colored People (NAACP), and Milton (Galamison) need to talk. He said that they agreed to meet at midnight tonight and talk things over. Rustin mentioned that he is speaking tonight in New Jersey at an Americans for Democratic Action (ADA) banquet. Rustin said in regard to his meeting with King that everything is almost settled and that he is going to work on the 15th of March.

UNITED STATES DEPARTMENT OF JUSTICE

FEDERAL BUREAU OF INVESTIGATION

Houston, Texas
February 29, 1964

Re: ...

On February 25, 1964, ... Freeport, Texas, advised he had been informed by a ... that ... Jr., Freeport, Texas, had allegedly contacted an ex-convict relative to killing Robert Kennedy, the Attorney General of the United States, and Martin Luther King.

... advised ... had obtained this information from a source, whom he did not identify, who had reportedly obtained the information from the ex-convict who was not identified. He said he was advised that ... source indicated to him that ... had intimidated the ex-convict.

... advised he had no information as to where or when this attempt was to take place.

... if he would be interested in going to Alabama, or Mississippi, and help settle the "Nigger" situation. He said ... mentioned "they" had $10,000.00 on deposit for ten people. He said he was shocked by ... question and replied, "I'll have to think about it."

... advised that was the extent of his conversation with ... that no mention was made of any specific individuals and he has had no further discussion with ... since that time concerning the above.

... advised ... that he wrote Governor George Wallace, Alabama, during integration troubles in that state, at an unrecalled date, offering his services in any way possible to aid in keeping peace in the state. He said no specific type of aid was offered. He states he believes he told Governor Wallace ten or twelve people would come if he wanted assistance.

... stated his letter was answered by Governor Wallace, thanking him for his offer, but refusing same.

... advised he told several unrecalled people of his offer to Governor Wallace and of Governor Wallace's reply to him.

... advised he never mentioned any money to anyone he talked to and never mentioned the killing of Robert F. Kennedy, Martin Luther King, or anyone else.

The Attorney General   March 3, 1964

Director, FBI

COMMUNIST PARTY, USA
NEGRO QUESTION
COMMUNIST INFLUENCE IN RACIAL MATTERS
INTERNAL SECURITY-C

Recent observations by Special Agents of this Bureau and information from confidential informants who have furnished reliable information in the past reveal the continuing association between Martin Luther King, Jr., and Stanley David Levison.

On February 28, 1964, arrangements were made for King, Levison and Clarence Jones to meet in New York City the next morning to discuss the problem of a filibuster relative to civil rights legislation. They were to also discuss whether or not the Southern Christian Leadership Conference, which is headed by King, should go ahead with its plans to hire Bayard Rustin as its Northern Coordinator. At 8:58 A.M. on February 29, 1964, our Agents observed Levison enter the lobby of the Sheraton-Atlantic Hotel in New York City. He made inquiry as to the room number for Martin Luther King and was informed that King was in Number 1631. At 9:17 A.M. Levison entered an elevator which later stopped on the 16th floor. At 9:18 A.M. Jones entered the Hotel and took an elevator which also stopped on the 16th floor. Levison and Jones were observed to depart the Hotel at 11:25 A.M. and King departed at 11:41 A.M.

On February 29, 1964, Levison told an associate that he, Levison, had conferred with King regarding Rustin, at which time King indicated that he might change his plans as to the hiring of Rustin because some individuals had expressed themselves with disfavor concerning King's association with Rustin.

Jones told King that "we" have been "overhauling" and going over the records of the New York Office (of the Southern Christian Leadership Conference {SCLC} office) in connection with mailing procedures and the (mailing) lists. Jones mentioned in connection with this that "our friend" (Stanley Levison) and Miss Adele Cantor (an employee of the SCLC) would like very much to go down to Atlanta on Friday and Saturday, and King replied that those dates would be all right with him. Jones said he would notify the people (Levison and Cantor) about

Friday, and King told Jones to have them call him so he could have them picked up.

King stated in regard to the Rockefeller affair on Saturday, "we" are rebuilding three churches in Georgia and that he was wondering if the money collected could go to church rebuilding. Jones stated that it would be all right. King mentioned that they had raised $76,000 and that they need over $90,000. Jones mentioned that the "Rockefeller people" are so tax conscious that they put tax considerations above all other considerations. Jones stated that they would rather give the money to the SCLC and not to King's church. Jones remarked that the money could be given directly to the building fund and there would be no question about a tax deduction. King indicated that the way it is arranged at the present time the check would be made out to the Urban League and that they would make the distribution. King mentioned that the name of the fund is the Mt. Olive Baptist Church Building Fund and that Nelson Rockefeller is familiar with it because he gave $10,000 to it. King said that he talked to Rodman Rockefeller (who is the son of Governor Rockefeller) and he stated that Rodman wanted to guarantee him $6,500 and the remainder was to go to the (Urban) League no matter how much money was collected. King said he told Rodman that he could not do it that way because the League did not have trouble collecting money and that they were tax exempt and that he could not use his time collecting money for organizations other than his own. King mentioned that "apparently you have little dissension in the League," and Jones indicated that there was and stated that "they" (the Urban League) want all of the money. Jones stated that (Rodman) Rockefeller indicated to him that unless he (Jones) could furnish him a tax exempt organization to which a contribution could be made in order to contribute to King, then the contribution would only be token. Jones said that Rockefeller should be happy contributing to the Mt. Olive Fund because there would be no question as to the tax exemption.

Jones advised King that he and Joan Daves had discussed the possibility of discussing King's picture rights (regarding the book) with Harry Belafonte and 20th Century [sic] Fox. King said that would be fine.

On February 26, 1964, the same confidential source furnished information which indicated that Clarence Jones contacted Stanley Levison on that date. Jones indicated to Levison that he had spoken to King. Levison mentioned in regard to the article for "The Nation," that he has not sent the substitute material to "The Nation" but would send the material today. Levison told Jones that he should call "The Nation" and tell them that the substitute material is being sent because the use of the original material might cause some problems with King's publishers over the copyrights of King's forthcoming book. Jones stated that Friday would be fine with King. Levison mentioned that he is not feeling well, and he stated the day he meets with King will depend on how he is feeling at the end of the week.

On February 26, 1964, the same confidential source furnished information which indicated that Clarence Jones contacted a representative of "The Nation" on that date. In regard to the feature article by Martin Luther King, Jones was told that the type is set and that the magazine is ready to go to the press. Jones said that he will have to discuss this matter with King and with the publishers of King's forthcoming book. Jones also said that he realizes it is too late to kill the publication of the article and that it is all right for "The Nation" to print it.

On February 26, 1964, the same confidential source furnished information which indicated that Clarence Jones contacted Stanley Levison on that date. Jones said that he had been in touch with "The Nation" and that it is too late to kill King's article and submit a substitute article. Levison indicated he feels that "The Nation" realized the value of an article which is going to be published in a book at a later date. Levison said he will take the substitute article to "The Nation."

Memorandum

TO: Mr. W. C. Sullivan   DATE: March 4, 1964

FROM: Mr. F. J. Baumgardner

SUBJECT: MARTIN LUTHER KING, JR.
         SECURITY MATTER—COMMUNIST

This memorandum recommends that an extremely discreet contact be made . . . Marquette University to prevent its awarding of an Honorary Degree to Martin Luther King, Jr.

We recently learned that Marquette University, Milwaukee, Wisconsin, is considering the awarding of an Honorary Degree to King. The University had proposed giving King a Degree on 6/7/64 but King was unable to make that date since he had another commitment on the same day. At the present time negotiations between Marquette and King are in a state of suspense relative to the selection of a date. Marquette, however, is favorable disposed toward giving King such a degree.

Marquette is the largest Jesuit university in the country and the Director, on 6/11/50, at Milwaukee, was presented with an Honorary Degree on behalf of Marquette University. . . . can be relied upon completely if we were to make any information available on a strictly confidential basis.

OBSERVATIONS:

It is shocking indeed that the possibility exists that King may receive an Honorary Degree from the same institution which honored the Director with such a Degree in 1950. We ought to take positive steps to head this off if at all possible within the framework of the security of our information and sources. By making pertinent information concerning King available . . . at this time, on a strictly confidential basis, we will be giving the University sufficient time to enable it to take positive action in a manner which might avoid embarrassment to the University.

[Section 10]

MARTIN LUTHER KING, JR.

The daily newspaper, "Orlando Sentinel" of **March 7, 1964,** carried the following:

"2,000 Hear King Push Mix Now

"Braving chilling winds and temperatures in the 50's about 2,000 Negroes with a sprinkling of whites filed into Tinker Field grandstand last night to hear Dr. MARTIN LUTHER KING, JR., make another of his fiery speeches for 'integration now.'

"The non-violent action proponent repeated many of the statements he had made earlier in the day to a group of Negro pastors from all over Florida and added advice as to what the Negro must do to bring about total immediate integration.

"KING and earlier speakers urged the Negro to exercise his right to vote. He told of the difficulties encountered by the Negro attempting to register in some areas, but said in other places the Negro failed to register merely because of 'complacency, indifference and laziness.'

"Rapping sharply at office holders who KING said were avowed segregationists, he told his audience, 'There is no reason for Florida to have a governor or senators who are segregationists.'

"One of the speakers, who also presided over the rally, was the Rev. CURTIS J. JACKSON, a candidate for Orlando City Commission who asked for the support of both Negro and 'liberal white' voters.

''KING, who received a standing ovation as he came out on the infield, opened his talk with the statement that the wind of change is 'sweeping out an old order and sweeping in a new order in America.' He said, 'In spite of loud noises from places such as Alabama and Mississippi, segregation is on its deathbed and the only thing left to be seen is how expensive its funeral is going to be made by segregationists.'

''He told his Negro listeners that they had a number of challenges to meet and among these is one to make full and constructive use of the freedom they possess.''

To: Mr. W. C. Sullivan   3/20/64

From: Mr. F. J. Baumgardner

COMMUNIST PARTY, USA
NEGRO QUESTION
COMMUNIST INFLUENCE IN RACIAL MATTERS
INTERNAL SECURITY—COMMUNIST

The 3/9/64 issue of ''The Nation'' contains an article on pages 230–234 entitled ''The Hammer of Civil Rights'' by Martin Luther King, Jr. ''The Nation,'' of course, is the infamous magazine which has a long record of being anti-Bureau and frequently in favor of communists and communist causes.

The article is generally a summary of King's views on recent developments in the civil rights movement and attempts at directing the reader to further action necessary. Neither the Director nor the Bureau are mentioned. However, near the end of the article certain statements appear which may be significant if only by reason of the fact that the Bureau is not mentioned.

King claims that there is genuinely a new South but that it cannot surface without the shelter of Federal power and order. He claims that the dignity of the Federal Government would be enhanced if it arrayed a trained force of Federal marshals. He notes that the country abounds in specialists in law enforcement and suggests that the Administration summon to the White House a conference of experts to deliberate with the highest officials of Government. Participants should include the President and the National Security Council. He suggests as among other participants, heads of the Treasury law-enforcement agencies and

in connection with this suggestion states that there is a need to know
what is going on in conspiratorial racist circles. He claims that many
of the shocking bombings might have been avoided if such knowledge
had been available.

He is led to the suggestion of Treasury agencies because the Bureau
of Narcotics is extensively experienced in effectively working within
secret groups and points out that the alcohol-tax unit of Internal Revenue is probably more familiar with the rural South than is any other
agency "because for years it has been tracking down 'moonshiners.' "

[Section 11]

UNITED STATES GOVERNMENT
Memorandum

TO: Mr. Mohr   DATE: April 8, 1964

FROM: C.D. DeLoach

SUBJECT: MARTIN LUTHER KING, JR.
           SECURITY MATTER—COMMUNIST

Mr. Baumgardner's memo to Mr. Sullivan 4/2/64 recommended that
I orally brief . . . in accordance with an attached "Top Secret" summary
indicating Reverend Martin Luther King's communist connections . . .
The purpose of such action was because Reverend King had been invited to make the commencement address and receive an honorary degree from Springfield College, Springfield, Massachusetts. . . .

I called upon . . . at 10:30 A.M., 4/7/64 in his office. At the beginning
of our conversation I told . . . that my remarks should be held in the
strictest of confidence. He agreed to this. I then mentioned that he had
long been a supporter of the FBI's and, therefore, the Director wanted
me to brief him concerning a matter of potential embarrassment to a
college he obviously was very personally interested in. . . . was told
that captioned individual was to receive an honorary degree and make
the commencement address at Springfield College at the end of this
scholastic year, June 1964. He was advised that King for some time
has been maintaining a close liaison with a number of secret members
of the Communist Party. I told him that King had received guidance

and counsel and had relied greatly upon one of these members. I told
. . . also that King . . . I further mentioned that Reverend King, in some
of his activities, . . .

. . . told me he was shocked to receive this information. He stated it
was hardly believable. He said if it were not for the integrity of the
FBI he would disbelieve such facts. I told him that our information was
very obviously truthful and based upon indisputable facts.

. . . told me that while he wanted to respect our confidence, this
information placed a great burden upon him. He stated he felt duty
bound to tell . . . I reminded . . . that I had advised him of the above-
mentioned facts in strict confidence. He then inquired if I would speak
to . . . He described . . . as a very outstanding individual who could be
trusted implicitly. I told the . . . I preferred not to speak with . . . about
this matter and that I wanted him, . . . to know that under no circumstances should this information be attributed to the FBI. . . . assured me
that he would treat our information on a confidential basis; however,
he might possibly have to take . . . into his confidence.

I had been back in my office approximately 30 minutes when . . .
called me. He stated that . . . was in his office at the time, having
dropped by . . . inquired if I would see . . . right away. I told him that
I was tied up on other matters and it would be impossible. He next
inquired if I could see . . . at 8:00 A.M. on the morning of 4/8/64. I told
. . . I couldn't do this inasmuch as I had a commitment to attend a
breakfast meeting of a civic group. He then closed the conversation by
stating . . . would call me and arrange an appointment. I asked . . . if
he had disclosed the remarks made during our previous conversation
. . . He stated that he had inasmuch as he wanted to make it absolutely
certain that Reverend King did not appear at Springfield College. I told
him that under the circumstances then that I would see . . .

. . . After making an appointment, came by my office at 4:00 P.M.,
4/8/64. He opened the conversation by stating that he fully recognized
the necessity to keep the information concerning King in strict confidence. He stated he wanted us to know that he would maintain this
confidence and would not advise anyone of this information. He pointed
out that he had been very shocked when . . . told him of these facts
and had insisted that Reverend King be prevented from making the
commencement address at Springfield College. . . . who impressed me
as being a very sensible, intelligent individual, stated that due to the
fact that he will keep this information confidential, it would be impossible . . . to "uninvite" King to make the appearance at Springfield College. . . . I told . . . at this point that any action he took in this regard

was entirely up to him but that no information was to be attributed to the FBI and that we were to be kept strictly out of this matter. He stated he fully recognized this fact and no one would ever know that the FBI had given . . . this information. . . . immediate steps to prevent Reverend King from receiving an honorary degree. He said he wanted to think about the possibility of preventing King from making the address but at this step of the game he did not see how it could be done.

. . . expressed a desire to shake hands with the Director some day. . . . the Director two invitations in the recent past to receive an honorary degree and make the commencement address at Springfield College. However, the Director's schedule had caused him to not accept these invitations. I explained the Director's heavy schedule and the fact that he was reluctant to leave Washington while Congress was in session.

Upon leaving, . . . assured me that no information would be released and none would be attributed to the FBI. I told him that we would, of course, deny any such information had been furnished. At this point he advised me that, of course, his main reason for coming to the FBI was to determine if we could suggest any course of action he might take. I told him we could suggest nothing, that any action taken was entirely up to him.

ACTION:

For record purposes.

UNITED STATES DEPARTMENT OF JUSTICE

FEDERAL BUREAU OF INVESTIGATION

Cincinnati, Ohio
April 17, 1964

RE: MARTIN LUTHER KING

. . . furnished information to the Dayton Resident Agency of the FBI that . . . , a parolee under supervision of his office had reported that date to his office and while in his office furnished the following information:

While he . . , was walking . . . in Dayton, at about 9:30 P.M. . . . he walked by a vehicle and heard someone call his name. He walked back to this car, which was a 1961 Chrysler New Yorker, four door Sedan, black, with Illinois license plates, numbers not obtained. The vehicle was occupied by a white man he recognized as being . . . under whom he, ... served in Korea. This person's last name was recalled as ... but first name not recalled. The second individual, a Negro and driver of the Chrysler, was recognized to be a member of the same company in Korea, but of a different platoon. His name was not recalled. ...

The driver asked him ... if he were interested in making some money. ... asked who they were and they reminded they were former Army acquaintances. He got in the back seat of the Chrysler and rode with these two men to a place where they parked ... west of Dayton. Enroute to that location they informed him they knew he was on parole, knew his current activities and the names of his girl friends. After arriving at the place, they parked, the Negro acquaintance reminded him, ... of statements he, ... had made against the U.S. while he was in confinement in Korea, both before and after receiving a sentence of 10 years in General Courts Martial in ... He was tried at that time on charges of assaulting a non-commissioned officer, AWOL, threatening a commissioned officer and disobeying an indirect order. At that time he, ... was bitter because of the courts martial and felt he was being prejudiced and the action would not have been taken if he had not been a Negro. Comments he recalled making included statements that he had been taught to kill and he could be of great value to the Russian KGB. During the period he was very outspoken in his criticism of the U.S. and everyone in his company would have known about these statements, which he feels is the reason these two former military acquaintances in Korea contacted him at this time.

According to ... these acquaintances again asked him if he was still interested in making large sums of money and he replied that it depended upon what he had to do. ... then stated, "We are trying to unite Negroes to give up passive resistance and start violence." ... also commented that since the death of Medgar Evers had caused a more militant attitude among the Negroes, the death of Martin Luther King would cause a new and more militant flare of violence and a closer unity among the Negroes. At this point ... offered to give him, ... $25,000 if he would accept a "contract" to kill Martin Luther King, and in addition offered him political asylum in any Satellite country. ... asked for time to think the proposition over and requested advice as to where to contact them. They told him that he was not to contact them, but they would contact him, ... They did not furnish ... a time for next contact, nor did they indicate their residence, employment or other information that might lead to their present whereabouts. These acquaintances did not disclose any details of the plot or how the money would be paid or the source of the money. From his association with these acquaintances during military service he could not recall any information as to their residence addresses, families or employment in the U.S.

... was interviewed at the Dayton Resident Agency of the FBI on April 15, 1964, and furnished the same information as to the alleged contact as that received from ... In this interview, ... suggested that in the event he were again contacted by these same acquaintances or others in this matter that it would be helpful if the FBI could persuade his parole officers to relax the parole restrictions presently on him to allow him ''more freedom of movement.'' ... commented that he believed these persons contacting him felt they could trust him to carry out any request they might make. ... also commented that the Chrysler driven by these individuals was equipped with hi-fi record player located under the dash and a telephone in the glove compartment. He said he observed a gold dancing monkey figurine fastened on the dash, which he believed to probably be an aerial as he did not observe an aerial attached to the outside of the vehicle although the car was equipped with a radio.

... furnished the following descriptions of these former acquaintances:

... white male, about 43 years of age, 6'1" tall, 190 pounds, ...

Name unknown, Negro male, age about 34, 5'9" to 10" tall, 200 pounds, dark complexion, ...

... stated that while serving the sentence imposed by the General Courts Martial he was afforded treatment at the ..., for a psychiatric condition he described as ''paranoidal schizophrenia, with homicidal tendencies.'' He stated that after this treatment he was transferred to the ... where he on several occasions became violent and injured personnel before he could be subdued and calmed with tranquilizer injections. He stated he still has this tendency toward violence if he is ''pressed'' by anyone. ...

''This parolee is a person with little or no regard for parole supervision, as well as a person with no initiative and motivation toward employment. It would appear to this officer that this individual is out to get something for nothing and enjoys the role of living a parasitic sort of life.'' The file also shows ''At one time he ... was diagnosed as having acute psychotic mental disorder. Fourteen months ago (prior to September 12, 1963), he was pronounced cured.''

... stated that his office records show ... was incarcerated at ... primarily for psychiatric diagnosis and therapy, and at one time was diagnosed as having acute psychotic mental disorder. Also that ... has furnished false information to his parole officer on numerous occasions, has little or no regard for parole rules or supervision and rebels against authority. . . . stated he believes the information furnished by . . . that he was contacted and given a proposition to kill Martin Luther King is false, but he is unable to determine what . . . is attempting to accomplish by furnishing such information.

. . . parole officer . . . who has frequent contact with . . . family, advised it was necessary for him to recently have . . . confined in the . . . because he was living with various women and is currently residing with a widow woman, . . . He described . . . as highly unreliable and is considering having . . . committed to a state mental hospital because of his violations of parole rules and because of his emotional instability . . . mentioned that . . . with whom . . . is supposed to reside, has reported that . . . came to her home one night and stated to her that he had just killed a man who had tried to attack a woman down the street. . . . went to the location where the man was supposed to be lying dead in the street and she determined that the information . . . had furnished to her was false. . . . described . . . as a ''pathological liar.'' . . . stated that from his experience with, and knowledge of . . . he would place no credence whatsoever to the information furnished by . . . that he had been contacted by two former acquaintances who proposed that he kill Martin Luther King. . . . stated that if he does not have . . . committed to a mental hospital he plans to closely supervise . . . and check his activities about every other day.

DECODED COPY

____AIRGRAM   ____CABLEGRAM   XXXRADIO
____TELETYPE

URGENT 4-24-64
TO DIRECTOR
FROM SAN FRANCISCO 2.2006

FOR IMMEDIATE PERSONAL ATTENTION ASSISTANT DIRECTOR W. C. SULLIVAN, COMMUNIST PARTY, USA—NEGRO QUESTION, COMMUNIST INFLUENCE IN RACIAL MATTERS, IS-C; MARTIN LUTHER KING, JR., SM-C
  RE SAN FRANCISCO TEL THIS DATE
  AT 10 A.M. PRESS CONFERENCE, HOTEL SENATOR, SACRA-

MENTO, ATTENDED BY THREE LOCAL TV STATION REPRESEN-
TATIVES AND APPROXIMATELY TEN NEWS MEN. QUESTION
WAS ASKED OF KING IF HE WOULD ELABORATE ON DIREC-
TOR HOOVER'S STATEMENT REGARDING INFILTRATION OF
COMMUNISTS INTO CIVIL RIGHTS MOVEMENT. KING SAID HE
THINKS IT UNFORTUNATE THAT HOOVER MADE THAT STATE-
MENT. HE THINKS MR. HOOVER SHOULD HAVE SAID THAT
COMMUNIST PARTY HAS NOT BEEN ABLE TO INFILTRATE
CIVIL RIGHTS LEADERSHIP.

QUESTION ASKED IF THE HARD CORE OF CIVIL RIGHTS
LEADERSHIP COMMUNIST MOTIVATED. KING REPLIED IT IS
NOT COMMUNIST LED, INSPIRED OR INFILTRATED.

QUESTION ASKED IS DR. KING SYMPATHETIC WITH COM-
MUNIST PARTY. KING REPLIED THAT HE IS NOT INFLUENCED
BY COMMUNIST PARTY AT ALL AND DOES NOT AGREE WITH
THEIR PRINCIPLES. HE IS A CHRISTIAN. ASKED ABOUT SHOP-
INS IN SAN FRANCISCO BAY AREA. KING REPLIED THAT HE
BELIEVES AT TIMES IT IS NECESSARY, BUT FIRST STEP IS NE-
GOTIATION. QUESTION ASKED ON HIS AGREEMENT WITH
STALL-IN'S TO WHICH HE REPLIED THAT WHILE HE CON-
DONES CIVIL DISOBEDIENCE HE DOES NOT CONDONE DE-
STRUCTION OF PROPERTY.

TO QUESTION REGARDING MUSLIM MOVEMENT, KING RE-
PLIED THAT HE DOES NOT AGREE WITH IT, BUT THAT IF
CIVIL RIGHTS BILL DOES NOT PASS THERE WILL PROBABLY
BE MORE VIOLENCE IN CIVIL RIGHTS MOVEMENT AND MORE
PERSONS MAY JOIN THE MUSLIM TYPE OF ORGANIZATION.
HE SAID THAT THE FBI HAS STATED THAT THERE ARE ONLY
100,000 BLACK MUSLIMS. HE DOES NOT THINK THERE WILL
BE MORE GAINS UNLESS CIVIL RIGHTS BILL FAILS.

FINAL QUESTION WAS AGAIN IN REGARD TO CHARGE OF
COMMUNIST PARTY IN NEGRO MOVEMENT, WOULD IT BE
NECESSARY TO PURGE COMMUNISTS FROM CIVIL RIGHTS
MOVEMENT. KING ANSWERED THAT IF THEY KNOW ABOUT
COMMUNISTS IN THE SOUTHERN CHRISTIAN LEADERSHIP
CONFERENCE THEY ARE REMOVED, BUT SINCE THEY ARE
NOT AN INVESTIGATIVE AGENCY THEY MAY NOT KNOW
ABOUT THEM.

RECEIVED: 6:02 PM FN

To: Mr. W. C. Sullivan   May 11, 1964

From: Mr. F. J. Baumgardner

COMMUNIST PARTY, USA
NEGRO QUESTION
COMMUNIST INFLUENCE IN RACIAL MATTERS
INTERNAL SECURITY—COMMUNIST

Martin Luther King, Jr., appeared as the guest on the 5-10-64 Columbia Broadcasting System (CBS) television program "Face the Nation." Paul Niven was moderator; panelists were Benjamin Bradlee of "Newsweek" and Dan Rather. We had prior information that this program was arranged with King by Marquis Childs of CBS. Only about the last five minutes of this 2-hour program were devoted to the subject of communist influence in the racial movement. The following comments were made by King in response to questions put to him.

Niven opened this phase of the program by stating that it had been alleged that King has been slow to sever ties with the communists even after warnings to do so by the Government. King responded by stating he was glad the question was asked. He then went on to state that communism is based on things that he could never accept and that there is a provision in the constitution of the Southern Christian Leadership Conference (SCLC) which says that no communist can be a member. King claimed that he was very vigilant in enforcing this provision of the constitution of his organization. King claimed that there has only been one case (he did not mention the name) and in that instance asked for the resignation of the man. King acknowledged that one or two communists might "drift" into his organization but there is definitely no infiltration. When King was asked as to possible infiltration in the civil rights movement in general, he gave the same reply as he did for the SCLC by stating that a communist may drift into the movement but there is definitely no infiltration. By infiltration he explained he meant having people at a policy-making level. When one of the panelists stated that King's position is in opposition to the head of the FBI, King replied that it was unfortunate that such a great man as Mr. Hoover has led himself to make such an allegation as was regarding communist influence in the Negro movement. He said that he had hoped the FBI would come out and say this it is amazing that so few Negroes have become communists. King was asked if the Justice Department had told him of anyone to remove from his organization that he has not followed through on. He remarked that there was only one and he removed that individual.

Comment:

King's obvious reference was to the "removal" of Hunter Pitts O'Dell from the SCLC. As expected, King lied about being warned of anyone else because he had been warned about Stanley Levison and has nevertheless maintained a close association with Levison.

Most of the program was devoted to the general subject of civil rights and the civil rights bill pending in the Senate. The following information was developed during the questioning of King.

There will continue to be demonstrations whether or not the bill passes, as its passage is only one step; there must be demonstrations to test compliance. King has not discussed the matter of demonstrations with the White House. He said he was appalled at efforts by the Government to emulate the bill; refused to name Government officials but said they included those of the Justice Department. King has talked with Senate leaders regarding the bill but not during the past few weeks; he plans to talk to these leaders in the next few days. King claimed that he and the other principal Negro leaders have conferred and want the bill as passed by the house. They will not compromise on important sections of the bill; he feels it would be better to have no bill at all than have the important sections deleted.

King said he plans to attend both national party conventions this summer and will be active in connection with the seating of delegates. His movement may lead a march at these conventions. King believes that if the Presidential elections were held today, President Johnson would carry the South overwhelmingly. He does not intend to campaign for any candidate and does not know yet whether or not he will publicly endorse anyone. He never has in the past. He believes that the vast majority of the people are in favor of the civil rights bill. He said that there is a danger that the Republican Party may become the "white man's party" in this country. He would definitely not endorse Senator Goldwater. He plans on some "direct" action in the event the bill is watered down but has made no final decision as to the type of action. He has no plans for another march on Washington this year and stated he is not at liberty to say what type of action is to take place. He emphasized, however, that he is not saying there will be drastic civil disobedience; it will be of a non-violent nature.

RECOMMENDATION:

For information.

UNITED STATES GOVERNMENT
Memorandum

TO: Mr. DeLoach   DATE: 5-11-64

FROM: M. A. Jones

SUBJECT: REVEREND MARTIN LUTHER KING, JR.
APPEARANCE ON "FACE THE NATION"
SUNDAY, MAY 10, 1964,
12:30 P.M., CHANNEL 9, WTOP-TV

Captioned individual is President of the Southern Christian Leadership Conference and was interviewed by a panel of reporters on captioned program.

REFERENCES TO THE DIRECTOR:

King was asked about communist infiltration of the Negro civil rights movement. He said that to him infiltration implied that a large number of communists would be found in leadership positions or on a policy-making level. This is not the case in the civil rights movement.

He went on to say that communism is not freedom but rather is totalitarian in nature. Consequently, communism is incompatible with the civil rights movement. He said that if there were communists in the movement, he would like to know so he could get rid of them. He admitted that there may be one or two individuals who drift into Negro organizations but they are certainly not holding down jobs of leadership.

He was asked about the Director's recently released statement to the effect that some communists were participating in the movement. He said again that this was not true and that it was "unfortunate that such a great man as J. Edgar Hoover" would "aid rightists" by such a statement. He said he would hope rather that the FBI would come out with a statement to the effect that it was amazing that so few Negroes, in view of the treatment they have received, have turned to communism.

He said that the Justice Department had informed him concerning only one communist known to be participating in King's organization and King said that when given this information he promptly expelled this man from the organization.

OTHER COMMENTS:

He indicated that Negro organizations still plan demonstrations in Alabama to "expose the hypocrisy of Governor Wallace" and that other demonstrations will occur elsewhere whether or not current civil rights legislation passes Congress. He explained that even with the passage of the pending bill, it will still be necessary to enforce these new laws and he felt that demonstrations would be necessary to insure this.

He expressed surprise that some Justice Department officials and Senators had indicated they were no longer going to maintain the strong positions they had taken on civil rights legislation just a few weeks ago and that they now appeared ready to compromise and agree to "crippling proposals" being advanced by Senator Dirksen.

He said that if the Presidential election was held today, President Johnson would carry the South with few exceptions. He said there is a definite danger that the Republican Party will become the "white man's party" unless liberals within that organization assert leadership.

He hedged on previous statements attributed to him that there would be demonstrations in Washington if the civil rights bill appeared to be in trouble and he admitted that no plans had been made for such demonstrations as of this time.

RECOMMENDATIONS:

None. For information.

[Section 12]

FBI

PLAIN TEXT   5/15/64
AIRTEL   REGISTERED MAIL

TO: DIRECTOR, FBI (100-3-116)

FROM: AC, CINCINNATI (100-14244) (RUC)

SUBJECT: CP, USA
         NEGRO QUESTION
         COMMUNIST INFLUENCE IN RACIAL
         MATTERS
         IS-C

Re Cincinnati teletype, 5/9/64; and Bureau airtel to Cincinnati, 5/14/64.

Enclosed for the Bureau are six copies of a letterhead memorandum containing information concerning appearance of MARTIN LUTHER KING, JR., at Cincinnati, Ohio, on 5/8/64. Two copies of the letterhead

memorandum are being furnished Atlanta for information, and one copy
is being furnished New York for information.

. . . Radio Station, was interviewed on 5/8/64, by SA . . . Contact
with . . . was initiated because at approximately 5:00 P.M. . . . 5/8/64,
SA . . . was advised by . . . former Special Agent, currently . . . Cincinnati, Ohio, that he had just heard part of a local radio broadcast, during
which KING was quoted as having made statements critical of the FBI.
It is noted that . . . advised radio station . . . Cincinnati, did not carry
the remarks made by KING and there was no subsequent newspaper
publicity in the Cincinnati, Ohio, area given to the remarks made by
KING as set forth in the letterhead memorandum.

UNITED STATES DEPARTMENT OF JUSTICE

FEDERAL BUREAU OF INVESTIGATION

Cincinnati, Ohio
May 15, 1964

RE: MARTIN LUTHER KING, JR.

. . . Radio Station, Cincinnati, Ohio, advised a Special Agent of the
Federal Bureau of Investigation that on this afternoon he covered a
news conference held by Martin Luther King, Jr., at the Cincinnati
Gardens, Cincinnati, Ohio. . . . stated the news conference was held in
connection with a speech to be given by King at 8:00 P.M., May 8, 1964,
at Cincinnati Gardens before the convention of the African Methodist
Episcopal Church (AME).

. . . stated that during the interview with King, a reporter asked King
if he could make any statement concerning the fact that J. Edgar Hoover, Director of the FBI, had been recently quoted as stating that Communists were attempting to infiltrate racial organizations. . . . stated that
King appeared to take offense to this question and became angry. King
said the question was ridiculous and it was ridiculous to say that Communists were infiltrating racial groups. According to . . . King stated he
wished the FBI and Director Hoover would pay more attention to the
horrible situations regarding civil rights violations in the United States,
such as church bombings.

. . . advised that after the news conference with King was concluded,
he observed an individual, who was obviously an AME official, ap-

proach King. The AME official told King in words to the effect that King had not yet said anything about fund-raising. . . . said King replied in words to the effect that the AME official should not worry as he would take care of the fund-raising. King was heard to remind the AME official that half of the funds raised would go to AME and the other half would go to King for the Southern Christian Leadership Conference.

UNITED STATES DEPARTMENT OF JUSTICE

FEDERAL BUREAU OF INVESTIGATION

New Haven 10, Connecticut
June 9, 1964

RE: MARTIN LUTHER KING, JR.

. . . advised that King arrived in Middletown during the morning of June 7, 1964. He delivered the baccalaureate address at graduation ceremonies, Wesleyan University, the same morning. He was also awarded an honorary degree as Doctor of Divinity. In the early part of the afternoon, he left Middletown by private car for New York City, where he was to receive an honorary degree . . . from Jewish Theological Seminary, New York City.

The June 8, 1964, edition of the "Hartford Courant," a daily newspaper published in Hartford, Connecticut, contains an article concerning KING's appearance at Wesleyan University, and the following is quoted concerning remarks made by KING:

"On our mountain of complacent adjustment, the Commandment 'Thou shalt not steal' has been changed to 'Thou shalt not get caught,' and if you are going to lie, lie with finesse. All of us are moving through a wilderness (using the parallel of Moses leading his people to the promised land) but many of us don't want to face the disciples [sic], the ordeals, the sacrifices needed to move through the wilderness to the promised land of brotherhood, the promised land of justice. We must move from this mountain of complacent adjustment and unobtainable goals. Too often we get bogged down on these symbolic mountains and we must move on to individual and collective fulfillment."

He spoke of "a symbolic mountain, ethical relativism, reducing morality to human appetites, customs and the time in which we live. We have come to the point where it is survival of the slickest and if you are going to lie, lie with finesse. Dress your mate in the garments of love. But it is time to move to the mountain where right is right and wrong is wrong and never the twain shall meet. The symbolic mountains of practical materialism, indifference concerning poverty in our nation and in the world, racial segregation, corroding hatred and crippling justice,'' also concerned the Georgia minister.

"Poverty is not a new problem but what is new is that for the first time we have the resources and the techniques to do something about it. There are 30 to 40 million people in the world in the vast ocean of poverty caught on the wave of materialism. If we are to be a great nation we must rise out of our apathy and indifference toward poverty and do away with it. We must remember those who are economically secure in our affluent society can never be what they ought to be until those who are economically insecure are what they ought to be.''

Dr. KING then talked about, ''The means to ends, both in relation to segregation and to peace. Violence has never brought about lasting peace. We must come to see that it is either non-violence or non-existence, both in our country and in international relations. The alternative to disarmament is a civilization plunged into the abyss of annihilation. Segregation is the Negro's burden and America's shame, whether it is the legal segregation of the south or the de facto segregation of the north. It is morally wrong and sinful, based on human laws out of harmony with natural moral laws. The arc of the moral universe is long but it bends toward justice. May God grant every member of this graduating class the desire and the will to work against this evil system. This problem must be solved through a sort of massive divine discontent. Help us to move from all of these mountains. Help us to move out with determination toward a brotherhood that transcends race or color, a brotherhood based on peace, brotherhood and justice.''

At a press conference afterward, he spoke briefly on the segregation problem in the north. He said if the north isn't careful, the south will surpass it in human relations. In the north, the problem is to get at the more subtle forms of segregation that may become so deeply entrenched they will be hard to get at all. It all depends on goodwill and active response. There is a need for greater participation, a need for thrust and action by the white community, a need for voices of goodwill to speak out to solve the evil of segregation.

FEDERAL BUREAU OF INVESTIGATION

U.S. DEPARTMENT OF JUSTICE

COMMUNICATIONS SECTION

JUN 9, 1964

TELETYPE

FBI WASH DC

1116AM URGENT 6-9-64 LRA

TO ATLANTA JACKSONVILLE

FROM DIRECTOR 100-106670 1P

MARTIN LUTHER KING, JR. SM-C

. . . BLUFFTON, GEORGIA, TELEPHONICALLY CONTACTED THE BUREAU DURING THE EVENING HOURS OF SIX EIGHT SIXTY FOUR RELATIVE TO THE SUBJECT. HE ADVISED SOMEONE HAD BETTER GET KING OUT OF ST. AUGUSTINE, FLORIDA, BEFORE HE GETS KILLED. HE STATED HE WAS NOT THREATENING KING OR [sic] DID HE HAVE ANY SPECIFIC INFORMATION AS TO WHO MIGHT KILL KING, HOWEVER, KNOWING THE TEMPERAMENT OF THE PEOPLE IN THE SOUTH, HE FELT KING'S LIFE WAS IN JEOPARDY.

IT IS NOTED . . . APPEARED TO HAVE BEEN DRINKING AND DURING THE CONVERSATION USED CONSIDERABLE PROFANITY . . .

BUREAU FILES CONTAIN NO INFORMATION IDENTIFIABLE WITH . . .

ATLANTA, ABOVE IS FOR YOUR INFORMATION.

JACKSONVILLE, ALERT LOCAL AUTHORITIES.

END

June 10, 1964

Honorable Walter W. Jenkins
Special Assistant to the President
The White House
Washington, D.C.

Dear Mr. Jenkins:

A confidential source who has furnished reliable information in the past furnished the following information concerning a contact had between Clarence Jones and Wyatt Walker on June 8, 1964.

Walker voiced concern over the safety of Martin Luther King, Jr., in view of threats which have been made on King's life. Walker said that King is returning to St. Augustine, Florida, on June 10, 1964, and that he should have protection. Walker indicated that what was needed was to have some outside pressure brought to bear on President Johnson and Attorney General Kennedy.

Jones stated that a commitment must come from the Department of Justice that all reasonable steps will be taken to protect King's life. Jones also stated that the only pressure which will move Attorney General Kennedy will be that which comes from prominent people. Walker suggested that they contact James Baldwin and people like him. Jones agreed with this but stated he would also like to get some people in the city government of New York City and other civic-minded people. Jones indicated that he would work on something to be sent to the Justice Department in connection with the safety of King.

On June 9, 1964, Walker contacted our Atlanta, Georgia, Office and advised that King and other Southern Christian Leadership Conference officials were to depart Atlanta on the morning of June 10, 1964, en route to St. Augustine, Florida. Walker explained his reason for making contact with the FBI in Atlanta was that the Southern Christian Leadership conference office in St. Augustine had received two local calls threatening to assassinate King and that the house where Southern Christian Leadership Conference personnel, including King, were staying in the St. Augustine area had been shot into and burned. Walker said that there apparently had been no investigation by the local police or Federal officers and he expressed regret concerning this. He claimed to have already advised the Department of Justice in Washington, D.C. He also claimed that there has been a complete breakdown of law and order.

Walker admitted that to his knowledge no complaint had been made to the St. Augustine Police, State of Florida officials, or the FBI at St.

Augustine. Walker was advised that the information he had furnished did not appear to be a Federal violation coming within the jurisdiction of the FBI and information concerning threats against the life of King should be furnished to local law enforcement authorities. He was also advised that if he had any information which he believed related to civil rights violations at St. Augustine, he should report the information to our Jacksonville, Florida, Office.

An Associated Press news release from St. Augustine dated May 29, 1964, reported that local authorities were aware of and had conducted investigation relative to the firing upon a cottage which King had rented in the St. Augustine area. Investigation was also conducted by local authorities concerning a fire of unknown origin in King's cottage.

Wyatt Walker is the Executive Assistant to King. James Baldwin is a well-known author. Clarence Jones has been identified as a person in a position of leadership in the Labor Youth League in late 1953 or early 1954. . . .

The information above was also sent to the Attorney General by the Director in a memorandum under the same date and caption.

FBI

June 11, 1964

AIRTEL

To: SAC's, Jacksonville (PERSONAL ATTENTION)

From: Director, FBI (100-106670)

MARTIN LUTHER KING, JR.
SECURITY MATTER-C

ReBuairtel 6/9/64 which emphasized the instructions as to advising appropriate authorities when specific information is received relative to a threat on the life of Martin Luther King, Jr.

ReATtel to Bureau and Jacksonville 6/9/64 which advised of contact made with Atlanta Office by King's Executive Assistant, Wyatt Walker. He referred to the local threatening calls made at St. Augustine, Florida, as well as damage to the house where King and Southern Christian Leadership Conference personnel stayed. He expressed concern over what he claimed was apparently no investigation by authorities.

For information of receiving offices a United Press International news release of 6/9/64 reported upon King's stating he had been threatened with death if he returned to St. Augustine. He reportedly told a reporter that he talked with the Department last week and was assured the FBI would investigate complaints of violence against him and other Negroes.

The purpose of instant airtel is to re-emphasize again the absolute necessity for alerting local authorities to all information received about threats to King which do not come within the Bureau's jurisdiction. Of course, if a matter arises within the Bureau's jurisdiction, the appropriate action must be promptly taken. Be alert to situations which might result in embarrassment to the Bureau because of any claims of Bureau inaction or delay. Keep the Bureau promptly advised of all developments pertinent to this matter.

NOTE:

The publicity King is receiving makes it evident that he will not hesitate to attempt to place the Bureau in the middle and thus embarrass the Bureau if he can. While we have already issued the necessary instructions on handling complaints relative to threats on King's life, it is believed that instant airtel should go forward as a re-emphasis, particularly in view of the volatile situation at St. Augustine and acts of violence which have developed and including the firing upon King's cottage.

UNITED STATES DEPARTMENT OF JUSTICE

FEDERAL BUREAU OF INVESTIGATION

San Diego, California
June 11, 1964

TALKS BY REVEREND MARTIN LUTHER KING, JR. AT SAN DIEGO STATE COLLEGE AND CALIFORNIA WESTERN UNIVERSITY, SAN DIEGO, CALIFORNIA, ON MAY 29, 1964

... that at 2:00 P.M. on May 29, 1964, Reverend MARTIN LUTHER KING, JR., spoke to a near-capacity crowd of approximately 1,500 people in the Open Air Theater at San Diego State College, San Diego, California.

KING emphasized the importance of passing the civil rights legislation now in Congress and of defeating the initiative to nullify present California civil rights statutes which will be on the November ballot. He pointed out that man's scientific genius has made the world one in a geographic sense, but now man must make the world one in terms of brotherhood and peace. He said people must get rid of the idea that there are superior and inferior races. KING called for immediate action to rid the country of segregation. He said civil rights leaders realize that integration can be achieved only when all men truly want it, but that legislation is needed to change men's habits, after which the change of heart will follow. KING urged passage of the civil rights bill now pending in the Senate, warning that its defeat might bring peril to the nation and that the evil forces keeping the racial problem in existence might become malignant and bring the races an incurable cancer.

There were no incidents or arrests at this meeting.

... that at 8:00 P.M. on May 29, 1964, Dr. MARTIN LUTHER KING, JR., addressed an estimated 11,000 people at California Western University in San Diego, California. Attendance figures accounted for 9,000 people in the Golden Gym and another 2,000 listening over loud-speakers in the open-air Greek Theater.

KING stated, "It is a descration of the American heritage to have so perverted the intent of the framers of our Constitution, that freedom has been withheld from whole sections of our populace because of racial diversity. It is a defiance of our law to refuse to grant its protection equally and impartially to all our people." KING told the story of Rip Van Winkle with a modern connotation: "Too many caucasians are sleeping through a revolution. By the time they awake, tragedy that could have been avoided will have caught them in its wake."

Local ministers were asked to take their proverbial role of leadership because "an apathetic church is betraying its trust." Sponsors of the program were Western Christian Leadership Conference, County Council of Churches, San Diego Ministerial Association, Associated Student-body of California Western University, and United Church Women of San Diego. The Choir of Calvary Baptist Church presented appropriate selections.

Literature was distributed to those entering the campus by persons believed to be John Birchers. This literature showed a group photograph of KING and others captioned "MARTIN LUTHER KING ... AT COMMUNIST TRAINING SCHOOL" and underneath this photograph was a paragraph which stated as follows:

"The above picture was made by an employee of the State of Georgia, at the Highlander Folk School in Monteagle, Tennessee, during the Labor Day weekend of 1957. The photographer was sent to the school by the Georgia Commission on Education. The school was abolished by an act of the Legislature of the State of Tennessee at a later date because it was charged with being subservive [*sic*]."

The San Diego Police department was cognizant of these public functions.

UNITED STATES DEPARTMENT OF JUSTICE

FEDERAL BUREAU OF INVESTIGATION

New York, New York
June 16, 1964

Re: Communist Party, United States
of America–Negro Question
Communist Influence in Racial Matters
Internal Security-C
Malcolm X Little
Internal Security—Muslim Mosque, Incorporated

On June 12, 1964, a confidential source, who has furnished reliable information in the past, furnished information that a woman, whom the source could identify, contacted Clarence Jones on that date. Jones indicated that Martin Luther King would not be able to make the meeting since King is still in jail, but Jones mentioned that he has been authorized to speak for King. She mentioned that Wilkins (Roy Wilkins, Executive Secretary of the National Association for the Advancement of Colored People) (NAACP) and Jim (James Farmer, National Director of the Congress of Racial Equality) (CORE), are sending representatives, and she said that Young (Whitney Young, Executive Director of the Urban League) and Malcolm (Malcolm X Little) will be there.

On June 13, 1964, the same confidential source furnished information that Harry Belafonte contacted Clarence Jones on that date. Belafonte told Jones that he was not going to the meeting that day because Ruby Dee "is too dangerous," but he said that he wanted Jones to go and to advise him of the proceedings.

On June 13, 1964, the same confidential source furnished information that Ruby Dee contacted Clarence Jones on that date. She asked if

Jones would be available for the meeting that day (June 13, 1964), and Jones indicated that he would be there. Ruby Dee mentioned that Whitney Young (Executive Director of the Urban League) and Malcolm X would be there and that A. Philip Randolph (President of the Brotherhood of Sleeping Car Porters and Vice-President of the American Federation of Labor-Congress of Industrial Organizations) (AFL-CIO) and James Farmer (National Director of CORE) are sending representatives. Jones mentioned that Belafonte (Harry Belafonte) would not be able to attend because he is busy recording. Jones indicated that Martin Luther King would not be able to attend because he is still in jail.

On June 13, 1964, the first confidential source furnished information which indicated that Clarence Jones contacted Ossie Davis on that date. Jones said that in "reflecting on today's conference the most important thing discussed was Malcolm X's idea that we internationalize the question of civil rights and bring it before the United Nations." Jones stated that he thought Malcolm X had the best idea of all those discussed at the conference on "the question of the civil rights movement in the United States today." According to Ossie Davis, Malcolm's idea is to bring the Negro question before the United Nations to internationalize the whole question and bring it before the whole world. Jones stated that "we should present the plight of the Negro to the United Nations General Assembly in September of this year." Ossie Davis said, "This time we won't make the same mistake William Patterson made ten years ago." According to Jones, Malcolm X should "assume the responsibility of making the foreign arrangements as he's been there." Ann Jones (the wife of Clarence Jones), stated that Clarence told her that the meeting was thrilling and that Malcolm X impressed everyone with his weighty thoughts on the civil rights question.

It is to be noted that Martin Luther King was arrested in St. Augustine, Florida, in connection with his attempt to integrate public places in St. Augustine.

UNITED STATES DEPARTMENT OF JUSTICE

FEDERAL BUREAU OF INVESTIGATION

New York, New York

June 26, 1964

Re: Communist Party, United States
of America—Negro Question
Communist Influence In Racial Matters
Internal Security-C

On June 25, 1964, a confidential source, who has furnished reliable information in the past, furnished information that Martin Luther King, Jr., contacted Clarence Jones on that date. King mentioned that "they" (the Southern Christian Leadership Conference (SCLC) and those demonstrating against segregation in St. Augustine, Florida), are having a tough time in St. Augustine. He stated that there is a complete breakdown of law and order, and King remarked that the Klan (the Ku Klux Klan) "is making a showdown down here and the federal government has not done a thing."

King told Jones that forty people were beaten that evening, and he added that this was the worst night which they had ever had. King remarked that the Klan (Ku Klux Klan) is very close to the police (in St. Augustine). King indicated that the demonstrators are the people being beaten and that they are also the people being placed in jail.

King remarked that the reporters (newspaper reporters covering the situation in St. Augustine) say that if federal troops are not brought in "it is going to be bloody." In this connection, King said he is going to have many telegrams poured into the White House. Jones replied that Johnson (President Johnson) is very sensitive to public opinion, and he remarked that King is the most powerful Negro leader. Jones instructed King to continue to make sharp statements to the press blaming the federal government for not doing more.

King stated that they (the Ku Klux Klan) feel that they can beat us into submission, and King added that he is afraid someone will be killed. Both men agreed that President Johnson is preoccupied with the election and Mississippi (the situation in Mississippi where three civil rights workers have been missing since June 21, 1964). King stated he will tell the press that the government is not protecting them. According to Jones, the "hard core" in the South will not respect the Civil Rights Bill, and they agree that the government will have to enforce it.

Jones stated that he will get some people to work sending telegrams. King indicated that he is considering having a march on the White House to protest actions in St. Augustine and Mississippi.

[Section 13]

UNITED STATES DEPARTMENT OF JUSTICE

FEDERAL BUREAU OF INVESTIGATION

New York, New York
July 7, 1964

Re: Communist Party, USA
Negro Question
Communist Influence in Racial Matters
Internal Security-C

On July 5, 1964, a confidential source, who has furnished reliable information in the past, furnished information that Clarence Jones contacted Dora (Dora McDonald, Martin Luther King's secretary) on that date. Jones indicated that he had been working on a speech which King is scheduled to give to the Platform Committee of the National Republican Convention (which is scheduled to begin on July 13, 1964, in San Francisco, California). According to Jones, the speech will mention the activities in the civil rights field over the past four years such as boycotts, sit-ins, and other protests, and it says that these have not been sufficient. According to Jones, the speech goes on to say that these events were given legislative recognition in the passage of the Civil Rights Bill, and that the success of the Civil Rights Bill will depend on the compliance or degree of compliance and how much the economic condition of the Negro is improved.

According to Jones, in his speech King will suggest that the Republican Party consider the following: compliance with the Civil Rights Bill, police brutality and the harassment of civil rights workers, and automation and unemployment. Jones stated that King will suggest under compliance with the Civil Rights Bill that the President make use of his powers by appointing United States Marshals to observe in the offices of voter registration in any problem areas and to accompany to the office of voter registration any group of five or more persons who have been threatened, and supplementing this he will recommend that the powers of the United States Department of Justice and the Federal Bureau of Investigation (FBI) be more vigorously and creatively employed.

Continuing, Jones mentioned that King, in his speech, will say if the Communist Party (CP) and other subversive organizations can be successfully infiltrated why cannot an intelligence surveillance be maintained on the terrorist groups and persons subverting the United States Constitution by arson, murder, and bombing. According to Jones, King will further recommend that the right to vote be guaranteed by creative use of the Executive power and the use of every power at the disposal of the FBI to expose the activities of the vigilantes and white citizens council groups which are terrorizing Negroes.

[Section 14]

On July 5, 1964, [a confidential source] furnished information that CLARENCE JONES contacted DORA MCDONALD on that date to dictate a speech which MARTIN LUTHER KING, JR., was to give before the Platform committee of the Republican Party in San Francisco on 7/7/64. The transcript is not being made the subject of a letterhead memorandum in view of the fact that the conversation is being set out verbatim, and it is felt that if the information is disseminated in this fashion the source of the information might be revealed.

It is to be noted that in the event that this information is disseminated, it should be classified ''Secret'' in view of the sensitive position which the source . . . has with respect to the racial situation in the New York area.

I am pleased to have this opportunity to address the Platform Committee of the National Convention of the Republican Party. During the past four years since my appearance before this committee in Chicago, Illinois, profound and revolutionary changes have occurred within our country as well as throughout the world. In Africa and Asia millions of colored peoples have swelled the ranks of the world march toward human rights. In the United States twenty million

Negroes, in accelerated cadence have joined in the world wide struggle to eliminate the immoral practices of discrimination and segregation based on race and color.

In 1960, I and other representatives of Negro and civil rights groups fought to interpret to the conventions of both political parties the meaning and implications of the then current wave of student sit-in demonstrations which had occurred in many cities throughout the South. The sit-ins like the bus boycott of Montgomery, Alabama, the subsequent freedom rides coupled with the slow pace of school desegregation and the disillusionment and disappointment of Negroes with both political parties on the issue of civil rights were sparks from the embers for freedom smoldering from within twenty million black Americans. In 1963, the 100th Anniversary of the Negroes liberation from chattel slavery, these embers erupted into blazing conflagrations in Birmingham, Alabama; Danville, Virginia; Jackson, Mississippi; and other parts of our nation. Unlike four years ago, however, the meaning of the so-called Negro revolution of 1963 became clear for all to see and was given legislative recognition in the recently enacted Civil Rights Bill.

With the passage of the new Civil Rights Bill, many are already asking "What more does the Negro want?"; "Will demonstrations continue?" No single answer can easily be given to those questions since any answer depends upon the degree of compliance and the extent to which the economic condition of the Negro is improved. In this connection, I would like to suggest that those matters now requiring the most urgent attention and consideration of this committee and of the Republican Party as a whole are:

    I. Compliance with the newly enacted Civil Rights Bill

    II. Police brutality and harassment of persons seeking to remove discriminatory barriers from our society.

    III. Automation and unemployment.

I. Compliance With the Civil Rights Bill

The Negro revolt of 1963 against the continued injustices of racial discrimination and segregation will be infinitesimal compared to the civil strife which would ensue if the enactment of the new Civil Rights Bill receives the same kind of resistance interposed to the implementation of the 1954 desegregation decision. The failure of ardor of the two major political parties to make it unequivocally clear at their national conventions that they are committed to immediate enforcement of this new legislation is to invite national disaster and discord. The burning desire of millions of Negro Americans for *all* their freedom *here* and *now* has become crystallized into a new militancy and determination which says to all America that there will be no social tranquillity, peace, cessation of demonstrations until every vestige of racial injustice is eliminated from American society. It would be a tragedy and an irony of history if the party of Lincoln should now, some 100 years after the Proclamation of Emancipation omit from its platform and an unambiguous [*sic*] declaration of commitment to the enforcement of all sections of the Civil Rights Bill. Accordingly, I recommend that your platform statement command the attention of the American people to complete compliance with the Civil Rights Bill and that your committee state that under our system of government the civil rights legislation is the law of the land and constitutional pending a judicial determination of any claimed unconstitutionality by the United States Supreme Court. (Note: Martin may want to word that a different way; he may not even want to invite that kind of statement about unconstitutionality.)

II. Harassment of Persons Seeking (Jones Instructed Her To Go Back And Pick Up The Title Under The Other II)

Today Negro citizens in many parts of the South particularly in Alabama and Mississippi find that they must risk their very lives in order to exercise alone or in concert with other citizens their constitutionally guaranteed right to vote. The undisputed facts of brutality, murder, bombings, police harassment, and interference with voter education and registration efforts among Negro citizens in many of our southern states requires the extension and exertion of more not less Federal Powers in these areas. While under our system of government local law enforcement within the several states is traditionally within the province of local police officials. This reservation of power in the states is subject to the constitutional guarantees of the 14th and 15th Amendments. Negro citizens look to the Executive Branch to prevent the continued interference with rights secured them under our Federal Constitution. It is, therefore, natural that Negroes throughout our country in looking at the flagrant, brutal violations of constitutional rights in Mississippi; St. Augustine, Florida; in Alabama, and elsewhere ask themselves: "If the United States Government can protect the right to vote in South Korea, South Viet Nam, West Germany, only to mention a few and indeed is ready to risk war over missile bases in Cuba, why is that same government helpless, lethargic and ineffective to protect the rights of Negro citizens in Mississippi?"

The recent disappearance of three civil rights workers in the State of

Mississippi and other instances of police harassment point to the necessity for vigorous and creative use of the power of the Executive Branch of the government to protect federal rights in locally hostile environs.

As you know I am not a lawyer but I have been advised by several legal authorities that there exists ample statutory authority for the federal government to act in Mississippi and other parts of our country without the necessity of federal troops to insure that federally guaranteed rights are respected in every state of this union. Title 10, Section 333, of the United States Code, annotated provides that "the President by using the militia or the armed forces, or both, or *by any other means,* shall take such measures as he considers necessary to suppress, in a state, any insurrection, domestic violence, unlawful combination, or conspiracy:

> "(1) so injure the execution of the laws of the state, and of the United States within this state, that any part or parts of its people is deprived of the right, privilege, immunity or protection named in the Constitution and secured by law, and the constituted authorities of that state are unable, or refuse to protect that right, privilege, or immunity, or to give that protection; or (2) opposes or obstructs the execution of the laws of the United States or impedes the course of justice under those laws."

Pursuant to the authority vested in the President of the United States under the above quoted section, the President could appoint a special panel of United States Marshals to serve as field observers in the offices of local voting registrars in any area where there is a claimed denial or deprivation of the right to vote guaranteed to all citizens under the 15th Amendment to our Federal Constitution. Such a panel of Marshals would be in addition to the present national staff attached to the various judicial districts throughout the Continental United States. This proposed staff or panel of voting rights Marshals could be specifically trained to carry out their duties under their Presidential appointment. In addition to serving as observers, such Marshals could be empowered to physically accompany five or more persons claiming interference and deprivation of their right to vote to the office of the local registrar. Any and all such claims of interference and denial of the opportunity to register or vote would have to be supported by a sworn affidavit by the person claiming such denial or interference on appropriate forms provided by the special panel of voting rights Marshals. None of the Marshals specially appointed by the President under Title 10, Section 333, mentioned earlier, shall be empowered in any way to interfere with the local administration of voting registration and election requirements of the respective states within which any claimed denial or interference with the right to vote is made. I urgently recommend that this Platform Committee include within the platform of the Republican Party a recommendation for the establishment and appointment of such a panel of voting rights Marshals.

Supplementing the use of executive power under Title 10, Section 333, just described, the powers of the United States Department of Justice and the Federal Bureau of Investigation must be more vigorously and creatively employed. In view of the instances of murder and brutality which have occurred in Mississippi, the recent unexplained disappearance of three young civil rights workers in that state, the numerous unsolved bombings of Negro homes and churches in Alabama, Georgia, and Louisiana, including the infamous murder of four Negro girls attending Sunday School in Birmingham in September 1963, Negroes are justifiably asking: If our government is capable of gathering intelligence information in a matter of hours from all parts of the world and has been able to successfully infiltrate and maintain a constant intelligence surveillance of the United States Communist Party and other subversive groups, is it not also capable of maintaining an intelligence surveillance of the terrorist groups and persons subverting the Constitution of the United States by arson, murder, and bombing of civil rights activities.

In light of the above considerations, therefore, I urge this committee of the party of Abraham Lincoln to make it unmistakably clear to all Americans that: 1. the exercise of the right to vote shall be vigorously safeguarded by the creative use of the executive powers under Title 10, Section 333, of the United States Code, annotated. 2. the Republican Party recommends the use of every power at the disposal of the FBI to expose the activities of vigilantes and white citizen council groups seeking to terrorize and intimidate Negroes from exercising their constitutional rights.

III. Automation and Unemployment

The newly enacted Civil Rights Bill brings the American Negro to the threshold of becoming a full (fledged?) citizen participant in our society. While technological changes and structural unemployment brought about by automation are color blind, the objective economic position of the Negro in society causes him as a group to be harder hit by automation. Negroes are still at the bottom of the economic ladder. They live within two concentric circles of segregation. One imprisons them on the basis of color, while the other confines them within a separate culture of poverty.

Our nation is experiencing a complex manpower revolution engendered by accelerated labor force growth, dramatic shifts in the composition of the labor force, increasingly rapid technological change and rising educational and skill requirements. Automation is eliminating jobs from our economy at the rate of 40,000 per week or 2,080,000 a year. The Senate Subcommittee on Employment and Manpower of the Committee on Labor and Public Welfare in its recent report entitled ''Toward Full Employment,'' 88th Congress, 2nd Session, advises us that: ''the forces which have spawned the manpower revolution have created a situation in which the economy must generate an average of 3 1/2 million new jobs a year throughout the rest of the decade just to keep unemployment from rising beyond its persistent level of only 5 1/2 per cent of the work force. An additional two to three and one half million jobs would be needed to reduce unemployment to 4 per cent of the labor force and another 3/4 of a million to reach 3 per cent.''

In addition to the foregoing factors, 20 per cent of the families or over 40,000,000 families have annual incomes under $3,000. Poverty in modern America tends to be concentrated [sic] among disadvantaged groups. Those in poverty are not suffering from unemployment alone. According to the 1964 economic report of the President, while 44% of poor families have no employable family head, the head of 49% of families with annual incomes under $3,000.00 does have a job. Full time employment, however, at less than $1.50 per hour, is not sufficient to produce the annual income necessary to keep a family from extreme poverty.

One half of all Negro families in the United States are poor by the $3,000.00 annual income definition. The ''employment'' rate for Negroes has been persistently double that of the entire labor force. This higher employment rate is found in every age and sex group in all industries and in all regions. (Source Senate Subcommittee on Employment and Manpower). The proportion of Negro males 25–54 years of age outside of the labor force rose from 42 to 64 per cent per 1,000 between 1949 and 1963, whereas the proportion rate of white males of the same age not in the labor force actually declined from 33 to 28 per cent per 1,000.

In 1962, almost one out of three non-white workers had not completed elementary school as compared with 1 in 10 among whites. A fifth of non-whites and a third of whites had finished high school. In 1959, the medium annual income of all the white population who had income was $3,207.00, whereas for Negroes it was slightly over $1,518.00. The average Negro with four years of college education can expect to earn less in his lifetime than the white eighth-grade dropout. In short, Negroes in America are unemployed the longest, have lower earnings when they are employed, have less education and on the average benefit less financially from the education they do obtain.

The question confronting the platform committee of the Republican Party, therefore, is not "What more does the Negro want now that the Civil Rights Bill has been passed?" but rather, "What can the Republican Party do to make freedom real and substantial for our Negro citizens?"

I am specifically proposing here and now that this Platform Committee in its platform statement being drafted on behalf of the Republican Party include an endorsement and support of the broad principles of such a bill. My legal advisers stand ready to meet with any representative of government on the details of the proposed Bill of Rights to the disadvantaged.

UNITED STATES DEPARTMENT OF JUSTICE

FEDERAL BUREAU OF INVESTIGATION

New York, New York
JUL 28 1964

Communist Party, USA
Negro Question
Communist Influence in Racial Matters
Internal Security-C

A confidential source, who has furnished reliable information in the past, advised on July 26, 1964, that the Reverend Martin Luther King, Jr., President of the Southern Christian Leadership Conference (SCLC) and Bayard Rustin conferred on that date. King sought Rustin's advice as to what his role should be as leader in the non-violent revolution in relation to the riots in Harlem and Rochester, New York. In this regard, King said Mayor Wagner of New York City desired to discuss the situation with him tomorrow night (July 27, 1964). King said he had set a tentative date to met the mayor for July 27, 1964, but was not certain it was the correct thing to do in view of the situation. Rustin told him that the situation in New York was quiet at that time.

Rustin told King that he had appeared on a national television program on that date (July 26, 1964). He said the program on the National Broadcast System was participated in by James Farmer (National Director of the Congress on Racial Equality) (CORE), Cleveland Robinson (Secretary-Treasurer of District 65, Retail, Wholesale and Department Store Union, American Federation of Labor—Congress of Industrial Organizations, AFL-CIO), and a representative of the National Association for the Advancement of Colored People (NAACP). Rustin said everyone took the position that Mayor Wagner had been derelict in the performance of his duties.

Rustin, according to the source, expressed the opinion that there was a serious problem concerning King's meeting with Mayor Wagner, unless King could be critical, as all other leaders maintained that he was not doing enough. Rustin also felt that King should be free to make a statement to the press following the meeting, otherwise he (King) would really be in a "box." King said he agreed with Rustin and felt that he should be free to criticize the Mayor, and tell the press that he told Mayor Wagner that he thought the demands of the Negro community were just demands and that he needed to act on them immediately. Rustin told King that he should say something similar to the following: "Law and order do not exist in a vacuum; to the degree that you have justice—to that degree can law and order be maintained, and where justice is non-existent frustration will break out in some form, either Negroes being unjust to themselves, preying on themselves, using violence on themselves, or someone else, and the root of the problem is to get rid of the situation." Rustin said King should "urge Mayor Wagner to face the housing, school and job problems, and that many Negro leaders in New York City were united in seeing these as the major problems. Rustin said that anything short of this would spoil King's image. King said that Rustin was exactly right and that he just wanted to be sure that their positions coincided since the Mayor had talked about having an off the record conference. Rustin told King that he should not do that (having an off the record conference) and definitely should be free to make a statement to the press in which he could urge the Mayor to move on with more housing, to integrate the schools and to find jobs for the unemployed. King asked Rustin's opinion as to what else was needed by him at that time, to which Rustin replied he would have to give some serious thought to the matter.

According to the source, King and Rustin considered the feasibility of King making an appearance and speech to end the violence in New York City, as he had done in some southern communities. King said he felt it would be a mistake because some of the groups might be determined to repudiate him and he would not get a chance to speak. To this Rustin agreed and said, "They are dangerous dogs who will lash out at anything."

Rustin inquired as to when King would be in New York City, prompting King to remark that he could not leave for New York before 5:50 P.M. on July 27, 1964. He said he would arrive in New York at about 8:20 P.M. on that date, and would see the Mayor at about 9:30 P.M. on that date. Rustin remarked that he would like to meet King at the airport and discuss things with him on the way into the city. King said he would inform Rustin in the morning (July 27, 1964) as to the exact time he would arrive.

King asked Rustin about the office (Freedom Democratic Party Office in New York). Rustin replied that he wanted to talk to King about that as he had determined that "this combination cannot work. Ella (Ella J. Baker, Student Non-Violent Coordinating Committee, SNCC) is not going to permit the project to be carried out." Rustin said in view of this why should "we" get into something at that level, which looked as if it was going to be big but, was not.

UNITED STATES DEPARTMENT OF JUSTICE

FEDERAL BUREAU OF INVESTIGATION

New York, New York
July 30, 1964

Communist Party, United States of America
Negro Question
Communist Influence in Racial Matters
Internal Security-C

A confidential source, who has furnished reliable information in the past, advised on July 28, 1964, that Bayard Rustin conferred with an unidentified male on that date. Rustin remarked that "we" (Reverend Martin Luther King, Rustin and others) were with Mayor Wagner of New York City, from 10:00 P.M., July 27, 1964, until 2:30 A.M., July 28, 1964, and from 1:00 P.M., July 28, 1964, until early evening, July 28, 1964.

Rustin said the Mayor had agreed to go to Washington, D.C., on Monday (August 3, 1964) to request ten million dollars to aid people in the ghetto (Harlem). Rustin said "we" have convinced the Mayor that he should report that the problem (riot in Harlem) was economic; therefore he is trying to find 1,500 jobs by Monday for young Negroes in the ghettos.

Another point under negotiation with the Mayor, Rustin said, is the establishment of a civilian commission to investigate alleged cases of police brutality. Rustin said this proposed commission would be comprised of Negroes, Puerto Ricans and whites. He said, however, that Police Commissioner Murphy was fighting this to the bitter end.

Rustin was asked by the unidentified male why Mayor Wagner had asked King to come to New York City. Rustin answered that Mayor Wagner could not negotiate with the Negro leaders in New York because they were "stupid and crackpots;" furthermore, Rustin said Wagner wanted the "umbrella" of King's name in the negotiations. He said some Negroes in Harlem were screaming that King had no right to come to New York because conditions here were none of his business.

On the night of July 23, 1964, the same confidential source advised that Rustin and Martin Luther King had conferred during the night. King inquired if Rustin had heard any results of the conference between the Mayor and Police Commissioner Murphy. Rustin replied, "Murphy is impossible; this indicates to me that they are putting up a real fight." King said the Mayor was still meeting with the Commissioner, and that he (King) had been requested by the Mayor to stand by. King said it was urgent that "we" meet with him.

As regards any agreement reached between the Mayor and him, King said several problems were involved, namely: his (King's) fear of criticism from Harlem Negro leaders, and the possibility that he would be placed in the role of "Uncle Tom." Rustin agreed that King should not be placed in the role of a negotiator.

UNITED STATES DEPARTMENT OF JUSTICE

FEDERAL BUREAU OF INVESTIGATION

New York, New York

August 3, 1964

Communist Party, United States of America

Negro Question

Communist Influence in Racial Matters

Internal Security-C

On July 31, 1964, a confidential source, who has furnished reliable information in the past, advised that one Don Alexander, who represented himself to be associated with radio station WLIB in New York, conferred with Bayard Rustin on that date. Alexander apprised Rustin that Mayor Wagner of New York City, had just announced his rejection of the demands of the civil rights leaders for the establishment of an independent civilian police review board, and wanted Rustin's remarks as a consequence. Rustin said he had maintained from the very beginning (commencement of the Harlem disturbance) that two things were necessary to insure racial peace: that a police review board be established and that Lieutenant Thomas Gilligan of the New York City Police Department be suspended. (Police Lieutenant who shot and killed a Negro youth, James Powell, July 16, 1964).

Rustin said it was obvious that ''we'' (Negro leaders) cannot go to the Negro community and ask that they refrain from demonstrating unless the city officials of New York are going to accede to these demands. If the Mayor had not seen fit to act, that was tragic, Rustin said. He said under these circumstances he would not urge anyone in New York to respect the requests of civil rights leaders not to demonstrate.

''The New York Times,'' July 20, 1964, page 1, column, reported that major civil rights leaders conferred in New York City, on July 29, 1964, and agreed to recommend to their members to observe a ''broad curtailment if not total moratorium'' on all mass demonstrations until after the November 3, 1964, Presidential elections.

Alexander asked if his understanding was correct that a good likelihood exists that many groups (civil rights) will be staging mass demonstrations in view of the Mayor's actions. Rustin replied "we" shall do something that is meaningful, and if that includes a mass demonstration, he would be in favor of such action.

According to the source, Alexander said many of the leaders on the local civil rights level had disagreed with the tactics on the part of the national leadership, which ordered a curtailment of demonstrations until after election day. Rustin said if Negroes receive their demands, he would be happy to curtail demonstrations, but said demands cannot be curtailed in a vacuum. He said they must be curtailed in relation to whether "we" are getting results, therefore he would not support one side or the other.

Alexander asked if the decision of the civil rights leaders to curtail demonstrations was arrived at from the point of view that mass demonstrations created a great amount of anti-Negro sentiment. Rustin replied that there are many white people in the middle, who find certain types of mass demonstrations under certain circumstances, and certain types of rioting tend to pull them in support of the Goldwater forces. He said he thought part of the reason to curtail the demonstrations was in order to prevent Goldwater from being elected President. To elect Goldwater, Rustin said, would prevent the implementation of the Civil Rights Act. He said he thought the leaders were trying to hold out something which looked as if "we" were trying to be reasonable, but added "we" can only be reasonable if they (City officials) meet "our" demands.

In response to a question of Alexander as to what Rustin's impression of Commissioner Murphy, New York City Police Department, was, Rustin said Murphy did not intend to give one inch, and that he was the chief culprit and should be dismissed immediately. The grounds for Murphy's dismissal, Rustin said, should be: that he used more "violence" than necessary during the riots; that he continues to permit crime in Harlem; and has failed to move against Lieutenant Thomas Gilligan.

During the night of July 31, 1964, the same confidential source advised that Bayard Rustin was in contact with Reverend Martin Luther King, Jr., on that date. The reason for the contact, the source said, was to consider the statement of Mayor Wagner of New York City, issued that date (announcing the rejection of their demands for the establishment of a civilian review board to review police brutality cases). Rustin told King that the general feeling in New York was that his statement was "not enough, as we told him."

King said he was getting many calls asking for his comments on the Mayor's statement. Rustin replied that there was only one thing for him (King) to say and that was "that you (King) made it clear when you came to New York that you felt that one thing that would bring peace and harmony was the nine point program which included the review board and that you were very sorry that the Mayor did not see his way clear to do it."

Rustin also said King should expect to be asked questions as to whether he thinks people in New York should break the moratorium on demonstrations. Rustin advised King to answer that by stating, that he was not in New York and that that was up to the people in New York.

[Section 15]

UNITED STATES
Memorandum

TO: Mr. W. C. Sullivan   DATE: August 13, 1964

FROM: Mr. F. J. Baumgardner

SUBJECT: MARTIN LUTHER KING, JR.
           SECURITY MATTER-C

We advised the White House on 8/8/64 that Martin Luther King, Jr., President of the Southern Christian Leadership Conference, wanted to meet with the President to discuss certain problems in connection with the moratorium on racial demonstrations, which King felt dictated the necessity for a conference between himself and the President.

On the morning of 8/13/64, SAC Roney of the New York Office called and said that at 10:48 A.M. . . . advised King was in conversation with Bayard Rustin, currently active in the civil rights movement in New York City and known to have had previous communist affiliations. It appears they were discussing King's continued efforts to meet with the President on the civil rights matter.

During the conversation, King said that he talked to Presidential Assistant Lee White on the night of 8/12/64. White told King the President was tied up and wouldn't be able to see him. He wondered whether King would discuss the matter with the President on the telephone, King told Rustin that he felt the President was trying to avoid him. King felt that the President did not want to meet personally with King for fear it would get back to the South that the President was dealing with King. King told Rustin he thought they should put up a fight and instructed Rustin to get in touch with White and let him know that King feels the President is avoiding him. King told Rustin that he thought the President should know that King doesn't like it. King commented that the President needs the Negro vote and added "We have no way to go, but we can certainly stay home."

ACTION: We are advising the White House by letter concerning King's comments to Rustin. We are following this matter closely and will keep you advised of pertinent developments.

UNITED STATES DEPARTMENT OF JUSTICE

FEDERAL BUREAU OF INVESTIGATION

New York, New York
August 14, 1964

Community Party, United States of America
Negro Question
Communist Influence in Racial Matters
Internal Security-C

A confidential source, who has furnished reliable information in the past, advised on August 13, 1964, that he learned that Bayard Rustin and the Reverend Martin Luther King, Jr., were in conference on that date. According to the source, King told Rustin that he had talked with Lee White (Special Assistant to President Johnson) last night and was informed by him that the President was tied-up today and tomorrow (August 13–14, 1964), and wondered if he could confer with him (King) on the phone. King said after thinking about it, he believed "this" was important enough that he talk to President Johnson face to face and not over the phone.

It is noted that on August 7, 1964, the same confidential source advised that Bayard Rustin and King conferred on that date, and King was advised to send a telegram to President Johnson requesting a meeting with him for this week. The purpose of the meeting, that telegram stated, was to consider the moratorium on demonstrations and the possibility of further conflict in urban centers.

In continuing their conference, King said he had the impression that he (President Johnson) was not only trying to avoid the issue, but also avoid meeting him face to face for fear that it would get back to the South that he (the President) was dealing with him.

King, the source said, thought he (the President) was trying to avoid meeting him in Washington, where the press could let the nation know he was meeting with him. He said this was the reason he (the President) first proposed they meet in New York. This, King said, made him a little sensitive.

Rustin told King that his position was correct for two reasons: because he would not derive any satisfaction over the telephone; and secondly, because "those young people must know you are putting up a fight for them."

King apprised Rustin that he was told by Lee White that the President would see Joe Rauh (Counsel to the United Auto Workers, American Federation of Labor—Congress of Industrial Organizations) on Monday or Tuesday (August 16–17, 1964).

King said the first suggestion was that "some man who advises the President on this thing" would come to New York and talk to him but said he rejected that. He said he advised that the matter was of such importance that he desired to discuss it with the President in person, not on the telephone. He said as an after-thought that he should have indicated to White that he felt the President was not only trying to avoid the issue, but also avoid seeing him. "I really think," King said, "this is what it is, I don't think the President is so busy that he could not see me on one of the most pressing issues he had to face." King said he was of the opinion that "this political thing has these fellows afraid" and he was afraid for the South to see him sitting with him and talking to him at this time.

In reply to King's observations, Rustin was of the opinion that "we" must wage a fight, adding that Joseph Rauh cannot "put it over, he has tried again."

King instructed Rustin to contact Lee White and let him know his (King's) feelings; let the President know that he feels this is "down right avoiding him and the issues." Furthermore, King was of the opinion that the matter was so important the President should deal with it himself rather than through some assistant. King said that President Johnson should know that he does not like it, adding that if "we" do not wage a fight "they" will just run over us in the next two months. "Lyndon Johnson," King said, "needs the Negro vote. He feels that we have no way to go but we can certainly stay home."

The same confidential source advised on August 13, 1964, that Bayard Rustin and Lee White, Special Assistant to President Johnson, were in conference on that date. According to the source Rustin told White that the Reverend Martin Luther King, Jr., had talked with Rustin and other Negro leaders in New York City and that there was a sense of distress because King was asked to see the President not only on his own behalf but on behalf of a number of others. Rustin continued that King had very definitely gotten the impression that the President did not want to see him in Washington. White stated the President was willing to see King yesterday, August 12, 1964. Rustin commented that he had pointed this out to King, but that King had the impression that the President didn't want to see him in Washington for some reason, at this time.

Rustin continued that he wanted to report this to White just to keep channels open.

White stated that if there is any feeling of that sort he would much rather hear it.

Rustin asked White to talk to King again. Rustin continued that almost all of the men who were involved in this moratorium signing (against demonstrations) feel that they are in a very peculiar position and that someone should talk with the President. Rustin added that Mr. Joseph Rauh was one of the persons who had urged King to see the President. Rustin went on to say that the leadership does not choose to pass on to the President their point of view through Mr. Rauh. Rustin again stated that it would be a good thing if White again talked to King.

White commented that this was especially true if that is the feeling in King's mind that the President is trying to avoid him.

Rustin stated that to put it correctly, King had the impression somehow from the conversation, that the President didn't want to see King in Washington at this time. Rustin continued that that was the way King had told it to him. Rustin stated that King had asked him to relay this to White, "to do what you will about it." Rustin went on to say that he thinks it's frightfully important because "we" have a very peculiar problem at this end, at this time. Rustin continued that "we'll be much more capable of trying to realize a sensible conclusion of this matter, if King is able to say that he has spoken with the President. Rustin added "that's the simple problem and I want it to be very fair with you, I'm not so sure we're going to be able to handle it anyway."

UNITED STATES DEPARTMENT OF JUSTICE

FEDERAL BUREAU OF INVESTIGATION

Philadelphia, Pennsylvania
August 17, 1964

MARTIN LUTHER KING, JR.,
SPEAKS IN PHILADELPHIA,
AUGUST 10, 1964

The Philadelphia Inquirer, a daily newspaper, in its issue of August 11, 1964, page 2, contained an article captioned "King Calls Violence Futile." This article reflected that Reverend MARTIN LUTHER KING, described as "apostle of non-violent resistance in the civil rights field," told 3,000 Negro college women Monday night, August 10, 1964, that violence and war are obsolete in the nuclear age.

KING addressed that 41st meeting of the Alpha Kappa Alpha Sorority in Irvine Auditorium at the University of Pennsylvania. He condemned the recent rioting in Harlem and Rochester, N. Y. He stated that violence is not only immoral but also impractical. He stated, however, that so long as there is segregation and discrimination the causes of violence will remain present.

He called for "massive programs" to rid the nation of its Negro ghettos.

KING stressed love as the chief means of ending segregation. He stated that Negroes "can love the oppressor while hating the action of oppression." In regard to the 1964 Presidential Election, KING stated "If it is GOLDWATER in '64, it will be hot water in '65, bread and water in '66, and no water at all in '67."

He urged increased Negro voter registrations.

The Philadelphia Inquirer also carried an article on the same page stating that CECIL B. MOORE, President of the Philadelphia Chapter of the National Association for the Advancement of Colored People, stated Monday, August 10, 1964, that public . . .

UNITED STATES DEPARTMENT OF JUSTICE

FEDERAL BUREAU OF INVESTIGATION

New York, New York

August 25, 1964

Re: Communist Party,
United States of America—
Negro Question
Communist Influence in
Racial Matters
Internal Security-C

A confidential source, who has furnished reliable information in the past, advised on August 21, 1964, that he had learned that Bayard Rustin, Martin Luther King, Jr., (President of the Southern Christian Leadership Conference) and Andrew Young (Executive Assistant to King) were in contact on that date. They took the opportunity to consider the Democratic National Convention (opening in Atlantic City, New Jersey, August 24, 1964) and whether Rustin thought King should attend.

Rustin advised King that he should appear tomorrow (August 22, 1964) at 2:00 P.M. and put up a fight to get them seated (Freedom Democratic Party delegates from Mississippi). After that, Rustin opined, it seemed that King might be in a position that he might not want to be in. In explaining to King and Young just what he meant, Rustin said that in the event President Johnson did something unacceptable to the "left youngsters," they would demonstrate, and if King were there, they would expect him to join them, and should he refuse, the press would ask for an explanation. Regardless of what King might say, Rustin said, it would be interpreted by them (youngsters) as harmful to their efforts. He said King should not be in that position, and that one way to prevent it was to leave tomorrow (August 22, 1964) after his appearance.

In continuing, Rustin said if King were in Atlantic City and something should happen, people like Walter Reuther (President of the United Auto Workers and Vice President of the American Federation of Labor—Congress of Industrial Organizations, AFL-CIO) would ask his support in stopping the "youngsters" from doing "kookie things."

For that reason, Rustin said, he (Rustin) would not go to the Convention.

According to the source, Rustin told King and Young that he had been called by "youngsters" in Atlantic City, New Jersey, requesting that he call King and ask him to telegram Attorney General Robert Kennedy and request his support (in seating the delegates from the Freedom Democratic Party). In this regard, Rustin advised King to do whatever he could to strike a blow for freedom.

King, Rustin said, should make his appearance at the meeting of the Credential Committee on August 22, 1964, then he would return to New York City, to Atlanta, Georgia, or go any place he desired to go. In the evening King desired to return to the Convention he could consider going on Monday or Tuesday, Rustin stated, provided there was to be a peaceful demonstration to seat the delegates. In this regard, King said he had been assured by James Farmer of the Congress of Racial Equality (CORE) that demonstrations would be peaceful. To this, Rustin said Farmer did not have control of CORE, therefore, he could not control what happened. Rustin said this was because Farmer had given his "left wing" such freedom to do what they wanted, that nobody paid any attention to him.

Furthermore, Rustin said that CORE had sent the biggest "kook" down to Atlantic City to organize demonstrations. According to the source, Rustin identified this person as Herb Callender (Chairman of the Bronx Chapter of CORE).

Rustin told Andrew Young that he should attend the Convention to act as King's representative. This, Rustin said, would permit people to relay requests and messages to King through Young, who could then inform them that King was unavailable due to an accident. Rustin said King's injury might be the most fortunate thing to ever happen to King. King said he was using a crutch in order to get around. This prompted Rustin to advise King to go to Atlantic City on a crutch. By doing that, Rustin said, the people from the Student Non-Violent Coordinating Committee would interpret it as a great token.

With regard to King's appearance before the Credentials Committee, Rustin told him that Joseph Rauh (counsel to the United Auto Workers and counsel to the Freedom Democratic Party) would expect him to talk for about fifteen minutes. Rustin told King to make a real emotional appeal for the Freedom Delegates and to read a statement which Andrew Young had prepared. The following is in essence what was contained therein:

"That no state had gone to such extremes to prevent participation of

Negro citizens in political life as the state of Mississippi," and enumerated such things as "literacy tests, economic reprisals, police intimidation and church burnings," to support the allegation, and said that "as a consequence, citizens of that state had come to the Convention in a moral appeal for recognition and representation in the Democratic Party. The seating of the delegation from the Freedom Party has political and moral significance far beyond the borders of Mississippi or the halls of the Convention, for there the very idea of representative government is at stake." In conclusion, the statement urged the seating and recognition of the Freedom Democratic Party delegates.

Rustin, the source said, was highly complimentary of the statement, but instructed Young to add the following: "that to all who love democracy and freedom, nothing was so symbolic as whether the right decision was made to seat the delegates."

King told Rustin that since neither he nor Rustin would be in Atlantic City during the Convention, they should try to get together in New York City to discuss what they planned to do before the election.

The same confidential source advised on August 22, 1964, that Bayard Rustin was in contact with one Cortland (phonetic) on that date. Rustin told Cortland that Martin Luther King was going to appear before the Credentials Committee of the Democratic Party on that date, to present his testimony.

Rustin said King was also willing to send a telegram to Attorney General Kennedy (seeking his moral support in seating the delegation from the Freedom Democratic Party). In light of that, Cortland read the following telegram which was to be sent in the name of King to Kennedy:

"Four years after the Convention in which your brother took up the fight for full civil rights throughout the United States, we call upon you to carry that fight forward by voicing your support for the Mississippi Freedom Democratic Party. Your experience as Attorney General has made you the man in the country who is most aware of the moral imperative to support the Mississippians in their serious effort to change the human condition. Your voice on this issue would carry a great moral and political weight in favor of a democratic decision on the floor of the Convention. Your statement of support will encourage all who work for the liberal cause in both the North and the South.

Rustin approved the statement and told Cortland to release it from the office of the Freedom Party in Atlantic City, New Jersey, when the right opportunity arose.

[Section 17]

UNITED STATES DEPARTMENT OF JUSTICE

FEDERAL BUREAU OF INVESTIGATION

New York, New York
October 16, 1964

Re: Communist Influence in
Racial Matters
Internal Security-C

On October 15, 1964, a confidential source, who has furnished reliable information in the past, advised that Bayard Rustin was in contact with A.J. Muste on that date. Rustin said his purpose in contacting Muste was to discuss plans concerning Martin Luther King's trip to Europe to accept the Nobel Peace Prize. In that regard, Rustin said he had been asked by King to accompany him (to Oslo, Norway) for the purpose of handling arrangements for him. Rustin, the source said, remarked that King did not trust any of the people "around him" to be knowledgeable enough to know whom he should or should not contact when he goes over to accept the award.

Rustin, in commenting on King's request, said he thought he should go, but was faced with a problem as to where he could get the money which would be needed for transportation, as well as other expenses incidental to the trip. In regard to his expenses, Rustin said he thought "we" should appeal to some of "our friends" (Rustin's and Muste's friends) to raise the money.

With regard to King's use of money that he will receive with the award, Rustin said Coretta King (wife of Martin Luther King) desired that Martin place in trust $5,000 for each of their children's education, but that King opposed the suggestion. As a consequence of their indecision as to what to do with the money, Rustin said Martin King had invited him down to Atlanta on Monday, October 19, 1964, to discuss what the money should be used for.

Rustin told Muste that he was of the opinion that King should make a decision and an announcement to the effect that of the $54,000 award, he was going to set aside $30,000 for the Southern Christian Leadership Conference (SCLC) for the express purpose of teaching the doctrine of non-violence. He said this could be accomplished through the establishment of institutes in this country for the purpose of acquainting young people with the tactics and philosophy of non-violence. As to the remaining $24,000, Rustin said he was of the opinion that it should be placed in trust for the children of the Kings. This, Rustin said, would benefit the children because Martin was not a wealthy man. He said his only reservation about the trust for the children was whether it would appear to the public that the Kings were trying to take care of their own (alluding to King's provision for his children).

Muste said in reply to Rustin's feelings about the children of King, that he did not think King should provide for them but instead, should give all the money to the SCLC. This, Muste said, would not subject King to criticism for taking a part of the money for himself. Rustin said he was of the opinion that if King does give away part of the money, then it should go exclusively to the SCLC for the purpose of teaching non-violence, and for nothing else. He said the SCLC could raise funds for its regular budget. Muste agreed, stating that King received the Prize for advocating non-violence, therefore, should apply the money for that purpose.

Rustin, in commenting on his forthcoming meeting with King, said King wanted him to help prepare a speech which he would make (apparently in regard to his decision about what to do with the money). In that regard, Rustin asked Muste to prepare a few thoughts that he could use when he meets King.

According to the source, Rustin and Muste concluded their contact with a promise of Muste that he would help Rustin raise the money with which to make the trip with King.

The April 14, 1957, issue of "The Worker," an east coast Communist publication, page 16, column 1, described A.J. Muste as the dean of the Socialist pacifists.

UNITED STATES GOVERNMENT
Memorandum

TO: Mr. W. C. Sullivan   DATE: November 2, 1964

FROM: Mr. F. J. Baumgardner

SUBJECT: MARTIN LUTHER KING, JR.
            INTERNAL SECURITY—COMMUNIST

By telephone calls from our Atlanta Office 10:45 A.M. and 11:40 A.M., today (11-2-64), we learned of the following information through a highly sensitive source. Martin Luther King, Jr., just learned this morning of a campaign which has been initiated to encourage people to vote for King for president as a write-in candidate 11-3-64. The campaign is taking several forms, including telegrams being sent to Negroes throughout the country; efforts to gain radio time to urge people to vote for King; and the circulation of handbills in larger cities encouraging a vote for King. The handbills reveal distribution by "Committee for Negroes in Government," Louisville, Kentucky. (No record of this organization Bufiles.)

According to our source, King interpreted the actions described above as an obvious attempt to cancel out the Negro vote and to confuse Negroes in their voting. King believes that the campaign was initiated by Goldwater forces because any votes for King by Negroes would obviously diminish the number of such votes for President Johnson.

King held an immediate press conference in Atlanta, Georgia, this morning in which he told the press of the foregoing and denied having any connection with the campaign. He urged people not to pay any attention to the efforts to have people vote for him.

ACTION:

The foregoing information was immediately telephonically furnished to Mr. DeLoach's Office so that he might alert the White House. This is for your immediate attention. Letters to the White House and to the Acting Attorney General are being expeditiously prepared.

[Section 18]

UNITED STATES GOVERNMENT
Memorandum

TO: Mr. DeLoach   DATE: 11-19-64

FROM: M. A. Jones

SUBJECT: DIRECTOR'S BRIEFING OF WOMEN
          REPORTERS ON 11-18-64

BACKGROUND:

In connection with the Director's briefing of the woman reporters yesterday, the Director has requested documentation on several matters including the ages of the individuals convicted in the McComb, Mississippi, case; date and place of conviction of Bayard Rustin ... and whether or not he has been or is in the Communist Party; the Albany, Georgia, statements by Martin Luther King; and the five Agents and their birthplaces at Albany, Georgia.

DOCUMENTATION:

McComb, Mississippi, Case:

There follows the names and ages of the individuals sentenced in the McComb, Mississippi, bombing case:

Hilton Dunaway—Age 26   Jimmy Preston Wilson—Age 38
Murphy Duncan—Age 44   Paul Dewey Wilson—Age 25
Gerald Lawrence—Age 21   John Paul Westbrook—Age 20
Emory Allen Lee—Age 35   Ernest Frederick Z ck—Age 25
Billy Earl Wilson—Age 22

Bayard Rustin:

Rustin was born 3-17-13 at West Chester, Pennsylvania, and was educated Wilberforce University and the City College of New York. He was a member of the Young Communist League, a cited organization, from the late 1930's to the early 1940's. The July 11–18, 1964, issue of the Saturday Evening Post, in an article entitled "The Wolf of Civil Rights," points out that Rustin was "an organizer for the Young Communist League." He admits his membership in the American Student Union in 1939 (cited as a communist front by the House Committee on Un-American Activities) but claims he withdrew from the organization in 1940 to embrace the Quaker religion. Rustin has been referred to as an expert on civil disobedience and a leading exponent of pacifism. He has been active in numerous picket lines and demonstrations and has been an agitator against military conscription and racial segregation for which he has been arrested on several occasions. Since 1942, he has been a field representative for the Fellowship of Reconciliation and has been Executive Secretary of the War Resisters League. He is considered an orator of national prominence. He has also been a secretary to Reverend Martin Luther King. Rustin has reportedly attended Communist Party conventions in 1957. He has traveled to Africa with pacifists to protest against hydrogen bomb tests by French authorities (1959) and accompanied American pacifists to England to protest production of nuclear weapons (1958).

Martin Luther King's Statement in Albany, Georgia:

Considerable publicity was given to statements made by Martin Luther King concerning the situation in Albany, Georgia, at the time he highly criticized the FBI. His statements were made on 11-16-62 during an interview in the Robing Room of the Riverside Church in New York City where King had just preached a sermon. King was quoted as stating, "Because FBI Agents have sided with segregationists, they have not investigated beatings and other intimidations of Negroes who are fighting for equality in Albany, Georgia, or surrounding areas." Another statement of King's was, "One of the great problems we face with the FBI in the South is that the Agents are white southerners who have been influenced by the mores of the community." He is also quoted as stating, "Everytime I saw FBI men in Albany, they were with the local police force."

Five Agents in Albany, Georgia:

In connection with Martin Luther King's criticism of the FBI taking sides with the segregationists in Albany, Georgia, and that the Agents are white southerners who have been influenced by the mores of the community it is noted that four of the five Agents were Northerners.

[Section 19]

UNITED STATES GOVERNMENT
Memorandum

TO: W. C. Sullivan   DATE: 11/19/64

FROM: F. J. Baumgardner

SUBJECT: MARTIN LUTHER KING, JR.
           SECURITY MATTER—COMMUNIST

At 1 P.M., 11/19/64, SAC Roney of our New York Office called to furnish information concerning a proposed reply King will make to the Director's statement concerning him which appeared in the 11/19/64 issue of the "Washington Post."

We learned from . . . the following conversation which took place today between Harry Wachtel and Bayard Rustin, advisers to King. Wachtel said he had drafted something he felt King (Dr. Martin Luther King, Jr.) should release. Rustin asked Wachtel if he thought King should make a statement and Wachtel said he should. There is set forth as follows the text of the proposed statement as drawn up by Wachtel.

"I have not seen the exact text of J. Edgar Hoover's press interview in which, among other things, he attacked the Warren Commission report and questioned my integrity. No amount of name-calling or slanders can serve as a smoke screen to hide the signal failure of the FBI to adequately perform its duties whether they elate to the events leading up to the assassination of President Kennedy, protection of Negroes against violence in the South or in the control of the Klu [*sic*] Klux Klan and other extreme rights groups. While I resent the personal attack on my integrity I will not allow Mr. Hoover to blur the real issue, namely, that during a reign of terror and violence in many southern communities, the Negro people received neither aid nor comfort from the FBI. Also immaterial is the place of birth of Federal FBI Agents. What really matters is that the Negroes in southern communities have learned from bitter experience that the FBI did not act in these communities to protect them against brutality and violence. Just as no amount of snide comment can overcome the criticism by the Warren Commission of the FBI's role in the tragic events of last November, neither can Mr. Hoover's outburst erase the dismal record of the FBI in the

South on brutality, bombings, murder and church bombings. The distemper of Mr. Hoover does, however, establish one thing clearly to the American people and that is that he has outlived his usefulness as the head of the FBI or as a public servant. I am confident that this public display of distemper will not go unnoticed by the President.''

Rustin then replied to Wachtel that he liked the statement with two exceptions. One is that Wachtel should drop the part about King being resentful because King is not resentful. Rustin said that the second thing he was against was the conclusion. Rustin said King does not want to inject himself or allow himself to be injected by this incident into something involving the President. Wachtel then asked Rustin if he was against both parts of the last statement, namely, the part about Hoover having outlived his usefulness and the part about the President noticing the distemper. Rustin said he was in favor of taking both parts out. He said that instead they could say ''The question which now confronts us is whether a person of such intemperance can any longer serve as a public servant.'' Rustin said it is strong and also because King is not a person who says this person has to go, etc. Wachtel said he agreed with the charges and said to Rustin that he had written the statement in anger. Wachtel said he would call Dora McDonald, King's secretary, in Atlanta to let King know that we will be together from 2 to 3 P.M. today and that he, King should avoid the press until he speaks to us. Rustin said all King should say is that he will have a statement later on.

OBSERVATION:

As you know, Bayard Rustin has publicly admitted having been associated with the communist movement in the past. Harry Wachtel is not known to have been a Communist Party member; however, there are indications he may also have been associated with the communist movement in the 1940's and we presently are conducting investigation to determine this.

The significant thing involved here is not that these individuals have jumped quickly to King's defense, but rather that they are seizing the opportunity, in line with a long-held communist objective, to launch a campaign to oust the Director as head of the FBI.

The important thing at this point is to follow this matter closely to determine the degree to which King follows their advice in regard to issuing the statement prepared by Wachtel for we will then have further evidence of the extent to which King is being used by communist sympathizers in support of communist objectives.

For the time being, we should hold dissemination of the information in abeyance until we see which way King moves. Then we can put the whole picture together and make appropriate dissemination.

ACTION:

I told SAC Roney to call our Atlanta Office and advise them of this development. I told him to instruct the Atlanta Office to be alert to any additional information which may be developed through their sources and to keep the Bureau advised expeditiously.

[Section 20]

FEDERAL BUREAU OF INVESTIGATION

U. S. DEPARTMENT OF JUSTICE

COMMUNICATIONS SECTION

NOV 19 1964

WESTERN UNION

BIA025 1053A EST NOV 19 64 AB034

A LLM73 PD FAX ATLANTA FA 19 1034A EST

J EDGAR HOOVER

FEDERAL BUREAU OF INVESTIGATION WASHDC

I WAS APPALLED AND SURPRISED AT YOUR REPORTED STATEMENT MALIGNING MY INTEGRITY. WHAT MOTIVATED SUCH AN IRRESPONSIBLE ACCUSATION IS A MYSTERY TO ME. I HAVE SINCERELY QUESTIONED THE EFFECTIVENESS OF THE FEDERAL BUREAU OF INVESTIGATION IN RACIAL INCIDENTS, PARTICULARLY WHERE BOMBINGS AND BRUTALITIES AGAINST NEGROES ARE AT ISSUE, BUT I HAVE NEVER ATTRIBUTED THIS MERELY TO THE PRESENCE OF SOUTHERNERS IN THE FBI. THIS IS A PART OF THE BROADER QUESTION OF FEDERAL INVOLVEMENT IN THE PROTECTION OF NEGROES IN THE SOUTH AND THE SEEMING INABILITY TO GAIN CONVICTIONS IN EVEN THE MOST HENIOUS [sic] CRIMES PERPETUATED AGAINST CIVIL RIGHTS WORKERS. IT REMAINS A FACT THAT NOT A SINGLE ARREST WAS MADE IN ALBANY, GEORGIA, DURING THE MANY BRUTALITIES AGAINST NEGROES. NEITHER HAS A SINGLE ARREST BEEN MADE IN CONNECTION WITH THE TRAGIC MURDER OF THE FOUR CHILDREN IN BIRMINGHAM, NOR IN THE CASE OF THE THREE MURDERED CIVIL RIGHTS WORKERS IN MISSISSIPPI. MOREOVER, ALL FBI AGENTS INEVITABLY WORK WITH

LOCAL LAW ENFORCEMENT OFFICERS IN CAR THEFTS, BANK
ROBBERIES, AND OTHER INTERSTATE VIOLATIONS. THIS
MAKES IT DIFFICULT FOR THEM TO FUNCTION EFFECTIVELY
IN CASES WHERE THE RIGHTS AND SAFETY OF NEGRO CITI-
ZENS ARE BEING THREATENED BY THESE SAME LAW EN-
FORCEMENT OFFICERS. I WILL BE HAPPY TO DISCUSS THIS
QUESTION WITH YOU AT LENGTH IN THE NEAR FUTURE. AL-
THOUGH YOUR STATEMENT SAID THAT YOU HAVE AT-
TEMPTED TO MEET WITH ME I HAVE SOUGHT IN VAIN FOR
ANY RECORD OF SUCH A REQUEST. I HAVE ALWAYS MADE
MYSELF AVAILABLE TO ALL FBI AGENTS OF THE ATLANTA
OFFICE AND ENCOURAGED OUR STAFF AND AFFILIATES TO
COOPERATE WITH THEM IN SPITE OF THE FACT THAT MANY
OF OUR PEOPLE HAVE SUSPICIONS AND DISTRUST OF THE
FBI AS A RESULT OF THE SLOW PACE OF JUSTICE IN THE
SOUTH.

UNITED STATES GOVERNMENT
Memorandum

TO: Mr. Mohr   DATE: 11-20-64

FROM: C. D. DeLoach

SUBJECT: ACTING ATTORNEY GENERAL
         NICHOLAS deB. KATZENBACH
         REMARKS CONCERNING DIRECTOR
         MIAMI, FLORIDA, 11-20-64

At 3:50 P.M. today SAC Frohbose of the Miami Office telephoned
and talked with Mr. Wick. He said Mr. Katzenbach had just finished a
press conference in the United States Attorney's office in the Federal
Building in Miami. Mr. Katzenbach is in Florida to speak before the
University of Miami Law School alumni tomorrow.

At the conference, said Frohbose, were several Federal Judges, other
Federal officials and, of course, TV, radio, wire service and local press
representatives.

At the press conference Mr. Katzenbach was asked if he thought J.
Edgar Hoover should retire after making remarks concerning King. Mr.
Katzenbach answered by stating Mr. Hoover should not retire, that he

has complete confidence in Mr. Hoover and he is one of the great Americans and a devoted public servant. Katzenbach said that he hoped and prayed that Mr. Hoover would stay on.

The press asked what Mr. Katzenbach thought of Mr. Hoover's statement calling King a notorious liar. Katzenbach said he would not add nor detract from Mr. Hoover's statement and he would not comment on it further.

Mr. Katzenbach was asked if Martin Luther King's statement that the FBI is not investigating civil rights matters in the South is true. Mr. Katzenbach said King's statement is not true. He said the FBI has solved many cases and is investigating cases and will continue to investigate civil rights cases wherever they may be. He said the FBI as well as Katzenbach do not want cases to go unsolved.

UNITED STATES GOVERNMENT
Memorandum

TO: Mr. Mohr   DATE: December 1, 1964

FROM: C. D. DeLoach

SUBJECT: MARTIN LUTHER KING
     INFORMATION CONCERNING

An individual who identified himself as Dr. Andrew Young, Executive Assistant to Martin Luther King, called from New York City at 12:05 P.M. today and asked to speak with me.

Dr. Young stated I probably knew what he was calling about. I told him I did if he was calling with reference to Reverend King's request for an appointment with Mr. Hoover. I mentioned that the Acting Attorney General had called this morning about this matter and that I had just advised the Acting Attorney General that Mr. Hoover would see Reverend King at 3:30 P.M. today. Dr. Young stated this would press them a bit, however, he thought they could make it.

Dr. Young stated that Reverend King wanted to talk about law enforcement in the future. He stated they have several programs at Selma, Alabama, and in the Blackbelt County's surrounding Selma. He stated this might be a bad time for Reverend King to be discussing matters; however, they feel that they have been negligent in that they have contacted the Department in the past and have not sat down with the FBI.

Dr. Young stated that Reverend King merely wanted to sit down with Mr. Hoover and discuss matters. He stated that Reverend King did not desire to complain but merely to find out what type of protection the FBI will offer Negro citizens when they attempt to exercise their rights in the future. I interrupted Dr. Young at this point and stated I felt certain that both he and Reverend King fully understood that the FBI did not have the authority or jurisdiction to "protect" anyone and that if Reverend King was seeking a change in policy in this regard he should talk to the Acting Attorney General and not Mr. Hoover. Dr. Young made no reference to this statement but spoke up again and stated that there had been a breach and misunderstanding between Reverend King's organization and the FBI in the past and that this was a matter they did not want to encourage.

Dr. Young assured me that Reverend King did not want to mention anything that has come up in the past. He stated, as a matter of fact, people are harassing them to death and they cannot get any work done in their office because they have to answer questions concerning the FBI. He then added that Reverend King was most anxious and willing to meet with the Director and particularly wanted to do so before he departed for Oslo, Norway.

I interrupted Dr. Young again at this point and told him that it was useless for them to request a "peace meeting" with us as long as the crusade of defamation against Mr. Hoover and the FBI was to be carried on by Reverend King and his organization. Dr. Young stated that he understood this. He stated that actually "they" feel that the FBI had done a very sound investigating job. He added that the current misunderstanding is something that should be cleared up. He then asked me if I knew of any conditions for the meeting. I told him that the only condition desired was that there be an understanding that the campaign of slander and defamation against the Director of the FBI by Reverend King and his organization, behind our backs, be dropped. Dr. Young replied, "yes." He then asked if there would be any objections if he and Reverend Abernathy accompanied Reverend King. I told him there would be none. He asked again the time of the appointment and I told him 3:30 P.M. today. He again stated that this would press them, however, he thought they could make it.

Dr. Young asked me if the FBI planned to make any announcement concerning the meeting. I told him that we would make no announcement at this time. He inquired as to whether Reverend King should make an announcement. I told him this was entirely up to Reverend King.

At 12:25 P.M. today we received a call from the wire services indicating that Bayard Rustin had just announced in New York that Reverend King would meet with the Director at 3:30 P.M. this afternoon. It was quite obvious that this group already had their press release prepared with the exception of the time element.

[Section 21]

December 1, 1964

MARTIN LUTHER KING'S CRITICISM OF THE DIRECTOR AND FBI

CURRENT ATTACK:

On November 19, 1964, Martin Luther King, Jr., sent a telegram from Atlanta to FBI Director J. Edgar HOOVER concerning Mr. Hoover's remarks to the press the previous day. Set forth below is an analysis of this telegram.

King States: He has questioned the FBI's effectiveness but has never attributed this merely to the presence of Southerners in the FBI.

Facts: In November 1962, in discussing racial disturbances in Albany, Georgia, King was widely quoted in the press as stating that one of the greatest problems regarding the FBI in the South is that the Agents are white Southerners who have been influenced by the mores of the community. This is, of course, absolutely false, and it is noted that four of the five Agents then assigned to Albany, Georgia, were Northerners.

King States: Not a single arrest was made in Albany, Georgia, during the many brutalities against Negroes.

Facts: During the summer of 1962, there was a continuing series of mass racial meetings, marches and demonstrations by Negroes in the Albany, Georgia, area. This resulted in numerous multiple arrests of Negroes for lying down in the street, blocking traffic and disorderly conduct. During this period, numerous allegations of civil rights violations

were made to FBI Agents and Department of Justice officials. In every instance the Department of Justice was advised of the complaint and the results of any investigation
conducted. Any additional investigation requested by the
Department was immediately and thoroughly run out and
the results furnished to the Department. The Department
of Justice did not see fit to prosecute any of the incidents
arising out of these demonstrations.

During this same period, however, prosecution was brought against
Denver Edgar Short, Jr.; Deputy Marshal; Sasser, Georgia, which is
about 20 miles from Albany. Short allegedly intimidated voter registration workers on August 30, 1962, and FBI investigation developed that
Short cursed the victims, ordered them out of town and fired his gun
in the direction of their tires. A U.S. District Court petit jury acquitted
Short of civil rights charges on January 25, 1963.

It is also noted that on 9-17-62, FBI Agents arrested four white
subjects in the vicinity of the I Hope Baptist church, a Negro church
near Dawson, Georgia, and about 30 miles from Albany, which had
been burned that day. In the absence of a Federal violation, confessions
obtained by FBI Agents were made available to local authorities resulting in a seven year sentence for each of the three adult subjects and
three years probation for the fourth subject who was a juvenile.

On 1-4-62 FBI Agents arrested Jack Phelix Smith and a detainer was
placed against Douglas Howard Parker, a state prisoner, on civil rights
charges in connection with the burning of the Shady Grove Baptist
Church near Leesburg, Georgia, on 8-15-62. This was a Negro church
approximately 12 miles from Albany. Smith and Parker are white. A
Federal Grand Jury failed to indict, the FBI evidence was made available to state officials who presented the case to a local grand jury which
also returned no bill.

King States: Not a single arrest has been made in connection with the
              bombing in Birmingham or the three murdered civil rights
              workers in Mississippi.

Facts: The Sixteenth Street Baptist Church, Birmingham, Ala-
              bama, was bombed 9-15-63 killing four Negro children.
              The FBI immediately launched the most intensive type
              of investigation which is still vigorously continuing. The
              investigation was prejudiced by premature arrests made by
              the Alabama Highway Patrol, and consequently, it has not
              yet been possible to obtain evidence or confessions that
              would insure successful prosecution although the FBI has

identified a small group of Klansmen believed to be responsible.

The FBI launched a massive investigation following the disappearance of the three civil rights workers in the vicinity of Philadelphia, Mississippi, on June 21, 1964. The FBI located their bodies in an earthen dam and has developed information identifying those responsible. Intensive investigation is continuing to develop the case for prosecution as quickly as possible.

It should be noted that FBI recent investigations in Mississippi have produced the following positive results: (1) Eleven arrests in McComb on state charges involving bombings and other violence. Nine of those arrested have pleaded guilty or nolo contendere and received probationary sentences; (2) Seven arrests in Natchez on state charges involving shooting incidents and a beating; (3) Two subjects arrested on state murder charges 11/6/64 in connection with the killing of Henry Hezekiah Dee and Charlie Eddie Moore; (4) Seven arrests for racial violence by the Sheriff of Pike County who stated this resulted from his success in practicing FBI methods he observed during the FBI's recent investigations; and (5) FBI Agents have arrested five present and former law enforcement officers in Neshoba County on charges of police brutality. They are presently awaiting trial.

King States: FBI Agents work with local officers on criminal cases making it difficult for them to effectively function where Negroes are threatened.

Facts: This is a shopworn canard, the falsity of which is clearly illustrated by the FBI's currently effective cooperation with local officers in Mississippi, FBI's arrest of five officers in Neshoba County, Mississippi, FBI's effective cooperation with local officers in the Georgia church burning investigations, the Penn murder case and many other cases in all parts of the country.

King States: He has no record of a request from the Director to meet with him.

Facts: In November 1962, FBI officials sought to make an appointment with King to straighten him out with regard to his public remarks concerning the FBI's performance in Albany, Georgia. King was never available on the telephone and left instructions with his secretary on 11/28/62 that he would call the FBI when he was willing to arrange an interview. He made no further response.

<u>King States:</u> He has always made himself available to Atlanta FBI
Agents.

<u>Facts:</u>   In July 1961, it was necessary for the FBI to contact King
in connection with a special inquiry investigation for the
Peace Corps. An appointment was made through King's
secretary for his interview 7/22/61; however, King kept
the FBI Agent waiting for one hour past the appointed
time and stated he was behind in his paperwork and had
completed some of it before admitting the Agent.

In June 1962, the FBI made efforts to obtain an appointment with
King in connection with a case involving a Peace Corps applicant.
Beginning on approximately 6/5/62, King's secretary kept stating that
he was not available for interview although it was known to the FBI
that he was in his office daily. On 6/8/62 Wyatt T. Walker, King's
assistant, advised the Atlanta Office that he and King were proceeding
to Shreveport, Louisiana, in connection with the voter registration drive
and that the Little Union Baptist Church in Shreveport had received a
bomb threat. At that time, Walker was informed that FBI Agents had
been urgently trying to make an appointment with King and Walker
stated an appointment would be made. On 6-8-62, King telephoned the
Atlanta Office from Shreveport to inquire as to why the Agent wanted
an appointment and to advise of the bomb threat previously furnished
by Walker. King consented to interview which was conducted 6-9-62.

King was also interviewed by the Atlanta FBI office on 7-24-62 in
connection with racial incidents at Albany, Georgia, involving alleged
violation by King of a temporary restraining order issued by the U.S.
District Court to stop demonstrations. The interview was conducted in
the U.S. courtroom where King had appeared for a hearing.

On 11-30-62, when FBI Headquarters officials were attempting to
arrange an interview with King, the Atlanta FBI office contacted King's
secretary to make such an appointment at King's convenience. The
Agent was advised that King was writing a book and could not be
reached. King's secretary was requested to have King contact the Atlanta Office on an urgent matter but he never made such a contact.

On 6-25-63 the Atlanta FBI Office attempted to contact King to
advise him of a threat against his life. Efforts to contact him were at
first unsuccessful, but after a delay of some hours, King's secretary
informed him of the Bureau's interest in talking to him and arrangements were made for an Agent to contact King by telephone.

In connection with this whole matter, it should be kept in mind that the FBI's function is purely investigative in nature. It is not empowered to offer protection to anyone, at any place, at any time.

PREVIOUS ATTACKS:

Generally, King's previous attacks against the Director and the FBI in the civil rights field have been similar to those outlined above. As an example is the criticism carried in the New York Times of November 19, 1962; in essence King claimed the FBI in Albany, Georgia, sides with the segregationists. He also said the FBI has not done an effective job in investigating beatings of Negroes in Georgia. His remarks were made after giving a sermon at the Riverside Baptist Church in New York City.

December 1, 1964

ORGANIZATION OF THE CURRENT
ATTACK AGAINST THE FBI
BY MARTIN LUTHER KING

On November 19, 1964, the day after the Director's press conference, Martin Luther King, Jr., contacted his secretary, Dora McDonald, at the Atlanta, Georgia, office of the Southern Christian Leadership Conference (SCLC), according to a reliable source. She told him his telegram to Mr. Hoover regarding the Director's criticism of King was going out to the press. King stated he wanted to issue a statesmanlike "covering statement" in connection with the telegram.

King declared the nature of the follow-up statement would be that he cannot conceive of Mr. Hoover's labeling King a liar unless he (Mr. Hoover) was under extreme pressure and apparently had faltered under the tremendous burdens, complexities and responsibilities of his office. King said he would state he cannot become involved in a public debate with Mr. Hoover and that he has nothing but sympathy for the Director who has served his country so well. King told his secretary the telegram and the statement will be the only comment he will personally issue in this matter. He told her, Mr. Hoover should retire because he is "too old and broken down."

King instructed his secretary to have Randolph T. Blackwell, Program Coordinator of SCLC, go over the press release and telegram. He stated the release should be given to those who are "for us," naming Catherine Johnson of Associated Press or United Press International, one Don McKee, and Ted Poston of the "New York Post."

King later talked to his aide, Bernard Lee, the source advised, and told Lee to be sure all Negro news media get the release. He told Lee to call "Jet" magazine, a Negro publication, and to give a copy of the release to one John Herbert in New York. Lee told King, in answer to a question as to what was wrong with Mr. Hoover, that he thought the Director was getting old and is a "scared cow."

King directed Lee to have Bayard Rustin in New York and Walter Fauntroy, SCLC representative in Washington, D.C., contacted and told to start criticism of the FBI in those areas. He said he already had started in Miami, Florida. He instructed that Slater King, a civil rights leader in Albany, Georgia, should be contacted since he would welcome an opportunity to make a statement against the FBI and the Director. Blackwell did this later that day. King declared people in the western states who are SCLC members must be contacted to have them begin the attack against the FBI. King told Lee that telegrams to Mr. Hoover should also be sent to the President.

King declared that Blackwell and Cordy T. Vivian, director of Affiliates of SCLC, should handle the attack on the FBI so it would not appear that King was fighting the Director over a personal matter. He said the President should censure Mr. Hoover and it would be a good idea for all telegrams to the President to request this.

On the same date, according to the source, King told Vivian this is the time to attack the whole FBI. He declared that he cannot be the one who does it, stating "we" need people in the South to make statements about the laxity of investigations and law enforcement, especially concerning civil rights. People in the North are needed to protest Mr. Hoover's charge against King. King suggested telegrams be sent to the President urging Mr. Hoover be censured and urging he be retired because "he is old and getting senile."

The source reported Vivian suggested the attack be based on Mr. Hoover's ineffectiveness in civil rights; that he is past retirement age and would have been out last year except for certain people asking that he stay on. King disagreed, asserting he wanted Mr. Hoover "Hit from all sides."

Later on November 19, 1964, the source related that Wyatt Walker, a former SCLC executive now employed by a firm in New York City, contacted Vivian. He was told by Vivian to "get things going" in New York. Vivian told Walker to handle the east coast and said Tom Kilgore, an official of the Western Christian Leadership Conference in Los

Angeles, California, was to handle the west coast. Vivian instructed Walker to get telegrams sent to the President, Department of Justice and the FBI demanding that Mr. Hoover apologize to King.

Vivian told Walker that this is an opportunity to mount an attack against police brutality. He said the FBI will try to defend itself with the statement that it is an investigative agency and that people making the protests should know what to expect from the FBI. Vivian later contacted Kilgore and give him similar instructions.

According to a highly confidential Atlanta informant, one Reverend Hodge, location unknown, contacted Vivian and wanted methods SCLC was using against Hoover. Vivian advised SCLC files failed to indicate Hoover ever tried to contact King. Vivian gave Hodge the following points to get across concerning Hoover and the FBI:

(1) FBI has been ineffective in that no persons have been brought to trial (In Albany only Negroes went to jail.);

(2) FBI is only investigative arm which Vivian claims is ridiculous in that investigations have not been good enough for convictions and reports are available only to FBI and Department of Justice. (For example, one of SCLC staff members was shot at Greenville along with two other people and nothing was done about it.);

(3) Hoover never tried to get in contact with King to verify statement;

(4) King did not tell people to contact FBI;

(5) FBI has jurisdiction whenever civil liberties have been violated. Vivian claimed Director had no evidence to support Director's statements against King. Vivian further claimed King does not want to debate the Director but it is their job as subordinates to handle the criticism against Hoover and the FBI. Vivian claims the Director's statement concerning pressure groups is vague and full of generalities and Hoover is more interested in John Birch Society, Minutemen and Ku Klux Klan but will not attack them. Vivian claimed ''we'' had statements sent from all civil rights leaders to the President from James Farmer of CORE, Wilkins of NAACP and Jack Greenberg of African Union.

The source continued that Vivian claimed the main points to drive home are that the investigations and reports of the FBI can only be seen by Justice Department and he feels reports are inadequate.

Identities of Individuals Mentioned:

Randolph T. Blackwell, according to a confidential source in 1953, had been a member of the Communist Party (CP) in the District of Columbia, and another source indicated Blackwell attended a Labor Youth League (cited by the Department of Justice) Convention.

A confidential source advised in November 1947, that Cordy T. Vivian was a member of the CP in Peoria, Illinois, and had been active in CP affairs for some time.

Bayard Rustin, in July 1964, issues of "The Saturday Evening Post" was said to have gone to New York in 1938 as an organizer for the Young Communist League and as such had the job of "recruiting students for the Party." He reportedly left the Party in 1941.

ATTEMPTS TO CONTACT MARTIN LUTHER KING

On November 19, 1962, the "New York Times" quoted King to the effect that the FBI had not done an effective job in Albany, Georgia, and one of the greatest problems with the Bureau in the South was that the Agents were white Southerners. (Actually, four of the five Agents assigned to Albany, Georgia, were Northern born.) With regard to this matter, it was approved that Assistant Directors Sullivan and DeLoach make an appointment with King to straighten him out concerning the unfounded criticism he reportedly had made.

On November 20, 1962, Mr. DeLoach attempted to reach King by telephone to arrange an interview. The Atlanta operator advised that there was no telephone at the residence usually occupied by King. Then the operator tried to reach King at the Ebenezer Baptist Church in Atlanta; however, an individual there stated that King was away on two weeks' vacation and could not be reached. Upon being asked if King was near a telephone, this person replied affirmatively but stated King did not wish to be disturbed.

Mr. DeLoach then called the Atlanta Office and instructed ASAC F. V. Hitt (now on inspection staff) to telephonically locate King and tell him (1) that Messrs. DeLoach and Sullivan wanted to sit down with him any time he was in the Washington or New York area; and (2) that the desired conversation did not involve an investigation of King but stemmed from a desire to talk to King.

The Atlanta Office then succeeded in contacting King's secretary on November 30, 1962, and was advised that King was at a "hideaway" writing a book and could not be reached during the week of November 30th. The secretary further advised that the following week King would be traveling in Alabama. The secretary was requested to have King contact the Atlanta Office with regard to an urgent matter; however, King never made his contact. (By letter dated November 20, 1964, SA ... has remarked that when he attempted to contact King to make an appointment request by Mr. DeLoach, King and his staff completely

ignored the FBI even though they were told the request to talk to him
was a matter of utmost urgency.)

OTHER DIFFICULTIES OF ATLANTA OFFICE IN
CONTACTING KING

On about July 18 to July 20, 1961, attempts were made to make an
appointment with King to interview him in connection with the special
inquiry investigation of Theodore Edward Brown for the Peace Corps.
On July 19th or July 20th, King's secretary stated that "Dr. King can
see you on Saturday afternoon but you don't work Saturdays, do you?"
His secretary was advised that the Agent would be at King's office any
time King would be available. A definite appointment was made for 2
P.M. Saturday afternoon, July 22, 1961. The Agent appeared at King's
office at approximately 1:50 P.M., where he waited for an hour before
being admitted to King's office. King stated he was sorry to keep the
Agent waiting but he was behind in his paperwork and had completed
some of it before admitting the Agent.

In June 1962, efforts were made to obtain an appointment with King
in connection with a case involving Shirley Blackwell Cummings, a
Peace Corps applicant. Beginning on approximately June 5, 1962,
King's secretary kept stating that he was not available for interview
although it was known to us that he was in his office daily. On June
8, 1962, Wyatt T. Walker, King's assistant, advised the Atlanta Office
that he and King were proceeding to Shreveport, Louisiana, in connection with the voter registration drive and that the Little Union Baptist
Church in Shreveport had received a bomb threat. At that time, Walker
was informed that Agents had been urgently trying to make an appointment with King, and Walker stated an appointment would be made. On
June 8, 1962, King telephoned the Atlanta Office from Shreveport to
inquire as to why the Agent wanted an appointment and to advise of
the bomb threat previously furnished by Walker. King consented to
interview which was conducted on June 9, 1962.

After being unable to contact King on July 23, 1962, the Atlanta
Office interviewed him the next day in connection with racial incidents
in Albany, Georgia, involving alleged violation by King of a temporary
restraining order issued by the U. S. District Court to stop demonstrations. The interview was conducted in the U. S. courtroom where King
had appeared for a hearing.

On June 25, 1963, the Atlanta office attempted to contact King to
advise him of a threat against his life. Efforts to contact him were at

first unsuccessful, but after a delay of some hours, King's secretary informed him of the Bureau's interest in talking to him and arrangements were made for an Agent to contact King by telephone. (It will be recalled that in connection with other threats against King's life, the Jackson Office was instructed in July 1964, to provide coverage during King's visit to Mississippi. They performed this assignment in line with a request from the President; and, interestingly, Sheriff Lawrence A. Rainey of Neshoba County, Mississippi, wrote to the Director on July 28th to inquire about the authority by which FBI Agents furnished protection to King during King's visit to Philadelphia, Mississippi, on July 24, 1964. The Bureau recommended that Rainey's letter not be answered, after a copy of it had been received by the White House and subsequently to our attention.)

FBI ACCOMPLISHMENTS IN THE CIVIL RIGHTS FIELD

Every civil rights complaint is given thorough, prompt and impartial attention. Special Agents handling these cases are highly trained investigators who have completed advanced training courses which qualify them to conduct civil rights investigations. At Bureau Headquarters, a select staff of men with great experience and knowledge of this type of investigation supervise the cases.

The duty of maintaining law and order in civil rights demonstrations, preserving the peace and protecting life and property is the primary responsibility of local and state law enforcement agencies. The FBI is solely an investigative agency as distinguished from a police agency, and as such, is without authority to maintain the peace or furnish protection. It is the duty of the FBI, however, to furnish factual data to the Department of Justice so that a determination can be made as to whether there is any basis for Federal action under the civil rights statute.

Our work in the field of civil rights is increasing. In fiscal year 1960, the FBI handled 1,398 civil rights cases. In fiscal year 1963, the number of cases jumped to 2,692 and in fiscal year 1964, it increased to 3,340.

Although a substantial number of arrests and convictions have resulted from our investigations in these matters, the effectiveness of our work in this field can never be precisely assayed on the basis of such statistics. Perhaps the greatest value of our work in this field lies in the results of our intelligence and liaison programs which can never be traced to direct prosecutive action. We continuously gather information on a day-to-day basis which indicates that some violent action is either being definitely planned or that a situation will occur which has a high potential for violence.*

The fact that we vigorously investigate civil rights violations undoubtedly serves as a deterrent to discourage violations on the part of law enforcement officers and spurs these officers to immediately and vigorously investigate civil rights situations that otherwise might be ignored.

Liaison with Governors and ranking state officials has also been effective. Also, although we may not have jurisdiction in a particular case the cooperative facilities of the FBI Laboratory and Identification Division are made available.

It is also noted that on July 10, 1964, the Director traveled to Jackson, Mississippi, to open a new FBI office in that city. With this office, we feel we can more efficiently and effectively meet our growing responsibilities.

There follows thumbnail sketches of some of the FBI's more recent specific accomplishments in the civil rights field.

Racial Discrimination and Intimidation of Voters

Under the Civil Rights Acts of 1957 and 1960, the Attorney General was empowered to institute civil actions seeking injunctive relief against racial discrimination and intimidation in voting. We have conducted investigations under these in 168 counties in six southern states. As a result, 67 suits have been filed in the States of Alabama, Florida, Georgia, Louisiana, Mississippi and South Carolina. As a result of suits filed based on our investigations into discrimination in voting, thousands of previously disenfranchised Negro citizens have been enabled to register for voting.

Assaults Upon Voter Registration Workers in Mississippi

Rabbi Arthur Joseph Lelyveld and two other white voter registration workers were assaulted by two white men in Hattiesburg, Mississippi, on June 10, 1964. Local authorities were furnished with the results of our investigation which identified two local white men who perpetrated the assault. The subjects were prosecuted on charges of assault and battery, fined $500 each and each was sentenced to 90 days in jail. The jail sentences were suspended pending good behavior.

---

*Such information is immediately disseminated to appropriate authorities.

Two white civil rights workers accompanied by a young Negro were assaulted in Jackson, Mississippi, on July 22, 1964. FBI investigation identified a local Klansman as having struck one of the victims with a club. Results of our investigation were furnished to local authorities. The subject pleaded guilty to local assault charges and was fined $50.

Three voter registration workers were intimidated and one was assaulted at Itta Bena, Mississippi, on June 25, 1964. FBI Agents arrested three local white men on June 26, 1964, for violation of Federal Civil Rights Statutes. A Federal Grand Jury at Oxford, Mississippi, considered this case on July 17, 1964, but failed to indict although the intimidation and the identities of the subjects were clearly established.

Civil Rights Act of 1964

The Civil Rights Act of 1964 added tremendously to the work of the FBI. Approximately 1,800 reports and memoranda concerning alleged violations have been prepared by FBI Agents since the Act became effective on July 2, 1964.

Based on extensive FBI investigations, a three-judge Federal Court in Atlanta, Georgia, found the Act Constitutional and enjoined the Pickrick Restaurant and the Heart of Atlanta Motel from racial discrimination. The Heart of Atlanta Motel case has been heard by the Supreme Court and a decision is expected momentarily. Another case which has been heard by the Supreme Court involves a restaurant in Birmingham (Ollie McClung Case) which case was heard by a three-judge Federal Court and the Act was ruled unconstitutional, regarding this specific restaurant. A decision is expected momentarily on this case also and on the decision of this case and the Heart of Atlanta Motel Case rests the fate of the effect of the Civil Rights Act. Based on FBI investigations, suits have been filed against restaurants and motels in Florida and numerous restaurants in Alabama that discriminate. Additional court actions are anticipated in South Carolina, Georgia and Alabama. A federal suit now pending seeks to restrain the Mayor of Greenwood, Mississippi, and other public officials from interfering with the right of Negroes to attend a theater and for failing to provide adequate police protection in the operation of a theater.

On July 23, 1964, three white men, Willie Amon Belk, his son, Jimmy Allen Belk, and Sam Allen Shaffer, Jr., were arrested by FBI Agents at Greenwood, Mississippi, on charges of conspiracy to violate the Civil Rights Act of 1964. The arrests followed a thorough, intensive and immediate investigation concerning the beating of Silas McGhee, which occurred on July 16, 1964. The facts in this matter will be presented to a Federal Grand Jury in January 1965.

School Integration Matters

During August and September 1964, the FBI investigated desegregation of public schools in 18 possible trouble spots in southern states. In connection with these investigations, we determined plans or activities of Klan and other hate groups which might have interfered with desegregation or resulted in acts of violence, and this information was disseminated to local authorities.

Three Civil Rights Workers Murdered

The FBI conducted an all-out investigation concerning the disappearance of Michael Schwerner and two other civil rights workers in the vicinity of Philadelphia, Mississippi, on June 21, 1964. The victims' burned-out automobile was located by FBI Agents on June 23, 1964, and the bodies of the three murdered victims were found in an earthen dam on August 4, 1964. Arising out of this investigation the FBI established other civil rights violations and on October 2, 1964, a special Federal Grand Jury returned indictments against Sheriff Lawrence Andrew Rainey and three other local law enforcement officers and a former sheriff of Neshoba County, Mississippi. All five subjects were arrested by FBI Agents and are awaiting trial on police brutality charges not connected with the murders. While the FBI is certain as to the identities of the subjects responsible for the murders of the three civil rights workers, intensive investigation is being conducted to develop suitable evidence. Today (12-1-64) representatives of our Civil Rights Section are discussing with Assistant Attorney General Marshall possibilities of prosecution of the subjects regarding the murders.

Murder of Lieutenant Colonel Lemuel A. Penn

On 7-11-64 Lieutenant Colonel Lemuel A. Penn was murdered near Colbert, Georgia. FBI investigation resulted in the arrest of four subjects by FBI Agents on 8-6-64. Complete details of FBI investigation were made available to the State for prosecution of the subjects on murder charges. Two of the subjects were acquitted in local court on 9-4-64; a third subject has not yet been tried in local court but is still under indictment for murder and the local case against the fourth subject has been dismissed.

On 10-16-64 indictments were returned by the Federal Grand Jury at Athens, Georgia, charging six men with conspiracy to injure, oppress, threaten and intimidate Negro citizens in the free exercise and enjoyment of rights and privileges secured to them by the Constitution. These individuals were Denver Willis Phillips, George Hampton Turner, Herbert Guest, Cecil William Myers, Joseph Howard Sims and James S. Lackey. Guest, Lackey, Myers and Sims were the four men arrested by the FBI in connection with the murder of Penn. A second indictment on 10-16-64 charges Guest with possession of a shotgun having an over-all length of less than 26 inches which had not been registered by Guest with the Secretary of Treasury or his delegate. All except Lackey were 11-30-64 on a Federal indictment—pleas of not guilty rendered to the charges. Trial is set for 1-11-65.

Bombing of Home of Iona Godfrey

FBI investigation established that William Sterling Rosecrans, Jr., a 30-year-old Klansman, had participated in the home bombing of Iona Godfrey, a Negro in Jacksonville, Florida, on 2-16-64. Godfrey's six-year-old son was attending a white school under a Federal Court Order. Rosecrans pleaded guilty to obstructing a court order and was sentenced on 4-17-64 to seven years by the U. S. District Court. Five other Klansmen, who allegedly were involved in the bombing, were also arrested by FBI Agents, but one of these subjects was acquitted in U. S. District Court and the jury was unable to reach a verdict regarding the other four. Retrial of latter four began November 16, 1964, and resulted in acquittal of all four on 11-25-64.

Bombings in McComb, Mississippi

Intensive FBI investigation was conducted in connection with a series of bombings in the McComb, Mississippi, area from June to September 1964. Through the diligent efforts of the FBI and the Mississippi Highway Patrol, nine white men were tried by Circuit Court Judge W. H. Watkins at Magnolia, Mississippi, in connection with charges that they were involved in bombings of homes and churches at McComb. The nine entered pleas of guilty and nolo contendere. After a 30-minute lecture Judge Watkins suspended their sentences and placed all on probation. Judge Watkins, who was appointed by former Mississippi Governor Ross R. Barnett, cited the defendants' youth and good families in taking this action. He stated also that in committing these crimes they had been "unduly provoked and undoubtedly ill advised." It may be noted that four of the bombers were aged 44, 38, 36, and 35.

Murder of Two Negroes

Two Mississippi white men were arrested 11-6-64 in connection with the murder of Henry Hezekiah Dee and Charlie Eddie Moore, two Negroes from the Meadville, Mississippi, area. The lower portions of the bodies of these two Negroes were found in the Old River backwater of the Mississippi River on 7-12 and 13, 1964. The white men, James Ford Seale, aged 29, and Charles Marcus Edwards, aged 31, were charged under warrants issued by Meadville Justice of the Peace Willie Bedford, with willfully, unlawfully, feloniously and with malice aforethought killing the Two Negroes on or about 5-2-64. Dee and Moore were last seen alive on 5-2-64. One of the subjects, Edwards, is a self-admitted Klansman.

Murder of Medgar Evers

In connection with the murder of Medgar Evers; a field secretary of the National Association for the Advancement of Colored People on 6-12-63, Byron de la Beckwith is under state indictment. Local prosecution is based upon an investigation which traced a rifle which local authorities believe could have been the murder weapon to Beckwith. The FBI traced the rifle's telescopic sight to Beckwith and, further, identified a fingerprint found on the sight with Beckwith's. He was tried twice (2-7-64 and 4-17-64) in State court, but jury could not reach verdict in either case. Local district attorney has indicated he will not try Beckwith again without new evidence.

Plot to Dynamite Building Occupied by Civil Rights Organization

The combined efforts of FBI Agents and the Mississippi Highway Safety Patrol resulted in the arrest of James Rutledge at Meridian, Mississippi, on 10-8-64 on State charges of feloniously possessing explosives. Rutledge was in possession of a large quantity of dynamite and literature of the Ku Klux Klan at the time of his arrest. The arrest resulted from information developed by the FBI which indicated the dynamite was to be used to damage a building occupied in the Neshoba County, Mississippi, area, by the Council of Federated Organizations.

The FBI immediately instituted an investigation following a recent explosion adjacent to the Bishop Denis J. O'Connell High School in Arlington, Virginia. The FBI obtained confessions implicating three former students in the bombing and on 10-29-64, the three appeared before an Arlington County Juvenile Judge. Two of the youths who were aged 17 were found guilty of a misdemeanor and the third youth, aged 18, was found guilty of contributing to the delinquency of a minor. The three subjects are awaiting sentence. The subjects were prosecuted locally as there was no Federal violation.

On June 20, 1964, indictments were returned by the Federal Grand Jury in Nashville, Tennessee, against seven officers of the Nashville-Davidson County Sheriff's Office and the Rutherford County Sheriff's Office. The indictments charged police brutality in violation of a Federal civil rights statute and the officers are presently awaiting trial in U. S. District Court, Nashville, Tennessee.

UNITED STATES GOVERNMENT
Memorandum

TO: Mr. Mohr   DATE: December 1, 1964

FROM: C. D. DeLoach

SUBJECT: MARTIN LUTHER KING

Following is a transcript of the brief statement which Reverend Martin Luther King made to newsmen immediately after leaving the Director's Office this afternoon. While this is not a verbatim account of the statement, it is as near accurate as possible:

I am pleased I had the opportunity to meet with Mr. Hoover this afternoon and I might say the discussion was quite amicable. I sought to make it clear to Mr. Hoover that the plight of Negroes in the South is such that there must not be any misunderstanding between the FBI and civil rights leaders but must be a determination to defend the rights of all.

We talked specifically about those areas where SCLC will be working in the months ahead. We discussed areas where there will be strong resistance to the implementation of the civil rights bill. We made it clear that we found our most difficult problems in Alabama and Mississippi and in these communities there are areas where we see a great deal of potential and sometimes actual terror.

I sincerely hope we can forget the confusion of the past and get on with the job the Congress, the Supreme Court and the President have outlined as America's most crucial problem; namely, the job of giving and providing security and justice to all the people in the world.

NBC's Russ Ward and one of the NBC men equipped with a tape

recorder followed King down the hall and on through the courtyard where his car was parked. According to the NBC technician, King was talking with them all the time. He said that King expressed "the usual pratter" [*sic*] and the only statement of any consequence was something to the effect that arrests in the Mississippi murder case could be expected within the next few days.

The Director next spoke of civil rights violations. He told the reporters he wanted to dispel a number of myths concerning FBI jurisdiction and the assignment of personnel in such cases. He stated it was a common belief in some circles that Special Agents in the South were all, without exception, southern-born Agents. As a matter of fact, 70% of the Agents currently assigned to the South were born in the North. He stated that the "notorious" Martin Luther King had attempted to capitalize on this matter by claiming that all Agents assigned to the Albany, Georgia, Resident Agency, were southern-born Agents. As a matter of fact, 4 out of 5 of the Agents assigned to the Albany, Georgia, Resident Agency were northern born. The Director stated he had instructed me to get in touch with the Reverend King and line up an appointment so that King could be given the true facts. He stated that King had refused to give me an appointment and, therefore, he considered King to be the most "notorious liar" in the country.

The Director stated he wanted to make it clear that the FBI is not a "police agency." We do not guard anyone; we are "fact finders"; the FBI cannot "wet nurse" anyone. The Director explained that the FBI has had remarkable success in civil rights cases, although, to hear Martin Luther King talk, the FBI has done nothing. The Director stated that we have been able to penetrate the Ku Klux Klan and that as a result we know what the Klan is doing currently and what they plan to do in the future. He added that in the case of the 3 murdered civil rights victims in Mississippi he had instructed that FBI Agents interview all members of the Ku Klux Klan to put them on notice that the FBI was going to thoroughly investigate violations of the law. He added that Governor Johnson of Mississippi had fired 5 or 6 officers who had been members of the Klan. The next question asked for Mr. Hoover to give them more details about Martin Luther King. He stated, off the record, "He is one of the lowest characters in the country." There was an immediate inquiry as to whether he could be quoted on the original statement that Martin Luther King was a liar and he stated, "Yes—that is public record."

UNITED STATES GOVERNMENT
Memorandum

TO: Mr. Mohr   DATE: December 1, 1964

FROM: C. D. DeLoach

SUBJECT: ...

           ...

           APPOINTMENT—FBI HEADQUARTERS

           . . .

At his request, I met with . . .

Upon seeing . . . , I told him I was glad to have the opportunity to get together with him despite the unfair criticism that he and Reverend King had launched against the Director and the FBI during the past several days. I told him I wanted to straighten him out on such criticism. . . . laughed and replied that he personally had not been guilty of any serious criticism against the FBI and that he hoped that I would understand that he wanted to continue to be friends rather than enemies.

. . . told me that he had heard from a number of newsmen that the FBI planned to expose Reverend King . . . and prevent this action being taken if at all possible. He stated he knew that King had made a sudden decision to come down also and that he hope that King's meeting with the Director had been an amiable one. I told him that it had been.

I told . . . that we, of course, had no plan whatsoever to expose Reverend King. I told him that our files were sacred to us and that it would be unheard of for the FBI to leak such information to newsmen. I told him I was completely appalled at the very thought of the FBI engaging in such endeavors. I told . . . the FBI had received rumors of this nature from a number of sources and that we felt that there obviously was some substance to these rumors. I mentioned . . . that undoubtedly King has numerous enemies and that most certainly someone had apparently done quite a job on King.

. . . told me that he was glad to hear that the FBI did not plan to expose King. He stated this had a number of civil rights leaders quite worried inasmuch as if King were exposed this would possibly ruin the entire civil rights movement. I again repeated that we had never entertained the idea to expose Reverend King; however, I wanted . . . to definitely know the campaign of slander and vilification against the Director and the FBI should stop without any delay. I told him that if this war continued that we, out of necessity, must defend ourselves. I mentioned that I hoped it would not be necessary for the FBI to adopt defensive tactics. ... got the point without any difficulty whatsoever. He immediately assured me that there would be no further criticism from him. He stated he felt certain there would be no further criticism from King.

... told me that he was greatly relieved to have this conversation. ...

I reiterated ... once again that our door was always open for discussion but that he should definitely keep in mind that if this group wants war they could certainly find it fast. He stated that he wanted to part as friends and that he hoped that we could continue the pleasant relationship that we started over two years ago in New York City in our various discussions. I assured him that this would be possible as long as the unfair criticism did cease.

ACTION:

For record purposes.

UNITED STATES GOVERNMENT

Memorandum

TO: Mr. Mohr   DATE: December 2, 1964

FROM: C. D. DeLoach

SUBJECT: MARTIN LUTHER KING
APPOINTMENT WITH DIRECTOR
3:35 P.M., 12-1-64

At Reverend King's request, the Director met with King; Reverend Ralph Abernathy, Secretary of the Southern Christian Leadership Conference (SCLC); Dr. Andrew Young, Executive Assistant to King; and Walter Fauntroy, SCLC representative here in Washington, at 3:35 P.M., 12-1-64, in the Director's Office.

I met King and his associates in the hallway outside the Director's office. An attempt was made to rush directly through the reception room, however, King slowly posed for the cameras and newsmen before proceeding.

Upon being introduced to the Director, Reverend King indicated his appreciation for Mr. Hoover's seeing him then stated that Reverend Abernathy would speak first. Reverend Abernathy told the Director it was a great privilege to meet the distinguished Director of the FBI—a man who had done so much for his country. Reverend Abernathy expressed the appreciation of the Negro race for the Director's fine work in the field of civil rights. He stated that the Negroes had problems, particularly in the South, and, therefore, had requested a discussion with the Director at the very time their people were continuing to "raise up from their bondage."

Reverend King spoke up. He stated it was vitally necessary to keep a working relationship with the FBI. He wanted to clear up any misunderstanding which might have occurred. He stated that some Negroes had told him that the FBI had been ineffective, however, he was inclined to discount such criticism. Reverend King asked that the Director please understand that any criticism of the Director and the FBI which had been attributed to King was either misquote or an outright misrepresentation. He stated this particularly concerned Albany, Georgia. He stated that the only time he had ever criticized the FBI was because of instances in which Special Agents who had been given complaints in civil rights cases regarding brutality by police officers were seen the following day being friendly with those same police officers. King stated this, of course, promoted distrust inasmuch as the police sometimes "brutalized" Negroes.

Reverend King stated he personally appreciated the great work of the FBI which had been done in so many instances. He stated this was particularly true in Mississippi. He added that FBI developments in that state have been very significant. The FBI is a great restraining influence. Reverend King denied that he had ever stated that Negroes should not report information to the FBI. He said he had actually encouraged such reporting in many instances. He claimed there were good relationships in many communities, especially Atlanta, Georgia, between Negroes and the FBI. He stated he would continue to strongly urge all of his people to work closely with the FBI.

Reverend King stated he has never made any personal attack upon Mr. Hoover. He stated he had merely tried to articulate the feelings of the Negroes in the South in order to keep a tradition of nonviolence. He added that the Negro should never be transferred from a policy of nonviolence to one of violence and terror.

Reverend King said that the Director's report to the President this summer on rioting was a very excellent analysis.

Reverend King advised that Negroes are currently laboring under a very frustrating situation. He stated that, "We sometimes are on the verge of temporary despair." He added that it was a challenge and a duty for him to keep the Negro from coming to a boiling point. He stated that sometimes the cries coming from the Negro represent a real feeling of lonesomeness and despair. He, however, has pointed out that the path to success is nonviolence rather than violence.

Reverend King stated he has been, and still is, very concerned regarding the matter of communism in the civil rights movement. He stated he knew that the Director was very concerned because he bore the responsibility of security in the nation. Reverend King stated that from a strong philosophical point of view he could never become a communist inasmuch as he recognizes this to be a crippling totalitarian disease. He stated that as a Christian he could never accept communism. He claimed that when he learns of the identity of a communist in his midst he immediately deals with the problem by removing this man. He stated there have been one or two communists who were engaged in fundraising for the SCLC. Reverend King then corrected himself to say that these one or two men were former communists and not Party members at the present time. He then identified ''Jack O'Dell'' as an example. He stated that he has insisted that O'Dell leave his staff because the success of his organization, the Southern Christian Leadership Conference, was far more important than friendship with O'Dell.

The Director interrupted King to state that the FBI had learned from long experience that the communists move in when trouble starts. The Director explained that communists thrive on chaos. The Director mentioned that his riot report to the President reflected the opportunistic efforts of communists. He then stated that communists have no interest in the future of the Negro race and that King, of all people, should be aware of this fact. The Director spoke briefly of communist attempts to infiltrate the labor movement.

The Director told King and his associates that the FBI shares the same despair which the Negroes suffer when Negro leaders refused to accept the deep responsibility they have in the civil rights movement. He stated that when Negroes are encouraged not to cooperate with the FBI this sometimes frustrates or delays successful solution of investigations. The Director told King that he had personally gone to Mississippi to meet with Governor Paul Johnson inasmuch as there had been practically no liaison between the Department of Justice, the President and the State of Mississippi beforehand. The Director stated that upon meeting Governor Johnson the Governor explained honestly that he was a segregationist, however [sic] abhorred violence. The Director stated that he had told Governor Johnson they had a common meeting ground inasmuch as he was in Mississippi to put an end to violence and brutality. The Director told Governor Johnson that he would like to do this in collaboration with the State Police, however, if the FBI could not receive such cooperation we would do it on our own. The Director then made reference to water moccasins, rattlesnakes and redneck sheriffs, in that order, who still exist in Mississippi who represent the trashy type of characters who are promoting civil rights violations. The Director told King that he had trained twenty representatives of the Mississippi State Highway Patrol and that this had represented a good move to promote better cooperation and solution of civil rights cases.

The Director told Reverend King that the FBI had put the "fear of God" in the Ku Klux Klan (KKK). He told King that we knew of the identity of the murderers of the three civil rights workers and that these murderers would soon be brought to trial. The Director then spoke of the terror in Mississippi backwoods and of the fact that sheriffs and deputy sheriffs participate in crimes of violence. He summarized by telling King that we, therefore, are under the same strain that sincere Negro leaders are under. The Director added that the KKK constantly damns the FBI and that we have currently been classified as the "Federal Bureau of Integration" in Mississippi.

The Director told King that many cases, which have been brought about as a result of FBI investigation, must be tried in State Court. He spoke of the difficulty in obtaining a verdict of guilty in instances in which white juries are impaneled in cases involving white men. The Director spoke of the KKK involvement in the Lemuel Penn case just outside of Athens, Georgia. He stated this was an outrageous miscarriage of justice in that the defendants, despite the open and shut evidence on the part of the FBI, had been acquitted.

The Director made it clear to Reverend King and his associates that the FBI could not state whether a conviction would be obtained or not in the case involving the murdered three civil rights victims. He stated, however, that the FBI has excellent evidence in this case. The Director then explained that it was most necessary for the FBI not to "jump the gun" unless we had sufficient evidence in which a case could be brought to trial.

The Director made reference to Reverend King's allegation that the FBI deals or associates with law enforcement officers who have been involved in civil rights violations. He stated emphatically that, "I'll be damned if the FBI has associated with any of these people nor will we be associated with them in the future." The Director explained that the FBI, not only because of the very nature of the law but also because of the background of our investigative employees, was in full sympathy with the sincere aspects of the civil rights movement. He stated that the FBI constantly needs cooperation and assistance in order to solve cases. He added that he made it a point, several years ago, to transfer northern Special Agents to southern offices. He stated that, for the most part, northern-born Agents are assigned civil rights cases in the South. The Director added that he feels that our Special Agents, regardless of where they are born, will investigate a case impartially and thoroughly. He mentioned, however, that it was unfair to the Agent and the FBI to "have a strike against him" in that criticism had been leveled over the fact that southern Agents would not give Negroes a "fair shake." The Director stated that such criticism was entirely unjustifiable and that no case had ever been brought to our attention proving such a fact.

The Director made reference to the recent case in McComb, Mississippi, in which nine men had been charged with burning churches and violence against Negroes. He stated this again was a miscarriage of justice. He added that the judge's decision in releasing the defendants because they had learned their lesson and were entirely wrong and that it caused some people to question where the youth really began. He explained that some of the defendants had been in their 40's. The Director added that a deal probably, of course, had been made, however, this would certainly not represent any deterrent to future actions of violence by these men.

The Director explained that there is a great misunderstanding today among the general public and particularly the Negro race as to what the FBI can and cannot do in the way of investigations. The Director emphasized that the FBI cannot recommend prosecution or declination of prosecution. He stated that Agents cannot make "on the spot" arrests. He stated that the FBI merely investigates and then the Department of Justice determines whether prosecution be entertained or not. The Director added that the question is sometimes raised why prosecution is not scheduled sooner. He stated this, of course, was not the responsibility of the FBI in any way whatsoever. He pointed out that our civil rights investigations are conducted in a very thorough and expeditious manner once the Department has authorized such investigations.

The Director spoke of the FBI's successful penetration of the KKK. He stated that the FBI has interviewed all members of the KKK in Mississippi and has served notice to these members that if trouble occurs we plan to come to them first. He stated our penetration of the KKK has been successful as the manner in which we infiltrated the communists and the Soviet espionage services. He stated that our progress in infiltrating the KKK has been so rapid that Klan members now suspect each other and are fighting among themselves. The Director mentioned that we have two confessions in the killing of the three civil rights workers. He added that the Klan in Mississippi has failed to meet for some time because the members of this organization are apprehensive as to the identity of FBI informants in their midst. The Director stated he had personally been an enemy of the KKK for a long time.

He spoke of the FBI's case in Louisiana in the late 1920's in which FBI evidence successfully culminated in the conviction of the top Klan leader. He stated the KKK fully concentrated on Negroes, Jews and Catholics, however, concentration now is strictly on the Negro race.

The Director explained that in Alabama the FBI cannot deal with the Highway Patrol because of psychoneurotic tendencies of the Alabama Governor. He stated that the State of Georgia has a good Governor and that the Georgia Bureau of Investigation, while not comparable to the Mississippi Highway Patrol, has cooperated with the FBI.

The Director told Reverend King and his associates that FBI representatives have held several thousand law enforcement conferences in which southern police officers have been educated as to civil rights legislation. He stated this has clearly assisted law enforcement, particularly the FBI, however, admittedly, this represents slow progress, but progress nevertheless. He added that this educational campaign will be continued and that it will eventually take hold. The Director gave the example of a Mississippi Sheriff who recently broke a case as a result of FBI training.

The Director made it very clear to Reverend King and his associates that FBI Agents conduct very thorough interviews in civil rights cases. He stated he would like to know immediately if any of our Special Agents ever act in a supercilious manner or if they mishandle a complaint regarding civil rights. He stated that if the facts reflect that our Agent is in the wrong he will be called on the carpet fast. The Director asked that Reverend King or any of his representatives feel free to call the FBI at any time they have such complaints.

The Director told Reverend King he desired to give him some advice. He stated that one of the greatest things the Negro leaders could accomplish would be to encourage voting registration among their people. Another thing would be to educate their people in the skills so that they could compete in the open market. The Director mentioned several professions in which Negroes could easily learn skills. The Director also told King he wanted him to know that registrars in the South were now more careful in their actions. He stated that there were less attempts now to prevent Negroes from registering inasmuch as the FBI is watching such actions very carefully. The Director told Reverend King that the FBI was making progress in violations regarding discrimination in eating places. He gave as a specific example a restaurant in Atlanta, Georgia, in which surveillances have taken place to ascertain if out-of-state cars are being served at this particular restaurant. The Director stated he personally was in favor of equality in eating places and in schools. He stated emphatically, however, he was not in favor of taking Negro children 10 or 12 miles across town simply because their parents wanted them to go to a school other than those in their specific neighborhood.

The Director told Reverend King that in due time there will be a complete change in the mores of community thinking in the United States regarding the racial problem. He stated that meanwhile the FBI will continue to handle its responsibility in a thorough and impartial manner. He reiterated that the FBI cannot encourage prosecution in Federal Court despite the fact that some local courts cannot be trusted. He added that some judges cannot be trusted.

The Director praised the Georgia papers that declared the verdict of the Penn case to be a travesty of justice. He added that the Jackson, Mississippi, papers had contained several editorials deploring violence against Negroes and participation in church burnings. The same editorials declared that this was no way to solve racial problems. The Director stated that his statements made at a press conference in Jackson, Mississippi, this summer to the effect that he was in Mississippi to see to it that an end was put to the violence of bombings and burning churches had had some effect upon backwoods terrorists.

The Director told King that he wanted to make it very clear that the question is often raised as to whether the FBI will protect civil rights workers or Negroes. He stated that he has in the past and will continue to answer such questions on the basis that the FBI does not have the authority nor the jurisdiction to protect anyone. He stated that when the Department of Justice desires that Negroes be protected this is the responsibility of U.S. Marshals. The Director reiterated that the FBI is strictly an investigative agency and cannot and will not extend itself beyond legislated jurisdiction. The Director repeated very emphtically that while our investigations are very definitely thorough and impartial he wanted to state once again that if Reverend King or any of his associates ever knew of a Special Agent showing bias or prejudice he wanted to know about this matter immediately.

The Director explained that we have civil rights cases not only in the South but also in the northern cities. He gave examples of New York and Chicago. He stated that there have been some cases in Miami, Florida.

The Director spoke once again of the necessity of the Negro educating himself in order to compete in manual and professional skills. He mentioned the examples of a shoeshine boy in Miami, Florida, who turned out to be, after questioning by the Director, a graduate of Howard University. This shoeshine boy, a Negro, explained to the Director that he could not get a job above the level of shoeshine boy because of the color of his skin. The Director stated this, of course, was wrong and that under no circumstances did he, or anyone in the FBI, share the opinion that the Negro, or any other race, should be kept down. The Director spoke of his pride in Negro Agents and particularly mentioned Special Agent Aubrey Lewis, the former Notre Dame track star who is currently assigned to the New York Division.

The Director spoke of a Miami Special Agent who was transferred to that Office from St. Louis. This Agent explained to the Director on one occasion that he was first a little upset about being transferred to Miami because he felt his race would be against him. He stated, however, much to his surprise, that the white people in Miami treated him with the greatest of courtesy while people of his own race referred to him as a "fink" simply because he was a representative of law enforcement.

Reverend King interrupted the Director at this point and asked if this same Negro Agent is still assigned to the Miami Division. The Director replied in the affirmative. The Director stated that at a recent dinner Father Hesburgh, the President of Notre Dame University, explained to the Director that his institution had difficulty getting Negroes on the football team because their grades were never high enough. The Director told Reverend King that same thing is true of Negroes who apply for the position of Special Agent. He stated in most instances they lack the qualifications, however, we were very happy to hire any Negro who was qualified for the position. The Director told Reverend King that we, of course, could not let down our qualifications simply because of the color of a person's skin.

The Director told Reverend King and his associates that the problems that he and the Negro leaders have is a mutual problem. He stated in most instances in civil rights matters we have learned that "you are damned if you do and you are damned if you don't." The Director stated nevertheless the FBI would continue to do its job. He stated that we additionally are very proud of 10 or 11 Indian Special Agents and of a number of Special Agents who have Mexican blood in them. He stated the color of a man's skin makes no difference to the FBI whatsoever, however, we do merit the cooperation and assistance of all groups and it is most unfair when these groups are taught not to cooperate with the FBI.

The Director mentioned that he wanted to make it very plain that the FBI will not tolerate any of our personnel being slapped around. He gave an example of the Lombardozzi case in New York where one of our Agents was jumped by five hoodlums outside a church. He stated these hoodlums were immediately taught a lesson. The Director mentioned that in the war with hoodlums, for every man we lose we make certain, through legal means of course, that the hoodlums lose the same number or more.

The Director proudly spoke of the ability of Agents to outshoot and outfight hoodlums and other individuals who attempted to take advantage of our personnel. He stated the KKK is afraid to "mix" with our Agents. He mentioned that the Klan was "yellow." He stated they are brave as long as they have the majority with them but afraid when they face an equal number.

The Director spoke of the Mack Charles Parker case in Poplarville, Mississippi. He stated that our evidence in this case had been turned over to Governor Coleman, the then Governor of the State. He mentioned that Governor Coleman was a decent type of individual who had immediately seen to it that a State Court received evidence contributed by the FBI. The Director mentioned that our evidence in this case was excellent, however, the Grand Jury refused to indict the subjects involved in the lynching of Parker.

The Director told Reverend King that in many instances our Agents have been spit upon, then have been refused food and lodging and many things are done to thwart hard-hitting investigations by the FBI. He stated that nevertheless we continue to gather evidence in an expeditious and thorough manner.

Reverend Abernathy stated that the Negroes have a real problem in tearing down the current system of segregated voting tests in the South. He stated it was most important that there be kept alive in the Negro communities a ray of hope. He stated that the Negro people should not be allowed to fall into an atmosphere of despair.

The Director explained that this was a very important point. He stated that real progress has been made in higher wages, voting registration and housing matters. The Director pointed out, however, that such progress has not been emphasized by the rabble-rousers who constantly attempt to stir up the Negroes against the whites. The Director gave as an example the communist, Epton, in New York City. The Director stated that Epton is sometimes pointed to as a person the Negro should emulate because of his militancy. The Director stated this was wrong and it is also wrong to "mislead" the Negroes.

Reverend Abernathy stated that the SCLC does not want Negroes like Epton in their movement. He stated that Reverend King, more than anyone else, has prevented people like Epton and the Muslims from taking over the civil rights movement. Reverend Abernathy stated that actually the Negroes are a part of the Federal Government, therefore, anything that represents the Federal Government is an encouragement to the Negro. He added that even the side [sic] of a post office building or a Federal courtroom is an encouragement to the Negro. He mentioned that when a Negro receives information that a case in which he has been brutally mistreated is going [to] Federal Court he feels encouraged over the fact that he will get a fair trial. Reverend Abernathy continued that the same problem is true when a Negro sees an FBI Agent. He stated that the Negro feels open encouragement inasmuch as the FBI will not only fairly handle his case but will serve as a great deterrent of violence.

The Director stated that the KKK today is represented by common white trash. He stated that the Klan was actually worse than the Communist Party inasmuch as the Klan resorts to violence while the communist usually emulate termites in their activities.

The Director reiterated that King and his associates should feel free to call him at any time when they have knowledge of possible civil rights violations. King replied that over the past few years he has noted amazing signs of progress in the civil rights field. He stated he has been very surprised to see some communities comply with the new civil rights statutes. He stated there still are some pockets of resistance particularly in the South. He added that the SCLC is planning to stimulate voting registration activities in Selma, Alabama, in the near future. He mentioned that some members of his organization have been successful in infiltrating this white community and have learned there is a great potential for violence in Selma.

The Director interrupted King and briefly detailed five cases in which the FBI has gathered evidence in Selma, Alabama. The Director mentioned that these cases came about as a result of FBI investigation and that we were continuing our investigations in Selma, Alabama. He mentioned that one case would come to trial on December 9, 1964.

The Director particularly made reference to the fact that we have three excellent cases in Selma at the present time.

Reverend King inquired as to whether his representatives should notify the FBI when they arrive in Selma, Alabama. He quickly corrected himself that he knew his representatives should contact the FBI upon arrival, however, he asked the Director what would be the possibilities of FBI Agents being in Selma, Alabama, inasmuch as there appeared to be a potential for violence. The Director specifically asked Reverend King when his activities would take place. Reverend Abernathy indicated such activity would take place around January 1, 1965. The Director clearly explained that FBI Agents would be in Selma, not for the purpose of "protecting" anyone, but for the purpose of observing and reporting to the Department of Justice any possible violations of civil rights that might occur. Reverend King expressed appreciation in this regard.

Reverend King stood up and stated he wished to express his personal thanks for a most fruitful and necessary meeting. The Director told Reverend King that he should get in touch with us anytime he felt it was necessary.

Reverend King mentioned that there were representatives of the press in the Director's reception room. He turned to me and asked if the FBI planned to make any comment regarding the meeting. I told him that the Director has instructed that we make no comment whatsoever. Reverend King asked the Director if there would be any objections if he read a short prepared statement to the press. The Director told Reverend King this, of course, was up to him.

In proceeding to the reception room, Reverend King pulled a press release, hand-written in ink, out of his right coat pocket. This press release obviously had been prepared prior to the time Reverend King arrived at FBI Headquarters. A previous memorandum has been sent through reporting verbatim the comments by King in the Director's reception room.

ACTION:

It is suggested that the attached letter be sent to the President concerning the meeting between the Director, Reverend King and his associates.

The General Investigative Division, Civil Rights Section, should take due note of the proposed activities in Selma, Alabama, and should instruct the appropriate office to make certain that Agents are on hand to observe activities in Selma, Alabama, on or around January 1, 1965.

December 2, 1964

The President
The White House
Washington, D. C.

My dear Mr. President:

In response to his request to see me, I conferred for about an hour with the Reverend Martin Luther King in my office yesterday afternoon. He was accompanied by the following members of the Southern Christian Leadership Conference of which he is President: Reverend Ralph D. Abernathy, Treasurer; Andrew J. Young, Program Director; and Walter E. Fauntroy, Director of the organization's Washington, D. C., office.

The meeting was most amicable and King indicated that he had requested to see me in an effort to clear up any misunderstandings that we might have. He apologized for remarks attributed to him criticizing the FBI and me with specific reference to Albany, Georgia. He stated that in this connection he had either been misquoted or there had been an outright misrepresentation.

He said that while some Negroes have complained to him that the FBI has been ineffective in investigating civil rights violations, he personally discounts such complaints and said he appreciated the fine work the FBI has been doing in this regard.

He said he had been critical of the FBI only in connection with instances where our Agents, who had been furnished complaints involving police brutality, were, thereafter, observed being friendly toward these same officers. He said situations like this serve to breed Negro distrust for the FBI. I advised Reverend King that I was aware that allegations of this nature had been made and that I looked into the matter. It was determined that these charges were without basis.

Reverend King categorically denied ever having made a personal attack on me and also denied that he had ever instructed Negroes not to cooperate with the FBI. I told him that when Negroes are encouraged not to cooperate with the FBI, the solution of cases is delayed and sometimes frustrated. He said, to the contrary, he encouraged such cooperation. He explained that Negroes in many areas are frustrated. He said he feels it is his duty to keep them from expressing their frustrations through violence. Reverend King made reference to my report to you on the rioting that took place in some of our modern cities last summer. He indicated he considers it an excellent analysis of the situation.

Communist infiltration of the civil rights movement was discussed. Reverend King stated that as a Christian he could never accept communism and that he shared my concern with the problem. He described communism as a "crippling, totalitarian disease." He said that while there are "one or two" former communists currently engaged in the fund-raising activities for the Southern Christian Leadership Conference, he does not tolerate communists in his organization. He cited the communist background of Hunter Pitts O'Dell and noted that he considered the success of the Southern Christian Leadership Conference more important to him than his friendship with O'Dell. Consequently, he claimed, O'Dell is no longer associated with his organization.

The problems confronting the FBI in civil rights investigations were explained to the Reverend King in detail. I made it clear to him that cases developed as a result of FBI investigation must often be tried in local courts where there are difficulties involved in getting white juries to convict white defendants in connection with civil rights matters. I cited some of our experiences in this regard.

He and his associates were advised of the recent conferences held for local law enforcement officers throughout the United States for the purpose of fully acquainting them with civil rights legislation and their responsibilities in connection with same. I told him that the results of this campaign have been encouraging in the cooperation received.

I pointed out to him that there is a great misunderstanding today among the general public and particularly the Negro race as to the FBI's role in civil rights matters. I emphasized that the FBI is an investigative agency, that it cannot recommend prosecution or make-on-the-spot arrests where Federal Laws have not been violated. He was advised that the FBI will not protect civil rights workers or Negroes because the FBI does not have the authority or jurisdiction to do so. He was also advised that the FBI cannot and will not exceed its authority. Reverend King was told that our investigations are conducted in a thorough and impartial manner, but if he or any of his associates knew of a Special Agent who had shown bias or prejudice, I wanted to know about it immediately.

Reverend King indicated that the Southern Christian Leadership Conference is planning to engage in voter registration activities in Selma, Alabama, on or about January 1, 1965, and that he has learned that there could be violence. I told him that our Agents would be on the scene, not for the purpose of rendering protection, but to observe and report to the Department of Justice any possible violations of civil rights that may occur.

Reverend King expressed his gratitude for having the opportunity to meet me. He said he felt our meeting had been a productive one, and I told him to feel free to get in touch with me any time he thought it necessary to do so.

Respectfully submitted,
J. Edgar Hoover

UNITED STATES GOVERNMENT
Memorandum

TO: Mr. A. H. Belmont   DATE: December 15, 1964

FROM: Mr. W. C. Sullivan

SUBJECT: ...

      ...

NEW YORK, NEW YORK

The captioned person I have been developing as a contact for the past couple of years. In a memorandum a few months ago, I set forth my conversation with him wherein I alerted . . . concerning certain basic facts on Martin Luther King. Since that time he has taken measures to gradually separate the . . . from the support of him. Further, he has sent the Bureau on a very sensitive and confidential basis a long list of names of persons who participated in . . . which we needed badly to have relative to our investigations.

Late this afternoon . . . will be in the city and I will meet with him again, at which time I will circumspectly reiterate the truth that Martin Luther King is a serious liability to the civil rights movement in this country. I will also learn from . . . about any other developments which he has been able to sponsor to curtail the activities of King.

UNTIED STATES GOVERNMENT
Memorandum

TO: Mr. A. H. Belmont   DATE: December 16, 1964

FROM: Mr. W. C. Sullivan

SUBJECT: MARTIN LUTHER KING, JR.
           SECURITY MATTER-C

Last evening, . . . while en route from the South, stopped at the National Airport for a couple of hours to discuss with me the subject of Martin Luther King. As I have reported in previous memoranda, he has been informed concerning certain basic facts relating to King . . . and his connections with communism.

Last night . . . told me that he has been working on this matter whenever the opportunity presented itself and he said he wanted the FBI to know that steps have been taken by . . . to make certain from this time on that Martin Luther King will never get ''one single dollar'' of financial support from . . . . . . told me that since our first conversation he has heard from some other sources concerning King . . . In view of this, he felt that he was free to discuss the matter with a few key . . . clergymen, including . . . who has been active in the civil rights movement. Naturally, . . . they were horrified and . . . said that he could not see how a Christian clergyman could give any more support to a man like King. . . . also told me this week he intends to confer with . . . for the purpose of persuading . . . that the Negro leaders should completely isolate King and remove him from the role he is now occupying in civil rights activities. In . . . opinion, the most effective way to dethrone King and get him out of the public eye is to have the important Negro leaders united in their determination to do this.

. . . in a few weeks will be leaving . . . will return from there in about 2 or 3 months. I will meet again with him at that time.

As I have previously said, . . . is a very fine man in every respect. He has a most sensitive conscience and he is a person on whom considerable reliability can be placed. I know the extent of his concern about King and I feel positive that he will try to do as much as he can to remove King from the powerful social position he now occupies. . . . deplored to me very strongly the fact the King was able to be named ''Man of the Year'' by ''Time'' magazine, was the recipient recently of the Nobel Prize, secured an audience with the Pope, and has been the recipient of different awards from both Protestant and Catholic groups. I agreed with him most heartily and said it was too bad those people responsible for giving such recognition to King were not more circumspect. He replied that it was probably due to their lack of knowledge concerning King's communist connections and . . . but he believes this condition is being corrected, at least among the clergymen.

UNITED STATES DEPARTMENT OF JUSTICE

FEDERAL BUREAU OF INVESTIGATION

New York, New York
December 23, 1964

Re: Martin Luther King, Jr.
Security Matter-C

A confidential source, who has furnished reliable information in the past, advised on December 21, 1964, that Martin Luther King, Jr. (President of the Southern Christian Leadership Conference, SCLC), was in contact with Clarence Jones on that date. Jones told King that he had a recent discussion with Walter Fauntroy (Director of the Washington, D. C., office of the SCLC), regarding King's getting involved with the "challenge of the Mississippi Democratic Freedom Movement." Jones said he had studied it and thought it was a good legal and creative position.

With regard to the Mississippi Democratic Freedom Movement, "The New York Times," December 21, 1964, described the movement as a challenge to the seating of Mississippi all-white representatives in Congress.

The source, in continuing, said, Jones and King discussed a way for King and the SCLC to become involved, prompting Jones to remark that he and King should give thought to getting together, perhaps in Washington, D.C., before January 4, 1965, to discuss the matter. King acknowledged his interest in becoming involved, adding, however, that he had had problems with the Student Nonviolent Coordinating Committee (SNCC) and the Council of Federated Organizations (COFO), in the past. Jones said they should see if King could get involved, but not through them (SNCC and COFO). He suggested his (King's) involvement on an independent basis, prompting King to reply that they should think it through and find out the best thing to do.

Jones and King discussed whether they (SCLC) should have their own program in Mississippi. King remarked that they have good grass roots there. King asked of Jones what "they" wanted him to do, causing Jones to answer "they want you to get involved, but it is feared that you will steal the show." Jones said he would determine what King could do of value.

With regard to a possible something before the 4th of January, 1965, King said he would inquire of Fauntroy as to whether it was feasible. He said he would be in Atlanta most of the time during Christmas. Jones said in view of that, "they" could go to Atlanta. According to the source, King was agreeable.

During their contact, King and Jones also considered questions pertaining to the tax laws applicable to his award for receiving the Nobel Peace Prize. In that regard, King said he was of the impression that he could give $6,000 to the SCLC tax free, but did not know about the $17,000 for the Unity Council (United Council of Harlem Organizations). Jones said in that regard, that he had a long discussion with "our friend" after "your" (King's) father saw him in New York, and he (Jones) discussed it with him. Jones said he would check with his tax authority and let King know the answer.

Excerpts from Electronic Surveillance File 1964

2/27/64

Roy Bennett to Stanley Levison.

Bennett and Levison discuss the Civil Rights Bill that is presently before the U.S. Senate. Bennett says that the President of the U.S. is really in favor of the Bill passing and that the ADA and other Liberal Groups have put down the groundwork of organization as to how this Bill can be passed. Bennett says that enough Senators will be present at all times to get the Bill through the Senate if the Southerners falter. Levison says that Martin Luther King, Jr., has been giving consideration to going on a hunger strike while the Civil Rights Bill is being debated. Bennett suggests that this might not be a good idea as King most likely will starve to death as the debate on the Civil Rights Bill will last for quite a while. Levison says that some of the Negro civil rights people might ask that all children and all adult supporters of the civil rights movement go on a hunger strike while the Civil Rights Bill is under consideration by the Senate. Bennett says that the ''Hunger Strike idea'' may not help the civil rights movement in the United States and that King won't do anything foolish because he always ''confers with the big wheels before he does anything for national publicity.''

3/11/64

Levison called his wife and stated he was at Penn Station having just arrived from Atlanta, Georgia, and that he would be home shortly.

Stanley Levison to Clarence Jones.

Levison said he didn't know that Jones said that Wyatt Walker informed him that he is going to be Director of the New York office. Jones said that Wyatt was concerned that he couldn't be Director and Bayard Northern Coordinator. (Wyatt claimed that this is the reason that the decision on Bayard is going to be vetoed.) Levison said the decision is not to be vetoed. Levison said, in a nutshell, what I agreed on with Martin—and Wyatt had no part in this, is it would not be wise to take Bayard on now with a filibuster. There is no question that he should be hired after the filibuster. Levison said he made the point with Martin that Bayard would have to be paid at once—not only because it is proper, but also because he wanted it pinned down. Levison said he violently objected to the Wyatt thing—he could see that Wyatt and Bayard couldn't get along. However, Martin is anxious not to have

311

Wyatt as an enemy, he doesn't want Wyatt to leave under circumstances where he will be hostile. Martin said that Wyatt and Bayard will be subject to the same committee. Jones said that Wyatt wanted to make it clear that Bayard would be responsible to him. Levison said he won't be—they will both be responsible to the committee. Levison said that if Wyatt leaves SCLC he wouldn't hesitate to tell him where he stands. Levison is afraid that Wyatt will stay with SCLC to its detriment.

3/14/64

Jones telephoned Levison and advised it did not appear that Rustin wanted a job with SCLC or anyone else if he couldn't have a free hand and that he (Jones) thinks that Rustin will go to work for CORE or for Phil Randolph . . . Levison states he is inclined to think at this point it would be better not to hire Rustin because it would be buying an awful lot of trouble and that Rustin's assets outweighed his liabilities only if he would submit to discipline.

3/16/64

Call from Stanley Levison to Clarence Jones.

Jones advised Levison that he had heard that Bayard Rustin had received an $11,000 grant from the Urban League. Jones was not sure of the exact nature of the grant but he said it had something to do with civil rights and poverty. Levison stated that this would suggest that he could not work with "us." Levison stated that there was something very political about Rustin's actions re[garding] the Socialist's party. Levison stated that his rejection of any political link may have turned Rustin away from them. Jones stated that he felt Rustin may not have made this decision on his own but that it may have been from others. Levison agreed and stated that he thought Rustin went to Black Mountain and returned with a directive.

1965

1965

[Section 22]

[Section 27]

March 24, 1965   Report
March 24, 1965   Report

[Section 28]

March 27, 1965   Memorandum: Miami
March 29, 1965   Memorandum: New York
March 30, 1965   Memorandum: Washington

[Section 29]

March 31, 1965   Memorandum: Philadelphia
March 31, 1965   Memorandum: Newark
March 31, 1965   Memorandum: Buffalo
April 1, 1965   Airtel: Director to
                            Baltimore/Charlotte/Philadelphia
April 2, 1965   Letter to Mr. J. Edgar Hoover
April 2, 1965   Memorandum
April 2, 1965   Memorandum: Charlotte
April 7, 1965   Memorandum: Mobile

[Section 30]

April 8, 1965   Memorandum: Birmingham
April 12, 1965   Memorandum: Jacksonville

[Section 31]

April 24, 1965   Memorandum: Indianapolis

[Section 32]

May 4, 1965   Memorandum: Charlotte
May 6, 1965   Memorandum: Philadelphia

[Section 33]

May 13, 1965   Letter to Mr. Hoover

May 17, 1965   Memorandum: San Antonio
June 3, 1965   Memorandum: Cincinnati

[Section 36]

June 23, 1965   Teletype: New Orleans to Director
June 30, 1965   Letter: Governor Mark Hatfield to Harry
                       Wachtel
July 8, 1965   Teletype: Chicago to Director

[Section 37]

July 10, 1965   Transcript: TV Broadcast
July 15, 1965   Memorandum: Sullivan to Belmont

[Section 38]

August 6, 1965   Airtel: Director to Atlanta/New York

[Section 40]

August 16, 1965   Memorandum: New York
August 17, 1965   Memorandum: New York
August 17, 1965   Memorandum: Charlotte
August 17, 1965   Memorandum: Miami
August 20, 1965   Memorandum: San Francisco
August 23, 1965   Memorandum: Los Angeles
August 27, 1965   Memorandum: New York
August 30, 1965   Memorandum: Washington

[Section 41]

September 3, 1965   Memorandum: Los Angeles to Director

[Section 43]

August 30, 1965   Memorandum: Jones to DeLoach

[Section 46]

October 12, 1965   Teletype: Savannah to Director
October 12, 1965   Memorandum: Chicago
October 29, 1965   Memorandum: Chicago

[Section 47]

November 11, 1965   Teletype: St. Louis to Director
November 12, 1965   Memorandum: St. Louis to Director

[Section 48]

November 24, 1965   Letter to Mr. J. Edgar Hoover
December 2, 1965   Memorandum: Baumgardner to Sullivan

[Section 49]

December 7, 1965   Airtel: New Orleans to Director
December 7, 1965   Memorandum: Mobile

[Section 22]

UNITED STATES GOVERNMENT
Memorandum

TO: Mr. DeLoach   DATE: 1-8-65

FROM: M. A. Jones

SUBJECT: MARTIN LUTHER KING

... has forwarded tear sheets from one of the December issues of "Lo Specchio," an Italian-language weekly published in Rome, Italy, which carried a story by Paolo Cappello. The story dealt with King's stop in London before arriving in Oslo and relates how King and his entourage toured London nightclubs which included a stop at one of the most expensive and exclusive restaurants in the British capital, Mirabelle. Before the evening was over King and his party allegedly spent as much money "as a poor Negro makes in six months." The last stop of the night took place in one of the best-known nightclubs in London where King and his group ate and drank until daybreak and apparently consumed a very large amount of champagne.

The article is very cleverly and well written, and in addition to pointing out King's drinking and high living while in London, considerable space is also given to his contacts with leftist groups while in the British capital. The author also identifies the leftist backgrounds in the individuals mentioned and belittles King's position on international politics such as the China-India controversy over land boundaries. Paolo Cappello, the author, aptly points out how some London observers questioned whether the eating and drinking Mr. King was the same person who delivered a sermon the previous day from London's St. Paul's Cathedral in which he "harped on the strings of kindheartedness, moderation, and piousness" for a good half-hour.

Bufiles contain no references identifiable with Paolo Cappello. "Lo Specchio" carried a favorable article in October 1961, about the Director and the FBI and while we would ordinarily have written a letter of appreciation in this instance, it was not done as it was determined that its Editor, George Nelson Page, a former American citizen, had denounced [sic] his citizenship and joined the Fascists in Italy in the early 1940s. He was later interned by allied military authorities in Italy after that country's occupation.

It appears the article carried by "Lo Specchio" contains excellent public source material for our contacts in this country who would be interested in the true background of Martin Luther King.

[Section 23]

UNITED STATES GOVERNMENT
Memorandum

TO: Mr. Belmont   DATE: January 19, 1965

FROM: A. Rosen

SUBJECT: REGISTRARS OF VOTERS,
         DALLAS COUNTY, ALABAMA,
         VOTING DISCRIMINATION,
         CIVIL RIGHTS; ELECTION LAWS

THREAT AGAINST MARTIN LUTHER KING
   With regard to the allegation made . . . concerning a threat against the life of Martin Luther King, it is noted that this information was

first received early on 1/17/65 from Mr. Robert Owen, Departmental Attorney, who said that he had received the information from ... inquiry was made of Owen as to the original source of the information and he said he did not at that time know ... source for the information. Owen called later on 1/17/65 and said that he had received additional information and that ... original source was promptly interviewed ...

We are conducting extensive investigations at present to locate and interview other persons named by ... when the alleged threat was made. One of these persons ... was interviewed 1/18/65. ... stated that he attended the National Citizen's Council Conference at Montgomery, Alabama, 1/15–16/65 ... He refused to furnish specific information about the meetings except he stated affirmatively that he heard nothing about any threats of violence to Martin Luther King at any of the meetings.

January 22, 1965

Honorable Bill D. Moyers
Special Assistant to the President
The White House
Washington, D. C.

Dear. Mr. Moyers:

... a representative of this Bureau to communicate the following information to the President ... who expressed great admiration of the President, advised that in the recent past he has learned from several sources about the ... Martin Luther King, Jr. ... explained that he was shocked to learn of this and immediately realized what serious consequences King's misbehavior could have for the civil rights movement in which ... has been actively interested for years.

... made three points: (1) that from diverse sources he has learned of ... and of King's deceiving of sincere, good people in this Nation who have been supporting King; (2) that he regrets greatly that a banquet is being given in King's honor next week in Atlanta, but the arrangements have now reached the point it is probably not possible to prevent the banquet; and (3) that he believed that the very best thing that could happen would be to have King step completely out of the civil rights movement and public life for he feels that if this is not done, sooner or later King will be publicly exposed.... believed that an exposure of King will do irreparable harm to the civil rights movement in . . . and others are so interested and have worked so hard for; and likewise it will do injury to different citizens of the country who have been supporting King, . . .

. . . told this Bureau's representative that if it had not been necessary for him to leave Washington, D. C., immediately, he would have liked to convey this message to the President in person. However, in view of the necessity for his hasty departure, he asked that his views be transmitted to the President by the FBI.

Sincerely yours,
J. Edgar Hoover

February 3, 1965

Honorable Bill D. Moyers
Special Assistant to the President
The White House
Washington, D. C.

Dear Mr. Moyers:

On January 2, 1965, Reverend Martin Luther King, Jr., appeared in Selma, Alabama, where he announced the beginning of a statewide drive to enable Negroes to register for voting. Since that time, there has been a continuing series of demonstrations by Negroes seeking to register to vote in Selma, and many demonstrators have been arrested on such charges as violating the city's parade ordinance, disorderly conduct and refusing to obey an officer.

On February 1, 1965, King led a group of approximately 264 Negroes from a church in Selma toward the county courthouse. They were confronted by J. Wilson Baker, Commissioner of Public Safety, who stated they were violating a city ordinance by parading without a permit. The group continued approximately three blocks when they were again confronted by Commissioner Baker who placed the entire group under arrest.

The group was taken to the City Hall where Commissioner Baker told King and Reverend Ralph Abernathy, an associate of King's, that they were not under arrest and advised them to leave the building. King and Reverend Mr. Abernathy then held a press conference on the steps of the City Hall, and they were instructed by a police officer to leave the premises. When they refused to do so, they were arrested and charged with violating the city's parade ordinance. All others arrested have been released on bond, however, King and Reverend Abernathy remain in jail in Selma in lieu of a $200 bond each.

On February 3, 1965, we received information from a reliable source to the effect that Andrew Young, an assistant to King in New York City, held a discussion with Clarence Jones, an attorney in New York who is an advisor to King. Young and Jones discussed a request from King that "show people" visit him in Selma, and it was indicated that this might be arranged for February 4, 1965.

Young and Jones also discussed a request of King's that Young make a personal call to the President to have him intervene in some way. Young indicated that he did not think he would be able to speak directly to the President but thought that he could discuss the matter with Mr. Lee White.

Jones advised Young that it should be made clear to the President they do not want troops in Selma but are requesting that the President set the issue straight before the nation regarding the right to vote without obstruction, chastise Alabama for obstructing the right to vote and take legislative or executive action to clear up the confusion in this area.

Jones also suggested to Young that the President dispatch a small force of United States Marshals specially deputized by the President or the Attorney General and he alleged that the United States Marshal at Selma is afraid of Sheriff James Clarke.

Clarence Jones was a member of the Labor Youth League in the mid 1950s. The Labor Youth League has been designated as subversive pursuant to Executive Order Number 10450.

It is suggested that the above information may be of interest to the President, and the Attorney General is also being advised.

Sincerely yours,
J. Edgar Hoover

[Section 24]

UNITED STATES DEPARTMENT OF JUSTICE

FEDERAL BUREAU OF INVESTIGATION

New York, New York

February 8, 1965

Re: Communist Influence in Racial Matters
Internal Security-C

A confidential source, who has furnished reliable information in the past, furnished information on February 4, 1965, indicating that Clarence Jones received information on that date which revealed that Harry Wachtel wanted him (Jones) to attend a meeting of the "Research Committee" (a meeting of Martin Luther King's advisors) on February 5, 1965. According to the source, the meeting was to take place at Wachtel's office, 575 Madison Avenue, New York City, between the hours 12:30 and 5:30 P.M.

Wachtel, according to the source, had received a message from Andrew Young (Program Director of the Southern Christian Leadership Conference, SCLC), in Selma, Alabama, on February 4, 1965, that the meeting should be held as planned, adding, however, that Martin Luther King would not attend but would be represented by him (Young).

During the late evening of February 4, 1965, the same confidential source advised that Clarence Jones and Andrew Young were in contact on that evening. Young advised that neither he nor King would attend the "Research Committee" meeting scheduled to be held on February 5, 1965, in Wachtel's office. Young said that was due to the expected visit of several Congressmen in Selma, Alabama, on the same date.

Another confidential source, who has furnished reliable information in the past, advised that Harry Wachtel and Clarence Jones were in contact on February 5, 1965, regarding the scheduled "Research Committee" meeting for that date. Wachtel said in that regard that he was certain that King and Andrew Young would not attend, and that only Bayard Rustin (Organizer of the March on Washington), Cleveland Robinson (Secretary-Treasurer of District 65, Retail, Wholesale and Department Store Workers Union; American Federation of Labor—Congress of Industrial Organizations, AFL-CIO), Walter (Walter

Fauntroy, Director of the Washington office of the SCLC), Mike Harrington (National Committee member of the Socialist Party) and he (Wachtel) would attend.

Wachtel and Jones also took the opportunity to discuss a letter which appeared in "The New York Times" on February 5, 1965, which solicited funds in behalf of King and the SCLC. In that regard, Wachtel said he was a "little unhappy that he had not been in on the composition of the letter, and how big a bomb it would have been if King had been released from jail." Wachtel said he desired that King get out of jail, but Jones said he trusted King's timing and urged Wachtel not to worry about it.

With regard to the letter in "The New York Times," which Wachtel and Jones discussed, it is noted that on February 5, 1965, "The New York Times," page 15, carried an advertisement captioned, "A Letter From Martin Luther King from a Selma, Alabama, Jail." In the letter, King opens with a statement that little did the King of Norway realize when he presented him the Nobel Peace Prize that in less than sixty days he would be in jail, adding that he (King of Norway) and the world will be shocked because they are little aware of the unfinished business in the South.

King continues: "By jailing hundreds of Negroes, the City of Selma, Alabama, has revealed the persisting ugliness of segregation to the nation and the world."

King, in answering a question as to why they were in jail, said, "Have you ever been required to answer 100 questions on government, some abtruse even to a political science specialist, merely to vote? Have you ever stood in line with a hundred others and after waiting an entire day seen less than ten given the qualifying test?"

King said: "We are in jail simply because we cannot tolerate these conditions for ourselves or our nation."

A plea for funds is then made by King in behalf of the SCLC.

According to the source, Jones and Wachtel also discussed the efforts being made to unseat the Mississippi Congressional delegation because of their state's refusal to permit Negroes to vote. In that regard, they commented over the fact that Bayard Rustin was "getting the red smear." Jones said it was not "red baiting" but simply a statement of the record and that people had to make their own decision.

Wachtel quoted Rustin as saying, "Look, I may be a liability but I'm good." To this, Wachtel remarked, "This guy's a liability and he's not good, period."

With reference to the meeting of the "Research Committee," on February 5, 1965, at 12:55 P.M., Special Agents of the Federal Bureau of Investigation observed Bayard Rustin enter the building at 575 Madison Avenue, New York City, and take the fifth floor elevator; at 1:35 P.M., the Special Agents observed Cleveland Robinson enter and take the elevator to the fifth floor.

It is noted that Wachtel's office is on the fifth floor of the building at 575 Madison Avenue, New York City.

On February 6, 1965, a confidential source, who has furnished reliable information in the past, advised that Bayard Rustin was in contact, on that date with Harry Wachtel.

Wachtel advised Rustin that Lee White (Special White House Assistant) had contacted Wachtel and stated President Johnson was disturbed and annoyed with King's recent statement that he would see President Johnson on February 8, 1965. According to White, President Johnson is tied up on February 8, 1965, and that King could meet with Attorney General Katzenbach on February 8, 1965.

Wachtel said a second tentative plan would be for King to telephone President Johnson, February 6, 1965, and then see Katzenbach February 8, 1965. Wachtel said that King could issue a statement that he had just talked to the President.

The final course of action was not known by the source.

During the afternoon of February 7, 1965, the first source mentioned heretofore, furnished information that Harry Wachtel and Clarence Jones were in conference on that date regarding a meeting of King and President Johnson. Wachtel said he had been in touch with Lee White at the White House about King's coming trip to Washington. In that regard, Wachtel said that trip had opened a "hornets' nest for the President," and that King's statement about a meeting with the President would have to be very carefully worded.

Wachtel said the White House desired certain words such as "not definite, hopeful, in view of circumstances'' used by King in his statement about meeting the President.

King, according to Wachtel, was to see the President some time after his meeting on Tuesday with the Vice President and Attorney General, but said that fact had to be kept in complete secrecy. If it got out, Wachtel said, the President would not see King.

Wachtel, in pursuing the matter further, said he hated to see the Viet Nam crisis, but at least it showed he (Lee White) did not lie yesterday when he said the National Security Council expects to meet on Monday and Tuesday.

King, according to Wachtel, ''now knows that when he is dealing with the President, he is not dealing with a friend, but with a Texan.''

The same source furnished information on February 7, 1965, indicating that Stanley Levison visited Clarence Jones at his home on that date. The source was unable to advise what the visit pertained to.

Late during the same date, the source advised that Clarence Jones prepared a press release for Martin Luther King on events in Selma, Alabama, and then conferred with Harry Wachtel, seeking his comments on the release. The release prepared was as follows:

''Recent events in Selma, Alabama, have disclosed the persisting barriers to enfranchisement of Negroes in the South. If the rate of registration manipulated in Selma were to prevail, it would take several decades to register eligible Negroes. The mandate of the American People and the intention of Congress are subverted by these conditions. There is a clear and urgent need for new and approved Federal legislation and Executive action to eliminate these undemocratic barriers. To pursue this objective, conferences in Washington are being planned. The pressure of international affairs have made impractical a Monday conference with the White House. However, on Tuesday, I will be meeting with Vice President Humphrey in his capacity as Chairman of the newly formed Council for Equal Opportunity, and the Attorney General, Nicholas deB. Katzenbach. Following the preliminary explorations of the issue, plans will be made for further discussion on appropriate levels where the programs we believe to be indispensable for solution of problems can be examined.''

With the concurrence of Jones, Wachtel expunged the words executive action and inserted law enforcement in lieu thereof, and made additional changes to read as follows after the word undemocratic barriers:

''To pursue this objective conferences in Washington have been scheduled. The pressure of international developments has made impractical the scheduled Monday conference. However, on Tuesday, I will be meeting with Vice President Humphrey in his new capacity as Chairman of the newly created Council for Equal Opportunity, and with Attorney General Nicholas deB. Katzenbach. I am in communication with the White House concerning a possible meeting with the President. While there are no definite arrangements for such a meeting, I am hopeful that such a conference will be held on Tuesday. Following the preliminary explorations of the issue, plans will be made for further discussion on appropriate levels where the programs we believe to be indispensable for solution of problems can be examined.''

FBI

Date: 2/9/65

AIRTEL

TO: DIRECTOR, FBI (100-106670)

FROM: SAC, MOBILE (100-1472)

SUBJECT: MARTIN LUTHER KING, JR.
          SM-C

Re Bureau airtel to Mobile 2/5/65.

. . . Selma, Ala., advised . . . that MARTIN LUTHER KING did not mail any letters from the Selma jail during his recent incarceration there. . . . said, however, that numerous people visited KING in the jail and could have carried out letters for him. . . . said that as far as he knows KING was not searched when placed in the jail, and thus, he does not know whether or not KING had any letters with him [when] he entered the jail.

Concerning the report that the FBI had appealed to KING to leave Selma, this is absolutely false. KING was not interviewed by any Bureau personnel while in Selma. He was photographed on 1/18/65 after he was assaulted by a white mail [sic] at Hotel Albert in Selma. The photographing agent, SA . . . spoke to KING notifying him that he wanted to take his photograph but did not identify himself and did not interview KING or comment other than notifying him that he was taking his picture, to which KING readily agreed.

UNITED STATES GOVERNMENT
Memorandum

TO: DIRECTOR, FBI (100-106670)   DATE: 2/9/65

FROM: SAC, MOBILE (100-1472)

SUBJECT: MARTIN LUTHER KING, JR.
           SM-C

The Mobile Office was advised by . . . Selma, Alabama, that he is in possession of a telegram dated 2/4/65 at Milwaukee, Wisconsin, addressed to the Chief of Police, Selma, Ala., which reads as follows:

"I HAVE PROOF LUTHER KING MET WITH COMMUNISTS IN HOTEL ROOM AT OSLO, NORWAY. ALSO KING PAID $500 TO HOTEL CLERK AT FINLAND CITY FOR PUBLICATION TO HAVE BREAKFAST SERVED IN BED BY WHITE WAITRESS IN BIKINI SUIT. NORWEGAN SEAMAN GAVE ME SIGNED DOCUMENTS."

The above is being furnished for whatever action the Bureau may deem advisable.

UNITED STATES DEPARTMENT OF JUSTICE

FEDERAL BUREAU OF INVESTIGATION

Kansas City, Missouri
February 16, 1965

At 6:40 P.M., February 15, 1965, the Kansas City, Missouri, Office of the Federal Bureau of Investigation was telephonically contacted by a male identifying himself as . . informed that parties unknown to him were trying to recruit him to kill President Johnson and Dr. Martin Luther King, Jr.

. . . claimed that he formerly resided at . . . Kansas City, Missouri, but now lives in a downtown Kansas City, Missouri, hotel which he refused to identify, for the reason that he would be in danger from the recruits if it were learned he had contacted the FBI by telephone.

. . . said that he has worked a route for the . . . and while running this route he was approached by a stranger who told . . . that . . . had

been chosen to assassinate the President and Dr. King, and that if ...
attempted to contact authorities, ... would be sorry. The stranger allegedly told ... that ... would be met at the bus station (not identified
by ...) where ... would receive further instructions. The bus station
meeting was to be at 10:00 A.M., February 16, 1965.

... said he had no telephone, that he was calling from a pay telephone, Plaza 3-9317, and would call the FBI back at 7:30 P.M., February
15, 1965, to arrange for an interview by the FBI later the night of
February 15, 1965.

... said his derogatory views concerning both "targets" were well
known, as well as the fact that he was once a rifle expert in the
Army.... said he does not wish to commit such a crime and is seeking
any way out.... did not telephone, and has not further contacted the
FBI Office.

On the early morning of February 16, 1965 ... on the instructions of
her supervisor.... telephonically furnished the following information,
without mentioning ...

... has been employed ... He was an alcoholic, has adjusted well
to ... and has worked steadily, missing only two nights in working at
the ... said that ... began driving trucks for ... on February 2, 1956,
and so far as is known, has been rational during his entire employment
and a non-user of alcoholics.... has additional descriptive and background information concerning ...

A confidential source informed on the early morning of February 16,
1965, that telephone number Plaza 3-9317 is a non-published pay telephone at Katz Drug Company, 3200 Troost, Kansas City, Missouri.

The above-named ... may possibly be identical with a ... the subject
of a National Stolen Property Act case, involving worthless checks in
January 1948. The Houston, Texas, FBI office was origin. Information
available reflects that ... was born ... Texas, was a white male, six
feet tall, weighing 205 pounds, and was formerly a member of the ...
Texas Fire Department, from ... last known address in ... was ... his
wife ... but her whereabouts were unknown ...

A WASH DC

FBI MOBILE
12:28 PM CST   URGENT 2/18/65   FLK
TO DIRECTOR/44-12831/
FROM MOBILE/44-557/
REGISTRARS OF VOTERS OF DALLAS COUNTY, ALABAMA, VOTING DISCRIMINATION. CR-EL.
RE MOBILE TELETYPE TO THE BUREAU, FEBRUARY SEVEN-TEEN, LAST, AT ELEVEN FIFTY SEVEN P.M., CST.
. . . ADVISED . . . REV. MARTIN LUTHER KING AFTER LAST NIGHT/S [sic] MEETING AT BROWNS CHAPEL AME CHURCH, AT WHICH TIME KING TOLD HIM THE PLAN PREVIOUSLY MENTIONED TO MARCH ON THE OFFICE OF GOV. GEORGE WALLACE IN MONTGOMERY, ALABAMA, ON FEBRUARY TWENTY TWO, NEXT, HAS BEEN CANCELED, AS KING INDI-CATED MORE TIME WAS NEEDED TO DEVELOP THE DETAILS OF THIS DEMONSTRATION. KING INDICATED TO . . . HE TEN-TATIVELY PLANS TO RETURN TO SELMA, ALA., ON THE NIGHT OF FEBRUARY TWENTY ONE, NEXT, OR THE EARLY MORNING OF FEBRUARY TWENTY TWO, NEXT. KING STATED THAT A MASS MEETING IS DEFINITELY PLANNED FOR LOWNDES COUNTY, ALA, ON THE NIGHT OF FEBRUARY TWENTY THIRD, NEXT; HOWEVER, OTHER PLANS FOR THE SELMA AREA ARE UNDER CONSIDERATION, AND DEFINITE PLANS NOT FINAL. . . . STATED REV. RALPH ABERNATHY INDI-CATED THAT LOCAL NEGRO ORGANIZATIONS IN SELMA WILL SOON MAKE DEMANDS ON CITY AND COUNTY OFFI-CIALS TO HAVE NEGRO DEPUTIES AND NEGRO POLICE OFFI-CERS HIRED IN SELMA, AND THAT REFUSAL TO DO THIS WOULD BE MET BY CONTINUED DEMONSTRATIONS AND ECO-NOMIC WITHDRAWAL, WHICH ABERNATHY EXPLAINED WOULD MEAN LIMITED PURCHASING BY NEGROES FROM WHITE PERSONS WHO WOULD OPPOSE THE MEASURES.
DALLAS COUNTY BOARD OF REGISTRARS MADE THE AP-PEARANCE BOOK AVAILABLE AS OF NINE THIRTY A.M., CST, TODAY, AT WHICH TIME THERE WERE TWELVE WHITES AND TWENTY FIVE NEGROES IN LINE. NUMBER ONE FOUR ONE TWO WAS THE FIRST NUMBER ISSUED.
CONTEMPT OF COURT HEARING FOR CORDY TINDELL VIV-IAN IS STILL SCHEDULED FOR TWO THIRTY P.M. IN DALLAS

COUNTY CIRCUIT COURT. BRIAN LANDSBERG AND GEORGE RAYBORN, DEPARTMENTAL ATTORNEYS ON THE SCENE AT SELMA BEING ADVISED OF PERTINENT DEVELOPMENTS.

[Section 25]

FEDERAL BUREAU OF INVESTIGATION
U. S. DEPARTMENT OF JUSTICE
COMMUNICATIONS SECTION
FEB 24 1965

TELETYPE

FBI WASH DC
FBI LOS ANG.
1206 PM URGENT 2/24/65
TO DIRECTOR 100-106670
FROM LOS ANGELES 100-57229 2P
MARTIN LUTHER KING, JR., SM DASH C.

SOURCE WHO HAS FURNISHED RELIABLE INFORMATION IN THE PAST, TODAY ADVISED THAT . . . HAD RECEIVED TELEPHONE CALL FROM ANONYMOUS MALE AT APPROXIMATELY ELEVEN FIFTEEN P.M. FEBRUARY TWENTY THREE LAST. CALLER . . . THE CHRISTIAN NATIONALIST ARMY IS PLANNING TO KILL MARTIN LUTHER KING AT A MEETING HE IS TO ATTEND IN LOS ANGELES ON THE NIGHT OF FEBRUARY TWENTY FOUR INSTANT. . . .

. . . LAPD . . . AND . . . BEVERLY HILLS PD, ADVISED OF FOREGOING. THEY STATED EVERY PRECAUTION WILL BE TAKEN IN EFFORT TO INSURE NO INCIDENTS OCCUR.

[Section 26]

February 24, 1965

PRESS CONFERENCE with DR. MARTIN LUTHER KING held at International Airport, Crown Room of Satellite No. 6, Delta Airlines, on February 24, 1965, 11:40 A.M.

I'd like to make an initial statement. I am THOMAS KILGORE JR., Director of the West Coast Bureau of DR. KING's movement, SCLC.

DR. KING is here for a few days and for fund raising events for the occasion one of his appearances will be in the Palladium tomorrow at 12 o'clock sponsored by the World Affairs Council and we are happy now to present DR. KING for you to raise questions and do whatever you would like.

DR. KING, do you consider the life of ELIJAH MUHAMMAD is in danger at this particular time?

Well, I think we must face the fact that there are some very ghastly and nightmarish aspects of violence taking place at this time and it does seem to be a feud between some of the Black Nationalist groups. Consequently, I think we have to face the fact that there is probably some danger [to] the life of ELIJAH MUHAMMAD. I think this is very unfortunate. I think this whole episode and as I said, this ghastly nightmare of violence and counter-violence is very unfortunate and must be condemned by all people of goodwill.

DR. KING, what could it possibly lead to if worse came to worse?

Well, it just continues to degenerate and darken nights of violence. I think it has to stop somewhere. It isn't good for the image of our nation. It isn't good for the Negro cause. It isn't good for anything that we hold dear in our country and our democracy. I believe firmly in non-violence. I think we have got to learn to disagree without being violently disagreeable and this whole philosophy of expressing dissent through murder must be vigorously condemned.

DR. JAMES FARMER has indicated that he believes this is part of an international conspiracy. Do you have any comment on this?

Well, I don't know about that. I have no knowledge to follow through or make such a statement. This may well be but my knowledge doesn't reveal this and I don't try at this point to even further a speculation as to who assassinated MALCOLM X. The Police Department of New York, I assume, is vigorously investigating this and I think until the investigation is finished I would withhold any statement about the person or persons who perpetrated this dastardly act.

DR. KING, you have just come from Selma. What is the feeling of the Negro in general about this thing that is going on now as far as the Black Muslims are concerned. Do they have a feeling about it?

Well, I think the general feeling in the Negro community, that this is very unfortunate and that we have such large problems to deal with in getting rid of racial injustice that it is both impractical and immoral to be fighting among ourselves. I think this is the general attitude that prevails among the people that I have had a chance to talk with about it.

DR. KING, is there a present threat to your life?

Well, I get threats quite often. This is almost a daily and weekly occurrence. I mentioned in Selma just the other day that I had received information from reliable sources that there would be an attempt to take my life and that there was an attempt when I was in Marian, Alabama, which is in Perry County, about a week ago but at the time I was surrounded by a number of people and I was never clear enough to be a target and we got some anonymous threats on Monday when I returned to Selma; so that this continues and it's something that we get, as I said, ever so often.

Did this information come to you from a well placed source like the FBI?

Well, no it didn't come from the FBI. This information did come from investigative agencies though. Particularly the incident in Marian. This came from sources from within the investigative machinery of the State.

Now, when you say the threat on your life. You're not talking now about from the Black Muslims or the Nationalists. You're talking about white segregationists.

Oh yes, from segregationists.

DR. KING, have the threats on you life been increasing, the number of them. Have they been increasing?

Well, they always increase when we get in the heat and height of the movement. They tend to decrease in periods when we are not in an intensified development but I think that whenever we have been in the midst of a determined struggle, whether it was in Birmingham or St. Augustine Florida, or Albany, Georgia, or now in Selma. The threats tend to increase at that time.

May I ask you this. What is your understanding of the specific legislation that is being drafted now in the Justice Department that would apply to such situations that exist in Selma?

I don't have the details on this legislation. Some of my lawyers will be talking with the Attorney General today about it. I talked with Attorney General Katzenbach on Monday about the registrars but only in general terms and he said that they were reaching the point now that they wanted to finalize it and in a few days it would be presented to the President but as far as specifics, I can't say at this time. I would hope that it will include a provision for federal registrars and certainly a provision that will get rid of the so-called literacy tests and I think these federal registrars, if the bill is to be meaningful, must be appointed by and responsible to the President. The present bills that we have which came through the 1957, 1960, and 64 sections of the Civil Rights Bill on voting rights at points tend to institutionalize the difficulties and it does provide a provision that federal referees can be appointed by federal judges. Now we have a case right now in Marian, Alabama, where they have a federal referee but Judge Thomas appointed a federal referee from Hale County, one of the adjoining counties and he done registered more Negroes than the registrars, so that these—we made a system now whereby federal registrars will be responsible to and appointed by the President himself.

Is it your understanding that the President wants this?

Well, in my recent conversations with the President, I get this impression. Now he hasn't made any definite promise to me and he hadn't formulated a bill in his mind at that time and he made it clear that he would rely on the Justice Department to study this in depth and to make a recommendation but he strongly feels that something must be done beyond the present bills that we already have.

DR. KING, do you feel there is a possibility that something might happen to you some time? Have you made arrangements for someone to carry on—something like the President and Vice President have if anything happens?

Oh, yes, we have in our movement many dedicated, intelligent and dynamic leaders. We have this in my own organizations and we have definitely discussed these things very realistically. We are not fooling ourselves about the dangerous possibilities that we face.

Q. Could one of your men fall heir to your particular leadership?

K. Well, I would say the Southern Christian Leadership Conference—
Dr. Ralph Abernathy is the closest associate that I have and my closest advisor and the man who articulates the meaning of our movement extremely well and who is dedicated absolutely to the philosophy of non-violence, and is a great leader in his own right.

Q. Dr. King, what is your attitude toward the threats that you received?

K. Well, I guess I have learned now to take them rather philosophically. I think this cause is right and because of my deep feeling about the rightness of the cause, it gives me courage to carry on, and I think that one has to conquer the feeling of death if he is going to do anything constructive in life and take a stand against evil, and I go along with the view that one who has not found something so true and so meaningful and profound that he will die for it is not fit to live, so I am prepared to face anything that comes in standing up to this struggle with the great belief and the great feeling that unmerited suffering is redemptive.

Q. Do you feel that the civil rights investigation out of Washington has accomplished anything at all? And if it has, what?

K. I think it accomplished a great deal; first, they brought the attention of the nation to the situation in Selma, and brought to the people of Selma and the Black Belt Counties in general, the kind of expression of support that gave them a new sense of hope. I think the third thing that came out of it was the fact that these Senators were—these Representatives were absolutely convinced that there were glaring injustices and denials on the question of voting rights in Selma, Alabama, and, on the basis of that, some went back and introduced bills so that we already have some bills that have been introduced by members of the House and I think that with the bills introduced and the Administrative Bill that will soon come, we can get the best elements out of all these and will emerge with a very strong bill.

Q. Dr. King, I wonder if you will not identify the high government official who said there is a threat against your life, if you will tell us why you don't identify him?

K. Well, I am not at liberty to identify. Many of these things come confidentially and in order to continue that investigation it is necessary so often not to reveal these things, so I would not like to reveal any names.

Q. You insist it was a high federal official who informed you?

K. Well, I can say that the Attorney General called me on Monday and expressed great concern about my safety and made it very clear that they are concerned.

Q. Did he give you information about the threat on your life?

K. Well, I didn't go into that with him. These things are not too pleasant to discuss so I didn't want to go into great detail. I usually like to talk with some of my aides about it and after that I got three additional calls which tended to confirm the fact that threats had been made.

Q. Yesterday a group of Republican Senators asked this question: what is the White House doing to meet the need of universal registration laws that were pointed up by you in Selma? I wonder if you will answer this question?

K. Well, I am very happy to see these very outstanding Republicans take this courageous and necessary stand on the immediacy—the need, rather—of immediate legislation. I think there is action going on and I think the Administration is serious about this—I am sure that the Attorney General is serious when he said they are moving to the point of formalizing some bill to present to Congress. But I guess all of us need a little prompting at times and I hope that the strong statement made by the outstanding Republicans will cause the Administration to move a little faster, because I think it is urgent to get this legislation immediately, and we certainly don't want to see it drag out in Congress and we don't want to see a filibuster, and we don't want to see this be put off in order to deal with some other issue that may be important—this is just as important as any other issue facing our nation today.

Q. Dr. King, it would appear in the reports that we have out of the South that not as many people have showed up in the last few days for the demonstrations for voter registration. Is there a diminishing interest among folk down there?

K. Oh, not at all; I think it is as strong as it has ever been. The fact is that we have outdone ourselves and we have turned out more people than we really anticipated by this time. We have gotten more than 2,200 Negroes in Selma to appear to sign what is called the "appearance sheet." We were aiming at 3,000 by July and we already have 2,200, so it means that by touching that many people, we don't have as many people to follow along now to sign the "appearance sheet." It means we must get into the community to find the people who have not signed it.

Q. You are not depressed that only a couple of hundred have shown up from time to time in the last few days?

K. Oh, not at all. I think the enthusiasm is as high as ever—the determination is as great, and I have no doubt about the fact that the Negroes in Dallas County are going through with this and they are determined to get the vote and they aren't going to stop until it happens.

Q. Will you be going back to Marion [sic] soon?

K. I will be going back Monday of next week to hold demonstrations there.

Q. Dr. King, would you be good enough to repeat what you said at the beginning about the whole Black Muslim situation of violence?

K. Yes, this ghastly nightmare of violence and counter-violence is something that must be condemned by all people of goodwill in this nation. I don't think violence solves any social problem; it only creates new and more complicated problems. I think it is also necessary to say that the assassination of Malcolm X was an unfortunate tragedy and it reveals that there are still numerous people in our nation who have degenerated to the point of expressing . . . murder, and we haven't learned to disagree without being violently disagreeable.

I think it is even more unfortunate that this great tragedy occurred at a time when Malcolm X was re-evaluating his own philosophical presuppositions and moving toward a greater understanding of the non-violent movement and toward more tolerance of white people, generally.

But I think one must understand that in condemning the philosophy of Malcolm X, which I did constantly, that he was a victim of the despair that came into being as a result of a society that gives so many Negroes the nagging sense of "nobodyness." And just as one condemns the philosophy, he must be as vigorous in condemning the continued existence in our society of the conditions of racial injustice, depression and man's inhumanity to man.

I think there is a lesson that we can all learn from this all over the nation and that is that violence is impractical and that now, more than ever before, we must pursue the course of non-violence to achieve a reign of justice and a rule of love in our society, and that hatred and violence must be cast into the unending limbo if we are to survive.

Q. Dr. King, do you intend to attend the funeral?

K. No, because of the engagement that I have here. But I will certainly extend my sympathy to his wife and to his family and, as I said, this has come as a great shock to so many of us and altho [sic] we had constant disagreements, I had a deep affection for Malcolm X and I am very sorry about the whole thing.

Q. Is there any real fear in your mind that more and more Negroes are becoming "disaffected" with non-violence?

K. No, I think—on the contrary, Negroes are now more convinced than ever that non-violence is the most potent weapon available to an oppressed people in their struggle for freedom and for human dignity, and I think more and more people are coming to see that this is the most practically sound and morally excellent way to deal with the problem.

I don't think anybody should feel that the violence that is presently taking place is an indication of the feeling of a large segment of the Negro community. I think this represents a very small, fanatical minority and nothing like a majority of the Negroes. The Negroes, by and large, are peace-loving and willing to at least follow the technique of non-violence in their struggle for voting rights.

Q. Is anything short of massive federal intervention going to make any substantial change in the situation in Alabama?

K. I must be honest enough to say that realism impels me to admit that the changes in Alabama and Mississippi will not come from within.

I cannot see the changes coming short of massive federal action. I think the feelings are too great, the sickness too deep, the mass neuroses too pervasive to really bring about the change within in terms of the benevolence of the white power structure, but I think, with strong massive action from the federal government on many fronts, the people will inevitably yield to what comes down from our national leadership.

Q. Are you satisfied, sir, that this dedication of this administration is sufficient?

K. Well, I would certainly say that the President is committed on civil rights. I have no doubt about that. He has made it clear that he is committed to the implementation of the civil rights bill and that he sees the moral implication of this whole struggle to make integration a reality in America. So, up to now, I have no gripes with President Johnson. I think he has moved on with dedication on the matter of civil rights.

Q. Dr. King, inasmuch as there remains this superficial contradiction between your remarks, even today, and the Justice Department, that there has been some kind of misunderstanding as to who initiated the mention of the death threat to you . . .

K. Well, I don't—I didn't know there was any misunderstanding or contradiction.

Q. This morning the L.A. Times was quite clear that the Justice Department said that you initiated the suggestion that there was a plot on your life and not they.

K. Well, now, I never did say that the Justice Department initiated the suggestion. I never named the person who initiated the suggestion. When I was speaking in a mass meeting on Monday night when I mentioned this, I never gave any names, so I think the Justice Department is saying that because Mr. Katzenbach merely called me and expressed, as I said, great concern for my safety, but at that time he didn't go into any details that I got about half an hour later in two other conversations.

Q. I have one more question. Dr. King, in the terribly consistency of this . . . if something should happen to you, since you are the focal point of this non-violent group, at which point then would that non-violence turn to violence? Have you thought about that?

K. Well, I certainly hope that nothing happens to me but I will be the first to say that if something ever happens to me, I would hope that the people who have tried to follow my leadership and have committed themselves to my philosophy would be as committed to it then as ever. I don't believe in retaliatory violence and if something happens to me or any leader in the non-violent movement, I would never advocate Negroes turning to violence as a retaliatory approach to the problem.

When you get in a non-violent movement, the one thing that you commit yourself to is the fact that you are standing up for truth and justice and what is right, and you are willing to face death, if necessary. We teach this day in and day out that we must be willing to accept blows without retaliation—and we are constantly beaten in this movement—and we go to the point of saying that if physical death is the price that some must pay to free the white brothers and their children from a permanent psychological death and a permanent death of the spirit, then nothing can be more redemptive, so I would feel and certainly hope that if anything should happen to any of us in the non-violent movement, that Negroes would react to this as non-violently as they have to the mobs in Mississippi and Alabama.

Q. I would like to ask, Dr. King, if your organization gives any consideration to the possibility of another so-called "long hot summer," as we had last summer and, if so, have you made plans to quell or hold it down, or keep it from starting in the first place?

K. Well, one has to understand the meaning of "the long hot summer." I don't ever want to feel a long, hot, violent summer, but I think we will continue to have rather hot non-violent summers until this problem is solved, and we must face the fact that although we have made strides and we have made real progress, we still have a long, long, way to go, not only in the South but in the North, and I think some of our most nagging problems in the future will be in the big cities in the North in the area of jobs, and schools, and housing, and I think that as long as these problems are there, we are going to have protest activities and demonstrations and it will keep the heat alive. My only hope is that our heat will always be non-violent and disciplined and carried out in a dignified manner.

I just wanted to make a statement to thank the City Council and the County Board of Supervisors for declaring today and tomorrow MARTIN LUTHER KING DAYS. It is always a great pleasure to come to Los Angeles and we have gotten some of our greatest support, both financially and morally, from this great city and this great state, so I am deeply grateful to the Mayor and City Council and the County Board of Supervisors for this warm expression of support.

Page B-1
Herald-Examiner
Los Angeles, California

Date: 2/26/65

Threats—Dr. King Guarded

Dr. Martin Luther King, Jr., continued under heavy guard today after threats yesterday including one to dynamite the Hollywood Palladium where he spoke.

More than 100 policemen last night surrounded the Sunset Boulevard block where the integrationist and Nobel Prize winner attended a benefit premiere of "The Greatest Story Ever Told" at the Pacific's Cinerama Theater.

After the film, detectives surrounded Dr. King and hastily escorted him from the lobby into a waiting limousine containing a guard with a walkie-talkie. The limousine pulled away preceded by a motorcycle escort and followed by two cars of detectives.

HEAVY GUARD

While the movie was being shown an officer walked about a ledge of the theater at 6360 Sunset Blvd., and about 15 uniformed policemen stood outside the lobby. Detectives, motorcycle officers and other uniformed policemen cruised the block on which the theater is situated.

The police force included more than 30 plainclothes officers and 20 motorcycle officers. No incidents were reported.

Another large police detachment will surround and infiltrate Temple Israel of Hollywood where Dr. King will speak tonight.

The temple at 7300 Hollywood Blvd., will bristle with patrolmen and detectives carrying out tight security measures, as Dr. King, president of the Southern Christian Leadership Conference, speaks at 8:30 p.m.

Dr. King's appearance highlights the temple's observance of Brotherhood Week. The holder of 125 citations and awards for his civil rights activities will share the pulpit with Dr. Max Nussbaum and Rabbi Meyer Heller, the congregation's spiritual leaders.

Irving Briskin, congregation president, said today the public is invited to hear the speakers and attend the services, which will be held in the sanctuary.

The heavy police protection began with Dr. King's arrival here and continued to surround the peaceful civil rights worker yesterday when he addressed 2,000 persons in the Hollywood Palladium.

RAPS 14 VOTE

Despite the tight security measures taken by authorities, Dr. King insisted he was enjoying his Southern California stay. "My few days here are a refreshing contrast to Selma, Ala.," he told his audience.

But he rapped California's recently mandated Proposition 14, which nullified the Rumford Housing Act, declaring:

"We are a long, long way from realizing the American dream if we cannot learn to live together."

He also spoke of the voter registration problem in Selma, pointing out that part of his peaceful action program calls for earning the right to vote for Negroes "all over this nation."

Dr. King hinted at the possibility of an economic boycott in Mississippi, saying:

"I think if we were to do this, there would be a change overnight."

I-12 Los Angeles Times
Los Angeles, Calif.

Date: 2/27/65

Dr. King Vows to Intensify His Drive in Selma

BY ERIC MALNIC
Times Staff Writer

Dr. Martin Luther King Jr. vowed here Friday night to "return Monday to Selma" and "intensify efforts" to gain registration for Negro voters there.

Dr. King's statement defied the recent declaration by Joe Smitherman, mayor of the Alabama town, that the community can and will settle its racial turmoil only if Dr. King and other "outsiders" stay away.

Dr. King's pledge to return to Selma came after a sermon at the Temple Israel in Hollywood in which the Negro leader displayed anew his increasing militancy—although specifically non-violent militancy—in his fight for Negro civil rights.

He told an overflow crowd at the temple that mankind must not get "caught up in unattained goals, but must move on to the promised land of justice and brotherhood."

'Some May Be Jailed'

In that journey to the promised land, he said, "some of us may get scarred up a bit, some may end up in jail cells, some must even face death—but 'We shall overcome.' "

Scores of police officers surrounded the temple at 7300 Hollywood Blvd. while Dr. King spoke, reflecting the continued anxiety over telephoned threats on the integration leader's life during his stay here.

The anxiety was intensified by the knowledge that an alleged racist, Kieth [sic] Gilbert, who police say took part in the theft of a cache of dynamite, had yet to be apprehended and was considered "armed and dangerous."

However, there were no incidents or expressions of hostility by the crowd of more than 1,500 that gave Dr. King a warm welcome at the Hollywood temple.

In addition to calling for intensified efforts in the field of civil rights, the recent Nobel Peace Prize winner urged his audience to move forward in the drive to end poverty and physical violence.

"The poor, the underprivileged, the tortured—even the least of these—is our brother," Dr. King said.

"A great nation is a compassionate nation," he said. "Love is the highest good—he who loves has discovered the ultimate meaning of reality."

The Negro leader said he will leave Los Angeles Sunday to return to Selma.

III-5 Los Angeles Times
Los Angeles, Calif.

Date: 2/27/65

Dynamite Theft Suspect Eludes Police Search

An alleged racist who reportedly participated in a raid on a dynamite magazine Thursday night was being sought by lawmen throughout California Friday.

Officers were warned that because of Keith D. Gilbert's past conduct, and because he may be armed and still carrying some of the stolen explosives, he must be considered "dangerous."

Most of an estimated 1,400 pounds of dynamite taken from a powder company magazine was recovered Thursday night in Gilbert's garage apartment at 419 Western Ave., Glendale.

Along with the explosives, investigators found a small arsenal of weapons, several cases of ammunition and stacks of Minutemen tracts.

Three Under Arrest

Three men who police say were involved with Gilbert in the dynamite theft have been arrested. Stephen Lowe, a 20-year-old sailor, was arrested Friday morning at a friend's home in North Hollywood. The other two, Rodney Chesney, 42, and his nephew, Ronald Bartell, 24, were arrested Thursday afternoon.

The latter pair were released on bail Friday night after being charged with misdemeanor traffic violations.

A warrant was issued Friday for the arrest of 26-year-old Gilbert, a former gunshop owner and exponent of right-wing causes.

Police said Gilbert and others stole the explosives in a pre-dawn raid at the Hercules Powder Co. property in Magazine Canyon near Sylmar.

The theft came a day after Dr. Martin Luther King, the civil rights leader, arrived here for a series of talks.

Heavy guard placed around Dr. King after his arrival Wednesday because of threats on his life was tightened even further.

Guard Still in Effect

The taut security measures for Dr. King remained in effect Friday as the Negro leader spoke at Hollywood Temple Israel.

But police said Gilbert, awaiting trial on March 8 for allegedly attempting to shoot a Negro publicist in September, may have fled this area.

Police said they traced Chesney and Bartell, both of 9867 Wheatland Ave., Sunland, through a license number jotted down by a power company employe [sic] who saw the explosives being loaded into the back seat of a car.

They, in turn, led officers to the stolen dynamite, ammonium nitrate and blasting caps in Gilbert's apartment in Glendale.

When last seen, the 150-pound, 5 foot 9 inch Gilbert was wearing a gaudy plaid shirt and khaki trousers.

A-5 Herald-Examiner
Los Angeles, Calif.

Date: 2/28/65

Dr. King's Guard at Maximum

Dr. Martin Luther King Jr. continued under heavy protection here today as he prepared for the final round of appearances, including the leading of worship at the Victory Baptist Church.

Police expected some 2,500 worshipers at the church, at 4802 McKinley Ave., to hear Dr. King's sermon.

Adding to police worries was the failure of law officials to locate a man described as "armed and dangerous," with "a real hatred for Negroes," Keith D. Gilbert, 27, of Glendale.

'NO ULTIMATE'

Gilbert is wanted in connection with the theft of 1,400 pounds of dynamite on Thursday and is already awaiting trial on a charge of shooting at a Negro.

"There is no such thing as ultimate protection," said Lt. Charles D. Reese, 37, who is in charge of the protection detail. "However, we are giving Dr. King every ounce we can afford."

The church where Dr. King will speak is near the headquarters of several "extremist Negro groups."

To handle the number of people expected to attend the services, loudspeakers will carry Dr. King's voice outside to the sidewalk and parking lot.

TWO HELD

Police have two men under arrest for the theft of the dynamite, Clyde Young, 22, a salesman, and Lewis Stephen Lowe, 20, a sailor, and have issued an all-points bulletin for Gilbert's arrest.

Dr. King is scheduled to tape a television interview with Negro author Louis Lomax later this afternoon and to fly back to Selma, Ala., tomorrow to continue the Negro voter registration drive there.

RE: UNKNOWN SUBJECT; ANONYMOUS
   TELEPHONE CALLS, CHICAGO,
   ILLINOIS, MARCH 6 AND 7, 1965

At 9:05 A.M., March 6, 1965 ... Office of Deputy Superintendent, Chicago Police Department, advised the Chicago Office of the FBI that a short time earlier this date the Chicago Police Department had received an anonymous telephone call to the effect that Chicago's Mayor Richard J. Daley would be killed if any harm was done to Martin Luther King, Jr., in Alabama today. The anonymous caller then hung up.

It should be noted that information concerning receipt by the Chicago Office of the FBI of the anonymous telephone threat against Martin Luther King has been made available by the Chicago Police Department to various press media in Chicago. ... advised that the telephone call threatening the life of Mayor Daley was undoubtedly prompted by the wide-spread press and radio dissemination of this information. ... advised that the Chicago Police Department has no suspects in this matter, however, were providing heavier protection for Mayor Daley as a result.

At 1:30 P.M., March 7, 1965, an anonymous male individual telephonically contacted the Chicago Office of the FBI and stated that he was going to get an airplane out of O'Hare Airport, Chicago, between 2:00 and 3:00 P.M. this date, destined for Alabama. The caller stated that he had a gun and that he had a man in Alabama who has Reverend Martin Luther King spotted. The caller continued that he did not care for "these comments against the President of the United States," then hung up.

UNITED STATES DEPARTMENT OF JUSTICE

FEDERAL BUREAU OF INVESTIGATION

Chicago, Illinois
March 8, 1965

UNKNOWN SUBJECT; ANONYMOUS TELEPHONE
CALLS, CHICAGO, ILLINOIS, MARCH 6 AND 7, 1965,
THREATENING THE LIFE OF MARTIN LUTHER KING, JR.
RACIAL MATTERS

At 3:05 A.M., March 6, 1965, an anonymous male individual telephonically contacted the Chicago Office of the Federal Bureau of Investigation (FBI). This individual stated that he was "head of the KKK in Chicago," adding that he had already paid one of his men $2,500 to riddle Martin Luther King with bullets on the following day, Sunday, March 7, 1965, when King marches on the capital. This is believed to be a reference to Montgomery, Alabama.

This caller also stated "Anyone who tells the President what to do is going to get it." No explanation for this latter remark was offered and the caller then hung up.

FEDERAL BUREAU OF INVESTIGATION
U.S. DEPARTMENT OF JUSTICE
COMMUNICATIONS SECTION
MAR 17 1965

TELETYPE

FBI WASH DC

FBI CHICAGO
1255 PM CST URGENT 3/17/65 JLS
TO DIRECTOR, ATLANTA, MOBILE AND MOBILE (SELMA)
FROM CHICAGO (157-NEW) 2P

. . . CHICAGO, ILLINOIS: THREAT TO KILL MARTIN LUTHER KING, MARCH SEVENTEEN INSTANT, RM, RACIAL MATTERS

AT SIX ZERO FIVE A.M. MARCH SEVENTEEN INSTANT, SUB-JECT TELEPHONICALLY CONTACTED CHICAGO OFFICE AND STATED QUOTE MARTIN LUTHER KING IS A MAN TO BE WATCHED. WHERE IS HE GETTING THAT GARBAGE. I'D BLADE HIM IF HE GOT IN MY WAY ENDQUOTE. WHEN ASKED WHAT HE MEANT BY BLADE HIM, SUBJECT STATED QUOTE I'D KILL HIM IF HE GOT IN MY WAY, YES, I'M A THREAT TO HIM. I'M NOT PREJUDICES. HAVE YOU GOT THAT WRITTEN DOWN? I'M SINCERE. I HAVE NO MALICE AGAINST THE MAN. THE MAN HAS AGITATED TOO LONG. I DON'T WANT A MAN LIKE THIS. I HATE SPOOKS. HE BELONGS HOME AND HAS NO RIGHT AGITATING ENDQUOTE. SUBJECT SOUNDED AS WHITE MALE, DRUNK AND AT TIMES INCOHERENT.

FBI

3/17/65

AIRTEL

To:
     SACs, Mobile
     Atlanta

From: Director, FBI (100-106670)

ANONYMOUS THREAT TO KILL
MARTIN LUTHER KING—SELMA,
ALABAMA ON 3/20/65

ReCGtel to Bureau, Mobile, Atlanta and Selma 3/17/65 captioned as above which reported that the Chicago Police Department had received an anonymous telephone call wherein the caller stated "I will kill Martin Luther King in Selma, Alabama, on next Saturday. I have made this threat previously, but this time I will keep it."

Mobile and Atlanta Offices are instructed to immediately advise local police authorities at Selma, Alabama, and Atlanta, Georgia, of the information contained in retel.

For the future guidance of the Mobile and Atlanta Offices, and to obviate the necessity for communications such as instant airtel, the following policy should be followed relative to information received concerning threats against King. In all instances, unless the Bureau indicates otherwise, the Atlanta, Georgia, Police Department which covers the permanent residence of King should be advised of the information concerning the threat. This applies even though the threat indicates that some action will be carried out in an area away from Atlanta. In addition, whenever the area where the threat is to be carried out is known, the local law enforcement agency covering that area should be advised.

Until further notice from the Bureau, the foregoing policy should be followed. Any deviations must be only with Bureau approval. Neither King nor representatives for him should be advised of the information concerning the threats.

[Section 27]

RE: MARTIN LUTHER KING, JR.

An article appeared in the Cleveland "Plain Dealer," **March 24, 1965,** edition, page 11, columns 1 through 5, captioned "King Warns

Oppression of Negro Can Destroy U.S.'' This article stated that Dr. MARTIN LUTHER KING, JR., a 36-year-old Nobel Peace Prize winner, President of the Southern Leadership Conference [sic], spoke at a testimonial dinner in his honor at the Hotel Sheraton-Cleveland, Cleveland, Ohio, on March 23, 1965. This article stated that KING in his address warned that the ''seeds of the country's destruction lie in oppression of the Negro. He said that now more than ever before, the United States is challenged to maintain its strength through justice and brotherhood.

''More than 2,200 persons, who paid $10 or $25 a plate to hear Dr. KING, frequently interrupted him with spirited applause, especially when he alluded to the civil rights march from Selma, Alabama, to Montgomery.

''Money realized from the dinner will be used to finance civil rights activities such as the Alabama march, which, Dr. KING said, will have cost $50,000 when it is completed tomorrow.

''Dr. KING's theme last night was 'The American Dream.'

'' 'America,' he said, 'is a dream unfulfilled. Now more than ever before, America is challenged to realize this dream.

'' 'We must act now before it is too late. We cannot afford not to live up to the American dream.'

''This can be accomplished, Dr. KING said, only through a realization that 'all men are heirs of the legacy of dignity and worth.'

''He said, 'the time has come when we all must learn to live together as brothers or all perish together as fools.'

'' 'Individuals cannot live alone,' he said. 'Neither can nations. All life is interrelated. I can never be what I ought to be until you are what you ought to be, and you can never be what you ought to be unless I am what I ought to be.'

''Dr. KING called for 'massive action' all over the nation to stamp out segregation. He urged his audience to flood Washington with mail in support of the voter registration bill proposed by President JOHNSON.

''He called JOHNSON's speech asking for such legislation 'the most passionate, eloquent and unequivocal plea for justice ever made.'

''Dr. KING praised the 'ground crew' of the civil rights movement, such as the Alabama marchers.

'' 'They're the ones I accepted the (Nobel) prize for,' he said. 'In a real sense, they are the heroes of this struggle.'

''Dr. KING was introduced by the Rev. O.M. Hoover, chairman of the dinner. Both intend to join the Alabama marchers early today.

"Mayor RALPH S. LOCHER greeted Dr. KING. He had proclaimed yesterday as Dr. Martin Luther King Jr. Day.

"Gov. JAMES A. RHODES spoke with Dr. KING over the telephone in the afternoon. The governor told him that a last minute change advancing the dinner from tonight to last night made it impossible for him to attend.

"WILLIAM O. WALKER, publisher of the Call & Post, Negro weekly here, and state industrial relations director, presented Dr. KING with a $100 check from Gov. RHODES.

"WALKER is a native of Selma. His parents formerly owned the cafe from which the Rev. JAMES J. REEB of Boston walked before he was beaten to death March 9.

"Dr. KING's flight to Cleveland yesterday was delayed by bad weather. When he arrived he looked tired. His voice was soft at an afternoon press conference, but was strong and clear last night.

"At the press conference, Dr. KING said he never allowed 'fears for my life to take possession of me . . . because I know that our cause is basically right, and it will be triumphant. It will be triumphant no matter what happens to me.'

"Last night's dinner was sponsored by a committee representing a cross-section of Greater Cleveland's community, civic and religious life. Councilman JOHN W. KELLOGG, R-18, was coordinator. Toastmaster was W. WILLARD BROWN, director of the University Circle Research Center."

RE: MARTIN LUTHER KING, JR.

An article appeared in the Cleveland "Plain Dealer," **March 24, 1965,** edition, page 6, column 1, captioned "Two Priests Here Joining Alabama Rights March." This article reflected that the Reverend EDWARD J. GRIFFIN and the Reverend THOMAS J. GALLAGHER, two priests of the Cleveland Catholic Diocese, are joining the civil rights march in Selma, Alabama. According to the article these two priests left here last night aboard Dr. MARTIN LUTHER KING's chartered jet.

The article stated "a spokesman for the diocesan chancery said the two had permission to join the march. This will be the first time a Cleveland priest has participated in a civil rights demonstration in the South, although several took part in the march in Washington in August 1963.

"Father GRIFFIN, assistant pastor at Holy Family Church, Parma, is active in several community relations groups here. Father GAL-

LAGHER is chaplain of the Catholic Interracial Council in Akron and an assistant at St. Hilary Church there.''

. . . advised on March 24, 1965, that EDWARD A. SPELIC, 2948 Lorain Avenue, Cleveland, was released by the Cleveland Police Department on this date without being charged.

. . . advised on March 24, 1965, that Dr. MARTIN LUTHER KING, JR., left Cleveland Hopkins International Airport at 12:55 A.M. on March 24, 1965, on a chartered jet plane for Montgomery, Alabama, by way of Pittsburgh, Pennsylvania, and Atlanta, Georgia.

[Section 28]

UNITED STATES DEPARTMENT OF JUSTICE

FEDERAL BUREAU OF INVESTIGATION

Miami, Florida
March 27, 1965

Re: . . .
THREAT AGAINST THE PRESIDENT

At 12:20 P.M. on Saturday, March 27, 1965, . . . telephonically contacted the Miami FBI Office and identified himself as . . . Miami Beach, Florida. He stated that he wished to furnish information concerning a threat against the lives of President Lyndon B. Johnson and Reverend Martin Luther King. In furnishing this information . . . indicated that he had not personally heard the threats described herein below but that various guests in his hotel had told him of the threats.

According to . . . a white male, approximately 27 years of age, 5 feet 6 inches tall, having blond hair and a fair complexion, registered at the . . . 1965, under the name of . . . Texas, and was assigned room number 119, where he was still residing as of March 27, 1965. . . . stated that . . . informed him that he had actually been [in] the Miami area for a week prior to the time he checked into the . . . According to . . . is employed as a cook at . . . which is a concession serving the . . . private beach area as well as an adjoining public beach. . . . confided that . . . is a heavy drinker of intoxicants and while not working usually spends his time at . . . Bar or . . . Bar, both of which are situated on . . . Miami Beach, Florida.

. . . stated that two guests of the hotel whom he identified as . . . and . . . both of whom are from Toronto, Canada, complained to . . . that . . . told them he was glad President Kennedy was assassinated and further informed that in the event President Johnson or Reverend Martin Luther King come to Miami, he would be the man that would shoot them. . . . stated that . . . has repeated these threats to . . . and . . . on more than one occasion, during the past week, March 23 through 27, 1965.

. . . stated that in view of these threats against the President, he and one of his employees took upon themselves to enter the room number 119 . . . while . . . was not in. In the room they located under a lounge chair a revolver, which . . . was not able to describe in any more detail.

UNITED STATES DEPARTMENT OF JUSTICE

FEDERAL BUREAU OF INVESTIGATION

New York, New York
March 29, 1965

Re: Martin Luther King, Jr.
Security Matter-C

On March 28, 1965, Reverend Martin Luther King, Jr., was interviewed on the National Broadcasting Company television program, "Meet the Press." King stated that the march from Selma to Montgomery, Alabama, was one of the most powerful and dramatic civil rights display that has ever taken place. He said that the march had a two-fold purpose: 1. To protest police brutality in Alabama and 2. To secure the right of the Negro to vote.

King stated that there can be no respite in demonstrations as long as conditions exist in Alabama that call for demonstrations. He said there is a moral obligation to continue demonstrations so that the issues can be kept before the people of the United States.

According to King there are barriers which remain in Alabama that must be destroyed, namely the unhampered right for all to vote in Alabama, removal of the poll tax, an end to brutality by all law enforcement agencies and equal opportunity for the Negro in the anti-poverty program.

King stated that he did not consider that he violated the law by marching in Selma, in defiance of a court injunction, since attorneys had advised that it was an invalid order. King said there are two types of laws according to his thinking: 1. The just law which [one] has a moral obligation to obey and 2. The unjust law which [one] has a moral obligation to defy. King said he does not believe in defying or evading laws, but stated the chief norm in his actions is to accept the penalty if his conscience tells him the law is unjust.

King said that he plans to call for nation-wide economic withdrawal from Alabama, a boycott of Alabama products and to bring pressure on Governor Wallace of Alabama for his reign of terror.

Concerning a charge of Communist Party infiltration of the Civil Rights movement, King said he saw no evidence of this since all civil rights organizations state in their bylaws that there can be no member of the Communist Party either as an official or as a member.

Concerning a charge that he in 1958 attended a Communist training school known as the Highlanders Folk School, King denied that it was a Communist training school and indicated that he had only spent one hour there to present a speech on the 25th anniversary of the school.

King concluded his remarks by stating that the civil rights movement will continue to be non-violent in nature.

UNITED STATES DEPARTMENT OF JUSTICE

FEDERAL BUREAU OF INVESTIGATION

Washington D.C. 20535
March 30, 1965

UNKNOWN SUBJECT
MARTIN LUTHER KING, JR.—VICTIM
RACIAL MATTERS

... advised on March 29, 1965, that while he was on duty at ABC News, Washington, D.C., the night of March 28–29, 1965, he received a telephone call from an unidentified individual who stated that he and his group were going "to get" Martin Luther King.

... stated he received this call at approximately 12:15 A.M., March

29, 1965, and that the unknown caller talked approximately ten minutes. During this time the caller did not indicate who he was, who his group was, nor when or where they would "get" King. . . . stated he believed this telephone call was a local call and that the person speaking was believed to be a man and that he had a "Southern accent."

. . . stated this individual had apparently been listening to the television program, "Meet the Press," during the evening of March 28, 1965, on which Martin Luther King had appeared. According to the information in . . . office this program had originated at NBC, Washington, D.C., but that King had appeared through NBC, San Francisco, California.

. . . Metropolitan Police Department, and . . . Secret Service, have been notified of the above matter. (Both Washington, D.C.)

[Section 29]

UNITED STATES DEPARTMENT OF JUSTICE

FEDERAL BUREAU OF INVESTIGATION

Philadelphia, Pennsylvania
March 31, 1965

ALLEGED PLOT TO ASSASSINATE
MARTIN LUTHER KING

. . . was arrested on a local traffic charge in . . . Maryland, by the Maryland State Police (MSP). It was subsequently determined that . . . was a fugitive and was wanted in the State of Pennsylvania where he had escaped from the custody of the Sheriff's Office, . . . prior to appearing in court on assault and battery charges.

While in custody of the MSP, . . . was interviewed by Special Agents of the Federal Bureau of Investigation (FBI) and advised as follows:

On approximately March 12, 1965, at Columbia, South Carolina, . . . met with . . . (last name unknown) and . . . (last name unknown). After determining that . . . was opposed to the racial demonstrations in the South, . . . and . . . offered . . . and . . . $400 each if they would accompany them to Georgia and $50,000 additional if they would assassinate MARTIN LUTHER KING.

During the above interview, . . . claimed to have received "mental" discharge from the United States Marine corps; to have recently been injured in a Greyhound bus accident; and to suffer hallucinations and amnesia after which he cannot understand which of his memories are fact and which are fantasy.

Philadelphia files indicate . . . was born [in] . . . Virginia; he is presently married and his wife . . . and family reside in . . . Pa. . . . has been sought and arrested by the FBI on numerous occasions for interstate transportation of stolen property, interstate transportation of stolen motor vehicle, theft from interstate shipment, and desertion. . . . was arrested on . . . 1954, at . . . Pa., as a deserter and it was subsequently determined through fingerprint comparison that he had fraudulently enlisted in the Army . . . he was interviewed at this time and he advised he was unable to recall the fraudulent enlistment and/or the subsequent desertion. He claimed at the time to have been under the care of . . . Pa., a psychiatrist, since 1950 and to have suffered severe epileptic "fits" prior to and during that time. During his interview he exhibited U.S. Army discharge dated . . . 1953, from Camp Pickett, Virginia; U.S. Marine Corps discharge dated . . . 1953, from Parris Island, South Carolina; and another U.S. Army discharge dated . . . 1949, place of discharge not indicated. . . . claimed that all aforementioned discharges were for medical reasons in view of his mental condition.

. . . 1953, . . . psychiatrist who had treated . . . in the past and who was then his physician, advised Agents of the FBI that . . . suffers from a petit mal form of epilepsy known as "fugue state." . . . said . . . condition was precipitated by the taking of alcohol, after which he undergoes periods of confusion and amnesia as long as 30 days, during which time he commits anti-social acts resulting from dual personality.

. . . advised that when . . . has a seizure, he can be led to anything short of violence. . . . stated he felt subject's condition is genuine since it would be difficult to mimic symptoms as well as mimic the proper reaction to treatment for his mental condition. . . . advised subject's father paid $115.00 per week while . . . was being treated at . . . however, he did not think subject's father was shielding . . . since he asked to have his son permanently placed in a State mental institution. The father advised . . . that he was tired of making restitution for the many crimes committed by his son. At the time of . . . last visit to . . . on . . . 1957, he advised that . . . was in a "fair state of mental repair"; however, . . . was in need of "constant psychiatric attention."

. . . in which institution . . . was incarcerated several times, advised on March 30, 1965, that it was generally known that . . . was a "mental case''; however, ... file at the prison failed to reflect any report of mental examination.

UNITED STATES DEPARTMENT OF JUSTICE

FEDERAL BUREAU OF INVESTIGATION

Newark, New Jersey
March 31, 1965

... advised that ... came to the ... Hospital on ... and stated a neighbor of his ... had recommended this hospital as a place where he might receive psychiatric examination and possibly treatment.

... stated ... was given a preliminary interview by ... He stated ... told ... he felt he might need psychiatric examination. He further stated he did not like people and wished he had been a Nazi in Germany during the time the Nazis were in power.

He stated, according to ..., he would like to get a gun and shoot the Reverend Martin Luther King. He said the Ku Klux Klan was closer to the American way than the policies advocated by President Johnson. He also said, according to ..., he hated many leading Americans in government including Chief Justice Earl Warren.

... stated ... arranged for an interview of ... on ... 1965, by a psychiatrist at the institute, but ... had not shown up for the appointment.

... stated ... also advised he had served three years in prison on a charge of carnal abuse. ... stated this individual, in all probability, does need psychiatric help, and his statements indicate he may be suffering from paranoiac and schizophrenic tendencies. He stated he might be dangerous because of these tendencies.

... advised the records of this agency contain an arrest record for ... whose addresses were ... She stated this individual was born on ... She said he had ... She said he had been arrested on ... 1953, in ... New Jersey on a motor vehicle violation for which he was fined $100 and ten days in jail. She said he also was arrested by the New Jersey State Police at ... New Jersey, on ... 1956, for being disorderly and assault and battery, for which he received a $100 fine and five days in jail. She stated he was also arrested on ... 1960, in ... New Jersey, for contributing to the delinquency of a minor and was convicted on ... of the charge of carnal abuse for which he received a three to five year sentence ...

UNITED STATES DEPARTMENT OF JUSTICE

FEDERAL BUREAU OF INVESTIGATION

Buffalo, New York
March 31, 1965

On March 31, 1965, . . . New York State Police, advised the Buffalo Office of the FBI that he had interviewed . . . on March 30, 1965, and had obtained from WASHBON the signed statement set forth below:

"While I was serving a sentence for Attempted Breaking & Entering a Automobile at . . . Florida from April, 1964, through October, 1964, I shared my cell with . . . who stated that he was finishing a life sentence after having it cut by some big wheel in Washington.

"During my contact with . . . he stated that he was a member of a syndicate or mob and when he was younger he had a lot of jobs including shooting 6 colored people. He also made bombs for this gang, now that he is older about all he does is make bombs.

"I told him that I wouldn't mind doing one job that would bring me $5 or $10,000 and then stop. He told me that when I got out he could set me up with the type of people to pull these kinds of jobs. He said once you get into it they would never let me go & advised me not too [sic].

"He told me that I could go on a job with him. He said he had been contacted by a group that offered him $20,000 to shoot MARTIN LUTHER KING. He was suppose to do this job when he got out of jail. He said he could choose his helpers and offered me $5,000 in small bills and cash before leaving his house. He couldn't tell me many of the plans until the time the shooting was to take place. The plans would be delivered to him in a sealed envelope with the money. After the shooting we would drive to the closest town and separate and he would drive to his home and I could go where ever I wanted to as he did not want two people in the car.

"He talked about this on several occasions and tried to impress on me that nothing would go wrong. He said I should contact him at his home, . . . Florida. This would be after we were both out of prison. He said that if he was not home when I got there to tell his wife, . . . that . . . from Miami had sent me. His wife knew about his activities and I think she was a big wheel in the group. If I said . . . sent me she would know it was all right to talk.

"He continued to stress the point that nothing would go wrong because when these people set something up it would go like clock work.

"When I got out of prison I never contacted . . . and decided to go back to . . . N.Y. with my folks. He impressed on me not to tell anyone about things we discussed in prison."

FBI

4/1/65

AIRTEL

To: SACs, Baltimore (Enclosure)
                      Charlotte
                      Philadelphia (Enclosure)
From: Director, FBI

MARTIN LUTHER KING, JR.
SECURITY MATTER-C

ReBAtel to Bureau, Atlanta, Miami, Charlotte, Philadelphia and Savannah and teletypes from Charlotte, Philadelphia, Savannah and Miami, all 3/30/65, all captioned "Alleged Plot To Assassinate Martin Luther King, RM."

Baltimore teletype reported that one . . . was in custody of local authorities in Maryland and was to be returned to . . . Pennsylvania . . . as he was an escapee from local authorities there. . . . related a lengthy tale concerning an alleged plot to assassinate King in which he claimed he was involved. He indicated that he has had service in the Army and Marine corps and had a "mental" discharge from the latter. He claimed that he has suffered hallucinations and amnesia and cannot separate fact from fantasy. He claimed that he had obtained a machine gun in connection with the alleged plot and that his story concerning possession of the gun could be verified because on approximately 3/4/64 he was stopped by a local law enforcement officer near Sanford, North Carolina, and pointed the gun at this officer. He also related an allegation that he met with Jack Ruby and Lee Harvey Oswald in Fort Worth, Texas, 1962. The Baltimore teletype closed with an instruction for Atlanta to advise local authorities; for Philadelphia to obtain a background as to . . . mental condition at . . . and for receiving offices not to conduct investigation unless advised to the contrary by the Bureau until information concerning . . . mental condition was determined.

Bureau files reveal that . . . has been involved for many years in connection with violations of the law, both local and Federal. He has had several terms of military service and has been a deserter in the past. . . . contains the report of Special Agent . . . dated 7/15/54, concerning . . . The report has pertinent data concerning . . . mental state. Philadelphia airtel 6/28/54 in the same case also contains pertinent mental-condition data.

. . . contains the most recent investigation of . . . wherein he was a . . . fugitive, . . . His fugitive status was cleared by his recent local arrest in Maryland. Information in this file reveals that . . . has given a variety of birth dates over the years and has traveled about the country a good deal.

ReCEtel reported investigation at Sanford, North Carolina, which failed to verify the claim of . . . that he had encountered a local officer near Sanford as alleged.

RePHtel reported a summary of information verifying the mental difficulties . . . has experienced over the years.

In view of the reported mental condition of . . . and apparent lack of any Bureau jurisdiction related to the alleged plot concerning King, no further investigation should be conducted. It is necessary, however, for the Bureau to make appropriate dissemination concerning the threat and . . . mental condition. The following instructions, therefore, should be promptly carried out by the indicated offices and requested material submitted by return airtel.

Baltimore should submit a letterhead memorandum including the information concerning the alleged plot relative to King's life; data concerning . . . local incarceration; mental condition factors as related by . . . and his claim concerning the Sanford, North Carolina, incident. Do not include Ruby-Oswald information.

For your information, extensive investigation by the Bureau in the past failed to confirm any claim that Oswald and Ruby were known to each other prior to the assassination of President Kennedy.

Charlotte should submit a letterhead memorandum reporting investigation conducted at Sanford, North Carolina.

Philadelphia should submit a letterhead memorandum containing details as to . . . current incarceration; all available information concerning the mental condition of . . . (thoroughly review your files for this information); and a brief summary of the military record of . . . as revealed in your files.

It is noted that referenced Baltimore teletype should have been sent to Tampa rather than Miami and subsequently Miami sent a copy of the Baltimore teletype to Tampa by air mail. In the event Tampa has any pertinent information, it should submit same by a letterhead memorandum.

All offices preparing letterhead memoranda should designate a copy for Atlanta and in view of Atlanta's previous advice to local authorities, Atlanta should now also furnish local authorities a brief summary concerning the mental condition of . . .

TRUE COPY

Atlanta, Ga
April 2, 1965

Mr. J. Edgar Hoover,
Director of F.B.I.
Washington, D.C.

Honorable Mr. Hoover:

The Newsweek magazine issue of Dec. 9th, 1964, carried a story about you and your statement that Rev. Martin L. King Jr. was a notorious liar. I have followed that worthy character and read all about his associations with subversive individuals which were printed in Georgia and Alabama but not in the press in the north and west.

People in Georgia have pictures of him in attendance at a Communist training school near Monteagle, Tenn. We know of his Communist associations and of having two on his Southern Christian Leadership Conference payroll.

We also know Bayard Rustin put on the huge Washington D.C. parade in 1963 for Core leaders and Board members Martin Luther King Jr. and NAACP leaders and Board member A. Phillip Randolph. We also know Bayard Rustin same communist helped Martin Luther King draw up his acceptance speech for his Nobel Peace prize in Oslo Norway last December.

We are mighty suspicious same Bayard Rustin was back stage and Kingpin of King's overnight invasion from the northern into Selma when he and his aides purposely provoked police into action by disobeying orders about three times for an interstate march on Montgomery solely for propaganda purposes. We also suspect King and Bayard Rustin had plans weeks ahead of staging a 25,000 demonstration in Montgomery Ala. and for King to break laws in Selma.

For 48 years I dont remember of a segment of our citizenry wanted to travel along a busy interstate highway thereby endangering their own lives and innocent travelers on a busy highway. Prior to 1961 no segment of citizens ever had that intestinal brass. If they had they would have been promptly told to act the part of responsible and sensible citizens.

However a federal judge allowed it. Now the communist techniques of street demonstrations was permitted and condoned again in 1965 and legally extended to busy interstate highways with army guard.

I further contend a huge Communist plan to infiltrate into the lives, communities and states in the entire south, Illinois, Michigan, Ohio and Pennsylvania was kicked off in Selma and Montgomery Alabama.

There are sufficient laws on the books of our country to insure proper voting rights and if done in the Christian free world way as done in the western countries and the United States instead of by the Marxist atheist way as done in Selma and Montgomery there would have been no strife, hatred, violence and death. Therefore with King's being the "front man," *he is morally responsible for all that which happened as well as stirring up strife again in the south* where Civil Rights was peacefully accepted. Only one death resulted in July 1964 near Athens, Ga. and 3 businesses going to court.

I further contend King is getting north and south in an unnecessary state of some bad feelings. If all went well between wites and negroes he wouldnt let it be. He would find something to start something going. The Ku Klux Klan never was any good and stirred up internal trouble not necessary. At the same time they are not subversive as the Communist in wanting to undermine every level of our country and the moral fabric of our citizens as well. We dont need the Klan. At the same time if King had not started breaking local laws in Selma but done everything in an upright responsible way a good constructive citizen and leader would do, there would have been no strife and hatred, violence and three deaths. Even the Klan would have remained underground.

I am for integration and rights for all citizens to vote whether illiterate or not. The illiterate should be of sound mind and vouched for by two credible witnesses in their community. I have wired Senator Dirkson [*sic*] to try to get this into the new law.

It can all be worked out O.K. if King is kept out of the streets and all done in an orderly Christian free country way of doing it.

That is off my mind. I was indignant about the way Newsweek

covered you in the fashion of a scandal monger and the unwarranted criticism by the New York Times, New York Herald Tribune, Washington Post and Los Angeles Times. The Newsweek did not give you one favorable comment.

Therefore besides sending in a reply to Newsweek I also sent a copy to the four critical newspapers mentioned. In addition to that, I also sent copies to the Chicago Tribune, Detroit News, Jackson Clarion Ledger, Jackson Miss, the Saturday Evening Post and Red Book magazine. In all, I let seven newspapers and three magazines know I didnt like the unwarranted attack on you by Newsweek, New York Times, New York Herald Tribune, Washington Post and Los Angeles Times. I enclosed the reply by Newsweek

I remember well when the F.B.I. was formed and you were appointed by Judge Stone in 1924 to take charge. I have followed the F.B.I. and you from its infancy to the sound organization it is today. You are to be commended for a job efficiently and honorably done and for being a good public servant.

I wanted to join the FBI in 1927, but my wife vetoed it. We were married Jan. 26, 1924 and I am a World War One U.S. Marine from 1917–1921 vintage.

When my wife was against me joining the F.B.I. I joined my state National Guard from March 1927 to Nov. 1935.

My allegiance to the flag and my country have never left me and I hold membership in the American Legion for 44 years. I couldn't sit down and keep quiet last December when the "get Hoover clique" started. I thought I would let you know I stuck out my neck for you. I should have done so at the time.

I can't sit down and keep quiet either regarding Rev. King Jr. I say no matter what our problems are—let us do the work in a Christian free world way as opposed to the Marxist athiest way in the streets and the underground. I know you cannot reply on King and subversion.

> Yours truly
> [Signature deleted]

UNITED STATES DEPARTMENT OF JUSTICE

FEDERAL BUREAU OF INVESTIGATION

April 2, 1965

Re: Communist Influence In
Racial Matters
Internal Security-C

Communist Infiltration
The Southern Christian
Leadership Conference
Internal Security-C

On March 31, 1965, a confidential source, who has furnished reliable information in the past, advised that Bayard Rustin (organizer of the March on Washington, August 1963, and advisor to Martin Luther King, the President of the Southern Christian Leadership Conference (SCLC) was in contact with Tommy Smith (a personal friend and confidant of Rustin) on that date. Rustin told Smith that he would be in Baltimore, Maryland, on April 1 and 2, 1965, to attend a meeting of the Administrative Board of the SCLC.

Rustin told Smith that he was "trying to bail out King on that stupid boycott thing" (alluding to the appeal by King that Alabama be boycotted because of what King called "a total breakdown of law and order and a reign of terror.") In that regard, Rustin said, that one of his (King's) aides "who doesn't have much sense put this on the wires and sent telegrams all over the country without notifying King." It was at that time, according to Rustin, that King asked him what he should do. According to Rustin, he told King to say that the boycott matter was being discussed and that it would be decided during the Administrative Board meeting whether to go through with the boycott.

UNITED STATES DEPARTMENT OF JUSTICE

FEDERAL BUREAU OF INVESTIGATION

Charlotte, North Carolina
April 2, 1965

THREAT TO KILL MARTIN LUTHER KING
MARCH 24, 1965
RACIAL MATTERS

On March 30, 1965, . . . Durham, North Carolina, voluntarily came to the Durham Resident Agency of the FBI for interview. At the commencement of the interview, he was advised he was not required to furnish any information but that any information he did furnish might be used against him in court. He was also advised of his right to counsel by an attorney of his own choice or anyone else prior to furnishing any information whatever.

. . . reiterated that he was . . . About 7:15 P.M., Tuesday, March 23, 1965, he received a telephone call at his home from an individual identifying himself as . . . This caller told . . . he had been referred to . . . by an . . . The caller then went on to say he was en route to Alabama and asked if he could get any support from . . . or . . . He said he was going "looking" for MARTIN LUTHER KING as he did not like him.

. . . said he asked the caller if he was seeking to incorporate . . . or . . . in a conspiracy to harm MARTIN LUTHER KING. The caller said he was not seeking assistance from . . . to get to Alabama but wondered if . . . would back him up if he were caught. . . . said he told the caller that neither . . . nor . . . would help him. He added, however, that perhaps other people might come to the caller's assistance. He said he did not identify anyone who might come to the caller's assistance but explained that he meant should the caller actually harm MARTIN LUTHER KING there were probably people around who would, in fact, come to his financial aid.

. . . said the caller then continued to talk as if he might be mentally upset, indicating he hated MARTIN LUTHER KING and all his assistants. The caller went on to say he was going to Alabama and "bust" him wide open. The caller continued he had served about twenty-five years in jail and was not afraid to go back

The caller then indicated he desired to meet with . . . He indicated that even though ... would not assist or support him, he still had other things to speak to him about. ... said he could think of no other way to get rid of the caller so he agreed to meet the caller at 10 A.M., ... 1965, at ...

... stated at the time he made this appointment he had no intention whatever of keeping it but did so only to get rid of the caller.

... stated on ... 1965, he had not gone to ... and had not met ... said he had discussed the matter with ... and ... had recommended that ... furnish the information to the FBI. Furthermore, about 2 P.M. on ... 1965, ... saw ... who told ... that a gray-haired man had been in the ... on ... near ... about 10:30 A.M. that day looking for ... This man said ... had an appointment with him but had failed to appear.

... told ... this person seemed to be "off his rocker."

... emphasized he had never seen nor met ... in person. His only contact was the one telephone call above described. During this conversation, ... had never mentioned any money and ... categorically denied ever giving ... any money whatever or reason to believe he would receive any from him.

... said his personal position was that he would regret and resent anyone killing MARTIN LUTHER KING as he had not desire to make a martyr of KING.

... advised he owned a ... He did not have or operate a ...

... further advised he was not a normal customer or ... and he was not acquainted with the operators of this establishment. He admitted that he had on one occasion stopped at this establishment for a cup of coffee with ... however, he had not been at this establishment on ... 1965.

The following physical description of ... was obtained by interview and observation:

Sex	Male
Race	white
Born	...
...	North Carolina
Height	5'9"
Weight	180 pounds
Hair	Black
Eyes	Brown

On ... 1965, ... Durham, North Carolina, stated that on ... 1965, ... told him of receiving a telephone call at his home on ... 1965, from an individual identifying himself as . . . who had spoken to . . . of seeking help to go to Alabama to kill MARTIN LUTHER KING. . . . said he had suggested that . . . furnish this information immediately to the FBI.

. . . said he felt the caller had been drunk and was trying to raise money for additional drinking. . . . denied any acquaintance with . . .

On . . . advised he had an acquaintance with . . . He recalled that on about . . . 1965, about 6:30 P.M., . . . was at the . . . drinking beer and "pretty high." . . . started speaking about the Ku Klux Klan and wanted to know who to get in touch with this organization. . . . said he would like to meet the leader of this group and was told the leader resided in . . . North Carolina. . . . then went on to say he would not mind going to Alabama to kill MARTIN LUTHER KING.

On . . . said . . . had departed from Durham about Thursday morning . . . 1965. He indicated he was going by bus to the vicinity of Charlotte, North Carolina, to seek treatment at some kind of college for alcoholics. . . . advised his uncle had been drunk for approximately six weeks. He added so far as he knew his uncle was not in possession of any firearms.

On . . . advised her brother had been drinking heavily for the past two months. He left Durham . . . 1965, to go by bus to an alcoholic center near Charlotte, North Carolina, where he had received treatment approximately three times previous. She understood this treatment would last for sixty days. She noted . . . had been broke and she had given him the money for a bus ticket.

So far as . . . knew . . . had never made any threats against the life of MARTIN LUTHER KING or anyone else. She said in her opinion . . . did not own any firearms.

On . . . advised her records reflected that . . . 1965 . . . reported . . . had recently returned to Durham from Charlotte where he had been employed in . . . stated . . . was drinking excessively and she sought assistance.

. . . advised her files further reflected that during . . . 1964 . . . had personally come to . . . and sought admission to the . . . Her records further reflected he had, in fact gone to this . . . 1964, and completed the course there.

. . . *SHOULD BE CONSIDERED ARMED AND DANGEROUS AS HE HAS ADMITTED POSSESSION OF A PISTOL AND IN VIEW OF HIS PAST RECORD. HE SHOULD BE CONSIDERED AS HAVING POSSIBLE SUICIDAL TENDENCIES IN VIEW OF HIS REPORTED ATTEMPTED SUICIDE . . .*

UNITED STATES DEPARTMENT OF JUSTICE

FEDERAL BUREAU OF INVESTIGATION

Mobile, Alabama
April 7, 1965

PROPOSED SPEECH IN MOBILE, ALABAMA, IN
MAY 1965 BY MARTIN LUTHER KING, PRESIDENT
SOUTHERN CHRISTIAN LEADERSHIP CONFERENCE,
ATLANTA, GEORGIA

AT MOBILE ALABAMA:

. . . advised that it had been rumored in Mobile that there would be
a voter registration demonstration in Mobile on Thursday, April 15,
1965. He said that it had been reported that Reverend J. E. Lowery, a
representative of the Southern Christian Leadership Conference (SCLC),
Birmingham, Alabama, and a former resident of Mobile, would come
to lead the demonstration which demonstration would be an SCLC affair. He said that local Negro, Edwin Moorer, had been claiming to be
connected with the SCLC and was probably the one who was making
plans for the demonstration.

. . . advised that no demonstration of any kind is planned for Mobile.
. . . said that Edwin Moorer is a local Negro, but has no connection
whatever with SCLC, although he has been collecting money throughout
the Mobile area and reportedly has been claiming he is working with
SCLC. . . . stated that during the night of April 6–7, 1965, he had
received a call from C. T. Vivian of SCLC Headquarters, Atlanta, Georgia, saying that word of Moorer's activity had gotten back to SCLC
Headquarters. Vivian instructed . . . to disavow Edwin Moorer publicly
and to announce that Moorer has no connection whatever with SCLC.
. . . will notify Moorer that if he persists in claiming connection with
SCLC and collecting money or performing other activities under the
name of the SCLC the organization will attempt to prosecute Moorer
criminally.

. . . said that he had heard the rumor about an SCLC voter demonstration for Mobile Thursday, April 15, 1965, but that this rumor was the
work of Edwin Moorer and there is no truth whatever in the rumor and
there is no demonstration planned for that date or anytime insofar as
he is currently aware.

... said that he had received notice, however, that Reverend Martin Luther King would come to Mobile, Alabama, to make a speech sometime during the first part of May 1965. He said that he does not know the date King is to come to Mobile, but said that he would furnish this information when received by him. He said that it is tentatively planned that King will speak in Mobile, stay overnight, and leave the next morning. ... said that he does not feel there will be any problem in connection with King's appearance in Mobile and it is expected that King will make his usual public speech concerning voter registration and related matters. ... said that if King was not allowed to come into Mobile and make his speech without interference, that the entire staff of SCLC workers would come into Mobile for demonstrations, which ... is not in favor of. He said he feels certain there will be no problem; however, in connection with King's appearance for a speech as the city administration and police agencies of Mobile would not try to interfere with King's visit, but would be interested only in maintaining order.

[Section 30]

UNITED STATES DEPARTMENT OF JUSTICE

FEDERAL BUREAU OF INVESTIGATION

Birmingham, Alabama
April 8, 1965

RE: UNKNOWN SUBJECTS;
<u>THREAT TO KILL MARTIN LUTHER KING, JR.</u>

... advised that five people were planning to kill MARTIN LUTHER KING, JR., at Birmingham, within the next day or two, and that a reward of $15,000 was being offered to the assassin. ... stated that he, himself, was asked to be one of the assassins, that he was from Washington, D.C., and was "employed" by the Federal Narcotics Bureau.

... Washington, D.C., was interviewed at the Sheraton Hotel on ... , 1965, ... He advised that while awaiting an appointment with Attorney ... in ... office on the ... Birmingham, Alabama, at approximately 8:00 A.M., ... 1965, he overheard four men in the corridor outside ... office discussing MARTIN LUTHER KING, JR., and he heard one of the men say that KING should be killed, as he is grooming himself for the presidency and that he is an agitator and should be put out of the way. He stated that the four persons gave him the impression that they were attorneys in Birmingham. He heard one person offer $4,000 toward a fund for an assassin. He heard another offer $6,000 and a third person stated he would make up the difference for $15,000 for an assassin.

He stated that when in Washington, he is used by the Narcotics Bureau of the U.S. Department of the Treasury to investigate narcotic violations in the Washington area. He stated that he is paid in cash by the Government for his work. He also said that he has a brother in Birmingham ...

On March 11, 1965, the above information was furnished to ASAC HARVEY HENDERSON, Secret Service Agency, Department of the Treasury.

... Federal Bureau of Narcotics, was also advised of the above information and it was determined that ... was unknown to the Federal Bureau of Narcotics in Washington, D.C.

UNITED STATES DEPARTMENT OF JUSTICE

FEDERAL BUREAU OF INVESTIGATION

Jacksonville, Florida
April 12, 1965

RE: ...
PANAMA CITY, FLORIDA

Special Agent ... United States Secret Service, Washington, D.C., telephonically advised the Federal Bureau of Investigation April 4, 1965, that on that day he received a collect call, which he refused to accept, from the captioned individual. He said the captioned individual definitely sounded intoxicated and merely mentioned that he had information regarding an assassination attempt on Martin Luther King.

... Panama City, Florida, Police Department, advised ... who is also known as ... and ... has been arrested on several occasions by the Panama City Police Department and the Bay County sheriff's Office, Panama City, for charges of driving while intoxicated, disorderly conduct, drunk, and uttering a forged instrument [sic], and from fingerprints submitted this man has been identified by the Federal Bureau of Investigation. . . .

. . . advised he has talked with this individual on several occasions and has been impressed this man constantly drinks to excess and appears to be mentally incompetent and to have hallucinations.

. . . was located at the . . . Panama City, April 3, 1965, and at that time he advised SA . . . that he had been drinking that day. He said he had telephoned "LBJ" and told him that Martin Luther King was going to be assassinated on "Saturday." He stated he would refuse to furnish any information on his source of information and he said he was not involved, and he then said that Governor Wallace of Alabama was going to kill King on Saturday and had told him that he was going to kill King at Selma. He said . . . knew all about this and he had talked to . . . about it.

. . . advised he has had no personal association with . . . for almost 30 years and knew from reputation that . . . is a drunkard, . . . said he had heard of no plot to assassinate Martin Luther King and would attribute any such comment from . . . as a drunken hallucination.

[Section 31]

UNITED STATES DEPARTMENT OF JUSTICE

FEDERAL BUREAU OF INVESTIGATION

Indianapolis, Indiana
April 24, 1965

. . . South Bend, Indiana, senior student at . . . High School, South Bend, advised a Special Agent of the FBI on April 23, 1965 that . . . a senior student at . . . School, in February or March 1965, told her privately in American Government class that he believed that he was pre-destined to take over the world in 25 years or so. . . . stated that if he had the power, he would kill Reverend Martin Luther King, President Lyndon B. Johnson and Bernard Baruch, in this order.

. . . stated that in conversations she had with . . . in American government class during the 1964–1965 school year, . . . had indicated that he believed all Negroes, Jews, and possibly Catholics should be exterminated. . . . indicated he felt that anyone who disagreed with him should be exterminated. . . . when "doodling" in his notebook, constantly draws swastikas. He has stated that both of his parents are of German descent, and he feels that anyone who is not of pure German blood is worth nothing. He has stated that if he marries he will marry only a girl of pure German descent. He terms the American Government class a "propaganda class."

. . . stated she believes that . . . was not joking when he made these statements, but was completely serious.

[Section 32]

UNITED STATES DEPARTMENT OF JUSTICE

FEDERAL BUREAU OF INVESTIGATION

Charlotte, North Carolina
May 4, 1965

RE: ALLEGED PLOT TO ASSASSINATE MARTIN LUTHER KING, WILSON, NORTH CAROLINA, MAY 16–23, 1965
RACIAL MATTERS

. . . advised . . . obtained the following information from a source he considered to be reliable.

This source advised . . . he had just returned from a Ku Klux Klan meeting consisting of approximately six hundred members in Johnson County, North Carolina, near the Nash County line. He stated that during the week of May 16–23, 1965, Evangelist ORAL ROBERTS is scheduled to appear in Wilson, North Carolina. During this same period a Negro Singing is to be held in the baseball park at Wilson. Thousands of Negroes are expected to be in attendance and these two events are expected to be covered by radio and television. Dr. MARTIN LUTHER KING is scheduled to be in attendance at the singing and reportedly has already reserved rooms at the Holiday Inn Motel in Wilson and the Holiday Inn Motel in Rocky Mount, North Carolina. This source stated that a bounty has been placed on the life of Dr. KING, and $100,000.00 is to be paid to his killer. This alleged killer is reported to be from Green Pond, a community in Nash County, North Carolina. This man reportedly has been picked and screened to do this job and the funds to pay for killing Dr. KING are from the Ku Klux Klan organization country wide. Several white priests and people from other states are expected to accompany Dr. KING on this reported visit to Wilson.

. . . stated that . . . has confirmed that the park has been leased for a Negro Singing Convention sometime during the week of May 16–23, 1965, exact date not certain.

. . . was interviewed, and he verified the above information as furnished to him. He stated that the source of his information, whom he would not care to divulge at this time, appeared to be intoxicated at the time he gave this information to . . .

. . . Chief of Police, Wilson, North Carolina, and Chief Deputy Sheriff . . . Wilson County Sheriff's Office, Wilson, North Carolina, were both advised of the above information. Both stated that to their knowledge MARTIN LUTHER KING had made no plans to visit their city.

. . . Special Agent in Charge, 111th Intelligence Corps Group, Charlotte, North Carolina, was advised of the above information on May 3, 1965.

A confidential source advised on April 7, 1965, that information was received that MARTIN LUTHER KING, JR., leader of the Southern Christian Leadership Conference, will make an appearance some place in North Carolina during the month of May 1965. This information was not specific as to when or where KING would appear, but the United Klans of America, Knights of the Ku Klux Klan, Inc., (UKA), will be on hand at the time of KING's arrival if this date and time can be established. The Klan, if it does appear at the time of KING's reported arrival, will not harm KING but will gather in large numbers in a get-together of their own at the place designated for KING's appearance.

UNITED STATES DEPARTMENT OF JUSTICE

FEDERAL BUREAU OF INVESTIGATION

Philadelphia, Pennsylvania
May 6, 1965

MARTIN LUTHER KING, JR.

. . . advised that MARTIN LUTHER KING, President of the Southern Christian Leadership Conference (SCLC), participated on May 1, 1965, in a panel discussion which was part of a seminar under the general title "The Rule of Law in a Changing Society." The seminar commemorated Law Day U.S.A. According to . . . KING's speech was moderate and more or less conciliatory.

The Philadelphia Inquirer on May 2, 1965, in reporting on the Law Day U.S.A. Seminar, quoted KING as saying "Justice at times proceeds with a halting gait and the law has often been slow to speak for the poor, the dispossessed and the disfranchised." KING told the group that "only a few years ago labor unions were chattels in the eyes of the law." KING paid tribute to the legal profession for "its many contributions to the civil rights movement."

The Philadelphia Sunday Bulletin, in its edition May 2, 1965, contained an article on page 1, captioned "KING Chides Extremists at Law Day Rally." The article reflected that DR. MARTIN LUTHER KING, a featured speaker at a Law Day U.S.A. observance, warned that if white extremists have their way, the South will be reduced to anarchy. KING said that many Southerners claim his civil rights movement is as lawless as the deeds of segregationists. Denying the charge, he said that the really lawless are those who bomb churches, kill and beat demonstrators, then hide from authorities.

The end result of such tactics, which KING attributed to the Ku Klux Klan and white extremists, would be anarchy because, he said, the guilty refuse to accept the legal penalty.

In contrast, KING asserted, his supporters demonstrate openly and willingly accept the penalties.

"We defy openly and willingly go to jail," the clergyman said. "Our aim is to persuade."

KING defended his plan for a boycott of goods produced in Alabama, comparing it to the action of the colonists against the British tea taxes and the boycott of British goods during THOMAS JEFFERSON's Administration in protest against the impressment of U.S. seamen.

KING called for more active involvement by Americans, warning that a "dangerous silence" now prevails over too large a section of the population.

"I have no despair about the future," he said. "I am convinced that we Negroes will win our freedom all over America. Our destiny is tied up with the destiny of America."

The Evening Bulletin, in its edition of May 3, 1965, contained an article on page 14, captioned "KING Criticizes U.S. Churches for Failure to Provide Leadership in Civil Rights." The article reflected that Rev. Dr. MARTIN LUTHER KING, JR., on May 2, 1965, criticized the churches, including Negro churches, for failing to provide the leadership in such social causes as the civil rights movement.

DR. KING said the church is "the most segregated institution in America," and that 11 o'clock on Sunday morning is "the most segregated hour in America."

KING said too many ministers "hide behind their stained-glass windows" and he accused some churches of being too often the "tail lights instead of the headlights" in the drive for social betterment.

DR. KING spoke in dedication ceremonies for the new $1-million Bright Hope Baptist Church, 12th Street and Columbia Avenue. Nearly 3,500 attended.

There were some 1,800 persons in the church proper and another 1,700 in a lower auditorium and the gymnasium watching the proceedings on a closed-circuit television.

KING said he thinks of himself as a Baptist minister first and in the tradition of the Southern Baptist ministers gave a rousing sermon that left his audience standing and cheering.

DR. KING, who, with his father, is co-pastor of the Ebenezer Baptist Church in Atlanta, Ga., said he considers his civil rights work as only an extension of his ministry.

"Any religion that talks of the soul and not of the conditions that can corrupt and damn the soul is dried, dead, do-nothing religion," KING said.

DR. KING said that too often in recent history the church has "left men disappointed."

KING noted that the apartheid policy of racial separation in South Africa has the support of the Dutch Reformed Church.

But, KING said, many churches in the United States are equally guilty because they often ignore such problems as civil rights.

"We suffer in this country," KING said, "not only from the violence of the bad people, but from the silence and indifference of the good people."

But, KING said, there are signs that the churches are waking up. He noted the large number of priests and nuns and ministers who joined the march from Selma to Montgomery, Ala.

DR. KING said many Negro churches suffer from either "freeze up" or "burn up."

Those that freeze up, KING said, are the ones that have become too dignified, who boast of the important people in their congregations and who are ashamed to sing the old songs of the Negro heritage.

The ones that burn up, KING said, are those "with more religion in their hands and feet than in their hearts" and where sermons are judged "by their volume and not their content."

On May 3, 1965, Source-2 advised that DR. MARTIN LUTHER KING attended a luncheon sponsored by the Locust Club, a private social organization composed of private businessmen, at which time he addressed approximately 70 attendees and received from $7,000 to $8,000 in contributions for his efforts in the South.

The Philadelphia Evening Bulletin, in its edition of May 4, 1965, in an article on page 3, captioned "Racial Frustration Breeds Violence, KING Warns Here," reflected that DR. MARTIN LUTHER KING addressed 600 civil rights and civic leaders attending the Golden Slipper Square Club banquet at the Bellevue-Stratford Hotel on the evening of May 3, 1965. The article reflected that DR. KING received the club's 1965 "Humanitarian Award" and a check for $1,000 to support the program of the SCLC, which he heads.

The article reflected that DR. KING warned that Negroes will listen to those advocating violence if non-violent demands for civil rights are not met.

KING said lack of retaliation by Negroes in the South for church bombings and brutality is proof that the theory of nonviolence is deep-seated and catching on.

DR. KING said his warning of violent reprisal pertained to Negroes hit hardest by segregation.

"They feel they have nothing to lose," KING said.

Expressing appreciation on behalf of the "thousands and millions of people who have engaged in this struggle," the Nobel Peace Prize winner said,

"If democracy is to live, segregation must die. It's a new form of slavery. We must get rid of segregation, not only to get rid of the communist challenge, but to improve our image abroad."

DR. KING said the Negro has come a long way in his stride toward freedom.

"But I must balance this by saying that we have a long, long way to go," KING said.

"Just 25 years ago a year hardly passed when Negroes in the South weren't lynched by brutal mobs. This has just about ceased today, but there are other things just as bad."

DR. KING cited church bombings, burnings, the death of civil rights workers, restrictive voting laws and economic reprisals.

KING said that more than 200 Negroes in Alabama were fired from their jobs last month because they wanted to register to vote.

KING blamed the administration of Governor WALLACE for this and other "atrocities."

The Philadelphia Daily News, in its edition of May 4, 1965, contained an article concerning KING's speech at the Golden Slipper Square Club, and indicated that KING received a $1,000 check and a miniature Torah, which contains the Hebrew text of the five books of Moses. The article stated that the $1,000, plus $7,000 which had been given to DR. KING earlier by 60 Jewish communal leaders at a Locust Club luncheon, will be used, he said, to aid the fight for Negro voting registration in Alabama and Mississippi.

[Section 33]

TRUE COPY

May 13, 1965

Dear Mr. Hoover:

I would like to congratulate you on your 40 years as Chief of the Federal Bureau of Investigation and for the fine job you have done.

Also would you please help in identifying the person in the picture I am enclosing. It shows a Negro looking like the Rev. Martin Luther King at a communist training school in Monteagle, Tennessee, about 7 years ago. He has probably changed somewhat by now, perhaps putting on some weight. Of course a person looks different from different angles, but I looked at a lot of pictures of him, and they all resemble the picture at that communist meeting.

I have read recently where you felt the communists were starting to infiltrate the Negro Civil Rights Movement. Also I read an article by Joseph Alsop saying the Southern Leadership Conference headed by Rev. Martin Luther King has been infiltrated by the communists. I felt if the picture of the man who looks like the Rev. Martin Luther King was really him attending a communist meeting then he should be thoroughly discredited.

The communist party which really advocates the overthrow of our government should be outlawed.

I feel and I know a lot of other people feel that the Negro Problem is getting out of hand.

Also the communist, socialist, and liberal influence in this country is slowly eroding the freedoms of the individual that once made this country proud and great. If we continue the way we are, we will eventually end up under communism.

I am the father of seven children, 3 boys and 4 girls, so I am very much concerned with the situation as it is today.

Please let me know if you feel the Negro identified as No. 1 in the picture I am enclosing is really the Rev. Martin Luther King.

Respectfully,
[Signature deleted]

UNITED STATES DEPARTMENT OF JUSTICE

FEDERAL BUREAU OF INVESTIGATION

San Antonio, Texas
May 17, 1965

ALLEGED THREAT TO LIFE OF
MARTIN LUTHER KING, JR.

... telephonically contacted the FBI Office, San Antonio, Texas, regarding alleged assassination plan of MARTIN LUTHER KING, JR., related to him by an unknown individual at the ... Temple, Texas, earlier that evening.

Attempts to interview ... and details concerning the allegation made by him that same evening were conducted with negative results due to his intoxicated condition. It was decided to hold further interview in abeyance until the following morning.

... confidentially advised that evening that her husband frequently becomes intoxicated at which time he misunderstands or misinterprets what people are saying to him. She was of opinion that due to his past behavior little credence should be given to his story.

... was recontacted at which time he advised that at approximately 4:00 P.M. he went to the ... Temple, Texas, and started drinking. After approximately fifteen or twenty minutes an unknown male, approximately 55 to 60 years old, 6' tall, short gray-black hair, 190–200 pounds, wearing an old flannel shirt and khaki pants, came into the bar and sat next to him. After a few minutes MOORE started talking to this individual about Texas and other topics. After a few minutes this man inquired if ... was in the Army at Fort Hood as a member of CID (Criminal Investigation Detachment). ... told him that he was not and "never would be." The other man then began to talk about a "Mr. KING." He said Mr. KING was telling Mr. JOHNSON what to do and that

KING would be running the United States next. . . . then said, "no, he'll be stopped before then." The man then asked . . . if he was acquainted with military artillery and other military weapons and what . . . qualifications were on them . . . told him he could "split a match right down in half." The man then again asked if . . . was in CID. . . . replied, "No, but I am in CIA." . . . explained that he was not really in the CIA, but he just said this to string this man along. The man then said, "You are from Panama." . . . replied, "No, I am from Arkansas, but I have been in Panama." . . . again explained that he was never really in Panama, but he was again stringing this man along. . . . said he then got disgusted with this man and tried to terminate the conversation. After approximately ten or fifteen minutes the man again spoke to . . . making some unrecalled remark about KING and KING's assassination. . . . asked this man if he knew the movements of this "so called Mr. KING." The man replied that he knew every move KING made and the time and place. . . . replied, "Well, if you know all this, and I am the assassinator, what is my possibility of getting out of it after it's did, and how much money is involved." . . . again explained that he was stringing this man along, but this time in an attempt to develop some information regarding a possible assassination of KING. The man replied that there was no money involved at the present time. . . . told him, "Well I have to look after the security and welfare of my family. If I did it, I would have to have $50,000 and a way out." The man said there was a way out, but no money.

. . . advised that at this point the man went to the men's room, and he, . . . started to leave the club. As he was leaving he asked the man how he could get in touch with him and this man replied "I'm here all the time." . . . said he then immediately went to his home in . . . and called the FBI in San Antonio requesting that an Agent contact him.

During the course of the above interview . . . repeatedly changed his story and exhibited great difficulty in recalling what had taken place the evening before. He admitted to having at least five or six beers and to being prone to easy intoxication. . . . further admitted that during the course of his discussion with the above individual, he steered the conversation toward the possible assassination of KING in an attempt to determine if any such assassination plan existed. He was unsuccessful in doing so.

In view of the above, no further investigation is being conducted by the San Antonio Office of the FBI.

UNITED STATES DEPARTMENT OF JUSTICE

FEDERAL BUREAU OF INVESTIGATION

Cincinnati, Ohio
June 3, 1965

RE: PROPOSED ACTIVITY BY NATIONAL KNIGHTS
OF THE KU KLUX KLAN UPON MARTIN LUTHER KING,
JR.'S VISIT TO ANTIOCH COLLEGE, YELLOW SPRINGS,
OHIO, JUNE 18–19, 1965

... a source who has not furnished sufficient information in the past
to establish extent of reliability, advised as follows:

William Hugh Morris, *Emperor, National Knights of the Ku Klux
Klan (NKKKK)*, plans to burn a forty-foot cross near Yellow Springs,
Ohio, (location unknown to date) on Friday evening, June 18, 1965.
Morris is traveling to Tennessee, Georgia, Mississippi and Louisiana
sometime this week to recruit persons to travel to Ohio for this activity.

On morning of June 19, 1965, Klan members will carry "charred
crosses" and station themselves at entrances around Antioch College
and Yellow Springs, Ohio, vicinity. This activity is to protest "left
wing" activities at Antioch College and [the] fact Martin Luther King,
Jr., is speaking at Antioch College commencement exercise June 19,
1965.

Morris indicated that the purpose of his activity is for free national
publicity which he believes will enhance the Klan cause.

Characterizations of the NKKKK are attached hereto.

APPENDIX
NATIONAL KNIGHTS OF THE KU KLUX KLAN, INC, (NKKKK)

A source advised that on May 22, 1960, the National Grand Council
of the Knights of the Ku Klux Klan met at Atlanta, Georgia, to discuss
consolidation of the Klan's unity of effort and activities to establish a
National Fund, and a National Secretary, and to design a new flag. The
meeting was attended by representatives of the Federation of Ku Klux
Klan, Alabama; Association of Arkansas Klans, Arkansas; Florida
Knights of the Ku Klux Klan, Florida; Southern Knights of the Ku
Klux Klan, Florida; Association of Georgia Klans, Georgia; Knights of
the Ku Klux Klan, North Carolina; Association of South Carolina Klans,

South Carolina; Dixie Knights of the Ku Klux Klan, Tennessee; and Hyksos Klan, Texas.

This source advised that at a consolidation meeting at Atlanta Georgia, September 2–5, 1960, at which the North Carolina and Texas Klans were not represented, it was resolved and passed that their name be changed to National Ku Klux Klan.

A second source advised in March 1964, that several meetings of Klan groups were held during the period 1960 to 1963 in an effort to unite the Klan groups under a single leadership.

The organization was granted a charter in DeKalb County, Georgia, November 1, 1963, under the same National Knights of the Ku Klux Klan, Inc., as a "patriotic, secret, social, and benevolent order."

A third source advised in December 1963, that the organization had issued a statement of its program which indicated the organization to be anti-Negro, anti-Jewish, anti-Catholic, and anti-foreign born.

The third source advised in August 1964, that the organization has a headquarters in Tucker, Georgia, and the day-to-day operations are under the direction of James R. Venable, Chairman.

APPENDIX
NATIONAL KNIGHTS OF THE KU KLUX KLAN
OF OHIO, INC. (NKKKK)

On October 8, 1964, Karen Crabtree, Clerk, Secretary of State's Office, Columbus, State of Ohio, advised public records from this office indicate a charter was granted to the NKKKK of Ohio on October 5, 1964, by the State of Ohio. The charter was filed under Certificate Number 10194, and the Corporation Number is 334111.

The purpose of the corporation is to operate as a realm [sic] organization within the State of Ohio and in accordance with the Constitution and laws of the National Knights of the Ku Klux Klan, Inc., Atlanta, Georgia. Second, to promote patriotism toward the civil government, honorable peace among men and nations, love among ourselves, liberty, justice and patriotic association for the mutual benefit of all mankind.

The incorporation papers were signed by Flynn R. Harvey, Grand Dragon. Flynn R. Harvey, 418 Josephine Drive, Columbus, Ohio; William K. Smith, 3482 Maple Grove Drive, Grove City, Ohio; and Bobby J. Stephens, 2973 Reaver Avenue, Grove City, Ohio, are the corporation trustees.

On October 23, 1964, Frederick W. Lenty, Corporation Counsel, State House, Secretary of State's Office, State of Ohio, advised that the National Knights of the Ku Klux Klan of Ohio, Inc.'s charter granted October 5, 1964, was revoked October 22, 1964, for the official reason that the National Knights of the Ku Klux Klan Organization was on the U.S. Attorney General's subversive list. Mr. Lenty said the actual purpose for revocation of the charter was not because the National Knights of the Ku Klux Klan is on the U.S. Attorney General's subversive list, but because it was felt the existence of a state-granted charter would encourage the Klan to make the claim it was "state sanctioned" and therefore entirely legitimate.

In actuality the Ku Klux Klan and not the National Knights of the Ku Klux Klan has been designated by the U.S. Attorney General pursuant to Executive Order 10450.

[Section 36]

FBI NEW ORLS

4-2 PM CST 6-23-65 URGENT DAO

TO DIRECTOR 62-109078

AND ATLANTA

FROM NEW ORLEANS 62-3721
. . . THREAT AGAINST THE PRESIDENT.
. . . POLICE, MONROE, LOUISIANA, ADVISED THE MONROE FBI RESIDENT AGENCY ON JUNE TWENTY THREE, SIXTY FIVE, THAT ON JUNE TWENTY TWO, SIXTY FIVE, . . . MONROE, LOUISIANA, TURNED IN A WALLET TO THE MONROE POLICE DEPARTMENT. . . . TOLD THE POLICE DEPARTMENT THAT HE HAD FOUND THE WALLET AT . . . RESTAURANT, . . . WEST MONROE, LOUISIANA ON JUNE TWENTY TWO, SIXTY FIVE.
. . . ADVISED THAT IN LOOKING THROUGH THE WALLET HE FOUND A LOUISIANA DRIVERS LICENSE . . . CALHOUN, LOUISIANA. THE INFORMATION ON THE DRIVERS LICENSE SHOWED . . . DESCRIPTION WAS WHITE MALE, BROWN HAIR, BLUE EYES, ONE HUNDRED FIFTY POUNDS, FIVE FEET SIX INCHES IN HEIGHT.
. . . MARTIN SAID THERE WAS ALSO A SOCIAL SECURITY CARD IN THE WALLET IN THE NAME OF . . . SOCIAL SECURITY

NUMBER ... ALSO SAID THAT HE FOUND IN THE WALLET WHAT APPEARED TO BE A LETTER. HE SAID THAT THIS LETTER WAS FOLDED UP AND APPEARED TO HAVE BEEN IN THE WALLET FOR A CONSIDERABLE LENGTH OF TIME. ... ADVISED THAT THE CONTENTS OF THIS LETTER WERE AS FOLLOWS: "DEAR IMPERIAL WIZART OF THE KU KLUX KLAN, I AM WILLING TO EXTERMINATE MR. JOHNSON'S BOSS (MARTIN LUTHER KING) FOR THE SUM OF FIVE MILLION DOLLARS IF YOU WILL KINDLY PAY IMMEDIATELY THIS SUM. HE WILL BE RID OF IN THE NEXT MONTH IF YOU SO AGREE. THANK YOU, ... AND ... P.S. I WILL KILL PRESIDENT JOHNSON FOR AN EXTRA ONE MILLION DOLLARS.
SINCERELY, ...

OFFICE OF THE GOVERNOR
STATE CAPITOL
SALEM 97310

June 30, 1965

Mr. Harry H. Wachtel
Wachtel & Michaelson Law Offices
575 Madison Avenue
New York, N.Y. 10022

Dear Mr. Wachtel:

Your letter of June 1, 1965, reached me just before our Western Governors' Conference here in Oregon for which I was the host Governor, which accounts for my delay in replying.

You imply that I have misunderstood Dr. Martin Luther King's views on civil disobedience. You forwarded his speech before the Bar of New York City on April 21, 1965, and cited certain specific passages. I have studied his speech, giving particular care to the parts you cite. I find that I am not laboring under any misunderstanding. Rather Dr. King and I seriously disagree. I am not alone in disagreeing with Dr. King. Many thoughtful and conscientious Americans, including the President of the American Bar Association, share my deep concern.

To understand our disagreement you must clearly comprehend the background and identity of views [sic] from which our divergent conclusions are reached. I have done everything in my power as a legislator and as a governor to promote the civil rights and liberties of all Americans, red, yellow, white and black. As a legislator, it was my privilege to co-sponsor civil rights legislation, and as Governor I have twice urged the passage of further extensions of Oregon's fine civil rights statutes. Moreover, I supported the repeal of the anti-miscegenation law in Oregon. I have supported and fully administered our laws prohibiting discrimination in housing. I believe I can say with humility that no Oregon Governor has done more for civil rights than I have and certainly no state has less discrimination than Oregon. Dr. King and I both believe in the same civil rights goals and both of us have worked hard and long in this cause. Furthermore, both of us are practicing, sincere Christians belonging to the same segment of Protestant belief. You can see that little separates us other than the color of our skin, which both of us ignores as completely immaterial.

Yet I disagree with Dr. King's open advocacy and constant use of civil disobedience. I take the stand that, where we have legal processes for changing laws, we have no right to violate those laws. On the other hand, Dr. King said in his speech to the New York City Bar, in substance, (p. 21), that even where all people have the actual right to vote, he thinks that "whenever unjust laws exist people on the basis of conscience have the right to disobey those laws." He goes on to say (p. 24) that even where the voting rights are assured and the laws are just, the people have the right to disobey the law to call attention to the extra-legal injustices. In effect, Dr. King says that, when directed by one's own conscience and one's subjective sense of justice, one has a right to disobey a law either to change the law or to protest other injustice, regardless of the availability of the democratic process for correcting the law or the injustice.

His stand is an open invitation to anarchy. If every person obeyed only those laws he thought were just, society and civilization would disappear in a holocaust of civil destruction. Believers in euthanasia would commit murder. Sincere believers in California's Proposition 14 principle would negate our Oregon civil rights laws. Our jails would overflow. Our courts would be swamped. Society, as we know it, would disappear.

Democracy can only succeed if the majority's conscience and sense of justice, as embodied in our laws, controls the acts of all citizens, assuming effective voting rights for all qualified voters. Only under this system can civil law and order be maintained. Only under this system can mayors and governors and presidents protect the rights of all citizens.

Dr. King has lived his life in the front line of a battle. I, too, have been in that front line, but I also have sat in the seat of authority and been charged with maintaining law, order, progress and prosperity for all citizens. If Dr. King could sit where I sit for only a short time, he would realize the impossibility of allowing individual conscience to control law observance. For instance, though I long have advocated the doing away with the death penalty, I refused to commute death sentences until the law was changed by our people. I did so because I believe that governors, perhaps above all others, are bound to support the law. I took an oath to that effect. Dr. King would see, as I do, the destruction of democracy and this great republic in the civil disobedience he espouses. He would also see how close civil disobedience is to riot, violence to slaughter.

By divine blessing, we Americans have been granted the sacred privilege of living in freedom in a functioning democratic republic. We always have available to us the orderly, peaceful, and protecting process of the law. Where local prejudice and a tradition of discrimination exist, and it is not possible to correct a wrong through a change of ordinance or by other governmental process, then the state processes can be used. If the same prejudice and practice prevent correction at the state level, then the Federal Government should and can act. When we need a new law enacted or an old law changed, the majority can accomplish the desired result peacefully at the ballot box. Until the change takes place, we must obey the present law, if constitutional. If it is not constitutional, we can have it done away with by our courts. If it is illegally enforced or ignored, we have peaceable recourse to our courts. Were this not so, all of us would be slaves of the few and powerful. Because it is so, we are free.

Civil disobedience weakens our system of law and order and thereby weakens our freedom. We strengthen our freedom by obeying the law, not by disobeying. We cannot strengthen a minority's rights by destroying the majority's rights and freedom. We have gained the Negro nothing, if in obtaining his equality with white Americans we so injure our democracy that all Americans' freedom is destroyed.

Our government is not the despotism of Hitler's Germany, nor is it the absolutism of Nebuchadnezzar. Dr. King's analogies to Naziism or absolute monarchies do not apply to our great democratic republic where the courts are strong and independent, where all do, or by proper legal process can, obtain the right to vote, where the rights of all are obtainable because our people obey the law and the courts.

Dr. King attempts to justify his acts by citing the crimes of lawless southerners, in the killing of Mrs. Liuzzo and the massacre of Reverend Reeb. These are crimes, legally as much as morally, and must be punished. But these wrongs, these crimes, do not justify another crime. Murder does not justify civil disobedience. Nor does a riotous tea party in Boston Harbor two centuries ago to protest a voiceless tyranny justify a crime in 1965 in a land as free as ours.

No, if civil disobedience prompted by individual conscience becomes the accepted means of changing the law in this country instead of the due and deliberate actions of the legally constituted representative assemblies of our government, then, our freedom will disappear in the destruction of our properly enacted laws and our properly constituted civil authorities. The freedom, the equality, and the opportunity which Dr. King seeks for his people will be a hollow shell, a valueless goal, submerged in the lost freedom and the denied rights of all Americans.

I will continue to fight for the civil rights and equal opportunity of all people. But I shall do so within the framework of our democratic form of government, legally and without stint, ever conscious that I must preserve at the same time the freedom of all Americans or the Negroes' rights will become an equality in slavery.

Sincerely,

Mark Hatfield

Governor

FBI WASH DC

FBI CHICAGO
1007 AM CDST URGENT 7/8/65 JLS
TO DIRECTOR AND ATLANTA
FROM CHICAGO (100-35356)

ANONYMOUS THREAT TO KILL MARTIN LUTHER KING, CHICAGO, ILLINOIS, JULY TWENTY FOURTH, NINETEEN SIXTY FIVE.

AT SIX FORTY FIVE AM, JULY EIGHTH INSTANT, . . . (PROTECT) ADVISED THE FBI, CHICAGO, THAT HE RECEIVED A CALL FROM AN UNIDENTIFIED MALE STATING THAT HE WAS GOING TO KILL MARTIN LUTHER KING. THIS INDIVIDUAL DID NOT INDICATE TIME, DATE, OR PLACE. . . . STATED CALLER

INDICATED HE WAS CALLING FROM O'HARE FIELD, CHI-
CAGO, AND IN . . . OPINION WAS INTOXICATED.

AT SEVEN THIRTEEN AM, JULY EIGHTH INSTANT, UN-
KNOWN MALE CALLED CHICAGO OFFICE OF FBI INQUIRING
IF THE FBI IS GOING TO PROTECT MARTIN LUTHER KING
AND ADDED NOT TO PUT WHITE MEN IN FRONT "BECAUSE
WE DON'T WANT TO KILL WHITE MEN." CALLER INDICATED
THEY INTEND TO KILL KING ABOUT THE TWENTY FOURTH
OF JULY, WHEN HE IS IN CHICAGO.

[Section 37]

TRANSCRIPT OF CHANNEL 2, KNXT-TV, LOS ANGELES PROGRAM "NEWSMAKERS," 7/10/65, 6:30 P.M. to 7:00 P.M. FEATURING MARTIN LUTHER KING, JR.

"Now more than ever before, we must supersoothe the course of
non-violence to achieve a reign of justice and a rule of love in our
society. Hatred and violence must be cast into an unending void if we
are to survive."

Those are the words of tonight's newsmaker, the President of the
Southern Christian Leadership Conference, a recipient of the Nobel
Prize for Peace, Dr. MARTIN LUTHER KING, JR. Tonight in our
studios in an unedited and unrehearsed broadcast, Dr. KING will be
the object of incisive questioning on a variety of subjects by our KNXT
panel, anchored by MAURY GREEN and backed up by Channel 2
newsmen PAUL UDELL and SAUL HOLBERT on "Newsmakers."

Dr. KING, last week you called for a negotiated settlement of the
war in Vietnam and other civil rights leaders immediately disagreed.
JAMES FARMER of CORE said that involving the civil rights movement in foreign policy could fragment the Negro community and ROY
WILKINS of the NAACP reacted this way on the CBS program "Face
the Nation": "We think we have enough Vietnam in Alabama to oc-
cupy our attention. We'll leave foreign policy to the United States and
enter our objections as citizens who know very little about it, but as
for a major drive in this direction, our major drive is for the enjoyment
of civil rights by the Negro citizens of this country. We don't believe
in dividing our energies; we don't have that many energies." Dr. KING,
in view of the strong reaction by other civil rights leaders, countered
to your opinions, have you had any second thoughts on your statement?

KING: No, I haven't. I'm just as firm now as ever before on the statement I made a few days ago concerning the need for a negotiated settlement in the whole struggle in Vietnam. I must make it clear that I did not advocate at that time a unilateral withdrawal on the part of the United States. I think that there must be a negotiated settlement involving all parties involved in that very tragic conflict. I think it is necessary to say that Mr. WILKINS and Mr. FARMER have good points when they say that we have neither the energies nor the resources in the civil rights movement to go all out in the peace struggle, but I think that we must see that I'm much more than a civil rights leader. I happen to be a Minister of the Gospel. I'm the pastor of a church and in that role I have a priestly function as well as a prophetic function, and in the prophetic role I must constantly speak to the moral issues of our day far beyond civil rights, and I was speaking in this particular situation in terms of my own personal witness to the terms of peace. This is a burning issue of our time and I feel that it is necessary for me to continue to speak on it. I can never overlook the fact that as we struggle to develop an integrated society that we must be as concerned about survival and we must be as concerned about the existence of the world in which to be integrated as we are about the kind of integrated society that we talk about.

I think the question raised here was whether you do not alienate those persons who agree with you on civil rights, but disagree with you on Vietnam; alienate them from your cause, at a time when you cannot afford to alienate anyone.

KING: I don't think that this will happen. I'm sure that there are many people who will disagree with me on this and disagree with others, but I think as President JOHNSON said in his speech at John Hopkins University on Vietnam some months ago that there is room for healthy debate on this issue and I'm sure that the people who cannot quite go along with my point of view wouldn't be alienated from the civil rights struggle. In a real sense, there can be no peace in the world unless there's justice and there can be no justice without peace. I think in a sense these problems are inextricably bound together. I have not called for an organized effort on the part of the civil rights movement to engage in demonstrations around the peace question. I simply said that as devotees of civil rights, we must be as concerned about world peace, because in the final analysis this is the most pressing issue confronting our age and I think every concerned citizen of good will must be concerned about the threat of nuclear annihilation and if this war continues to be escalated, then this threat becomes an even greater and more ominous possibility.

Well, Dr. KING, you equate civil rights and peace and in the civil rights area you demonstrate and you've indicated that you are considering that the Southern Christian Leadership Conference is considering demonstrating in favor of peace in Vietnam. Have you decided to do so?

KING: No, I think that was a false report altogether. I never said anything about organizing demonstrations around the Vietnam situation. I merely said that I will have to speak out on this issue, because it is a burning issue of our time and there would be a need at points to engage in teach-ins to inform the public, but I have no plans to engage in demonstrations around this. I have not recommended it to the Southern Christian Leadership Conference and as the press reported wrongly, we were not in a meeting, a board meeting, or a convention of the SCLC when I made this speech. I was merely speaking to an audience sponsored by the Virginia unit of the Southern Christian Leadership Conference and as I said, I was giving a personal witness rather than an organizational resolution.

Dr. KING, on another subject, Reverend REESE from Selma, Alabama, has been accused by the authorities there of, in effect, taking money, I believe out of the till of the civil rights movement. What do you think of this charge?

KING: Well, let me make it clear in the beginning, I firmly believe that civil rights organizations, and all organizations that are dependent on the public for their funds, must be absolutely responsible in the handling of these funds, and this is why I insist on thorough and meticulous records of the Southern Christian Leadership Conference and the thorough auditing of every penny that comes into our organization. The Dollars Counter-Voters League happens to be an affiliate of SCLC but it is an autonomous unit that handles its own money. I would say on the question of Reverend REESE that this is still in the realm of accusation and accusation must not be confused with truth. He still has a right on the basis of the long tradition of our system of jurisprudence to be considered innocent until he is proven guilty and I'm willing to go along with this presumption of innocence until the facts are in. I have demonstrated our good faith in SCLC and I believe in fair play and justice by calling for and already initiating a sort of independent investigation of the facts and examination of the whole situation there. I've already asked several of our men to go in to start this investigation because I am not unmindful of the fact that in a hostile setting like

Selma, Alabama, one can be the victim of persecution rather than prose-cution, and I am not unmindful of the fact that the same grand jury that indicted him and the same forces that arrested him are the same forces that have been extremely negligent about dealing with and assur-ing the rights of Negroes and about bringing to the Hall of Justice the murderers of civil rights workers and Negroes in Selma, Alabama.

Well, Dr. KING, are you suggesting that the charges may be an attempt to embarrass the civil rights movement?

KING: This is a possibility. We've had this to happen before and I'm sure that it can happen again. We must see that in Selma, Alabama, when we started our campaign there, there were only 300-and-some Negroes registered to vote. Today, more than 6,000 Negroes have signed the so-called appearance book, which means that in the next few days with the passage of the voting bill and the presence of federal examiners in the Selma community, you will have (not audible) 6,500 Negroes registered to vote. This becomes a real power factor in Selma, Alabama, and I'm sure by those forces who have determined to block this and to smear the movement in order to confuse the Negro commu-nity and to confuse the issues so much that this vote will continue to mount and I have no doubt that it will continue to mount as the days unfold.

We'll continue our questioning of tonight's Newsmaker, the Reverend Dr. MARTIN LUTHER KING, JR., in just a moment when we'll take a closer look at the Reverend KING, the Nobel Prize winner and the man.

He did not get the prophetic name of MARTIN LUTHER until he was six years old. His father, a minister before him, changed it from the name MICHAEL that young KING was given when he was born in Atlanta, 36 years ago. Young MARTIN LUTHER gravitated somewhat reluctantly into the ministry and was ordained in his father's church when he was 18. He married a promising young singer, CORETTA SCOTT, when both were students in Boston, where KING received his Ph.D. KING might have remained just an active local minister at a parish in Montgomery, Alabama. He could have enjoyed life with his wife and four children, and played sand lot ball and the other sports he enjoyed so much, had it not been for an incident in Montgomery in December 1955 when ROSA PARKS, the seamstress on the right here, refused to give up her bus seat to a white person and the Montgomery bus boycott was born. KING was its leader, articulating the longings of his people, and the leader he has remained, marching with them, going to jail with them. His latest arrest in Selma, Alabama, was his

17th. Facing danger to himself and his family, this was the home of Reverend KING's brother, shattered by a bomb in Birmingham. He was one of the leaders of the famous 1963 march on Washington, meeting later with President JOHN F. KENNEDY. At 35, he went on to be the youngest man ever to receive the Nobel Prize for peace. Since then, he has led demonstrations in dozens of cities, has conferred with President JOHNSON, and has made his views known to the world in books with such titles as "Strength to Love," "Stride Toward Freedom," and "Why We Can't Wait."

Dr. KING, you have already announced that you plan personally to lead massive civil rights demonstrations here in Los Angeles shortly. Why has this city been chosen as a target for such action?

KING: Well, we have several cities in mind for summer activity in the North, and this is because the problems of the North are very serious and they're growing more serious every day in the area of race relations. These problems are really threefold. The problem of housing discrimination, the problem of de facto segregation in the schools and the lack of quality integrated education and the problem of job discrimination and poverty within the Negro community. Los Angeles has been chosen specifically because I have been invited here by the local Negro leadership working so passionately in the area of justice generally, but trying to make the poverty bill meaningful and real in particular. There is a feeling and I think it's a justifiable feeling that this bill, as proposed by the Mayor and the City Council, will not be properly administered because it excludes from participation in decision making on the policy level the very people who have been the victims of poverty and economic insecurity, and the poverty program must not, in any community, become a political football. It must not become a bill that is used by any of the forces in the political power structure for various ends, but it must be a bill that serves the purpose that it came into being to serve; namely, the bringing into the mainstream of our whole nation and American life those who have been excluded because of poverty.

Dr. KING, so far the civil rights movement here in Los Angeles has really not been able to mount massive civil rights demonstrations. Do you think that this poverty issue has a different dimension? What makes you think that there can be large demonstrations on this point?

KING: I think that many people are concerned about the problem of poverty and concerned about the poverty bill being adequately and properly dealt with and administered. I'm not only speaking of Negroes at this point because along the way and along the years, some of our strongest and most vocal allies have come from the white community and I'm sure that there are many white allies that will join with thousands and thousands of Negroes in protesting this issue. Poverty is a reality. It is something we can't overlook and it is something many people will be outraged about when they discover that it is not being properly dealt with.

Doctor, the basic charge against the type of argument which you advanced regarding those people that are poverty stricken having a voice in the administration program is that by virtue of being poor, it does not guarantee that you are able to see how the program should be directed. Do you believe the poor do have this insight into the direction of such a program?

KING: Oh, I think so, very definitely. First, because one is poverty stricken does not mean that that individual does not have basic intelligence. As I've gone through the Appalachian regions of our country, and even the delta of Mississippi where you've had a lack of educational opportunities, I've been amazed at the basic intelligence of individuals who've been deprived of so much, and I think that these victims of great deprivation are much more intelligent than many people realize, and I think they can make decisions. Since they have been the victims of poverty, I think they, more than anybody else, will know the programs that will help them, and they, more than anybody else, it seems to me, would have the capacity to participate in the decisions that will determine their destiny.

Is one of the reasons to revive or stimulate interest by Los Angeles Negroes in civil rights programs and thereby perhaps stimulate a flow of contributions?

KING: Well, I don't believe that the basic purpose of this drive is to stimulate contributions for the civil rights movement. I've talked to local leaders. I think they are motivated, first by deep love for American democracy and also by a commitment to the poverty program and its importance, but above all, they are motivated by a desire to see the program properly administered. There are many issues that can be dealt with on the question of civil rights in California, and it goes far beyond the poverty issue: [issues like] the fact that there is widespread discrimination in housing and the fact that this state turned the clock of history back, so to speak, by repealing a fair housing law, then all the questions of segregation in the schools and the question of job discrimination, as well as the problems of joblessness generally, growing out of automation and cybernation. There are many issues that can arouse this community a great deal and I think the poverty issue is now the pressing

one because of the urgency of it and because the grant is the thing that
is now standing before this community.

We'll continue our questioning of tonight's Newsmaker, Dr. MAR-
TIN LUTHER KING, JR., in just a moment.

Dr. KING, the Southern Regional Council reported only a few days
ago that unreasoning blind hatred of whites is on the increase in the
Negro community in the South, and we've had the information of an
organization recently called the Deacons which buys and uses guns, or
intends to use them if necessary. Now in Bogalusa, Louisiana, we've
just had an incident in which apparently the Deacons were involved
where a white man was shot. You, yourself, are an advocate of non-
violence. Do you approve of the Deacons?

KING: I would say that I understand the deep frustration and the
discontent and the seething desperation of Negroes who find themselves,
as we so often do, in situations where there is no protection from law
enforcement agencies and where the mobsters and the Klansmen and
the other persons who will use violence against us are aided and abetted
by law enforcement agencies, so I'd like to make it very clear in the
beginning that I understand this and I do not want to speak with the
kind of self-righteousness at this point that will cause me to fail to
sympathize with those who, out of deep frustration and discontent, turn
to violence. On the other hand, I'm still convinced that violence in our
struggle is not only immoral and I think that is true, but also impractical.
Consequently, I would have to say that the approach of the Deacons is
an impractical approach. I say that for two or three reasons. First, when
you develop a violent campaign, you confuse the issue and you get
people talking about reign of violence and Negroes turning to violence
and they forget to talk about the fact that segregation is an issue, that
injustice pervades the community and this is a main issue. The second
thing is that the line of demarcation between defensive violence that
the Deacons talk about and aggressive violence is very thin and when
you begin to teach people to use violence even defensively in a movement, you put them in the position of unconsciously or consciously
turning to violence in an aggressive sense. I'm sure that people want
to defend themselves. I don't need to preach that in anybody. I don't
think anybody needs to do it. That will be individual acts of individuals
who will defend themselves when they are caught in these situations
but the Deacons, I think, make the mistake of trying to develop a
movement around defensive violence and I think this is its impractical-
ity. The other thing is that we can't win a violent campaign. Many of
our opponents would welcome our turning to violence and they would

use this as an excuse to wipe out many innocent people. We have neither the techniques nor the instruments of violence, and we must never forget that we are 10 per cent of the population in the United States; and we must never forget the other thing as I've said so often— we are seeking to live with an (inaudible) condition the very people that are our opponents today, and we must be sure that we engage in the kind of struggle that will bring about creative tension, that will develop wounds that will heal rather than develop into festering sores that will not heal.

Dr. KING, our time is getting a little short. I wonder if you could give us a brief answer to a rather personal question. You, yourself, have become a symbol of non-violence and of the civil rights movement. You, yourself, have been threatened many times. Are you worried about this? Are you concerned about your personal safety?

KING: Well, I don't worry about it. Naturally, I'm concerned about my personal safety and it is true that every day I live under the threat of death. I get numerous letters of a threatening nature and numerous calls, but I think ultimately one has to be philosophical about this and I don't think I could function if I moved around every day worrying about the fact that something will happen and realism impels me to admit that something can happen—assassinations can take place, but it's my feeling that if an individual has not developed some cause, some truth, some principle that he is so committed to that he will die for it, he isn't fit to live. I think that unmerited suffering in the final analysis is redemptive.

Thank you, Dr. KING. Our time's up. Goodnight.

Reverend MARTIN LUTHER KING, JR., was tonight's Newsmaker.

UNITED STATES GOVERNMENT
Memorandum

TO: Mr. A. H. Belmont   DATE: 7/15/65

FROM: Mr. W. C. Sullivan

PROVIDENCE, RHODE ISLAND
LETTER TO THE PRESIDENT

By memorandum to the Attorney General dated 7/9/65, Lee C. White, Special Counsel to the President, the White House, forwarded a letter to the President dated 7/4/65 from . . . Providence 6, Rhode Island, with the question, "How do you suggest we handle this one?" . . . letter was in turn forwarded to Mr. DeLoach by memorandum from the Attorney General dated 7/13/65 with the question, "Do you have any suggestions which the Attorney General might make to Lee White?"

. . . letter charges that at a recent briefing session held at The National War college a Mr. Sullivan of the FBI stated openly that it was widely known that the Reverend Martin Luther King was a homosexual. . . . stated that the libel cannot be answered or withdrawn and that Mr. Sullivan's action was unforgivable and called for immediate disciplinary action.

On 6/28/65, Assistant Director Sullivan addressed the annual Defense Strategy Seminar, The National War College, Washington, D.C., on the subject, "Internal Security." Members of the Seminar held security clearance through Secret. Mr. Sullivan's address and the question and answer period which followed it was a classified discussion which included material classified Secret. Mr. Sullivan did not mention King in his address. In the question and answer period following his address, the role of King in the civil rights movement was brought up for discussion. Mr. Sullivan pointed out that subversive elements can and do exploit personal weaknesses to attain their objectives. He stated that King had two sides. He said that some of King's activities . . . of this, King could well become a great liability to the civil rights movement and a real albatross around the neck of the Negro people. Mr. Sullivan summed up his remarks by saying that because of King's shortcomings, it is most unfortunate that King has risen to a position of such importance in the racial situation. At no time did Mr. Sullivan state that King was a homosexual.

. . . Director of the Defense Strategy Seminar, advised through Liaison on 7/14/65 that records of the Seminar do not list . . . as having been present at the Seminar.

OBSERVATIONS:

According to the Director of the Defense Strategy Seminar, . . . is not listed as having been in attendance at this Seminar. Those in attendance at the Seminar held security clearance through Secret and Mr. Sullivan's address was a classified discussion including material classified through Secret. It appears obvious that . . . letter is based on hearsay information obtained from an unknown source. . . . donations to the Southern Conference Educational Fund and his participation in Fair Housing legislation indicated that he is involved in civil rights activities and undoubtedly is an admirer of King.

RECOMMENDATIONS:

(1) That the attached letter and memorandum be sent to Lee C. White suggesting that he may wish to reply to ... advising him that Mr. Sullivan spoke at The National War College in June 1965, but that this was a classified discussion and therefore his remarks could not be disclosed to ... However, he, White, had ascertained that Mr. Sullivan made no statement that Martin Luther King is a homosexual.

(2) That the attached letter be forwarded to the Attorney General with a copy to the Deputy Attorney General furnishing him with copies of the letter and memorandum sent to Mr. White.

[Section 38]

FBI

8/6/65

AIRTEL

To:　　　SACs, Atlanta (100-5586)
　　　　　　New York (100-136585)

From:　　Director, FBI (100-106670)

MARTIN LUTHER KING, JR.
SECURITY MATTER-C

Washington, D.C., newspaper accounts of subject's visit with the President 8/5/65, revealed the following:

King said that the President invited him to the White House to get his thoughts on an autumn civil rights conference to be called "To Fulfill These Rights." King said that he will submit a report to the President outlining problems the Negro now faces and that it would draw on the "studies and experiences we have had on our Northern tour." King also said that he would recommend either legislation or expanded Executive Order on housing.

As recipient offices are aware, much of King's writings and many of his ideas are generated by others, including individuals with present and former subversive backgrounds. Recipient offices should be extremely alert to information available through established sources which would indicate assistance by these subversives given to King relative to the report he is to prepare for the President and for any other material or items which he will use at the forthcoming autumn civil rights conference.

The Bureau should be kept promptly advised of all pertinent information developed, and that which may be disseminated should be submitted in an appropriate form.

[Section 40]

UNITED STATES DEPARTMENT OF JUSTICE

FEDERAL BUREAU OF INVESTIGATION

New York, New York
August 16, 1965

Re: Communist Influence In Racial Matters
Internal Security-C

On August 13, 1965, a confidential source, who has furnished reliable information in the past, advised that Dora McDonald (Secretary to Martin Luther King, President, Southern Christian Leadership Conference, SCLC) and Stanley Levison were in contact on that day concerning the rioting in Los Angeles, California. In that regard, McDonald said King had been contacted by a radio station in Los Angeles, who urged that he issue a statement appealing to the Negroes to end the rioting. She said that King, in turn, had requested that she contact him (Levison) and request that he prepare a statement dealing with the matter. According to the source, Levison prepared the following statement:

"I know that you have grievances that are hard to live with—I know that any Negro can reach the end of his patience and want to strike out and strike back. But it is not courage nor militancy to strike out blindly. Our enemies have always hoped that we would lose our heads and riot against the guilty and innocent alike. This enables them to argue that we haven't decency or good sense. I speak to you as one who had to march with other Negroes against guns, clubs, dogs and whips and who won victories over cruel and barbarous sheriffs and klansmen. We won victories because we had a greater weapon—disciplined cool heads, and iron determination not to provoke into violence. Our adversaries have always known what to do when we lost our heads—it gave them a chance to beat our heads. They have never known what to do when we refused to be sucked into the trap of violence.

"Tonight the whole world is watching you. If you want all America to respect you, if you want the world to know that you are men, put down your weapons and your rocks. Get a committee together and draw up demands. If you want my help I will sit with you and plan how to improve your conditions.

"Negroes in the South were not less oppressed than you and we have run Jim Crow from thousands of places without using a rock or a bullet. We made millions of white Americans sick and ashamed of their practices and by our discipline won many to our side. You are naming yourselves, not the segregationists. Tonight in the South, the segregationist is delighted. He has made you lose your temper and for a few moments of emotional excitement and relief you are conducting yourself without reason, without a name and without a goal. You are not an army of Negro people if you fight without reason. Our people are not rioters and are not looters. Come back to our ranks where there is a room for honest courage and militancy, where real and permanent victories have been won and will be won in the right way.

"The man who cools off, who puts down his weapon and stands up with only his body is the man of courage. Don't let us down here in the South. Don't discredit brave Negroes in jails in Johannesburg. Don't set yourself back. You can still win a great victory by halting the fighting because there is more honor and dignity in looking the other side squarely in the eye and demanding your rights than there is in struggling in blind fury. In the name of brave Negroes who have died in the South over the past ten years of bitter struggle, I appeal to you to end the hostilities so that together we can march forward for real gains for our people everywhere."

A confidential source, who has furnished reliable information in the past, advised on August 14, 1965, that Bayard Rustin (organizer of the March on Washington), and Martin Luther King were in contact on that date. Their contact, according to the source, dealt with the rioting in Los Angeles. King told Rustin that he was on his way to Puerto Rico to deliver a speech, and that upon arrival he would issue a press release dealing with the situation in Los Angeles, therefore, wanted Rustin's suggestions on the matter. Rustin suggested to King that the following points should be contained in any statement to the press:

"That we deplore resorting to violence no matter who is engaged in the violence because it is wrong and socially destructive. That while we deplore violence, we also deplore the concentration of the ghetto life which leads, with the absence of jobs, bad education and slums, to the hopelessness and despair where the Negro youth, out of these conditions, feels that they have no stake in American society.'' Rustin suggested in reference to that point that King make mention of President Johnson's conference scheduled to be held in November 1965, which will deal with the whole ghetto and family life problem, by stating that he hoped new and stirring ideas would emerge from the conference.

In continuing his suggestions, Rustin said that King should point out that, ''Rightly or wrongly, whether or not there was, in fact, police brutality in Los Angeles, almost every Negro in every family has, at one time or another, felt that he has been maltreated by the police; therefore, in addition to the social problems, in every city there needs to be a civilian review board. This board is to protect the policeman when he is right and to protect the citizen when the policeman is not right.''

King and Rustin both remarked that they had been asked to go to Los Angeles to help suppress the riots, but both opined that they would not be able to be of much assistance since the situation had deteriorated to such a point that it was a job for the National Guard. They ended their contact by speculating on whether or not they would be of any help subsequent to the riots.

The same confidential source furnished information on August 14, 1965, which disclosed that Rustin and Roy Wilkins (Executive Secretary of the National Association for the Advancement of Colored People, NAACP) were in contact on that date concerning, among other things, the rioting in Los Angeles, who had done nothing (to end the riots), were putting pressure on King to come to Los Angeles to aid in quelling the riots. Rustin said King was going to Puerto Rico to speak, but had airline tickets to travel to Los Angeles on his way back from Puerto Rico. Rustin said King would do nothing but create more confusion and embarrass himself if he went to Los Angeles. Wilkins concurred, adding that if King did go to Los Angeles, he would be regarded as an emissary sent to quiet the rioters.

The source advised on August 14, 1965, that Rustin and Harry Wachtel were in contact on the above date. During their contact, Wachtel spoke in regard to the rioting in Los Angeles, stating that he was not unhappy because the ''power structure acts as if they are only dealing with King and they are not dealing with guys who are easily incited, who live in stinking conditions.'' Rustin said he had dissuaded King from going to Los Angeles at this time.

UNITED STATES DEPARTMENT OF JUSTICE

FEDERAL BUREAU OF INVESTIGATION

New York, New York

August 17, 1965

Re: Communist Infiltration of the Southern
Christian Leadership Conference (SCLC)
Internal Security-C

On August 13, 1965, a confidential source, who has furnished reliable information in the past, furnished information which disclosed that Stanley Levison and Dora McDonald (Secretary to Martin Luther King, President of the SCLC), were in contact on that date. According to the source, McDonald related to Levison that King desired him (Levison) to prepare the answers to twelve questions dealing with Vietnam which were put to him (King) by the "New York Times." Mcdonald said the "Times" inquiry was precipitated by King's recent statement on Vietnam.

The "New York World Telegram and Sun," August 13, 1965, page 2, contained an article captioned, "Dr. King Urges Vietnam Talks." The article notes that King, while addressing the convention of the SCLC (held in Birmingham, Alabama, August 9–13, 1965), urged opposing sides in the Vietnam conflict to negotiate and end the struggle's cycle of "mistrust, violence and war."

According to the source, Levison furnished to McDonald the answers to the twelve questions which she had given him, and they were as follows:

Question: In his statement, King noted several peace organizations had approached him regarding Vietnam. What specific groups were they?

Answer: Among others, National SANE, Women Strike for Peace, Student and Faculty Group in Berkeley, California.

Question: What is the text of the letter King is sending to President Johnson and Ho Chi Minh?

Answer: When the text is finalized, a copy will be made available.

Question: How will the letter be sent?

Answer: These details have not been planned as yet.

Question: Should the United States stay in Vietnam if South Vietnamese ask us to leave?

Answer: I believe we would have no moral or jurisdicial basis for
remaining if a sovereign government demands that we leave
its territory.

Question: Can he be more specific regarding his attitude on escalation
of the war?

Answer: Escalation is expressed in so many degrees and is related
to escalation on the other side so that I can discuss it only
in concrete terms. It is impossible to generalize.

Question: King said he is not blaming either government for the war.
Who is to blame?

Answer: There is blame on both sides because each has made responses too readily through means of violence without an
earnest search for reduction of violence. I am encouraged
by the restraint President Johnson has manifested and in
words and I believe the exercise of restraint will ultimately
lead faster to constructive negotiation than will the flexing
of the muscles of military power which the whole world
knows we possess in terrifying abundance.

Question: What specific proposals would King have to make?

Answer: I have not formulated specific proposals for ending the war
and I am not sure I have competence in that area.

Question: Is King seriously thinking of going to Vietnam and under
what circumstances?

Answer: I have no plans to go to Vietnam.

Question: Will King's letter also be sent to the United Nations?

Answer: There are no plans for a letter to the United Nations because
it is not a combatant nor any ally of any combatant. This
does not imply that it has no role. Its role is substantial but
different.

Question: Will King contact United States officials regarding his
plans, that is, Governors, Senators, Congressmen or
Diplomats?

Answer: I have no body of plans which could be the subject of
discussions. I am expressing a point of view which will be
self-explanatory and I sincerely hope useful for those who
have the responsibility to make plans.

Question: King states he is following a path of non-violence, but Reverend James Bevel recently made statements indicating he

is more militant. Can King reconcile this and is Bevel speaking for the SCLC or as an individual?

Answer: The emphasis James Bevel places on peace activity in relation to civil rights activity differs from mine because I am not presently proposing any change in the direction or the character of our civil rights work. He has the right to express his analysis and has done so.

Question: Reverend Bevel stated the civil rights movement is legislated out of business. Will King comment on this?

Answer: I do not agree with James Bevel's view that the civil rights movement has been legislated out of existence. We still have so far to go I cannot see the end of the road even now. I see the need for a multiplicity of additional legislative reforms which will take years of struggle to fully achieve.

It is noted that James Bevel is Field Secretary of the SCLC.

UNITED STATES DEPARTMENT OF JUSTICE

FEDERAL BUREAU OF INVESTIGATION

Charlotte, North Carolina
August 17, 1965

MARTIN LUTHER KING, JR.
SECURITY MATTER-C

On August 14, 1965, at approximately 11 P.M., . . . Asheville, North Carolina, telephonically furnished the following information.

. . . said something about trying to talk to someone at the FBI in Washington but his conversation was unintelligible. He said "I know I am crazy and I am half drunk." He said something about overhearing a man, whose name he did not know, say something about having two 8 millimeter rifles which would pinpoint a target [at] 500 yards. When asked what he was talking about, he said "I guess he was talking about the S.O.B. who is coming to Montreat next week." . . . said that he could explain better when he was sober and asked that he be contacted later.

On August 16, 1965, . . . advised that he did not have any specific information, but that several days ago he walked out of his office and two men were sitting on a bench and one of the men made a statement that he had two 8 millimeter rifles, and that if anyone wanted to use one on MARTIN LUTHER KING, he would be glad to loan him one. ... stated that the man doing the talking was a white male, age about 30, slender build, and was wearing blue pants which looked like part of a bus driver uniform. He stated that he could not furnish any better description of that man, and that he could not furnish any description of the other man except that he was also a white man. ... said that he thinks he has seen the man who did the talking before, but could not place him. He stated that if he could obtain any further information he would make that information available.

On August 16, 1965, this information was furnished by ... was furnished to Chief Deputy Sheriff ... Asheville, North Carolina.

UNITED STATES DEPARTMENT OF JUSTICE

FEDERAL BUREAU OF INVESTIGATION

Miami, Florida
August 17, 1965

RE: MARTIN LUTHER KING, JR.
SECURITY MATTER-C

On page 1 of the August 15, 1965, issue of "The Miami Herald," daily Miami newspaper, an article reflected that on August 14, 1965, KING, while en route to Puerto Rico to address a religious convention, stated the Los Angeles riots were "absolutely wrong, socially detestable, and self-defeating."

According to the article, KING later stated at San Juan that he favored use of the full force of the police power to quell the situation in Los Angeles.

KING added that he hoped the riots would not spread, but due to joblessness and housing conditions, every northern community is a potential powder keg.

On pages 1 and 2A of the August 16, 1965, issue of "The Miami Herald," an article reflected KING stated upon his arrival in Miami from Puerto Rico, that within the next few days he will go to Los Angeles to help restore Negro leadership in that riot-torn community.

KING stated he had been in constant touch with Negro leaders in Los Angeles since the rioting erupted Wednesday night.

According to KING, the trouble in Los Angeles resulted from the lack of a vibrant, non-violent program that gives oppressed people a chance to vent their fury without violence. KING said he is honestly compelled to admit that discontent is so deep and widespread that he feared other outbursts.

KING said the Negro rioting will not delay his plans to write both sides of the Vietnam conflict in hopes of bringing about a settlement.

He scoffed at a Republican Congressman's proposal that he stay at home and help put down the Negro riots instead of embarking on a peace mission to North Vietnam.

KING said he had no desire or intention to negotiate but "the orgy of bloodshed" in Viet Nam poses a threat to world survival and it is the proper concern of "a minister of the Gospel and an American citizen."

UNITED STATES DEPARTMENT OF JUSTICE

FEDERAL BUREAU OF INVESTIGATION

San Francisco, California
August 10, 1965

UNKNOWN SUBJECT;
Governor EDMUND G. BROWN,
California-Victim

Information was received on August 18, 1965, from John McInerney, Governor's Office, Sacramento, California, to the effect that an anonymous postcard was received on the morning of August 18, 1965, addressed to Governor Edmund G. Brown marked "Urgent." This card was postmarked at Los Angeles, California, during the afternoon hours of August 17, 1965. It stated, "Dear Sir, King will be shot!!! even by one of his so as to create greater havoc. Remember you have been told!"

UNITED STATES DEPARTMENT OF JUSTICE

FEDERAL BUREAU OF INVESTIGATION

Los Angeles, California
August 23, 1965

MARTIN LUTHER KING, JR.
SECURITY MATTER-C

... advised on August 19, 1965, that King was scheduled to meet with Los Angeles Mayor Samuel W. Yorty and Police Chief William H. Parker around noon on August 19, 1965, for a conference.

The "Los Angeles Times," a daily Los Angeles metropolitan newspaper, home edition, for August 20, 1965, Part 1, Page 1, carried an article captioned "King assailed by Yorty after Stormy Meeting." The article stated that Mayor Yorty, Police Chief Parker, and nine other persons, not identified, but described as mainly civil rights figures and aides to Yorty and Parker, held a two hour and 45 minute meeting with King in Mayor Yorty's office on August 19, 1965.

Mayor Yorty was quoted as stating after the conference that King had performed "a great disservice to the people of Los Angeles and the nation." Yorty criticized King for "talking about lawlessness, killing, looting, and burning in the same context as our police department." The Mayor staunchly defended Parker against Dr. King's suggestion that many Negroes want Parker to resign.

The article quoted Bayard Rustin, a deputy to Dr. King who attended the meeting, as stating that some of the participants used "crude" language and that the longest and most heated debate concerned King's demand for a civilian police review board. Another official present, not identified, stated that much of the argument at the conference "was over unfounded charges of police brutality."

Yorty was quoted as stating, "I don't think that it's wise for Dr. King to try and simplify all the complex issues that led to the riot and personify them in Chief Parker" and that Dr. King "shouldn't have come here."

King was quoted as stating that the rioting had an economic cause and this could be alleviated if Mayor Yorty could obtain sufficient anti-poverty funds.

King stated that Yorty and Parker would not permit him to visit arrested rioters in Lincoln Heights Jail, and he suggested that Yorty should tour the Watts area so that residents could tell him personally of their grievances. Mayor Yorty stated that he refused to let Dr. King visit the jail because he did not want to set off a prison riot.

King was quoted as stating that an independent police review board could "do a lot to ease tension by investigating specific charges of brutality." Yorty stated that a police review would tend to duplicate the present five member police commission which, he noted, includes a Negro, a Mexican-American, and a Jew. Yorty was further quoted as stating even if Parker wanted to resign he would refuse to accept the resignation.

. . . advised on August 19, 1965, that King had planned to visit the Watts area of Los Angeles where the rioting centered again on the afternoon of August 19, 1965, but for some reason canceled his plans. . . . did not know the reason but surmised it might have been because of the prolonged conference King had with Mayor Yorty and Chief Parker that day and that time did not permit.

. . . advised further on August 20, 1965, that the proposed meeting between King and Los Angeles labor leaders on August 20, 1965, was not held. Bayard Rustin had hoped to arrange such a meeting but it did not materialize. Apparently time did not permit arranging such a meeting on short notice. . . . did not know the identity of the labor leaders that King had hoped to meet with.

The "Los Angeles Times," home edition for August 21, 1965, Part 1, Page 4, carried an article "L.A. Lacks Leadership on Rights, King Says."

The article quoted Dr. Martin Luther King as stating at a press conference at the International Hotel, Los Angeles, on August 20, 1965, that he had failed to find any "statesmanship and creative leadership" to resolve the situation in the South Los Angeles riot-torn district.

When asked whether he was referring to Mayor Yorty and Governor Brown, King replied, "I think the governor has been moving in a forthright and committed way but I am not going to get into any name calling." He added he had not seen on the city level the kind of "sensitive and determined leadership capable of solving the problem."

King stated that he had been in contact with the White House on the morning of August 20, 1965, and had an appointment to talk to President Johnson by telephone that night from Atlanta about the Los Angeles situation.

King was further quoted as stating, "There are serious doubts that the white community is in any way concerned or willing to accommodate their needs. There is a growing disillusionment and resentment (by

Negroes in the Watts area) toward the Negro middle class and the leadership it has produced.''

King was further quoted as stating that the Negroes' fight is for "dignity and work, and this is the reason why the issue of police brutality looms so high. The slightest discourtesy on the part of an officer of the law is a deprivation of the dignity which most of the residents of Watts came North seeking.''

King was further quoted as stating, "There is a unanimous feeling among Negroes that there is police brutality." King added that while most Negroes want Police Chief Parker removed he had not heard any recommendations for a replacement for Parker.

A source, who has furnished reliable information in the past, advised on August 20, 1965, that at his press conference on that date King had also stated that he felt that the underlying cause of the riots in Los Angeles were basically economic and grew out of the depths of despair of the Negro. This source further advised that the riots in Los Angeles were of national significance and that while these riots constitute a "crisis" for the non-violent movement he still felt that the majority of people in the Watts area maintained an attitude of non-violence.

. . . advised on August 20, 1965, that King and his aide, Bernard Lee, departed Los Angeles at approximately 3:05 P.M. on the afternoon of August 20, 1965, by Delta Airline Flight 804, which was due to arrive at Atlanta, Georgia, at 9:52 (on the same date).

UNITED STATES DEPARTMENT OF JUSTICE

FEDERAL BUREAU OF INVESTIGATION

New York, New York
August 27, 1965

Re: Communist Influence
In Racial Matters
Internal Security-C

A confidential source, who has furnished reliable information in the past, advised on August 25, 1965, that Bernard Lee (Personal Assistant to Martin Luther King) was in contact with Stanley Levison on that date. Lee stated that he was contacting Levison on behalf of King, who desired that Levison review an article which he (King) was writing for

"The New York Times" magazine (Sunday's edition). Lee said that King wanted to determine whether or not the article was perceptive enough and if not, wanted him to make the necessary changes. Levison agreed to the request and said that he would make whatever changes were necessary.

Later, on August 25, 1965, the same source advised that Martin Luther King contacted Levison concerning the article which is to appear in "The New York Times," and also in regard to other matters. After discussing the article, they concurred that the article would receive nationwide attention, prompting King to comment that the article should contain a message to the effect that one way to respond to "that" (Los Angeles riot) was to take a completely negative attitude, whereby the civil rights leaders and everyone else would be blamed for the trouble. King said he had been accused since he had urged people to break laws during the civil rights demonstrations. In an effort to explain his position more clearly, King said that he was trying to get across the fact that a crisis like "that" (Los Angeles riot) could be both a danger point as well as an opportunity. "This is the time," King said, "to seek the causes and face the fact that we haven't done enough to right wrongs." He said, "Now is the time to make a new national commitment on the whole question of civil rights."

Levison, commenting on King's belief that a new national commitment should be made, said "such a statement could be expressed in the form King had used before, that non-violence can make its effective contribution only when there is a creative and cooperative response on the other side from the power structure."

According to the source, one other important matter was considered before King and Levison ended their conference. King said he had a feeling that there was a need to re-evaluate "our whole programmatic thrust" in the next few months, particularly their work in the North. He said that was necessary since there had been accusations that the Los Angeles riot had been caused because civil rights leaders had not carried their program to the isolated people.

It was agreed that in view of King's feelings that an urgent consultation with his advisers was needed, specifically Young, Bayard Rustin, Levison and Clarence Jones, that a meeting be held in Atlanta at the Hilton Inn on August 26, 1965, through the morning of August 28, 1965.

The conference ended with a promise by Levison that he would contact Rustin and Jones to see whether or not they could attend the meeting.

The source advised on the night of August 25, 1965, that Stanley Levison made arrangements to fly to Atlanta, Georgia, on August 26, 1965, aboard Eastern Airlines Flight 101Y, which was scheduled to leave Kennedy International Airport at 9:30 A.M. and arrive in Atlanta at 10:38 A.M. The source said Levison would be met at the Atlanta airport by Andrew Young (Executive Director of the Southern Christian Leadership Conference).

UNITED STATES DEPARTMENT OF JUSTICE

FEDERAL BUREAU OF INVESTIGATION

Washington, D.C. 20535
August 30, 1965

MARTIN LUTHER KING, JR.

On August 29, 1965, the Reverend Martin Luther King, Jr., President, Southern Christian Leadership Conference (SCLC), was interviewed on CBS Television program "Face the Nation" at Washington, D.C. This news interview was conducted by Lew Wood, CBS News Correspondent, Rowland Evans, Columnist, New York Herald Tribune Syndicate, and Martin Agronsky, CBS News Correspondent.

At the outset Dr. King indicated he had been so busy with the Civil Rights Movement that he had not had a chance to write a letter to Ho Chi Minh. He indicated he thinks it is very urgent to work relentlessly for a negotiated settlement of the dangerous and tragic conflict in Viet Nam and he wanted to use whatever concern that he could muster at this point to express his desire along with [the desire of] numerous people all over the world to bring an end to that conflict.

Statements made during the program are substantially as follows. Questions asked by the above newsmen are indicated by the letter "Q" and answers given by Dr. King are indicated by the letter "A."

Q: Dr. King, many Negro and white civil rights leaders, also responsible men of our Government, have indicated their concern that by your use of your own prestige and the Civil Rights Movement to seek independently a Vietnamese peace, you might end with weakening, dividing, and even negating the strengths of the Civil Rights Movement in this country. How would you respond to that criticism?

THE FBI FILE   407

A: I would certainly say I don't think this is true. First, I must make it clear that my expressions on the war in Viet Nam grow out of something much larger than participation in the Civil Rights Movement. I happen to be a minister of the Gospel and I take that ministry very seriously and in that capacity I have not merely a priestly function but a prophetic function and I must ever seek to bring the great principles of our Judeo-Christian heritage to bear on the social evils of our day and I happen to feel that war is obsolete and that it must be cast in to unending limbo. If we continue to escalate this war we move nearer to plunging the whole of mankind to the abyss of annihilation and I will continue to speak when I deem it timely and necessary on this issue not as a civil rights leader. I have no intention at this point, for instance, to enter into the peace struggle. I don't think we have the resources or the energy. The civil rights issues are still before us in a big and certainly complex way and we have got to work on that front, but as a minister of the gospel and one greatly concerned about the need for peace in the world and the survival of mankind I must continue to take a stand on this issue.

Q: Dr. King, you said a moment ago that you were so busy with the Civil Rights Movement you hadn't had a chance to write your letter to Ho Chi Minh. What is going to change that situation in the next few months? Why won't you be too busy with the Civil Rights Movement, particularly with the trouble in the northern cities?

A: I think we had certain emergency situations; certainly the Los Angeles situation was an emergency much more than other situations we faced in the past. Now I think we will get a let-up from that, and from other conditions from other events that will be that ominous in proportion. I think that as a result of the kind of let-up that we will get at that point I would have a chance to give more thought and a little more time to this issue of writing letters to those leaders.

Q: The question of the Logan Act, which prevents ordinary citizens outside of the Government from negotiating in any international relations on behalf of our country, seems to enter into this question. At least it has been brought up. Are you aware of the Logan Act and has it influenced your decision to write letters to Ho Chi Minh and so forth?

A: I am aware of that Act. I must say that when I mentioned the fact that when I was contemplating writing these letters I did not know about the Logan Act. After that it was called to my attention. I haven't had a chance to look at that Act in all its legal ramifications. I have had one or two of my lawyers take a look at it and it seems to me that the kind of thing that I am concerned about is no different from an individual writing an open letter on this issue to the New York Times or other newspapers. I have no desire to negotiate. I could not do it if I wanted to. My only concern is that there will be a negotiated settlement and this is the basic thing that I will say in the letters and I don't see how this will conflict with the Logan Act because I will not be seeking to negotiate on my own.

Q: Then you won't do it in the area of civil disobedience?

A: No, sir, I am not contemplating any civil disobedience at this point.

Q: Do you contemplate going yourself to Viet Nam?

A: Up to now I have not contemplated going to Viet Nam. I have been invited several times to go with various groups but I have not been able and I couldn't find the time to go. I don't have any plans to go at this time. Now it depends on developments; something may occur that will cause me to feel that I should reverse my point of view and go, but as it stands now I don't have any plans.

Q: Dr. King, a very distinguished Negro leader in this country, the Assistant Secretary of Labor, George Weaver, who is Head of the Bureau of International Affairs in the Department of Labor, makes another point upon your concern about the Vietnamese peace situation. He says that Americans who have called for peace talks could give the impression that large numbers of American people are not behind the President's Vietnamese policy and might cause the enemy, to quote Mr. Weaver, to miscalculate our determination to fulfill our commitments to resist aggression and that that result could be devastating.

A: I think we must say that part of the sacred heritage of our nation is a right to take a stand on the basis of freedom of speech for what conscience tells one is right. Nothing could be more tragic at this time, it seems to me, than for individuals to confuse dissent with disloyalty. I think we need creative dissent. Even President Johnson has called for healthy debate on this issue. We all know that our President has a very difficult job at this point and I am not in a position now of affixing blame on our President or on anybody. I just think the problem must be solved because I am

THE FBI FILE 409

concerned about our children, I am concerned about our men who are in battle and the Vietnamese children and people, and I think that the only course is to work with all the energy that we can develop to bring an end to that conflict.

Q: Dr. King, have you discussed this question in any degree with President Johnson?

A: Yes, I have talked with President Johnson.

Q: Does President Johnson approve of this basic position?

A: Of course, there are differences. President Johnson has made it clear that he feels he is doing what he has to do in the situation and I am not self-righteous at this point. He can understand the moral dilemma of those who feel the need of escalating the war so that I don't feel that I can stand with any pretense and say that I have the answer. I am only saying that my concern is so great that I am willing to take a stand and call for all of the work that we can do to solve this problem.

Q: Have you ever had any encouragement either from the President or from Arthur Goldberg, our Ambassador to the United Nations, in the peace enterprise that you are now engaged in?

A: I must say that President Johnson has not urged me at any point to withhold my statements, to cease speaking at this point. Now, I have not talked with Ambassador Goldberg. I plan to talk with him on Tuesday. He invited me to talk with him about peace in general and about Viet Nam in particular and I plan to do that.

Q: Have you a specific proposal to make to him on how you can bring about a negotiation?

A: I will be thinking about this for the next day or two before going, but at this point I don't have a specific proposal and as I said he invited me to the meeting so he has probably done some thinking about it. I don't know the nature of the agenda at this time.

Q: Dr. King, I would like to ask you about the statement that the Reverend James Bevel made at the time the President signed the Voting Rights Bill. He said and I quote that "[Johnson] signed the Civil Rights Movement out of existence" upon signing that bill into law. Do you agree with that?

A: I don't know the context in which Jim Bevel made that statement and I did not hear and I would not want to be in position of disagreeing with the whole context of his statement. On the specific statement I certainly don't feel that the Civil Rights Movement has been signed out of existence. I wish I could be that optimistic because we all want to see this problem solved and that great day when the brotherhood of man is such a reality that we won't even need civil rights organizations. The fact is that instead of signing the movement out of existence we must face the fact that in the next few years we will have some hard problems in civil rights that will demand all of our resources and resources of all of the forces of goodwill in our nation.

Q: Would you enumerate those problems?

A: I think we still have problems in the South, the problem in spite [sic] of the fact that we have made tremendous strides in public accommodations as a result of the 1964 Civil Rights Bills and great strides because of the Voting Bill of 1965. But legislative acts can only declare rights, they never thoroughly deliver them. We have got to go out and work hard to implement these bills. There is still a great deal of brutality in man's inhumanity to man all across the South. People are still being murdered, they are still being shot. Homes and churches and even automobiles, as we saw in Mississippi just the other day, are still being bombed, so we still have problems in the South which we must grapple with. I think in the North the problems are even more difficult precisely because they have not been so overt in the past because they did not have legal structures and because they were not out in the open. In the area of employment which I see as the most difficult problem—the economic problem. In the area of housing and in the area of schools we are going to have some tough and very difficult problems.

Q: Are you satisfied that our Government is doing everything possible to meet those problems, that it is aware of them?

A: I think our Government has a great concern here and I certainly think that President Johnson has done a most admirable and great job in the area of civil rights and that he understands the depths and dimensions of the problem. I don't think we have had a more eloquent analysis of the plight of the Negro at this hour than the speech which he gave at Howard University where he even went into the sagging, disintegrating family life within the Negro community and I think that the Government is doing a good deal. I think it is necessary that we all realize that it is necessary to expand our already existing programs. The Poverty Program will be most helpful, the education program too. These are creative beginnings and we need much larger programs in the economic and educational areas.

Q: Dr. King, I want to get into that speech that the President made at Howard University. Have you read the Moynihan (phonetic) Report, so called, about the Negro family in the northern city?

A: I have read excerpts in the newspapers.

Q: It is a rather sensitive area but in the question of illegitimate births, the Negro families have had a very difficult time in the North.

(The discussion then continues in regard to birth control and population problems.)

Q: It has been more than a week Dr. King, since you left those of us who were covering your visit to Los Angeles. You've had time to reflect on your investigations there. Have you come up with any new ideas as to why Los Angeles happened and, secondly, are we going to have more Los Angeleses before it is all over?

A: My ideas are about the same. I have tried to study the problem as thoroughly as one could study the problem in the few days that I visited there. I am thoroughly convinced that the economic problem is basic. Of course, there are other problems but one must not overlook the fact that 34% of the Negro people in Watts happen to have been unemployed and the housing conditions were bad and school conditions [*sic*]. All of this is in the midst of a very wealthy and beautiful community as far as housing is concerned. It was not just poverty, but poverty in the midst of plenty, poverty in the midst of an affluent society and this even deepened the frustrations of the Negro community. I must honestly say that while I would be the last one that would want to predict violence—I hate it so much that I like to avoid talking about it—but honesty impels me to admit that if there is not a massive program on the part of the Federal Government and local, state, and city governments to improve the lot of the Negro masses, we will find other Los Angeles situations developing in this country and even in more serious proportions.

Q: Dr. King, looking at the whole spectrum of the racial crisis in this country and in line with the observations which you have just made about other Los Angeleses, what cities seem to you the most threatened and have the greatest potential to erupt in the manner in which Los Angeles has just done?

A: I think almost any of our large northern cities. I think cities like New York with its Harlem, and Bedford-Stuyvesant, Philadelphia, Chicago, Detroit, Cleveland, and even Washington, I think are the most likely. I think Washington must be included. These are the most serious cities as far as potential explosions are concerned.

Q: Dr. King, in Washington, D.C., do you think that this is linked to the question of home rule? Do you think that if Congress fails to give Washington home rule that this could produce a situation similar to Los Angeles, a major crisis?

A: Yes, I certainly do. I know from my conversations with numerous people in the Washington community and because of a recent visit here that there is a deep feeling within the Washington community about the whole issue of home rule and it is really connected with the whole Rights to Vote Movement all across the South. I feel that Congress would do our nation a grave injustice and would set forth the conditions that may bring into being an unfortunate conflagration if something isn't done soon to bring home rule into being.

Q: Do you intend, Dr. King, to dramatize your feeling by arranging again a march on Washington to bring that home here?

A: If something isn't done I made it clear to the Committee when I was here that I would be willing to come back. They asked me to come back if things are not changed or if something isn't done by Congress to deal with this issue and I said that I would be willing to do it, so if in the next few weeks we don't see home rule emerging, I think it will be necessary to dramatize this issue, not in a small march but in a massive march on Washington, similar to our march a few years ago.

Q: Dr. King, after a hundred years the Negro seems to have gained his just rights or they have at least legally been granted him. Most Negroes are assuming these rights with responsibility but there are some recent events such as the Los Angeles riots and Watts the other night where it is alleged Negroes at a rally shouted, "Kill for freedom," and then there were armed Negro groups like the Deacons in Louisiana. This raises the question of a new-found boldness, even aggressiveness towards violence among certain elements of the Negro group. Have you considered this problem and does it represent a danger to you?

A: I have considered this problem, naturally. I have committed myself to a philosophy of non-violence and I believe it is a philosophy which is most practically sound as well as morally excellent. I don't think we help ourselves by resorting to violence whether it is the aggressive violence of a riot or the retaliatory violence in a southern situation, but I do feel that we must understand the condition that brings this kind of violence into being. Now I am so concerned about it that I plan to double or triple my efforts around the country to try to get over the meaning and power of non-violence. I think that many people will fail to understand that non-violence is more than a do-nothing method of cowardice. It is a positive and powerful method and I plan to go into communities all over this country to try to get this over.

[Section 41]

UNITED STATES GOVERNMENT
Memorandum

TO: DIRECTOR, FBI   DATE: 9/3/65

FROM: SAC, LOS ANGELES (100-106670)

SUBJECT: MARTIN LUTHER KING, JR.
SM-C

00: ATLANTA

Enclosed herewith for the Bureau, Atlanta and New York is one Xerox copy each, for information, of a Statement by Dr. Martin Luther King, Jr. on Arrival in Los Angeles, August 17, 1965.

New York is furnished a copy inasmuch as this statement appears to be primarily the five-point program suggested by BAYARD RUSTIN as set forth in New York radiogram to Director, Atlanta and Los Angeles dated 8/27/65 captioned CIRM IS-C.

Statement by Dr. Martin Luther King, Jr. on Arrival in Los Angeles
August 17, 1965

I have come to Los Angeles at the invitation of a number of concerned individuals and major organizations that have been, like myself, deeply involved in the struggle for civil rights and human dignity.

Let me say first of all that I profoundly deplore the events that have occurred in Los Angeles in these last few tragic days. I believe and have said on many occasions that violence is not the answer to social conflict whether it is engaged in by white people in Alabama or by

Negroes in Los Angeles. Violence is all the more regrettable in this period in light of the tremendous non-violent sacrifices that both Negro and white people together have endured to bring justice to all men.

But it is equally clear, as President Johnson pointed out yesterday, that it is the job of all Americans ''to right the wrongs from which such violence and disorder spring.'' The criminal responses which led to the tragic outbreaks of violence in Los Angeles are environmental and not racial. The economic deprivation, social isolation, inadequate housing, and general despair of thousands of Negroes teaming in Northern and Western ghettos are the ready seeds which give birth to tragic expressions of violence. By acts of commission and omission none of us in this great country has done enough to remove injustice. I therefore humbly suggest that all of us accept our share of responsibility for these past days of anguish.

I should like to state in quite more specific terms why I make this journey in the interest of reconciliation and future cooperation between the races.

First, I have come to minister to the thousands of innocent Negro people who have done no wrong or who have [not] thought in any way to use violence, yet whose community had been disrupted by rioting, the destruction of institutions they daily need, and many of whom have lost their work. This has been for them, not merely the hardship springing from the disruption of their physical community; it has been a spiritual disaster deepening their despair and hopelessness.

Secondly, I have come to minister to the small degree that I can—to those who have been involved in the rioting. Our Christian effort must be to redeem them and to leave no stone unturned, despite their guilt, to help them find a useful place in building a good society in which they can share as equals. In this connection I shall, as a first step, seek to visit with them in prison and to urge officials to find ways for them to help reconstruct the damage they have done.

Thirdly, I would like to confer with the many segments of the white community that have been the staunch allies of the Negro people in our struggle. Surely if millions of Negroes across this country are dismayed, deeply hurt, and bewildered by these past few days, it stands to reason that our white friends are also. The strength of the Negro-white alliance for justice will be maintained only if we are in constant dialogue, understanding past mistakes, evolving new programs, and providing ways and means to avert any such recurrence of violence.

Fourthly, I would like to work with the local leadership of Los Angeles in proposing programs for the eradication of those problems relating to housing, schools, jobs, and police behavior that were directly or indirectly related to the disorder.

Fifthly, if the local leadership feels that it will be helpful, I am prepared to sit with them in discussions with the public officials on the role and responsibility of governments and to evaluate with them a program that will eliminate such future occurrences in Los Angeles or in any other city of our nation.

[Section 42]

UNITED STATES GOVERNMENT
Memorandum

TO: Mr. DeLoach   DATE: 8-30-65

FROM: M. A. Jones

SUBJECT: MARTIN LUTHER KING
               "FACE THE NATION"
               TV PROGRAM
               WTOP—AUGUST 29, 1965

Martin Luther King was interviewed on "Face the Nation" at 12:30 P.M. on Sunday.

The interview opened when he was questioned concerning his intentions to enter the issue of peace in Vietnam. He was asked if he realized that private citizens are prohibited through the Logan Act from participating in international affairs. He said he did not know of the Act when he made a statement that he contemplated writing letters to international leaders concerning the war in Vietnam. He said he is not planning to go to Vietnam but something may occur in the future which would cause him to reverse his stand. He claimed that part of his heritage as an American is to take a stand on basic issues and that dissent should not be confused with disloyalty. He indicated that Ambassador Goldberg had invited him to discuss the peace issue in Vietnam with him.

He was asked if he can anticipate any difficult problems in the civil rights movement within the next few years. King asserted that although great strides have been made through legislation, these acts only declare rights they do not deliver. He feels that the employment provisions of the act will pose the greatest problems. King admitted that President Johnson has done a great job on civil rights but that the solution will require much larger programs than have been enacted.

He was asked concerning the high rate of illegitimate births among Negroes and whether he would favor a Government birth control program to solve the problem. King asserted that this is not only a Negro problem but a worldwide issue and that the Government should deal with the causes which have robbed the Negro male of his manhood.

[Section 46]

FBI SAVANNAH
1:32 AMEST URGENT 10/12/65 CJD
TO DIRECTOR /173-2172/AND ATLANTA
FROM SAVANNAH/173-186/ 2 PAGE

UNKNOWN SUBJECT; ALEXANDER H STEPHENS INSTITUTE, CRAWFORDVILLE, GEORGIA, PUBLIC EDUCATION, CIVIL RIGHTS ACT, SIXTY FOUR.

DR. MARTIN LUTHER KING JR. ARRIVED AT FRIENDSHIP CHURCH, CRAWFORDVILLE AT EIGHT TWENTY PM. HE SPOKE FOR ABOUT ONE HOUR STATING THAT CRAWFORDVILLE WILL BE THE SYMBOL OF INTEGRATED EDUCATION, JUST AS BIRMINGHAM WAS THE SYMBOL OF LUNCHROOM INTEGRATION AND SELMA REPRESENTED THE FIGHT FOR VOTER REGISTRATION. HE STATED THAT THERE WILL BE NO PEACE IN CRAWFORDVILLE UNTIL THE TALIAFERO COUNTY SCHOOLS ARE INTEGRATED. KING HAS NOT DECIDED YET IF THE NEGROES WILL MARCH TO ATLANTA. HE STATED THAT THE WHOLE NATION IS LOOKING TO CRAWFORDVILLE AND NO ONE, FROM THE STATE HOUSE DOWN TO THE STATE TROOPERS, CAN "TURN YOU ROUND." AFTER KING SPOKE, AN ESTIMATED EIGHT HUNDRED NEGROES MARCHED FROM THE FRIENDSHIP CHURCH TO THE COURTHOUSE FOR ANOTHER SPEECH BY REVEREND ANDY YOUNG, EXECUTIVE DIRECTOR OF SOUTHERN CHRISTIAN LEADERSHIP CONFERENCE. AFTER SINGING FREEDOM SONGS THE NEGROES MARCHED BACK TO THE FRIENDSHIP CHURCH. KING DID NOT PARTICIPATE IN

THE MARCH TO THE COURTHOUSE BUT LEFT AFTER HIS SPEECH, HEADED TOWARD ATLANTA. HE DID NOT SPEAK IN WARRENTON, GA., PRIOR TO THE CRAWFORDVILLE MEETING AS PREVIOUSLY ANNOUNCED. THE MEETING IN CRAWFORD-VILLE AT FRIENDSHIP CHURCH ENDED AT MIDNIGHT.

AT SEVEN FIFTY SEVEN PM TEN ELEVEN SIXTY FIVE A KLAN MEETING STARTED AT THE COURTHOUSE SQUARE IN CRAWFORDVILLE. A FEW WERE WEARING WHITE ROBES. A KLANSMAN FROM ALABAMA PRAISED GOVERNOR WALLACE OF ALABAMA AND URGED THOSE PRESENT TO APPLY FOR KLAN MEMBERSHIP. A WOMAN WAS THE NEXT SPEAKER, FOLLOWED BY J. HOWARD SIMS FROM ATHENS, GA. ABOUT ONE HUNDRED WERE PRESENT AT THIS KLAN MEETING. IT ENDED AT EIGHT FIFTY ONE PM.

UNITED STATES DEPARTMENT OF JUSTICE

FEDERAL BUREAU OF INVESTIGATION

Chicago, Illinois
Oct. 12, 1965

ELIJAH MUHAMMAD

The October 9, 1965, issue of the "Chicago Sun-Times," a Chicago, Illinois, daily newspaper, contained an advertisement on page 30 captioned "Kup's Show." This advertisement reflected that the following individuals would appear as guests on that show at midnight October 9, 1965, over WBKB-TV, Channel 7:

Elijah Muhhamad, leader of the "Black Muslims" (national leader of the Nation of Islam (NOI)
Mrs. Jeane Dixon, clairvoyant
Dick Gregory, entertainer
Dr. Fred Schwartz, leader of an anti-Communist crusade
George Schaeffer, television producer
Jay Richard Kennedy, author
Dan Boorstin, author

The NOI is described in the appendix pages of this communication.

It is public knowledge that "Kup's Show" is a Chicago-based panel type televised discussion show covering a variety of subjects lasting approximately three hours and telecast over WBKB-TV, Chicago. Irving Kupcinet, Chicago newspaper columnist and television moderator, presides over the show.

ELIJAH MUHAMMAD

The October 10, 1965, production of "Kup's Show" pertaining to Elijah Muhammad began at midnight, October 9, 1965, and was monitored by a Special Agent of the Federal Bureau of Investigation. Pertinent statements made by Elijah Muhammad are set forth hereinafter.

Elijah Muhammad did not participate in the television panel discussion but was interviewed separately by Irv Kupcinet at Muhammad's residence, 4847 South Woodlawn Avenue, Chicago, Illinois. He was interviewed from 12:00 midnight until 1:10 A.M. in a question-answer type of interview.

Muhammad thanked God whom he also referred to as Allah who came to him in the person of one W.D. Farad 34 years ago and gave Muhammad a message for the black man which is why Muhammad calls himself the Messenger of Allah.

Muhammad stated the black man has lived in America under the white slave master for 400 years and now wants something for himself, to be himself, and to be on his own. He added that for a black man to oppose this would result in his ultimate death as a social and economic force.

He stated regarding civil rights that Martin Luther King and other Negro civil rights leaders lack knowledge of the black race and fail to realize now is the time the black man should work to be independent and be on his own. He said civil rights leaders seek to be like the white man and want to be his equal in a white country. Muhammad pointed out that as the black man was of a different color than the white man and of a different race he should be on his own and not integrate. He said the black man has served his term of slavery and should not have to beg the white man for a job or to be his servant, adding the black man should seek a more prominent status on his own. Muhammad stated that was achieved in America by and for the white man, not the black man. He said by the government seemingly giving more things to the black man such as its poverty programs and similar health programs it only meant that the white slave master, as he gets wealthier, can afford to dole out a little more proportionately for the black man but that such programs do not in any way elevate the black man. He said the government had an obligation to give the black man a state of

[his] own and money for 25 years in which to operate in order that the black man can become completely self-sufficient.

Muhammad said he had no power himself to bring about such change, but that Allah had such means. He added that Allah also knows when separation will take place. He said the time has come for Allah to intervene to separate the black man from his white slave master.

Muhammad stated that in America there was only a small proportion of black men as compared to the white man. He refused to name what state he would like if offered to him. He said the white man in America would lose his self-respect if he yielded to the unreasonable demands of the civil rights leaders, as America cannot possibly agree with all of their demands.

Muhammad said in America intermarriages are not good, jobs for the black man were not available and in America the black man is not as good as the white man. The NOI desires, according to Muhammad, a state for themselves and equipment with which to operate it on a businesslike basis.

He stated that such prominent black men as Dr. Ralph Bunche, Jackie Robinson and the like only serve the white man and do nothing to better their black brothers.

Muhammad stated that like Moses and Jesus stated in the Bible, the black man was deaf, dumb and blind, adding that if that sounded like Governor Wallace of Alabama it still was true.

Muhammad stated that the education the black man has received will help him to go for himself, but doesn't mean that he should be satisfied and perform his services for the white man. He said such educated Negroes should separate from the white man and utilize their education for the black man when he gets his own state. He added that the black man would need modern tools, machinery, buildings and land in this connection.

He said the black man has lost his birthright and there is no record of his ancestry in America. He added that all the NOI wanted was freedom, justice and equality for the black man.

Regarding hate, Muhammad stated that according to Moses and Jesus a human being has to hate evil people, adding that such was in the Bible. He said in the Bible even brothers hated each other. He said some brothers couldn't live together and this included black and white and even Red China. Muhammad said you couldn't expect the Negro to follow the Bible if white Christians do not do so, adding that Christianity is anti-Negro.

Muhammad stated that Allah has stated all white men are devils, but that there are various degrees of deviltry and that some whites are better than others. He said Jesus stated the human race were followers of the devil and He was crucified for it.

Muhammad stated Martin Luther King was wrong in his approach to civil rights and said he was misguided as white men and black men could not get along together. He said the black man must trust in God, not Martin Luther King, adding that the Nobel Prize was no honor to King as he had done nothing for his people.

Muhammad said he never advocated boycotting white businesses, but only that whenever possible the black man should buy from black people. Muhammad added it would be very silly for him if he needed a suit to go without one if he could buy one from the white man.

Regarding the bearing of arms for America, Muhammad stated after a Muslim receives the teachings of their religion it is then up to them individually to determine if they desire to serve in the Armed Forces.

Muhammad thanked Kupcinet for the opportunity to present his views to the public.

APPENDIX

NATION OF ISLAM, Formerly Referred
to as the Muslim Cult of Islam,
Aka. Muhammad's Temples of Islam

In January, 1957, a source advised ELIJAH MUHAMMAD has described his organization on a nationwide basis as the "Nation of Islam" and "Muhammad's Temples of Islam."

On May 7, 1965, a second source advised ELIJAH MUHAMMAD is the national leader of the Nation of Islam (NOI); Muhammad's Temple of Islam No. 2, 5335 South Greenwood Avenue, Chicago, Illinois, is the national headquarters of the NOI; and in mid-1960 MUHAMMAD and other NOI officials, when referring to MUHAMMAD's organization on a nationwide basis, commenced using either "Mosque" or "Temple" when mentioning one of "Muhammad's Temples of Islam."

The NOI is an all-Negro organization which was originally organized in 1930 in Detroit, Michigan. MUHAMMAD claims to have been selected by Allah, the Supreme Being, to lead the so-called Negro race out of slavery in the wilderness of North America by establishing an independent black nation in the United States. Members following MUHAMMAD's teachings and his interpretation of the "Koran" believe there is no such thing as a Negro; that the so-called Negroes are slaves of the white race, referred to as "white devils," in the United States; and that the white race, because of its exploitation of the so-called

Negroes, must and will be destroyed in the approaching "War of Armageddon."

In the past, officials and members of the NOI, including MUHAM- MAD, have refused to register under the provisions of the Selective Service Acts and have declared that members owe no allegiance to the United States.

On May 5, 1958, the first source advised MUHAMMAD had, upon advice of legal counsel, tempered his personal statements and instruc- tions to his ministers concerning the principles of his organization in order to avoid possible prosecution by the United States government; however, he did not indicate any fundamental changes in the teachings of his organization.

On May 3, 1965, a third source advised MUHAMMAD had, early in July 1958, decided to de-emphasize the religious aspects of the teach- ings of Islam and to stress the economic benefits to be derived by those Negroes who joined the NOI. This policy change, according to MUHAMMAD, would help him acquire additional followers and create more interest in his programs.

UNITED STATES DEPARTMENT OF JUSTICE

FEDERAL BUREAU OF INVESTIGATION

Chicago, Illinois
October 29, 1965

ANONYMOUS THREAT TO KILL MARTIN LUTHER KING, JR., CHICAGO, ILLINOIS OCTOBER 28, 1965 SECURITY MATTER-C

At 7:00 P.M. on October 28, 1965 ... Associated Press (AP), Chi- cago, Illinois, advised the Chicago Office of the Federal Bureau of Investigation that he had just received a telephone call from an anony- mous male (AM) individual. The man called the Associated Press and wanted to know if they had a columnist that could do a story for him. ... stated that they did not have such a columnist and the man explained that he wanted to give the "Ku Klux Klan side of the story." He stated that he is a member of the Ku Klux Klan and has been since he has been 12 years old. He stated that he was very sensitive about what they are doing to the Ku Klux Klan and mentioned that he is a veteran of two wars and was in the Army and also in the Navy. ... stated that the male individual gave his Army Serial Number as RA 905 504. The man then said that recently he overheard a conversation in Chicago and believed that the people involved in the conversation ''were not crazy'' and he overheard them saying ''Martin Luther King, a Communist nigger, will not live to see the end of this year.'' He went on to say that he understood that King will die but the Ku Klux Klan will not have anything to do with it. ... advised that he receives many crank calls, but this individual, who did not furnish his name, seemed serious.

At 7:15 P.M. on October 28, 1965, an anonymous male telephonically contacted the Chicago Office of the Federal Bureau of Investigation and stated that he is a member of the Ku Klux Klan and is anxious to go to Washington, D.C., to testify in behalf of the Ku Klux Klan. He stated ''Martin Luther King will be knocked off before New Year's Eve.'' When asked who will do this, he replied, ''He will be knocked off by his own people.'' When asked where he heard this, he said he ''heard it in a place in downtown Chicago recently.''

[Section 47]

7-51 PM URGENT 11-11-65
TO: DIRECTOR AND ATLANTA
FROM: ST LOUIS
  MARTIN LUTHER KING, JR. SM-CV.

..., MO., TELEPHONICALLY ADVISED THIS DATE THAT WHILE VISITING UNIDENTIFIED TAVERN IN ST. LOUIS NOVEMBER TENTH LAST, AN UNIDENTIFIED WHITE MALE, IN HIS FORTIES, WELL DRESSED, FIVE FEET EIGHT INCHES, ONE HUNDRED SEVENTY POUNDS, DARK EYES, CUT SCAR OVER RIGHT CHEEK, OFFERED HIM FIVE THOUSAND DOLLARS AND TRANSPORTATION COSTS SOUTH TO KILL REV. KING. HE GAVE HIM FIFTY DOLLARS CASH AND AGREED TO MEET ... IN ... NOVEMBER TWELVE WITH TWENTY FIVE HUNDRED DOLLARS DOWN, REMAINDER PAYABLE AFTER KING'S DEATH. ... STATED HE WAS JUST QUOTE BLOWING OFF UNQUOTE ABOUT HIS DISLIKE FOR NEGROES AND HE DOES NOT DESIRE TO BECOME INVOLVED IN ANY MURDER.

... IS IN RURAL AREA. IN VIEW OF FIFTY DOLLAR CASH PAYMENT, SA'S DISPATCHED TO INTERVIEW ... PERSONALLY AND ALERT LOCAL S.O. AND TOWN MARSHAL. PRIOR TO THEIR ARRIVAL, ... CALLED AGAIN AND STATED SAME UN-IDENTIFIED MAN HAD JUST LEFT HIS HOME AFTER GIVING HIM TRANSPORTATION MONEY SOUTH, DIRECTING HIM TO LEAVE TONIGHT AND ADVISING HIM HE WOULD BE MET ON ARRIVAL BY PERSON WHO WOULD SHOW HIM WHAT TO DO. HE WAS UNABLE TO OBTAIN AUTO LICENSE OR OTHER IDEN-TIFYING DATA.

CITY MARSHAL, ..., MO., AND SHERIFF, ... MO., BOTH STATE ... PSYCHONEUROTIC WITH HISTORY OF CONFINE-MENT IN A VA HOSPITAL AND STATE INSTITUTION. ... RE-PEATED STORY TO INTERVIEWING AGENTS AND AGAIN STATED HE WILL NOT PROCEED TO ATLANTA AND HAS NO INTENTION OF HARMING DR. KING.

LOCAL AUTHORITIES HOWEVER, BELIEVE HIM POTEN-TIALLY DANGEROUS.

SECRET SERVICE LOCALLY AND SLPD ADVISED.

LHM FOLLOWS.

The LHM (letterhead memorandum) that followed indicates that the subject was informed he would be met at the bus terminal and [told] him where to go and what to do. ... was told that his contact would recognize him and say, "The Sewanee is going dry." ... was to reply, "No, it has raised a foot."

The memorandum continues as follows.

... stated that he personally has no guns and that in his discussion with the unknown subject he told him he is proficient in the use of a hunting knife. It was agreed tentatively that this would be used as the assassination weapon.

... asserted that he has no intention of proceeding to Atlanta nor does he desire to participate in any assassination of Reverend King. He stated his comments at the St. Louis tavern were general in nature and do not reflect any desire on his part to commit a violent act. He went on to say, however, that should Reverend King come to the ..., Missouri, area and stir up trouble by demonstrations, he might possibly set up an ambush "and put a rifle slug in him."

... and ... Missouri ... both stated on November 11, 1965, they have both known ... for some time and he has long suffered hallucinations. Both pointed out that six months ago . . . mother, . . . Missouri, called the Sheriff's Office and stated her son had lost his mind and she desired that he be picked up. Sheriff . . . and his men proceeded to . . . and chased . . . for approximately four miles. During that time he ran through brambles and his clothes were almost torn from his body. En route he ran through a country church, upsetting everything inside, and then wound up at the family cemetery plot. Here the Sheriff's posse found him, talking to buried relatives as though they were alive.

Following this he was placed in the state mental institution . . . Missouri, but was soon released.

These officers further said that several months ago . . . poured gasoline on the outside of his house and announced he was going to kill some members of his family and anyone who tried to stop him. When law enforcement officers arrived, he was spraying the inside of the house with a garden hose to put out an imaginary fire.

Furthermore, according to . . . within the past month he called . . . and the local conservation officer, saying he had just killed three deer out of season and they were in his basement. When . . . and the conservation officer went to his residence, no deer could be found. This was obviously a product of his imagination.

. . . stated that late in the afternoon of November 11, 1965, he interviewed . . . wife, as well as neighbors, and they advised him no one had visited the . . . residence that afternoon. . . . stated that after . . . called him and outlined . . . story of the assassination plot, he decided to take . . . into protective custody and said he was confining him overnight in the County Jail. He said he would make a decision in the morning as to whether he would return him to . . . asylum . . . or to his home. He stated that he understands . . . has been a patient at . . . Hospital in St. Louis, Missouri, and also a patient of the Veterans Administration. . . . asserts he is classified 4F with the local draft board . . . Missouri.

Both . . . and . . . stated they are convinced that the alleged plot against Dr. King was conjured up by . . . On the other hand, they feel that he is a potentially dangerous man who could commit an act of violence. . . . stated that . . . can throw a hunting knife with unusual ability. On one occasion, when officers went to his home, he threw a hatchet across the room and sank its blade in an adjacent door frame, evidently as a warning.

. . . further said that . . . was on welfare but earns money buying and selling furniture and appliances. He regards . . . as a burglar and a thief. . . . drinks to excess, and when he does, beats his wife badly. He pointed out that when he took ... into protective custody on November 11, 1965, ... did have $50 in $10 bills, plus approximately $28 in $4 and $1 bills and change. When interviewed by Special Agents of the Federal Bureau of Investigation, he insisted that the $50 was the money he had obtained from the unknown subject.

[Section 48]

November 24th, 1965

Mr. J. Edgar Hoover,
Chief Administrator Office of F.B.I.,
U.S. Department of Justice Bldg.,
Washington, D.C.

Dear Mr. Hoover:

We recently ran in our paper a couple of short news items relative to some activities of Rev. Martin Luther King. We had two objections registered to this, both suggesting that Mr. King was not the kind of man that we would be quoting, or in any way holding up even to seeming honor and respect. One lady has written stating the following:

"When clerics in positions of high authority project the name of M. L. King as one who speaks for the church, and who is honored by the church, the Christians of the world are being misled and deceived by pharisaical hypocrisy as evil and devastating as that which existed in the time of Christ.

"The personal life of Martin Luther King is so scandalous that it is being kept under wraps in the secret files of the F.B.I. . . . His Executive Secretary's record is in police courts for homosexualism, and it is a matter of photostatic evidence."

These are unpleasant and serious charges. The other correspondent suggested that Mr. King was backed by Communists. You will, of course, know whether there is anything about Mr. King which you can share with me, either in confidential manner or for publication—the latter is what I should prefer. If the charges made by my correspondent are completely foundless [sic], I should like to be able to say so on your authority if possible. On the other hand if there are some grounds for these serious charges, I should, if possible, know, even if the information is something which cannot be publicized. My reason for wishing to know, is clearly that I might govern myself to some respect in such publicity as I give to Mr. King.

Any information which you may be in a position to share with me would be very much appreciated.

Yours very truly,
[Signature deleted]

UNITED STATES GOVERNMENT
Memorandum

To: Mr. Sullivan   DATE: 12/2/65

From: F. J. Baumgardner
            MARTIN LUTHER KING, JR.
            SECURITY MATTER-COMMUNIST

You will recall that we had received second-hand information that . . . had stated that according to her brother, a banker . . . Martin Luther King, Jr., has a numbered account with a balance of over one million dollars where this banker is employed. It has been previously recommended, and the Director approved, that we initiate a discreet investigation to attempt to corroborate this allegation, after which we could consider further action to discredit King either through counterintelligence channels or by turning the information over to the Internal Revenue Service for possible criminal prosecution.

We are proposing that . . . be interviewed and on a confidential basis his cooperation be solicited. Our approach to him . . . His help is being sought in a matter relating to the Nation's security. Mention will be made to . . . that there has been publicity in the past in the press that some . . . have numbered accounts and that we have information that one of these account holders may be King. If . . . is cooperative (and we have no reason to believe otherwise) and with our assurance of anonymity, we should be able to obtain the information we desire first hand. We believe that at this time a direct approach to . . . is the best course of action open to us as he is no longer affiliated . . . bank, which fact should encourage his cooperation, and because he is the individual who originally made the allegation concerning King.

[Section 49]

FBI

Date:12/7/65

AIRTEL

TO: DIRECTOR, FBI (100-106670)
FROM: SAC, NEW ORLEANS (100-16800) (RUC)
SUBJECT: MARTIN LUTHER KING, JR. SM-C

Re Bureau airtel, 12/3/65.

. . . was contacted by SA's . . . in accordance with instructions contained in re Bureau airtel. . . . at the outset of this interview with . . . he was informed of the identity of the interviewing Agents and advised that the matter about which the interviewing Agents desired to make inquiry of him was of a very highly confidential nature. Accordingly, . . . was informed that any information or assistance he could furnish would be held in strict confidence by the Bureau and his identity would be protected. Likewise, he was asked to hold in strict confident the context of this interview. He readily agreed to the foregoing and indicated he was desirous of cooperating to the fullest extent in assisting the Bureau in any way he could. It was then made known to . . . that he was being contacted as a result of his past extensive experience in banking circles and, more particularly, in view of his recent affiliation . . .

It was pointed out to . . . that there had been previous publicity that . . . have numbered accounts. He was also advised that the Bureau has information that one of the holders of such numbered accounts . . . may be MARTIN LUTHER KING, Jr. It was pointed out to . . . that the Bureau is not investigating the legitimate activities of KING in the civil rights field but that the Bureau's interest, rather, pertains to communist attempts to influence the civil rights movement.

In response to inquiry, . . . specifically stated that he has no information that MARTIN LUTHER KING, Jr., presently has, or, at any time in the past, has had a numbered account . . . advised that he had previously . . . and can positively state that while he held that position, there were no numbered accounts at that bank. Accordingly, he stated it would not have been possible for KING to have had a numbered account . . .

. . . did mention that he had heard some comment during the early part of 1965 or in 1964 on the occasion of one of the several visits of MARTIN LUTHER KING, Jr., . . . that King probably was putting money in a numbered account . . . explained, however, that he had placed no credence in that comment as he recalls that it was merely a wild conclusion that had been previously drawn by someone whose identity he does not now recall. . . . considered the aforementioned comment as being without substantiation and typical of the many such remarks that one may hear . . . concerning any well-known person who may visit . . .

It was . . . opinion that if KING did have a numbered account, it would logically be placed with one of the legitimate banking institutions . . . rather than in one of the less reputable banking institutions where it would be risky to place large amounts of money . . .

In view of the statement by the Bureau re Bureau airtel that the Bureau has been unable to penetrate numbered accounts . . . was queried concerning the identity of any person who would be knowledgeable concerning numbered accounts. . . . indicated that there would be people who would have information . . . concerning the identity of such persons, and he recommended that . . . as a person who would be knowledgeable concerning the identities of various people who have numbered accounts . . . and, further, as a person who would be in a position to acquire information from other sources concerning the identities of persons having numbered accounts.

. . . remarked that . . . loyal United States citizen . . . emphasized the point that . . . is a very tactful man who can maintain a confidence and who would be very discreet should the Bureau desire to make inquiry of him concerning this matter, and, he added, any other matters in which the Bureau may have an interest.

. . . suggested that if the Bureau did decide to make inquiry of . . . concerning this or any other pertinent matter, that the Bureau may desire to advise . . . that he was being contacted on the recommendation of . . . is cognizant of the sensitive nature of which an inquiry as well as its international implications, but persisted in his comment that he felt that . . . would be a good source for the Bureau should the Bureau have a need to obtain information in any specific instance regarding numbered accounts . . .

. . . was thanked for his cooperation in this matter.

UNITED STATES DEPARTMENT OF JUSTICE

FEDERAL BUREAU OF INVESTIGATION

Mobile, Alabama
December 7, 1965

MARTIN LUTHER KING, JR.

Visit of Martin Luther King, Jr., to
Greenville, Alabama, and Accompanying
Demonstration, December 6, 1965

A Negro mass meeting was held at the Harrison Street Baptist Church, Greenville, Alabama, December 6, 1965. The meeting was led by Martin Luther King, who is President of the Southern Christian Leadership Conference (SCLC). King arrived at the Harrison Street Baptist Church at 1:17 P.M., CST, and after a short meeting with local leaders, talked to a crowd of 350. The talk covered general racial problems in the State of Alabama, and he warned of "not being lulled to sleep by the two convictions last week." King noted that there are still many problems concerning racial activity in the South, and that it would be necessary to continue demonstrations and other racial activity. Andrew Young, who is Vice President of the SCLC, accompanied King on this visit to Greenville.

King ended his talk at 2:30 P.M., at which time a march was formed in front of the church and 350 people paraded in columns of two through the Negro neighborhood until 2:40 P.M., [when] they were met at the corner of Parmer and South Park Street by City Solicitor Elisbe Poole and 40 well-armed city and county police. At this time the paraders were led by Reverend Samuel B. Wells, R.B. Cottonreader, and Leon Hall, all of the SCLC, Atlanta. The Negroes sang and protested strongly against not being allowed to march to the county courthouse. Leon Hall was the most vocal of these individuals, and was shocked by an electric baton used by City Solicitor Poole. A Greenville city police officer tapped an unknown marcher in the stomach with his baton. However, there were no other incidents. Andrew Young arrived at the scene at 3:00 P.M., CST, and turned the marchers around; however, [Young] said that there would be marches on a continuing basis until such time as "the Negroes of Greenville are allowed the freedom of the white man." He further advised that a large mass meeting would be planned for Friday, December 10, 1965, at the Harrison Street Baptist Church.

Excerpts from Electronic Surveillance File 1965

8/13/65

"Andy" calls Stanley Levison.

Andy: Let me read to you what I've got. "The Southern Christian Leadership Conference is based on the faith that all men are sons of God and therefore all men are brothers. This concept of brotherhood knows no national limitations. Men of Asia are no less brothers than men of Europe. The war in Vietnam is a serious challenge to our concept of brotherhood. We therefore encourage Doctor Martin Luther King, Jr., our President, and, the Staff of the Southern Christian Leadership Conference, to proclaim our philosophy of non-violence and assert its relevance in international conflict such as now rages in Vietnam. We further urge that Dr. King and the Staff make possible a mature, non-violent understanding of the issues of this world-shaking dilemma to the members of our affiliated groups since many of these groups in southern communities have access to only the most conservative warmongering viewpoints in their local press. However, we must still affirm that the primary function of our organization is to secure full citizenship rights for the Negro citizens of this country and that our major contribution to world peace and brotherhood is to create a truly democratic society here in America. Our resources are not sufficient to assume the burden of two major issues in our society. We would therefore urge that the effort of SCLC in mass demonstrations and action movements be confined to the question of racial brotherhood. In the event of continued escalation of the Vietnam conflict, however, we respect the right of Dr. King and the administrative committee to alter this course in the interest of the survival of mankind and turn the full resources of our organization to the cessation of bloodshed and war. This we feel to be our bounded duty as ministers and laymen and adherents to the way of love and the philosophy of non-violence.

Stanley: You've got everything from the standpoint of concepts in it that need to be said.

Andy: The part Martin didn't like was where I said "we therefore encourage." He said that yours was more "commending" Martin Luther King.

Stanley: Where you said you encourage Martin Luther King or encourage the affiliates?

Andy: We therefore encourage Dr. MLK, our President, and the Staff

of SCLC to proclaim our philosophy of non-violence and assert its
relevance.

Stanley: I like what you said about the primary purpose of the organization is racial brotherhood in the United States. And you left yourself
a perfectly proper opening in the event of, you said, escalation of
the war. I would tend to add "in the event of perilous escalation."
Because escalation has so many degrees. And I think we're all agreed
that it's when it gets to be really perilous. So I think you dealt with
that very soundly. As far as the ideas are concerned I think you've
got a very good balance.

*Stanley Levison places a call to the Thomas Jefferson Hotel,
Birmingham, Alabama and asks for Miss Dorothy Gaines (phonetic). (No answer). Levison then asks to speak with Mrs. MacDon-
ald in Dr. King's suite. He is connected with her.*

Stanley: I've been on the phone with Andy a couple of times about the
Draft Resolution on Vietnam. Andy had asked me for the first draft
that was written and I couldn't find it. I just located it and wondered
if I could dictate it to you so you could give it to him. I know he's
over at the (doesn't finish sentence). This convention is inspired by
the appeal of all the living Nobel Peace Prize laureates calling for
an end to the hostilities in Vietnam. The text of that statement is as
follows. Then just leave a blank because I think he has that. "We
applaud the action of our President, Martin Luther King, the 1965
Nobel Peace Prize winner, in signing the statement and we fully
endorse its sentiments. We call on all organizations to join with us
in formally endorsing the appeal, recognizing that without international peace in the nuclear age the quest of humanity for a full life
and a moral existence can become meaningless in a few terrifying
moments of total planetary destruction. We may have the power but
we have no right to decree the end of the human race because nationalist egotisms dominated our sense of humanity in one insane instance
of the thousands of years of the life of man." That's it.

8/25/65

Bernard (phonetic) calling for Dr. King to Stanley Levison saying
that Martin is doing an article for the *New York Times Magazine* on
the L.A. riots. Andy has done the draft and he (King?) wanted you to
take a look at it to see if it was perceptive enough.

Martin Luther King calls Stanley Levison.

Martin: Bernard (phonetic) told you about this article, didn't he?

Stanley: Yes. And as a matter of fact, I talked to Andy yesterday about something else and he mentioned it to me.

Martin: I'd like you to look it over. I think it's basically a good job, but there may be some things missing which should be there. Maybe it isn't as analytical as it should be.

Stanley: I will look at it carefully. I think it's the kind of article that will get a lot of attention.

Martin: Right. I think the other thing missing is at the end a kind of message to the power structure and the white America, that there are really two ways to respond to this. One is a kind of negative alarm that begins to accuse everybody from civil rights leaders on down . . . I know that it's been said in the South a great deal; that I'm really responsible for them because I taught people to break laws and led all these mass demonstrations. And once you teach people to be lawless, you know these arguments. . . . What I'm saying is that in a crisis like this it can be both a danger point and an opportunity. And this is the time to seek the causes and everybody humbly face the fact that we haven't done enough to right the wrongs. This is a time now to make a new national commitment on the whole question of civil rights.

Stanley: It could be expressed in the fashion that you've spoken of before, that non-violence can make its effective contribution only when there's a creative and cooperative response on the other side from the power structure.

Martin: Andy was just on the other phone. And he was saying that he read the *Time* and the *Newsweek* analyses and as a consequence felt that some things should be included that he did not include. Have you seen those articles?

Stanley: No.

Martin: They're not good articles. They're rather negative. Of course, I expected that. Now maybe from that there's something that needs to be said.

Stanley: I'll go over them . . .

Martin: The other thing. I haven't asked Bayard about this, but since the riots we just feel that there is a need to kind of reevaluate our whole programmatic thrust for the next few months, particularly re- garding our work in the North. Because Chicago has been pleading with us to come on in. So we just feel that we've really got to sit down and do a lot of work and thinking before I make any kind of commitment to Chicago. And whether we really decide to concentrate for the next few months in the South and not do anything in the North, we're damned, but if you do you've got some problems. For instance, there are those who say now that civil rights leaders, this is the *Newsweek* article, they're accusing us that Los Angeles is a demonstration of the failure of civil rights leaders to carry the movement to these isolated, forgotten people. And it's the failure of the bourgeoisie of the middle class leadership to really get over to them. And they just pulled single things out. For instance, when I was there it was very interesting how the small hostility that I encountered really was transformed into the most cheering (phonetic) situation I've ever been in. But they take two or three hecklers, and they take this as an absolute repudiation of their leadership; overlooking the overwhelming response. The greatest response I got when I was in Watts was when I told them that we can't hate all white people; that some of our greatest allies, people who had died for our freedom, were white people. And they just went wild over that.

Stanley: That's very interesting. That should be pointed up.

Martin: Yeah. They cheered at that point more than at any other point. An overwhelming response. Andy points that out in the article.

Stanley: That's important. This thing needs discussion though because there's no question that a decision to move into these areas will be treated by the press as a contention that you're going to produce miracles. And this is where you have to be cautious. Because even if you produce less than a miracle, you just produce excellent results, they'll attack you. And you've got to weigh the effects of that attack against what is produced. You see, what I'm concerned about collaterally to all of this is the effect on the necessary fundraising. There's no question in my mind that California will have an effect on the direct mail fundraising; because so much of it is North and white that it's bound to put a chill on it for a while. . . .

9/12/65

Conference call to Stanley Levison from Martin Luther King, Andy Young, Harry Wachtel, Clarence Jones, Cleve[land] Robinson, Wyatt Walker and Walter Thompson (phonetic).

King: Hello, this is Martin. The only one missing is Bayard Rustin. I want a little advice from all you distinguished wise Americans.

Levison: Flattery will get you nowhere.

King: Well we are having a staff retreat down here in South Carolina. I want to discuss the matter on my stand on Vietnam and the conference with Goldberg the other day. I think you all know my view on the wrongness of our foreign policy and my deep convictions and the truth of conscience matter that it is. I don't mind being a minority of one as I have been but I am mindful of the criticism I have been taking. I think we have to admit that what is developing is that the administration feels that I am going too far and it is a battle with the administration and I'm absolutely convinced that the statement of Senator Dodd—I don't know if you read it. ... I'm convinced that Lyndon Johnson got Dodd to say this because I am convinced that these are his convictions and that the administration and President Johnson urged him to do this. I am convinced that the press is being stacked against me on this position. I have already gotten unkind editorials on what I said. The criticism that effects me more is the one that says that I am power drunk and that I feel that I can do anything because I got the Nobel Prize and it went to my head and that the true motive of my statements are never revealed and the statement that I am stepping out of my bounds. No, I really don't have the strength to fight this issue and keep my civil rights fight going. They have all the news media and T.V. and I just don't have the strength to fight all these things. I just don't have the strength to fight these two battles and there has to be a real fight on my part. I may feel a sense of guilt about the civil rights movement because this would take too much of my time to fight this and I feel that I couldn't get the backing of the civil rights leaders on my position such as Roy Wilkins and Whitney Young. The other thing is the deeper you get involved the deeper you have to go and take stands and speeches and appearances and I'm already overloaded and I'm almost emotionally fatigued. ... So what first of all can be done to give the national public a realization of the fact that I am not out here alone? Second, how to deal [with] the Dodd Statement. Third, I would like to get your opinion on the letters, of the letters that I have proposed writing to the leaders, of the various involved nations. There again I have gotten criticism and statements that I am meddling and stepping out of the area of my ability. The Atlantic Constitution wrote an article [that] said I continue in this folly of this letter writing. They call me the single most powerful Negro leader in the country and that I know I can't talk as an individual. I also feel that Ho Chi Minh and Cho En Lai are not going to respond affirmatively regarding these letters and that will make me look worse so I have to find out how I can gracefully pull out so that I can get on with the civil rights issue because I have come to the conclusion that I can't battle these forces who are out to defeat my influence. . . .

Wachtel: . . . When Martin spoke to the press he said that civil rights demand all his time now but they won't print that now. The three points that Martin made are there, to negotiate with the Viet Cong, to halt the bombing and to recognize Red China. These points are there and he is not going to withdraw from these points he made and he is not going to repeat them. So he now requires as Stan Levison said to do in civil rights that which will tell everyone I have spoken my part and I never purported to lead this struggle and now I am going back to my regular work.

Young: I think that Senator Dodd and Whitney Young somehow need to be confronted.

Wachtel: Right, but not by Martin.

Levison: No, not by Martin.

Wachtel: Right, someone else must answer his detractors whether it be someone like Edward Daulberg (phonetic) or Spike or . . .

Young: I think the most effective criticism of Dodd should come from the state of Connecticut, someone like Bill Coffin (phonetic) and possibly Lou Pollock, the Dean of the Yale Law School. Wyatt, you know all those boys.

Wyatt: Yes, I can get to them.

Levison: Who has the third man?

Young: Rev. Dick Battles, and somebody for Yale who can really jump on Dodd.

Wachtel: He's the Dean of Yale Law School Pollock and a good friend of Goldberg. We should get one of them and then let the one get the others.

King: The average mind is not sophisticated enough to analyze who Dodd is and that he is the strongest supporter of the FBI and its invasion of privacy and the Un-American Activities Committee and an extreme isolationist and all that, but they don't know that, consequently many people are misled, many good people who read this and would say yes Martin is going too far. Some Negroes would say this. All I'm saying is that as a citizen I have a right to say this, as a moral leader to deal with a question that deals with the survival of mankind. . . .

I don't agree that I need to withdraw, I only need to withdraw temporarily.

Wachtel: You don't have to withdraw, Martin, just sit back and let the bombshell you dropped have its impact.

King: Let me suggest for your consideration: I suggest that Wyatt contact Bill Coffin, Lou Pollock and Dick Battles [to] have them draw up a strong letter to Senator Dodd and have a press conference on that letter. . . . Then Harry and Cleve get with Bayard early and go over this whole conversation and then Bayard and Cleve get to Phil Randolph and he should have a press conference too, directly answering Whitney Young.

Wachtel: Right, we will get to him.

King: I think that Harry should feel out Bobby Kennedy.

Wachtel: O.K.

King: I don't think he will endorse the admission of Red China but he may endorse my right to speak on it.

Wachtel: And non-military solutions which is his position.

King: Yeah, o.k., let's try him. Let's also line up Senators Morse, Church, McGovern. Walter can you do that?

Thompson: Yes, I know Morse.

Robinson: Morse may want to put into the record certain things he could reply to Dodd on the floor of the Senate and put it in the record.

King: I think he will reply to Dodd. Now, the fourth point. Harry will you contact in the morning the *New York Times*. And fifth, Andy will you contact the Christian Century [?] and I think it will come through at this point.

Young: I think between Clarence and Stan [we] could get the *Saturday Review*, *The Nation* and Norman Cousins, *The Progressive*.

Levison: Yes.

Wachtel: We don't want to become a national question.

King: I think we have as much right to become a national headline as Dodd did and I think that Lyndon Johnson pushed Dodd to do it. . . . If I have to answer Dodd I'm going to do it in a high moral tone. . . . I think we have to tell these fellows that this is an attempt to undermine the civil rights through me.

9/28/65

Operator calls Stanley Levison with a conference call from Dr. King. She has Bayard Rustin, Andy Young, John Barber, and Harry Wachtel and King. John Barber is King's new Executive Assistant [who] just got in yesterday. Wachtel and Levison don't know him.

King: . . . I have got to make a speech on the fifteenth of October in Philadelphia celebrating the 50th anniversary of the Women's International League of Peace and Freedom. I don't see how on that platform I could avoid talking about peace and Vietnam and Pakistan. Newsmen of Philadelphia have already called me and pressured me for statements.

Rustin: You have a bigger problem that Stanton Lynn [Staughton Lynd] is on the platform with you and I say you should not be there for it. I'm to be on the platform and I am indisposed and so should you be.

All those on the phone say that Stanton Lynn is a bad person to be with.

King: Well, I don't want to get in bad with Lynn. He is a friend of mine.

Rustin: So have I, Martin. I have signed a paper that young men should not go into the draft but my position is not like his. Lynn is in favor of tearing up draft cards and you are not. If Martin goes on that platform with Stanton Lynn the newspapers will attack you to no end.

Wachtel: Could you let someone go and read Martin's speech?

King: Well, Coretta could read the speech.

Young: This may be an opportunity for Martin to clear the air on his thoughts of peace.

Wachtel: I think it would look as if Martin is running.

Levison: Well there were two stories that defended Martin. One was in *Bridgeport Herald* and the other was in the *Amsterdam News*. The one point was that Martin had to speak out on peace like he had to do on civil rights.

Rustin: As I understand the last questions how far one was going to be drawn in on a debate of the peace question.

Wachtel: Yes, but the Philadelphia engagement could be something that could trigger a larger problem.

King: I could always arrange not to get there until time just before the speech and leave right after so I would not have to answer his speech at all. One of the most scathing editorials I had seen was in the *Philadelphia Inquirer* and I think that if I could get there and leave immediately and not have a press conference that I could serve the purpose.

. . .

Rustin: I frankly, Martin, do not like the notion that you are putting it in the terms of why Martin King has to speak out on peace. I think you could use Stanley's approach that in the civil rights struggle the greatest enemies are not those against us but those who are silent and then switch it to the problem of 20,000,000 keeping quiet and then you could appeal to the people to take a stand on foreign policy.

Barber: Wouldn't this give the press a chance to criticize him.

Rustin: Well, the reason the Pope doesn't get criticized is that he does not get specific.

King: Yes, I thought I should be less specific. I think a moral statement is necessary at this time. This would show that my prime work at this time would be in the civil rights struggle.

Rustin: Well, I would like to give a few points to be taken down. 1) That additional reason why Dr. King wants to see peace is that there are grave problems of hunger and poverty all over this world and that when people are involved in war even though they may have money to do all of these things, their money goes into the greatest conflict in their mind which is war. So when we have peace we can rebuild a democratic society. 2) The continuation of war obscures the needs of people domestically, it is that the extreme continues and the money which should really be used for the construction of housing and the destruction of slums and the building of quality integrated schools is cut off . . .

King: John, I'll give you two or three basic points I wanted to have expanded, to give the press before I speak on the platform with Lynn.

Levison: Martin can tell the press he doesn't share all of Lynn's views and doesn't want to discuss them now.

King: Better still, I can tell them I haven't had time to study Lynn's views and don't want to comment on them now.

Rustin: You mustn't get there while Lynn is speaking. Stay in your room until you're ready to speak.

King: Should I say in this speech how wrong we are in Vietnam, the public doesn't realize this, how immoral this is. I think someone should outline how wrong we are. Uh, I don't know if I'm the person to do this.

Levison: Martin we've just gone over this and decided that you're not the person to do this.

King: O.K. I'll go along with this. O.K. then, John, Andy, I'll be seeing you very shortly. So long Stan, Harry. (conference ended)

1966

1966

[Section 49]

January 6, 1966	Memorandum: Louisville

[Section 52]

February 24, 1966	Teletype: Chicago to Director

[Section 53]

March 5, 1966	Memorandum: Chicago
March 9, 1966	Memorandum: New York

[Section 57]

May 9, 1966	Memorandum: Baumgardner to Sullivan
May 9, 1966	Airtel: Chicago to Director

[Section 59]

June 8, 1966	Memorandum: Chicago
June 10, 1966	Teletype: Charlotte to Director
June 12, 1966	Teletype: Chicago to Director
June 14, 1966	Memorandum: Chicago

[Section 60]

June 17, 1966	Informative note: RDS
June 17, 1966	Radio: St. Louis to Director
June 19, 1966	Teletype: Detroit to Director
June 29, 1966	Memorandum: Baumgardner to Sullivan

[Section 61]

| July 26, 1966 | Memorandum: Charlotte |
| July 28, 1966 | Airtel: Chicago to Director |

[Section 62]

August 5, 1966	Memorandum: Dallas
August 16, 1966	Airtel: Louisville to Director
August 16, 1966	Teletype: Chicago to Atlanta
August 19, 1966	Teletype: Milwaukee to Director
September 6, 1966	Teletype: Chicago to Director

[Section 63]

| September 8, 1966 | Memorandum: Baumgardner to Sullivan |
| September 20, 1966 | Report |

[Section 64]

| October 20, 1966 | Teletype: New York to Director |

[Section 65]

November 1, 1966	Memorandum: Norfolk
November 1(?), 1966	Memorandum
November 14, 1966	Memorandum: Baumgardner to Sullivan
November 22, 1966	Memorandum: DSS to Tolson

[Section 66]

| December 20, 1966 | Memorandum: New York |

[Section 49]

UNITED STATES DEPARTMENT OF JUSTICE

FEDERAL BUREAU OF INVESTIGATION

Louisville, Kentucky
January 6, 1966

Martin Luther King, Jr.
Security Matter-C

. . . advised a Special Agent of the Federal Bureau of Investigation
as follows:

A one-day civil rights conference is scheduled to be held in Louisville, Kentucky, on December 16, 1965, primarily for the purpose of
obtaining support for the passage of civil rights legislation by the Kentucky Legislature, scheduled to convene in Frankfort, Kentucky, on
January 4, 1966. The December 16, 1965, conference is co-sponsored
by the Kentucky Conference of the NAACP and the Kentucky Christian
Leadership Conference, an affiliate of the Southern Christian Leadership
Conference (SCLC). Among scheduled speakers at the conference are
the Governor of Kentucky, Ned Breathitt, the Reverend Martin Luther
King, Jr., the Reverend C. T. Vivian of the SCLC and James Farmer,
Director of the Congress of Racial Equality. Reverend King is scheduled
to speak on the evening of December 16, 1965, at the Zion Baptist
church in Louisville, which is pastored by Reverend King's brother, the
Reverend A. D. Williams King.

News articles appearing in the December 17, 1965, issue of the Courier-
Journal and Louisville Times, daily Louisville, Kentucky, newspapers,
and the December 23, 1965, issue of the Louisville Defender, a weekly
Louisville, Kentucky, newspaper containing information primarily relating to Negro matters, reported that December 16, 1965, civil rights
conference in Louisville was held as scheduled without any adverse
incident having occurred.

In its article regarding the conference, the Louisville Defender reported that Reverend Martin Luther King in his address before the
conference had said that the current civil rights revolution is the most
important period of change in the nation's history and that Americans
must accomplish several goals if the revolution is to succeed. He listed

the following: 1) We must reaffirm the immorality of racial segregation, that segregation is not only unsound but morally wrong and sinful. 2) Work passionately and tirelessly to abolish poverty in the nation and the world. 3) Continue to develop mass action programs to get rid of the last vestiges of segregation in America.

It was further reported in the Louisville Defender article that Reverend King brought applause from his audience when he remarked, "It may be true that legislation cannot integrate but it can desegregate . . . it may not change hearts but change habits of men . . . it may not make a man love me but it can restrain him from lynching me . . . well, I think that is pretty important." Further, Reverend King had said that he was alarmed at indications that "war on poverty" may be cut back to finance the war in Vietnam and that should such happen, the United States would win the war in Vietnam and lose the war on poverty in this country. Reverend King urged that it be made clear to the government that "we cannot go back on poverty."

. . . advised a Special Agent of the Federal Bureau of Investigation that to his knowledge, there had been no one who had in any way attempted to interfere with the December 16, 1965, civil rights conference in Louisville, . . .

[Section 52]

WASH DC

FBI CHICAGO
955 PM CST URGENT 2/24/66 JLV
TO DIRECTOR (100-106670)
FROM CHICAGO (100-35356)

MARTIN LUTHER KING, JR., SM-C

REMYTEL TODAY.
LOCAL NEWS MEDIA REPORTING CIVIL RIGHTS GROUPS
LED BY KING CONTINUED WITHOUT INTERFERENCE RENOVA-
TION OF WEST SIDE "SLUM BUILDING" AT ONE THREE TWO
ONE SOUTH HOMAN [sic] AVENUE, CHICAGO. FURTHER
LOCAL JUDGES, LAWYERS AND REAL ESTATE OFFICIALS
BLASTED AS ILLEGAL THE ACTION OF KING IN ASSUMING

WHAT THEY CALLED "TRUSTEESHIP" OF BUILDING. USDC
JUDGE JAMES B. PARSONS QUOTED IN PART AS STATING "I
DON'T THINK IT IS LEGAL; IT IS THEFT." ALSO "I AM NOT IN
AGREEMENT WITH CIVIL DISOBEDIENCE OR THE FLOUTING
OF GOOD LAWS. THIS IS A REVOLUTIONARY TACTIC."

LATE BULLETIN REPORTED COUNTY PUBLIC AID DEPART-
MENT WILL WITHHOLD RENT PAYMENTS FOR TWO RELIEF
FAMILIES IN BUILDING IF CIVIL RIGHTS GROUPS WHO HAVE
"ASSUMED TRUSTEESHIP" OF BUILDING REFUSE TO TURN
THE RENTAL MONEY OVER TO BUILDING OWNER.

[Section 53]

UNITED STATES DEPARTMENT OF JUSTICE

FEDERAL BUREAU OF INVESTIGATION

Chicago, Illinois
March 5, 1966

MARTIN LUTHER KING, JR.

. . . advised the Chicago Office of the Federal Bureau of Investigation
(FBI) that Doctor Martin Luther King, Jr., President, Southern Christian
Leadership Conference (SCLC), arrived in Chicago at 12:05 P.M., March
2, 1966, accompanied by Reverend Bernard Lee, aide to King. King
and Lee arrived in Chicago from the Atlanta Headquarters of the SCLC
and indicated to police representatives at O'Hare Airport that they
planned to return to Atlanta on March 4, 1966.

. . . advised that his information concerning King's itinerary reflects
that he was to spend the afternoon of March 2, 1966, in meetings with
representatives of his SCLC staff here in Chicago, was to attend an
early evening social reception on Chicago's north side, and subsequently
to continue with staff meetings for the remainder of the evening. There
was no information available concerning contemplated activities on the
part of King for March 3–4, 1966.

. . . advised that his information concerning King's activities as of
this time was to the effect that King has been ill for several days with

a severe cold and has participated in no scheduled activities of any kind. . . . advised that there was no information available which reflected that King, under a doctor's care, would leave Chicago on March 4, 1966.

. . . above, advised that Doctor King departed Chicago at approximately 4:00 P.M. on this date, from O'Hare Airport, en route to Atlanta. Just prior to King's departure, he is reported to have taped an appearance on "Kup's Show," a local television conversation program, to be shown during the early morning hours on March 6, 1966, at Chicago . . .

In monitoring of the television program "Kup's Show," . . . it was observed that Doctor King appeared for approximately fifty minutes . . . General discussion took place concerning the local civil rights campaign of King. It was stated at the inception of the program that King had been ill recently and had interrupted his recuperation to make this television appearance.

King had stated during the program in response to a series of questions from the moderator, generally as follows:

He had brought the SCLC campaign to Chicago because of the urgent problems of racial injustice here. King felt that there was more such injustice now in the large northern cities than in the south, and Chicago, with its vast slums and ghetto areas, represents the classic example of the economic, educational, social and human problems of the northern Negroes.

A second reason given by King for concentrating on Chicago was the existence here of the Co-Ordinating Council of Community Organizations (CCCO), a grouping of local civil rights organizations, experienced and effective, and the lack of such an organization or organizations in other large northern cities. Consequently, the SCLC, initially upon its arrival in Chicago, was able to utilize the services of the CCCO as a nucleus of local support and utilize the already existent facilities of this group. King continued that the civil rights movement generally has a strong emotional attachment to Chicago because so many Chicago people, both lay and clergy, have activated themselves in the past in the southern civil rights movement.

King advised that issues which will be points of concentration in Chicago are those of employment, schools and slums, which he described as not just housing conditions, but general conditions of economic exploitation. He emphasized that the SCLC campaign was not an anti-Daly campaign, this is a reference to Chicago's Mayor Richard J. Daly. King welcomed Daly's efforts and programs which were in any way directed toward the removal of conditions which serve to exploit and inhibit the activities and well-being of the Negroes in Chicago.

Regarding the recent remark attributed to him to the effect that in order to get things done, tensions in Chicago must be raised, King explained that by this he meant that history generally reflects that change has never come without creative tension. He felt that situations must exist, or be created, to make people examine issues which they would rather ignore, then recognize that something must be done to change or rectify these situations. He likened this condition to a boil which is often concealed, but when brought to a head, is subsequently lanced or cleaned, then heals itself. The tensions which he referred to were not intended to be interpreted as an indication of violence and any situations which are created in Chicago would be non-violent type situations.

King believed that it was possible that more northern Negroes than southern Negroes were receptive to violent type tactics to improve their conditions, but he believed the great mass of Negroes rejected this approach. He felt the non-violent movement could succeed in Chicago and stated that all local civil rights leaders of stature have rejected violence as a tactic to be utilized in solving the Negro's problems. Regarding his recent meeting with Elijah Muhammad, identified as the leader of the Nation of Islam, he recalled that since he had started coming to Chicago some time ago, it had been his practice to meet with all types of people representing all types of groups. His meeting with Muhammad was in response to invitations given him in the past by Muhammad but which he had never been able to accept. He stated that he had no illusion about the reality of a joint program of any kind with Muhammad's organization but felt that he had the responsibility, as the leader of a non-violent movement, to visit with Muhammad to see if there were any possible areas in which the two could cooperate in a manner which would be beneficial to the Negro people. King had no explanation for Muhammad's subsequent severe attacks on him, in which King had been referred to as a "lover of white people," but was not in any way concerned by such attacks. He stated that it was his feeling that the philosophy of Muhammad's organization was under-standable, since it was based upon the frustrations long suffered by the Negro people, but felt that to substitute a black tyranny for a white tyranny was simply to replace one evil with another. He noted that what he is striving for is freedom for all, both black and white, as individuals and reiterated his belief that American society as constituted today possesses the tools to make integration work. He concluded that the philosophy of Muhammad was not realistic, that the Negro was unmistakably a part of America and has contributed in great measure toward making this country what it is today.

King's attention was then called to the assumption of the "trusteeship" of a slum building on Chicago's west side, a trusteeship which his organization, the SCLC, had assumed, together with several local civil rights groups. He was asked for comment concerning the serious criticisms leveled at him by many elements in Chicago subsequent to this activity.

King stated that this is a problem similar to many which he has faced in the South. He noted that his organization feels sincerely that they are obligated to engage in activities which in such instances are not legal in a strict sense, but represent moral issues which cannot be avoided. He stated that insofar as this particular building was concerned, he and his organization had been faced with the making of a moral decision growing out of an immoral situation. He noted that the tenants in this particular building, many with very young children, had had no heat, light or water for days, plaster was falling from the building walls, and the building was infested with rats. The tenants here had tried numerous ways to get help, but had been unable to get any relief for these conditions. He stated that his organization felt the moral responsibility to provide immediate help for these people and he personally as well as others in his organization were willing to go to jail if necessary as a result of their actions. King agreed that it was possible his action here might not be perfectly legal, but stated that it is his position that along with property rights goes the responsibility to maintain property in decent, livable conditions for human beings.

King denied that he was making any effort to bring disunity to the community. He praised the local Chicago Police Department for its past patience in dealing with civil rights problems and concluded that the Negroes, through legislative activities, have made great strides toward equality through the past several years ...

The March 5, 1966, edition of the "Chicago Sun-Times," a daily Chicago newspaper, contained an article concerning the slum building at 1321 South Homan [sic] Avenue ... John B. Bender, age 81, had filed a civil suit on March 4, 1966, against King, ...

Bender's attorney stated that Bender agreed with the objectives and intentions of King but felt that the law was just as important as civil rights and the objectives of King could only be accomplished under the jurisdiction of the court.

UNITED STATES DEPARTMENT OF JUSTICE

FEDERAL BUREAU OF INVESTIGATION

New York, New York
March 9, 1966

Martin Luther King, Jr.
Security Matter-C

On March 4, 1966, the Public Information Department of the Educational Broadcasting Corporation, 304 West 58th Street, New York City, the operators of WNDT, Channel 13, released a schedule of program which [indicated] ... Martin Luther King would be interviewed on the subject of Vietnam ... by Arnold Michaelis, ... a noted television producer ...

Hereafter, follows a resume of King's remarks as heard by Special Agents of the Federal Bureau of Investigation, who observed the show on the night of March 8, 1966:

King, in opening the thirty minute television show, said that war was considered a social evil which has ominous possibilities for the total destruction of mankind. In Vietnam, King said, "we" (the United States) have taken a stand against people seeking self-determination. He said there is wrong on both sides and that the wrong on "our" side (the United States) should not be ignored.

King noted that Premier Diem (a former Premier of Vietnam, who was slain) came into power and as a result of oppressive measures the Viet Cong came into being. He said the United States watched the war escalate during the following years. He said that "we" (the United States) must accept the fact that Communism is with "us," adding, however, that he had a great philosophical opposition to Communism.

King said he felt at one time war could be a "negative good," in that it could block the spread of a negative evil force, like Hitler, for instance. He said he then arrived at a "Pacifism" stage and concluded that war could no longer serve as a negative good because of its destructive capabilities.

He said the United States must go through a re-evaluation of its entire foreign policy, and said that sectional concerns must be transformed into ecumenical concerns. He said "we" must have disarmament. He said it is a case of non-violence or non-existence.

Furthermore, King said "we" must recognize that the world must live together. It (the world) must become one in terms of brotherly concern. Whatever effects others directly concerns "us" (the United States) indirectly, he said.

King noted that Hitler in "Mein Kampf" also talked about peace. He said too often "we" think of peace as a goal we seek rather than as a means by which "we" arrive at that goal. King said "we" (the United States) talk about world peace in lofty terms, but we are using war to get there.

In answer to a question by Michaelis as to what he would do if he was authorized to speak for the United States, King said he would depend more on moral power than on military power. He said the United States must do something to create an atmosphere for negotiations, must make some good-faith moves.

President Johnson, he said, was not a "warmonger" as he inherited a great deal of the problem. He said if the United States was in favor of unconditional talks, it should make moves to lessen tensions and also stop the bombings in Vietnam.

He said if the United States was willing to negotiate, there was no point in saying that it would not negotiate with the Viet Cong. If the United States could get rid of its pride, he said, it would not hurt morally or militarily to pull out of Vietnam. France, he said, pulled out of Algeria without winning a military victory and it did not damage its position.

King said he was not calling for unilateral withdrawal from Vietnam but instead, had called for negotiations. He said the United States would not pull out, but said events had reached the point where all sides must give a little.

Hanoi and China have been recalcitrant about negotiating. In that regard, he said he was concerned about interpretations being placed on Chinese statements and felt that if the United States would make it clear that it wanted to negotiate and was not seeking to destroy Vietnamese life and property, something would happen whereby negotiations would be possible for the United States. He said the United States had once before turned down an offer to negotiate.

In commenting on the effectiveness of the United Nations, King said there could not be a real United Nations until the largest nation in the world (China) was in it.

He said there was a need for leadership at this time. In amplifying, King said the administration (the Johnson administration) states that polls show support for its policies. He said, however, that policies should not be molded as a result of what polls reportedly reflect.

He said it was difficult for leaders to break out of their official "molds." The ultimate test of a leader, according to King, is not where he stands in a moment of convenience but, instead, where he stands in a moment of crisis. As an example, he noted the action of President Lincoln (in his Emancipation Proclamation).

When asked if he would go to see Ho Chi Minh or to China, King said he had not gone that far yet. He said he had talked to President Johnson about Vietnam on two occasions and made known his strong convictions.

In concluding his remarks, King said that although he had convictions regarding Vietnam, it did not mean that he was disloyal to the United States.

[Section 57]

UNITED STATES GOVERNMENT
Memorandum

To: Mr. W. C. Sullivan   DATE: 5/9/66

From: Mr. F. J. Baumgardner

           MARTIN LUTHER KING, JR.
           SECURITY MATTER-C

As you are aware, we have obtained considerable information identifying Martin Luther King as . . . however, for public consumption, King endeavors to create the image of a substantial member of the clergy and a faithful and devoted husband and father.

In this regard, the New York office made available a tape of an interview by Hugh Downs of Martin Luther King on the NBC "Today" show which took place on 4/18/66. Excerpts of this interview are set out below which indicate his hypocritical attempts to further his public image as a respected member of the clergy.

In answer to a question by Downs about loose sex relations and problems of the youth and what King thought the clergy could do about this, King responded in part: "Well, I think the clergy and the church should plunge right into this problem and deal with it, in what I consider an intelligent moral manner. In the past, too often the church has taken a kind of prohibitive attitude on the whole question of sex, a hush-hush attitude, rather than trying to honestly discuss sex and deal with the problems surrounding it. I think the only answer is for the church through its channels of religious education and other methods to bring this issue out into the open and reaffirm once more that what God creates is good and that it must be used properly and not abused. I think it is also necessary to bring out at this point that sex is basically sacred when it is properly used and that marriage is man's greatest prerogative in the sense that it is through and in marriage that God gives man the opportunity to aid him in his creative activity. Therefore, sex must never be abused in the loose sense it is often abused in the modern world.''

The complete transcript of the interview of King by Downs is attached.

Handwritten at the bottom of this page—and initialed "H"— is the notation: "This is positively nauseating coming from a degenerate like King."

NBC "TODAY" SHOW, APRIL 18, 1966

Hugh Downs: Dr. King, in view of the way that so many clergymen and other religious people have taken part in the civil rights and other movements, do you think that this ... that the churches and clergy are reasserting the moral responsibility, the moral leadership in a nation that is considered largely materialistic in outlook?

Dr. King: Yes, I definitely feel that the church is gaining new life on this question in reasserting moral leadership. I have thought all along that the church being the moral guardian of the community had to take a basic forthright stand on the issue of civil rights. Naturally, there have been moments when I have been disappointed with the stand of the church, but I think in the last few years the church has been amazingly relevant on this issue and this has been most encouraging.

Hugh Downs: Do you think this means the commitment on the part of the clergy to eradicate the evil in inequality throughout the world?

Dr. King: I think it does, I must make a distinction here between what I see on the one hand as basic creative stands on the part of the church in general, church bodies, and the stand on the part of the individual congregations. [There is] a gulf between church bodies taking a stand on this issue and [the] many church local congregations, many of them still all too slow. But I think the major denominations within Protestantism, and certainly the Roman Catholic Church, and the Jewish Synagogues generally are committed to take a greater stand on all of the social evils that face our days.

Hugh Downs: How far does the responsibility of the clergy go in matters of both domestic and international affairs of the nation?

Dr. King: Well I think it goes all the way. I see the church as a conscience of the community, the conscience of the nation, the conscience of the state, and consequently, the church must be involved in all of the vital issues of the day, whether it's in the areas of civil rights, whether it's dealing with the whole question of war and peace. I think the church has in many instances been all too silent on the issue of war. I think it goes into the area of dealing with the economic problems that people face not only in our nation, but all over the world. Because poverty is still a great reality in our world today and I think the church has to address itself to all of these contemporary problems.

Hugh Downs: I want to ask you in a moment about poverty and about war and peace, but right now I would like your opinion on whether you think the civil rights movement would have gotten as far as it has to date without the active participation of the clergy?

Dr. King: No I really don't think so, I feel that the Negro himself must initiate many moves to end the long night of oppression, segregation and discrimination, but I don't think the problem itself can be totally solved until there is a kind of grand alliance of what I call the coalition of conscience working together and the Negro cannot solve this problem by himself. He is ten per cent of the population. He needs allies over and over again in the white community, and I think we've definitely gotten further with this kind of cooperation from the church.

Hugh Downs: When it comes to issues of war and peace, how far do you think a clergyman should go in the matter of asserting leadership? I have in mind particularly now the conflict in Vietnam. What can the clergyman do? What should he do?

Dr. King: I think the clergyman first must in his messages and through his congregation seek to get to the ideation of roots of war, so to speak, and seek to take a general stand against war itself. There have been too many instances where individual clergymen and the church in general gave a kind of moral sanction to war as if it was a holy venture, and it is my strong feeling that we have got to make it clear that war itself is the enemy of mankind, and as President Kennedy said, "unless we put an end to war, war will put an end to mankind." Along with this, I think we got to deal with specific wars and speak to the nation and the world honestly about them, and this is why I am very happy that the National Council of Churches for instance, Pope Paul and many Jewish rabbis of the country, have come out in very vocal and forthright terms [and] are calling for a negotiated settlement in this situation, calling for the recognition of Red China in order to ease tensions in Southeast Asia, calling for cessation of the bombings in the north, and other things that are vitally necessary I think to bring about peace in that very turbulent situation.

Hugh Downs: The population explosion probably hit hardest at the poor. To what extent do you think the Government should finance birth control?

Dr. King: I think the time has come that this must be done on levels much larger than private agencies can reach. I think that birth control is now a necessity not only in our nation, but all over the world, particularly in the larger nations like China and India, in many nations in Asia and Africa and all over South America, and I think that if it is to be dealt with, it must be on a level that really grapples with the enormity of the problem and this means that the Government would have to be involved. This means that more and more of the United Nations will have to deal with this problem because the population explosion is the (illegible) greater threat to mankind as the problem of war [*sic*]), so that it has to have planned structured methods that work to deal with it.

Hugh Downs: After some of the evils that hit young people now, the loose sex relations and problems of the quite young and apparently the age is getting younger, bodily, what do you think the clergy can and should do about this?

Dr. King: Well, I think the clergy and the church should plunge right into this problem and deal with it, in what I consider an intelligent moral manner. In the past, too often the church has taken a kind of prohibitive attitude on the whole question of sex, a hush-hush attitude, rather than trying to honestly discuss sex and deal with the problems surrounding it. . . . I think the only answer is for the church through its channels of religious education and other methods to bring this issue out into the open, and reaffirm once more that what God creates is good and that it must be used properly and not abused. I think it is also necessary to bring out at this point that sex is basically sacred when it is properly used and that marriage is man's greatest prerogative in the sense that it is through and in marriage that God

gives man the opportunity to aid him in his creative activity. Therefore, sex must never be abused in the loose sense it is often abused
in the modern world. I think the other thing that is necessary to say
here is that it is necessary to move to the causal basis of sexual
promiscuity, the deep anxieties and frustration and confusion of modern life which lead to the abuses, and the church must not only work
on the level of condemnation, but it must seek to get at the causal
basis and work to remove these causes and deal with the psychological problems that bring the looseness into being, rather than making
a general condemnation and not be concerned about the causal basis.

Hugh Downs: There is a lot of discussion in magazines and among
theologians of a concept that says God is dead. What would be your
answer to people who say God is dead?

Dr. King: Well, naturally in a kind of general sense I cannot go along
with the idea God is dead. I am a theorist, and I believe firmly in
the reality and the existence of God. I don't think there is any way
to prove this through some metaphysical philosophical argument. In
other words, I think there are intimations of God in nature and history
rather than any positive proofs. I think this answer comes through
revelation and through real experience. On the other hand, I welcome
this argument about God is dead to a degree, because I think it will
cause many people to re-evaluate their conceptions of God. I do feel
that many people have had their small conceptions of God. They
have seen God as little more than an anthropological being who
walks in the Garden of Eden in the cool of the evening, and they
have seen God in a very narrow tribal context, and this argument,
this debate within theological circles, I feel, will do a great deal to
cause many people to realize that certain conceptions of God are
dead and they need to be dead and the other thing is that it is
important for me to say at this point that I feel that there is a greater
and more dangerous type of atheism that we must be concerned about
than the argument about God is dead. That's theoretical atheism to
a degree. But I'm concerned about practical atheism, and that is
living as if there is no God, but it is my conviction that anyone who
feels that life has meaning, and that there are value structures in the
universe, and anyone who has an ultimate concern believes in God.
The only atheist to my mind is the person who says that there are
no values in the universe, and I do find people living as if there is
no God, as if there are no values and I'm more concerned about this
kind of practical atheism than I'm concerned about the theoretical
atheism that will come and go. This is not a new idea, ever since

the days of nature there has been a discussion of the idea of God being dead and certainly many many instances, the name of God has appeared in the obituary column of philosophical journals and ideas of our world, but in spite of this, God the great reality, the principle of concretion that created force for good in the universe always ends up breathing again.

Hugh Downs: Thank you, Dr. King.

FBI

Date: 5/9/66

AIRTEL

TO: DIRECTOR, FBI (100-106670)

FROM: SAC, CHICAGO (100-35356)

SUBJECT: MARTIN LUTHER KING, JR.
SM-C

... Regular sunday sermonettes [are] being presented by KING over Chicago WAAF-AM. ... The broadcasts are jointly sponsored by the Seaway National Bank, 8555 South Cottage Grove Avenue, and the Joe Louis Milk Company of Chicago. ... on 4/10/66 and 4/17/66. ... As a review would indicate, the broadcasts contain no information of a controversial nature and are predominately religious in content.

The broadcasts made by KING of 4/24/66, 5/1/66 and 5/8/66 have been monitored and are similar in content and direction ... The theme of the 5/8/66 broadcast was "I say unto you, love your enemies, bless them that curse you ...''; that of 5/1/66 was "Father, forgive them for they know not what they do," and that of the broadcast of 4/24/66 concerned the ability and power of God to subdue the powers of evil.

No criticism or reference to the FBI was made in the course of any of these broadcasts and no direct reference was made to activities such as demonstrations or specific civil rights activities as such. In view of this, Chicago will continue to monitor these broadcasts and in the event any are found to contain pertinent data of interest to the Bureau, the Bureau and Atlanta will be promptly advised.

[Section 59]

UNITED STATES DEPARTMENT OF JUSTICE

FEDERAL BUREAU OF INVESTIGATION

Chicago, Illinois
June 8, 1966

MARTIN LUTHER KING, JR.

AUBREY JAMES NORVELL;
JAMES HOWARD MEREDITH-VICTIM
CIVIL RIGHTS—ELECTION LAWS;
CIVIL RIGHTS ACT OF 1965

. . . advised the Chicago Office of the Federal Bureau of Investigation
(FBI) on June 7, 1966, that information available to his Unit reflected that
Dr. Martin Luther King, Jr., President, Southern Christian Leadership
Conference (SCLC), had arrived in Chicago during the morning hours of
this date. . . . advised that this information was to the effect that King had
engaged in brief conferences with representatives of the local SCLC lead-
ership, then had departed almost immediately from Chicago for Memphis,
Tennessee, where he was to meet with James Meredith, hospitalized in
Memphis as a result of having been shot near Hernando, Mississippi, during the course of an intended march from Memphis to Jackson.

. . . continued that Frank Ditto, Head of the Oakland Committee for
Community Improvement, a local Chicago civil rights group, had departed Chicago for Memphis, as a result of the Meredith shooting,
however, . . . had no information concerning the plans for further action
on the part of either King or Ditto upon their arrival in Memphis.

In connection with the above, a local Chicago newspaper, the ''Chicago Daily News,'' edition of June 7, 1966, contained an article reflecting that the Union To End Slums, described as an affiliate of the
SCLC, has called for a rally in Chicago on June 10, 1966, to raise
funds to send bus loads of marchers to Mississippi as a result of the
Meredith incident. This meeting was to be held at the Chicago SCLC
Headquarters, 3101 West Warren Avenue.

A representative of this group was quoted as having stated it is hoped
that buses can be chartered ''to send hundreds of civil rights volunteers'' to join a march there to be led by Dr. King.

This article continued that other civil rights organizations had begun mobilizing scores of volunteers, clergymen, students, teachers, and housewives from Illinois and surrounding states to join the march. The article reflected that although a few local leaders within the civil rights movement were urging a mass march on the Mississippi State Capitol at Jackson to rival last year's Selma, Alabama, march, most have adopted a wait-and-see attitude ...

On June 8, 1966, Matthew Ahmann, National Director, National Catholic Conference for Interracial Justice, (NCC) Chicago, advised that he has been in contact with various NCC offices throughout the United States and the NCC has not yet determined what course of action it will take concerning the Mississippi march.

Ahmann advised the NCC is prepared to devote the same effort to Mississippi as was given to Selma, Alabama, when they recruited thousands of priests, nuns, and lay workers throughout the United States to participate in the Alabama march.

Ahmann advised that the desires of the various civil rights organizations will be considered as well as the possible desirability of clergy participating to preclude violence. He anticipated a decision being made within the next few days.

FBI WASH DC

FBI CHARLT
1100 AM EST URGENT 6-10-66 BSH
TO DIRECTOR, ATLANTA, CHICAGO, JACKSON, AND MEMPHIS,
FROM CHARLOTTE (157-3134)
THREAT TO KILL MARTIN LUTHER KING BY JAMES WILLIAM "CATFISH" COLE, KINSTON, NC, JUNE TEN, NINETEEN SIXTY SIX, RACIAL MATTERS.

... ASSOCIATED PRESS (AP) REPRESENTATIVE, CHARLOTTE, NC, ADVISED TODAY THAT AP REPRESENTATIVE, KINSTON, NC, HAD REPORTED ALLEGED THREAT MADE BY COLE AGAINST MARTIN LUTHER KING.

INQUIRY TODAY REFLECTS ... FREE LANCE REPORTER, KINSTON, NC, RECEIVED CALL FROM COLE JUNE NINE, LAST, AND MET WITH COLE AT COLE'S REQUEST AT APPROXIMATELY TWELVE TEN AM TODAY.

... ADVISES THAT WHEN HE MET COLE AT KINSTON, NC,

COLE HAD PREPARED A WRITTEN STATEMENT WHICH . . .
COPIED VERBATIM AS FOLLOWS:

"I'M GOING TO MISSISSIPPI FOR THE PURPOSE OF MAKING
SURE MARTIN LUTHER KING, JR. NEVER REACHES HIS DESTI-
NATION. I'VE SEEN TOO MANY PEOPLE BUNGLE THE JOB OF
KILLING KING, I'M NOT GOING TO BUNGLE IT. I'LL KILL HIM
MYSELF IF NO ONE BEATS ME TO IT. I'VE SEEN THAT NEGRO
RUNNING UP AND DOWN THIS COUNTRY RUNNING OUR WAY
OF LIFE TOO LONG. I CAN AND WILL PUT A STOP TO THAT
NIGGER. I HOPE I CAN GET SEVERAL OF THEM, BUT I KNOW
I'LL GET KING. I WILL LEAVE KINSTON THIS WEEKEND. I
WILL GO ALONE, I DON'T NEED ANY HELP FOR THIS LITTLE
JOB. THE TRIP IS FINANCED BY FRIENDS AND SUPPORTERS
OF JAMES W. 'CATFISH' COLE.''

ORIGINAL STATEMENT PREPARED BY COLE NOT OBTAINED
BY . . .

COLE AND VEHICLE NOT AT COLE'S USUAL PLACE OF BUSI-
NESS WHEN CHECKED THIS AM. EFFORTS CONTINUING TO LO-
CATE AND INTERVIEW COLE.

APPROPRIATE INFORMANTS AND SOURCES BEING CON-
TACTED TO VERIFY COLE'S PLANS.

APPROPRIATE LOCAL AND STATE AUTHORITIES, MILITARY
INTELLIGENCE AND SECRET SERVICE ADVISED.

FOR INFORMATION OF OTHER OFFICES, JAMES W. ''CAT-
FISH'' COLE IS GRAND WIZARD OF NORTH CAROLINA
KNIGHTS OF THE KU KLUX KLAN. BUREAU WILL BE AD-
VISED OF ALL DEVELOPMENTS.

ATLANTA, IF POSSIBLE, FURNISH KING'S ITINERARY TO
JACKSON AND MEMPHIS.

FBI CHICAGO
?800 PM CDST URGENT 6-12-66 HRF
TO DIRECTOR (100-106670) AND ATLANTA (100-5586) MEMPHIS
AND JACKSON
FROM CHICAGO (100-35356)
MARTIN LUTHER KING, JR. SM-C; PLANNED CIVIL RIGHTS
MARCH FROM SOLDIERS TO CITY HALL CHICAGO, ILL. TO BE
LED BY MARTIN LUTHER KING, JR. SIX TWENTY SIX SIXTY
SIX RM.

... ADVISED KING DEPARTED CHICAGO THREE P.M. THIS DATE APPARENTLY FOR ATLANTA, GA.

KING ANNOUNCED JUNE ELEVEN LAST CIVIL RIGHT RALLY SCHEDULED FOR SOLDIERS FIELD SIX TWENTY SIX NEXT POSTPONED TO JULY TEN NEXT BECAUSE OF QUOTE NATIONAL EMERGENCY END QUOTE IN MISSISSIPPI.

CHICAGO NEWS MEDIA REFLECTS QUOTE FIRST ANNUAL GANGS CONVENTION END QUOTE HELD JUNE ELEVEN LAST AT CHICAGO HOTEL WITH APPROXIMATELY FIFTY LEADERS OF CHICAGO'S STREET GANGS PRESENT. KING CALLED UPON GANG LEADERS TO QUOTE ORGANIZE TOGETHER END QUOTE WITH HIS CIVIL RIGHTS GROUP TO FIGHT POVERTY, SLUMS AND QUOTE THE POWER STRUCTURE THAT MAKES THEM POSSIBLE END QUOTE. MEETING CHAIRED BY REVEREND A.R. SAMPSON WHO IS DESCRIBED AS IN CHARGE OF SCLC'S ATTEMPT TO INVOLVE GANG MEMBERS IN CIVIL RIGHTS ACTIVITIES THIS SUMMER. MILITARY, SECRET SERVICE AND USA ADVISED.

UNITED STATES DEPARTMENT OF JUSTICE

FEDERAL BUREAU OF INVESTIGATION

Chicago, Illinois
June 14, 1966

MARTIN LUTHER KING, JR.

... advised the Chicago Office of the Federal Bureau of Investigation on June 9, 1966, that Dr. Martin Luther King, Jr., President, Southern Christian Leadership Conference (SCLC) arrived in Chicago, at O'Hare International Airport, at approximately 10:12 P.M. on this date, via Delta Airlines Flight 762, from Memphis, Tennessee. ... advised that King arrived from Memphis, participating there in the Voter's Registration March in progress from Memphis to Jackson, Mississippi, returning to Chicago in this instance for an anticipated 2–3 day stay to coordinate local SCLC activities. King was met at O'Hare Airport by Albert Raby, Head of the Coordinating Council on Community Organizations (CCCO), which organization is now affiliated here with the SCLC. At present there was no information available to O'Malley concerning King's activities during his stay in Chicago.

On June 10, 1966 . . . advised the Chicago Federal Bureau of Investigation (FBI) Office concerning King's activities here, that on the evening of this date King was to appear at a SCLC Rally being held at the Warren Avenue Congregational Church, 3101 West Warren Avenue, which rally was for the purpose of raising funds to send an as yet undetermined number of bus loads of demonstrators from Chicago to Mississippi, to support the Voter's Registration March in progress there. On June 11, 1966, King is to participate in a SCLC Workshop to be held at Chicago's Sheraton Hotel, revolving around the participation of Chicago Negro youth and street gangs in the SCLC freedom movement here. Space has been reserved at the Sheraton Hotel for this workshop by the Unitarian-Universalist Church, Midwest Region Office, 5711 South Woodlawn Avenue, Chicago. . . . continued that during the day of June 11, 1966, King is to appear at a luncheon sponsored by the Midwest Regional United Automobile Workers Union, where WALTER REUTHER, UAW President, is also to be a speaker. . . . concluded that although no specific departure time for King from Chicago has been established, the Chicago Police Department is assuming that King will depart Chicago, most probably for Memphis, Tennessee, during the evening hours of June 11, 1966.

Concerning the above activities of King, a confidential source, who has furnished reliable information in the past, advised on June 11, 1966, that King did not appear as scheduled at the June 10, 1966, fund-raising rally at the Warren Avenue Congregational Church. The source advised that King is in Chicago at the present time, however, it was determined that during the evening hours of June 10, 1966, he was detained at another appointment, place or nature unknown, and was unable to appear at this affair.

On June 13, 1966 . . ., advised that information only recently available to his Unit reflects that during the morning hours of June 11, 1966, King and a number of his SCLC aides, together with CCCO representatives, met at the Corpus Christi Church, 4926 South Parkway, Chicago. At this meeting the decision had been made to postpone the June 26, 1966, mass rally planned for Chicago by King and the SCLC, the rally now scheduled to take place July 10, 1966. No additional changes were made in the plans for this rally as to content and organization, however, it was felt that because of the pressure built up during the past week of events in Mississippi, surrounding the shooting there of James Meredith, such a postponement was necessary.

Concerning the June 11, 1966, appearance of King at the UAW luncheon, LaSalle Hotel, Chicago, an article in the June 12, 1966, edition of the "Chicago Tribune" a daily Chicago newspaper, contained in summary the following information:

King and Reuther were the principle speakers at the Region 4, UAW affair, both commenting on the similarity between the labor and civil rights movements in this country. Reuther called upon his union to help build "the great society" by raising human rights above property rights. King stated that the civil rights and labor movements are inextricably bound together, and that the forces which are anti-labor are in almost all cases also anti-Negro. He praised the UAW for "embodying principles of civil rights," noting that many of the foremost civil rights weapons, such as the sit-in, the picket line, and the demonstrations are being used in the civil rights movement because of the past successes unions have had with these tactics. King announced further that the proposed civil rights freedom rally, which was to have been held at Soldiers' Field, followed by a march on Chicago's City Hall, on June 26, 1966, has been postponed to July 10, 1966. He commented in this connection that the march presently being held in Mississippi took precedence over all other events in the civil rights movement.

Further concerning the postponement of the June 26, 1966, rally and march in Chicago an article in the June 12, 1966, edition of the "Chicago Sun Times" specifically related to this matter. King was quoted as having stated as follows: "The cowardly attempt on the life of James Meredith has created a national emergency, which has focused our immediate energies on Mississippi. This in no way diminishes our effort to end the slums in Chicago ... which is an extension of Mississippi. In Mississippi, Negro civil rights workers are physically lynched or mistreated. In Chicago, Negroes are spiritually murdered and mistreated." King added that it has always been basic to the civil rights movement to meet an act of violence with an immediate massive display of non-violent direct action.

In connection with the June 11, 1966, SCLC Workshop at the Sheraton Hotel in Chicago, the June 12, 1966, edition of the "Chicago Sun Times" contained an article entitled "Gang Leaders Asked to Join King's Movement Here." The article in summary set forth the following:

On Saturday, June 11, 1966, King called upon approximately 50 leaders of Chicago street gangs to "organize together" with the civil rights group, the SCLC, to fight poverty, slums, "and the power structure that makes them possible." The gang leaders had gathered together for a "first annual gangs convention." A picture of an unjust society was painted for these gang leaders, who were asked to join together to fight those evils non-violently. Chief among the evils detailed for them were those of slums, poverty, and police brutality . . .

. . . This meeting was coordinated by the Reverend A. R. Sampson, described as one of Dr. King's chief Chicago lieutenants, who is in charge of SCLC's attempt to involve gang members in civil rights activities . . . Various speakers urged gang members to realize that they are not each other's enemy. The real foe was said to include Chicago's Mayor Daley, the Chicago Police Department, local school administrators, slum landlords, businessmen and the like. It was pointed out that when a case of police brutality or a fatal slum fire takes place "the man on top is as responsible—he is as guilty, as much a criminal—as one of us who puts a blade on someone." Sampson proposed the establishment of a Community of Police Service (COPS) to "pressure the system" for a change in the attitude and approach of the Polich Department to the gangs.

The article quoted King as stating to those present "if we are to deal with our problems, we have to get power and power in Chicago is being so well organized that we can get the most powerful political organization in the country to say 'yes' when it wants to say 'no.' " King also was noted as having invited all gang members to participate in the July 10, 1966, mass rally and subsequent march on Chicago's City Hall. He stated that the marchers at this time will place a number of demands before Chicago's Mayor Daley for improvements in the city's approach to those minority groups, calling for a "massive Marshall Plan" for Chicago's poor.

During the course of the workshop the Urban Training Center, a local cooperative project of ministerial groups, volunteered its service to the gangs . . .

[Section 60]

INFORMATIVE NOTE

Date_____6/17/66_____

Information received 6/13/66 that professors at Berkeley, California, were preparing a white paper protesting U.S. action in Vietnam. One Mattison, St. Louis, Missouri, had a representative of "National Emergency Committee of Persons Concerned About Vietnam" contact Martin Luther King's headquarters at Atlanta to solicit his signature to a letter urging [that] President Johnson study [the white] paper. Whether King will sign letter still not known.

We have no information concerning above committee. San Francisco was requested 6/13/66 to identify committee and St. Louis was requested [to] identify Mattison.

Above information furnished Internal Security and Civil Rights Divisions of Department, State Department and military intelligence agencies. When identifying data regarding committee received from San Francisco, complete information will be furnished White House, Attorney General and Deputy Attorney General.

Matter being closely followed at Bureau.

RDS:amr

DECODED COPY

__AIRGRAM   __CABLEGRAM   xxRADIO
   __TELETYPE

....

R-49

URGENT 6-17-66 10:35 AM

TO DIRECTOR (100-106670)

FROM ST. LOUIS (100-17801) 171315

MARTIN LUTHER KING, JR., SECURITY MATTER—COMMUNIST
   REBUAIRTEL JUNE 13, LAST.

LYND MADISON BELIEVED IDENTICAL WITH GORMAN LINDSAY MATTISON, EMPLOYED WASHINGTON UNIVERSITY, ST. LOUIS, MO. CONFIDENTIAL SOURCE ADVISED JUNE 16 LAST THAT MATTISON HAS SPEARHEADED PREPARATION OF "A CITIZENS' APPOSE [sic] WHITE PAPER, THE POLITICS OF ESCALATION." SIX HUNDRED COPIES PRINTED. THIS 99 PAGE BOOKLET STATES IT WAS PREPARED BY SCHOLARS AT UNIVERSITY OF CALIFORNIA AT BERKELEY AND WASHINGTON UNIVERSITY IN ST. LOUIS. DESIGNED TO SHOW ERROR OF U.S. POLICIES IN VIETNAM. COVER LETTER ALSO PREPARED DIRECTED TO PRESIDENT AND SIGNERS BEING SOLICITED INCLUDING MARTIN LUTHER KING, JR. MATTISON CURRENTLY IN WASHINGTON, D.C. TO OBTAIN SIGNERS AND PLANS TO APPROACH U.S. SENATOR ROBERT F. KENNEDY. WHITE PAPER TO BE RELEASED ON OR ABOUT JUNE 26.

DECODED COPY

__AIRGRAM   __CABLEGRAM   __RADIO
  xxTELETYPE

....

12:45 AM URGENT 6-18-66 CWH
TO DIRECTOR AND ATLANTA
FROM DETROIT 180240

MARTIN LUTHER KING, JR., SECURITY MATTER-C. 00:
ATLANTA

ANONYMOUS MALE ON JUNE 17, 1966, AT APPROXIMATELY
3:30 PM, TELEPHONICALLY ADVISED DETROIT DIVISION THAT
HE IS EMPLOYEE OF CADILLAC MOTOR COMPANY, DIVISION
OF GENERAL MOTORS, PLANT NUMBER ONE, CLARK AND
MICHIGAN AVENUE, DETROIT, THAT ELEMENT OF KKK EM-
PLOYEES OF CADILLAC PLANT ONE INTEND TO ASSASSINATE
MARTIN LUTHER KING, JR. KING IS SCHEDULED TO APPEAR
AT FREEDOM DAY RALLY SPONSORED BY LOCAL UNION,
CIVIC AND CHURCH ORGANIZATIONS AT DETROIT ON JUNE
19, 1966. ANONYMOUS CALLER HEARD THAT . . . AN EM-
PLOYEE OF PLANT ONE, CADILLAC, IS POSSIBLY INVOLVED
IN THIS REPORTED ASSASSINATION. CALLER STATES KLAN
ASSASSINATION IS TO BE AT COBO HALL, DETROIT, BUT
EXACT PLANS UNKNOWN TO HIM. FOR INFORMATION OF AT-
LANTA AND BUREAU, . . . HAS BEEN IDENTIFIED BY DETROIT
INFORMANTS TO BE . . . ALSO KNOWN AS . . . WHO RESIDES
. . . MICHIGAN, EMPLOYED . . . CADILLAC MOTOR COMPANY.
SEE DETROIT REPORT DATED JUNE 15 LAST . . .
   . . . ADVISED KING TO ARRIVE DETROIT 12:07, SUNDAY,
JUNE 19, METROPOLITAN AIRPORT, DETROIT, VIA DELTA AIR-
LINES, FROM ATLANTA, GEORGIA. UNION OFFICIALS, DE-
TROIT, PICKING UP KING AT AIRPORT, DRIVING TO
SHERATON CADILLAC HOTEL, DETROIT, ROOM 3122. KING
SCHEDULED TO SPEAK COBO HALL, EXHIBITION HALL B, BE-
TWEEN THREE TO SIX PM. DEPARTURE TIME OF KING UN-
KNOWN, POSSIBLY NEXT DAY, AM.
   DETROIT PD, MICHIGAN STATE POLICE NOTIFIED OF AL-
LEGED ASSASSINATION OF KING AND FURNISHED ALL AVAIL-
ABLE BACKGROUND . . . DETROIT PD PLANNING PHYSICAL
SURVEILLANCE OF . . .

UNITED STATES GOVERNMENT
Memorandum

TO: Mr. W. C. Sullivan   DATE: June 29, 1966

FROM: F. J. Baumgardner

SUBJECT: MARTIN LUTHER KING, JR.
         SECURITY MATTER-C

The Chicago Office, by airtel dated June 23, 1966, has furnished information received from the Chicago Police Department relative to predictions made by a Reverend Clifford M. Royse, Director of the Chicago Psychic Center, Chicago, Illinois. Royse has made several predictions including "a warning of the greatest for the leader, Martin Luther King assassination." Also included among fifty predictions for 1966, which were allegedly made in October 1965, is the statement "a warning of a stroke for FBI Chief J. Edgar Hoover, leaving his job open to a younger, thinner, taller man, possibly from the Midwest."

In making his prediction concerning King, Royse also described the individual which he pictures as the person who will kill King. A Chicago Police Department artist prepared a sketch of this individual based upon the description furnished by Royse. Royse states that his predictions are based on extrasensory perception and psychic mediumship.

The files of the Bureau and the Chicago office contain no information relative to Royse. Chicago is withholding any dissemination of the above information pending an evaluation by the Bureau.

RECOMMENDATION:

It is recommended that no dissemination be made of the above information since to do so may be placing us in the position of supporting the predictions of this unknown psychic medium. Attached for approval is an airtel to the Chicago office advising that no local dissemination should be made.

[Section 61]

UNITED STATES DEPARTMENT OF JUSTICE

FEDERAL BUREAU OF INVESTIGATION

Charlotte, North Carolina
July 26, 1966

SCHEDULED APPEARANCE OF
DR. MARTIN LUTHER KING, JR.
AND STREETWALK OF UNITED KLANS
OF AMERICA, INCORPORATED, KNIGHTS
OF THE KU KLUX KLAN (UKA), BOTH
RALEIGH, NORTH CAROLINA
JULY 31, 1966
RACIAL MATTERS

Reference is made to memo submitted at Charlotte, North Carolina, June 30, 1966, captioned "Scheduled Appearance of DR. MARTIN LUTHER KING, JR., Raleigh, North Carolina, July 31, 1966, Racial Matters."

. . . advised that he had received information that it was announced at a regular meeting of the Mt. Holly, North Carolina, unit of the United Klans of America, Incorporated, Knights of the Ku Klux Klan (UKA) on July 17, 1966, that Dr. MARTIN LUTHER KING, JR. was to be in Raleigh, North Carolina, on July 31, 1966, and that officers of United Klans of America wanted all Klansmen possible to be present. Informant stated that it was announced that they "want two whites present for every nigger."

. . . advised that Klansmen are being urged to attend a streetwalk in Raleigh, North Carolina, on July 31, 1966, in opposition to scheduled appearance there of Dr. KING on that date.

. . . advised that a streetwalk had been arranged by United Klans of America in Raleigh, North Carolina, about 2 P.M., July 31, 1966, and that all Klansmen are being urged to attend the streetwalk and a Klan rally which was scheduled later in the day at Clinton, North Carolina.

None of the above informants furnished any information indicating that any type [of] violence would take place or that the Klan would interfere with Dr. KING's scheduled appearance in Raleigh.

... advised ... host to Dr. KING in connection with his scheduled appearance in Raleigh, North Carolina, July 31, 1966. ... advised that he has not received any information indicating any violence or any action against Dr. KING is contemplated, but that he is concerned for Dr. KING's welfare while in the Raleigh, North Carolina, area. ... was advised that he should make his concern known to local and state authorities, Raleigh, North Carolina. He was further advised that in the event any information was received by the FBI indicating possible action against Dr. KING in connection with his scheduled appearance in Raleigh, North Carolina, that Dr. KING would be notified along with appropriate state and local officials.

On July 26, 1966, ... Raleigh, North Carolina, Police Department; ... Sheriff, Wake County, North Carolina; ... North Carolina State Bureau of Investigation, Raleigh, North Carolina; and ... North Carolina Highway Patrol were apprised of scheduled appearance of Dr. MARTIN LUTHER KING, JR. on July 31, 1966.

A characterization of the United Klans of America, Inc., Knights of the Ku Klux Klan, is attached as an appendix to this memorandum.

APPENDIX
UNITED KLANS OF AMERICA, INC.
KNIGHTS OF THE KU KLUX KLAN (UNITED KLANS)

Records of Superior Court of Fulton County, Georgia, show that this Klan organization was granted a corporate charter on February 21, 1961, at Atlanta, Georgia, under the name United Klans, Knights of the Ku Klux Klan of America, Inc.

A source advised on February 27, 1961, that United Klans was formed as a result of a split in the U. S. Klans, Knights of the Ku Klux Klan, Inc. According to the source, the split from a leadership dispute, and the United Klans has the same aims and objectives as the parent group. These are the promotion of Americanism, white supremacy, and segregation of the races.

The first source and second source advised in July 1961, that United Klans, Knights of the Ku Klux Klan of America, Inc., merged with Alabama Knights, Knights of the Ku Klux Klan. The merged organization established headquarters in Suite 401, the Alston Building, Tuscaloosa, Alabama. The organization is directed by ROBERT SHELTON, Imperial Wizard, and is the dominant Klan group in the South with units in several southern states.

On August 14, 1961, the second source advised that the organization formerly known as United Klans, Knights of the Ku Klux Klan of America, Inc., would be known in the future as United Klans of America, Inc., Knights of the Ku Klux Klan. The second source said the name was changed by a resolution adopted at the National Klonvocation held July 8, 1961, at Indian Springs, Georgia.

The second source advised that at a meeting at Prattville, Alabama, on October 22, 1961, a majority of the Klaverns of the U. S. Klans, Knights of the Ku Klux Klan, merged with the United Klans of America, Inc., Knights of the Ku Klux Klan.

On August 17, 1964, a source advised that the North Carolina organization of the United Klans of America, Inc., Knights of the Ku Klux Klan became affiliated with the national organization of the same group in the spring of 1961. The State Headquarters are at the residence of North Carolina Grand Dragon JAMES ROBERTSON JONES, Granite Quarry, North Carolina, who is subordinate to the national organization with headquarters in Tuscaloosa, Alabama.

The organization in North Carolina has the same aims and objectives as the parent group; that is, advocacy of segregation of the races and white supremacy.

On August 4, 1965, the same source advised that the status, leadership, and affiliation of the North Carolina organization have not changed.

FBI

Date:7/28/66

AIRTEL

TO: DIRECTOR, FBI (100-106670)

FROM: SAC, CHICAGO (100-35356)

SUBJECT: MARTIN LUTHER KING, JR
            00:Atlanta

. . . advised the Chicago Office he had met with . . . known firearms expert . . . during April 1966, at the National Rifle Association Convention, Chicago, Illinois.

. . . showed . . . a two-shot .22 caliber Magnum load Derringer and concealment holster which was fitted into the left sleeve of a suit coat in a manner designed to evade a common frisk search. . . . told . . . that this was a pistol of the type that the . . . had sold to MARTIN LUTHER KING, JR., as a personal defense weapon.

. . . suggested . . . be contacted for the details of the sale of this gun to KING and advised that his name, . . . could be used in contacting . . . In all other contacts, the source of this information should be protected.

LEADS

NEW HAVEN

AT HAMDEN, CONNECTICUT. Locate and interview . . . regarding the sale of this gun to MARTIN LUTHER KING, JR.

[Section 62]

UNITED STATES DEPARTMENT OF JUSTICE

FEDERAL BUREAU OF INVESTIGATION

Dallas, Texas
August 5, 1966

MARTIN LUTHER KING, JR.

On the morning of August 4, 1966, a woman, who refused to furnish her name or any other information which would help to identify her, telephonically contacted the Dallas Office of the Federal Bureau of Investigation and stated, ''I just wanted you to know Martin Luther King is coming to Dallas in September so you could shoot him.'' She added, ''I hope somebody kills that black son-of-a-bitch.''

On August 5, 1966 . . . Dallas Police Department, Dallas, Texas, advised that Martin Luther King, Jr., is to be in Dallas to speak to a church group on September 25, 1966.

FBI

Date: 8/16/66

AIRTEL

TO: DIRECTOR, FBI (100-106670)

FROM: SAC, LOUISVILLE (100-4583) (RUC)

SUBJECT: MARTIN LUTHER KING, JR.
          SM-C
          OO: ATLANTA

Re Chicago airtel dated 7/28/66, and New Haven airtel dated August 9, 1966.

. . . on August 16, 1966, advised as follows:

He has no knowledge of . . . ever having sold any type of weapon to MARTIN LUTHER KING, JR., and he personally would have nothing to do with such a sale. . . . could not remember . . . or ever having met or talked to . . . He stated he had never made any statement to anyone to the effect that . . . had sold MARTIN LUTHER KING, JR., any type of weapon.

. . . also attending the . . . advised that he has no knowledge of . . . ever having sold MARTIN LUTHER KING, JR., a weapon. He said he is sure he would have heard had such been the case. He pointed out that it is possible for anyone to buy . . . arms from dealers.

. . . exhibited a Derringer-type pistol .22 caliber using a magnum load. He stated that he had seen concealment holsters designed to fit in the arm of suit coat. He indicated he believed these holsters were made by . . . New York City, who makes concealment holsters for various weapons.

. . . indicated he had one of these concealment holsters for the magnum .22 caliber Derringer and it is possible that this holster was observed by . . . at the National Rifle Association Convention in Chicago.

. . . indicated that he knew . . . but that he, . . . had never made any statement to . . . regarding having sold a weapon of any kind to MARTIN LUTHER KING, JR.

8/6/66

PLAIN

TELETYPE   URGENT

TO: SAC, ATLANTA (100-5586)
FROM: SAC, CHICAGO (100-35356)
    THREAT TO KILL MARTIN LUTHER KING BY . . . CHICAGO,
ILLINOIS, EIGHT THIRTEEN SIXTY SIX.
    . . . CHICAGO PD, ADVISED NINE THIRTY PM AUG. THIR-
TEEN THAT AT APPROXIMATELY EIGHT THIRTY PM AUG.
THIRTEEN . . . WM, AGE FIFTY FOUR, RESIDING . . . CHICAGO,
TELEPHONICALLY CONTACTED TWENTIETH DISTRICT PD
STATING HE WILL KILL KING IF KING GOES TO WINNEMAC
PARK, LEAVITT AND FOSTER, CHICAGO. . . . STATED . . . TOLD
HIM HE WANTED TO BE ON RECORD SHOULD KING APPEAR
IN WINNEMAC PARK AND BE KILLED. . . . STATED . . . AP-
PEARED SOBER AND RATIONAL. CHICAGO PD INVESTIGAT-
ING. CHICAGO INDICES NEGATIVE ON . . . NOTED NO
MARCHES HAVE BEEN HELD NEAR WINNEMAC PARK AND
KING NOT CURRENTLY IN CHICAGO. ATLANTA AND JACKSON
ADVISE PD, MILITARY, USA, SECRET SERVICE ADVISED.

FBI MILWAUK
4 52 PM CDT URGENT 8/19/66 DLS
TO   DIRECTOR (100-106670) AND ATLANTA (100-5568)
FROM   MILWAUKEE (157-112) (P) 1 PAGE

MARTIN LUTHER KING, JR., RACIAL MATTER.

    ON AUGUST NINETEEN INSTANT . . . MILWAUKEE PD, FUR-
NISHED A XEROX COPY OF AN ANONYMOUS LETTER RE-
CEIVED BY HIS DEPARTMENT ON AUGUST ELEVEN LAST.
LETTER CONTAINS THREAT TO KILL KING WITH HIGH POWER
RIFLE WITH SCOPE IN EVENT KING COMES TO MILWAUKEE.
LETTER MAILED FROM MILWAUKEE AND SIGNED ONLY
"WHITE POWER."
    MILWAUKEE CONTEMPLATES NO INVESTIGATION RE THIS
MATTER SINCE MILWAUKEE PD HAS INITIATED AND IS CON-
TINUING INVESTIGATION.

FBI WASH DC

FBI CHICAGO
1234 PM CDST URGENT 9-6-66 HRF
TO DIRECTOR AND ATLANTA
FROM CHICAGO (100-35356)

SUBJ: ALLEGATION BY ... AKA ... OF PLOT TO KILL MARTIN
LUTHER KING, JR., CHICAGO, ILLINOIS, NINE SIX SIXTY SIX.
INFORMATION CONCERNING ...

... WHO FURNISHED VARIOUS SPELLINGS FOR NAME, CON-
TACTED CHICAGO OFFICE TWELVE ZERO FIVE A.M. NINE SIX
INSTANT ADVISING THAT LAST NIGHT (NINE FIVE LAST) HE
"JOINED THE NAZIS" ... THEN FURNISHED CONFLICTING
AND NEBULOUS STORIES CONCERNING OFFER MADE TO HIM
TO KILL KING, WHEN KING RETURNS TO CHICAGO IN EX-
CHANGE FOR SAFETY OF ... WIFE AND CHILD.

DESCRIBED SELF AS VETERAN OF ONE ZERO ONE AIR-
BORNE DIV., NATIVE OF OHIO, AND EXPERT "VARMINT"
SHOOTER, WITH HIGH-POWERED RIFLE COLLECTION.

WHEN ... PRESSED FOR DETAILS, VARIED STORY AND IM-
POSSIBLE TO GET LOGICAL, COHERENT STORY. IN GENERAL,
FOLLOWING EMERGED: DISCUSSION IN ... INN HELD EARLY
EVENING NINE FIVE LAST CONCERNING RACIAL UNREST IN
CHICAGO.... PRESENT, AS A WHITE, FEMALE ... TOO ... TO
MEETING IN ... A RESIDENT AT ... AND THREE OTHERS,
TWO OF WHOM MALES, PRESENT AT MEETING, BUT IDENTI-
TIES UNKNOWN, ... FIRST ADVISED THAT AT MEETING HE
WAS ASSIGNED TO SHOOT KING, IN RETURN FOR FAMILIES
SAFETY. LATER STATED THAT HE WAS TOLD BY ... HIS FAM-
ILY WOULD BE KILLED IF HE DID NOT ATTEND MEETING,
THIS PRIOR TO MENTION OF KILLING KING. FINALLY ... AD-
VISED HE WAS TOLD HE MUST "COOPERATE" BEFORE SUN-
RISE, SO HE "JOINED" THEM, BUT DENIED KNOWLEDGE
THEY WERE NAZIS. DESCRIBED HIMSELF AS SYMPATHETIC
TO JOHN BIRCH SOCIETY IDEAS, BUT NO NAZI.

WAS ADVISED FBI DOES NOT AFFORD PROTECTION TO INDI-
VIDUALS AND OFFERED NO OBJECTION TO INFORMATION OR
IDENTITY BEING FURNISHED TO CHICAGO PD, OR SUBSE-
QUENT POLICE INTERVIEW. DURING CONTACT ... HUNG UP
ON ONE OCCASION, WAS SUBSEQUENTLY RECONTACTED AT
PHONE NO., FURNISHED BY HIM AS THAT OF ... INN.

[Section 63]

UNITED STATES GOVERNMENT
Memorandum

TO: Mr. W. C. Sullivan   DATE: September 8, 1966

FROM: F. J. Baumgardner

MARTIN LUTHER KING, JR.
SECURITY MATTER-C

. . . advised that King held a conference on September 6, 1966, at New York City with several individuals including his principal advisers, Stanley Levison, Lawrence Baddick, Harry Wachtel, Bayard Rustin, and Clarence Jones, all of whom have subversive backgrounds.

The purpose of the conference was to consider an open letter Rustin prepared over King's signature to Negro youth imploring Negroes to adhere to non-violence. Levison disagreed with a statement in the letter concerning funds for poor school children and jobs for youth. Levison said President Johnson had been asked "ninety times" for jobs but nothing had come of it. Levison said the time had come when King should threaten President Johnson that if no action is forthcoming by May 1967, a march on Washington, D. C., would be organized.

Participants were unable to agree on a final draft of the letter. It will be reworked by Rustin for King's approval on September 11, 1966, and allegedly read over the National Broadcasting Company on September 12, 1966.

FEDERAL BUREAU OF INVESTIGATION
Date:___9/20/66___

. . . Grenada, Mississippi . . . furnished the following information voluntarily after being advised of the identities of the interviewing Agents:

He was advised by . . . whom he declined to identify, on September 17, 1966, that . . . had been approached by two unknown white men on that same date with a request . . . in advance of a murder.

. . . advised that . . . related to him that the two men confided in him that they were actively involved in a plot to kill Reverend MARTIN LUTHER KING, and they desired . . . in advance . . .

... did not discuss the matter any further with the two men and informed them that he would not have anything to do with them or their proposition.... then contacted ... and related the above information to him in what ... considered a strictly confidential ... relationship.... stated that in view of the nature of their relationship, he felt that it would be a direct violation of ... to disclose the name of ... but in the event of an incident, he would disclose the identity of ...

... stated that he was now aware of the identity of the two men who approached ... however, he felt that they were most likely local residents of Grenada.

He also stated that he would recontact ... to try to influence him to make direct contact with the FBI to furnish the information to that agency.

[Section 64]

FBI NEW YORK /6/
312PM URGENT 10/20/66 JAM
TO DIRECTOR 100-106670
FROM NEW YORK 100-136585 3P

MARTIN LUTHER KING, JR., SECURITY MATTER-C
A CONFIDENTIAL SOURCE, WHO HAS FURNISHED RELIABLE INFORMATION IN THE PAST, ADVISED ON OCTOBER SEVENTEEN, SIXTY SIX, THAT CLARENCE JONES, ATTORNEY FOR MARTIN LUTHER KING, JR., TOLD PAUL O'DWYER (NEW YORK CITY ATTORNEY AND BROTHER OF FORMER MAYOR WILLIAM O'DWYER), THAT HE HAD BEEN GIVEN AN ASSIGNMENT BY MARTIN LUTHER KING, JR., TO ATTEMPT TO REACH JIMMY HOFFA (HEAD OF THE TEAMSTERS UNION) TO ARRANGE A MEETING BETWEEN HOFFA AND KING. JONES SAID HE DID NOT WANT ANY PUBLICITY ATTACHED TO THIS, THAT KING IS VERY SENSITIVE ABOUT ANY KNOWLEDGE OF THE MEETING BECOMING KNOWN UNTIL HE HAS HAD A CHANCE TO HAVE THE MEETING, AND THAT WAS WHY HE CONTACTED O'DWYER. O'DWYER PROMISED TO HELP. JONES STATED THAT KING WOULD GO TO WHERE HOFFA IS AND THAT HE, JONES, WOULD ALSO BE PRESENT AT THE MEETING.

ON OCTOBER NINETEEN, SIXTY SIX, THE SAME LEARNED
THAT ON THAT DATE O'DWYER TOLD JONES THAT HOFFA
WANTED TO KNOW THE PURPOSE OF THE MEETING. JONES'S
COMMENTS INCLUDED THE FOLLOWING:

KING HAS FELT FOR SOME TIME THAT MOST OF THE SUP-
PORT OF THE CIVIL RIGHTS MOVEMENT HAS COME FROM
THE SAME UNIONS SUCH AS DISTRICT SIXTY FIVE OF THE RE-
TAIL, WHOLESALE AND DEPARTMENT STORE UNION, THE
PACKING HOUSE WORKERS UNION, AND CERTAIN LOCALS OF
THE UNITED AUTO WORKERS UNION. KING SAID THAT HIS
CONVERSATIONS WITH PERSONS AROUND THE TEAMSTERS
UNION SEEM TO INDICATE THAT THE UNION MIGHT BE
MORE WILLING TO SUPPORT CIVIL RIGHTS THAN PEOPLE BE-
LIEVE. KING IS PARTICULARLY IMPRESSED WITH THE FACT
THAT THE TEAMSTERS UNION HAS ABOUT FOUR HUNDRED
FIFTY THOUSAND NEGRO MEMBERS AND WANTS TO HAVE A
FRANK DISCUSSION WITH HOFFA ON GREATER
INVOLVEMENT.

THERE HAVE BEEN CONFLICTING OPINIONS WITHIN THE
SOUTHERN CHRISTIAN LEADERSHIP CONFERENCE AS TO
WHETHER KING SHOULD GO TO THE TEAMSTERS. SOME SAY
HOFFA WILL USE IT AND THAT THEY SHOULD NOT IDENTIFY
WITH THIS UNION. THERE ARE OTHERS WHO SAY HOFFA HAS
HAD HIS LEGAL DIFFICULTIES BUT IS STILL PRESIDENT OF
THE UNION.

THE EARLIER THE MEETING BETWEEN HOFFA AND KING
THE BETTER BECAUSE KING IS RATHER DISGUSTED WITH
THE AMERICAN FEDERATION OF LABOR, CONGRESS OF IN-
DUSTRIAL ORGANIZATIONS' LEADERSHIP. KING FEELS THEY
HAVE NOT REALLY MOVED INTO THE AREA AND THAT THIS
IS PARTIALLY THE REASON FOR THE WHITE BACKLASH.

[Section 65]

UNITED STATES DEPARTMENT OF JUSTICE

FEDERAL BUREAU OF INVESTIGATION

Norfolk, Virginia
November 1, 1966

RE: SCHEDULED APPEARANCE OF
DR. MARTIN LUTHER KING
SOUTHERN CHRISTIAN LEADERSHIP CONFERENCE
NORFOLK, VIRGINIA
OCTOBER 30, 1966

On October 31, 1966, a source, who has furnished reliable information in the past, advised that there were approximately 2,000 persons in attendance on October 30, 1966, at the New Calvary Baptist Church, Norfolk. The source advised that Dr. Martin Luther King, Atlanta, Georgia, delivered an address prior to the installation of Dr. Reid as the Minister of the church. Dr. King was accompanied by Reverend C. W. Harris and Mr. Bernard Lee. Reverend Harris is President of the Virginia State Unit of the SCLC, Hopewell, Virginia. . . .

"It is midnight in our world today. The darkness is so deep we hardly know what way to turn. Nations are engaged in a contest for world supremacy. Viet Nam reminds us that the clouds of war are close at hand. Our nation, through its refusal to work out a plan to end the war in Viet Nam, is bringing about world War III. . . .''

At a news conference following this lecture, Dr. King was reported to have said that the white backlash is surfacing and that latent hostilities are coming out in the open now. He said it was easy enough to go along with equal voting rights and public accommodations because they are not on a personal level. Now we are dealing with the hard issues—the basic class issues—which are the most difficult yet.

Dr. King said Negroes are actually in worse condition than they were 25 years ago and one of the problems in the Negro community is getting Negroes to see that their condition is getting worse instead of better. Dr. King said the Negro unemployment rate is higher than ever and the economic plight is worse than ever. He stated the black power movement advocated by Stokely Carmichael of the Student Non-Violent

Coordinating Committee was just part of a healthy debate within the Negro movement. He further stated, "We hope to emerge with a united strategy because I think our goals are all the same. Black power has not destroyed our movement in any way." Dr. King said the civil rights movement is not slowing down, and "it's going to have to speed up."

November 1 (?), 1966
In reference to a memorandum captioned MARTIN LUTHER
KING, Jr., SECURITY MATTER-C DATED 10/27/66, the following
is noted:

The specter of communist influence on King is not a new development. The nationally syndicated columnist Joseph Alsop referred to it in April 1964, in a column concerning King's employment in the SCLC of an individual named Jack O'Dell. Alsop stated that King had been warned by Government officials that O'Dell was a "genuine communist article," and warned too that an even more important associate of his was "known to be a key figure in the covert apparatus of the Communist Party."

Such associations and, more particularly, guidance from such individuals could well explain King's failure to take a strong stand in opposition to McKissick and Carmichael. They have been exhorting their followers not to support the Administration's action in Vietnam, to refuse serving if drafted, and to tear apart our cities with violent acts of civil disobedience. These demands well serve communist aims to bring about a communist victory in Vietnam and to divide the masses along class lines to foment disorder in the streets.

Such guidance would help to explain also why King split with men like Wilkins, Randolph and Young on the issue of whether civil rights leaders should be speaking out on matters of foreign policy or whether their role should be confined to civil rights matters. It will be recalled that King attempted to project his views to criticism of fighting in Vietnam but the responsible civil rights leaders took a stand in opposition to him.

It would appear that King's advisers have a broader goal than the civil rights movement in this country. There is talk that King will travel extensively abroad to areas such as Latin America to speak out in behalf of the poor, Negro and white alike, in underdeveloped countries.

Perhaps being the recognized leader of 22 million Negroes in this country is not enough. If the image of him can be projected as the "savior" of the downtrodden throughout the world, his prestige and influence will grow to a degree which will enable him to dictate demands in a voice that will ring loud and clear through the halls of Congress and in the White House. Much would depend on the background of his advisors and the nature of the demands they would be whispering in his ear.

Should that come about, the religious groups, foundations and others who have contributed millions to support King and his activities could find that their generous support had spawned a monster seeking to devour them.

The saddest part of all is his dreams of true equality and justice in a united country free of prejudice and bigotry shattered.

To repeat, Martin Luther King, Jr., could be the great American tragedy of our times.

UNITED STATES GOVERNMENT
Memorandum

TO: Mr. Sullivan   DATE: 11/14/66

FROM: F. J. Baumgardner

MARTIN LUTHER KING, JR.
SECURITY MATTER—COMMUNIST

Attached for your approval for dissemination are copies of a letterhead memorandum containing the following information:

... advised on 11/11/66 that Clarence Jones, a former member of the Labor Youth League, a communist-front organization, and Stanley Levison, a long-time communist, were in conference. Both of these men are advisors to Martin Luther King, Jr., president, Southern Christian Leadership Conference, Jones advised that King met James Hoffa, President, International Brotherhood of Teamsters, Chauffeurs, Warehousemen and Helpers Union, on 11/10/66 in Washington, D. C. Hoffa agreed to support King's organization by giving it $50,000 periodically. In return, King would support Hoffa when Hoffa enters the labor dispute between two labor organizations trying to organize hospital workers in Chicago, Illinois. Hoffa indicated he would do this even though his Union may only get fifteen to twenty per cent of the hospital workers as Union members.

According to Jones, Hoffa wants to have an association with the civil rights movement.

Jones further advised that during the meeting a committee was organized to handle matters of mutual concern between the Teamsters Union and King's group. Hoffa appointed one of his aides as the chairman of this committee.

OBSERVATIONS:

At the proper time, we will consider appropriate counterintelligence action to further expose this liaison between King and Hoffa. However, at the moment, no action of this kind will be taken because we should not risk jeopardizing the delicate source from which this information was obtained.

11/22/66

MR. TOLSON:

. . . called and said that Mr. Hoffa told him that he had learned through the grapevine that the President had been told that he had given Martin Luther King $50,000 for the civil rights movement. He said Mr. Hoffa stated he would not give 50¢ and that the President had gotten the opposite impression of how he felt and thought about King. He said Mr. Hoffa did not know who furnished this report to the President.

. . . stated that Mr. Hoffa further stated that he would like for him . . . to let Mr. Hoover know that he, Hoffa, could not agree more with Mr. Hoover about Martin Luther King and to tell Mr. Hoover "that the real big boss got a report from somebody that the Teamsters are going to give Martin Luther King $50,000 and this report is erroneous."

. . . said Mr. Hoffa asked him if he should issue a press release and he, . . . told him he could not advise him, but if he stirred up something he might be doing King a favor.

DSS

[Section 66]

UNITED STATES DEPARTMENT OF JUSTICE

FEDERAL BUREAU OF INVESTIGATION

New York, New York
December 20, 1966

Martin Luther King, Jr.
Security Matter-C

On December 16, 1966, a confidential source, who has furnished reliable information in the past, advised that he had learned that Stanley Levison and Andrew Young (Executive Director of the Southern Christian Leadership Conference (SCLC) had conferred on that date. According to the information which the source was able to ascertain, Levison and Young talked about a testimonial for James Hoffa (President of the International Teamsters Union) which Hoffa's local in Detroit, Michigan, was to have on December 20, 1966.

In that connection, Levison and Young discussed a telegram they were preparing for King which was to be read during the banquet. In essence, the greeting, as proposed for the telegram from King to Hoffa, would contain a statement that King would not make any effort to judge Hoffa (alluding to Hoffa's conviction and the impending jail sentences) since he (King) had been confined on several occasions, therefore, could understand how a vigorous man would have real difficulties facing confinement.

The source said Levison thought the greeting to Hoffa should also make some mention of Hoffa's accomplishments in the field of civil rights, spelling out that the Teamsters Union has over one million members who are Negroes.

This document contains neither recommendations nor conclusions of the FBI. It is the property of the FBI and is loaned to your agency; it and its contents are not to be distributed outside your agency.

Excerpts from
Electronic Surveillance File
1966

5/28/66

Levison calls direct to number for King. Coretta King gets on the phone and says that Martin is in Washington for the "Face the Nation" program tomorrow at 12:00. General conversation.

Mrs. King says she is interested in collecting the speeches and papers of Martin to keep their own history. She states that no other Negro has achieved Martin's prominence and stature and he deserves a library of his own. She says that she is upset because Boston University has the manuscripts of King and the family has nothing.

Levison: If he signed something that becomes active at his death he can change it. I'm glad you mentioned this to me it is the first I knew of it, I will talk to Martin about it.

Mrs. King: I think that Martin's Papers should be in the South anyhow.

Levison: Yes, that's right I think I will talk to Martin and it might be good to get some kind of a foundation interested in this. . . .

Jones, Fauntroy, and Levison on the line with King.

King: I've got to be on "Face the Nation" tomorrow and wanted to run through it with you. The most important question is Student Non-violent Coordinating Committee, the Black Nationalism, and the Black Panther Party; second, the Alabama elections; and then the Washington conference. And I guess the other thing will be Chicago and Viet Nam. So I wanted to get some of your thinking in the area. We should get a statement if they ask about SNCC and the Black Panther Party and Black Nationalism.

Levison says that Martin should always remember that the press always makes him a moderate and that he should urge non-violence but militant attitude and urge the Negro not to take abuse and that the economic and political means and . . . a brotherhood is the end.

King: Yes, the thing that should be brought out is that we have been militant, tough and non-violent. One other thing that we have to show the public is that their isolationism breeds such reactions as SNCC has.

Levison: Yes, on the one hand you have to make it clear that you are no part of a separatist trend. The more you use the word separatist

481

rather than nationalist the better. You hope to achieve unity in the Negro movement and you don't want to be pitted against others even if they are mistaken and you will undertake the task of handling the differences . . .

Jones: Well, I read yesterday the attack on the recommendations of the conference and the fact that the SNCC isn't going to take part in the government processes to care for the American Negro and the fact that such groups as SNCC are negative and will not even try will hurt the whole group.

King: Well couldn't I say it that way and that they could be at the conference and make some constructive beginnings because the government will listen to that.

Levison: Martin, maybe you could bring up an illustration of the late 40s and President Truman's committee that came through with many recommendations and they even pointed out that the Federal Government was the biggest violator of segregation and now the Administration has committees which have unearthed important conditions and spot lit them, but in the absence of a militant movement that compels the government to act, nothing is usually done.

King: I think that is a very good way to say it.

Fauntroy: Martin, I think one question you will get is where is the money going to come from: the billions of dollars.

Levison: I think one answer would be where did the money come from for a war? The answer is that it was necessary and so was the beautifying of the highways, etc. . . .

King: Yes, and if the point can be made that if Negro employment was as high as the white employment it could add money to the economy by 27 billion. Now about the long hot summer I always feel uncomfortable predicting riots and violence. How should we deal with this? . . .

Levison: You say that social science doesn't allow you to predict riots but that where injustice is located it could be there.

King: I don't believe the Alabama elections will come up. What about HUAC and the petition of 100 and nine thousand persons from 48 states urging an investigation of the SCLC and communist influence and me. I will just handle that like I did before. Now anything else?

Levison: Viet Nam.

Jones: The text of your remarks should be what you said at that resolution from SCLC; you should stick to that. The thought that the South Vietnamese Government retributions against their own people and the Buddhist right to engage in non-violent demonstrations.

Levison: One additional point regarding Negroes and the war and the burden of the war is heavier on them than on others because of the economic status of the Negro and the fact that more Negroes are at the front than other Americans and they are making a bigger contribution than anyone else and it's an unfair position for them. You can say the percentage of Negroes is double to the number in the army, unemployed, etc. . . .

King: What about MacNamara's statement on the Peace Corps and the Poverty Corps and the Draft.

Jones: I think you should comment favorably on that it would be better to do that than going to war and kill someone. Can't you start with the basic problem of non-violence and carry it to not killing another human being because it is violence?

King: Yes, that we do not see violence and murder as the true method of resolving social problems.

Levison: Yes, and about government service you could say you can agree if the government provides equal opportunity and equal justice but if not then it is unequal to call on anyone and that the government is unfair to Negroes and underprivileged whites in this draft thing. . . .

7/12/66

Dr. Martin Luther King calls Stanley Levison.

King: In light of the weather we had a good turnout at the Chicago rally. We had at least 60,000 people there, and the stadium was more than half full. They estimated 30,000, the police did, but the Negro commander policemen estimated 60,000 people but they would not use his figure. I think it went well . . . Did they have anything today on the meeting with Mayor Daley (Mayor of Chicago)?

Levinson: Last night there was a story, which said you were going to initiate demonstrations in connection with open housing because after meeting with Daley you felt you obtained nothing in the way of a commitment or promises from him.

King: I am calling about the starting point of the "action program" and as usual we are confronting our financial problems. I am convinced that the money is here in Chicago. It's a matter of organizing it. Most of the churches here will support us. The social clubs, there are three or four thousand of them. If we could get 1,000 of them to give 10 or 25 dollars, fraternities and sororities would give this out of guilt because these are middle-class Negroes who will not demonstrate but will give money. You have your businessmen and they are responsive. You have barbers and beauticians. I'm in a meeting now discussing it. We believe firmly there is 50,000 dollars here waiting for you if you organize. At the rally two or three churches brought 200 and 500 dollars.

Levison: You mean you did not take up a collection Sunday?

King: No. We couldn't take it in the stadium. We passed out envelopes in the buses but it was unorganized. I was wondering if we could get Bill Stein to take a stab at this. To spend a month or six weeks out here. And if there are situations where we need a front man we could provide a Negro for that. He (Bill) could structure this and we need someone who has had experience in fundraising ... He (Bill) would be the full-time man with other people giving the necessary suggestions. There is a lot of money in the white community that we haven't tapped. I went to two suburban meetings, 99% white and in both places they raised several hundred dollars and over a thousand at one place. They will give if you can just get to them. Guilt makes you give in many instances. I think we have it here, a gold mine, but we haven't tapped it ...

7/15/66

Levison and Andy.

Andy described the Chicago riots as the ''most frustrating damn situation I've ever been in.'' Andy explained that ''the people we're working with are so much a part of the problem and so hostile toward the police that we have as much fight to keep them from encouraging the riots.'' Andy told Levison that the attitude of some of the community organizations, who really could stop the riots, is so hostile that they share in the riots vicariously. And admitted that ''they're not horrified at the thought of Negroes rioting'' and likened the situation in this regard to the one which prevailed in Watts. Levison asked Andy, ''Isn't it necessary for you to take a position which doesn't make it appear as if you're assuming too much responsibility for putting a lid on it but that you actually throw the gauntlet to Daley? In other words, it's Daley's riot, not your riot. If Daley wants to sit on his behind and do nothing, he is the precipitator. It seems to me your role ought to be attacking Daley and making the attack sharp because Daley can't afford this.''

Levison predicted that the riots in Chicago would cause Daley to lose ''his comfortable position with his Negro vote and his Negro organization,'' all of whose members ''must be shaking in their boots.'' Andy took issue with Levison's appraisal of the affect of the riots on Mayor Daley and explained that ''Mayor Daley's control of the Negro middle-class mind on the South Side is what does it.'' Andy asserted that the hostility is directed against the Chicago police and not against Mayor Daley in the same way that the anger in the Chicago school situation was directed against Superintendent Willis and not against Mayor Daley.

Andy told Levison that ''the rioters are really the wild, young kids and the intellectuals are the ones that give them support and plant ideas.'' Levison suggested that a large section of the population in Chicago including part of the Negro middle class, is not unhappy about the riots and feel that ''they're giving them what they deserve to get.'' Andy again disagreed and insisted that the main block of the Negroes in Chicago did not feel this way. Andy also pointed out that ''Daley is in a very good position, even with us, because we have to say that Wilson is a damn good Police Commissioner'' but added that the head of the Police Fraternal Society in Chicago had charged yesterday that Martin Luther King had caused the current riots by teaching people disrespect for law and order through his advocacy of non-violence. Levison told Andy that ''they grab a situation in order to cut you down with it'' and insisted that ''you have to grab it and lay the responsibility at the door at which it belongs.'' Levison contended that, while the focus of the emotion (in the riots) might be directed against the police, it was the function of Andy's group to point out that the police are only a part of the municipal apparatus and the municipal leadership has done nothing about the whole body of grievances of the people. Levison emphasized that Andy's group had to turn the riots against Mayor Daley because ''they're going to turn it against you.'' Levison told Andy, ''I think the most dangerous situation you're in is not so much the one where people will be convinced that Martin Luther King is responsible for the riots but where they'll believe that he could have stopped them and he didn't. You've got to place the onus in this thing on Daley for failing to do what need to be done. Then, your meetings and everything else become constructed because they were demands that he do what needed to be done and he didn't do it.''

9/6/66

Conference call from Dr. Martin Luther King to Stanley Levison, Harry Wachtel, Ralph Cranton (phonetic), Bayard Rustin, Walter Thorcase (phonetic), Clarence Jones, Junius Briggs, Lawrence Redick, and Cleveland Robinson.

Rustin opened the conversation saying that he felt that the time had come for King, backed up by Phil Randolph, to speak to the Negroes of this country, but to speak to them from the position of militancy, and to speak to them from the point of view of defending them while urging them, for tactical reasons, to hold on to the message they have won. Bayard feels that the "Open Letter to Young Negroes" should be read now and then they could discuss it. While the letter is directed to young Negroes and may have some effect upon them, there is a political necessity far beyond young Negroes, which is, to let that nine-tenths of the population which we might convince that we are sincerely trying to make social changes by peaceful means; not be in the position of stopping their support, by which he doesn't mean financial, but moral.

Bayard said the letter would be sent to two categories: a) Boys Clubs, Boy Scouts, Girl Scouts, settlement houses, basketball teams, etc., where Negroes between the ages of 16 through 25 can be reached, b) Negro ministers, Negro press, Negro college presidents, high-school principals, fraternal organizations, women's clubs, Elks, Masons, unions with large organizations (the AFL-CIO are prepared to make it available in hundreds of thousands to their unions, urging them to reprint it in their magazines and newspapers) libraries, PTAs etc. . . . Bayard doesn't want King to read the letter alone, he wants Philip Randolph to back him up in case there is any fallout as there are not too many people prepared to attack Randolph.

Bayard reads the letter:
I write you not just as an older civil rights leader, but as a father deeply concerned about the future of my own children, Oakie and Martin, Dexter and Bunny. I write you as one whose skin is also black and who therefore knows your anguish and hopelessness in the face of continued discrimination, broken promises, and token progress. Never since I joined the freedom movement have I felt as much grief and distress as in these days. When around the country we see our cities transformed into racial battlefields. As the new school term opens I know that hundreds of thousands of you want to desperately return to school but you do not have the money to do so. I know that hundreds of thousands of you want nothing so much as to find decent jobs that will make it possible for you to buy the necessities and some of the nice things in life that make dignity possible. But I also know that many of you have walked the streets day after day after day only to find that no work is available for you. In this connection, I, yesterday, wired President Johnson urging him to make available enough funds so that all poor young persons in our society

could return to school. I also urged the President to place immediately before Congress a bill to create public works to provide meaningful employment for every able-bodied young person who needs it, whatever his present skills, his training, his color, may be. For I am convinced that the tragic ordeals we have passed through on the streets of our cities this summer are the results of the fear, the frustration, and the hopelessness on both sides that springs from our nation's failure to make it possible for all youth, especially Negroes, to obtain quality integrated education and dignified work. Since 1955, I have taken part in many struggles to make your life, and that of my children, more meaningful. In the course of these struggles in Montgomery, in Birmingham, in Selma, in Chicago, we have made some degree of progress, I believe, because we did not give in to bitterness, hatred and to violence. For this very reason I am convinced that thousands of people of every color and creed, moved by the justice of our cause, and the soundness of our methods, rose up to join in our quest for freedom. We must not now be so foolish to let a tiny minority of hateful bigots provoke us into emotional behavior, into actions which will destroy our movement and will separate us from others in this society whose help we sorely need. We must not fall into this racist trap. On the other hand a very small minority of you, overwhelmed by the injustice, have forsaken non-violence, and engaged in disorder. The vast majority of you have adhered to peaceful means. I implore all of you to remember that molotov cocktails, and looting and hatred, cannot, and will not, solve the problems we really care about. They cannot make jobs, or decent homes or good schools. Not for you today, not for your children tomorrow. I do not ask you to cool it, on the contrary, I urge you to become active in the freedom movement and to make it an irresistible power. I urge you to be prepared to use your energy in non-violent mass action protests in your community. You can march in the streets and make this nation aware of your grievances, you can mobilize your elders to go to the polls and put their voting power, the only real power, to work for you. You can organize at the grass roots level and demand police protection and respect. You can call for justice and freedom now. The fate of the rest of the Negro people may well rest in your young hands, it is up to you. Finally, let me congratulate you for your sense of discipline and responsibility in the face of grave frustrations and often brutal provocation. Here again I understand. I understand from the treatment I recently received in the streets of Chicago how painful such frustrations and provocation can be. Since the 1960 sit-ins, Negro youth have been the backbone of our movement. I implore you to continue your place of honor in the movement as our most courageous and clear-headed force.

Sincerely, Martin Luther King

King feels that the Negroes will think that this letter should be aimed at the white people. King is worried about being called an Uncle Tom. King doesn't want to give the Negroes forces that they have to deal with, a limb with which to hang him . . . Junius has arranged with NBC to get prime time to deliver the letter. Larry says it should be cut down . . . Junius doesn't want it delivered at a press conference because they will chop it up, he feels that it should be delivered in its entirety . . . feels it should be delivered the day before school opens. Ralph says they should get the idea that knowledge is power into the letter . . . think with their heads and not with their stomachs. Levison doesn't like the part where King says he today asked President Johnson for jobs; he's asked the President ninety times before and there has been no action. Levison says to threaten him by saying that if no action is forthcoming by May 1967, King and Randolph will have a march on Washington. The others don't like the idea. Robinson wants something about the peace movement in the letter, he feels it is a basic ingredient at this time with all the Negroes in the armed forces in Viet Nam. (King starts talking and has trouble with his connection as the rest of them can't hear him clearly. One of them asks the FBI to please allow them to hear King.) Ralph says to tell them that they can't solve problems with rocks any more than nations can solve them with bombs. Everybody agrees that this is good . . .

10/1/66

Clarence Jones to Stanley Levison.

. . . Levison said King has been very depressed lately over events, that King told him he has been talking and making speeches and doesn't really know what he is saying. Levison continuing, said he told Martin, ''we need to sit down, talk, discuss, raise questions, examine some theory, and stop letting action send us on kind of mindlessly from day to day.'' . . .

Jones said . . . there is no person in the civil rights movement who ideologically really is offensively taking Stokely Carmichael on. Jones said he thinks that Stokely is repeating political havoc, and he must be isolated like he is a black Trotskyite. Stokely is absolutely insane, and nobody is really going after him with a hammer and tong; that there is too much toleration of him. Jones stated, there comes a time in a political movement when you have to call a spade a spade, and you have to fight for the supremacy of your theory; that if your theory is being attacked, you have to isolate those people who are trying to destroy it. Jones said some of the people he has been talking to have accused him of trying to make an argument to excuse white supremacy and racism, and that the problem is not Stokely but racism. Levison said that is nonsense ... and Jones responded that is sophistry.

Levison and Jones said that what happened in Georgia is incredible, and the apparent cause is racism which didn't have to happen if that idiot ... Stokely ... did not start a riot in Atlanta. (Maddox running for election in Georgia.) Levison and Jones agreed that Stokely must be politically isolated. Jones said if Stokely is not politically isolated, he just cannot see how there is any reasonable possibility of bringing about any successful alliance. Explained that a responsible political theory has to demonstrate that it can fight for its own position. Levison replied in his opinion, by leading a small group into battle at the wrong time, Stokely did more damage to the movement than a person who would have been a paid agent ...

10/11/66
Stanley Levison calls his brother Roy Bennett.
. . .
Stan: ... *The Times* yesterday had the story that we will consider expelling SNCC and CORE. It will be on the agenda because Bayard and NAACP and the director of the Jewish agencies wrote the statement. . . . I would suspect that to join with the NAACP when you're going to attack and isolate another element in the movement is suicidal for Martin. Often enough the press calls him a moderate and this would seal it.

Roy: I wondered about that part. It had the look of the right wing ganging up.

Stan: And there is a difference between CORE and SNCC. CORE is trying to break away and be more responsible and Carmichael isn't. Carmichael himself should be isolated while you should try to keep some of the elements that follow SNCC. Really what you're contending for is a substantial number of Negroes who are attracted to the slogan [Black Power]. That's who you don't want to alienate because they are the young upcoming activist group. It's almost like in the Soviet Union. There is an age breakdown here. The guys who

prepare a statement like this all have gray hair.... Clarence Jones
and I agreed that the slogan has to be done away with. The word
"black" is fine and Martin should have used it much more in the
past; black consciousness, black unity, and so forth. And the word
"power" is good. There is a whole section in his book "Why We
Can't Wait" on power and the importance of power, that he blue-
penciled, you know, because he did not like the word power, you
know.

Roy: Yeah, because it is not non-violent.

Stan: You can use those words but not together because now Black
Power has been associated with riots, violence and it's silly to hold
on to a slogan that's not terribly good anyway....

10/15/66

Bayard Rustin to Stanley Levison.

Stanley said when he asked Martin for a reason for his positive reply
to the question "do you endorse statement issued by other civil rights
leaders?" he replied, "I thought we agreed that that is what I would
say." Stan added he then reminded King of what he had told him
earlier stating, "he should say he finds nothing in it that he doesn't
agree with, but his own statement to the press was his feelings on the
matter." Stanley continuing, explained that the statement is a little different from the endorsement....

Bayard said King still has to make up his mind publicly and state
whether he [will] endorse the statement or not.... Levison explaining
King's position said, "the position is and could be that there is only a
certain margin of difference between King and the others, and King
differs only in the fact that he doesn't want to ignore or isolate those
who have an erroneous slogan at the present time." ...

Bayard then said he thinks that Martin Luther King will be in a jam
when hundreds of Negroes in the country will be endorsing and signing
a statement of this nature and his name isn't on it. In his opinion it is
a very serious mistake for King.

Levison explained it is his feeling that King will not sign the statement no matter how many were going to sign it.

Bayard: You can't continuously put yourself in the middle this way,
and that is what Martin has done again.

Levison: He wants to, and that is precisely the thing even if he is alone
in the middle, he doesn't care.

Bayard: It's bad with a large segment of white liberals, and it's also
bad with the Negro middle classes.

Levison: I am not convinced of that....

Stanley Levison to Rev. Andy Young.

Levison learned that Dr. King is in Atlanta. Levison read story in *New York Times* with headline: "Dr. King Endorses Racial Statement, Backs Negro Repudiation of Black Power Concept."

Young: Isn't that a shame.

Levison: In other words, you can't read this without assuming he didn't have a chance to sign it, and as soon as he did he endorsed it. John Morsell called Bayard this morning, and said Martin decided to sign it. Bayard called me, which is most unusual, he rarely ever calls me. I must assume he called me because he had a purpose. He said dozens, hundreds of people want to sign the statement. He said Martin is in a very difficult position now, he can hardly not sign it.

Young: Bayard did this to us.

Levison: I was convinced when he called me that he did it. I have been thinking about it, and I may have a quicker reaction than you. I think Martin has to write a letter to the *Times* in which he clearly defines where he stands. . . .

Young: . . . He should say that while he realizes the role of Urban League and NAACP, he never thought his role to be synonymous with theirs. Also, that while he understands the frustrations of the black people and their disillusionment with the administration, he is not ready to give up.

Levison: I think he has to say just that.

Young: In effect, he should say this is the reason he did not sign with the others because it was polarizing the civil rights movement. The ad in the *New York Times* should be headlined "Who seeks to divide us?" Maybe the ad should also go into the politics of the civil rights movement for the first time and call on whites and liberals and Negroes to stand together.

Levison: If you jump off to the approach "who seeks to divide us?" you are implying that it is the conservative wing.

Young: I am ready to say that it is the administration trying to divide us.

Levison: Oh, that I go along with you on. . . .

Stanley Levison to Martin Luther King Jr.

Levison points out *Times* article headed "Dr. King Endorses Racial Statement," which notes that King had not signed the original petition rejecting black power but did at a news conference today, join with his support of the petition, advanced by the NAACP. King replies "that just shows you how you can get in a bind.'' Levison says that he is convinced that Bayard did this and that Andy agrees that it was Bayard's doing.... Levison says he thinks Bayard wants to box you (King) in and ... "you are boxed in.'' Levison notes that Bayard maintains that King cannot take a middle position and Levison says that he told Bayard that a middle position is exactly what Martin must take. King asks Levison what can we do about this. Levison says first that a letter must be sent to the *Times* acknowledging that you endorsed the statement but adding that the endorsement was of the four principles that you had always accepted, however, the press has chosen to read this act as a rejection of black power concepts and the organizations ... this you cannot accept and must clarify what your position is—i.e., rejecting black power as a slogan and any injury it may cause but not rejecting the need for participation and power of Negroes and, of course not accepting the theory that any excommunication of certain groups should be carried out. King says "I think that's the only way out, but what bothers me is when I make these tactical errors it's usually when I'm trying to deal with Bayard.... I wouldn't have made that error if Bayard hadn't said if it comes up it would look bad for you to say anything against us,'' yet I could have said it. King laments "I dunno why I didn't think to ask. What should I say if they ask about this?'' ... Levison says, "You are going to have to rethink this business of treating Bayard as one of your advisors and rather treat him as if he's John Morsell or Roy (Wilkins) where you are on your guard.'' King says "It makes me look as if I don't have any integrity, especially after I told Floyd that I didn't sign the petition.'' ...

They agree to get out a letter in which Martin can clarify his position as different from CORE and SNCC but not so far that he cannot work with them showing that Martin cannot be pulled to either the conservative or the extreme side....

10/23/66

Stanley Levison to Rev. Jackson in Chicago, Illinois.

... Levison addressing Jackson by first name, Jesse.... Jesse said he addressed the American Jewish Congress yesterday, and he feels that relationship with this group has not been sufficiently appealed to; that it is necessary to cultivate a relationship with these Rabbis all across [the] country.... Levison [said] he is on the National Executive Board of the American Jewish Congress, and for the past couple of weeks the "Board" has been meeting with the new National President who is a Rabbi from Cleveland . . . Rabbi Lelyveld, who was beaten up in Mississippi. Levison said Lelyveld expressed the opinion that he "will not back up because of black power but on the contrary, he wants to understand it." Levison added Lelyveld had discussions with Floyd McKissick . . . and he is not like the typical white liberal who is running away or using black power as an excuse for diminishing his interest. Levison, continuing, said "the thing that surprised me is Lelyveld is almost an apologist for black power." Levison said when he argued that the term "black power" is not a good slogan but stressing at the same time the need for power and the need for black consciousness, Lelyveld argued back that the term "black power" is a good slogan. Levison said this means Lelyveld has a pretty advanced type of thinking. Levison said other Jewish groups gravitate towards NAACP because there is a case of middle class liking middle class and at any rate, in these areas, he can help a lot. That the area he likes to see tapped which hasn't been adequately tapped is the Negro community itself where there is money but no one has organized any type of mechanism for getting it, and the first one who does that is going to do something revolutionary. Levison explained that there are a lot of Negroes who are not church goers, don't belong to any social club that raised money for the movement and are ready to give something if they are approached. He said years ago he had some experience in organizing people to go door to door in a big development in the community, and every door they knocked on they got something. Jesse said he is working on a plan to bring the Negro press to a level of real acceptability and get them tied up to SCLC objectives, and for that he is calling a meeting Thursday. He is also getting together with some insurance representatives and leaders to explain to them that they along with the Negro preacher could have a substantial drive to increase the dividends for those companies. That a kickback percentage of the gross that would take place in a given time should go to SCLC. . . . Jesse then said, "every deal we come in to we [might] carve out our level of economic self-interest before we get involved.". . .

12/22/66

Harry Wachtel to Stanley Levison.

Wachtel asked Levison how it felt to have been part of a "bug." Levison asked what. Wachtel said the bugging of Dr. King in 1963. Wachtel said he is referring to the article by James Reston. Wachtel said that Martin played it wrong by saying that he knew about it. Wachtel said that Martin should have shown great indignation about it.

Wachtel said a citizen should not treat something like that so lightly. Levison said probably because we did know about it. Wachtel said he felt, and several people agreed with him, that when you have a guy doing an illegal act you should not be so sweet about it.

1967

1967

[Section 67]

[Section 69]

[Section 70]

[Section 73]

[Section 74]

[Section 77]

[Section 67]

UNITED STATES DEPARTMENT OF JUSTICE

FEDERAL BUREAU OF INVESTIGATION

New York, New York
February 21, 1967

Martin Luther King, Jr.
Security Matter-C

On February 18, 1967, a confidential source, who has furnished reliable information in the past, advised that he had learned that Martin Luther King, President of the Southern Christian Leadership Conference (SCLC); Stanley Levison, a New York City Attorney and a real estate man; Andrew Young, Executive Director of the SCLC, and Cleveland Robinson, Secretary-Treasurer of District 65, Retail, Wholesale and Department Store Union, AFL-CIO, were in conference on that date concerning the role of Martin Luther King and the peace movement.

King is desirous of taking a firm stand against the war in Vietnam and of becoming a leader in the peace movement, which is currently attracting the support of students and "white liberals." He is, however, apprehensive of losing a forthcoming Ford Foundation grant if the SCLC becomes involved with a radical group. James Bevel, Chicago SCLC leader, who is now leading a peace committee, has been pressing King for support in this matter, but King intends to stall him until March 6, 1967, when King will attend a research committee meeting, concerning this problem in New York City.

Young and Robinson favor overt action in this matter viewing [it] as a moral problem requiring leadership of the masses. Robinson wants King to contact ministers and lead a grass roots peace movement. Young favors influencing Walter Reuther of the AFL-CIO to join the peace movement. After Reuther joins the movement, Young advocated that King approach President Lyndon B. Johnson and advise President Johnson that King will no longer be associated with the administration and that he is going to fight against the military service and for the peace movement. The coalition of labor and civil rights, in Young's opinion, would force an administration to capitulation.

Levison is skeptical of overt action in this area. He feels the most effective stand for King is as the leader of the civil rights movement. King, from this position, could attract support from the peace movement and exercise his influence through such individuals as Senators Jacob Javits, Robert Kennedy and William Fulbright. Levison also advocates persuading Walter Reuther to join the peace movement through his brother, Victor Reuther.

This subject will be discussed more fully at the March 6, 1967, research committee meeting.

On February 20, 1967, this source advised that King, Levison, and Joan Daves, a publisher's representative in New York City who handles the books which King writes, and Hermine Popper, who is editing King's new book [*Where Do We Go From Here: Chaos or Community?*], were in conference.

Popper is of the opinion that the chapters in the book written by King and the chapters written by Levison are excellent, however, they are obviously written by two different people with two different points of view. She finds an inconsistency in the handling of such subjects as White America, middle-class Negroes, white liberals and Negroes' abilities in the economic sphere. She feels that these inconsistencies destroy the book's unity.

King and Levison disagree with her and feel that any differences are inconsequential and that no serious inconsistencies exist. Levison maintains that he knows exactly what King is thinking and adapts his thinking to King. Levison feels that any inconsistencies are due to poor formulation and not to a difference of thought or approach. Both Levison and King will reread their first drafts and submit minor corrections, but no major changes are anticipated.

[Section 69]

UNITED STATES DEPARTMENT OF JUSTICE

FEDERAL BUREAU OF INVESTIGATION

Los Angeles, California
April 13, 1967

DR. MARTIN LUTHER KING, JR.
SECURITY MATTER-C

The Los Angeles "Herald-Examiner," a major Metropolitan Los Angeles newspaper, on Wednesday, April 12, 1967, reported that Dr.

Martin Luther King, on April 12, 1967, accused the National Association for the Advancement of Colored People with misrepresenting his views on the Vietnam war. He told a news conference, which was held in Conference Room #8 at the Biltmore Hotel at 9:30 A.M. on April 12, 1967, that he favors a cessation of bombing, unilateral withdrawal of troops and an end to American participation in an "unjust war." He said it was true he believes the war is hurting the civil rights movement. "But," he said, "the NAACP has created a myth about my views on Vietnam, which confuses the clear issues." The article noted that King stated he was "saddened to think that the Board of Directors of the NAACP would join in the perpetuation of the myth about my views. They have challenged and repudiated a non-existent proposition." The article noted that in response to a question, King denied that he is or had ever been a member of the Communist Party, and according to the article, a moment later stated that though he is a "pacifist," he would have willingly fought against the Nazi menace in the 1940s.

A source who has furnished reliable information in the past, on April 12, 1967, furnished a copy of the prepared statement by Dr. King which was delivered before a press conference at the Biltmore Hotel in Los Angeles on April 12, 1967. The statement which was followed by a question and answer period by representatives of the news media, is set forth as follows:

I have lived and worked in ghettos throughout the nation, and I travel tens of thousands of miles each month which takes me into dozens of northern and southern Negro communities. My direct personal experience with Negroes in all walks of life, convinces me that there is deep and widespread disenchantment with the war in Viet Nam; first, because they are against war itself, and secondly, because they feel it has caused a significant and alarming diminishing of concern and attention to civil rights progress. I have held these views myself for a long time but I have spoken more frequently in the recent period because Negroes in so many circles have explicitly urged me to articulate their concern and frustration. They feel civil rights is well on its way to becoming a neglected and forgotten issue long before it is even partially solved.

Recently, a myth about my views on Viet Nam has confused these clear issues. The myth credits me with advocating the fusion of the civil rights and peace movements and I am criticized for authoring such a "serious tactical mistake."

I hold no such view. Only a few weeks ago in a formal public resolution, my organization, SCLC, and I explicitly declared that we have no intention of diverting or diminishing in any respect our activities in civil rights, and we outlined extensive programs for the immediate future in the south as well as in Chicago.

I am saddened that the Board of Directors of the NAACP, a fellow civil rights organization, would join in the perpetuation of the myth about my views. They have challenged and repudiated a non-existent proposition. SCLC and I have expressed our views on the war and drawn attention to its damaging effects on civil rights programs, a fact we believe to be incontrovertible and therefore, mandatory to express in the interest of the struggle for equality.

I challenge the NAACP and other critics of my position to take a forthright stand on the rightness or wrongness of this war, rather than going off creating a non-existent issue.

We do not believe in any merger or fusion of movements but we equally believe that no one can pretend that the existence of the war is not profoundly affecting the destiny of civil rights progress. We believe that despite the war our efforts can produce results and our strength is finally committed to that end. But it would be misleading and shallow to suggest that the role of the war is not hampering it substantially, and it can be ignored as a factor.

Loud and raucous voices have already been raised in Congress and elsewhere suggesting that the nation cannot afford to finance a war against poverty and in equality on an expanding scale [sic] and a shooting war at the same time. It is perfectly clear the nation has the resources to do both, but those who oppose civil rights and favor a war policy have seized the opportunity to pose a false issue to the public. This should not be ignored by civil rights organizations. The basic element in common between the peace movement and the civil rights movement are human elements.

I am a clergyman as well as a civil rights leader and the moral roots of our war policy are not unimportant to me. I do not believe our nation can be a moral leader of justice, equality, and democracy if it is trapped in the role of a self-appointed world policeman. Throughout my career in the civil rights movement I have been concerned about justice for all people. For instance, I strongly feel that we must end not merely poverty among Negroes but poverty among white people. Likewise, I have always insisted on justice for all the world over, because justice is indivisible and injustice anywhere is a threat to justice everywhere. I will not stand idly by when I see an unjust war taking place and fail to take a stand against it. I will continue to express my opposition to this wrong policy without in any way diminishing my activity in civil rights, just as millions of Negro and white people are doing day in and day out.

Q: Dr. King
King: Yes sir.
Q: What would you do sir, to bring the war to a halt?
King: I feel that the United States is superbly placed to initiate steps that I believe can bring an end to this war. The first thing I would suggest in line with that of many other people is the halting of the bombing. Secondly, I think we should take the initiative to bring about a ceasefire. I think unilaterally we can do that hoping that as a result of this it will create the atmosphere for negotiations. I think we should also begin the process of removing all military build-up in Southeast Asia . . . and stop interfering in Laos. I think the fourth thing that should be done is to make an unequivocal statement that the National Liberation Front should be a part of the negotiations, and also recognized realistically that many people in South Viet Nam follow the National Liberation Front, and that they must be a part in the future government. And finally I think we should just reconvene the Geneva [Convention, in other words abide by the Geneva Convention] by setting a date that we will remove our troops from Viet Nam, and I believe all of this will bring about a comment [sic] which will force Hanoi to negotiate.
Q: How then will we keep the civil rights moving at the same tempo, to bring the war to a halt, and what would you desire to see done there?
King: Well, I think many of the resources that we are putting in this war would be placed into programs that would certainly make equality and justice a greater reality for Negroes, and for all of the people of our country. We are spending about 35 billion dollars a year in Viet Nam, and we are not quite coming up to two billion in the skirmish against poverty, and until we get rid of this war and get rid of our obsession with it as a nation, these programs are going to continue to suffer, the programs dealing with poverty, the programs dealing with slums and getting rid of the blight of our cities, so that the resources in the war can well be turned and should be turned toward the ending of poverty and all of the conditions that make for our frustration and despair in our cities all over the country.
Q: Dr. King, we are talking about peace in Viet Nam, what about civil rights?
King: Well, I've tried to make that clear in this statement and I have

great respect for Dr. Bunche, but I certainly can agree with that. . . . I think I have not only a right but I think I have a responsibility to take a stand in both of these areas, and I don't think he weakens either. I said a few minutes ago that I am a clergyman and I take my responsibility as a clergyman very seriously and I think that along with the priestly function of the clergyman, there is a prophetic function, and that means that I must forever seek to bring insights of our _____ Christian heritage to _____ on the social evils of our day, and I think war is a social evil, consequently I must take a stand on this. I do it not out of anger . . . I do it out of great anxiety and agony and anguish of spirit in many points because I feel that this war is damaging the soul of our nation, and it is diverting attention from civil rights, so I do not see how anybody can fail to see the interrelatedness of the two issues.

Q: But in practical terms, doesn't this, number one, divide the civil rights movement to begin with, and secondly, lose the civil rights movement a great deal of support by those people who are in favor of war in Viet Nam?

King: I think the existence of the war in Viet Nam does much more to weaken the civil rights movement than my standing against the war in Viet Nam.

Q: (Cut off, cannot hear)

King: I think again the war in Viet Nam is a much greater injustice to Negroes in the Untied States than anything that I could say against the war, that is the only answer I can give to that. . . . Negroes are _____ in numbers, Negroes are 10% of the population of this country, and 22% of the deaths in Viet Nam. Negroes are experiencing spiritual and psychological death in the slums of our cities every day because the programs are not emerging to solve those problems, and they are not emerging in many instances because of the war in Viet Nam. Consequently, I would say that the injustice is being done to Negroes, and being done by the existence of this war, and not by any statement that I am making or any involvement that I may have in the peace movement.

Q: Dr. King, I'd like to put the question this way, sir. Some of your severest critics are basing their argument against you on the claim that your placing the principal blame for the war in Viet Nam on the United States rather than on the other side. Now, how do you deal with this argument?

King: Well, I deal with it only on the basis of the facts there is no doubt about the fact that we initiated the build-up of this war on land, on the seas and in the air. And, this is why I say that we must take initiative to end the war. There is no doubt about the fact that Viet Nam declared itself independent in 1945. We refused to accept or recognize Viet Nam at that time and this was before China, Communist China, came into being. After that for eight years we have supported the French and their attempt to recapture their former colony, and we supported it toward the end to the tune of more than 80% of the financial and supply build-up of that particular war, and even after the French started despairing of our reckless action we encouraged them to go on, and even after they were defeated and _____ we still were determined after the Geneva Accord in 1954, we participated in bringing to power Premier Diem who engaged in some of the most ruthless and oppressive actions known in that particular area of the world. We participated in helping Diem prevent the election of 1956 from taking place, so anybody can see that our hands are not clean in the situation. I am not white-washing Hanoi . . . I do not approve of violence, I am a non-violent believer devotee and I want this conflict to be solved non-violently, without violence, but we must admit that the United States has participated in this build-up and I think it is because of the misreading of history on our part, a kind of paranoid or morbid fear of communism.

[Section 70]

UNITED STATES DEPARTMENT OF JUSTICE

FEDERAL BUREAU OF INVESTIGATION

New York, New York
April 13, 1967

Communist Infiltration of the
Southern Christian Leadership
Conference (SCLC)
Internal Security-C

On April 11, 1967, a confidential source, who has furnished reliable information in the past, advised that information had come to his attention which disclosed that Stanley Levison and Dora McDonald, personal secretary to Martin Luther King, the President of the SCLC, were in contact on that date concerning a statement King was to make on April 12, 1967, in Los Angeles, California.

The statement King would make, according to the source, would try to explain his position on the Vietnam War in order to counter the adverse criticism he is receiving. The following is in substance the contents of a statement Levison gave to McDonald for transmission to King to be used by him:

King was to state that he had lived in ghettos in Chicago and Atlanta, and had traveled thousands of miles each month, which had taken him into Negro communities across the nation; that his direct personal experience with Negroes in all walks of life convinced him that the majority opposed the war in Vietnam. Their opposition, King would say, is based on two reasons: they are against the war itself and they feel it has caused significant and alarming diminishing concern to civil rights progress [sic].

In the speech prepared by Levison, King was to attribute his recent opposition to the war to many requests from Negroes that he articulate their concern and frustration. They (Negroes) feel, King was to say, that civil rights is well on its way to becoming a neglected and forgotten issue long before it is even partially solved.

With regard to the criticism King had received from the National Association for the Acvancement of Colored People (NAACP), the statement prepared by Levison would have King state that it was untrue that he advocated the fusion of civil rights and the peace movement; that he and the SCLC had expressed their views on the war and had drawn attention to its damaging effects on civil rights programs, but do not want a merger or fusion of movements.

The statement commented that the war is hampering the civil rights program, therefore, could not be ignored as a factor. The basic elements in common between the peace movement and the civil rights movement are human elements, Levison's statement observed.

In conclusion, the statement, as prepared by Levison, noted that King did not believe the nation could be a moral leader of justice, equality and democracy if it became trapped in the role of a self-appointed world policeman; and that he would reiterate his determination to express his opposition to this wrong without in any way diminishing his civil rights role.

UNITED STATES DEPARTMENT OF JUSTICE

FEDERAL BUREAU OF INVESTIGATION

New York, New York
April 14, 1967

Communist Influence in Racial Matters
Internal Security-C

On April 12, 1967, a confidential source, who has furnished reliable information in the past, advised that Martin Luther King, Jr., President of the Southern Christian Leadership Conference (SCLC), was in conference on that date with the following individuals: Harry Belafonte, prominent entertainer; Harry Wachtel and Stanley Levison, New York advisors to King; Andrew Young, Executive Assistant to King, and Cleveland Robinson, Secretary-Treasurer of Local 65 of the Wholesale-Retail Store Workers of America. The following is a resume of what transpired:

King prefaced his remarks by commenting that a campaign is under way to undermine his leadership in Negro communities because of his stand on Vietnam. King had in mind the criticism of Dr. Ralph Bunche, United States Representative to the United Nations, who reported to the press on April 12, 1967, that King should not try to lead both the civil rights movement and the crusade against the war.

Andrew Young reported that Bunche had agreed to meet with Dr. Benjamin Spock and King following Saturday's (March [sic] 15, 1967) march at the United Nations.

With regard to the criticism from Bunche, Belafonte remarked Bunche had never made a contribution to the civil rights struggle. As to the National Association for the Advancement of Colored People's (NAACP's) criticism of King, Belafonte said Roy Wilkins of the NAACP recently received an award from Secretary of State Dean Rusk, which accounts for the fact that they are in agreement.

Levison commented he was not in agreement that Saturday's event was the answer for King. It was his belief that the press will handle the event in the same manner as they handled other Negro reactions, but Levison said that Saturday would not be King's only chance to speak. It was his belief that Saturday's demonstration will be composed of ninety percent white people, and therefore, King's advisors must insure Negro community support for King. Levison urged that a newspaper advertisement be run following Saturday's demonstration asking whether King can be active in the peace fight.

Contrary to the opinions of his advisors, King thought Saturday would be most important since it will be the largest peace demonstration in the country. Wachtel agreed, but cautioned King not to rely on Saturday's demonstration as his opportunity to oppose the war, since many people will not respond due to the "red baiting atmosphere."

King, in trying to suggest ways to bring about harmony among Negroes, said he would try to meet with A. Philip Randolph, President of the Brotherhood of Sleeping Car Porters, and other Negro leaders to explain his position. He reiterated his belief that the criticism of him is an effort to get him and to undermine him, and offered proof of this by pointing to criticisms of him whereas no Negroes will attack Congressman Adam Clayton Powell.

Wachtel, in agreeing with King's conclusion, said that they may even pull "J. Edgar Hoover's old stuff" out of the bottom of the bag.

The conference ended with an agreement to meet again on Saturday night, April 15, 1967, at Belafonte's house, and that King should confer with Dr. Bunche and A. Philip Randolph.

Following the aforementioned conference, King and Levison conferred privately since King wanted Levison's observations free from the others. In order to insure success on Saturday, Levison suggested having spots on the radio and will confer with Robinson about it. Levison cautioned against having these radio spots appeal to Negroes to follow King on Saturday because most Negroes do not want to become identified with this demonstration.

King's speech, to be delivered at the United Nations on Saturday, April 15, 1967, was discussed, particularly the length of it. Levison asked King to cut out the parts dealing in history, defense, and the United Nations. King agreed and asked Levison to prepare a paragraph stating that even though many people feel the United States should unilaterally withdraw from Vietnam and that no damage would be done to the United States' position and would, in fact, heighten prestige, King has concluded it will not be done, so his concern be to bring the war to an end.

Levison advised King to retain the part in the speech that fifteen million Americans oppose the war in addition to those who are half-hearted about United States involvement.

In trying to arrive at a decision as to what course King should follow after Saturday, Levison advised him to unite with people who have been isolated following their criticism of the United States, so he would be aligned with those who have power and who make a difference rather than be aligned with a fringe element as he is now.

According to the source, Levison feels that King's peace position is so far advanced that it has isolated him the same way Paul Robeson's pro-Soviet position isolated him.

UNITED STATES GOVERNMENT
Memorandum

TO: Mr. W. C. Sullivan   DATE: April 14, 1967

FROM: C. D. Brennan

MARTIN LUTHER KING, Jr.
SECURITY MATTER-C

PURPOSE

The purpose of this memorandum is to recommend that either Assistant to the Director DeLoach or Assistant Director Sullivan be approved to personally contact and brief Governor Nelson Rockefeller of New York concerning the communist influence on Martin Luther King, inasmuch as King is to meet shortly with Governor Rockefeller and King's communist advisors hope to take advantage of the forthcoming meeting to influence events in Latin America along communist lines.

BACKGROUND

Last week, through ... we learned that Stanley Levison, the concealed communist who is Martin Luther King's chief advisor, was in contact with an associate to whom he disclosed that he had recently talked to Rockefeller. This apparently is Governor Nelson Rockefeller of New York because Levison said the discussion concerned Venezuelan iron ore deposits about which Rockefeller enterprises are negotiating with the Venezuelan Government.

Levison also told his associate that Rockefeller was disturbed about Martin Luther King's position on Vietnam and wanted to meet King to discuss it. Levison told his contact this pleased him because it would give King the opportunity to present to Rockefeller King's views on Latin America which he feels has the potential of becoming the next Vietnam. According to Levison, King wanted to use the opportunity to advise Rockefeller on the steps that should be taken in Latin America supposedly to avoid this.

The following day April 6, 1967, the same source advised that Levison was contacted by Harry Wachtel about King's meeting with Rockefeller. As you know, Wachtel is King's other close advisor and Wachtel also has had past communist affiliations. Wachtel told Levison that arrangements had been made to have Martin Luther King met Rockefeller on either April 22 or April 24, 1967.

OBSERVATION

Martin Luther King has clearly become merely a puppet in the hands of Levison and Wachtel. He relies on both these individuals more than anyone else and they currently are directing most of his activities and shaping most of his public speeches in a way that goes straight down the communist line. These two men have guided King to a position whereby they are attempting to make him not only the acknowledged leader of the 22 million Negroes, but now the accepted leader of the vast anti-war effort in the country. Tomorrow, for example, King will play the most prominent role as the spokesman for the peace protesters in the demonstration in New York City. His recent vicious condemnation of the United States in a public speech shows how much of a communist puppet he has become and illustrates the danger he represents in the hands of the scheming communists.

Now Wachtel and Levison see an opportunity to project the communist line further into Latin American activities through King by attempting to have King influence Rockefeller in his thinking. The danger in this is that Rockefeller, through his vast Latin American holdings, is very influential in Latin American affairs, and if he buys any of King's ideas they will definitely represent the communist ideas of Levison and Wachtel.

On the surface Wachtel is a partner in the law firm of Rubin, Wachtel, Baum and Levine, 598 Madison Avenue, New York, New York, a very large and influential law firm. Levison on the surface is the owner and operator of the Park Management Realty Company, 1841 Broadway, New York, New York. Both of their past communist affiliations have been well concealed and today neither of them ostensibly have any connection with the Communist Party; nevertheless, from our experience they represent two of the most dedicated and dangerous communists in the country.

Once previously, in December 1964, King had occasion to have dealings with Governor Rockefeller and we arranged to have Rockefeller briefed by former Special Agent . . . concerning Levison's influence on King and . . . Either . . . did not make much of an impression or Rockefeller chose for reason of political expediency to ignore it inasmuch as

we learned in October 1965 that Rockefeller gave King a $25,000 dona-
tion, spoke in King's church in Atlanta, and had dinner with King's
father and his family.

Despite this, the stakes are too high in what is involved in the current
forthcoming meeting with King and Rockefeller for us not to do something to prevent the communists from influencing Rockefeller through
King. It is believed that we should again make an effort to brief Rockefeller, not only about King, but also in regard to the backgrounds of
Levison and Wachtel and that this time it should be done personally
through either Mr. DeLoach or Mr. Sullivan, either of whom could
handle this discreetly, prudently, tactfully and in a manner which would
insure that the FBI's interest would be completely protected and
assured.

UNITED STATES DEPARTMENT OF JUSTICE

FEDERAL BUREAU OF INVESTIGATION

New York, New York
April 19, 1967

Communist Influence in Racial Matters
Internal Security-C

On April 17, 1967, a confidential source, who has furnished reliable
information in the past, furnished the following information:

Stanley Levison and Gloria Cantor, the secretary to Harry Belafonte,
the well-known entertainer, were in contact on that date concerning an
affair which took place on Saturday afternoon, April 15, 1967, following
the demonstration at the United Nations protesting the war in Vietnam.
The affair, which was held at Belafonte's house, was attended by Cantor, Levison, Martin Luther King, Stokely Carmichael and others.

It was Levison's opinion, in summing up the results of the discussion
which took place at the affair, that progress was made since it was
agreed not to argue and criticize each other (Carmichael and King) on
matters not agreed to, but instead, to cooperate on common goals. Levison was of the opinion that Carmichael made a conscious effort to
be cooperative.

Cantor did not agree with Levison's statement that Carmichael was
cooperative, commenting that he was talking down to King. She does

not trust Carmichael; neither does Levison. However, Levison feels differently toward him because he (Carmichael) knows that the kind of program he wants to advance is impossible for him with or without King. What Carmichael contends, according to Levison, is that there can be no advances made in civil rights unless Negroes form an armed resistance group, and resist the draft and resort to violence. This is hopeless and stupid in Levison's eyes; Carmichael wanted to open a program of cooperation with King so that he could tour the country with King. It was Levison's conclusion that he just wanted to be with King so that he could draw an audience.

Cantor, according to the source, can be described as a hero worshipper of Martin Luther King, but recently she has formed some reservations in her own mind about some of his actions. In explaining, Cantor was disappointed to see King let Belafonte "push" him into an embarrassing situation during their discussion with Carmichael and other representatives of the Student Non-Violent Coordinating Committee (SNCC). Cantor was very sorry to see Belafonte side with SNCC rather than King. It is her feeling that due to Belafonte's pressure on him, King is beginning to think like SNCC.

Cantor then revealed to Levison that she was upset to see that Belafonte could lead King. She opined that this may be due to King's indebtedness to Belafonte, since Belafonte continues to pay for "his nurse" (King's). Levison acknowledged that he knew about it, but felt it was due to the fact the King has a constant struggle with expenses.

Levison tried to console Cantor by telling her that King would never think and act like SNCC. He went even further and disclosed that King had told him that Belafonte was drawn to SNCC emotionally, but he (Belafonte) trusted King's integrity much more than he did SNCC's. Levison revealed that other discussions between King and Carmichael would take place thereby affording an opportunity to test the sincerity of both Carmichael and Belafonte.

It was Levison's belief that the trouble in the civil rights movement is due to the feelings of the radicals that King has to be a conservative and that Carmichael has to be a radical. Levison opined that Carmichael would eventually end up in defeat since he has no program to speak of and what he has, is an usound one. In elaborating, Levison felt that one does not call for insurrection in a place where you are outnumbered and outgunned.

Statement by
Dr. Martin Luther King, Jr.
Atlanta, Georgia
Tuesday, April 25, 1967

On Saturday of last week there appeared an article in several prominent newspapers which reported on several groups and individuals urging that I become a candidate for the presidency of the United States
in the 1968 elections. I must confess that I was quite surprised by these
sentiments and find it very hard to take them seriously. I understand
the stirrings across the country for a candidate who will take a firm
principled stand on the question of the war in Viet Nam and the problems of the poor in urban ghettos, but I must also add that I have no
interest in being that candidate. I have come to think of my role as one
which operates outside the realm of partisan politics raising the issues
and through action create the situation which forces whatever party is
in power to act creatively and constructively in response to the dramatic
presentations of these issues on the public scene. I plan to continue that
role in the hope that the war in Viet Nam be brought to a close long
before the 1968 elections and that this present Congress find both the
courage and the votes to once again move our nation toward a truly
great society for every citizen.

It is understandable that this war is tending to create a fluid political
situation. Should this fantastically unwise and futile war continue to
escalate toward World War III, and perhaps humanity's extermination,
and should the campaign for racial equality be further starved, rebuked
and forgotten, our country inevitably will be facing national disaster.
Such circumstances may well cause profound and broad-based political
realignments and make relevant an independent candidacy. But even
so, I do not conceive of this as my role.

I reiterate, I have no interest in any political candidacy and I am
issuing this statement to remove doubts of my position on this subject.

[Section 73]

FBI

Date: 6/6/67

AIRTEL

TO: DIRECTOR, FBI

FROM: SAC, DALLAS (157-NEW) (P)

SUBJECT: ALLEGED OFFER OF $100,000
         BY WHITE KNIGHTS OF THE
         KU KLUX KLAN,
         JACKSON, MISSISSIPPI
         TO ANYONE WHO KILLS
         MARTIN LUTHER KING, JR;
         MARTIN LUTHER KING, JR.-VICTIM

OO-Jackson

On 6/2/67 . . . presently an inmate . . . was interviewed by SA . . . and
. . . SA . . . at which time a signed statement was obtained pertaining to
an alleged violation of . . . civil rights since being brought to jail in . . .
The Bureau has been advised of that matter under caption . . .

After obtaining a signed statement in the civil rights matter, . . . orally
furnished the following information, requesting that his identity be concealed as the source of the information.

. . . stated that while at . . . until his release . . . he became friendly
with another inmate identified as . . . According to . . . the FBI had tried
to "get" . . . on bank burglary charges but were unsuccessful and . . .
was presently in the penitentiary on charges of concealing three stolen
autos and was due for release sometime next year.

. . . said he had previously met . . . before going to the penitentiary
in . . . and he recognized . . . "in the joint."

. . . said that just before he was scheduled to be paroled from . . .
approached . . . stating that he knew . . . was going . . . soon as he
squared away two local detainers [sic] and . . . told . . . he needed him
to set things up for him.

. . . told . . . that $100,000 had been offered by the White Knights of
the Ku Klux Klan to be paid to anyone who would kill MARTIN
LUTHER KING, JR.

. . . stated that after he was squared away on his two . . . charges . . .

wanted him to contact . . . and ask her when she next writes to . . . at the penetentiary to tell him . . . had arrived . . . indicated he would write and tell . . . that . . . was "O.K."

If . . . wanted to try to "pull this" himself, . . . would put him in contact with two people identified to . . . only as . . . colonel in the National Guard . . . and a second person whom . . . cannot now identify. . . . stated, however, that the unidentified person, according . . . had recently been appointed Deputy U. S. Marshall . . .

It was . . . understanding that if he were willing to pull the job, he was to get in touch with . . . advise her, and she would thereafter put him in touch with the above two men, both of whom . . . understands are associated with the White Knights. . . . stated these men would insure payment if KING were killed.

. . . continued, saying that if he was not interested in doing the job himself, he was supposed to "case KING's place," (location not specified) in Atlanta, and check the layout. . . . pointed out he could do this rather easily, as before serving time he worked for . . . After getting the layout, . . . was to tell . . . the set-up so that when . . . was released from the penitentiary he could handle it himself. . . . stated he would get a percentage of the money received by . . . for casing KING's residence. . . . stated that based on his knowledge of . . . he believes . . . is perfectly capable of committing the plot. He stated . . . "hates Negroes and lets them know it in the pen."

. . . also claimed that another inmate . . . a nearby cellmate of . . . when he was at the penitentiary, has knowledge of the aforementioned plot.

. . . is from . . . and has worked as a . . . in Rock Island. He is presently . . . charge . . . had asked . . . to contact May to determine if . . . could build a long barrel and firing pin for a new type of .38 automatic pistol. . . . know that . . . is . . . and a friend of . . . According to . . . intended to use this long barrel pistol with the scope and firing pin to be made . . . in the killing of KING. . . . planned to dispose of the scope, firing pin, and long barrel, and replace the original barrel and firing pin and in this manner the gun could not be traced to . . .

. . . claims he contacted . . . about . . . proposal and . . . reportedly told . . . he did not want anything to do with the plan . . .

UNITED STATES DEPARTMENT OF JUSTICE

FEDERAL BUREAU OF INVESTIGATION

New York, New York
July 12, 1967

Communist Infiltration of
The Southern Christian
Leadership Conference (SCLC)
Internal Security-S

On July 11, 1967, a confidential source, who has furnished reliable information in the past, advised that Martin Luther King, Jr., was in conference with Chauncey Eskridge, Chicago attorney and advisor to the Southern Christian Leadership Conference and Stanley Levison, principal advisor to King, on that date concerning matters pertinent to the SCLC.

King asked Levison's advice concerning a proposed boxing match between Cassius Clay (Muhammad Ali), admitted Minister of the Nation of Islam (NOI) and former heavyweight boxing champion, and Jerry Quarry, a heavyweight boxer. This match would be held in California and the proceeds would be donated to the SCLC according to a proposal made by Clay to Eskridge on July 11, 1967.

Levison advised King that this would be acceptable to him. He pointed out that Clay is a Negro who is strongly opposed to the war in Vietnam and that in the public mind this would be the basis of their relationship. Levison pointed out that this was much more acceptable than King's decision to address a "New Left" Convention, since King will be pictured as being part of the New Left. King indicated he would accept Clay's offer.

The same source advised that Stanley Levison was in conference with Harry Wachtel, New York advisor to King, later the same day concerning King and the SCLC. Wachtel was quite upset about the announcement that King was to be the keynote speaker at the "New Left" Convention in Chicago on August 31, 1967, and asked how this situation arose. Levison felt that the slanting of the release was the work of Donald Janson, "The New York Times" reporter whom Levison characterized as vicious. Levison stated that King was persuaded to speak at the convention by the husband of Ann Farnsworth since Ann Farnsworth has contributed $100,000 to King and King was scheduled to be in Chicago at the time of the convention. Levison feels that King sold himself because of Farnsworth's contributions, but that Andrew Young, Executive Director of the SCLC, was also to blame.

FBI

Date: 7/21/67

AIRTEL

TO: DIRECTOR, FBI

FROM: SAC, KANSAS CITY (157-472) RUC

ALLEGED OFFER OF $100,000
BY WHITE KNIGHTS OF THE KU KLUX KLAN
JACKSON, MISSISSIPPI TO ANYONE WHO
KILLS MARTIN LUTHER KING, JR.;
MARTIN LUTHER KING, JR.—VICTIM

Re Dallas airtel to Bureau 6/6/67

Enclosed is one copy each of the . . . regarding . . . and . . . for Dallas and Jackson. Both inmates presently confined . . .

. . . was unable to identify any present or former inmate known as . . . those interviewed reported such person was not known to them.

. . . an interview . . . by SA . . . advised that he considered the story by . . . regarding an alleged plot to kill MARTIN LUTHER KING, JR., just one of the . . . "cock and bull stories"

. . . stated that he is not an associate of inmate . . . knows him only well enough to recognize him in the institution and has never talked to him. He added that he, . . . keeps to himself, trying to serve his sentence without being involved in the troubles of other inmates and that he is not acquainted with the associates of . . . He denied knowing the identity of any inmate known as . . .

According to . . . it is well known to all inmates in the institution that he is a capable machinist and that he does a great deal of mechanical drawing in connection with the work done in this institution. He added that when he became acquainted with former inmate . . . he learned that . . . had few friends among the other inmates. Further that . . . liked to talk about himself as well as about any subject, with anyone who would listen to him. He explained that . . . found him a good listener and would often spend several hours in the doorway of his, . . . cell, talking while he, . . . was working on his drawings. He added that he seldom did much of the talking but only agreed with whatever . . . had to say on whatever topic was being discussed.

. . . stated he does recall that on one occasion . . . had mentioned that one . . . and he assumed . . . was referring to . . . had informed there was a plot to kill MARTIN LUTHER KING, JR. for $100,000. He added that . . . stated that it was "all set up" but that he did not want to tell him too much about it. . . . stated he informed . . . that he did not want to know anything about the matter. He said he further told . . . that KING was probably so well guarded that a person could not "reach him with a ten-foot pole." . . . also recalled that . . . claimed that . . . had told him to get in touch with someone whose name he mentioned but which he does not now recall, . . . when . . . was released.

. . . went on to state that he indicated to . . . that he . . . had heard some similar comment regarding $100,000 being offered to kill KING. . . . stated this referred to an occasion several years ago when he was drinking in some bar in Raleigh, N.C. He explained that he was not acquainted with any of the occupants of this bar. He added that some of the occupants were discussing the current racial problems and one individual made the comment that "Someone had a good idea when they offered $100,000 to get KING killed."

. . . further stated that at no time had . . . ever requested him to make any part of a gun. He stated that . . . had once inquired if he . . . could make a gun and that he informed . . . that any machinist with any ability could make a rifle. . . . recalled that he and . . . at the same time were talking about what an advantage it would be for the military to have a rifle with longer magazine or clip that would carry more cartridges than the one presently used.

. . . advised that when . . . mentioned the alleged plot to kill KING he paid little attention to what was being said and passed it off as just another of . . . stories.

. . . advised . . . that he was not an associate of . . . that he knew no inmate associate of . . . who was known as . . . and that he had never heard any comment from any source regarding a plot or offer of $100,000 for the killing of MARTIN LUTHER KING, JR.

. . . stated that for a period of time when he first arrived at this institution he frequently ate at the same table with . . . but that although there was no friction between them they made other friends with whom they eat. He stated that he is aware that . . . dislikes colored people and avoids contact with colored inmates but that he is not outspoken on the subject. He added that he had never heard . . . make any type of threatening or critical remark to any colored inmate and he is not known to have had any trouble with such inmates. . . . stated that he did not know any of the present associates of . . .

UNITED STATES DEPARTMENT OF JUSTICE

FEDERAL BUREAU OF INVESTIGATION

Atlanta, Georgia
July 25, 1967

MARTIN LUTHER KING, JR.
SECURITY MATTER-C

On July 25, 1967 . . . advised Reverend MARTIN LUTHER KING, JR., President, Southern Christian Leadership Conference, held a press conference at 11 A.M. that date at the Ebenezer Baptist Church, Atlanta.

Reverend KING announced this conference related to his concern over the current racial strife throughout the nation. He said he had forwarded a telegram to President LYNDON B. JOHNSON expressing his thoughts and recommendations regarding this matter. Reverend KING then distributed to those present at the news conference copies of this telegram.

. . . furnished a copy of this telegram which reads as follows:

I LISTENED WITH GREAT ANTICIPATION TO YOUR STATEMENT OF LAST EVENING, FOR I TOO HAVE LABORED WITH HEAVY HEART THROUGH THE TRAGIC EVENTS OF THE PAST WEEKS. THE CHAOS AND DESTRUCTION WHICH NOW SPREADS THROUGH OUR CITIES IS A BLIND REVOLT AGAINST THE REVOLTING CONDITIONS WHICH YOU SO COURAGEOUSLY SET OUT TO REMEDY AS YOU ENTERED OFFICE IN 1964. THE CONDITIONS HAVE NOT CHANGED, AND THOUGH THE AIMLESS VIOLENCE AND DESTRUCTION MAY BE CONTAINED THROUGH MILITARY MEANS, ONLY DRASTIC CHANGES IN THE LIFE OF THE POOR WILL PROVIDE THE KIND OF ORDER AND STABILITY YOU DESIRE.

THERE IS NO QUESTION THAT THE VIOLENCE AND DESTRUCTION OF PROPERTY MUST BE HALTED, BUT CONGRESS HAS CONSISTENTLY REFUSED TO VOTE A HALT TO THE DESTRUCTION OF THE LIVES OF NEGROES IN THE GHETTO.

FIRST THE RENT SUPPLEMENT BILL WAS KILLED THEN THE MODEL CITIES PROPOSAL WAS DRASTICALLY CUT AND FINALLY EVEN A BILL WITH NO POLITICAL OR FINANCIAL IMPLICATIONS, BUT GREAT HUMANITARIAN ASPECTS, WAS LAUGHED OUT OF THE HOUSE AND CONGRESS REJECTED A SIMPLE BILL TO PROTECT OUR CITIES AGAINST RATS. THE SUICIDAL AND IRRATIONAL ACTS WHICH PLAGUE OUR STREETS DAILY ARE BEING SOWED AND WATERED BY THE IRRATIONAL, IRRELEVANT AND EQUALLY SUICIDAL DEBATE AND DELAY IN CONGRESS.

THIS IS AN EXAMPLE OF MORAL DEGRADATION. THIS HYPOCRISY AND CONFUSION SEEPING THROUGH THE FABRIC OF OUR SOCIETY CAN ULTIMATELY DESTROY FROM WITHIN THE VERY POSITIVE VALUES OF OUR NATION WHICH NO ENEMY COULD DESTROY FROM WITHOUT.

I DO NOT THINK WE ARE HELPLESS; WE ARE ONLY ACTING HELPLESSLY. I SHOULD LIKE TO OFFER A SINGLE PROPOSAL THAT I AM CONVINCED WILL BE AS EFFECTIVE AS IT IS JUST.

EVERY SINGLE OUTBREAK WITHOUT EXCEPTION HAS SUBSTANTIALLY BEEN ASCRIBED TO GROSS UNEMPLOYMENT, PARTICULARLY AMONG YOUNG PEOPLE. IN MOST CITIES UNEMPLOYMENT OF NEGRO YOUTH IS GREATER THAN THE UNEMPLOYMENT LEVEL OF THE DEPRESSION 30'S

LET US DO ONE SIMPLE DIRECT THING—LET US END UNEMPLOYMENT TOTALLY AND IMMEDIATELY. IN THE DEPRESSION DAYS THE NATION WAS CLOSE TO PROSTRATE ON THE BRINK OF BANKRUPTCY, YET IT CREATED THE WPA TO MAKE MILLIONS OF JOBS INSTANTLY AVAILABLE FOR ALL EXISTING LEVELS OF SKILL. THE JOBS WERE TAILORED TO THE MAN, NOT THE MAN TO THE JOB, IN RECOGNITION OF THE EMERGENCY. TRAINING FOLLOWED EMPLOYMENT, IT DID NOT PRECEDE IT AND BECOME AN OBSTACLE TO IT.

WHAT WE DID THREE DECADES AGO DURING AN ECONOMIC HOLOCAUST CAN EASILY BE DONE TODAY IN THE COMFORT OF PROSPERITY.

I PROPOSE SPECIFICALLY THE CREATION OF A NATIONAL AGENCY THAT SHALL PROVIDE A JOB TO EVERY PERSON WHO NEEDS WORK YOUNG AND OLD, WHITE AND NEGRO. NOT ONE HUNDRED JOBS WHEN 10,000 ARE NEEDED. NOT SOME CHEAP WAY OUT.

NOT SOME FRUGAL DEVICE TO MAINTAIN A BALANCED BUD-

GET WITHIN AN UNBALANCED SOCIETY. I PROPOSE A JOB FOR
EVERYONE, NOT A PROMISE TO SEE IF JOBS CAN BE FOUND.

THERE CANNOT BE SOCIAL PEACE WHEN A PEOPLE HAVE
AWAKENED TO THEIR RIGHTS AND DIGNITY AND TO THE
WRETCHEDNESS OF THEIR LIVES SIMULTANEOUSLY. IF OUR
GOVERNMENT CANNOT CREATE JOBS, IT CANNOT GOVERN.
IT CANNOT HAVE THE WHITE AFFLUENCE AMID BLACK POV-
ERTY AND HAVE RACIAL HARMONY.

THE TURMOIL OF THE GHETTO IS THE EXTERNALIZATION
OF THE NEGROES' INNER TORMENT AND RAGE. IT HAS
TURNED OUTWARD THE FRUSTRATION THAT FORMERLY
WAS SUPPRESSED IN AGONY.

THE NEGRO KNOWNS THAT A SOCIETY THAT IS ABLE TO PLAN
INTERCONTINENTAL WAR AND INTERPLANETARY TRAVEL IS
ABLE TO PLAN A PLACE FOR HIM. IN ITS CALLOUS REFUSAL TO
BE JUST THE CIVILIZED SOCIETY IS DRIVING A WEDGE OF DE-
STRUCTIVE ALIENATION INTO THE HOPE OF HARMONY.

TRANQUILLITY WILL NOT BE EVOKED BY PIOUS WORKS.
TO DO TOO LITTLE IS AS INFLAMMATORY AS INCITING TO
RIOT. DESPERATE MEN DO DESPERATE DEEDS. IT IS NOT
THEY WHO ARE IRRATIONAL BUT THOSE WHO EXPECT INJUS-
TICE ETERNALLY TO BE ENDURED. I AM CONVINCED THAT A
SINGLE DRAMATIC MASSIVE PROOF OF CONCERN THAT
TOUCHES THE NEEDS OF ALL THE OPPRESSED WILL EASE RE-
SENTMENTS AND HEAL ENOUGH ANGRY WOUNDS TO PER-
MIT CONSTRUCTIVE ATTITUDES TO EMERGE.

I REGRET THAT MY EXPRESSION MAY BE SHARP BUT I BE-
LIEVE LITERALLY THAT THE LIFE OF OUR NATION IS AT
STAKE HERE AT HOME. MEASURES TO PRESERVE IT NEED TO
BE BOLDLY AND SWIFTLY APPLIED BEFORE THE PROCESS OF
SOCIAL DISINTEGRATION ENGULFS THE WHOLE SOCIETY.

MR. PRESIDENT, THIS IS AN EMERGENCY STATE AS
SURELY AS WAS THE RECENT CRISIS IN THE RAILROADS OF
OUR NATION. UNLESS CONGRESS CAN BE MOTIVATED TO
ACT IMMEDIATELY UPON SOME CREATIVE AND MASSIVE
PROGRAM TO END UNEMPLOYMENT, WE FACE THE POSSIBLE
SPREAD OF THIS TRAGIC DESTRUCTION OF LIFE AND PROP-
ERTY. I URGE YOU TO USE THE POWER OF YOUR OFFICE TO
ESTABLISH JUSTICE IN OUR LAND BY ENACTING AND IMPLE-
MENTING LEGISLATION OF REASON AND VISION IN THE
CONGRESS.

[Section 74]

UNITED STATES DEPARTMENT OF JUSTICE

FEDERAL BUREAU OF INVESTIGATION

New York, New York
July 25, 1967

Communist Infiltration of the
Southern Christian Leadership
Conference (SCLC)
Internal Security-C

On July 24, 1967, a confidential source, who has furnished reliable information in the past, advised that Stanley Levison, New York advisor to Martin Luther King, Jr., furnished a press release to Dora McDonald, secretary to King, pertaining to the racial situation in Detroit, for release by King. The text of this release, as furnished by Levison, is as follows:

"As the flames of riot and revolt illuminate the skies over American cities there is an intense desire to restore normality. Normality means that Negroes should cease looting stores while the white society resumes looting Negro lives. While no one should condone anti-social acts of Negroes nor [sic] should White America rationalize its destruction and depredations of its black minorities. The storm warnings have been posted a hundred times far in advance but those who have the power to create solutions have created trivialities and diversions. If it is wrong for Negroes to loot and burn, it is even a more horrible wrong for white armed forces to shoot to kill for larceny. This is an example of the moral degradation, hypocrisy and confusion seeping through society which ultimately must destroy its positive values. I do not think we are helpless; we are only acting helplessly. I should like to offer a single proposal that I am convinced will be as effective as it is just. Every single outbreak without exception has substantially been ascribed to gross unemployment particularly among young people. In most cities for Negro youth it is greater than the unemployment level of the Depression 30's. Let us do one simple, direct thing—let us end unemployment totally and immediately. In the Depression days the nation was close to prostrate on the brink of bankruptcy. Yet, it created the WPA to make millions of jobs instantly available for all existing levels of skill.

The jobs were tailored to the man, not the man to the job. In recognition of the emergency. Training followed employment, it did not precede it and become an obstacle to it. What we did three decades ago during an economic holocaust can easily be done today in the comfort of prosperity. I propose specifically the creation of a national agency that shall provide a job to every person who needs work, young and old. White and Negro. Not 100 jobs when 10,000 are needed. Not some cheap way out. Not some frugal device to maintain a balanced budget within an unbalanced society. I propose a job for everyone, not a promise to see if jobs can be found. There cannot be social peace when a people have awakened to their rights and dignity and to the wretchedness of their lives simultaneously. If our government cannot create jobs, it cannot govern. It cannot have white affluence amid black poverty and have racial harmony. The turmoil of the ghettos is the externalization of the Negroes' inner torment and rage. It has turned outward the frustration that formerly was suppressed agony. The Negro knows that a society that is able to plan intercontinental war and interplanetary travel is able to plan a place for him. It is callous refusal to be just and civilized the society is driving a wedge of destructive ailenation into the hope of harmony. Tranquility will not be evoked by pious words. To do too little is as inflammatory as inciting to riot. Desperate men do desperate deeds. It is not they who are irrational but those who expect injustice eternally to be endured. I am convinced that a single dramatic, massive proof of concern that touches the needs of all the oppressed will ease resentments and heal enough angry wounds to permit constructive attitudes to emerge. I regret that my expression may be sharp but I believe literally that the life of our nation is at stake here at home. Measures to preserve it need to be boldly and swiftly qpplied before the process of social disintegration engulfs the whole society.''

UNITED STATES GOVERNMENT
Memorandum

TO: Mr. W. W. C. Sullivan   DATE: 7/28/67

FROM: C. D. Brennan

          MARTIN LUTHER KING, JR.
          SECURITY MATTER-C

PURPOSE:

Attached for your approval for dissemination are communications containing the following:

BACKGROUND

On July 19, 1967, . . . advised that Stanley Levison, long-time secret Communist Party member and advisor to Martin Luther King, Jr., President, Southern Christian Leadership Conference, was in contact with King concerning the recent racial riots. Levison suggested King advocate a new program which would be implemented by the federal government similar to the Works Project Administration of the 1930's. Also, Levison dictated a press release to King's secretary on 7/24/67, which King was to use the next day.

In addition on July 25, 1967, his advisors urged King to issue a statement that would not condemn violence in the cities but would in a sense condone it. He was also to rebut the statements made by the President the night of July 24, 1967.

This information was disseminated to the President, the Attorney General, and his staff.

In his press conference King announced he had sent a telegram to the President urging the creation of a national agency similar to the Works Project Administration. An examination of the telegram discloses that a large percentage was taken verbatim from the press release prepared by Levison. However, it is interesting to note that during the press conference King stated he condemned the present riots and did not condone violence. He also supported the President's use of Federal troops to deal with rioting in Detroit, Michigan.

OBSERVATIONS:

Although King used a large percentage of Levison's press release in his telegram to the President, he did not follow the subversive advisor's recommendations completely. It is felt this fact should be brought to the attention of the President and the Attorney General. The telegram sent to the President by King will be included in the letter to the Attorney General.

UNITED STATES GOVERNMENT
Memorandum

TO: DIRECTOR, FBI   DATE: 8/9/67

FROM: SAC, JACKSON (157-7990) (C)

SUBJECT: ALLEGED OFFER OF $100,000
BY WKKKK, JACKSON, MISS.,
TO ANYONE WHO KILLS MARTIN
LUTHER KING, JR.;
MARTIN LUTHER KING, JR.—VICTIM
RM
OO: JACKSON

Re Dallas airtels to Bureau dated 6/6 and 7/14/67; Kansas City airtel to Bureau dated 7/21/67.

Enclosed is one copy of an FD-302 showing the results of interview with . . .

Jackson indices are negative regarding . . . informants and sources have no knowledge of alleged offer to kill MARTIN LUTHER KING, JR., and no further information has been developed which would lend credence to . . . story.

In view of the information this far developed, there does not appear to be any basis for further investigation regarding captioned matter, and this case is being closed.

FEDERAL BUREAU OF INVESTIGATION

Date   8/9/67

. . . after being advised the identity of the interviewing Agent and the nature of the interview, was told that she did not have to make any statement and that any statements she did make could be used against her in a court of law. She was additionally advised that she had the right to contact an attorney prior to making any statement. . . . advised the following:

She is acquainted with ... who is presently serving time in the ... Penitentiary ... She frequently corresponds with him. Early in 1964 after becoming acquainted with her, ... rented a room at her residence where he stayed for several weeks. As far as she knows this is the only time ... has ever spent in Mississippi. She does not believe that ... is involved or ever has been involved in an Klan activities or associated with anyone who was in the Klan. She has never associated with anyone whom she knew to be involved in Klan activities and has never been involved in Klan activities herself. She does not know ... of the White Knights of the Ku Klux Klan of Mississippi (WKKKKOM) or anyone associated with the White Knights.

She stated that she does not know any of ... associates, does not know anyone by the name of ... nor has ... ever mentioned ... name. She does not know of any alleged offer of $100,000 by the WKKKKOM to kill MARTIN LUTHER KING, JR. She has never heard anything similar to this mentioned and claims not to be involved in any such plot, especially since she does not know anyone who is a member of the Klan, especially the White Knights. She does not know anyone by the name of ... in the National Guard at Jackson, or anyone recently appointed as U. S. Marshal at Jackson. She did state, however, that her brother's name is ... but he is not in the National Guard, not a member of any Klan group, and does not know ... The only person she knows in the U. S. Marshal's Office is ... She also knows ... with the U. S. Marshal's Office. She considered both of these persons to be respectable people, and she thought most assuredly they would have no association with any Klan group.

UNITED STATES DEPARTMENT OF JUSTICE

FEDERAL BUREAU OF INVESTIGATION

San Fransisco, California
August 11, 1967

MARTIN LUTHER KING, JR.

On August 10, 1967, at the Fairmont Hotel, San Francisco, California, Dr. MARTIN LUTHER KING, JR. addressed a convention of the National Association of Real Estate Brokers, which is composed of Negro members of the real estate profession throughout the country. KING spoke to approximately 370 delegates and his speech was later televised over KQED, San Francisco.

Dr. KING's topic was "Turning Neighborhoods Into Brotherhoods," and had three main points: (1) The Evil of Racism; (2) Poverty in the United States; (3) The War in Vietnam

Racism:

KING discussed the historical roots of racism beginning with slavery, talked about the Emancipation Proclamation, and then discussed the Negroes' present situation, stating that there has never been any real commitment by the white people concerning "black equality." He said racial injustice is "black man's burden and white man's shame." He stated that the roots of racism are very deep in this country and said "the plant of reedom has grown only a bud, not a flower."

Poverty:

In discussing poverty, KING talked about the world situation, India's poor people, Negro unemployment, that 50% of the Negroes in the United States were in substandard housing conditions, that in ghettos Negroes pay more for less, that Negro schools are inadequate, and that Negro children were trapped with no way out of poverty. He stated that whites move to the suburbs and ignore the Negroes. Sometimes, he said, Negroes have given up because they cannot support their families and in trying to escape they turn to dope and alcohol.

Riots are partly a result of these intolerable conditions. However, riots are self-defeating. He stated his motto is not "Burn Baby Burn, but Build Baby Build, Organize Baby Organize." One cause of riots, he announced, was the nice, gentle, timid, moderate, who is more concerned about order than justice and who is always trying to delay progress. He also lashed out at the middle-class Negroes "who have forgotten the stench of the black waters" and have abandoned their responsibility.

He stated another cause of riots is Congress who is hypercritical and insensitive, and more anti-Negro than anti-riot. He blamed the State Legislatures for refusing to pass fair housing bills, labor unions for keeping Negroes out of unions, and the white clergy for remaining silent. He stated a destructive minority can destroy the majority.

He stated that President JOHNSON is more interested in winning the war in Vietnam than in winning the war on poverty here at home and Congress is more concerned with rats then Negroes.

America, KING said, has plenty of money to solve its problems, but it needs a will and for the Negores, a massive program like the GI Bill of Rights.

Vietnam War:

KING stated that the Vietnam War was now more serious than anything else in the world. He deplored this war for wasting national resources and destroying lives and society. He said the war has isolated the United States morally and politically, and scarred the image of this nation. The war has directed attention away from civil rights.

The United States has built a climate of violence in the world that is contagious. The United States is fighting against freedom in Vietnam and refuses to recognize the Vietnam fight for independence. The United States is not fighting communism, it is fighting a nationalist movement. He said that if KY were in the United States he would be called an "Uncle Tom" for fighting against his own people.

KING said the United States should admit it made a mistake in Vietnam. He said one of President KENNEDY'S finest moments was admitting, after the Bay of Pigs invasion, that the United States had made a mistake. Therefore, "I call on President JOHNSON tonight to say to the nation and the world that we have made a mistake in Vietnam." KING said the war must stop or the United States is risking being transformed into an inferno "that even Dante couldn't imagine."

In summation of his three main points, KING urged his audience to continue to move forward in these areas and ended by saying, "If you can't fly, run; if you can't run, walk; if you can't walk, crawl; but by all means keep moving."

UNITED STATES DEPARTMENT OF JUSTICE

FEDERAL BUREAU OF INVESTIGATION

New Orleans, Louisiana
August 24, 1967

UNKNOWN SUBJECT, ALSO KNOWN AS . . .
THREAT TO KILL MARTIN LUTHER KING; . . .
—COMPLAINANT

. . . was interviewed regarding a plot to kill Martin Luther King.
. . . advised on August 23, 1967, that she received the first of ten

phone calls ... at 3:55 P.M. on August 22, 1967, at her office. Individual identified himself as ... and stated that he is a member of the KKK. The Klan Unit was not further identified. ... told ... that he was calling from a pay telephone at ... Shreveport, Louisiana. He said the entire Klan had a plot to kill Martin Luther King. The plan had been in formation for the past three months. ... stated he was the person who would actually kill King, but he would give no other details about the plot to ... over the telephone. ... said that he had "sold out" and that he had but two hours to live. He did not say what he meant by "sold out" or why he had but two hours to live.

... wanted ... to contact an official of the NAACP in Shreveport and have this official meet him at ... where ... would relate the details of the alleged plot to kill King. ... stated that he wanted to talk to an NAACP official and have this official contact higher authorities in the NAACP. ... stated that if he were to call a high-ranking official of the NAACP they would not believe ... who had gotten the information personally from ...

Between 5:00 P.M. and 5:30 P.M. on August 22, 1967, ... came into the office ... also talked to ... and agreed to go to ... and meet ... stated that ... never met ... because ... called ... about 5:45 P.M. on August 22, 1967, and told her that ... did not meet him. ... called ... for the last time at 5:50 P.M. on August 22, 1967, and told her that she should come to ... and meet him. ... did not go because she could not find anyone to go with her.

... stated that he would explain the details of the plot to kill King to the NAACP in Shreveport for $500. He stated that this money would be used to get his wife and family out of Louisiana because he was doomed in view of the fact that he had "sold out." He stated this was the only reson he wanted the $500. ... had no further contact with ... following the last phone call to her office at 5:50 P.M. on August 22, 1967.

... originally contacted ... the Community Relations Service, U.S. Department of Justice, Little Rock, Arkansas. ... called the Little Rock and New Orleans Divisions of the FBI on August 22, 1967, and stated that ... in Shreveport had information regarding a plot to kill Martin Luther King ... did not identify ... was located August 23, 1967.

... Police, Shreveport, Louisiana, advised of the above information on August 23, 1967.

[Section 77]

UNITED STATES DEPARTMENT OF JUSTICE

FEDERAL BUREAU OF INVESTIGATION

Mobile, Alabama
December 12, 1967

PARADE AND RALLY HELD BY
THE UNITED KLANS OF AMERICA,
KNIGHTS OF THE KU KLUX KLAN,
December 10, 1967
Montgomery, Alabama

A parade and rally was held by the United Klans of America, Knights of the Ku Klux Klan, on December 10, 1967, in Montgomery, Alabama, from 2:00 P.M. until 4:15 P.M.

. . . advised on December 11, 1967, that he estimated approximately 65 robed Klansmen participated in the march and rally. He said about 100 people participated in the march including about 30 females, teen-agers and children. One female was dressed in a Klan robe. There were three pickup trucks, one car and a Volkswagen station wagon in the parade. He estimated the crowd including spectators at about 150. He said one State Trooper overheard a Klansman remark, "There are more Montgomery City Policemen and State Policemen here than Klansmen."

James Spears, Grand Dragon of the State of Alabama, United Klans of America, spoke at the rally. Spears was critical of President L. B. Johnson, talked about the Communist conspiracy in the United States, and said that the Klan does not stand for violence. Spears stated the parade was to reassure the people as to the United Klan of America's ideals and that it stands for America. Spears commented on the poor turnout for the parade and rally.

. . . advised on December 10, 1967, and December 11, 1967, that there were no incidents or trouble during the parade and rally.

. . . advised he would estimate the participants and spectators for the parade and rally at about 150. . . . overheard . . . that he was very much disappointed in the turnout.

. . . information received . . . was furnished to . . . Director of Public

Safety, State of Alabama; . . . Montgomery Police Department; and . . . Prattville Police Department, Prattville, Alabama. Pertinent information was furnished to . . . Montgomery Resident Office, 111th Military Group (IV), Montgomery, Alabama.

. . . advised that three crosses were burned in the Montgomery area Friday night. The crosses were quickly extinguished. . . .

. . . advised that Doctor Martin Luther King was present in Montgomery, Alabama, on December 10, 1967, and spoke at a 90th Anniversary meeting of the Dexter Street Baptist Church for the morning service. He said this church is located one block from the location of the Klan rally, which scheduled to get under way at 2:00 P.M. He advised that the congregation at the church had dispersed by 2:00 P.M. and Doctor King and party departed Montgomery at 3:20 P.M., December 10, 1967, and there were no incidents or trouble in Montgomery during his and his wife's stay.

Excerpts from
Electronic Surveillance File
1967

1/5/67

Stanley Levison long distance, person to person, to Dr. Martin Luther King, Jr., at 746-5042 in Atlanta.

...King tells Levison ... that he got a call (from Harry Wachtel) saying that Norman Thomas and "he" (Wachtel?) and Al Lowenstein (phonetic) and Bill Coffin (phonetic) want to see him (King) for about a half an hour as "they" heard that he is going to be in town (New York City). ... King then tells Levison that he doesn't know what Thomas, Lowenstein and Coffin want but that his impression is that it's something about politics because Lowenstein was telling him that "a group of people" felt that he (King) should run for President in 1968. King says this would admittedly be not with idea of winning, confirming that it would be to give an alternative. King says he is sure it's possible that that's what they want to talk to him about. Levison comments that it's an interesting idea. King agrees. . . .

1/9/67

Dr. Martin Luther King called Stanley Levison.

Levison stated that he was disturbed over the fact that a number of people were talking about King's silence in connection with Adam Clayton Powell. ... Levison told King that "when a front of defense this broad is set up, despite all the reservations that you feel, I have a feeling that you can't stay out of it without being isolated in the wrong way. In other words, it will be very difficult to explain to the Negro community why you would stay out if Roy Wilkins, a whole series of churchmen, in fact, what amounts to the principal leadership . . ." (has spoken out on behalf of Powell). King agreed that he would have to make some kind of statement on the Powell case despite the fact that "I have terrible agonies of conscience about it." ... King referred to Powell's lack of integrity and his criticism of civil rights leaders but stated that he must try to make the statement as "well-balanced as possible and not give the impression that I condone what is the most blatant expression of parading immorality that Adam constantly does." King pointed out that his statement could not emphasize Powell's moral irresponsibility and, at the same time, still defend Powell's right to retain his committee chairmanship. King asserted that many of Powell's constituents do not feel that he has been irresponsible but see him only as a Negro who "has made it" in the white man's world. . . . Levison dictated the following statement to him:

> The attempt to deprive Congressman Powell of his seat or his chairmanship, no matter from what angle one views it, is discriminatory because the same standards have never been applied to any other chairman. On these grounds, I strongly defend his right to retain both his seat and chairmanship. The issue is a clear one. Congressman Powell's rights do not depend on his popularity. No matter how repellent some of his conduct may be, it is not a basis for taking away the seat which only his constituents can confer on him. Nor is it a basis for denying him his chairmanship on the grounds of denial have been developed to apply exclusively to him.

1/14/67

Conference call with A. Philip Randolph, Martin Luther King, Bayard Rustin, Stanley Levison, Andy Young, Ralph Abernathy. Call initiated by King.

Randolph: I was planning to get in touch with you Monday. I'm so glad you called. I wanted to talk with you about a conference composed of the civil rights leaders together with leaders in other areas for the purpose of evaluating what has happened with respect to Adam Clayton Powell, and also how to develop some plans so that this Committee which will report in the next five weeks may not carry out the complete crucifixion of our brother. And I wanted to be sure that our civil rights leaders saw your statement which was very strong and very timely. I have been watching the press and I have noted that it appears that among some of the Congressmen there was some surprise that the Negroes rallied to the Congressman; they sort of had the feeling that they were not going to rally. . . .

Rustin: . . . One of the problems with this whole setup is that Powell is not coming forward and telling anybody what he is doing, what he is thinking. And running around calling Negro leaders names, saying he's got all the niggers including Phil Randolph and stupid King in his pocket. I think we've got to sit down in New York on Monday and hammer out where we're going because this man is about to disrupt the whole movement. This Powell, for whom I want you to know I have very little sympathy.

King: . . . I have received a number of letters over the last few days from people who are outraged because I supported Adam. . . . They fell that Negro leaders have been very dishonest in supporting Adam Clayton Powell as strongly as we have without pointing out that Powell was responsible for this. It looks like we are supporting and condoning immorality in terms of conduct where it comes to the money questions and all of the other things that finally came out concerning Adam. Now you don't mind going out [of the] way and facing the criticisms and even the loss of support that I'm sure some of us are going to face financially as a result of this, if Adam appreciates [it]. But this is my problem, that I don't get in Adam the kind of penitence and appreciation for the support that makes you feel all right in doing it. And I just feel that somewhere along the way we need to take our defense off Adam Powell, away from Adam so much, and deal with the issue.

Randolph: I think you're right about that. Bayard knows that we always pointed out that we don't agree with everything Adam says or does. But we are concerned about the basic principle of the right of the people in the Congressional District who elected him to be represented by him in Congress. And to deny these people the right of representation is a violation of the Constitution as well as morally unjustifiable. . . . The people in the District should be the final arbiters of Adam's morality from the point of view of electing him. But some of our white friends, who are perfectly sound on civil rights and with no manifestations of racial bias, seem to feel, as you have indicated, that when we come to the rescue of Adam it's evidence of our lack of a sense of civic righteousness. And I think we have to make it clear to them that we're face to face with a situation here where we have a constitutional obligation to support Adam. And also that we feel they ought not to start with him or end with him in their process of reforming Congress. We're not opposed to reforming the rules of the Congress. . . . But we don't believe that they ought to start with Adam and end with Adam because it does have overtones of racial bias.

King: I agree absolutely with that. The only thing that I feel is happening now is the impression is given that we are trying to deify Adam Powell and that we aren't putting enough emphasis on the other side, the need for basic Congressional reform, the inexcusability of taking his Chairmanship and unseating him, and at the same time making Colmer of Mississippi Chairman of the House Rules Committee. And this is what we have to point out. But I think the problem is the idea getting across that we are just overlooking the fact completely, condoning the fact that Adam Powell's conduct has contributed. And it seems to me that we have to come out with some kind of balanced approach to this thing. Because we put ourselves in the bind of being a party to a notion that anything can take place, anything can be done, if it happens to be a Negro. . . .

2/18/67

IC to Stanley Levison, a conference call, from Martin Luther King in Miami. Also on the line were one Cleve in New Rochelle, [and] one Andy.

Martin called the conference . . . He says the issue is that Beval is working more with the peace movement and is talking of a march to the UN on April 15. Martin wants to know how far do "we" go on the peace thing. He has almost reached [the] conclusion that we are marking time in the battle of the ghetto with the war in Viet Nam going on. . . . Stanley says he has always agreed with Martin on his views regarding peace but he doesn't like the idea of Martin plunging into peace as he feels Martin's strength to [the] peace movement would be in his leadership in [the] rights movement. Stanley is afraid Martin will lose status if he becomes prominent in [the] peace movement and will then be ineffective in both movements. He cites Beval as an example. . . . Cleve says that rights must take a different course—we are coming to grips with naked reality—that economically we haven't made progress—it hasn't cost the nation any money—we need substantial funds from the government and they won't be coming as long as we have Viet Nam. Cleve thinks we should be in the peace movement. . . . Martin says he, Martin, is influenced by the moral issue, says America is morally bankrupt—lost its humanness. . . . Martin feels that one way to reassert his leadership is by standing up for major issues in the Viet Nam issue. . . . Martin said there is more discontent in the Negro community than most people realize and that he gets more cheers in Negro colleges when he opposes war in Viet Nam than he does when he talks about rights. He says they go wild about the Viet Nam Issue. . . . Stanley said he thinks Martin can be effective by putting his influence to work on the Walter Reuthers, the Bobby Kennedys, etc. . . , rather than becoming a small-time peace leader. . . .

2/27/67

Stanley Levison calls Martin Luther King at the San Francisco Hilton Hotel, area code 415, 771-1400. However, he places the call to Rev.

Bernard Lee instead of placing it to King. Martin Luther King answers the phone.

Levison: I tried to get you earlier but forgot that you don't register under your name.

King: That's right.

Levison: You got quite an article in the *New York Times,* Sunday ... A lot of people commented that two-thirds of the article was quotations of what you said and then gave one line to each of the Senators. I never saw anything so impressive. . . .

(At this point Levison reads the *Times* article, quoting King's advocacy of the U.S. withdrawing from Viet Nam.)

Levison: They no longer say that you have no right to speak on Viet Nam. This is the place for you to express your anti-war sentiments. When you are in this kind of company, your voice is bigger. When you're with four Senators, you are in the right place for somebody of your stature. Then you are recognized as someone with a spokesman's right to analyze. . . . I just don't see you involved in that thing on the fifteenth. You notice that they don't get involved in that. I'm talking about the Senators and people with a big constituency. They leave that for those who want to express themselves in that fashion. You can't do both, and when you have to choose one, choose the one where you are making much more influence felt. . . .

4/11/67

Conference call between Dr. Martin Luther King, Stanley Levison, Harry (phonetic), Andy (phonetic) and Ralph (phonetic), and Ton (sic). UNfemale heard to say she could not locate Cleveland and Harry Belafonte.

Dr. King stated that he thought they should have this conference call to deal with questions of strategy on this Viet Nam situation ... Let's deal first with the NAACP ... The problem is that not only are they making an attack but they are making it on grounds that are absolutely untrue. . . . Harry pointed out that the last paragraph in the resolution adopted by the SCLC expressly says our primary trust is still to secure equal rights for all men in this land. In other words they are lying. King said that is right, they are lying. They are saying that I am making an error in fusing the two movements, the civil rights and the peace movements. That was also the basic point of the *New York Times* article, that was the basic point of the *(Washington) Post* article, that was the basic point that Javits said. . . . Now I think it is time to stop the lie . . . King said he didn't want to get in the debate himself, there are times when he should be statesmanlike enough to rise above it, but this time he didn't feel he should step back. He said he planned to continue to give most of his time to civil rights, that he is absolutely opposed to this war and gives support to the forces that oppose it. King said he thought that something should be done to offset the idea that he is fusing the two movements.

. . . Levison said in order to get maximum attention, King should make a statement in the form of a press conference. King said somebody ought to denounce the NAACP. Levison said King should not do it by name and Harry said that Cleve or Harry B. could do it. . . . King said he should say in the statement there are those who feel the need of attacking his position and he would like to urge them to attack him on the rightness or wrongness of the war and not obscure the issue by creating a false impression and giving it to the American public. That would put them on the spot . . .

Stanley Levison dictates the following statement to Dora McDonald.
"I live in the ghetto in Chicago and Atlanta and I travel tens of thousands of miles each month which takes me into dozens of Negro communities across the nation. My direct personal experience with Negroes in all walks of life convinces me that they in a majority oppose the war in Viet Nam. First, because they are against war itself and second they feel it has caused a significant and alarming diminishing concern to civil rights progress. I have held these views myself for a long time but I have spoken more frequently in the recent period because Negroes in so many circles have explicitly urged me to articulate their concern and frustration. They feel civil rights is well on its way to becoming a neglected and forgotten issue long before it is even partially solved. However, recently a myth has confused these clear issues. The myth credits me with advocating the fusion of the civil rights and peace movements and I am criticized for authoring such a serious tactical mistake. I hold no such view. Only a few weeks ago in a formal public resolution, my organization, SCLC, and I explicitly declared that we have no intentions of diverting or diminishing our activities in civil rights. And we outlined extensive programs for the immediate future in the South as well as Chicago. It pains me that the board of directors of NAACP should have spent its time discussing the alleged merger plan and formally disapproved it. They have challenged and repudiated a non-existent proposition. SCLC and I have expressed our views on the war and drawn attention to its damaging effects on civil rights programs, a fact that we believe to be uncontrovertible, and

therefore mandatory to express in the interest of the struggle for equality. We do not believe in any merger or fusion of movements, but we believe that the existence of the war is not profoundly affecting the destiny of civil rights progress. We believe that despite the war our efforts can produce results and our strength is fully committed to that end. But it would be misleading and shallow to suggest that the role of the war is not hampering us substantially and it can be ignored as a factor. Loud voices have already been raised in Congress and elsewhere suggesting that the nation cannot afford to finance a war against poverty and inequality on an expanded scale and a shooting war at the same time. It is perfectly clear the nation has the resources to do both but those who oppose civil rights in favor of a war policy have seized the opportunity to pose a false issue to the public. This should not be ignored by civil rights organization (*sic*). The basic elements in common between the peace movement and civil rights movements are human elements. I am a clergyman as well as a civil rights leader and the immoral roots of our war policy are not unimportant to me. I do not believe our nation can be a moral leader of justice, equality and democracy if it is trapped in the role of a self-appointed world policeman. I will continue to express my opposition to this wrong policy without in any way diminishing my role in civil rights. Just as millions of Negro and white people are doing day in and day out.''

8/12/67

Stanley Levison, Martin Luther King, Harry Wachtel, Rev. Andy Young and Fauntroy.

King: I don't want to go on network programs like ''Meet the Press'' unless we discuss the questions that might be raised, . . . [like] the rantings of Stokely Carmichael and the guerrilla fighting. Someone said he had gone to Russia. . . .

Levison: Well Martin, I think you have to disagree with Stokely. At this point you can't be abridged with a fellow who goes to Havana and brandishes a rifle. . . . Stokely's evolution has gone to a point where he would cease to be any kind of leader at all.

. . .

Fauntroy: I think that Stokely's connection with communism will be a question and it is clear now more than it has been last year. I think you can get off the point by saying that Stokely did not create the conditions that exist: the slums, etc. . . .

Wachtel: I think that Stokely is making it easy to hide the issues of the slums.

Levison: I think it's a good point. Stokely is now being used to hide and confuse the real issues. If Stokely is not a CIA agent, he is acting as one.

Wachtel: I think, Martin, that you should say that Stokely's position is wandering away from the issues and as a leader of non-violence, you are disappointed.

Young: I think the whole [issue] of leadership should be let alone. I don't know if this is the time to criticize Stokely because to a lot of middle-class Negroes he is a Moshe Dayan hero.

Levison: Something like Powell.

Young: Yes. So maybe Martin should not blast Stokely because that would get to be the issue. They would then ask him if Stokely is a threat to his leadership and non-violence.

. . .

King: I think that the time has come to aggressively take Stokely and Rap Brown on. Not as a blast, but a compassionate disassociation.

Wachtel: You are giving him the J. Edgar Hoover treatment that he is being used and he is becoming less relevant to the real problems here [in] the ghetto. The rats that Congress is growing more racist and he is feeding the fires we want to be quelled.

Young: I have no reluctance to criticize Stokely, but it is a question of Martin's leadership.

Wachtel: I feel the ability to carry out a non-violent program are being interfered with by the positions of Rap Brown and Stokely.

Young: No, that's not true. The truth is that the Congress would not do anything even if the President would ask them.

King: Many people who would otherwise be ashamed of their anti-Negro feeling have now an excuse.

Levison: There is a difference with even Malcolm X and the position of Stokely.

Young: Now, I don't want to defent Stokely, but if all his statements were said and if something doesn't happen then that is true. The problem is that the press is calling for a planned rebellion.

Levison: Yes and he is calling for it now and not in the future.

King: He has also said that the U.S. must be destroyed. Andy, do you mean to agree with that?

Young: No, Martin. But you have said that if the U.S. doesn't change its ways then it would be destroyed.

King: But that isn't calling for the destruction of the U.S.

Wachtel: I think that Martin should answer that Stokely is making it difficult to cope with the real issues.

. . .

King: I think I should condemn Stokely's call to violence. Then move on to Stokely's association with communism. Maybe I should get into the fact that young people today, many of them are in a revolution of the system they live in, that America has lost the revolution feeling and they have to turn elsewhere to get it. Now what about the question that "Does not the trend reveal that your leadership is being rejected."

Young: You talk in numbers that you have more people involved in voter registration than in riots in Cleveland and more involved in the breadbasket work.

Levison: That's good, Andy, but Martin should say that on the basis of polls that Martin is 89 or 90% like the Harris poll.

Wachtel: I don't think it is becoming of you even if you are number one that you should prove it. You are not a consensus leader that is what you have said.

Levison: But, Harry, that is begging the question . . .

King: Couldn't I say that I never discuss my leadership because this is vain too much to even go into it.

. . .

Wachtel: The question of the President appointing a Mayor of D.C., and why, if you can get in your licks as a Negro.

. . .

King: I should say that Washington power is far from what it should be, that D.C. does not have home rule and they should as soon as possible, and then I can go on to say that the Mayor should be a Negro etc. . . .

Wachtel: Now the next point your Presidential candidacy and your speaking at the New Politics Convention (sic).

Young: You can say that both political parties are top heavy on policy making or maybe not go into that. But that you talk about the people at the grass level, the people interested in peace and civil rights.

Wachtel: And then you favor a new political party, Dr. King.

. . .

Young: . . . New Politics does not consider itself a third party.

Levison: I don't think Martin should . . . answer the question of if he is for a third party ticket. He is for grass roots people becoming interested in party and political life.

King: Sure, you have the New York Reformed Democrats, etc. . . . I think we could say that there is a continued coexistence of the right-winged Republicans and the Southern Dixicrats [that] makes it impossible to get a straight policy and that there needs to be a new approach.

Young: I think the questions "Where can Negro people turn." There has to be some kind of Independent politics.

Levison: That's a good statement. (Wachtel agrees.)

Wachtel: I would not support a new party but a candidate for peace and independent politics. Fulbright[?] has linked the war and the Negro. I think you, Martin, has (sic) to be politically strong.

Wachtel: Now the Presidential Commission on Riots.

Young: A waste of time.

Wachtel: Now, Martin, the fact that you are not on it they might discuss it as not handling the problem that we need more to cope with the problem. That the President did not discharge responsibility in dealing with the crisis.

King: ... The Commission should have developed an emergency program to deal with the problem.

Wachtel: ... I only have two or three more points: We get to the war in Viet Nam and Viet Nam election in the statements of Bishop Sheen and Gavin; that these statements are exposing the transparency of our position in Viet Nam. Then Javits, today calling for a total reappraisal of our position there.

King: I am coming more and more to a point of withdrawing from Viet Nam altogether. And I think if Bishop Sheen can say that we should withdraw I should come out with that statement.

Levison: But, Martin, all of us were for immediate withdrawal from the first day because we are against war in general but your position is not that of Bishop Sheen. His point is not your position but your concern of people to adopting the immediate withdrawal.

King: I do know that when I was in Algeria there were many people that were against our position in Viet Nam.

Wachtel: There are new reasons why withdrawal [is] important because what has happened this summer, and as Fulbright said we are loosing both wars and all persons are becoming sick of the war.

Levison: Yes Harry, we know a majority of the people want to see the end of the Viet Nam war but have enough people moved over to that side?

Wachtel: The answer is that the only way the war at home will be over with is to finish that war over there. ... You say you are for withdrawal [Martin], but you don't think it is practical now, that you are for withdrawal in your heart and you are encouraged by the state-

ments of Sheen, Gavin, Kennedy and Javits and it is time for a
fundamental reappraisal, etc. . . .

. . .

King: If you have a riot you get things.

Young: I don't think that is right, the problem is the non-violent movement has asked for changes that cost millions and you can't get that
by asking or by violence, that is the problem.

Fauntroy: The quest has to have the riots hurt the Negro. I would say
yes it has created fear in the minds of the whites.

. . .

King: How about have they hurt us?

Young: I think they make people retreat.

Fauntroy: I would say it remains to be seen, and if America moves to
the right then America has been hurt. But if there is a massive action
concern then history will say there is a help. I think it remains to be
seen. I think you can say you hope it brings America to its senses. . . .
The whole question is will the Negro go communist? I think a drown-
ing man will grab on to anything; that we are treating our Negroes
so badly that we may see a revolution right here.

Levison: I think that it isn't will Negroes be attracted to it but, the
conditions make people go to communism.

. . .

King: I think we have to take this position that the majority of the
people of America are against the war in Viet Nam.

. . .

Levison: Now the leadership thing. Andy was developing something I
like. First that the existence of non-violence does not wipe out violence. I think at this point you might discuss civil disobedience as a
higher stage for the northern ghettos.

Young: It won't work because when you do it on a big scale it isn't
recognized as such.

King: That I think non-violence has to be stepped up on a larger scale,
to be escalated so its impact would be greater than violence.

Levison: We have never used sit-ins at factory gates and in factories
[to] stop production. I think you have to get in the escalating of non-
violence to a greater stage.

Young: We haven't done anything since Birmingham and we have to
get to where we were.

Levison: For the cities we have to get higher, Andy.

Fontroy: Don't you think that Rap Brown and Stokely have set back
the Negro cause.

Levison: Yes, they will ask that; I would say you don't agree with that.

King: I think they have pulled the rug from under the non-violent leaders by not responding.

Andy: But, Martin, nobody gives away power.

Levison: That sounds like Whitney Young.

King: I could quote Kennedy when we get on the question of violence. "Those who make peaceful revolution impossible make violent revolution possible . . ."

Levison: That is good. But about Negroes going communist. I don't think that Martin has to say I am not a communist.

King: Isn't it true that this is not a basic question because Negroes have been in poverty so long and that they haven't turned communist at this point, that they will not now.

Levison: I think that the Negro was not militant before.

Young: No, I think that the Negro loves America and he does not want to go to Russia or China, he wants to stay here the "nigger ain't turning anywhere."

Levison: Andy, to say that the Negro loves America just doesn't sit with me.

Young: Negroes will not tear up the city for communism but for hunger and conditions, and the police—that most of these riots are police riots. The crisis has nothing to do with ideology but with hunger and that the Negro is determined to have a decent life in America and if he is denied that life, then go into that quote of Kennedy's. What time do you get in, Martin?

King: I get in at 1:40 A.M. in Baltimore and I'm staying at the Washington Hilton and the broadcast is at 1:00 P.M. tomorrow.

1968

1968

[Section 83]

April 23, 1968   Memorandum: New York

[Section 84]

May 21, 1968   Letter from J. Edgar Hoover
May 21, 1968   Memorandum: DeLoach to Tolson
May 28, 1968   Memorandum: Bishop to DeLoach
June 6, 1968   Letter to Mr. J. Edgar Hoover

[Section 78]

UNITED STATES DEPARTMENT OF JUSTICE

FEDERAL BUREAU OF INVESTIGATION

Miami, Florida
February 20, 1968

RE: WASHINGTON SPRING PROJECT
Reference is made to communication from this Bureau
dated February 19, 1968.

The "Miami Herald" a local Miami, Florida, newspaper on February 20, 1968, reported that Dr. MARTIN LUTHER KING, JR., opened a series of meetings in Miami, Florida, on February 19, 1968, designed to help Negro clergymen minister to the social economic needs of their congregations. This article reported that Dr. KING and Reverend ANDREW YOUNG, one of his top aides in the Southern Christian Leadership Conference (SCLC), said the five-day series of conferences will not include planning for civil rights or anti-war demonstrations.

It was also reported that Dr. KING and Reverend YOUNG both said they did not expect STOKELY CARMICHAEL and RAP BROWN, leaders of the Black Nationalist militancy to attend. However, Reverend YOUNG said, "If STOKELY and RAP come we won't throw them out." This article goes on to report that in addition to the 150 official delegates, about 50 more ministers are expected to attend the meeting, which are not open to the public.

It was reported that about 125 delegates attended a luncheon on February 19, 1968, and heard a talk by Dr. R. A. ABERNATHY, a Vice-President of SCLC. In addition, this article reports that three lectures, followed by workshop sessions, are scheduled for February 20, 1968.

. . . Ministers Conference at the Sheraton Four Ambassadors, Miami, Florida, opened on schedule on February 19, 1968. In welcoming the group, Dr. MARTIN LUTHER KING, JR., reiterated that the purpose of this conference was for discussion, study and training in connection with problems facing the Negroes in the big city areas.

He further stated that attention would be given to attempting to reconcile the term "black power" with the overall civil rights movement in the United States. During the opening conference, nonviolence was continuously stressed.

Dr. KING stated that over-integration could occur to the point that Negroes could lose their identity. He gave as an example the integration of the Methodist Church, however, this was not further explained.

The only remark that was made to the people in attendance relative to the "Washington trip" was that this conference in Miami would not be used for the purpose of recruiting people for the trip to Washington, nor would it be a topic of discussion.

On February 20, 1968, the entire group will be broken up into "workshop units" according to their interest and needs of the area from which various ministers came. All leaders are to take part in the activities of the workshop and report back to the entire assembly.

During the opening day of this meeting, only one item of dissension occurred and that involved some opposition to the fact that apparently DAN MONOHAN, who was formerly connected with Urban Housing, has been invited to address the conference in Miami. Some ministers disagreed with this invitation, however, Reverend ANDREW YOUNG stated that his presence could contribute to the conference, and that he should be heard.

. . . that several items of literature were being passed out to the delegates. Included in the literature was a leaflet captioned "The Southern Christian Leadership Conference" [which] outlines the purpose of the training program. In addition, a statement made by Dr. MARTIN LUTHER KING, JR., Atlanta, Georgia, on December 4, 1967, which statement relates to the Washington Spring Project, was also being passed out.

These two items are quoted as follows:

"THE SOUTHERN CHRISTIAN LEADERSHIP
   CONFERENCE
Dr. Martin Luther King Jr., President.

"MINISTERS LEADERSHIP TRAINING PROGRAM
   Rev. T. Y. Rogers, Jr., Director

"CRISIS OF THE CITIES: A CREATIVE ANGLE

" '. . . transforming the inchoate rage of the ghetto into a creative force for change . . .' "

"The Ministers Leadership Program is designed to train local leaders in the knowledge of the many problems which the residents of the ghetto face and in ways of solving these problems. Our focus is the Black Preacher and the Black church for we believe that the greatest potential power for controlling the forces which made and sustain as well as those which can change the structure of the ghetto, is within the Black church. We further believe that because of the central place for which [sic] the Black church holds in the Negro community, we can develop the kind of leadership which will develop programs to transfer control of the ghetto to those who reside there. Finally, the Southern Christian Leadership Conference is an extension of the church and therefore much of our emphasis should be on strengthening the witness of the church in areas of life where problems are greatest.

"The Ministers Leadership Training Program will be conducted in fifteen metropolitan areas of our nation. We have selected a minimum of eight and a maximum of twenty preachers from these fifteen areas, depending upon the size and population, who will participate in our program. Our program begins with an orientation workshop in Miami, Florida. This workshop is designed to acquaint the preachers who will participate in our program with the overall history and philosophy of the Southern Christian Leadership Conference and with the programs which demand our concern at present. This workshop is also designed to acquaint the participants with the nature and scope of the multiplicity of problems facing the resident of the ghetto. Our emphasis will be on detailed examination of the forces which make the ghetto a reality; the structures which maintain the ghetto; and the possibility of destroying the ghetto by reconstructing and changing ownership of the economic structures of the ghetto. There will also be an examination of the theology of the church, a look at the history of the Black church, and a redefining of the ethic of the Black church in terms of the problems faced by the Black churches today.

"To accomplish the above mentioned ends we have invited to this workshop persons with expertise in the problems of the ghetto. They will deal with the 'Making of the Ghetto,' 'the New Mythology,' 'Political Action and Political Coalition,' the 'Challenge of an Urban Ministry,' 'Jobs,' 'Welfare Rights,' 'Nonviolence and Social Change,' and other problems facing the poor.

"During the orientation workshop the cities will be organized. A convener will be chosen for each city with the exception of New York City which will have a convener for Brooklyn and Queens and another for Manhattan and the Bronx. Those sixteen conveners will call the men of their cities together once per week for study, discussion, learning, planning and executing programs. The conveners will serve as the link between the Atlanta office of the Ministers Leadership Training Program and the particular city involved, and will channel programs and information to the members of their group.

"In brief the goals of the Ministers Leadership Training Program are as follows:
"1. To sensitize Black preachers to the problems of the ghetto and the relationship of these problems to their ministers.
"2. To create a discipline for analyzing and understanding the forces which create and sustain the ghetto.
"3. To develop an understanding of the various methods of solving problems and to focus these methods on solving the problems of the ghetto.
"4. To lay the foundation for the organization and structuring of the ghetto to meet the needs of the people who live there.
"5. To create a common force of grass-roots people to effect positive change in the ghetto.

"The problems with which this program is concerned are poverty, employment, education, housing, police brutality, inter-group relations, health and welfare, community services and property ownership.

"The cities in which this program will be conducted are:

1. Atlanta
2. Birmingham
3. Chicago
4. Cleveland
5. Detroit
6. Baltimore
7. New York

8. Los Angeles
9. Memphis
10. Philadelphia
11. St. Louis
12. San Francisco
13. Washington, D. C.
14. Newark

15. Houston

"Co-operating agencies: Urban Training Center of Chicago, Metropolitan Applied Research Center of New York, Internship for Clergymen in Urban Ministry of Cleveland and Gammon Theological Seminary of Atlanta."

"Statement by Dr. Martin Luther King, Jr.
President, Southern Christian Leadership Conference
Atlanta, Georgia

"December 4, 1967

"Ladies and Gentlemen:

"Last week staff of the Southern Christian Leadership Conference held one of the most important meetings we have ever convened. We had intensive discussions and analyses of our work and of the challenges which confront us and our nation, and at the end we made a decision which I wish to announce today.

"The Southern Christian Leadership Conference will lead waves of the nation's poor and disinherited to Washington, D.C., next spring to demand redress of their grievances by the United States government and to secure at least jobs or income for all.

"We will go there, we will demand to be heard, and we will stay until America responds. If this means forcible repression of our movement, we will confront it, for we have done this before. If this means scorn or ridicule, we embrace it, for that is what America's poor now receive. If it means jail, we accept it willingly, for the millions of poor already are imprisoned by exploitation and discrimination. But we hope, with growing confidence, that our campaign in Washington will receive at first a sympathetic understanding across our nation, followed by dramatic expansion of nonviolent demonstrations in Washington and simultaneous protests elsewhere. In short, we will be petitioning our government [to] move against poverty.

"We have now begun perparations for the Washington campaign. Our staff will soon be taking new assignments to organize people to go to Washington from 10 key cities and 5 rural areas. This will be no mere one-day march on Washington, but a trek to the nation's capital by suffering and outraged citizens who will go to stay until some definite and positive action is taken to provide jobs and income for the poor.

"We are sending our staff into these key areas to meet with the local leadership of these areas to discuss their readiness to cooperate with us in this venture.

"In the coming weeks we will disclose our detailed plans on mobilizing this massive campaign, and on the specific proposals which we are formulating.

"Today I would like to tell you why the Southern Christian Leadership Conference has decided to undertake this task with the advice and participation we anticipate from other organizations and thousands of individuals.

"America is at a crossroads of history, and it is critically important for us, a nation and a society, to choose a new path and to move upon it with resolution and courage.

"It is impossible to under-estimate the crisis we face in America. The stability of a civilization, the potential of free government, and the simple honor of men are at stake.

"Those who serve in the human-rights movement, including our Southern Christian Leadership Conference, are keenly aware of the increasing bitterness and despair and frustration that threaten the worst chaos, hatred, and violence any nation has ever encountered.

"In a sense, we are already at war with and among ourselves. Affluent Americans are locked into suburbs of physical comfort and mental insecurity; poor Americans are locked inside ghettos of material privation and spiritual debilitation; and all of us can almost feel the presence of a kind of social insanity which could lead to national ruin. Consider, for example, the spectacle of cities burning while the national government speaks of repression instead of rehabilitation. Or think of children starving in Mississippi while prosperous farmers are rewarded for not producing food. Or Negro mothers leaving children in tenements to work in neighborhoods where people of color can not live. Or the awesome bombardment, already greater than the munitions we exploded in World II, against a small Asian land, while political brokers de-escalate and very nearly disarm a timid action against poverty. Or a nation gorged on money while millions of its citizens are denied a good education, adequate health services, decent housing, meaningful employment, and even respect, and are then told to be responsible.

"The true responsibility for the existence of these deplorable conditions lies ultimately with the larger society, and much of the immediate responsibility for removing the injustices can be laid directly at the door of the federal government.

"This is the institution which has the power to act, the resources to tap, and the duty to respond. And yet, this very government now lacks the will to make reforms which are demanded by a rising chorus across the nation. According to the Harris Poll, for example, a substantial majority of Americans believe that we must proceed at once to tear down and rebuild the slums, and a solid majority feel that everyone should have a job. Concerned leaders of industry, civil-rights organizations, labor unions and churches are joining in such groups as the new Urban Coalition to urge progressive economic measures at the national level. Many urban political leaders are ready to carry out enlightened programs if only the federal government will provide the needed financial support. Newsweek magazine recently devoted an entire issue to the problem of racism in America and set forth some sound proposals for dealing with this situation.

"I cite these facts merely to show that a clear majority in America are asking for the very things which we will demand in Washington.

"We have learned from hard and bitter experience in our movement that our government does not move to correct a problem involving race until it is confronted directly and dramatically. It required a Selma before the the fundamental right to vote was written into the federal statutes. It took a Birmingham to dramatize the economic plight of the Negro, and compel the government to act.

"Unrest among the poor of America, and particularly among Negroes, is growing rapidly. In this age of technological wizardry and political immorality, the poor are demanding that the basic need of people be met as the first priority of our domestic programs. Poor people cannot long be placated by the glamour of multi-billion-dollar exploits in space. Poor people who encounter racial discrimination every day in every aspect of their lives can not be fooled by patronizing gestures and halfway promises. Poor people who are treated with derision and abuse by an economic system soon conclude with elementary logic that they have no rational interest in killing people 12,000 miles away in the name of defending that system.

"We intend to channelize the smoldering rage and frustration of

Negro people into an effective, militant and nonviolent movement of massive proportions in Washington and other areas. Similarly, we will be calling on the swelling masses of young people in this country who are disenchanted with this materialistic society, and asking them to join us in our new Washington movement. We also look for participation by representatives of the millions of non-Negro poor—Indians, Mexican-Americans, Puerto Ricans, Appalachians, and others. And we shall welcome assistance from all Americans of goodwill.

"And so, we have decided to go to Washington and to use any means of legitimate nonviolent protest necessary to move our nation and our government on a new course of social, economic, and political reform. As I said before, the power to initiate this reform resides in Washington. The President and the Congress have a primary responsibility for low minimum wages, for a degrading system of inadequate welfare, for subsidies of the rich and unemployment and under-employment of the poor, for a war mentality, for slums and starvation, and racism. The survival of a free society depends upon the guarantee and survival of freedom and equality. This is what we seek.

"In the final analysis, SCLC decided to go to Washington because, if we did not act, we would be abdicating our responsibilities as an organization committed to nonviolence and freedom. We are keeping that commitment, and we shall call on America to join us in our forthcoming Washington campaign. In this way, we can work creatively against the despair and indifference that have so often caused our nation to be immobilized during the cold winter and shaken profoundly in the hot summer."

[Section 79]

UNITED STATES GOVERNMENT
Memorandum

TO: Mr. DeLoach   DATE: 2/29/68

FROM: T. E. BISHOP

SUBJECT: PARADE MAGAZINE
             QUESTION RE MARTIN LUTHER KING

On 2/29/68 . . . telephonically contacted me from New York. Parade Magazine is a Sunday supplement which is distributed with a number of newspapers, including "The Washington Post." Each Sunday it carries a "Questions and Answers" section which deals with gossip, rumor, etc., concerning prominent individuals. Both the questions and the answers, of course, are made up by the editors of Parade Magazine and the format is merely a way of getting out the rumor and gossip to the public.

. . . stated that they are contemplating utilizing the following question and answer in a forthcoming issue of Parade:

"Question: Is it true that the FBI has a complete file on Martin Luther King's sex life?"

"Answer: Not a complete file, but it has a great deal of titillating information about his sexual activities."

. . . asked me if the FBI would have any objection to the above question and answer being run. I told him that we most certainly would have an objection because it clearly intimates that the FBI is furnishing information to the public concerning Martin Luther King. I pointed out to him that under no circumstances would the FBI make any comment concerning such a question and, therefore, we would most strongly object if Parade Magazine used the question and answer in the above form.

I asked him what his source was for the answer set forth above. He hemmed and hawed and finally stated that he was using as his source the article by Richard Harwood which appeared in "The Washington Post" on 2/25/68 since the article had stated that the FBI had a record of King's sex life and had made this available to certain individuals. I told . . . that he had certainly utilized an unreliable source and that it ought to be obvious to any normal individual that Harwood's article was filled with lies and innuendos, and was intended to be an attack on the FBI. I advised . . . that the information in the article was completely inaccurate and none of it had emanated from the FBI.

. . . then advised that in view of my feelings, they would not utilize the above question and answer in its present form and that, as a matter of fact, he thought they would just forget the whole thing and not print anything along the above lines.

UNITED STATES DEPARTMENT OF JUSTICE

FEDERAL BUREAU OF INVESTIGATION

Washington, D.C. 20535
March 4, 1968

The San Francisco office of the Federal Bureau of Investigation advised that on February 27, 1968, . . . furnished the following information.

. . . has become acquainted with . . . whom he describes as "anti-Negro," "anti-left," and "anti-liberal."

. . . denounced all liberals and particularly Negro leaders. . . . recently revealed . . . that he had compiled a list of eleven persons that he wished killed through assassination. . . . offered to furnish . . . airline tickets, an untraceable weapon, not described but believed to be a rifle or explosives, if he would travel to an appropriate place, which was not revealed, to kill one of the unnamed persons on the list. . . . included the names of Senator Robert Kennedy and ten other persons, all of whom he believes to be Negro, including H. Rap Brown, Stokely Carmichael, and Martin Luther King.

. . . stated that . . . is a strong supporter of ex-Governor George Wallace . . .

In conversations during January or February, 1968, . . . was extremely critical of President Johnson and made the general statement that the President would be shot but stated no specific method or time. . . . gained the impression that . . . statement regarding the President may have had some connection with the Democratic National Convention. . . . did not ask . . . to assist in this project.

. . . stated that . . . had made no mention of any organization in which he is active, such as the Ku Klux Klan or the Minutemen.

. . . is described as a white male, American, 5'9" or 5'10", 180 pounds, . . .

[Section 85]

FEDERAL BUREAU OF INVESTIGATION

SUBJECT: MARTIN LUTHER KING, JR.,
            A CURRENT ANALYSIS

DATE: March 12, 1968

TABLE OF CONTENTS

I. INTRODUCTION

Since 1956, Martin Luther King, Jr., has occupied a prominent role in the drive for equal rights for Negroes in the United States. During this critical period in our Nation's history, much has depended on him as the individual Negroes in great numbers have looked to [him] for leadership in their drive to achieve equality. Much depends on him still in these times when racial tensions have created an atmosphere of fear and foreboding among many Negroes and whites alike. The course King chose to follow at this critical time could have momentous impact on the future of race relations in the United States, and for that reason this paper has been prepared to give some insight into the nature of the man himself as well as the nature of his views, goals, objectives, tactics and the reasons therefor.

Washington Spring Project

Martin Luther King, Jr., President of the Southern Christian Leadership Conference (SCLC), has stated publicly that he and 3,000 of his followers will march on Washington, D. C., this spring. He has announced that he will lead a massive civil disobedience campaign that will disrupt the normal course of business and, in fact, close down the Nation's Capital. He originally announced this project on August 15, 1967, in Atlanta, Georgia, on the occasion of the tenth anniversary of the SCLC.

King predicted that this massive civil disobedience will be more effective than riots. Concerning civil disobedience, King declared, "To dislocate the function of a city without destroying it can be more effective than a riot, because it can be longer lasting, costly to society, but not wantonly destructive.''

King has referred to this campaign as the ''Washington Spring Project'' and the ''Poor People's March,'' which is reportedly being staged to pressure Congress into passing legislation favorable to the Negro. It is King's contention that the Government of the United States does not move until it is confronted dramatically. To add to the dramatic confrontation, King has boasted he and his entourage are coming to Washington to stay; that his followers will conduct sit-ins, camp-ins, and sleep-ins at every Government facility available including the lawn of the White House. He has bragged that he will fill up the jails of Washington and surrounding towns.

Black Nationalist Terror

One serious danger in the confrontation lies in the proposed action of the black nationalist groups which plan to attempt to seize the initiative and escalate the nonviolent demonstrations into violence.

King has met with black nationalists and attempted to solicit their support. Stokely Carmichael of the Student Nonviolent Coordinating Committee (SNCC), an extremist Black Nationalist organization, has conferred with King. Carmichael endorses the objectives of King and advises he will not oppose or interfere with the ''Washington Spring Project's'' plans for nonviolence. However, he also states his role will be governed by what SNCC decides.

King is aware of the possibility of violence because one of his aides proclaimed recently to the press, ''Jail will be the safest place in Washington this spring.'' However, in spite of this potentially explosive situation, King continues his plans. He adroitly uses this possibility as a lever to attempt to pressure Congress into action by warning that the ''Washington Spring Project'' may be the last chance in this country for peaceful change with respect to civil needs.

Strong Communist Influence

Another complicating factor in the picture is the degree of communist influence on King. One of King's principal advisors is Stanley David Levison. Ostensibly only a New York City attorney and businessman, Levison is, in fact, a shrewd, dedicated communist. Levison has spent the major part of his life advancing communist interests.

Levison gravitated to Martin Luther King, Jr., in 1956. He has been as dedicated in his support of King as he has been in advancing communist goals. He has actively involved himself in fund-raising drives for King, served as his legal counsel in certain matters, suggested speech material for him, discussed with King demonstrations in which King was involved, guided him in regard to acceptance or rejection of various public appearances and speaking commitments, and helped him with matters related to articles and books King has prepared.

Levison edited most chapters of King's new book entitled "Where Do We Go From Here; Chaos or Community?" Levison wrote one chapter of this book and the publisher's representative complained to King and Levison that it was obvious certain sections of the book were written by different individuals.

Stanley Levison had told Clarence Jones, another advisor to King, that under no circumstances should King be permitted to say anything without their approving it. Levison also informed Jones that King is such a slow thinker he is usually not prepared to make statements without help from someone. Levison is actively participating in the planning for King's "Washington Spring Project."

Explosive Situation

The combined forces of the communist influence and the black nationalists advocating violence give the "Washington Spring Project" a potential for an extremely explosive situation.

II. FORMATION OF SOUTHERN CHRISTIAN LEADERSHIP CONFERENCE

Background of Founder

Martin Luther King, Jr., was born January 15, 1929, at Atlanta, Georgia. His name at birth was Michael Luther King, Jr. In 1935, his first name was changed to Martin. King received an A.B. degree in 1948 from Morehouse College, Atlanta, Georgia. He then entered Crozer Theological Seminary, Chester, Pennsylvania, where he was one of six Negroes among 100 students. He won the Plafkner Award as the most outstanding student, was President of the Senior Class, and received the J. Lewis Crozer Fellowship for graduate study at the university of his choice. King graduated from Crozer Theological Seminary with a Bachelor of Divinity degree in 1951 and did graduate work at Boston University, Boston, Massachusetts, where he secured a Ph.D. degree in 1955.

Upon graduation, he was offered the pastorate of two Baptist churches in the East and teaching posts in three colleges. King chose the pastorate at the Dexter Avenue Baptist Church in Montgomery, Alabama. After becoming established in his church, he founded the Montgomery Improvement Association and led local Negroes in the Montgomery Bus Boycott that attracted national attention. In March of 1957, he founded the Southern Christian Leadership Conference (SCLC) with himself as President. He still holds that position today. He is also co-pastor of the Ebenezer Baptist Church, Atlanta, Georgia.

Subversives Attracted

Stanley Levison was attracted to King and SCLC when King gained national attention. Levison soon developed a close relationship with King and was known in King's group as "Assistant Chief." In 1961, he was assistant treasurer of SCLC.

... Through Levison's influence, other subversives were attracted to SCLC. Hunter Pitts O'Dell, former National Committee member of the CPUSA, was employed by SCLC. In 1962, when King mentioned to Levison that he was thinking of adding an administrative assistant to his staff, Levison recommended O'Dell, who was then head of SCLC's New York Office. King said he liked the idea. At the time, King was well aware of Levison's and O'Dell's communist affiliations. ...

Communist Exposed

King was forced to get rid of Hunter Pitts O'Dell in October 1962, when several newspaper articles exposed O'Dell's connection with SCLC and his communist affiliations. King still tried to hide O'Dell in his organization until July 1963, when he accepted O'Dell's "resignation." As King put it, O'Dell's release was not because of connections between O'Dell and the CPUSA but because of the emotional public response.

O'Dell continued his efforts to make his presence felt in the civil rights movement in behalf of the CPUSA. The Winter 1967, issue of "Freedomways," self-described as a review of the Negro freedom movement, lists O'Dell as Associate Managing Editor. Actually, "Freedomways" is a CPUSA-initiated and CPUSA-supported publication espousing the communist viewpoint of Negro problems.

King Speaks at Rally Honoring Communist

On February 23, 1968, King was the guest speaker at a rally of more than one thousand people at Carnegie Hall, New York City, sponsored by "Freedomways," celebrating the 100th anniversary of the birth of W.E.B. DuBois, famous Negro civil rights crusader who joined the Communist Party at age 93. Jack O'Dell, the popular name used by Hunter Pitts O'Dell, was also listed as one of the speakers at this affair.

On the following day, Stanley Levison confided to Clarence Jones that King performed very badly at the "Freedomways" rally. He commented: "King has never read anything as badly," and, "as though he did not understand what he was reading."

Former Communist Advisors

Bayard Rustin is a former advisor to King and a one-time assistant secretary of the SCLC. Rustin has publicly admitted affiliation with the communist movement in the late 1930's. He was also one of a selected number of observers permitted to attend the CPUSA's National Convention in 1957. . . .

Advisory Committee Established for King

On June 22, 1964, an advisory and research committee was formed, with King's approval, for the purpose of writing King's speeches and guiding his actions. Among the members of the group were Lawrence Reddick, Bayard Rustin, Clarence Jones, and Harry Wachtel.

. . . In addition to being on the Advisory Committee, Clarence Jones, a Negro attorney, is also General Counsel for the Gandhi Society for Human Rights, a fund-raising adjunct of the SCLC.

Prior to October 1966, King attempted to hide his association with Stanley Levison and used Jones as the intermediary. During the mid-1950's, Jones held a position of leadership in the Labor Youth League, an organization which has been designated as subversive pursuant to Executive Order 10450.

Clarence Jones married Annie Aston Warder Norton on June 3, 1956. She is the daughter of deceased publisher William H. Norton. Between 1947 and 1950 she was identified as a Communist Party club member at Sarah Lawrence College. In the early 1950's she was also active in the Labor Youth League. On April 5, 1955, she was observed as the driver of a station wagon which was used to transport Communist Party underground leaders in connection with an official Communist Party meeting. In 1956, she was described by a self-admitted communist as a "hard-core communist."

King Wins Nobel Peace Prize

In October 1964, it was announced that King, a 35-year-old Baptist minister, was being awarded the Nobel Peace Prize. On November 24, 1964, King contacted Jones and asked that Jones and Levison, among others, submit five-minute speeches which King could use in accepting the Nobel Peace Prize. King would select the best material from these speeches.

King's Attraction for Communist Advisors

Two previous aides of King were Cordy T. Vivian, who formerly served as Director of Affiliates of the SCLC, and Randolph Blackwell, who at one time acted as SCLC Program Coordinator. Both of these individuals are former members of the CPUSA.

During the early stages of development and formation of the SCLC, the following eight individuals helped shape and mold the policies of this organization, and, as noted, all have had communist affiliations:

Stanley David Levison	"Assistant Chief"
Clarence Jones	Advisory Committee
Harry Wachtel	Advisory Committee
Cordy T. Vivian	Director of Affiliates
Randolph Blackwell	Program Coordinator
Hunter Pitts O'Dell	Adminstrative Assistant
Lawrence Reddick	Advisory Committee
Bayard Rustin	Advisory Committee

Of these, Levison, Jones, and Wachtel continued to exert strong influence on King and the SCLC. In addition, at the tenth anniversary convention of SCLC at Atlanta, Georgia, on August 14, 1967, a brochure listed L. D. Reddick as historian of SCLC.

III. COMMUNIST OBJECTIVES

During the early 1960's the CPUSA was striving to obtain a Negro-labor coalition to achieve its goals in this country. At that time, the

CPUSA "Party Line" was: "Big business attacks on the rights of labor are continuing. In order to defeat this offensive, organized labor, assisted by communists, must launch a countercrusade, which can succeed only if it is based on the united action of the entire trade-union movement."

Also, communists had recognized the error of their way by proclaiming that the communist program for "self-determination" of the Negro in the "Black Belt" area of the South had been discarded. The new policy was to seek complete economic, political, and social equality for the Negro with all other American citizens. In a May 1961, issue, the communist newspaper, "The Worker," stated, "Communists will do their utmost to strengthen and unite the Negro movement and bring it to the backing of the working people."

Martin Luther King, Jr., and his organization were made to order to achieve these objectives. King and his group were demonstrating and conducting voter-registration campaigns to align the Negro movement solidly behind King.

The Peace Issue Appears

This activity continued with much fanfare until the passage of the Civil Rights Act of 1964 by the Congress. This was the most far-reaching civil rights act passed since the Reconstruction era. Now it was no longer newsworthy to demonstrate for Negro rights. The passage of this Act was one factor that took King off the front pages of the daily newspapers.

The second factor that had a bearing on King's lack of publicity and change of policy was the Gulf of Tonkin incident on August 2, 1964. Because of this, the United States took a more active role in the Vietnam War. The CPUSA then started to demand through its propaganda machine that the escalation of the war in Vietnam be stopped. The activities in Vietnam were now more important news than was the Negro freedom movement.

The CPUSA also realized that even though the peace issue was of primary importance, a secondary issue not to be forgotten was the freedom movement. Abandoning its previous efforts to form a Negro-labor coalition, the CPUSA now started touting a Negro-peace coalition that would form a massive movement to force the United States Government to change its foreign and domestic policies.

"The Worker," in April 1965, claimed that this coalition was starting to form when it stated, "The civil rights movement was coming to see the identity of interests of the Negro people's freedom movement with the anti-imperialist objective of ending the neo-colonialist war of the United States against the people of Vietnam.''

IV. THE EMERGENCE OF THE PEACE ISSUE IN KING'S GROUP

Role as a Peacemaker

King and his aides helped form this coalition of ''peace'' and ''freedom'' groups. They saw an opportunity to again propel King into the international spotlight by proposing he make peace in Vietnam.

On August 12, 1965, King announced publicly that he would appeal personally to President Ho Chi Minh of North Vietnam to join a conference to end the Vietnam war. He said he would also send letters to the leaders of South Vietnam, the Soviet Union, and the United States in this regard.

This move on the part of King was engineered by Bayard Rustin and Harry Wachtel. In early August they met and discussed how to inject King into the Vietnam issue. It was decided to have King write these world leaders utilizing King's prestige as a winner of the Nobel Prize. This action, they felt, would cast an image of King as a great moral leader and extend his influence beyond the civil rights movement.

Subsequently, a leading newspaper sent King 12 questions which would clarify his position on Vietnam. Upon receipt of these questions, King referred them to Stanley Levison to answer.

Because of the unfavorable public reaction to King's announcement, a conference with his top advisors was held in early September 1965, at which time it was decided that King would avoid the Vietnam issue. Bayard Rustin, Stanley Levison, Harry Wachtel, and Clarence Jones were in attendance at this conference.

Admiration Lost

In early 1966, King was lamenting to Harry Wachtel about a nationally known figure, who at one time was a heavy contributor to and admirer of King but was displeased because of King's stand on Vietnam. Wachtel reminded King, ''When we went into this Vietnam thing, we decided that he who controls the purse strings doesn't control our philosophy.''

Continued Pressure by Press

After the resumption of bombing of North Vietnam in February 1966, King conferred with Stanley Levison and Bayard Rustin concerning a statement for the press. King informed them that the press had been bothering him for a statement, but he dared not take any action until he discussed the matter with them. It was agreed that King would say he was deeply impressed by the large number of Senators who called for a cessation of the bombings. Levison reiterated that King should point out how much opposition there is to the bombings.

Anti-Vietnam War Resolution

Miami was the scene of the Southern Christian Leadership Conference executive board meeting in the Spring [of] 1966. During this two-day conference, the sessions ran into the early morning hours attempting to draft a resolution on the Vietnam war. While there appeared to be general agreement, Stanley Levison and Harry Wachtel continued to argue for a stronger resolution that would condemn participation by United States troops in Vietnam. The conference finally adopted a resolution calling on the Government to desist aiding the military junta in Vietnam and to seriously consider a prompt withdrawal.

"Face the Nation"

In May 1966, King was extended an invitation to appear on the Columbia Broadcasting System's program "Face the Nation." Prior to this appearance, King sought the advice of Stanley Levison and Clarence Jones. King wanted their thinking on the more important questions he might be asked. Levison noted the possibility that King might be questioned on the Vietnam war. Jones advised King to use the Southern Christian Leadership Conference resolution on Vietnam as his text. Levison suggested that King should also point out how unfair it was that Negroes were shouldering a heavier burden in the war and that more Negroes were in combat than other Americans.

When King appeared on the program, he suggested the United States stop bombing North Vietnam, negotiate with the Viet Cong, and recognize Red China.

Senate Hearings

Prior to his appearance before a Senate Subcommittee hearing on urban affairs in December 1966, King contacted Levison for counsel concerning his testimony. During this discussion, it was agreed that King must reiterate during his testimony that the war in Vietnam is standing in the way of the implementation of any of his civil rights projects and is an open invitation to confusion, chaos, disruptions, and riots.

During his subsequent testimony before this committee, he spoke critically of the war in Vietnam along these lines.

"The Nation" Symposium

In late February 1967, King spoke before a symposium sponsored by "The Nation" magazine concerning the problems of redirecting "American Power." After this speech in which King was highly critical of the United States involvement in Vietnam, Levison congratulated him.

Levison was pleased with the publicity King's speech received, commenting that King's appearance on a panel with four United States Senators was the appropriate occasion for him to express his antiwar sentiments.

Over the years a number of individuals who had been employed at one time or another by "The Nation" in editorial and writing capacities have been identified with the communist movement.

Riverside Church Speech

In early April 1967, King accepted an invitation to speak before the group, "Clergy and Laymen Concerned About Vietnam." This is an interdenominational committee formed to mobilize religious opinion against the war.

Prior to this speech, King and Andrew Young, Executive Director of SCLC, spent approximately eight hours in conference with King's top advisors in New York, New York. Stanley Levison and Harry Wachtel were present at this conference.

Later that same day, King spoke at the Riverside Church, New York, New York, before this group, at which time he was highly critical of the United States involvement in the Vietnam war. He referred to the United States Government as "the greatest purveyor of violence in the world today." He proposed a five-step process to extricate the United States from this conflict. Comments in the news media coverage of King's remarks pointed out that the five points are similar in concept to the conditions imposed by North Vietnam as a prerequisite to negotiations. It is interesting to note that King's proposals parallel the propaganda line which the Communist Party, USA, has been projecting regarding the war in Vietnam.

Spring Mobilization

At a conference in the Fall of 1966, of the Peace Mobilization Committee, it was tentatively decided to hold massive demonstrations on April 15, 1967, in New York City and San Francisco, California. Of the one hundred seventeen individuals in attendance, seventy-five were members of the Socialist Workers party or its youth group, the Young Socialist Alliance. The Communist party was represented by Arnold Johnson and James West, both of whom are members of the Communist Party, USA, National Committee.

This group subsequently changed its name to Spring Mobilization Committee to End the War in Vietnam. Reverend James Bevel, on leave from the Southern Christian Leadership Conference, was appointed Executive Director of this Committee.

On April 13, 1967, Levison and King were in contact to discuss the progress Levison was making in the writing of the speech King was to deliver on April 15, 1967, to a rally of the Spring Mobilization Committee at the United Nations. Levison discussed part of the speech which King enthusiastically accepted. King particularly liked the part indicating that the United States should unilaterally withdraw from Vietnam. He also enjoyed the part where he would appeal to the country to "demand insistently that our Government honor Hanoi's promise to negotiate if the bombings cease."

The CPUSA was delighted with King's actions in this regard. The recognized leader of 22 million Negroes had openly attacked his country's policy in Vietnam. He participated in the largest rally ever staged against the Vietnam war by being the keynote speaker. In his speech King again called for the withdrawal of United States troops from Vietnam. King was helping the CPUSA achieve its goal of uniting the Negro movement with the peace issue.

"The Worker" expressed the CPUSA's pleasure in the May 7, 1967, issue where it stated in part, "When Dr. King insists upon the connection between aggressive foreign policy and regressive domestic policy he insists upon what is true and consequential. When Dr. King points to the racism common in colonialism and jim crow he points to that which is historically demonstrable. When Dr. King affirms that the present war in Vietnam threatens all democratic and progressive advance in the United States and does so for economic, political, ethical and psychological reasons, again he is saying what every fact and every day's events confirm. Hence Dr. King, precisely as a leader in the struggle against jim crow, must be—and is—a leader in the struggle against war."

Being the astute advisor is, and to keep King from being openly aligned with the CPUSA, Levison advised King to align himself with those individuals who have power rather than be aligned with a fringe antiwar element. He was to make the new alignment after his April 15, 1967, speech.

King for President

The fringe element Levison referred to was attempting to persuade King to run for President on a peace ticket. On April 19, 1967, Levison and Wachtel conferred concerning King's political possibilities. According to Wachtel, a pacifist group was meeting that day in an effort to get King to agree to run for President with Dr. Benjamin Spock, the antiwar agitator, as his Vice Presidential candidate. Both Levison and Wachtel agreed that it was too early and that King should not agree to run at this time.

The CPUSA again seized the opportunity to cause dissension and unrest in the country by announcing they would support King and Spock on a peace ticket. At a May Day 1967 program in Berkeley, California, Gus Hall stated, "The Party forces should begin work right now to elect these two men because they are for peace in Vietnam."

Early in May 1967, Levison was still concerned with King's being identified with the peace movement rather than civil rights. When approached by peace groups attempting to get King to continue to run for President, Levison informed those representatives that King would talk on Vietnam on occasion to various groups, but that would be the extent of his involvement.

In an effort to evaluate his position, King and the SCLC held a retreat in Frogmore, South Carolina, on May 21, 1967, to determine the relationship of the SCLC to the peace movement. King and other top functionaries concluded that the SCLC would give no overt support to anti-Vietnam war demonstrations.

The Birth of Washington Spring Project

On July 19, 1967, Levison was in conference with King concerning the Newark, New Jersey, riot. Levison indicated he was concerned about King's failure to make any public statement concerning the racial disturbances. King informed Levison that he had been considering making a statement but did not merely want to condemn the riots but also to condemn the conditions which led to riots.

Levison suggested that King advocate a program with dramatic qualities similar to the Works Project Administration of the 1930s. This new program would be implemented by the Federal Government to employ the jobless youth. Levison continued that this program worked in a period when the United States was almost bankrupt and should work even better now that the country is almost sick with money. King agreed that Levison's idea had merit and he would publicly call upon the Federal Government to do something along this line.

King waited until the Tenth Annual Convention of the SCLC before he made these plans public. On August 15, 1967, he delivered an address at the convention urging new massive civil disobedience which would include general strikes, school boycotts, and a camp-in at Washington, D.C. All this would be to force Congress to take action to improve the lot of the Negro.

V. SOUTHERN CHRISTIAN LEADERSHIP CONFERENCE FINANCES

The foremost problem in conducting such a campaign is making financial arrangements to handle the costs. As he has in the past, King turned to Levison to help him handle this problem as well as all financing of the SCLC. At a retreat in September 1967, it was decided that SCLC would attempt to raise $1,500,000 during the coming year. It was contemplated that this money would be realized through the mail-appeal program of SCLC under the general supervision of Levison.

During the fiscal year July 1, 1966, to June 30, 1967, SCLC realized income in the amount of $901,021.52. The total expenses of SCLC for this period were $859,933.34. This indicated income exceeded expenses by $41,088.18.

A Tax Dodge

The SCLC set up Foundations to serve as tax exempt organizations that would solicit funds for SCLC. To this end the American Foundation on Nonviolence of New York City, and the Southern Christian Leadership Foundation of Chicago, Illinois, were established. As money is needed by SCLC, Harry Wachtel reportedly funnels the money from the American Foundation on Nonviolence to SCLC.

Funds from Firms and Foundations

In February 1967, the firm of Merrill, Lynch, Pierce, Fenner, and Smith, a stock brokerage firm, contributed $15,000 to SCLC. In August 1967, Edward Lamb of the Edward Lamb Foundation, Toledo, Ohio, donated some stock to SCLC which had a market value of $6,000. Edward Lamb is a well-known successful businessman in Toledo, Ohio.

It was learned in November 1967, that the Ford Foundation was about to give SCLC $230,000. This money was to train Negro ministers in 25 cities throughout the Nation to become qualified leaders in the ghetto areas.

Funds from Individuals

In October 1965, Governor of New York Nelson Rockefeller matched the $25,000 donation which King made to the Gandhi Society for Human Rights, another fund-raising adjunct of SCLC.

... During the year 1967, Annie Labouisse Farnsworth, also known as Mrs. Peter Farnsworth and heiress to the Clark Thread Fortune, donated $50,000 to SCLC. In January 1968, it was learned she was in the process of donating $100,000 to King's group.

Funds from Government Agencies

... It was also determined that in November 1967, the Department of Labor negotiated a contract with SCLC to train Negroes for employment in Atlanta, Georgia. Of the $61,000 involved in the contract, $13,000 went to SCLC and $48,000 went to the grocers in Atlanta for providing on-the-job training to the previously unemployed Negroes.

Funds for Washington Spring Project

In February, 1968, Levison was in conference with one of King's aides concerning methods of raising funds for the ''Washington Spring Project.'' Levison suggested that a meeting be held in the home of Harry Belafonte of approximately 60 individuals who have contributed

$1,000 or more to SCLC in the past. Levison advised that some of the people to be invited to this meeting would be Governor and Mrs. Nelson Rockefeller, Mary and Stephen Rockefeller, and Franklin D. Roosevelt III.

[Section 80]

UNITED STATES GOVERNMENT
Memorandum

TO: Mr. C. D. DeLoach   DATE: March 20, 1968

FROM: W. C. Sullivan

MARTIN LUTHER KING'S MARCH
ON WASHINGTON RACIAL MATTERS

We all know the great gravity of Martin Luther King's march on Washington next month. It could end in great violence and bloodshed. This being the capital city, it would do us irreparable propaganda damage around the world.

This Division has been preparing to carry out its intelligence responsibilities relative to this march in the most effective manner possible. We have been girding ourselves for this task ever since King's announcement to march on Washington. We should leave no stone unturned.

In view of the above, I would like the permission to talk confidentially to . . . and to . . . I know personally. I suggest this, because both . . . and . . . leadership in Washington give clear signs of being almost totally unaware of the lawlessness and the violence prone elements who will be involved in this march. I would like to make them discreetly aware of this particular factor. Further, I would like to sow the idea that as eminent church leaders they have an enormous responsibility relative to assisting and maintaining law and order. I want to drop the hint that it is not enough for these church leaders to approve publicly as they have done of the social-justice goals inherent in this march on Washington. I want to leave them with the thought that they will not be fulfilling their responsibilities unless they make it evident publicly that the church leaders of this city will not approve of any violence or lawlessness.

I feel very strongly that I can do some good here. Therefore, I do hope that the Bureau will not deny me the permission to see what I can accomplish in this extremely vital area. If I can bring something of this nature about on the part of these church leaders, it may make the work of this Bureau somewhat less heavy and difficult at the time of the march.

UNITED STATES DEPARTMENT OF JUSTICE

FEDERAL BUREAU OF INVESTIGATION

New York, New York
March 27, 1968

Martin Luther King
Security Matter-C

On March 26, 1968, a confidential source, who has furnished reliable information in the past, advised that Dora McDonald, Secretary to Martin Luther King, Jr., head of the Southern Christian Leadership Conference (SCLC), requested Stanley Levison to prepare a letter for colleges pointing out that King is not a candidate for the presidency and that there is no campaign material available. She said she wanted this letter, because due to the "Time" Magazine, College Presidential Poll in April, letters have been received from many colleges asking for campaign material and King's appearance at these colleges.

The source learned that later on March 26, 1968, Stanley Levison discussed with Martin Luther King, Jr., the request from Dora McDonald to prepare a letter stating King is not a presidential candidate. Levison suggested that King's position, on this college poll, should be to state that he, King, does not want to be included as a candidate because his candidates are those who are strongly opposed to the (Vietnam) war or those in favor of ending the war and those who support the principles of the President's Commission on Civil Disorders. Levison continued that as King sees it, there are only two candidates who reflect these points of view, namely, Senators Robert Kennedy and Eugene McCarthy, and King would prefer not to be a third candidate and split the anti-war candidates.

King agreed with this suggestion. He noted that he already determined that he would say he is not a candidate and is not interested in becoming one. He felt a better way to handle the requests would be to send some material such as some of his speeches.

Levison commented that if King were to be a candidate in the college poll he, Levison, could envision King polling a number of votes, along with Kennedy and McCarthy, which would result in President Johnson emerging the winner in the collegiate poll. Levison pointed out that, in taking the position he suggested, King would be "blessing both McCarthy and Kennedy," and not making a choice yet between them.

King stated this is the position he has followed thus far, that both are good, competent men, committed to the principles they are concerned about. He added, however, that they should be realistic enough to see that, if there is any possibility of stopping President Johnson, it will be Kennedy.

Levison agreed, stating that many liberals are being sentimental and not very wise because Kennedy will have a tough job in stopping President Johnson. He said it cannot be done "with a Galahad, like McCarthy." He added that he keeps pointing out that McCarthy was less progressive than Kennedy in the past. Levison agreed with King that McCarthy has not been as strong on civil rights as has Kennedy.

Levison and King agreed that President Johnson has his greatest strength among the working class and among Negroes, that McCarthy has no strength among these groups, but that Kennedy does. They agreed also that Kennedy will split the Negro vote with Levison adding that Kennedy also will split the working-class vote.

King expressed the opinion that at some point along the campaign trail Kennedy and McCarthy will have to get together. Levison then criticized McCarthy's stubbornness on this point, stating that he would have expected McCarthy to say he will finish up, do a tremendous job in Wisconsin, then withdraw.

FBI

Date: 3-29-68

AIRTEL

To: DIRECTOR, FBI (100-106670)

From: SAC, CLEVELAND (157-293) (P)

Re: MARTIN LUTHER KING
           SM-C

... Ohio, has corresponded with the FBI in Washington, D.C., and CV on several occasions in 1966 and 1967 seeking info re various organizations. ... in his letters indicated that he was 19 years of age in 1967 and was a member of the John Birch Society.

... submitted a letter to Senator FRANK J. LAUSCHE (Ohio) in Washington, D.C., in which he pointed out that he had been informed by a very reliable source that the "Rev." MARTIN LUTHER KING had ordered a shipment of 12,000 Remington automatic rifles; ... indicated he was aware of Dr. KING's extensive Communist background and ... expected that the Communists would take over this country by 1975.

The Bureau instructed CV to interview ... as to the source of this info and set out leads in an effort to verify this allegation.

... was interviewed on 1-5-68 and indicated he heard this allegation in a speech by Dr. PETER VARANOF, an officer of "Crusade for God and Freedom" at Mentor, Ohio.

VARANOF was contacted on 2-1-68 at Timberlake, Ohio, and he indicated he heard this rumor about the guns from ... Ohio.

... was also interviewed on 3-22-68 at ... Ohio, and he mentioned he heard the allegation from a member of his church, ... Ohio.

... Ohio, advised on 3-28-68 that ... whose name he refused to divulge who lives in the NY area told ... in approximately 2-67 about the purchase of guns by MARTIN LUTHER KING. This relative has a good friend named ... name unknown in NYC, ... Remington Arms Co., SI, Mass. ... while visiting the Remington plant about a year ago had occasion to see some shipping orders for some large quantities of guns, one order being for one of the Arabian countries and another was for MARTIN LUTHER KING for 10,000 shotguns, having 18" barrels. ... a short time later told ... about seeing this order; ... in a subsequent conversation told ... about these guns being purchased by KING.

Since ... has refused to furnish the name of ... who could in time furnish the complete name of . . . and his address, who originally started this allegation, CV feels that a check of the Remington Arms Co. could resolve this entire affair without any further interim interviews. Therefore BS is being requested to handle this phase of inquiry.

UNITED STATES DEPARTMENT OF JUSTICE

FEDERAL BUREAU OF INVESTIGATION

New York, New York
March 29, 1968

Martin Luther King, Jr.
Security Matter-C

A confidential source, who has furnished reliable information in the past, learned on March 28, 1968, that, late on that date, Stanley Levison and Martin Luther King, Jr., discussed the violence that occurred in Memphis, Tennessee, on March 28, 1968, following King's leadership of a protest march through downtown Memphis. King indicated that he had become so depressed over the developments in Memphis that he has considered calling off the Washington March (his self-described Poor People's Campaign, scheduled to begin in Washington, D.C., on April 22, 1968).

Levison told King that his depression was aggravated because he is physically exhausted as a result of his recent strenuous program. He counseled King not to be on the defensive over the events in Memphis but, on the contrary, [he] should take the position that the majority of people in the Memphis March did not join in the rioting that took place, proving the effectiveness of King's leadership and his policy of non-violence. Levison emphasized that the Washington March will be different in that King will have organized this march and his forces can stress the importance of non-violence. Levison suggested that Saturday morning (March 30, 1968) would be a better time to meet in Atlanta to discuss the Memphis incident rather than meeting on Friday night (March 29, 1968) because it will give King time to rest.

King agreed in every aspect with Levison's evaluation.

The source also ascertained that, prior to conferring with King, Levison spoke with the Reverend [Ralph] Abernathy, an aide of Dr. King's, who advised Levison that King has canceled a scheduled appearance in Washington, D.C., on March 29, 1968. Abernathy also noted that King is scheduled to be in Virginia on Saturday (March 30, 1968) but will probably cancel that appearance. Abernathy continued that it was a mistake for the King forces not to have a staff in Memphis to train people in non-violence. He said it also was a mistake on the part of the King forces not to have been more aware of the local situation.

UNITED STATES GOVERNMENT
Memorandum

TO: Mr. W.C. Sullivan   DATE: March 29, 1968

FROM: G.C. Moore

          COUNTERINTELLIGENCE PROGRAM
          BLACK NATIONALIST-HATE GROUPS
          RACIAL INTELLIGENCE
          (MARTIN LUTHER KING)

PURPOSE:
   To publicize hypocrisy on the part of Martin Luther King.
BACKGROUND:
   Martin Luther King has urged Negroes in Memphis, Tennessee, to boycott white merchants in order to force compliance with Negro demands in the sanitation workers' strike in Memphis.
   When violence broke out during the march King led in Memphis on 3-28-68, King disappeared. There is a first-class Negro hotel in Memphis, the Hotel Lorraine, but King chose to hide out at the white-owned and -operated Holiday Inn Motel.
RECOMMENDATION:
   The above facts have been included in the attached blind memorandum and it is recommended it be furnished a cooperative news media source by the Crime Records Division for an item showing King is a hypocrite. This will be done on a highly confidential basis.

Enclosure

DO AS I SAY, NOT AS I DO

   Martin Luther King, during the sanitation workers' strike in Memphis, Tennessee, has urged Negroes to boycott downtown white merchants to achieve Negro demands. On 3-29-68 King led a march for the sanitation workers. Like Judas leading lambs to slaughter King led the marchers to violence, and when the violence broke out, King disappeared.

The fine Hotel Lorraine in Memphis is owned and patronized exclusively by Negroes but King didn't go there from his hasty exit. Instead King decided the plush Holiday Inn Motel, white owned, operated and almost exclusively white patronized, was the place to "cool it." There will be no boycott of white merchants for King, only for his followers.

[Section 81]

UNITED STATES DEPARTMENT OF JUSTICE

FEDERAL BUREAU OF INVESTIGATION

New York, New York
April 1, 1968

Martin Luther King, Jr.
Security Matter-C

A confidential source, who has furnished reliable information in the past, learned on March 29, 1968, that on that date, Stanley Levison and Martin Luther King, Jr., discussed the position which King has found himself in as a result of the violence that occurred in Memphis, Tennessee, on March 28, 1968, at the time when King led a march through downtown Memphis. King told Levison that he feels they have to face the fact that, from a public relations point of view and every other way, "we are in serious trouble." He referred to the Washington, D.C., Spring campaign, known as the Poor People's Campaign, and said as far as it is concerned it is in trouble. King noted that it will be much more difficult to recruit people for the Washington campaign now because they (the Southern Christian Leadership Conference) (SCLC) are recruiting non-violent people and these people will hold back if they think they will be in a campaign that is going to be taken over by violent elements. King stated that this is not a failure for the SCLC because it has enough of a program to affirm its position but that it is a personal setback for himself.

King continued that persons such as Roy Wilkins (Head of the National Association for the Advancement of Colored People) and Adam Clayton Powell, and Negroes who are influenced by the press, will now feel that he, King, is finished, that his non-violence is nothing, that no one is listening to it. King reiterated that they had a great-public relations setback as far as his image and leadership are concerned.

Levison attempted to dissuade King from his point of view stating that it would be true only if King accepts "their" definition. He added that he felt it is a profound error King is making.

King noted that he did not accept it himself but that others will. Levison retorted that people would accept it for a few days, but, if events prove otherwise, will not accept it.

King noted that events will not prove otherwise unless they think soberly through this period. He said that somehow he had to reaffirm what the press will refuse to affirm. He referred to the Memphis incident stating that they all know it was just a few people who were involved. He added that it was a failure of the leadership in Memphis. King informed Levison that persons who were responsible for the violence came to see him on the morning of March 29, 1968. He said these persons were fighting the leadership in Memphis, the men who ignored and neglected them, the men who would not give them any attention, who ordered their telephones cut off. King added that he had no knowledge of all this, that the persons responsible for the violence were too sick to see that what they were doing during the violence was hurting him, King, more than it could hurt the local preachers.

King related that he was so upset and shocked over the Memphis violence that he was going to announce a personal fast as a means of appealing to the Memphis leadership, as well as those who participated in the violence, to come to him in a united front to take up the "cudgel" and get on with the movement. He said he felt this kind of spiritual move would be a way of unifying the movement, of transforming a minus into a plus. He added that he feels their Washington campaign is doomed.

Levison attempted to convince King that his reasoning was not correct. Levison said he was concerned over the "trap" King was placing non-violence in because King was saying that he must have 100% adherence to non-violence, which is an impossibility.

King commented that they could not get 100% adherence but that they must face the fact that a riot broke out in the ranks of the march, that "these fellows," in the line of march, would jump out, do something, and then come back and hide within the group. King said he is a symbol of non-violence and that the press is not going to say what Levison said. He said the symbol will be weakened and it will put many Negroes in doubt. He said he must do something that is a powerful act to unify forces and refute the press.

Levison stated that if it has this result he would agree but that he is bothered by the idea that King would be accepting the logic of the press that if King can control 99%, and not the 1% who are violent, he is a failure. He said they must find a way in which they do not accept this otherwise King will never be able to do anything unless he always spiritually reaches a level where he hypnotized every Negro alive.

King questioned how he could say that they can control the planned demonstrations in Washington, D.C., and at the same time conclude they are going to have 1% violence.

Levison counseled that King can say that he can control his followers and is not undertaking to control everybody else. He said King could take the position that his followers are non-violent and will do what they must do.

They agreed to discuss the matter in depth at a meeting in Atlanta, Georgia, in King's church office on the morning of March 30, 1968.

The same source advised on March 31, 1968, that on that date Stanley Levison commented on the meeting held in Atlanta, Georgia, on March 30, 1968. Levison's comments included the following:

At the Atlanta meeting they examined the whole Memphis incident and came up with a new approach. "We are going back to Memphis. We are going to prove that you can have mass action in the streets." Martin Luther King had decided not to go back to Memphis and not to go to Washington (for the Poor People's Campaign). It was the determination of the (SCLC) staff that changed King's thinking. King is going back to Memphis on Tuesday (April 2, 1968) and there will be a big march on Friday (April 5, 1968). The Memphis incident was caused by "a handful of kids" and it could have been controlled by "our guys" (the SCLC) had they been there.

He, Levison, made the point that they could not let "a couple of kids" keep "mass action" from being their weapon.

As for controlling the Washington, D.C., demonstrations, King knows he can control the youth. What has to be done is go to the high schools and tell them what the establishment wants them to do. Once they grasp this there is no chance of anything happening. What they (the SCLC) are afraid of in Washington is a double cross from Stokely Carmichael. and the answer to that is that "our job" (the SCLC) is not to stop violence but to be non-violent themselves. "Our position" is that "we" are going to go on because to be able to march in the streets is "our most important tool" and are not going on the streets because it may start violence. "Why do we have to be afraid of riots. It is their problem not ours."

The Atlanta meeting was good because it shows how much militancy there is in the SCLC.

Wilmington, N. C.
28401

Cong. Alton Lennon
House of Representatives
Washington, D.C.

Dear Sir:

During these days of crisis and civil disobedience, our citizens are becoming more and more alarmed with the lawlessness in our country.

About three weeks ago, Sen. Strom Thurmond urged that the official report from the F.B.I. on Dr. Martin Luther King be made public. I should like to urge you as an official representative from this state to support this move and that the American people be informed about the real Martin Luther King. As a public servant, I believe you to be interested in the welfare of this nation.

I should also like to urge you that the report on racial disorders from the F.B.I. be made public. I realize that it is important that certain information be withheld at certain times, but what could be more important than publicly exposing those who are subtly destroying this great nation of ours with a false front of Non-violence.

I should like to know your views concerning these matters and trust that you will urge this information be made public to the American people at once.

Respectfully yours,
[Signature deleted]

[Section 82]

To: MR. W. C. SULLIVAN   April 11, 1968

From: Mr. G. C. MOORE

COMMUNIST INFILTRATION
SOUTHERN CHRISTIAN LEADERSHIP CONFERENCE

PURPOSE:

Attached for you approval for dissemination are copies of a communication concerning a conference that was held speculating as to the future of the Southern Christian Leadership Conference (SCLC) since the death of its president, Martin Luther King, Jr.

RECENT DEVELOPMENTS:

Recently, Stanley Levison, long-time secret Communist Party member and principal advisor to the late Martin Luther King, Jr., was in conference with his wife concerning the future of SCLC, according to . . . These two agreed there was no one who could take the place of King but that King had more or less named Ralph Abernathy as his heir. Levison added that he would like to see Andrew Young, the current Executive Vice President of SCLC, take King's place.

At this meeting, it was also learned that the Field Foundation was going to give SCLC $300,000 but Mr. Levison added it would take a million dollars to keep the organization going. The Field Foundation was established in 1940 by Marshall Field, the retail tycoon of Chicago, Illinois. One of its objectives is to promote interracial harmony.

Later they discussed the "Poor People's Campaign" scheduled for April 1968, in Washington, D. C. Mr. Levison commented that it is unlikely that this campaign will transpire, especially in view of the recent rioting.

FBI

Date: 4/15/68

AIRTEL

To: DIRECTOR, FBI (100-106670)

From: SAC, NEW HAVEN (100-18410) (RUC)

Subject: MARTIN LUTHER KING
           SM-C
           00:AT

RE: Boston airtel to the Director, 4-10-68

On 4-15-68, . . . Remington Arms Company, Inc., Bridgeport, Conn., advised that MARTIN LUTHER KING had never ordered firearms from Remington Arms Company, Inc., or made inquiry concerning firearms.

According to . . . Remington Arms Company, Inc., has never received an order for 10,000 shotguns or rifles from any single individual.

FBI

Date: 4/15/68

AIRTEL

To: DIRECTOR, FBI (100-106670)

From: SAC, ALBANY (100-18761) (RUC)

Re: MARTIN LUTHER KING
           SM-C

           (OO: Atlanta)

           Re Cleveland airtel 3/29/68, and Boston airtel 4/10/68.

On 4/16/68, . . . Remington Arms, Inc., Ilion, N.Y., advised SA . . . that all guns sold by his company are manufactured at this plant and shipments of them are made to authorized distributors only. He stated no shipment of guns is made to individuals or to organizations and, therefore, no such shipment would have been directed at any time to Reverend MARTIN LUTHER KING.

He noted that a shotgun with an 18-inch barrel would be the Remington model 870, 12 gauge, which has been known as the riot gun now called the police gun. He stated that in 1966 there were 3,495 of these weapons sold, over 3,000 of which went to California Highway Patrol and during 1967 only 845 of these were sold all to known distributors.

UNITED STATES GOVERNMENT
Memorandum

TO: Mr. W. C. Sullivan   DATE: April 17, 1968

FROM: C. D. Brennan

ASSASSINATION OF MARTIN LUTHER KING

Since the assassination of Martin Luther King, we have been closely following the activities of Stanley Levison and leaders of the Communist Party, USA (CPUSA), to determine what effect this event has had on the efforts of both Levison and the Party to continue to exploit racial problems in this country. . . .

With regard to the reaction of the CPUSA, it is noted that as soon as news of the assassination was announced, the CPUSA moved, as expected, to exploit the situation to its own advantage. A special issue of "The Worker," east coast communist newspaper, was prepared eulogizing King and attacking racism in the U. S. Copies were shipped to each Party district for mass distribution. . . .

UNITED STATES DEPARTMENT OF JUSTICE

FEDERAL BUREAU OF INVESTIGATION

Chicago, Illinois
April 18, 1968

RACIAL DISTURBANCE
FOLLOWING ASSASSINATION
OF MARTIN LUTHER KING, JR.,
CHICAGO, ILLINOIS, BEGINNING
APRIL 4, 1968

Reference is made to Chicago memoranda, above captioned and that of "Assassination of Martin Luther King, Jr.," dated in the period April 9–12, 1968, and April 16, 1968.

It might briefly be noted that the above communications concerned themselves with major disturbances which took place in Chicago over the period of April 5–7, 1968, gradually subsiding from that point until the removal of Illinois National Guard (ING) forces and United States Army troops was effected, these forces having been ordered to Chicago during the initial phases of the disturbances to restore order.

On April 15, 1968, various Chicago sources advised, and Chicago's press media contained voluminous information concerning an unscheduled press conference held that date by Chicago's Mayor Richard J. Daley. During the course of this press conference Daley was critical of the actions of the Chicago Police Department (PD) and its Superintendent James B. Conlisk, Jr., for their actions in connection with the control of the previous disorders. Daley announced that he was forming a special blue ribbon committee of nine members to investigate the conduct of the PD, as well as the Chicago Fire Department (CFD) and ING forces during the course of these disturbances.

The committee appointed by Daley was to be headed by United States District Court (USDC) Judge Richard B. Austin and was to include the following individuals:

Franklin Kreml, member, Chicago PD
    Advisory Board

Charles Siragusa, Executive Director,
    Illinois Crime Commission

Daniel Walker, President of the
    Chicago Crime Commission

Justin Stanley, President
    Chicago Bar Association

Thomas Mulroy, former President of the
    Chicago Crime Commission

Ray Simon, Chicago Corporation Counsel

M. P. Vanema, President, Chicago Association
    of Commerce and Industry

William E. Petersen, President, Cook County
    Bar Association

According to local news media, at this press conference Mayor Daley had stated he had ordered Police Superintendent Conlisk, prior to the racial disturbances, to "shoot to kill" arsonists and to "shoot to maim or cripple" looters. Mayor Daley stated that as of this date he had reissued both orders to Superintendent Conlisk concerning any future riots. He had also ordered the use of the chemical Mace against teen-agers or other rioters and criticized the failure of PD to adequately utilize Mace during the disorders.

Daley advised the news media representatives at this press conference that he had discovered on this date, April 15, 1968, that these orders referred to previously had never been issued to Chicago police officers prior to or during the disturbance. In connection with the question put to Mayor Daley as to the possible removal of Superintendent Conlisk, he advised he would await the findings of the nine-man committee appointed by him before making any decision. As well as actions of city agencies and ING forces, the committee is to look into all ramifica-tions of the extensive arson activities during the recent disorders, the widespread determination of rumors and the extensive looting. An effort will be made by this committee to determine whether or not any con-spiracy was involved in any aspect of these disorders. Daley was quoted by various news media as follows, ''I said to Superintendent Conlisk very emphatically and very definitely that I wanted an order issued to the police at once, over his signature to shoot to kill any arsonists, or anyone with a molotov cocktail in hand to fire a Chicago building. I told Conlisk to issue an order to police to shoot to maim or cripple anyone looting any stores in our city.'' Daley stated that riot probers would also look into the fact that telephone lines in Chicago were jammed with calls during the disorders and that expressway traffic had seemed unusually heavy.

On April 15, 1968, a confidential source who has furnished reliable information in the past, advised that on April 12, 1968, Chicago's Mayor Daley had met with some 60 representatives of Chicago business and industry. Daley had requested these individuals to furnish 25,000 jobs for youths of the city during the coming summer to counteract the widespread unemployment of this age group during this summer time. This age group specifically would be inclusive of the years 16 to 21. Mr. Morgan Murphy, an executive of the Commonwealth Edison Com-pany, is to chair this committee which will be known as Mayor Daley's Summer Job's for Youth Committee.

During the late evening hours of April 15, 1968, . . . advised that a memorial march for King was held between the hours of 7:30–8:30 P.M. in the village. The march was sponsored by the Arlington Heights Human Relations Commission and some 250 persons, primarily Cauca-sian, participated. The affair was peaceful with no incidents or arrests having occurred.

... source, during the latter hours of April 15, 1968, advised that Chicago remained calm at the present time, that tensions continued to exist in the predominantly Negro-ghetto areas of the city, however, there had been no recent incidents which had transpired which could be related to the recent disorders.

On April 16, 1968, Chicago's news media continued to afford extensive coverage and commentary to the remarks made by Mayor Daley at his press conference the previous day.

Various news articles contained an order issued by Police Superintendent Conlisk to all commanding officers of the department as a result of the Mayor's instructions to him, the order is as follows: "Arson, attempted arson, burglary and attempted burglary are forcible felonies. Such as is necessary, including deadly force, shall be used to prevent the commission of these offenses and to prevent the escape of perpetrators. Commanding officers will insure the above and general order 67-14 will continually be reviewed at all role calls effective immediately, and continuing through April 22, 1964" [sic].

As a matter of information, it might be noted that general police order 67-14 was issued by a former Chicago police superintendent, O. W. Wilson, May 16, 1967, and is as follows: "Police are not to 1) fire into crowds; 2) fire over heads of crowds except on orders from officer above rank of captain; 3) fire warning shots where there is chance of injuring bystanders; 4) fire into buildings or through doors where person fired at is not clearly visible." Local press articles reflect considerable controversy had been aroused in the community as a result of the Mayor's remarks and instructions to the police superintendent. Various representatives of the Negro community and civil rights leaders were quoted as deploring the Mayor's comments with various representatives of other interested groups commenting in a laudatory fashion. For example, Reverend Jesse Jackson, National Director, Operation Breadbasket, economic arm of the Southern Christian Leadership Conference, referred to the Mayor's statement as [a] "facist's response." Jackson stated that he interpreted the Mayor's remarks to mean that police should have more regard for property and cans of food than human life.

John McDemott, Executive Director, Catholic Racial Council, was critical of the Mayor's comments, saying history would recall April 15, 1968, was the low point of Mayor Daley's attention. McDemott noted that race relations in Chicago are in an extremely delicate and critical condition with the situation at flashpoint, calling for a most careful and sensitive handling by the city's leaders. McDemott felt that the Mayor's request for more aggressive police reaction was like throwing a molotov cocktail at an ammunition dump.

Joseph J. Le Fevour, President, Fraternal Order of Police, was noted as having sent a telegram to Mayor praising his statements and comments.

In this same vein, Brigadier General Richard T. Dunn, commander of the ING, and in charge of ING forces in Chicago during the recent disorders, was quoted in the press to the effect that police behavior in general "indicated satisfactory performance" so far as he was concerned. Dunn stated that he was not in Chicago prior to the late evening of April 5, 1968, but after he became personally involved in the situation, actions of the police which he had observed, had all seemed perfectly proper to him. He was quoted as having stated "I personally saw police bringing looting to a halt in buildings out there."

... who has furnished reliable information in the past, ... advised on April 16, 1968, that Chicago's news media generally was having difficulty finding people involved in the upper echelons of industry or the community generally who would publicly back Mayor Daley's comment for a more aggressive response to disorders. This source advised that many individuals contacted for comments in this regard seemed to agree with the Mayor's firm stand, but felt, however, that the timing of his statement, together with the public criticism of the PD at this time, was highly inappropriate.

Chicago's sources generally knowledgeable concerning racial conditions on the west and south sides of the city, during the afternoon and evening April 16, 1968, were contacted and advised that although there are no known planned acts of violence, or demonstrations in these communities as a result of the Mayor's recent comments, his remarks were received with much displeasure and resentment. The sources advised that these comments have appeared to have increased the already existing tensions and anti-power structure attitudes of many residents of these areas.

In connection with another facet of the recent Chicago disturbances, it might be noted at this point that the Blackstone Rangers, a large and violent Negro youth gang operating on Chicago's south side, were reported by PD sources to be engaged in extortion activities against merchants and business establishments in that area, in an implied or indirect promise of protection of these merchants for contributions and donations to the Rangers. The PD reportedly has been making investigation into these charges.

In this connection a press conference was held on April 16, 1968, on Chicago's south side and at this press conference representatives of two south side Chicago businessmen's associations denied reports that the Rangers had been operating an extortion racket against local businessmen. A statement issued by these associations praised the Rangers for helping to keep down violence in the Woodlawn-Jackson Park area on the south side during the disorders. These spokesmen did concede, however, that there had undoubtedly been isolated extortions where some individuals had attempted to take advantage of the tense situation in this fashion.

During the late evening hours of April 16, 1968, . . . source advised that there had been several incidents of sniper fire reported in the area of Oak and Larabee Streets, on Chicago's near north side within the past hour or so. The sniping had been directed at Chicago firemen as they answered fire calls in this area, the fire calls proving to be false alarms. It appeared the alarms had been turned in for this area, with the sniping taking place when the fire trucks entered the vicinity of the fire boxes involved . . . were dispatched to escort fire apparatus in all future calls in this area during the course of the evening. The area was quiet as of this time and no injuries have resulted from the sniper fire. The source advised that these activities took place in the area of the near north side where disorders had occurred over the weekend of April 5–7, 1968.

On April 17, 1968, Chicago's news media continued to report extensively on the controversy which had arisen surrounding comments made by Chicago's Mayor Daley on April 15, 1968, concerning orders to shoot arsonists and shoot-to-stop orders against looters during disturbances.

In articles appearing in Chicago's newspapers in general circulation on this date, Mayor Daley was noted as having stated that his orders had been misunderstood and blown out of all proportion. The Mayor explained that his shoot-to-kill orders refer to "obvious" arsonists, continuing that "if they are burning the buildings down, they should be shot." The Mayor added that this order would apply to arsonists in future disturbances.

In reporting comments of various local personages and individuals familiar with the Chicago situation, various newspapers contain comments, pro and con, concerning the Mayor's recent remarks. Former Chicago Police Superintendent O. W. Wilson was reported to have supported Mayor Daley's comments, stating that the furor over his order was "an incredible misunderstanding." Wilson felt that Mayor Daley was proposing action within the framework of Illinois law, noting that the Mayor was not proposing shooting in lieu of arrest but was referring to the use of deadly force in effecting lawful arrest.

The "Chicago Tribune," a major Chicago newspaper, in an editorial on April 17, 1968, strongly supported Mayor Daley's position, pointing out that many homes might have been saved if more force had been used to crush the riot at its beginnings. The editorial pointed out that the orders to the police by Mayor Daley served notice on arsonists and looters that they would start further orgies of destruction at their own peril.

In an article appearing in another major Chicago newspaper, the "Chicago Sun-Times," on April 16, 1968, Professor Fred Inbau, Professor of Criminal Law at Northwestern University and President of Americans for Effective Law Enforcement, was noted as stating that police were justified in shooting to kill in certain instances. Inbau had stated "if the only way the police can prevent arsonists and looters from escaping is to shoot them, then shoot them."

Continuing in connection with the controversy which had arisen subsequent to Mayor Daley's press conference, a third confidential source, who has furnished reliable information in the past, advised that on April 17, 1968, Jesse Jackson, National director, Operation Breadbasket (OB), the economic arm of the SCLC, had held a press conference in Chicago. At this press conference, Jackson had announced that since Mayor Daley has declared war upon black people, through his orders to the Chicago Police Department, ministers affiliated with OB will stage a massive march and "prayer-in" at Chicago's City Hall, as well as marches into "uncivilized area," presumed by the source to mean white communities of Chicago, sometime in the near future. This activity would be in protest of the Mayor's comments. Jackson was unable to give any specific date as to when this activity would take place on the part of OB. He stated however, it would hopefuly be within the next week.

During the late evening of April 17, 1968, Chicago's press media carried stories which indicated that [the] Mayor had to some extent qualified his comments made at his press conference on April 15, 1968.

[Section 83]

UNITED STATES DEPARTMENT OF JUSTICE

FEDERAL BUREAU OF INVESTIGATION

New York, New York
April 23, 1968

Martin Luther King, Jr.;
Southern Christian Leadership Conference (SCLC)
Racial Matters

A confidential source, who has furnished reliable information in the past, ascertained on April 19, 1968, that, on that date, Tom Offenberger, who is associated with the SCLC, Atlanta, Georgia, and Stanley Levison, discussed the problems involved in controlling the rash of pictures, books and recordings of the speeches of Martin Luther King, Jr., which have been issued commercially since his death. Levison noted that a number of unauthorized books or booklets had been published and asserted they would track them down in an attempt to get something out of them. He revealed that he has concentrated on areas where he feels there is real money that will safeguard the organization (SCLC) or Coretta (King's wife). Levison emphasized that a book to be written by Coretta King is of central importance to her and that this must be a clear understanding among SCLC staff members as well as those people who were close to King, that they are not to write any books about King prior to the publication of Coretta's book. He said that Harry Belafonte is going to ask everyone on the SCLC staff to agree in writing on this point.

Levison mentioned that there are three projects under consideration on behalf of the organization (SCLC); one, a New York Madison Square Garden meeting in late May, two, a dinner to be held earlier of "big well-heeled people whom we feel might really give us big contributions" and three, a plan to solicit paintings from major artists which the SCLC could exhibit and then auction off.

Levison revealed that advertisements for contributions to the (King) Memorial Fund which he had recently placed under Harry Belafonte's name had resulted in receipts much less than had been expected.

Levison and Offenberger discussed the long-range approach of future fund-raising efforts of the SCLC. Levison opined that they would have to proceed on a membership basis in the Negro community and should utilize this moment to campaign for membership using the slogan "A Million to Replace One." Offenberger demurred at the idea of such a campaign but Levison pointed out that the fund-raising which has sustained the organization over the years was based upon King's unique personality, whereas the personality of Ralph Abernathy is "as ill-suited to the donors we have as you could possibly find." He described these donors as white middle-class intellectuals. He contended that these individuals needed a Martin Luther King and, while one might get by with a Coretta King as a successor, "you can't get by without somebody who is not an intellectual."

Levison estimated that as much as 75% of their list of contributors might be lost as a result of the change in leadership of the SCLC. He said the answer is to go where the new leadership has appeal, the (Negro) church community where it would be possible to build a membership at the present time. Levison stated that the SCLC should have gotten its income from the Negroes, in the first instance, and not the white people and was thus on the wrong basis all along.

Levison noted that the SCLC was co-sponsoring a conference in New York City on Monday (April 22, 1968) with the Institute for New Careers to discuss the legislative program they should be pursuing. He said the purpose of the conference would be to register their dissatisfaction with legislation already passed as "empty and utterly inadequate." Levison strongly recommended that Andrew Young (Executive Vice President of the SCLC) be advised of the conference and arrange to attend it as the SCLC representative.

(Regarding the meeting scheduled for New York City on April 22, 1968, the source previously advised that Stanley Levison had mentioned that a Dr. Frank Reisman [phonetic] wanted to hold a conference of organizations with the SCLC as a co-sponsor. He described Reisman as a neutral figure and as the head of an institute on new careers for Negroes of a quasi-professional nature which would involve assistants to doctors, teachers and professional men.)

Levison mentioned that Ralph Abernathy had received an invitation to speak before the convention of the Women's Business and Professional Clubs in Huntington, Long Island, New York, at the end of May 1968, and stressed that he should attend this convention. He identified this organization as the second largest Negro women's organization in the country.

Levison reiterated comments he had made previously that Coretta

King should not be subjected to too many interviews and should be careful of her public image. He said he is very much opposed to a lot of publicity at the present time.

He noted that the book division of "Ebony" Magazine wants to print some extracts but that this has to go through himself, Harry Belafonte and Joan Davis, a publisher's representative. Levison said he wanted to be sure that "we" control all the things which can mean some money and which they can do themselves.

Offenberger inquired about Abernathy appearing on "Face the Nation" and Levison said he was against it and that "Meet the Press" is worse. He said that "Issues and Answers" might be all right because in a "one on one situation" he (Abernathy) could handle himself. Levison added that they would cut Abernathy to pieces on "Meet the Press" and that on "Face the Nation" he might trip himself up. Levison said he would like to see Abernathy "hook onto" his own image as a militant, simple, straightforward person which he would negate by trying to be an intellectual on "Face the Nation" and getting tripped up. He said Abernathy is doing very well in creating the image of a person who is undaunted and is as fearless as King was. He commented that this can be extremely positive and that if Abernathy never emerges as an intellectual it would not matter.

Levison and Offenberger also discussed the opening of the SCLC's Poor People's Campaign on April 29, 1968, in Washington, D.C. Offenberger noted that, after a ceremony on May 2, 1968, at the Lorraine Motel in Memphis, Tennessee, where King was shot, there will be a march to Marks, Mississippi, to "pack up the people in Marks and get the mule train going." Offenberger noted that the Southern leg (of the march to Washington for the Poor People's Campaign), the Boston leg and the Chicago leg all start within a week. He stated that Bevel (Reverend James Bevel of the SCLC) was going to Memphis at once.

Offenberger, apparently alluding to Washington, D.C., mentioned the "shantytown will start going up" about May 13, that lumber and materials will be assembled beforehand "and you just kind of put the thing together." He said that by the end of the week (week ending May 18, 1968) people will be coming in from the different "wings" (of the march).

[Section 84]

May 21, 1968

...Richmond, Virginia 23235

Dear ...

Your letter of May 16th has been received and I want to thank you for your kind comments.

In response to your inquiry, the FBI has never made any statement to the effect that Martin Luther King was a communist. Information of this nature, whether substantiated or not, cannot be released because of a Department of Justice order regarding all matters of a confidetial nature.

Sincerely yours,

J. Edgar Hoover

UNITED STATES GOVERNMENT
Memorandum

TO: MR. TOLSON   Date: 5/21/68

FROM: C.D. DeLoach

APPROVAL OF WIRETAPS AND MICROPHONES
BY ROBERT F. KENNEDY -
Specific approval of wiretap on Martin Luther King

Article by Drew Pearson and Jack Anderson
Friday 5/24/68

Jack Anderson called and stated he wanted to speak in confidence. I told him if it concerned an official matter I could not agree with this stipulation. He stated he merely wanted to tip me off that Drew Pearson will have an article on Friday, 5/24/68, alleging that former AG Bobby Kennedy ordered the FBI to place a wiretap on Martin Luther King. He stated the article would probably hurt Kennedy a great deal.

I told Anderson we would have no comment concerning such an article; however, that I felt he was doing us a great disservice inasmuch as the article would certainly dry up Negro sources of information who have been friendly to the FBI.

Anderson stated he and Pearson were well aware of this fact; however, they felt that Kennedy should receive a death blow prior to the Oregon primary. I told him that, as he had been advised once before, the FBI would not become involved in bitter political struggles and that the record should be quite clear concerning this fact. Anderson said he well understood our position, and that he hoped Pearson's column would not affect the FBI too much. I told him that remained to be seen.

Anderson asked me if the FBI had disseminated a report concerning King's communist affiliations and sex life as of February or March 28, 1968. I told him I would make no comment. He stated he knew such a report was in existence and as a matter of fact he had read such a report. I asked for the identity of his source. He stated he must refuse to tell me. I told him we well knew that Ed Weisl, Jr., had advised him concerning specific information involving an old wiretap on King. I asked him point blank if Weisl had allowed him to read an FBI report. He stated he had already admitted to me on one occasion that Weisl was his source in the Department, but that he must refuse to reveal the identity of the source who had allowed him to read an FBI report. The conversation ended with this statement.

We did disseminate an FBI report on King dated 3/12/68. It may be that Anderson is bluffing or it may be that he is talking about this specific report. It would be my thought that he possibly knows the date of the report, but has not been given a chance to read it. We nevertheless should maintain a strict "no comment" in the event Pearson's article appears on Friday, 5/24/68.

UNITED STATES GOVERNMENT
Memorandum

TO: Mr. DeLoach   DATE: May 28, 1968

FROM: T.E. Bishop

           APPROVAL OF WIRETAPS AND MICROPHONES
           BY ROBERT F. KENNEDY

Mr. Carl Greenburg, Political Editor of the Los Angeles Times, called shortly after 2 P.M. today and advised that the Los Angeles times had just been furnished a statement by Frank Mankiewicz, Press Secretary to Senator Kennedy. According to Mr. Greenburg, this statement related to Drew Pearson's claim that Senator Kennedy authorized FBI bugging or wiretapping of Martin Luther King. Mr. Greenburg said that he wished the Bureau would have the benefit of this statement and also would appreciate any comment the Director might wish to make concerning it.

Mr. Greenburg was advised that the FBI had made no comment whatsoever regarding Drew Pearson's article. He did ask, however, if at all possible the attached statement be brought to Mr. Hoover's attention personally because as he said he was "more brutal" in his opinion than anything Kennedy had previously said concerning this matter.

RECOMMENDATION:

It is recommended that "no comment" be made concerning the attached Kennedy statement and that Mr. Greenburg be so advised by my office.

"Senator Kennedy has continuously stated that at no time while he was Attorney General did he approve or authorize any electronic survillances of anyone. Pursuant to policies in effect since President Roosevelt's Executive Order of 1940, he did, as Attorney General, approve a limited number of wiretaps in national security cases but, on each occasion, only at the written request of the FBI. Since leaving the Department of Justice, Senator Kennedy has not discussed any particular individual case and he will not do so now.

"It is unfortunate that Drew Pearson is permitting himself to be used in J. Edgar Hoover's continuing campaign against Martin Luther King—now apparently against the memory of Martin Luther King.

"The information that Pearson discusses in his column from the alleged surveillance was developed, according to him, in 1968, two Attorneys General and one President later and well after President Johnson's order forbidding such practices."

June 6, 1968

Mr. J. Edgar Hoover, Director
Federal Bureau of Investigation
Department of Justice
Washington, D.C.

Dear Mr. Hoover:

On Friday, May 24, 1968, the Statesville Record and Landmark carried a column by Drew Pearson which dealt with the wiretapping that had been carried out by the FBI. Mr. Pearson wrote "In this connection, this column has learned that, when Attorney General, Mr. Kennedy ordered a wiretap put on the phone of Dr. Martin Luther King." In the course of the rest of his column Drew Pearson proceeds to attack the morals of Dr. King. One paragraph reads "One report written February 20, 1968, quoted a confidential informant as claiming that Dr. King "Has been having an illicit love affair with the wife of a prominent Negro dentist in Los Angeles since 1962. King calls this woman every Wednesday and meets her in various cities throughout the country. The course related an incident which occurred some time ago in a New York City hotel, where King was intoxicated at a small gathering. King threatened to leap from the 13-floor window of the hotel if this woman would not say she loved him."

We the undersigned ministers of the Presbyterian Church U.S. would like to know what the true facts in this case are. If Mr. Pearson is guilty of character assassination we feel someone ought to call his hand and we believe that you as the Director of the Federal Bureau of Investigation are in a position to force a retraction if his alleged quoting from the FBI reports is not based upon fact.

We have no desire to deify Dr. King but we do not feel that this attack upon his memory ought to go unchallenged if there are no facts to substantiate it.

Please give this matter your serious attention and if it is possible please let us know what the facts really are.

Yours sincerely,
[Signature deleted]

Excerpts from
Electronic Surveillance File
1968—1969

3/26/68

Stanley Levison to Martin Luther King at 752-7000.

Levison: Dora wanted me to prepare a letter to go to the students groups that have been writing in about that *Time* presidential poll. I was talking to Andy the other night about what you're going to do in connection with the elections. And when Dora raised this it suddenly hit me that really the position you should take at this point seems to me, on this poll, is to tell them that you don't want to be included as a candidate because your test for candidates are those who are strongly opposed to the war or those who are in favor of ending the war and who, let's say, support the principles of the Kerne Commission Report fully. As you see it, there are only two candidates who do, McCarthy and Kennedy, and you'd rather not be a third one to split the anti-war candidates. . . . But you understand in taking this kind of position you're blessing both McCarthy and Kennedy. In other words, you're not making a choice yet between them.

King: That's the position I've followed so far; that both are good men, competent men, and committed to the principles that we are concerned about. Up to this point I haven't picked either man. I think we have to be realistic enough to see that if there's any possibility of stopping Lyndon it's going to be Kennedy.

Levison: That's right. That's my very strong position too. That an awful lot of nice liberals are being sentimental and not very wise. Because Bobby Kennedy is going to have one tough job stopping Lyndon. And it's just not going to be done with a Galahad like McCarthy. Also, the thing I keep pointing out is that McCarthy was less progressive than Kennedy before all this started.

King: McCarthy hasn't been as strong.

Levison: (Interrupts)—on civil rights.

King: Exactly.

Levison: That's what most people overlook. The other thing is that Lyndon Johnson has his greatest strength in the working class among Negroes.

King: That's right.

Levison: And McCarthy has no strength there, but Bobby Kennedy has a lot in those two groups.

King: A great deal. Bobby will greatly split the Negro vote.

Levison: That's right.

King: He's the only one really who can.

Levison: And he'll split the working class vote in half because the polls show that he's got 43% and Lyndon Johnson has 42%.

King: Is that so?

Levison: See, Lyndon Johnson has the benefit of having the hierarchy of the trade union movement but Bobby Kennedy has the popularity of a Kennedy in the working class. So those two terribly decisive groups, McCarthy is nowhere and Kennedy is strong.

King: That's right.

Levison: So this is what tipped me over to feeling it shouldn't be a contest of whose manners are better. . . . I'm also disenchanted with McCarthy because of his stubbornness on this. I would have expected him to say let me finish up and do a tremendous job in Wisconsin and then I'm going to withdraw. But he almost acts as though he's bitten by the Presidential but now.

King: That's right.

Levison: And that makes him much less a Galahad.

King: We'll make him Secretary of State.

Levison: I thought everybody wanted you to be Secretary of State (both laugh). Okay. I'll draft this letter along those lines.

King: If you need me I'll be around until tomorrow night. I have to go down to Memphis. . . .

4/4/68

Bill Stein to "Bea" and "Stanley" (Levison).

Bill asks if Stan is home. Bea says she will see how he is as she says Stan has been sick and has difficulty talking on the phone. Bill says he will give Bea the message then and tells her that Dr. King has just been shot in Memphis. Bea asks if Bill heard it on the phone. Bill replies negatively and tells Bea that they just broke into the Huntley-Brinkley newscast with the news. He tells Bea that King is in the hospital and they don't know how serious it is. Bea relays the news aside to Stanley.

Stanley then comes to the phone and speaks with Bill, who repeats to him what he had just told Bea, adding that King was shot in front of his hotel; that the police surrounded King's car, rushed him to a hospital, and that there is absolutely no knowledge of his condition. Stanley suggests that Bill call the *New York Times* in a little while as he says they might have some information on it, advising Bill to tell them that he is connected with King's organization. Bill agrees and says he will call NBC too as they have people down there. Stanley says that will be fine and asks Bill to let him know, explaining that he is really under the weather. Stan remarks that he really ought to get out there. Bill says he will keep on top of it and get back to Stanley.

"Bill" (Stein) to "Bea" and "Stanley" (Levison).

Bea answers the phone and Bill tells her that King is critical; that he is in St. Joseph's Hospital; and that he was shot in the face. Bea takes to tell Stanley, who is listening to the news. Stanley then comes to the phone and Bill tells him that he talked to the CBS news desk. He says they talked to St. Joseph's Hospital and that it looks very bad as King was shot in the face. Bill confirms that CBS news desk says they were told it looks very bad. Stanley advises Bill to keep in touch with them and to let him know. Bill agrees.

Bill Stein to Stanley Levison.

[Bill] told him he just heard on the radio that King has died. Stan said he has to think what has to be done.

Stanley Levison to "Harry" (Wachtel).

It is indicated that Harry already knows that King is dead. They agree that it is sad. Stanley says it was always a possibility and yet none of "us" ever wanted to think of it. Harry says that the night of "the benefit" King stayed at Harry's place until very late that morning and that "we" talked about nothing else for two hours. Levison says that about six months ago he told King that it was time that "we" got some professional bodyguards. But Levison says one could never get King to really do it because it just ran against his grain. Levison says this is not only a personal tragedy of the whole movement because who else has what King had? Harry agrees, adding: "Not one other living human being." Levison agrees and adds, "white or black."

4/5/68

Andy Young to Stanley Levison.

Andy and Stanley discuss Martin's successor and agree that "Ralph [Abernathy] is the only logical successor." Andy says that they are going to call a press conference later this morning to sort of straighten things out, and announce the establishment of the "Martin Luther King Fund to perpetuate his memory." ... Andy says that Bobby Kennedy called and put his plane at their disposal.

4/6/68

Stanley Levison to Bea Levison.

Bea asks Stanley about the radio report that the Field Foundation is going to give SCLC one million dollars. Stanley stated that the Field Foundation called SCLC but "said something about two hundred to three hundred thousand dollars." Stanley stated that it will take a million dollars to keep SCLC going. . . . Stanley states that Coretta is o.k. but that there is a lot of hostility between her and "the staff." Coretta is pushing for a memorial library but the staff is fighting it. Stanley went to Coretta's house and then to Daddy King's house "where most of the meeting took place." The people from Atlanta University came over. All the people that Daddy King respects—and they are all NAACP people. . . .

4/12/68

Will Maslow (phonetic) to Stanley Levison.

. . .

Will: Are you on the Board of Directors at SCLC?

Levison: No. I'm considered on the Executive Staff. Even though I don't get paid. The Executive Staff really makes policy.

Will: We had a memorial service here [in New York] and they put it on television. So we had the funeral in Atlanta and the service in the A[merican] J[ewish] Congress building on the same program. I don't know why they did it unless they wanted to show the Jewish angle. So let's keep in touch. I've been reading all the words about Atlanta. It must have been a very impressive thing.

Levison: Very impressive. The reaction of Atlanta was extraordinary.

Will: Do you think Abernathy will be able to do the job?

Levison: I'll put it to you this way. He'll do it better among Negroes than Martin King did because he's really one of them. He has less rapport with the whites.

Will: He doesn't speak as well.

Levison: No. Although he's not a bad speaker at all. It's less important that he mesmerize whites than he do it with Negroes. But his thinking is the same.

Will: Do Stokely Carmichael behave at the funeral?

Levison: Moderately. They agreed to have him come in the church.

Will: I read that he came in with eight bodyguards.

Levison: He insisted he wanted these other guys and they almost had a fight at the door. It was very nasty. But Abernathy will probably have less to do with him than King did. Because King had this self-confidence that enabled him to say I'll sit down and preach to him; which is what he used to do.

Will: I would think that Carmichael is the enemy of everything that King stood for.

Levison: That's why he would preach to him.

6/25/69

Stanley Levison and Andy Young.

Young: . . . I think that Kunstler is about to file a suit against the FBI but it includes Black Panthers, Women's Strike for Peace, SNCC, CORE, SDS, everybody to the left of us.

Levison: On wiretapping?

Young: Yes. Enjoining them against wiretapping them. Now the problem is that Kunstler is trying to get us in the soup but that's just not our company.

Levison: Yeah.

Young: And yet at the same time I got a letter from an editor of *Fortune* asking us why we hadn't said anything or done anything, and I think we do have to have a position or some kind of approach to this. . . . You know, your line is probably the other one that is tapped.

Levison: You think I don't know that. When they said that they had found a way—their problem was that he traveled so much, so they found a way, of course.

Young: I think we better get together when we can talk at length.

Levison: My approach has been one that you enunciated which was that we don't have anything to hide. We don't have telephone conversations to discuss conspiratorial actions to bomb the Statue of Liberty so when we talk about strategy in the movement, we talk openly, and if they want to record it, let them record it. Just for the record, not only with you but with them, I don't really have any connections I didn't have when they were tapping the wire. They know that . . .

1969—1971

1969—1971

[Section 86]

May 29, 1969	Letter to Mr. Hoover
June 8, 1969	Newspaper article
June 9, 1969	Memorandum: Eddy to Gale
June 15, 1969	Newspaper article
June 19, 1969	Newspaper article
June 19, 1969	Newspaper article
June 20, 1969	Teletype: New York to Director
June 21, 1969	Teletype: New York to Director

[Section 87]

June 24, 1969	Letter to Mr. J. Edgar Hoover

[Section 88]

June 24, 1969	Memorandum: Jones to Bishop
June 28, 1969	News release
August 6, 1969	Memorandum: Jones to Bishop

[Section 89]

February 12, 1970	News release

[Section 91]

August 10, 1970	Newspaper article
August 11, 1970	Newspaper article
August 17, 1970	Memorandum: Malmfeldt to Bishop

[Section 90]

August 17, 1990	Memorandum: Moore to Brennan

[Section 93]

October 21, 1970   Memorandum: Jones to Bishop

[Section 92]

January 22, 1971   Memorandum: Washington

[Section 86]

Northridge, Calif
91324

Mr. Hoover,

Most Americans have peacefully accepted the outcome of the investigation and trial of the killer of Martin Luther King. I haven't.

Ray didn't act alone, did he? What about the man named "Raoul" who simply disapeared [*sic*] from the proceedings? Why this reluctance to fully probe the truth?

Come to think of it—a lot of Americans are through with this peacefull [*sic*] acceptance—the handling and suppressing of the King case is just another factor in giving up hope for peaceful change. Please answer my specific questions.

[Signature deleted]

Received May 29, 1969

The Washington Post Times Herald
June 8, 1969

DIDN'T OK KING TAP, CLARK SAYS
By Ronald J. Ostrow and Nicholas C. Chriss
Los Angeles Times

Former Attorney General Ramsey Clark said yesterday that while he headed the Justice Department, the FBI had no authorization to wiretap or bug the Rev. Dr. Martin Luther King, Jr.

In an interview, Clark said: "The implication that people thought Dr. King was a security threat are outrageous."

Clark also denied that he ever had authorized the FBI to bug or wiretap Elijah Muhammad, leader of the Black Muslims.

Clark's statement raises the question of whether the FBI acted without authority in conducting electronic surveillance of the two Negro leaders while Clark was in office. It also suggests that the FBI may have violated the 1965 Executive Order by President Johnson providing that no wiretapping "shall be undertaken or continued without first obtaining the approval of the Attorney General."

The first official acknowledgement that Dr. King and Muhammad had been monitored came last week in Houston during a Federal court hearing on the appeal by former heavyweight champion Cassius Clay of his 1967 draft refusal conviction.

Clay contends that FBI eavesdropping on his conversations with Dr. King and Muhammad tainted his conviction.

Confirmation that Dr. King's home phone was tapped from 1964 until around the time of his assassination, April 4, 1968, came from FBI agent Robert Nichols. Asked if the tap continued until assassination date, Nichols nodded.

FBI headquarters issued a statement late Friday referring newsmen to Director J. Edgar Hoover's testimony before a House subcommittee on appropriations in the years 1965 through 1968.

Hoover testified then that the taps all were authorized in advance and in writing by the Attorney General then in office. A Justice Department spokesman termed Hoover's testimony "accurate in every respect."

Clark said he required the FBI, over whom he was the nominal superior, to give him every three months a list of individuals under electronic surveillance.

The names of Dr. King and Muhammad never appeared on such a list, he said.

The following notation, handwritten and initialed, appears on this entry in the file:

"Who did authorize the King and Muhammad taps?"

H

UNITED STATES GOVERNMENT
Memorandum

TO: Mr. Gale   DATE: June 9, 1969

FROM: A. B. Eddy

         CASSIUS MARCELLUS CLAY, JR.
         SELECTIVE SERVICE ACT

The information set forth in the Washington Post of June 8, 1969, concerning the testimony of FBI Agent Robert Nichols is erroneous. The Post article indicated that "confirmation that Dr. King's home phone was tapped from 1964 until the time of his assassination April 4, 1968, came from FBI Agent Robert Nichols. Asked if the tap continued until the assassination date, Nichols nodded."

Special Agent Nichols stated that he answered all questions orally, and that he never nodded his head in response to a question by the defense. According to Agent Nichols, he was asked by the defense if the surveillance of Dr. King was running up to April 1968, to which Special Agent Nichols responded that he did not know the exact date the surveillance was discontinued because he was not on the case after May 1965.

According to Assistant Special Agent in Charge (ASAC) Hetherington, the United States Attorney and the Assistant United States Attorney, both of whom were present in court, stated that Special Agent Nichols did not answer any question by nodding his head.

                    The Sunday Star
                    Washington, D.C.
                    June 15, 1969

                    CARL T. ROWAN

It is Time for J. Edgar Hoover To Go

A society is never in more peril than when the people lose the ability to identify a genuine threat to personal liberty.

This society is in a lot of peril if we may judge from the public reaction—or lack of it—to courtroom admissions of a variety of illegal FBI wiretaps and buggings of homes and hotel rooms.

A Justice Department official acknowledged in Federal District Court that Dr. Martin Luther King was under electronic surveillance in 1964 and 1965, and the FBI agent who supervised this surveillance told the court "it was my understanding that it went on after that."

The whole truth is that Dr. King's phones were tapped, his hotel rooms bugged, and he was personally shadowed right up to the time he was slain in Memphis on April 4, 1968.

Another FBI agent, C. Barry Pickett, told the court in Houston, Texas, that for four solid years he had listened eight hours a day, five days a week to the conversations of Elijah Muhammad, leader of the Black Muslims. Pickett employed both a telephone wiretap and a microphone planted in Muhammad's home.

These cases of electronic eavesdropping, which violate both federal law and a presidential executive order, were disclosed in a hearing on former heavyweight boxing champion Cassius Clay's effort to overturn a five-year prison sentence for his refusal to be drafted.

These buggings, which caught some Clay conversations in their "net," are but a fraction of the illegal wiretaps that have moved this country far closer to [being] a police state than most Americans realize.

Why the bland, indifferent reaction on the part of most Americans?

First, there is the general FBI justification for such tactics: "national security."

Former Attorney General Ramsey Clark, who states emphatically that the FBI had no authority to wiretap or bug Dr. King, asserts that "the implication that people thought Dr. King was a security threat is outrageous."

Still, that term "national security" is more powerful than "motherhood," for it evokes fear, and men still surrender more things—including liberty—out of fear than they do out of love.

The puzzling thing about Clark's statement is that he acts as though he is surprised to hear of the wiretapping and bugging of Dr. King. Could Clark possibly have been unaware that FBI officials were going before congressional committees and partly justifying large appropriations by titillating some congressmen and feeding anti-King ammunition to Southerners who despised the civil rights leader—all by way of revealing "tidbits" picked up through the wiretaps and buggings?

Was Clark unaware that certain FBI officials were roaming the country leaking to newspaper editors poisonous stories about Dr. King and what the buggings had allegedly revealed?

Everybody else in Washington of any consequence knew it, and many deplored it, but no one seemed to know how to go about making the FBI bend to the laws of the land.

There is a not-too-flippant assumption in Washington that J. Edgar Hoover has been FBI director for 45 years because all the recent Presidents have assumed that he knew too much about them to be replaced. So not only was he not replaced by any of the younger, very able FBI men in the normal course of things, but Presidents Johnson and Nixon have felt it wise or expedient to waive a law saying Hoover has reached the rocking-chair age.

Hoover ought to be replaced as FBI director—immediately.

As Washington agency heads go, Hoover may have done a better job than most. But the people of this country knew something when they limited the time one man might serve in the presidency. They saw personal fiefdoms as inimical to the democracy, the personal freedom that we have come to cherish.

If it is dangerous to have one man serve three full terms as President, it is far more dangerous to have one man take lifetime possession of a powerful police-investigative agency that prods into the deepest secrets of the most prominent, most honored citizens and has the power to discredit, even destroy, almost anyone. The kind of abuse of and contempt for the law manifest in the King and Muhammad eavesdropping become almost inevitable when a man is left in a key job as long as Hoover has been.

Were Hoover a more thoughtful man, or as concerned about the preservation of democracy and liberty as his speeches suggest, he would have resigned long ago. He would not keep putting Presidents in the political bind of deciding to keep him or get him out.

It is clear Hoover has no intention of resigning. So when does the President muster the courage to say: "Well then, thou good and faithful servant. Goodbye."?

The Evening Star
Washington, D.C.
June 19, 1969

King Wiretap Called RFK's Idea
Hoover Asserts Memo to FBI Cited Concern Over Marxism
(copyright 1969 by The Evening Star Newspaper Co.)
By JEREMIAH O'LEARY
Star Staff Writer

Wiretapping of Dr. Martin Luther King Jr.'s telephone was proposed to the FBI by then Attorney General Robert F. Kennedy in June 1963, and authorized by him in writing later that year, FBI Director J. Edgar Hoover told The Star today.

Hoover revealed the contents of two memorandums in one of which Kennedy expressed concern about possible infiltration of the race issue by Marxists and spoke of allegations that the Negro leader was closely associated with Marxist ideas and followers.

That memorandum to Hoover, dated June 1963, was written by Courtney Evans, then assistant director of the FBI and liaison man with the Justice Department. It reported the substance of a conversation Evans had just had with Kennedy in which the Attorney General asked about the feasibility of installing electronic devices on King's telephones. King headed the Southern Christian Leadership Conference.

Concerned About Allegations

Kennedy, according to the Evans memo, was concerned about reports that King was a student of Marxism, that he was associating with a New York attorney with known Communist connections, but that he did not openly espouse Marxism because of his religious beliefs. The Evans memorandum indicated Kennedy wanted to know if it was technically feasible to use electronic devices to prove or disprove these allegations.

The Evans memo said Evans replied to Kennedy that King was a man who traveled almost constantly and that it was extremely difficult to use wiretaps effectively in such cases.

Hoover told The Star that FBI officials also informed Kennedy at that time that they doubted the advisability of undertaking electronic surveillance of Dr. King because of possible political repercussions.

However, the second memorandum cited by Hoover shows that on October 7, 1963, the FBI chief reported to Kennedy that it was then technically feasible to apply wiretaps to King's telephones at two places, one of them at an unnamed location in New York.

That memorandum constituted the FBI's request for authority to proceed with the wiretap proposed by Kennedy four months before. The document bears in the lower left-hand corner the signature, "Robert F. Kennedy," and under the name the date "10-1-63."

Hoover did not indicate to The Star when the surveillance was started but said the taps were discontinued on April 30, 1965. At that time Nicholas Katzenbach was serving as Attorney General.

Asked about the results of the electronic surveillance today, Hoover declined comment.

The FBI director told The Star: "I have never authorized installation of technical electronic devices without written authority of the Attorney General."

Today's disclosures climaxed a long smoldering controversy over the role of the FBI, a subordinated bureau of the Justice Department, in using wiretaps or other electronic devices in investigative matters. The matter came to a head Sunday when Carl Rowan, a columnist for The Star, charged that the FBI had no authority to wiretap Dr. King's conversations. He quoted former Attorney Ramsey Clark, who succeeded Katzenbach, as saying "the implication that people thought Dr. King was a security threat is outrageous."

The Rowan charges prompted Associate FBI Director Clyde A. Tolson to write to Rowan early this week defending the legality of the King wiretaps.

"For your information," Tolson said in his letter, "the wiretap on Martin Luther King Jr. was specifically approved in advance in writing by the late attorney general of the United States, Mr. Robert F. Kennedy."

Tolson added that the monitoring device was "strictly in the field of internal security and therefore was in the provision laid down by the President of the United States."

Evans, now a Washington lawyer, was en route to Puerto Rico today and could not be reached for comment. However, Tuesday night Evans said he had no recollection of whether a wiretap authorization directed at King had ever been involved in his discussion with Kennedy.

Aides to Sen. Edward M. Kennedy, D-Mass, said today he would have no comment on Hoover's disclosure.

Friends of Robert Kennedy had suggested in recent days that, during 1964, in the period after the assassination of President John F. Kennedy, the attorney general's interest in some of his official affairs had flagged. However, the assassination came nearly six weeks after Robert Kennedy had signed the authorization for the King wiretap.

Hoover and Kennedy, after the latter became a New York senator, accused each other of being responsible for use of hidden microphones in investigations.

Evans figured in that controversy when Kennedy made public a February 1966, letter to him from Evans which made the point that the use of hidden microphones was not Kennedy's responsibility but suggested he may have directly approved the use of wiretaps on phones. That letter said the FBI sent national security wiretap requests to Kennedy for approval.

It is reliably reported that Kennedy was reminded by the FBI that it still had in its files the authorizations signed by him as Attorney General for telephonic wiretaps. However, Hoover did not disclose at that time any names of persons under wiretap surveillance with Kennedy's approval.

At that stage, Kennedy and Hoover broke off the public exchange of charges as if by mutual consent. This was regarded partly as due to Kennedy's realization that his signed authorizations were still in FBI files, partly to the FBI's desire not to have special attention drawn to its investigative techniques not to engage in a battle with the Kennedy forces that could have political overtones.

The Justice Department on Tuesday declined a direct answer when asked for documentation of Tolson's contention in his letter to Rowan. But earlier this month, a Justice Department spokesman said Hoover was "accurate in every respect" in his repeated statements that all wiretaps were being authorized in advance and in writing by the Attorney General during the time-span of the controversy.

A Justice department spokesman, asked today if Attorney General John N. Mitchell had given Hoover permission to discuss the contents of secret documents for the King wiretapping, replied simply, "no comment."

However, the spokesman recalled that the attorney general had declined to authorize disclosures in court of the basic authority for the wiretapping. Such disclosures had been demanded by defense lawyers in the Houston draft evasion hearing for former boxing champion Cassius Clay. It was during that hearing that the King wiretapping was officially revealed for the first time.

June 19, 1969
Clyde: Thought you'd appreciate the contribution of . . . to the follow-
ing. Regards.

Mike Royko

FBI's tapping of King phones

The FBI has a lot more explaining to do about its motives for spying on the late Dr. Martin Luther King.

It has publicly described as "malicious" a column written by Carl Rowan that criticized the tapping of Dr. King's phones.

Clyde Tolson, associate FBI director, says the wiretapping was done for "national security" reasons, with the approval of the late Robert Kennedy, then attorney general.

That doesn't even come close to telling it.

ONE THING IT DOESN'T EXPLAIN, is the following incident:

About four years ago, an ex-FBI agent I knew asked me to join him for a round of golf.

After the round, we sat in the clubhouse chatting. He worked the conversation around to Dr. King.

He told me the FBI had been using a variety of electronic eaves-dropping devices on Dr. King. Besides tapping his phone, they had planted listening devices in hotel rooms he used while traveling.

The result, he said, was a very thick file on Dr. King.

He gave me examples.

They were very personal things. They were things I'm sure Dr. King would not want anyone else to know about. If you bugged almost anyone's bedroom long enough, you would hear things that person didn't want anyone else to know about.

BUT NONE OF THE THINGS this ex-FBI agent told me reflected in any way on Dr. King's loyalty, his Americanism, or seemed to be remotely related to national security.

Nor did they reflect on his role as a leader in the civil rights crusade, a winner of the Nobel Peace Prize, or a figure of historic importance.

I asked the ex-FBI agent if his information was merely gossip or if he was sure about it.

He said he had visited J. Edgar Hoover in Washington and had been briefed on the contents of the King file.

It was not uncommon, he said, for trusted ex-agents to be let in on such things.

Obviously, I was supposed to be shocked by the things he told me. And I was. But not for the reasons he assumed.

The shocking part of it was that he was actually sitting there telling me such things.

They were none of my business, and they were none of his business. They were nobody's business but Dr. King's.

IT WAS PLAIN OLD MUD-SLINGING, on a level with the lowest scandal magazines and transom-peeking publications.

There was no doubt in my mind then, and none now, that it was being leaked to me for the purpose of discrediting Dr. King.

The same type thing, I have since learned, occurred in other cities, with other newsmen.

And it doesn't take much imagination to figure out why Dr. King and Hoover had engaged in a furious public quarrel. Hoover, quite clearly, did not like Dr. King.

That's why I suggest the FBI hasn't given an adequate explanation.

If the wiretapping was being done for national security, I presume that it should have been kept a big secret.

Secret? How much of a secret was it if a newspaper columnist in Chicago knew of the eavesdropping? Or if a former agent—a private citizen—could talk about it?

(For the record, the ex-agent was not a two-bit gumshoe given to flights of fancy. He was then a well known and highly respected investigator. He is today a famous and powerful man.)

AND IS THE PURPOSE OF SUCH official eavesdropping to gather spite material, transom-peeking tidbits that will be whispered in the ears of opinion-makers?

That, of course, is the greatest danger from Big Brother and his big ear.

If that's what Dr. King's file was used for, then I'll gladly second Rowan's suggestion that Hoover be replaced.

The scandal-sheet business should be left to private industry.

PM URGENT 6-20-69 AWS
TO DIRECTOR 100-106670 (CODE)
    ATTENTION DOMESTIC INTELLIGENCE DIVISION
FROM NEW YORK 100-136585

MARTIN LUTHER KING, JR. SM-C, 00: AT.

THE FOLLOWING INFORMATION WAS FURNISHED BY . . .
(CLASSIFY "SECRET") ON JUNE TWO ZERO, SIXTY NINE:

ON JUNE TWO ZERO, SIXTY NINE, CORETTA KING TOLD STANLEY LEVISON THAT ETHEL KENNEDY HAD CONTACTED HER THAT DATE TO SAY SHE WAS SORRY ABOUT WHAT HAS BEEN IN THE PAPER (APPARENTLY REFERRING TO THE ARTICLE CONCERNING THE AUTHORIZATION FROM ROBERT F. KENNEDY, WHEN ATTORNEY GENERAL, TO TAP MARTIN LUTHER KING'S TELEPHONES). CORETTA ADDED THAT ETHEL KENNEDY IMPLIED THAT SHE HOPED THIS WOULD NOT INTERFERE WITH THEIR FRIENDSHIP. CORETTA SAID SHE REPLIED THAT SHE UNDERSTOOD HOW THE PRESS CAN BE DIVISIVE AT TIMES AND THAT THIS DOES NOT COLOR HER ATTITUDE IN ANY WAY TOWARD THE (KENNEDY) FAMILY.

CORETTA ALSO TOLD LEVISON THAT ETHEL KENNEDY SAID "THEY" HAD A MEETING AT HER HOME THE PREVIOUS NIGHT AND TALKED ABOUT . . . [illegible] CORETTA SAID SHE DID NOT KNOW WHAT ETHEL WAS TALKING ABOUT AND DID NOT WANT TO ASK HER.

LEVISON COMMENTED THAT HE FELT CORETTA'S ANSWER WAS EXACTLY RIGHT BECAUSE THERE IS NO POINT IN ATTEMPTING TO ASSESS WHAT ROLE BOBBY KENNEDY PLAYED SINCE THERE IS NO WAY OF REALLY KNOWING.

CORETTA STATED THAT THIS WAS "SORT OF PASSING THE BUCK, AND THEY'RE TRYING TO PUT IT ALL OFF ON HIM." SHE ADDED THAT HE MAY HAVE AGREED AND GONE ALONG WITH IT.

LEVISON REMARKED THAT THEY KNOW KING, WHETHER HE FELT BOBBY KENNEDY WAS INVOLVED OR NOT, STILL MAINTAINED A FRIENDLY RELATIONSHIP WITH HIM. HE SAID IF KING FELT BOBBY KENNEDY HAD DONE ANYTHING, HE FORGAVE HIM NO DOUBT BASED ON THE CIRCUMSTANCES OF THE TIME, THE FACT HE WAS ALWAYS SUPER NERVOUS ABOUT HIS BROTHER (PRESIDENT JOHN F. KENNEDY). LEVISON SAID THIS IS THE ATTITUDE CORETTA SHOULD TAKE. HE SAID IF THE PRESS "WANTS TO DIG UP GARBAGE" IT SHOULD NOT BE ALLOWED TO INTERFERE WITH A CONSTRUCTIVE RELATIONSHIP.

CORETTA SAID THAT FOLLOWING HER CONVERSATION WITH ETHEL KENNEDY, THE PHONE RANG AGAIN AND THAT GIRL WHO ANSWERED SAID HOLD FOR SENATOR KENNEDY. CORETTA SAID, HOWEVER, THAT SHE WAS CUT OFF. SHE AND LEVISON AGREED THAT SENATOR (TED) KENNEDY MAY

HAVE FOUND OUT THAT ETHEL CONTACTED CORETTA AND DECIDED NOT TO GO THROUGH WITH THE CALL.

LEVISON CONTINUED THAT THE PRESSURE AT THIS POINT ... [illegible] MANY LIBERALS WHO RESENT FBI DIRECTOR HOOVER'S ROLE AND THAT HOOVER GAVE AN ANSWER. HE ADDED THAT HOOVER HAS BEEN ANSWERED BACK BY (RAMSEY) CLARK, AND THAT CLARK'S ANSWER WAS RIGHT.

LEVISON GAVE HIS OPINION THAT THE ENTIRE AFFAIR WILL "DRIFT AWAY" AND ADDED THAT "IT'S NOT THE KIND OF THING YOU CAN KEEP GOING." LEVISON FELT THE ENTIRE THING WILL BE FORGOTTEN BUT THAT FBI DIRECTOR HOOVER WILL BE BOTHERED BY IT BECAUSE IT LEAVES HIM AS THE MAN RESPONSIBLE.

CORETTA AGREED, STATING "I FEELS LIKE HE IS THE MOST GUILTY."

LEVISON COMMENTED THAT CORETTA'S SUGGESTION THAT SHE GET TOGETHER WITH ETHEL KENNEDY COULD BE FRUITFUL AND SHOULD BE DONE REASONABLY SOON. LEVISON SUGGESTED THAT CORETTA SET UP THE MEETING AND THAT THEY COULD TALK ABOUT IT BEFORE SHE AND ETHEL KENNEDY MET.

NO MEMO BEING SUBMITTED.

END.

WA 08
848 PM IMMEDIATE 6-21-6 DMW
TO DIRECTOR (100-106670) (PLAINTEXT)
    ATT DOMESTIC INTELLIGENCE DIVISION
FROM NEW YORK (100-136585)   5P

MARTIN LUTHER KING, JR., SECURITY MATTER—COMMUNIST (00-AT)

THE FOLLOWING INFORMATION WAS FURNISHED BY ... (CLASSIFY "SECRET") ON JUNE TWO ONE, SIXTY NINE.

ONE [sic] JUNE TWENTY FIRST, NINETEEN SIXTY NINE, HARRY WACHTEL, NEW YORK ATTORNEY AND SOUTHERN CHRISTIAN LEADERSHIP CONFERENCE ADVISOR, TOLD STANLEY LEVISON THAT THE GUESTS AT A PARTY ON JUNE TWENTY, LAST, WERE TRYING TO GUESS THE IDENTITY OF THE COMMUNIST-MARXIST-LENINIST LAWYER WHO HAD

BEEN TAPPED. WACHTEL SAID HE COULD ONLY ANSWER THAT IT WAS NOT HE. THE GUESTS DECIDED THAT IT WAS (WILLIAM) KUNSTLER, NEW YORK ATTORNEY. WACHTEL TOLD THEM HE DIDN'T KNOW, BUT THAT IT WASN'T CLARENCE JONES.

LEVISON TOLD WACHTEL TO TELL HIS (WACHTEL'S) CLIENTS WHO THE LAWYER REALLY WAS. LEVISON HAD ALREADY TOLD MOE FONER, OFFICER OF LOCAL ONE ONE NINE NINE, DRUG AND HOSPITAL WORKERS, NYC.

WACHTEL SAID THAT RAMSEY CLARK IS HITTING HARD AND THAT KATZENBACH IS SITTING THERE SAYING NOTHING. HE SAID THAT THEY HAVE PRETTY WELL ACKNOWLEDGED THEY ARE ALL INVOLVED, NOW THAT ROBERT KENNEDY PUSHED IT. WACHTEL SAID THE WHOLE TRUST IS NOW THAT KENNEDY DID NOT PUSH IT.

LEVISON SAID HE SAW (JAMES) WECHSLER, NEWSPAPER COLUMNIST, AND ASKED HIM WHAT KIND OF THING THIS IS. HE SAID HE TOLD WECHSLER THAT CIVIL LIBERTIES ISSUES WERE ALL RIGHT FOR HIM TO HAMMER ON, BUT WHAT WAS THIS. LEVISON TOLD WACHTEL THAT WECHSLER WROTE THE ARTICLE WHEN HE WAS DRUNK. LEVISON SAID THAT HE HAD TOLD MORE TO TELL WECHSLER TO LAY OFF THE SUBJECT.

WACHTEL SAID HE INTENDED TO CALL ON THE BASIS OF THE MIAMI HERALD THING AND POINT OUT THAT IT WAS DONE FROM NINETEEN SIXTY ONE ON.

WACHTEL SAID HE WAS NOT KEEN ON ACQUIRING TRANSCRIPTS OF TAPED CONVERSATIONS. LEVISON THOUGHT IT NAIVE TO THINK THEY TAPPED THE OFFICE AND NOT THE HOME. HE SAID THAT THEY WOULD TAP THE OTHER END TO GET MORE MILEAGE. LEVISON SAID THEY WOULD TAP HIM (LEVISON) AND NOT HIM. WACHTEL SAID "HAVE CERTAIN WAYS OF GETTING SOME VERIFICATION AND I HAVE INTENTIONS OF GETTING IT IF I CAN."

WACHTEL SAID THE TIMES HAD AN EDITORIAL ON BUGGING IN CHICAGO. HE SAID THAT WHAT THE FBI IS DOING STANDS ON ITS OWN AS WRONG.

LEVISON SAID THAT IN GENERAL WHAT IS NEEDED IS TO GET HOOVER TO BRING THE TAPES OUT, BUT THAT CORETTA (KING) DOES NOT WANT TO GO FURTHER.

LEVISON SAID HE KNOWS THIS GUY ARRINGTON (PHO-

NETIC) THAT HE IS SOME SORT OF PRODUCER. WACHTEL THEN SAID THAT HE WOULD NOT TELL LEVISON ANYTHING, BECAUSE THE LATTER'S LINES MAY STILL BE TAPPED.

LEVISON SAID THAT WECHSLER IS A SCHNUK FOR MAKING IT ALL PUBLIC. HE AGREED THAT CLARK IS A GOOD GUY FOR WHAT HE IS SAYING.

WACHTEL SAID HE TALKED TO CLARK A LONG TIME ABOUT WHAT WAS IN THE TAPES, AND THAT HIS FUNDA-MENTAL NOTION WAS THAT IT WAS NOT REALLY VERY CON-CRETE. WACHTEL SAID IT DEPENDS ON WHO IS SITTING UP THERE. HE SAID THAT IN CLARK'S TIME, IT MIGHT HAVE BEEN POSSIBLE TO HAVE A VIEWING (OF THE TRANSCRIPTS) UP TO THE POINT OF MAKING THE DECISION OF WHETHER OR NOT TO SHOW THEM (PUBICALLY [sic].

ON JUNE TWENTY ONE, SIXTY NINE, MOE FONER TOLD STANLEY LEVISON ABOUT THE MIAMI HERALD ARTICLE WHICH STATED THAT THEY HAVE PICTURES OF KING IN BED, ETC. LEVISON SAID THAT THERE ISN'T ANYONE IN PUB-LIC LIFE WHO ISN'T TAPPED.

LEVISON SAID THAT KING WAS GOING TO SUPPORT ROB-ERT KENNEDY FOR THE PRESIDENCY. HE SAID THAT THIS FACT WOULD APPEAR IN THE BOOK.

LEVISON TOLD FONER THAT HE AGREED WITH JIMMY'S (WECHSLER) FUNDAMENTAL PREMISES THAT MAYBE IT IS TIME TO GO INTO THIS. FONER SAID THAT THE PROBLEM WITH JIMMY IS THAT HE IS ONE OF THE FEW GUYS WHO HAS BEEN WILLING TO TAKE ON HOOVER IN THE OPEN. LE-VISON SAID HE THINKS THAT HE (LEVISON) AND JIMMY SHOULD HAVE LUNCH TOGETHER AS HE (LEVISON) HAS SOME CRITICISM ABOUT THE MATTER.

NYO HAS NO INFORMATION AS TO WACHTEL'S MEANS OF VERIFICATION AS SET OUT ABOVE.

NO MEMO TO FOLLOW.

END

[Section 87]

Freeport, Texas 77541
June 24, 1969

Mr. J. Edgar Hoover
Federal Bureau of Investigation
U.S. Department of Justice
Washington, D.C. 20535

Dear Mr. Hoover:

Thank you for your letter of June 20th explaining the FBI's position concerning the wiretapping of Dr. Martin Luther King's telephone.

I still would appreciate a clarification on the following: Robert Kennedy resigned as Attorney General in September 1964, but an FBI agent recently testified in federal court that *the wiretap continued until King's death in 1968.* If neither Nicholas Katzenbach nor Ramsey Clark gave permission for such a wiretap, where did the FBI get such authority between September 1964 and April 1968? Is it common practice for the FBI to carry on such activities without the knowledge of the Attorney General?

As a citizen of this country and as one who is concerned about the increasing invasion of privacy, I feel that you owe us further explanation.

Sincerely yours,
[Signature deleted]

[Section 88]

UNITED STATES GOVERNMENT
Memorandum

TO: Mr. Bishop   DATE: 6-24-69

FROM: Mr. A. Jones

SUBJECT: TAPE RECORDINGS FURNISHED
             BY . . .

             . . .

             WEST HEMPSTEAD, NEW YORK

Captioned individual has forwarded to the Director without cover letter two tape recordings which have been reviewed [by] the Crime Research Section.

One of these recordings is an excerpt from the President's news conference on 6-19-69 in which a reporter asked if the Director enjoyed the President's complete confidence and if any discussions had been had regarding "his tenure." The President replied that the Director did enjoy his complete confidence and there had been no discussions whatever regarding his tenure. The President said he also wanted to comment on the "controversy" on electronic surveillances which existed at the present time. He said he had checked personally and found that these surveillances had always been approved by the Attorney General and this was in line with the testimony which the Director had given on past occasions.

The second tape was an excerpt from a Columbia Broadcasting System news report in which former Attorney General Ramsey Clark was interviewed. It was on this occasion that Clark made his statement that he had denied the FBI authority to wire-tap Martin Luther King and also stated that he felt the time had come when Mr. Hoover should retire. A transcript of this interview has been prepared and is attached herewith.

INTERVIEW OF FORMER
ATTORNEY GENERAL RAMSEY CLARK
ON COLUMBIA BROADCASTING SYSTEM (CBS)
NEWS REPORT

ANNOUNCER: Two immediate successors to Robert Kennedy as Attorney General today defended the late senator in the wiretapping of the late Martin Luther King. Nicholas Katzenbach and Ramsey Clark disputed FBI Director J. Edgar Hoover's reported version of how the wiretapping began. John Hart questioned Clark.

HART: Mr. Clark, do you think that Robert Kennedy authorized this?

CLARK: There's two questions really: did he authorize it and did he initiate it. The implication that he initiated it to me is both terribly unfair and deceptive. It's unfair because both Bob Kennedy and Dr. King, who by implication is being put forth as perhaps a security risk, or at least in contact with security risks, are both dead—both murdered in the service of humanity and unable to defend themselves. It's also deceptive because the implication that there was any reluctance by Mr. Hoover or the FBI to wiretap Dr. King is wrong. He repeatedly requested my authority to wiretap him while I was Attorney General and I repeatedly denied the authority.

HART: This raises again the whole question, don't you think, of the raw files of the FBI, what is in there, and the control over them, and also the control of Mr. Hoover? Does anybody control him, and what do you think should be done about those files?

CLARK: Well, in a slightly different context, it certainly does raise the question of the FBI files. The FBI, to take parts of files, to select parts of files, to make a point that it's interested in, is wrong, absolutely wrong, and impermissible. It ought to reveal the whole truth or it ought to remain silent. In a case like this, it perhaps should remain silent.

HART: You're speaking about them publishing the entire memoranda?

CLARK: Well, perhaps more than a memoranda [*sic*]. There, you know, are many questions that have been raised in the public's mind that are not answered by the statements that have been made. The only statements that have been made are really defensive of the FBI and not divulging the truth.

HART: There are some people who are calling for Mr. Hoover's resignation. Is that required, do you think?

CLARK: It's . . . I think Mr. Hoover has participated in the building of what has been a great investigative agency. I think perhaps the time has come when he should retire both in the interest of his own career, which has been distinguished, and in the interest of the FBI, which has been a great investigative agency.

FROM KING FEATURES SYNDICATE, 235 EAST 45th ST., NEW YORK, N.Y. 10017
FOR RELEASE SATURDAY, JUNE 28, OR SUNDAY, JUNE 29, 1969

In WASHINGTON
BY RALPH de TOLEDANO
WHAT WAS IN THE KING WIRETAPS?

When the first accusations against Alger Hiss were made, the Establishment rose up in wrath to shout that they could not be true. How, its spokesman asked, could a man as respected and important be a member of the Communist conspiracy? Before the case had been fully developed, of course, it turned out that the original charges against Hiss were as nothing to what was proved in the Federal courts and sustained by the highest tribunal of the nation.

There were several lessons to be learned from this. The first: If Anglo-Saxon jurisprudence holds that a man must be considered innocent until proven guilty, this does not mean that those who make the accusations are, ipso facto, to be called liars and driven to an early grave. The witness, too, has rights. The second: Conspirators are successful precisely because they can convince the world that they are highly respectable and ultra-patriotic. Those of dubious political reputation are of no value to a conspiracy since they can deceive no one.

Those lessons, however, have not been learned. The discovery that Martin Luther King, Jr., under FBI electronic surveillance—at the instigation and with the authorization of Attorney General Robert F. Kennedy—quite naturally caused anguish to Dr. King's friends and admirers. But it would have been far more proper if those coming to the defense of the civil rights leader had coupled their outcries to demands for full and immediate exposure by the Justice Department of all the facts and the dossiers. Instead they called for the resignation of the FBI director, J. Edgar Hoover.

To date, none of Dr. King's frenzied defenders have pressed for a full disclosure of the reasons why Mr. Kennedy, a friend of Martin Luther King, and the FBI took the time and the trouble to bug the King telephone. Bobby Kennedy would never have given his approval had the FBI been interested solely in the civil rights activities of the late Dr. King. King's defenders have resorted instead to a whispering campaign against the FBI and the razz-ma-tazz of charges against Mr. Hoover.

If Attorney General Kennedy and the FBI were soley interested in reco.ding the gossip of the civil rights movement or its legitimate plans and operations, then they seriously erred. But the way to find out is to look at the summary of the tapes and the Martin Luther King dossier at the Justice Department. That would end the controversy once and for all. If the tapes and the dossier disclosed something touching on the national security, then attacks on J. Edgar Hoover would end.

It is, however, easier and safer to stay away from the substantive issue and direct attention and fire to the peripheral. It substitutes passion for logic, propaganda for evidence, and politics for the national interest. The anti-Hoover faction presumably believes it is right, yet it throws away the opportunity of possibly doing the FBI in the eye.

Nicholas Katzenbach, who was Kennedy's Deputy Attorney General, and later Attorney General in his own right, has rushed in with a rank denial that anything in the King file warranted the wiretaps. But Mr. Katzenbach forgets that it was he who studied the King record for the Attorney General—at the time that Mr. Hoover called the Negro leader one of the biggest liars in the country. And on the basis of that examination, he advised that no steps be taken to discipline the FBI director or to issue an official denial of Mr. Hoover's words.

To make these points, however, would be an exercise in futility but for one thing. Parts of the Martin Luther King story, unofficially gathered, have been floating around Washington and New York for a number of years. Those responsible for putting together this fraction of what is undoubtedly in the FBI file are not members of the fanatic right wing, not stiff-necked racists, but responsible members of the community. They have not attempted to publish the record nor to use it for political gain.

And they have held their peace over the years precisely because they have known what the Establishment's reaction would be—the cries, the denunciations, and the use of "innocence by association" to prove Dr. King's political purity. With the death of Dr. King, the files were closed and the need for publication ended. The integrity of the FBI and of those who have backed away from its investigation is now at stake. Hot-headed men and women are trying to use the current controversy to stir up hatred of men and government. Until the facts are laid before the American people, the controversy will continue, doing no one any good, least of all Dr. King's family.

UNITED STATES GOVERNMENT
Memorandum

TO: Mr. Bishop   DATE: 8/6/69

FROM: M. A. Jones

           RAMSEY CLARK
SUBJECT: TELEVISION APPEARANCE
           ON DAVID FROST PROGRAM

At 9 P.M., August 5, 1969, former Attorney General Ramsey Clark appeared on the David Frost television program on Station WTTG-TV (Washington channel 5). The first portion of Clark's appearance consisted of a question-and-answer session between him and Frost regarding electronic surveillance, Martin Luther King, and organized crime. . . .

In answer to the question of "How independent is the FBI?" the former Attorney General replied that he thinks the FBI operates with integrity; that when the FBI doesn't agree, it doesn't follow the rules with great enthusiasm—"but who does?"

Regarding the possibility of a conspiracy in the Martin Luther King murder case, Clark said he "would never stop looking for evidence of a conspiracy" but "on the other hand, I saw no evidence of one." When questioned about the source of James Earl Ray's money, Clark indicated "several" robberies were committed in England where Ray's fingerprints "were on the sack he pushed to the teller." Clark also said that he never knew an Attorney General to "instigate" a wiretap; and that as late as two days before King's death, the FBI had asked his approval for electronic coverage of King. He stated that Robert Kennedy thought King "was a great man—as do I."

[Section 89]

WASHINGTON CAPITAL NEWS SERVICE
February 12, 1970

NEW YORK (UPI)—FORMER ATTORNEY GENERAL RAMSEY CLARK TODAY CHALLENGED THE FBI TO REVEAL THE TRUTH ABOUT RUMORS "THAT TAPES FROM BUGS SECRETLY INSTALLED IN HOTEL ROOMS USED BY DR. (MARTIN LUTHER) KING WERE PLAYED TO PUBLISHERS, SENATORS AND OTHERS."

"THE PEOPLE OF THE UNITED STATES SHOULD KNOW WHETHER THIS IS TRUE. THEIR GOVERNMENT SHOULD TELL THEM," CLARK SAID.

CLARK ISSUED HIS CHALLENGE IN A COPYRIGHTED ARTICLE IN McCALL'S MAGAZINE RELEASED TODAY.

"THE RISK OF LEAKS, BLACKLISTS AND BLACKMAIL ARISING FROM THE EXISTENCE OF SO MUCH DATA IS EXTREMELY HIGH," CLARK SAID. "EAVESDROPPING BRINGS OUT THE WORST IN HUMAN NATURE. CLEARLY IRRELEVANT TO MOST CRIME—MURDER, MUGGING, ROBBERY, RAPE, BURGLARY, THEFT—IT IS USED TO SEEK UNKNOWN FACTS ABOUT KNOWN PEOPLE. OFTEN IT IS GUIDED BY THE PREJUDICES OF THOSE WHO WOULD OVERHEAR.

"THAT THE FBI WOULD TAP THE PHONES AND BUG THE HOTEL ROOMS OF DR. MARTIN LUTHER KING JR. SHOULD TELL US ALL WE NEED TO KNOW ABOUT THE DESIRABILITY

OF THOSE PRACTICES," CLARK SAID. HE SAID KING WAS "A PUBLIC MAN, HIS CONDUCT OPEN."

CLARK SAID, "THE RISKS OF SURREPTITIOUS POLICE SURVEILLANCE OF SUCH A LEADER ARE IMMENSE. IT IS THE ACT OF AN INCIPIENT POLICE STATE."

... THE FORMER ATTORNEY GENERAL SAID "EAVESDROPPING DESTROYS CONFIDENCE IN PUBLIC SERVICE AND IN SELF [sic]. IT CREATES A FEAR OF GOVERNMENT AND FELLOW CITIZEN. IT CORRUPTS THE INVESTIGATOR WHO USES IT AND COMPELS GREATER CUNNING AMONG THOSE WHO WILL COMMIT CRIME ANYWAY."

[Section 91]

Tucson Daily Citizen

August 10, 1970

King's Sexual Exploits
Said Used By FBI

New York (UPI)—Dr. Martin Luther King, Jr., toned down his criticism of the FBI after its director, J. Edgar Hoover, presented King with wiretapped tapes indicating King's extramarital affairs, Time magazine said yesterday.

King met with Hoover in the FBI director's offices in 1964, Time said, where Hoover "explained to King just what damaging private detail he had on the tapes and lectured him that his morals should be those befitting a Nobel Prize-winner.

"He also suggested that King should tone down his criticism of the FBI. King took the advice. His decline in black esteem followed ..." Time said.

The statements are in connection with a report of a new book on King called "The King God Didn't Save" by black novelist John Williams.

The book, with the conclusion that King was a failure, states that King "was a black man and therefore always was and always would be naked of power, for he was slow, indeed, unable to perceive the manipulation of white power, and in the end white power killed him."

Time said, "Most newspapers ignored the rumors and leaks to them of King's extramarital activities, but their existence undermined King's effectiveness just the same. The effect, says Williams, was one of slow political assassination; King was spared it only by the bullet of James Earl Ray."

The incriminating tapes came about, Time said, when the FBI, "suspecting that some of his associates had Communist connections . . . began tapping King's telephone and bugging his hotel rooms in 1963.

"From a security viewpoint, the wiretaps uncovered nothing. They established no links between King and the Communists. But, Williams reports, they did turn up an astonishing amount of information about King's extensive and vigorous sexual activities," Time said.

The Milwaukee Journal
August 11, 1970

Aides, Mrs. King
Challenge Story

New York, N.Y.—AP—Three colleagues of the late Martin Luther King, Jr., Monday denounced as "totally false" a Time magazine report that FBI Director J. Edgar Hoover confronted King with wiretap evidence revealing King's extramarital sex activities.

A fourth associate said Hoover should be suspended for "misuse, abuse and malfeasance in discharging his responsibilities" for the wiretap on King's phone.

The widow of the slain civil rights leader also issued a statement saying the Time story did not correspond with what her husband had told her.

Time stuck by its story.

Discussed Book

Discussing a new book about King, "The King God Didn't Save," by author John Williams, Time said Hoover, meeting with King in 1964, lectured King on his morals and suggested that he tone down his criticism of the FBI.

In a joint statement issued in Atlanta, Ga., the Rev. Ralph David Abernathy, King's successor as head of the Southern Christian Leadership Conference, the Rev. Andrew Young and the Rev. Walter E. Fauntroy, declared:

"As participants and witnesses to the discussions between Martin

Luther King, Jr., and J. Edgar Hoover, we are shocked by Time Magazine's totally false report.

"All three of us were present during the entire discussion and at no point did Mr. Hoover lecture Dr. King or even comment on his personal life."

Time "Discredits Self"

The statement said it was "blatantly untrue that Dr. King slowed down his activities because he felt threatened," and added:

"Time magazine discredits itself in seeking throw mud on man admired and loved by millions, black and white. It discredits itself in stooping to sensationalism through fiction and irresponsibility.

"We suggest that Time reread its own story on Dr. King's immortal contribution, published when he was named Time's Man of the Year (1964)."

Mrs. Coretta King's statement, also issued in Atlanta, said, "The conversation between my husband and Mr. Hoover, which he related to me, does not correspond at all with the Time magazine report."

A spokesman for Time said later:

"A careful reading of Time's article should make quite clear the magazine's admiration for Dr. King's work—for example, the observations that Dr. King's leadership brought conscience and cohesion to the cause of black equality and that he was the catalyst in the formation of a truly national civil rights movement.

"As for the facts in the article, Time stands by its reporting."

Blasts Hoover

In Chicago, the Rev. Jesse Jackson, national director of the SCLC's Operation Breadbasket program, charged the FBI with making the wiretap tapes as "an intentional defamation of character."

Jackson said Hoover, in letting the contents of the tapes become known, was trying "to undercut the trust and respect for the present civil rights leaders." He added:

"Mr. Hoover has stooped to the lowest rungs of viciousness and maliciousness in his underhanded dissemination of information regarding a deceased man."

Asks Investigation

Jackson urged that President Nixon suspend Hoover pending an examination of the FBI director by the civil rights division of the Justice

Department, black jurists, and lawmakers and white and black psychiatrists.

Time quotes Williams as saying the FBI began tapping King's telephone and bugging his hotel rooms in 1963, and while it uncovered no evidence of subversion it "did turn up an astonishing amount of information about King's extensive and vigorous sexual activities."

The wiretap on King's phone was disclosed last year in Houston, Tex., by an FBI agent testifying at a hearing on boxer Cassius Clay's refusal to be inducted into the Army. The agent was not allowed by the judge to say why King's phone was tapped.

UNITED STATES GOVERNMENT
Memorandum

TO: Mr. Bishop   DATE: 8/17/70

FROM: G. E. Malmfeldt
SUBJECT: CORRESPONDENCE AND TELEPHONIC INQUIRIES REGARDING AN ARTICLE IN "TIME" MAGAZINE 8/17/70 CONCERNING MEETING BETWEEN THE DIRECTOR AND MARTIN LUTHER KING IN 1964

The purpose of this memorandum is to recommend the handling of communications and telephonic inquiries regarding the wiretrapping of Martin Luther King and allegation that we engaged in blackmail in disclosing the results thereof.

We have received a number of letters regarding the article which appeared in "Time" magazine on 8/17/70 concerning the meeting between the Director and Martin Luther King in 1964. This article alleged the Director called King in and confronted him with wiretap information regarding King's extramarital activities. Some of the correspondents have asked if we blackmailed King while others have merely protested the wiretaps of him.

In order that we may be consistent in our replies to such correspondence, there are attached for the Director's approval: 1) a proposed letter wherein correspondent asks about blackmailing of King 2) a proposed letter wherein correspondent asks about our wiretapping of King 3) a proposed letter wherein correspondent is making reference to blackmail and inquiries about wiretapping and 4) a copy of an article by Jeremiah O'Leary which appeared in the 6/19/69 issue of "The Evening

Star'' regarding the King wiretapping. The latter is being furnished for the Director's information as it is noted this article sets forth our position on the wiretapping of King and is being utilized in connection with proposed letters numbers 2 and 3.

RECOMMENDATION: That the attached proposed letters regarding this matter be approved.

[Section 90]

UNITED STATES GOVERNMENT
Memorandum

TO: Mr. C. D. Brennan   DATE: 8/17/70

FROM: G. C. Moore

SUBJECT: JESSE LOUIS JACKSON
           RACIAL MATTERS

Pursuant to the Director's request, there is set forth below a summary write-up concerning Jesse Louis Jackson.

Jackson is National Director of Operation Breadbasket, the economic branch of the Southern Christian Leadership Conference (SCLC). It was organized for the purpose of exposing and correcting economic abuses suffered by Negroes and ghetto residents as a result of overcharging by ghetto store owners and to correct alleged discriminatory hiring practices. Jackson was born 10/8/41 in Greenville, South Carolina, and has attended North Carolina A&T College and the Chicago Theological Seminary. He is married and has three children. He joined the SCLC in 1966 and was with Martin Luther King, Jr. when the latter was assassinated. Jackson is frequently mentioned in the press as the heir apparent to King. He has led many civil rights demonstrations in the Chicago area. For the most part he has adhered to a non-violent approach; however, in the Summer of 1969 he spoke to a conference against fascism in Oakland, California, which was sponsored by the Black Panther Party (BPP). Also, in an article containing an interview with him which appeared in the November 1969, issue of ''Playboy'' magazine he indicated that he conditionally feels that violence is justified and expressed anti-police sentiments similar to those of the BPP.

On 8/10/70 Jackson held a press conference concerning an article in "Time" magazine regarding the meeting between the Director and King in 1964. During this conference he accused the Director of trying to "whitemail" King and called on President Nixon to "suspend" the Director. Jackson addressed the Atlanta Press Club, Atlanta, Georgia, on 8/13/70, and, referring to the recent "Time" article, declared, "The FBI says it doesn't have enough money for catching dope peddlers, but runs around making stag films." On 8/16/70 Jackson spoke at a Nation of Islam dinner in Chicago, Illinois. He called for all black leaders to join in his call for the suspension of the Director.

OBSERVATIONS:

It is obvious that Jackson is an opportunist and is attempting to enhance his image and gain nation-wide publicity by his recent actions. We can expect more of the same by him in the future and in view of this will remain alert for any situation we might be able to exploit through counterintelligence techniques.

ACTION:

For information. The above is submitted pursuant to the Director's request.

[Section 93]

UNITED STATES GOVERNMENT
Memorandum

TO: Mr. Bishop   DATE: 10/21/70

FROM: M. A. Jones

SUBJECT: "THE GOVERNMENT AND MARTIN LUTHER KING" BY VICTOR S. NAVASKY

The November 1970 issue of "The Atlantic" magazine carries the above-captioned article by Victor S. Navasky, who is described as one of the founders of the occasional satirical publication, "Monocle."

Allegedly, this article was taken from the author's forthcoming book (name unknown) on former Attorney General Robert F. Kennedy, which is to be published sometime next year. It appears this may be one of the means the author is using to obtain some advance publicity for his book.

Although it is pointed out that the author spent six years of "analysis and detective work" to reconstruct the facts surrounding the "tapping" of Dr. Martin Luther King, Jr.'s telephone, a review of the article quickly reveals that it is merely a rehash of prior arguments put forth by critics of the FBI as to whether the Bureau had received authority from the then Attorney General, Robert F. Kennedy, to install a technical surveillance on King, and if so, how was King's close friend (Kennedy) forced into doing such a thing.

The author attempts to develop this theme by noting what he refers to as the: (1) Kennedy version, (2) FBI version, (3) points at which the Kennedy version conflicts with the FBI version, and (4) the author's own version of what he feels actually happened. Although considerable space is devoted to explaining the Kennedy version, in which the author constantly alludes to information he has received from "Kennedy aides," "Kennedyites," and "Kennedy intimates," without naming any specific individual or source, limited coverage is extended to the author's FBI version.

KENNEDY VERSION:

In this section, the author explains that according to "Kennedy intimates," Attorney General Kennedy complied with the FBI's request for authorization to "tap" King's phone in October 1963, because: (a) the civil rights bill was coming up and if Dr. King were in any way tainted with communist connections, it would be used to defeat this bill; (b) to protect Dr. King by proving to the FBI that he was not being influenced by communist agents; and (c) to make the FBI, which had been wanting to tap Dr. King since 1961, "happy." At this point the author also noted that the rumors about Dr. King's active extracurricular sex life did not arise from the wiretap which Kennedy had authorized but rather from bugs installed "either by local police forces or on the FBI's own initiative without the specific authorization or knowledge of Attorney General Kennedy or anybody on his staff."

FBI VERSION:

In the "Washington Star," in which it was noted that Attorney General Kennedy first proposed tapping Dr. King's phone in June of 1963, and the fact that the Director had a memorandum of Courtney Evans (C.P. Evans to Mr. Belmont memo dated 7/16/63, captioned "Communist Influence in Racial Matters"), described as the FBI's liaison to the Attorney General, to prove it. The author also refers to our reporting to Kennedy on 10/7/63, that it was now technically feasible to apply wiretaps to King's telephone at the Southern Christian Leadership Conference Headquarters in Atlanta, and at an unnamed location in New York. In a satirical vein, the author notes that Mr. Hoover has a memo to "prove" the FBI's request to proceed with the tap "proposed" by Kennedy four months earlier (Memorandum from the Director to the Attorney General dated 10/7/63, captioned "Martin Luther King, Jr., and Communist Influence in Racial Matters"). Navasky notes that the FBI's version was, of course, attacked and discredited by individuals close to Kennedy as well as by Nicholas Katzenbach and Ramsey Clark.

KENNEDY VERSION CONFLICTS WITH FBI VERSION:

The author takes great pains to point out that the Kennedy version conflicts with the FBI version in two essentials: (1) Kennedyites say the tap was Hoover's idea and installed at his urging; and (2) they deny that Kennedy ever entertained doubts about Dr. King's loyalty. Here again the author relies on information received from Katzenbach and Ramsey Clark to support the Kennedy version.

AUTHOR'S VERSION:

The shallowness of the author's contention is immediately pointed out by his admittance that his own "inquiries haved not been entirely satisfactory," because of lack of cooperation from the FBI and limited cooperation from people close to Kennedy. He further notes a lack of complete confidence in his reconstruction by noting that "if there are any inaccuracies, it goes without saying that they were not intended."

In his version of what he feels actually transpired, the author notes that one can accept the Kennedy version with slight variations and goes on to discredit his interpretation of the FBI's version. He concludes by noting that the real explanation of why Kennedy went along with the FBI in tapping King's phone was the same reason given by some Justice Department alumni: "Because there would have been no living with the Bureau if he didn't." The author maintains that Kennedy authorized the tap not merely to avoid the then present problems of "living with the Bureau," such as having to face non-cooperation, risking an FBI torpedo aimed at the civil rights bill, inviting harassment from congressmen, columnists, and other legions of constituents who respond to Mr. Hoover's distress signals, but to protect the Kennedy Administration's reputation if they failed to tap King's phone and Mr. Hoover, at some distant date, used it against them.

VICTORY NAVASKY:

. . . In my memorandum to you dated 3/22/68, captioned "Victor S. Navasky, 27 Washington Square North, New York, New York, Request to Interview Assistant to the Director DeLoach," it was noted that Navasky had written to former Assistant DeLoach advising that he is writing a book on the Department of Justice under Attorney General Robert Kennedy, and noted that while his work will not be an "authorized" account, he hoped that Mr. DeLoach would afford him an interview in order to have the benefit of Mr. DeLoach's impressions and observations concerning the FBI's relationship with Mr. Kennedy during his tenure as Attorney General. Since it was felt that there was a good chance that Navasky's book would be a fast-commission book designed to extoll the accomplishments of Kennedy and possibly antagonistic toward the FBI, it was recommended and approved that Mr. DeLoach decline to be interviewed by Mr. Navasky.

In a subsequent letter to Mr. DeLoach, again requesting an opportunity to interview him, which request was denied, Navasky noted that he would be less than honest if he did not concede that as a result of his Yale Law School training and his past membership in the American Civil Liberties Union, he would approach his study with certain predispositions about some of the FBI's activities.

"MONOCLE" MAGAZINE:

Our files reveal that this is a magazine of political satire, which, in its Winter 1963–64 issue, carried a severe satirical attack against the Central Intelligence Agency. . . .

[Section 92]

UNITED STATES DEPARTMENT OF JUSTICE

FEDERAL BUREAU OF INVESTIGATION

Washington, D. C. 20535
January 22, 1971

WASHINGTON KING HOLIDAY COMMITTEE (WKHC)
RACIAL MATTERS

... advised that a meeting of the WKHC was held in Washington, D.C. (WDC), December 29, 1970, to formulate plans to celebrate January 15, 1971, the birthday of Dr. Martin Luther King, Jr., and to make this day a national holiday. According to source, petitions from throughout the country were to be presented that date to Congress for this purpose.

The source stated that the WKHC was founded following a meeting December 17, 1970, in WDC, between the Honorable Jon Conyers, Jr., Democrat, First District, Michigan and Mrs. Coretta Scott King, at which time the formation of a 90 member citizens' committee was announced. The group includes seven United States Senators, sixteen Congressmen, the Presidents of the National Council of Churches, United Auto Workers, State, County and Municipal Employees Unions, and other representatives from government, labor, business, religion and the arts.

Source further advised that in furtherance of the purpose of the WKHC, Mayor Walter E. Washington and City Council Chairman Gilbert Hahn, Jr., had drafted plans for the observance of the birthday of Dr. King, Jr., and would hold suitable memorial services in front of the District Building, 14th and E Streets, N.W., WDC, on January 15, 1971.

Source stated that Willie J. Hardy, a well known black community leader, is Chairman of the WDC WKHC and in her capacity as a Chairman formulated plans for city-wide observances in honor of Dr. King. The following is a schedule of the major events listed for January 15, 1971:

Time	*Scheduled Event*

8:00 A.M.   Breakfast—Holy Redeemer Catholic Church; New Jersey and New York Avenues.

9:30 A.M.   Memorial Service—Steps of the District Building, 14th and E Streets, N.W., WDC.

11:15 A.M.   Dedication of Martin Luther King, Jr., Food Co-Op, North Capitol and H Streets, N.W., WDC.

11:30 A.M.   Memorial Service O Bibleway Church, 1130 New Jersey Avenue, N.W., WDC. Keynote Speaker—Dr. Ralph David Abernathy of the Southern Christian Leadership Conference.

1:15 P.M.   Changing the name of Nicholas Avenue, S.E., to Martin Luther King Avenue, S.E.

2:00 P.M.   Pilgrimage to the Capitol from the Bible Way Church to present petitions to members of Congress.

6:00 P.M.   Parade from Florida Avenue, N.E., to K Street to H Street, N.E. (Parade Route—Starting Point: Trinidad Avenue, and Florida Avenue, N.E., west on Florida to K Street, West on K Street to 8th Street, South on 8th Street, to H Street, East on H Street, to 11th Street—Disband at Douglas Memorial Methodist Church, 11th and H Streets, N.E.)

7:00 P.M.   Memorial Service, Douglas Memorial Methodist Church, Reverend Walter E. Fauntroy, Principal Speaker.

8:00 P.M.   The Walton Singers—All Souls Unitarian Church, 16th and Harvard Streets, N.W.

Source advised that Dr. Ralph David Abernathy, President, Southern Christian Leadership Conference, and Mrs. Coretta Scott King would be present in WDC, on January 15, 1971, to participate in the march to the steps of the Capitol where petitions gathered from all over the United States requesting that January 15th be declared a National holiday would be presented to members of Congress.

Source further advised on January 11, 1971, that a joint news conference featuring Mayor Walter Washington, representing the District of Columbia Government, Mrs. Willie J. Hardy and Clarence Bennett, Co-Chairmen of the WKHC, was held at 2:30 P.M., that date, in the District Building to outline the events planned for the celebration of the 42nd anniversary of Dr. Martin Luther King, Jr.'s birthday.

Mayor Washington announced plans for city-wide and neighborhood ceremonies, religious services, meetings and other special events planned for January 15, 1971. The Mayor also advised that one of the city's major streets would be renamed Martin Luther King Avenue and that the renaming of the street would be marked by appropriate ceremonies. Mayor Washington announced that the necessary action to rename the street was being taken by the District of Columbia City Council with his full support.

Source stated the Mayor and City Council Chairman Gilbert Hahn, Jr., issued a joint proclamation urging citizens and organizations throughout the District to take part in memorial observances, and at the request of Chairman Hahn and the Mayor, the memorial activities in the District were planned and coordinated by Sterling Tucker, Vice Chairman of the Council and Julian Dugas, Director of the District of Columbia Department of Economic Development.

On January 15, 1971, Special Agents of the FBI observed the memorial service held in honor of the anniversary of the birth of Dr. Martin Luther King, Jr., which was held on the steps of the District Building, 14th and E Streets, N.W., WDC.

The service which was scheduled to begin at 9:30 A.M. did not commence until 9:50 A.M., at which time there were approximately three hundred people in attendance. The peak of the crowd, during the services, was estimated to be 4 or 5 hundred of which approximately 90 per cent were black.

Sterling Tucker, Vice Chairman of the D.C. City Council introduced the speakers, among whom were Gilbert Hahn, Chairman of the City Council; J. C. Turner, WDC AFL-CIO executive and Mayor Walter E. Washington, who delivered the keynote address memorializing and eulogizing Dr. King.

. . . after delivering a brief eulogy, Mayor Washington stated that just as Dr. King had a dream, so he, Mayor Washington had some dreams for Washington, D.C. He advised he wanted WDC to become a place of opportunity for both black and white . . . a place where little children could look to the sun.

Mayor Washington asked all to work in order to help make Dr. King's dream a reality and then stated that in this context it was important to him and altogether fitting that the new WDC library being constructed on G Street between 8th and 9th Streets, N.W., be dedicated to and named for Dr. Martin Luther King, Jr. He remarked that this memorial of brick and mortar would live through the ages and educate young people and was therefore a fitting memorial to King's life. Mayor

Washington concluded his address by stating he would leave the audience with the words of Dr. King:

"Don't tell them I was a Nobel Prize winner. Don't tell them that I
was a great preacher in a great church. Don't remind them of what
college I went to. Tell them I was a man."

. . . that the dedication of the Martin Luther King, Jr., Food Co-Op
took place at 11:15 A.M., as scheduled and was attended by approximately 100 people. Source stated that the dedication ceremony was very
brief and due to the cold weather, the crowd dispersed in an orderly
manner as soon as the ceremony ended.

. . . who also attend the Memorial Service held at the Bible Way
Church, 1130 New Jersey Avenue, N.W., WDC, advised that the service
did not begin until approximately 12:15 P.M., and was attended by at
least 2,500 persons. Source stated that the capacity of this church is
normally 2,000 people, but folding chairs were set up at the rear of the
church and along the aisles, additional people were standing at the rear
of the church and many people watched from a room in the undercroft
of the church which was equipped with closed-circuit television.

Source stated that Dr. Ralph David Abernathy, President of the
Southern Christian Leadership Conference was listed on the program
as the Keynote Speaker but an announcement was made that Dr. Abernathy had been detained in New York City because of a program being
held there in memory of Dr. King and would be late arriving in WDC.

In Dr,. Abernathy's absence, the Reverend Walter E. Fauntroy delivered the principal address. Source made available a taped recording of
this address, portions of which are set forth verbatim:

"I want to say a few words to memorialize this great man because
Dr. King was a man who dreamed what many people thought were
impossible dreams and yet he had a way of making them a reality.

"Let's travel back a few years to his first march on Washington,
August 28, 1963, and I hear again his melodic voice saying 'I have a
dream that someday this nation will rise up and live out the meaning
of its creed, that we hold these truths to be self-evident, that all men
are created equal.' . . . And I hear the affirmative come thundering
across this nation . . . 'That's not an impossible dream.' 'And I have a
dream that someday the sons of former slave owners will sit down
together at the table of government in this country'. . . . And I hear the
voices thundering back at Dr. King, 'It's an impossible dream'. . . .
'And I have a dream that someday the state of Mississippi . . . a state
sweltering in the heat of racial injustice will be transformed into an

oasis of peace and brotherhood,' and I hear them say that Dr. King is an impossible dreamer.

"Martin Luther King, Jr., the man whose life we honor today, was not simply a dreamer of impossible dreams. He had a way of transforming what people thought was impossible into a living reality."

Reverend Fauntroy reminded those present that Dr. King really believed in his dream and that "it was religious people . . . people who believed in God who followed Dr. King . . . Young people and old people, black people and white people, but they all had one thing in common . . . they believed."

Reverend Fauntroy then recalled a speech Dr. King made in which he said: "We come in the name of God. You can knock us down but we will keep on marching. You can beat us with your billy clubs but we will keep on marching. You can turn your vicious dogs on us but we will keep on marching. You can bomb our churches on Sunday morning and kill our children but we will keep on marching, because we want you to know that as we keep on walking there is something within us so that fire cannot burn us, billy clubs can't beat us, dogs can't bite us and bullets can't shoot us."

Continuing Reverend Fauntroy said, "If you are right, no one is too powerful. If you are right . . . you may be poor sometimes; if you are right you may be misunderstood sometimes; but if we are right, God will sustain us."

Reverend Fauntroy then recalled the visit of Dr. Martin Luther King, Jr., to see former President Lyndon B. Johnson at the White House in January 1965. Reverend Fauntroy stated that "Johnson had been re-elected by the largest majority of any President in this century and (Dr. King) told Johnson black people wanted a voting rights act which would protect black people in their right to register and vote across the South because we want the dignity and respect of our due. We want everybody across the South to know that we are somebody and we don't want to be gassed on the way to the polls and killed on the way back because we have the nerve to vote our convictions.

"President Johnson said, 'No, No, Dr. King. We can't do it. It would alienate the South. We have to wait for things to settle down, Dr. King said: 'I'll see you later.' ''

Reverend Fauntroy recalled how Dr. King went to Alabama even though all of his advisers spoke out against it and warned him there would be trouble. But, Reverend Fauntroy said, "Dr. King believed his dream and after having received the Nobel Peace Prize and having gone to Europe and having been acknowledged as what the world in truth knows. . . . that this black man was perhaps the most important man in the most important country in the most violent state in the history of mankind . . . after going to the mountain top and having the whole world recognize him . . . I hear him say 'I must go back. I must go back to Mississippi, back to Alabama, back to Georgia, until we have straightened out the problems that confront our people.' ''

Continuing, Reverend Fauntroy said: ''And we went to Selma, and the Bill Clarks (reference to Sheriff) were so foolish as to whip a group of people led by Hosea Williams and this led people all around the country to ask the President to do something and by March 16, 1965, the same President who told us it could not be done in 1964 told the nation and the Congress of the United States, 'We shall overcome,' and signed the bill. Today there are over 4 million new black voters on the voting rolls of the South.

''In 1963, Senator Herman Talmadge (Democrat, Georgia) referred to us as 'niggers.' He said, 'we gotta keep the niggers in their place' . . . But come 1965, after the Voting Rights Act of 1965, now that 300,000 black voters had registered in Georgia, he was ready to say, 'Well, I've got to get more concerned with the problems of the colored people.' When we had registered 500,000 new black voters in Georgia he was ready to say 'I am more concerned about the problems of my new brothers and sisters.' Between now and 1972 when we will have nearly 1 million new black voters on the books in the State of Georgia he will be heard to say, 'I am concerned about my black soul brothers.' '' Reverend Fauntroy cited the above as an illustration of how a dream can become a reality.

Reverend Fauntroy continued by stating: ''When King died he died leaving many legacies. He died dreaming of a day when you in this nation would be willing to do for the poor and the black what you have always been willing to do for the white and the affluent in the tradition of brotherhood, and that is, provide them an economic floor of security.

''You know, we have a way in this country of referring to public money when it is given to poor people in general, and black people in particular, as somehow being public welfare. But when you give it to the affluent in general and to white people in particular, they call it something else.

''I would say to Dr. King, and we often joked about this, 'We have a way of believing in capitalism for the poor and socialism for the rich.' Reverend Fauntroy then spoke of how the white immigrant was given the Homestead Act to enable him to have free land. He said this was done because "We needed that labor and we needed that creative input to the growing nation . . . but although we were willing to do it for the white affluent, we did not do it for the black and poor.

"After we got them out on the farms across the breadbasket of the nation, we found they were disenchanted. Some couldn't read, some could not write and some could not till the soil and so we must do something about this. Let us train them. But we won't call it public welfare. Let's call it a Land Grant College Act. And they trained them . . . trained them so well that they were growing too much and so we said, 'You are working too hard, farmers, and therefore, we are going to pay you to cut the work. We are going to pay you not to work.' But we won't call it public welfare. We'll call it the Soil Bank Program whereby every year we give to the farmers of this country 3.5 million dollars not to work.

"We've got in this country farmers like a fellow name of Sam Eastland who receives $171,000 a year not to work. And we go to the government and say we don't want to sit down, we want to work . . . give us a guaranteed minimum income . . . and Dr. King understood this. We spend millions of dollars to [subsidize] oil rich millionaires, [millions] of your tax money and my tax money . . . they don't call it public welfare . . . they call it the oil depletion allowance. And when we build suburbs around the country, they call it VA and FHA.

"Dr. King understood this and he said now is the time for the black and the poor . . . black people, white people, affluent people . . . the people who understand . . . to do for this country . . . do for its minorities what it has always been doing for its people of class. . . . The American Indian, black people, Spanish people, Mexican Americans, the Puerto Ricans . . . we must come together to build a new Populist Movement to move this nation to do for its poor what it has always done for its rich. And then he got the idea of a Poor People's Campaign and a new dream of uniting forces to build around the problems of the masses."

Reverend Fauntroy then stated that the idea of a Poor People's Campaign frightened those who disliked Dr. King and they plotted how he could be destroyed and plotted to kill him and said, 'then let us see what shall become of his dream.' "

Continuing, Reverend Fauntroy said: "Now they had good reasons for saying that because they knew that Dr. King was not just a prophet. He was a man. He not only dreamed the impossible dream but they remembered Selma and they remembered Birmingham; they remembered Montgomery and said, 'My goodness, if he said he's going to do it ... you can't fool the man this time. No Problem. Kill him!' ... And let us suppose that some prisoner somewhere on death row can bust out of jail and stalk King for a year and gun him down in cold blood ... and out of the city of Memphis without J. Edgar Hoover finding him ... and somehow travel to the East Coast, past Washington and Philadelphia and New York City into Canada and somehow get on a plane and make it over to England. Let us suppose that that wild beast is caught and let 'Oscar' burn a few buildings and having burned buildings in some of the largest cities and having just burned a few banks too, what shall become of his dream?

"As we pause here, at this moment, to memorialize this man and his life, have we started to ask ourselves ... what shall we do to make him live? ... What now shall become of his dream? I thank God for a day and age when students of Howard University have thought about the goodness of God. When they can pay tribute to the American great that have brought us through everything ... and they can be depended upon to lead us all. I thank God for this ... and regard it as the flesh and blood in the life and work of Dr. Martin Luther King ... for the men and wives of the thousands of people who have assembled in this church on this Friday afternoon and made it Sunday with our worship. I thank God. And if you are true, be true to the heavenly vision which Martin Luther King got on the mountain top ... and I know he got it when he said, 'Precious Lord, take my hand.'

"Dr. King died a troubled man. He was worried about that dream and the separation and the brutality that threatened to separate blacks and whites. He was worried about it. I know he must have been that night when he said, 'Lord, take my hand and lead me on.'

"He believed as he stood there on the mountain top that we would get there by and by, if enough people like you and me will go on together. I don't know about you but come what may, I'm going to work on the man's dream."

Reverend Fauntroy then said he would work to see the hungry fed, housed and clothed to see Dr. King's dream come true and that he would work until there was peace and power in this country. He closed his address by singing "The Impossible Dream."

... advised that Mrs. Willie J. Hardy then thanked Reverend Fauntroy for his moving address and asked all present to keep working on Dr. King's dream every day and make it come to pass. She then introduced Mr. Joseph Jackson, Lyricist President, Howard University Gospel Choir who recited a poem he composed entitled "Ode To The Memory of Dr. Martin Luther King, Jr."

Bishop Smallwood Williams, Pastor of the Bible Way Church was then introduced. He welcomed those present and then presented to the Reverend Walter Fauntroy a portrait of Dr. King which Bishop Williams had commissioned an artist to paint.

Bishop Williams related that while visiting a local art gallery he saw two pictures, one of the late President John F. Kennedy and the other, a likeness of the late Senator Robert Kennedy. Bishop Williams said he purchased these paintings and requested the art dealer to have a portrait painted of Dr. King since all three of these individuals had died at the hands of an assassin and all three died struggling to help the poor and the oppressed. Bishop Williams stated he hung the three pictures in his library as a constant reminder to him of the brotherhood and dignity of man but believed it fitting to present the portrait of Dr. King to a representative of the Southern Christian Leadership Conference (SCLC), so that it could be hung in the King Memorial Library in Atlanta, Georgia.

The SCLC is a publicly identified civil rights organization headquartered in Atlanta, Georgia, formerly headed by Dr. Martin Luther King, Jr.

... that after the benediction, which was given by Dr. Frank Reed, Pastor, Metropolitan AME Church, Washington, D.C., those present in the church departed and began to assemble for the march to the Capitol grounds which began at approximately 2:14 P.M., and was led by a mule-drawn wagon bearing petitions requesting that January 15 be declared a legal holiday.

... the Reverend Ralph Abernathy had not arrived when the line of march had formed and did not join the march until it neared the Capitol grounds at which time he was observed arriving by automobile. The line of march was stopped and Abernathy joined the front rank after which the marchers proceeded to the West front of the Capitol.

... at the West front of the Capitol, Abernathy gave a short address. Source made available a taped recording of this address, portions of which are set forth verbatim:

"As the President of the Southern Christian Leadership Conference and leader of the Poor People's Campaign, I sign this proclamation and declare this day the People's Holiday, and we are going to take this day as our holiday and we have come here today to testify and give Congress the opportunity to get in on the act.

"I want to just take a good look at some of the national holidays we observe. The first one is New Year's Day. Now what does that mean? Does that mean anything but food and football? And does it mean another year of the beginning of poverty or does it mean living with rats and roaches in a hypocritical nation that talks about democracy and practices something else?

"The second holiday is the birthday of George Washington. Now who is George Washington? some of you call him the Father of the Nation, but I call him a slave owner.

"And then we move on to Memorial Day, and on that day what do we do? We celebrate and commemorate those who were killed in the ungodly wars that America has participated in.

"And then we have Independence Day. Justice Douglas said a long time ago that Black people could not observe Independence Day because we do not have independence in this country . . . and now that we have obtained independence I would rather celebrate my independence on the birthday of Martin Luther King.

"And then we move on to Veterans' Day. That's another day when our super patriots jump up in their military regalia and put on their medals and parade through the streets trying to demonstrate the fact that this is the most militaristic nation to be found in the world.

"And then we move on to Thanksgiving Day. Now what is Thanksgiving day? That's when the pilgrims found some turkeys on the happy hunting grounds and killed them and cooked them and ate them with their Indian brothers before the white man took the country from the Indians.

"And the newest of all these days is Christopher Columbus Day. They will celebrate it this year for the first time. Now what in the world is Christopher Columbus Day? All I know is that he sailed across the Atlantic Ocean in some dirty ships and once he got over here he discovered that the Indians had already discovered America.

"And the final day of the national legal holidays is Christmas . . . when we ought to be thinking of peace on earth and good will toward men. Yet, a capitalistic society has taught us to think about a fake known as Santa Claus and to spend all of our money on junk and get in debt and stay in debt until the next Christmas. And then we are supposed to go about dreaming of a white Christmas. Well, we don't dream anymore . . . we live in reality and if we dreamed of Christmas at all if would be a black Christmas. So it is time for us to have a decent holiday and we have our own holiday. We've come to Washington today to ask Congress and tell them that we want to give them the opportunity to get in on the act and if they do not observe every January 15, we are going to observe it as a people.

"I don't know about you, but we live in a critically sick nation and there are one or two things we have got to do for this country.

"1) We got to work to get this city together and we got to do all within our power to see to it that the Nixon, Agnew, Rankin administration is a one-term administration. And we got to elect a young man or a young woman to office, whether they be 75 or any years of age, but they must think young and lead this young nation forward.

"2) Then the second thing that we have to do, as black people . . . we must get together. Therefore, I'm calling a national conference of black leaders and I want it to go all the way from the Black Panthers to the black people of the Church of Christ, Baptists, Presbyterians, Methodists and Catholics. Don't you know that you have let them oppress the Panthers? Man, they are going to suppress something else . . . if we let them get away with it. You are on that list."

The Black Panther Party is characterized in the appendix.

Dr. Abernathy then spoke of the indictment of the Berrigan brothers on a conspiracy charge and remarked that if they were conspirators then he was a conspirator, Reverend Fauntroy was a conspirator and Mayor Washington was a conspirator because everyone became a conspirator as soon as they stood up against the war machine in this militaristic society.

The Berrigan brothers have been publicly indentified as Catholic Priests, active in the anti-war movement, who were recently indicted by a Federal Grand Jury in Harrisburg, Pennsylvania, with planning to blow up underground heating systems for government buildings in Washington, D.C. and to kidnap Henry Kissinger, President Nixon's national security adviser.

Continuing, Dr. Abernathy said: "If we memorialize Dr. King, we can't do it with sad tears. We can't do it with sadness in our hearts. If we really want to memorialize Dr. King we must complete his unfinished work.

"If Dr. King could speak to us today . . . in fact he is speaking . . . I can hear his voice . . . and he is telling you to stop moaning here but to go to Galilee and find out what goes on in the world of men and tell them to get on the case. We must get together and we must do our thing and we must sock it to this nation.

"I've just picked up my petition and you pick up your petitions now and declare our legal holiday a national and regional holiday, but if Congress does not get in on the act, it's our day and we are going to observe it just as the Irish observe St. Patrick's Day by tying up traffic in New York and letting it be known that there is such a thing as Irish power in this country.

"Just like the Confederates observe their day in the South and let you know there is such a thing as slave power, black people are going to observe Martin Luther King's birthday along with white people of good will and let them know there is such a thing as black power.

"Right on. This is our government. A government of the people by the people and for the people and if this is socialism then I am a socialist. If it's communism that I'm a communist. But before you call me a communist call old George Washington . . . but whatever it is be assured I came to Washington to do my thing."

Reverend Fauntroy then announced that those present would present over three million petitions and Dr. Abernathy would lead the people by taking the petitions to the Senators and Congressmen present.

. . . the people who joined in the march then gathered up the petitions and walked up the steps of the West front of the Capitol where they were met by several Senators and Congressmen who received their petitions including Senator Birch Bayh, Democrat Indiana; Senator Adlai Stephenson, Democrat, Illinois; and Congressmen John Conyers, Jr. Democrat, Michigan.

. . . the activities described above ended at 3:53 P.M., without incident.

. . . while the line of march was being formed for the march to the West front of the Capitol, Mayor Walter E. Washington and City Council Chairman Gilbert Hahn, Jr., departed by automobile and took part in the ceremonies which renamed Nicholas Avenue, S.E., Martin Luther King Avenue.

. . . following a parade which began at Florida Avenue and K Street, N.E., at approximately 6:30 P.M., and ended at the Douglas Memorial Methodist Church, 11th and H Streets, N.E., at 7:00 P.M., a memorial service was held for Dr. King which was sponsored by the Near Northeast Community Improvement Corporation, a civic group which is located at 12th and H Streets, N.E.

. . . the memorial address was given by the Reverend Walter Fauntroy and was the same address he had given earlier in the day at the Bible Way Church.

All of these sources advised that the service, which was attended by about 1,000 people, ended at approximately 9:00 P.M. without incident.

None of the above sources saw Mrs. Coretta King at any of the functions held in WDC and the first source, mentioned above, advised on January 18, 1971, that Mrs. King had been unable to come to WDC because of memorial services and other activities in connection with Dr. King's birthday held in Atlanta, Georgia.

BLACK PANTHER PARTY (BPP)
also known as
Black Panther Party for Self Defense

According to the official newspaper of the BPP, the BPP was started during December 1966, in Oakland, California, to organize black people so they can take control of the life, politics, and the destiny of the black community. It was organized by BOBBY G. SEALE, BPP Chairman and HUEY P. NEWTON, Minister of Defense, BPP.

The official newspaper, called "The Black Panther," regularly states that the BPP advocates the use of guns and guerrilla tactics in its revolutionary program to end oppression of the black people. Residents of the black community are urged to arm themselves against the police who are consistently referred to as "pigs" who should be killed.

The newspaper, in its issue of September 7, 1968, had an article by the then Minister of Education, GEORGE MURRAY. This article ended with the following:

> "Black men. Black people, colored persons of America, revolt everywhere! Arm yourselves. The only culture worth keeping is revolutionary culture. Change. Freedom everywhere. Dynamite! Black power. Use the gun. Kill the pigs everywhere."

The BPP newspaper, issue of October 5, 1968, had an article introduced with the following statement: "We will dissent from American government. We will overthrow it."

DAVID HILLIARD, Chief of Staff, BPP, in a speech at the San Francisco Polo Field on November 15, 1969, said "We will kill Richard Nixon."

DAVID HILLIARD, in the "New York Times," issue of December 13, 1969, was quoted as follows: "We advocate the very direct overthrow of the government by way of force and violence."

In the issue of April 25, 1970, the BPP newspaper had an article by Minister of Culture EMORY DOUGLAS as follows:

"The only way to make this racist US government administer justice to the people it is oppressing, is ... by taking up arms against this government, killing the officials, until the reactionary forces ... are dead, and those that are left turn their weapons on their superiors, thereby passing revolutionary judgement against the number one enemy of all mankind, the racist U.S. government."

The BPP Headquarters is located at 1046 Peralta Street, Oakland, California. Branches of the BPP, and Committees to Combat Fascism, under control of the BPP, have been established in various locations in the USA.

1975—77

1975—1977

[Section 94]

January 17, 1975	Memorandum: McDermott to Jenkins
October 20, 1975	Memorandum: Deegan to Wannall

[Section 97]

December 4, 1975	Memorandum: Attorney General to Director

[Section 95]

December 4, 1975	Memorandum: Assistant Attorney General to Director
December 8, 1975	Memorandum: Director to Assistant Attorney General
December 9, 1975	Teletype: Director to All SACS

[Section 98]

December 16, 1975	Memorandum: Deegan to Wannall
December 18, 1975	Letter from Director
January 16, 1976	Airtel: New York to Director

[Section 100]

February 1, 1976	Newspaper article
March 4, 1976	Memorandum: Director to Attorney General

[Section 98]

March 9, 1976	Memorandum: Deagan to Leavitt
June 30, 1976	Teletype: Director to Kansas City, et al.
	[Section 99]
July 29, 1976	Teletype: Director to Atlanta, et al.

648

[Section 94]

UNITED STATES GOVERNMENT
Memorandum

TO: MR. JENKINS   DATE: 1/17/75

FROM: J.J. MCDERMOTT

SUBJECT: RON KESSLER
           WASHINGTON POST
           INQUIRY CONCERNING PERSONAL FILES
           IN FORMER DIRECTOR HOOVER'S OFFICE

C.D. DeLoach, Vice President, Corporate Relations, PepsiCo, Purchase, New York, telephonically advised today that captioned individual has called him 3 or 4 times inquiring concerning alleged secret files in the Director's office and tapes highlighting bedroom conversations of the late Reverend Martin Luther King.

DeLoach advised that he indicated to Kessler that he is sick and tired of false allegations that are being made regarding the Bureau and the late Director Hoover and there certainly must be better things the news media can do rather than to pursue malicious rumors that have no basis in fact.

DeLoach indicated that he acknowledged to Kessler that there had been tapes on Martin Luther King. He refused to divulge the contents of the tapes and advised Kessler in no uncertain terms that these tapes had never been played for anyone outside the FBI and that included newsmen and other Government officials. Along this line of questioning, Kessler asked about "pornographic photographs" that the Bureau allegedly had of King which had been offered to newsmen. DeLoach advised Kessler that we never had any photographs of this sort involving King and that if such photographs had existed, he would have known about them.

With regard to the subject of "secret files" in the late Director Hoover's office, DeLoach advised Kessler that in the interest of security, information that might have come to the attention of the Bureau concerning individuals of prominence was maintained in the Director's Office to preclude it being seen and the possible subject of discussion by young, inexperienced and curious file clerks. DeLoach cited, for example, the investigative file on . . . in connection with his . . . application for the position of Special Agent. DeLoach advised Kessler that the investigation was highly favorable, however, when . . . rose to prominence, the file was maintained in the Director's Office to insure its security. In response to a direct question by Kessler, DeLoach advised that he was not aware of any file on Eleanor Roosevelt in the Director's Office or anywhere else.

DeLoach said he emphatically advised Kessler that there were no "secret files" maintained on Senators or Congressmen in Mr. Hoover's office and pointed out to Kessler that he (Kessler) must have better things to do than pursue a matter as ridiculous as this.

UNITED STATES GOVERNMENT
Memorandum

TO: Mr. W. R. Wannall   DATE: 10/20/75

FROM: J. G. Deegan

SUBJECT: ARTICLE BY JACK ANDERSON AND LES WHITTEN
           CONCERNING MARTIN LUTHER KING, JR.
           SECURITY MATTER—COMMUNIST

This memorandum sets out detailed analysis of news article critical
of former FBI investigation of Martin Luther King, Jr., and recommends
we adhere to "no comment" position regarding allegations in the article, copy attached.

SYNOPSIS:

"The Washington Post" on 10/9/75, carried a column by Jack Anderson and Les Whitten in their "The Washington Merry-Go-Round" syndicated column with caption "Associates Ask Probe To Clear King's
Name." The article states in reference to the FBI and Martin Luther
King, Jr., that former Director Hoover personally ordered leaks regarding King's alleged sexual exploits and supposed Communist ties following the FBI's becoming aware King was being considered for the 1964
Nobel Peace Prize. Mr. Hoover supposedly labeled King as well as the
late Attorney General Robert F. Kennedy and former FBI official Quinn
Tamm as Mr. Hoover's most hated enemies. The article states that the
FBI conducted surveillance of King and bugged hotel suites. The following specific questions are set out and answered in the column:

Did Dr. King have secret Communist connections?; Did the FBI tape
a sex orgy involving Dr. King at Washington, D.C.'s old Willard
Hotel?; Did Dr. King, while in Norway to accept the Nobel Peace Prize,
chase a woman through an Oslo hotel?; Did Dr. King carry on a romance with the wife of a Los Angeles dentist?

Anderson refutes each allegation based on his supposed interview of
persons present. Our files do not support Anderson's charges except
that our files agree with his findings regarding the Oslo incident, and
we did surveill King occasionally and conduct electronic surveillances
of his hotel rooms occasionally. Anderson concludes "Thus the FBI's
attempt to besmirch the great civil rights leader, as Dr. King himself
predicted before his martyrdom, has backfired against the FBI."

Detailed response to each point as revealed by our files set forth in following Details.

OBSERVATIONS:

Each item referred to by Anderson is based on an incident covered in our files. Anderson deals with each item and dismisses it as refuted based on denials of the allegations by persons involved with King in each situation who, in each instance, deny or explain away the accusation. The obvious self-interest in such denials is ignored by Anderson.

RECOMMENDATION:

Any inquiry regarding this article to be responded to by "no comment."

DETAILS:

The 10/9/75, issue of "The Washington Post" carries the syndicated column of Jack Anderson and Les Whitten "The Washington Merry-Go-Round." This article has an added headline "Associates Ask Probe To Clear King's Name."

The article states that associates of the late Dr. Martin Luther King, Jr., have asked the authors to investigate the FBI's "smear charges" against King and to publish the authors' "honest findings." It is stated that Dr. King's widow, according to the associates, hopes the authors will clear Dr. King's name.

Anderson Allegation

The article claims that the FBI, sometime after 1964, began leaking stories about Dr. King's alleged sexual exploits and his supposed communist ties. The leaks allegedly were ordered personally by the late Director Hoover who "had developed a fierce hatred" for King. It is stated that Mr. Hoover was infuriated when he was advised "in a secret memo from his intelligence network" that Dr. King was expected to receive the 1964 Nobel Peace Prize. The article states "he was so infuriated that he scrawled words of outrage on the memo in blue pencil."

Bureau Files

Information regarding Dr. King obtained during the course of our investigation of him and the communist influence on him was disseminated in the normal course of business to appropriate officials and agencies in the Executive Branch, e.g., U.S. Attorney General and other Department of Justice officials, White House officials and occasionally the President. The files do not indicate a "whispering campaign" against King was ordered by Mr. Hoover or conducted by the Bureau.

The extent of Mr. Hoover's reactions to Dr. King's being nominated for and receiving the 1964 Nobel Peace Prize was as follows: Newspaper article 7/18/64, reported that Dr. King had been proposed for the 1964 Nobel Peace Prize. Mr. Hoover on the serial "What a farce!" (100-106670-398). In another article datelined 10/6/64, it was again reported that Dr. King was likely to receive the Nobel Peace Prize. Mr. Hoover on this serial, noted "King could well qualify for the 'top alley cat' prize!'" (100-106670-480). Mr. Hoover noted "Shameful!" when it was, in fact announced that Dr. King had been awarded the 1964 Nobel Peace Prize. (100-106670-484, 491). There is no indication in the file that Mr. Hoover initiated any specific action or intensified investigation as a result of Dr. King's receiving the Nobel Peace Prize.

Anderson Allegation

The article states that Herbert Jenkins, Atlanta, Georgia, Chief of Police, who was at that time president of the International Association of Chiefs of Police (IACP), visited Director Hoover. Mr. Hoover supposedly "suddenly, out of context . . . blurted that he had three enemies whom he hated more than anyone else in the world," former Bureau official Quinn Tamm, former Attorney General Robert F. Kennedy and Dr. King. The article continues by stating that the FBI kept Dr. King under surveillance and "even bugged his hotel suites." It is alleged that the FBI used the information obtained to start a "whispering campaign" against King.

Bureau Files

Herbert T. Jenkins, Chief of Police, Atlanta, Georgia, who had recently been elected president of IACP, had an interview with Director Hoover in the Director's Office on the afternoon of 1/18/65. Memorandum of J. J. Casper to Mr. Mohr dated 1/19/65, records this interview. Mr. Hoover did discuss at some length, his displeasure with Quinn Tamm, executive Director of IACP and the manner in which Mr. Tamm was handling his functions with the IACP. Mr. Hoover did not describe Mr. Tamm as an "enemy." The only reference to former Attorney General Robert Kennedy was the statement by Mr. Hoover that Mr. Kennedy had attempted to have Mr. Hoover lower the standards for FBI Agents as a possible means of increasing the number of Negro Agents employed by the Bureau. Mr. Hoover explained to Mr. Jenkins that he had told the Attorney General that he would not do this and that he would not drop the standards of Special Agents as long as he was Director of the FBI. The only reference to Mr. King is as follows:

"Mr. Hoover also discussed with Chief Jenkins his meeting with Doctor Martin Luther King. He pointed out that while he has only publicly called King a liar, he could have told of King's poor morals and communist connections." There is no statement of Mr. Hoover's describing anyone as his "enemy" or of his making any statements regarding his hating anyone.

Anderson Allegation
The statement that the FBI kept Dr. King under surveillance and "bugged his hotel suite" is not subject to dispute. The Bureau did surveill King on occasion and we did conduct electronic surveillance of hotel rooms occupied by King.

The following questions are raised in the article and answered therein:

Anderson Allegation
"Did Dr. King have secret Communist connections?" The article states that Dr. King "was in touch with a known Communist attorney in New York City who tried to influence the civil rights campaign." Anderson concludes that Dr. King did not let the Communists take over his movement and that Dr. King "remained a staunch anti-Communist." It is acknowledged that he accepted some of the attorney's anti-Vietnam War views.

Bureau Files . . .

Anderson Allegation
"Did the FBI tape a sex orgy, involving Dr. King, at Washington's old Willard Hotel?" The article states that "witnesses" who were with Dr. King at the Willard Hotel said that Dr. King used some "ribald" language but indulged in no sexual acts.

"There was evidence on the tape, according to those who heard it, that sexual intercourse occurred. But Dr. King was not one of the lovers. The man's voice was identified as that of an acquaintance."

Bureau Files . . .

Anderson Allegation
"Did Dr. King, while in Norway to accept the Nobel Peace Prize chase a woman through an Oslo hotel?" The article alleges that the FBI whispered such rumors around Washington, but that "witnesses"

state someone in King's party other than himself was involved with some prostitutes in the hotel, and that King was not so involved.

Bureau Files

Our files do not contain any information indicating that the FBI whispered rumors as referred to above around Washington. Our files do reflect that we had information that someone in King's party other than King was involved with some prostitutes in the hotel in Oslo, Norway. (100-442529).

Anderson Allegation

"Did Dr. King carry on a romance with the wife of a Los Angeles dentist?" The article states that "we spoke directly with both the dentist and his wife. Both agreed that she was Dr. King's close friend but not his lover."

Bureau Files ...

The article ends:

"Thus the FBI's attempt to besmirch the great civil rights leader, as Dr. King himself predicted before his martyrdom, has backfired against the FBI." This conclusion is not supported by our files.

[Section 97]

Office of the Attorney General
Washington, D.C. 20530

December 4, 1975

MEMORANDUM TO: DIRECTOR, FBI

FROM: THE ATTORNEY GENERAL

RE: MARTIN LUTHER KING, JR.

On November 24, 1975, I directed Assistant Attorneys General J. Stanley Pottinger and Richard L. Thornburgh to review the files relating to Martin Luther King at once in the light of recent testimony, and make a recommendation as to whether the assassination case should be reopened.

Mr. Pottinger's office is undertaking the initial review of all material in the Department of Justice in order to comply with my directive.

I have asked that this review be conducted thoroughly but with dispatch. Both Messers. Pottinger and Thornburgh understand, I believe, that this investigation is of the highest Departmental priority. I am sure that you will cooperate with them to facilitate their access to Bureau files both here and in the field, as they may request them, and to make available personnel of the Bureau for interviews and such other assistance as may be necessary.

I am also requesting that you assign one person responsible for assisting in this investigation.

[Section 95]

UNITED STATES GOVERNMENT
Memorandum

TO: Director   DATE: December 4, 1975
           Federal Bureau of Investigation

FROM: J. Stanley Pottinger
           Assistant Attorney General
           Civil Rights Division

<u>Martin Luther King, Jr.</u>

As you know, the Attorney General has instructed this Division and the Criminal Division to look at all actions taken by the Federal Bureau of Investigation with respect to Martin Luther King, Jr. I have assigned Deputy Assistant Attorney General James P. Turner and Criminal Section Chief Robert A. Murphy to assist me in this review. Therefore, I request that you make the following material available to this Division.

1. All material concerning Dr. King, his family, relatives and friends, and the Southern Christian Leadership Conference that has been provided to the Senate and House Select Committees on Intelligence.

2. All other material in your files relating to the same individuals and organization, either directly or indirectly, including, but not limited to:

a. All COINTELPRO proposals, actions and results of actions;

b. all requests, approvals and results, including tapes, transcripts and logs, of electronic surveillance, whether wiretap, microphone or otherwise;

c. all intelligence files.

3. The documents which are retained in the office of former Associate Deputy Attorney General Wilderotter (which documents we are presently reviewing).

4. Your complete file on the Investigation of the assassination of Dr. King, including internal administrative Bureau memoranda.

It should be clear that we are interested in reviewing every single item in your files which relates in any way to Dr. King, his family, friends, associates of SCLC. Please provide us with an inventory which indicates the file number or other identifying characteristic of each file, the location of those files, including those which might be in your field offices, and a brief description of what is in each file.

The Attorney General has assigned this task the highest priority. Therefore, please expedite this request.

TO: J. Stanley Pottinger   December 8, 1975
           Assistant Attorney General
           Civil Rights Division
FROM: Director, FBI

RE: MARTIN LUTHER KING, JR.

Reference is made to your letter dated December 4, 1975, in the above caption, your reference DJ 144-72-668.

This is to confirm a telephonic communication on December 5, 1975, between Mr. Robert A. Murphy of the Department and Deputy Associate Director James B. Adams of the Bureau. Adams sought clarifying information concerning those portions of the referenced letter pertaining to "friends and associates" of King, particularly as mentioned in the summarizing statement (page two, penultimate paragraph). It was agreed between Murphy and Adams that initially, we will make available the files relating to King, his immediate family and the Southern Christian Leadership Conference (SCLC), as well as the file concerning the FBI's investigation of the assassination of King. Insofar as "friends and associates" of King are concerned, as the review of the above-described files by the Civil Rights Division progresses, we will also make available additional files relating to "friends and associates" as the Civil Rights Division may designate and request same.

In the spirit of the completeness of your review which is so essential, we are also designating two additional files for immediate review as they contain numerous references to the Senate and House Select Committees on Intelligence. These two files are entitled "Communist Influence in Racial Matters" and "Communist Party, USA—Negro Question."

In order to expedite your review, it is suggested that you commence with those files we maintain at our Headquarters. Meanwhile, we will solicit the necessary inventories from our field offices for your further consideration.

This matter has been designated within this Bureau as of the highest priority.

CODE   **TELETYPE**

TO ALL SACS   DECEMBER 9, 1975
FROM DIRECTOR FBI (100-106670)
MARTIN LUTHER KING, JR., BUDED: DECEMBER 12, 1975

FOR INFORMATION OF ALL OFFICES THE DEPARTMENT OF JUSTICE HAS INITIATED AN EXTENSIVE REVIEW EFFORT "TO LOOK AT ALL ACTIONS TAKEN BY THE FBI WITH RESPECT TO MARTIN LUTHER KING, JR." IT HAS INSTRUCTED BUREAU MAKE AVAILABLE FOR DEPARTMENTAL REVIEW ALL MATE-RIALS CONCERNING KING, HIS FAMILY, RELATIVES, FRIENDS AND ASSOCIATES, AND THE SOUTHERN CHRISTIAN LEADER-SHIP CONFERENCE (SCLC) (ORGANIZATION WHICH WAS HEADED UP BY KING), AS WELL AS THE FILE RELATING TO THE ASSASSINATION OF KING. ("ASSASSINATION OF MARTIN LUTHER KING, JR.; CIVIL RIGHTS," CODE NAME MURKIN, BU-REAU FILE 44-38861.) MATERIAL TO BE MADE AVAILABLE TO INCLUDE, BUT NOT LIMITED TO, ALL COINTELPRO PROPOS-ALS, ACTIONS AND RESULTS OF ACTIONS; AND ALL RE-QUESTS, APPROVALS AND RESULTS, INCLUDING TAPES, TRANSCRIPTS AND LOGS, OF ELECTRONIC SURVEILLANCES, WHETHER WIRETAP, MICROPHONE OR OTHERWISE.

AS AN EARLY STEP IN THE DEPARTMENTAL REVIEW, IT HAS ASKED FOR AN INVENTORY OF ALL MATERIALS AVAIL-ABLE BOTH AT HEADQUARTERS AND IN ALL FIELD OFFICES.

THE PURPOSE OF THIS TELETYPE IS TO SOLICIT THE NECES-
SARY FIELD INVENTORIES. PRELIMINARY DISCUSSIONS WITH
THE DEPARTMENT HAS NARROWED THE REQUEST AS TO
"FAMILY, RELATIVES" TO INCLUDE ONLY IMMEDIATE FAM-
ILY. AS TO "FRIENDS AND ASSOCIATES," DEPARTMENT HAS
ADVISED THAT AS THE REVIEW PROGRESSES, IT WILL DESIG-
NATE THE SPECIFIC INDIVIDUALS IT IS INTERESTED IN FOR
REVIEW OF MATERIALS. THE FIRST SUCH INDIVIDUAL AL-
READY DESIGNATED BY THE DEPARTMENT IS STANLEY
DAVID LEVISON, BUFILE 100-392452. WHILE DEPARTMENT IS
APPARENTLY CONSIDERING FILE REVIEWS IN THE FIELD, ALL
THAT IS IMMEDIATELY DESIRED ARE FIELD INVENTORIES RE-
LATING TO PERTINENT MAIN FILES ONLY.

FOLLOWING ARE INSTRUCTIONS FOR PREPARATION OF IN-
VENTORIES BY ALL FIELD OFFICES.

[Section 98]

UNITED STATES GOVERNMENT
Memorandum

TO: Mr. W. R. Wannall   DATE: 12/16/75

FROM: J. G. Deegan

SUBJECT: MARTIN LUTHER KING, JR.

This informative memorandum to record for the file discussion held
12/15/75 by ... Intelligence Division, with Robert Murphy, Criminal
Section Chief, Civil Rights Division of the Department, concerning a
project under way involving Departmental review of King and related files.

Inasmuch as we have canvassed all field offices, at the Department's
request, for inventories of pertinent files, inquiry was made of Murphy
as to whether or not the Department visualized some time reviewing
field files. He stated that this might occur but, if so, it would likely be
on a limited basis. For example, Departmental personnel might visit
some key offices such as Atlanta and New York.

Attempt was made by ... to obtain some assessment as to how
long this project would continue. Murphy advised that early next week,

definitely before Christmas, the Civil Rights Division will furnish the Attorney General a status report which will emphasize the enormity of the task given them if all relevant files were actually to be reviewed. It is intended that the Attorney General be told that it is impossible for the limited number of personnel now assigned to this project (three individuals, including Assistant Attorney General Pottinger), to complete the task of reviewing all serials in all files unless they were given years to do so. Murphy visualized the possibility that the Attorney General might assign a staff of attorneys who would work on the file review for several months.

Because the Department requested as the first file to be reviewed that of King's former close adviser, Stanley David Levison . . . inquired as to the reason for the Department's extreme interest in this particular file and how it is visualized that the Levison investigation would have any bearing on the completeness of our investigation of the assassination of King. Murphy responded that its interest in the Levison case stems only from their interest in insuring we originally had a firm basis for the King investigation. Their interest is also tied in with an earlier suspicion that Levison might have been a Bureau informant. (This matter was covered in a prior memorandum reporting Pottinger's inquiry on this point and . . . dispelling any such thought to Pottinger.) Murphy indicated that if and when tapes are to be listened to, it is their intention that it be done only by Pottinger.

Murphy was advised that because the Department's original request in this matter dated 12/4/75 asked for inventories "in your field offices," we had canvassed only field offices, to the exclusion of Legats. He was told of our procedure on file destruction by Legats, but that there might be some material in some Legats' offices, particularly in Mexico City. He indicated that for the time our canvass of field offices only is sufficient and that we should take no action as to inventorying Legats' offices.

Finally, Murphy was briefed concerning certain material in our files in late 1963 and early 1964 which refer to some differences between Mr. Hoover and the then Domestic Intelligence Division on the King and related investigations. Murphy was told that some of Mr. Hoover's remarks written into the files were of a sarcastic nature and for a full understanding he should be aware of the atmosphere then existing between Hoover and then Assistant Director William C. Sullivan in that they apparently disagreed on the interpretation of communist.
<u>RECOMMENDATION:</u> influence in racial matters.

None. For information and record purposes.

December 18, 1975

Chicago, Illinois 60620

Dear . . .

I have been advised of your appearance at our Chicago Office on November 24, 1975, along with other members of the Dr. Martin Luther King, Jr. Movement, and the statements and demands made by you and your associates during your appearance there. I have also been informed that representatives of our Chicago Office explained to you and your associates our minority hiring policies, current recruiting efforts and offered to coordinate any efforts by your group to help recruiting.

Regarding the investigation of Dr. Martin Luther King, Jr., by the FBI, Mr. James B. Adams, Deputy Associate Director, FBI, stated during testimony before the Senate Intelligence Committee on November 19, 1975, that the FBI had a valid basis for investigating Dr. Martin Luther King, Jr., to determine the extent of communist influence being exerted upon him, but for reasons of national security and ongoing investigations we are unable to provide any specifics. When questioned concerning the basis for certain tactics employed during our investigation of Dr. King, Mr. Adams also testified there was no statutory basis or justification for such action. I refer to Mr. Adams' testimony inasmuch as I feel this is in answer to your statements and demands in relation to the investigation of Dr. King by the FBI, and my meeting with you is, therefore, not necessary.

Concerning your other demands relating to the President and the Attorney General of the United States and Congress, these demands, along with the facts concerning your appearance at our Chicago Office on November 24, 1975, have been forwarded to the Attorney General.

Sincerely yours,

Clarence M. Kelley
Director

NOTE:

Chicago teletype 11/24/75 captioned "Martin Luther King, Jr., Movement, Information Concerning" advised group of about 50 demonstrators calling themselves the Dr. Martin Luther King, Jr. (DMLK) Movement entered the Federal Building in Chicago (which houses FBI) on 11/24/75 and protested regarding FBI investigation of King. Group was headed by . . . who read statement of group's feelings about FBI investigation of King and demanded (1) President send a letter of apology to Mrs. Coretta King, widow of Dr. Martin Luther King, Jr. (2)

Attorney General send similar letter to Mrs. King (3) Mr. Kelley send similar letter to Mrs. King (4) Special session of Congress be called to deal with agencies "who spy, snoop on private citizens" (5) FBI, Chicago, set up an affirmative action program to deal with minority hiring. FBI, Chicago Office, representatives explained hiring practices, offered to coordinate any effort by group to help recruiting and stated other demands would be forwarded to FBIHQ. Group also requested to confer with Mr. Kelley and Chicago requested we consider directing suitable letter to . . . mentioning whether Director will see group. Letter sent to Attorney General 12/8/75 advising him of demonstration and statements and demands made by group in the event he wants to advise appropriate White House officials.

[FBI]

1/16/76

AIRTEL

TO: DIRECTOR, FBI

FROM: SAC, NEW YORK

SUBJECT: CITIZEN COMMITTEE FOR A DR. MARTIN LUTHER KING, JR., HOLIDAY

On 1/15/76, HOWARD BENNETT, National Chairman of "Citizen Committee for a Dr. Martin Luther King, Jr. Holiday," accompanied by WILLIAM BYRD, Vice Chairman of the Committee, appeared at the NYO.

Mr. BENNETT indicated the purpose of the visit was to find out what the Federal Bureau of Investigation was doing about the allegations that the killing of Dr. MARTIN LUTHER KING, JR., was a conspiracy. He was specifically interested in what had been done to identify the person who changed Dr. KING's room reservation from the first floor to the second floor at the Lorraine Motel, Memphis, Tennessee.

Mr. BENNETT and Mr. BYRD were advised that the Attorney General of the U.S. is currently reviewing the FBI investigation of Dr. KING's death. Mr. BENNETT stated he would make arrangements to see the Attorney General at some time in the future.

[Section 100]

Newsday: February 1, 1976
FBI Tied to King's Return To Memphis

By Les Payne
© Newsday, Inc.

The FBI continues to turn up in unexplained circumstances surrounding the assassination of Martin Luther King.

Newsday has learned that FBI informants actively participated in the rioting in Memphis in 1968 which drew the Rev. Dr. King back to the city where he was killed.

Several FBI informants and at least one undercover agent for the Memphis police department were among the most active members of a young, violence-prone black group which openly opposed King's peaceful march supporting the city's sanitation workers.

According to some witnesses, the 100-member group called the Invaders led the March 28 riots which attempted to discredit King's efforts. Following the riot, in which one youth was killed, scores injured and 238 arrested, King vowed that he would return to prove that he still could lead a nonviolent demonstration.

"Dr. King would never have returned to Memphis if the violence had not happened," said the Rev. Jesse Jackson, who was one of King's aides in the Southern Christian Leadership Conference. "We never intended to get bogged down in Memphis."

The Invaders created major disruptions among blacks supporting King, according to his aides. They criticized King for his nonviolent approach and urged local blacks to "burn, baby, burn." On April 4, the day King was killed, the groups met with him and his staff and threatened renewed violence unless they were given $750,000 to develop their community. "They just got louder and louder," one aide who was at the meeting recalled. "We told them we didn't have access to that kind of money. We had to put them out."

Two sources said FBI agents and Memphis policemen admitted that they had "penetrated" the Invaders with several informers. One of the informants reportedly planned a large portion of Police [*sic*] and FBI officials were regularly provided with detailed information about the group's plans, activities and of the group's violent confrontations [and its] meetings. "They knew everything that went on at Invaders' meetings," one source said. "It was as if they had a tape recorder there." The undercover Memphis policeman who joined the Invaders was at the scene of the violence on the day of the riot, several sources said. He is reportedly still a member of the Memphis force.

"Weston [not the real name of the undercover police agent] was very focal, very active," said a former leader of the Invaders who has talked to the policeman since he was discovered to be a member of the force. "He had a 7.62 Russian automatic rifle and he was armed every time we were armed. He was always suggesting actions that we should take; I never saw him physically attack anyone. But he was one of the most provocative members of the Invaders."

The Invaders, who wore jackets with their names printed on the back, were organized in late 1967. The youths were led mainly by college students of nearby Memphis State and LeMoyne colleges. The Invaders denounced the nonviolent strategy, but offered protection for King and his staff members. "They, like other blacks in the country, were naturally frustrated by the slow pace of change," said the Rev. Hosea Williams, Atlanta SCLC director. "We usually put them to work as parade marshals or security guards. They would never have hurt Dr. King. But those who infiltrated our groups, and we could never identify them, tried to exploit the youngsters' frustrations and neglect and turn them against us."

The FBI and Memphis police verified recently that they had informants among the Invaders in 1968. However, Henry Lux, who was the assistant police chief in Memphis, downplayed the group's role in the March 28 violence. Robert G. Jensen, who was the FBI agent in charge at the time, said, "I wouldn't be surprised if we had informers in the group. I'm sure there was adequate coverage of the Invaders."

It is reliably reported that the Bureau and Memphis police shared intelligence about the Invaders.

In addition to being involved with the March 28 violence, the Memphis police undercover agent was providing security for King at the Lorraine Motel on the day he was assassinated, according to knowledgeable sources. The officer was a member of the Invaders' four-man security force that had agreed to provide protection for King while he was in Memphis.

There have been a series of disclosures recently concerning covert FBI activities against King. This has led to a Department of Justice investigation. The inquiry started after the Senate Intelligence Committee discovered an FBI memorandum, dated March 28, 1969, which detailed a plan to portray King as a hypocrite for staying at a white-owned motel—the Rivermont Holiday Inn—where he fled after the violence erupted. The Justice Department investigated to see if the memo had anything to do with King's return to the black-owned Lorraine Motel, where he was killed. They found no evidence linking the FBI to a plot to have King return to the Lorraine Motel. However, Newsday has learned that the Invaders heatedly discussed King's stay at the white motel among themselves—some threatening violence over the issue.

A source at the Justice Department told Newsday that the FBI memo was part of then FBI Director J. Edgar Hoover's Counter-Intelligence Program (Cointelpro) against "Black Nationalist-Hate Groups." The plan, outlined in an FBI Domestic Intelligence Division memo, was put into effect March 4, one month before King was killed. It was designed to "prevent the rise of a 'messiah' who could unify . . . the militant black nationalist movement." An overall goal of Hoover's plan was to "discredit" black leaders and their movement among both blacks and whites.

The violence at Memphis, perhaps more than anything else, began to erode King's credibility among moderate blacks. King and his group were preparing to lead a nonviolent "Poor People's March" on Washington later that month. After the Memphis riots some nationalist black leaders attacked King for the violence. On the day before he was killed, NAACP leader Roy Wilkins attacked King in a story printed in the Memphis Press-Scimitar. Wilkins said he doubted that King could keep the Washington march nonviolent: "If a maverick of the rear ranks of the march decides to throw a brick through a window, there's nothing Dr. King up front can do to stop it."

Jensen, who was in charge of the FBI in Memphis, said that the "ultimate decisions [for Cointelpro] were made in Washington, D.C. and then they came to the field officer." He denied that his office ever received the hotel memo. "I have no recollection of a memorandum dated March 28," he said. "If it was an intra-office memo I wouldn't have seen it anyway. It would have come to us as general instructions."

The Senate Intelligence Committee said that it uncovered no evidence that the FBI was implicated in King's murder or any cover-up. The committee chairman, Frank Church (D-Idaho), has reportedly called for a federal special prosecutor to investigate the assassination to resolve "many unanswered questions," including whether the Bureau "vendetta" against King was related to his murder in Memphis.

Some of King's staff members over the years, have charged that the

Invaders were responsible for the riots which indirectly led, they say, to King's death in Memphis.

"The violence was definitely responsible for Martin's being in Memphis on April 4th," said Cong. Andrew Young (D-Ga). "The Invaders themselves have taken responsibility for the violence. Now if the FBI was involved with the Invaders, then it would bear looking into."

FBI officials deny any involvement in King's death. "The FBI did an excellent job in the investigation," Jensen said. "There are still a lot of theories, but no new evidence . . ."

However, former FBI agent Arthur Murtagh said that Hoover's relentless surveillance of King influenced the way individual agents approached the murder. For a time Murtagh directed the Bureau's intelligence unit in Atlanta which tapped the civil rights leader's telephone and bugged his rooms. "The Bureau under Hoover believed that King was a foreign Communist agent," he said. "He was the enemy. In this sort of atmosphere, the Bureau's investigating King's murder was like the CIA investigating the assassination of a Russian premier."

Murtagh said that some agents were "ecstatic" after King was shot. "When King was shot, an agent I knew in Atlanta went on a 30-minute high. We were in the Bureau's parking lot when the news came and this fellow kept saying, "They got Zorro [King's code name] . . . they got Zorro. They finally got that son of a bitch."

The Attorney General   March 4, 1976

Director, FBI

"NEWSDAY" ARTICLE CONCERNING
INVADERS AND DR. MARTIN LUTHER
KING, JR., DATED FEBRUARY 1, 1976

An article appears in the February 1, 1976, issue of "Newsday" captioned "FBI Tied to King's Return to Memphis" written by Les Payne (copy attached).

The article alleges that the FBI and the Memphis, Tennessee Police Department infiltrated the Invaders, a Memphis organization of young blacks. The Invaders allegedly were responsible for violence during a march in Memphis on March 28, 1968. The late Dr. Martin Luther King, Jr., was a participant in this march. It is alleged that because of the violence associated with this march Dr. King found it imperative to return to Memphis in April 1968, at which time he was assassinated. It is inferred that inasmuch as there were FBI and police informants in the Invaders, the FBI and the police were thereby possibly responsible for Dr. King's assassination based on the possibility that the March 28, 1968, violence was part of a conspiracy to compel Dr. King to return to Memphis and his death. It is alleged that the FBI informants and a Memphis Police Department undercover officer infiltrated the Invaders and were actively responsible for the violence associated with the Invaders.

A review of the files at FBI Headquarters and at the Memphis Field Office of the FBI has determined the following:

An umbrella black group was formed in Memphis in 1967 known primarily as the Black Organizing Project (BOP). One of its cells was the Invaders composed of young blacks. The Invaders were particularly militant. Leaders of the Invaders made inflammatory statements to the effect that it would be desirable for the city to burn.

On February 12, 1968, Memphis sanitation workers began a strike. Many rallies and marches were held in their support and the strike became a black cause. Dr. King and his organization, the Southern Christian Leadership Conference, supported this strike. On March 28, 1968, a mass demonstration was held in Memphis with Dr. King as a participant. The leaders of the Invaders actively urged students to skip school on that date and to participate in the march.

Shortly after the beginning of this march, with Dr. King at the head, young blacks toward the rear began breaking windows and looting. Dr. King immediately left the scene. Widespread looting occurred, three young blacks were shot, one fatally, approximately 60 were injured, five policemen received significant injuries and there were approximately 300 arrests. The National Guard was mobilized. The presence of a large number of uncontrolled youths, combined with the agitation of BOP/Invaders leaders, was considered the primary cause of the violence.

This violence was particularly distressing to Dr. King inasmuch as it was felt by him and his associates that this incident might be construed as an indication he could no longer effectively lead mass demonstrations without violence.

The FBI did not have informant coverage of the Invaders. There were five informants of the Memphis Office providing some degree of coverage of the Invaders or its leaders. One informant did become a member of the Invaders shortly after March 28, 1968, violence. He was present during the demonstration and reported on the activities of the leaders of the Invaders before and during the demonstration. Another informant was well acquainted with the BOP/Invaders leaders. He was also present during the demonstration and reported thereon.

Our files do not indicate that any of the FBI informants were involved in planning, inciting or participating in the violence. None were in any level of policy or leadership in the BOP or the Invaders.

The Memphis Police Department did have an undercover officer who had infiltrated the Invaders. He regularly reported on the activities of the Invaders. There is no indication in our files that the Memphis police officer was involved in the planning, instigating or performance of violence. This man has been publicly disclosed and he is no longer a member of the Memphis Police Department.

This is being provided for your information.

[Section 98]

UNITED STATES GOVERNMENT
Memorandum

TO: Mr. T. W. Leavitt   DATE: 3/9/76

FROM: J.G. Deegan

RESPONSE TO CRITICISM OF FBI
CONCERNING ACTIONS TAKEN AGAINST
MARTIN LUTHER KING, JR.

Purpose is to furnish External Affairs Division the attached list of public allegations against the FBI in our investigation of Martin Luther King, Jr., and appropriate responses, which may be useful in handling future King inquiries at FBI Headquarters and in the field.

BACKGROUND:
Memorandum from D.W. Moore, Jr., to Mr. Jenkins, 2/18/76, advised that a conference was held in Kansas City on 2/13/76, attended by Director, eight SACs and two representatives from the External Affairs Division. The purpose was to review ideas and procedures used by the field in promoting the best interest of the Bureau through local media. The SACs believed that one of the most difficult problems was re-

sponding to criticism of the Bureau's reported abuses regarding our activities against King. It was decided and approved by the Director that succinct and definite answers be provided to counter criticism of the Bureau's investigation of King.

The Intelligence Division has prepared the attached document which contains the major allegations raised by the Senate Intelligence committee and the media regarding our investigation of King. Included are responses which may be useful in handling any future questions concerning allegations in the King case. This information is provided for the use of External Affairs Division and for forwarding to SACs if such action is deemed advisable by External Affairs.

ACTION:

That the attached document be referred to the External Affairs Division for appropriate action.

MARTIN LUTHER KING, JR.

GENERAL:

In responding generally to questions and criticism regarding the FBI's investigation of King, it should be noted that our investigation should be viewed in context of the time involved—the early and mid 1960's— not today. Those were years of considerable racial strife throughout the nation when subversive and other disruptive elements were attempting to capitalize for their advantage on the social awakening in our country on the civil rights issue.

Media, congressional and public criticism of our investigation of King have occurred in the following major areas:

ALLEGATIONS:

(1) ALLEGATION: The FBI had no valid basis for investigating King.

RESPONSE: This is not true. The FBI had a valid basis for investigating King to determine the extent of communist influence being exerted upon him. However, for reasons of national security and ongoing investigations, the FBI is unable to provide any specifics. It can also be pointed out that this communist influence was of concern not only to the FBI, but also the President and Attorney General of the United States who spoke personally with King concerning the matter. It should be noted that the bona fide civil rights activities of King were never under investigation.

(2) ALLEGATION: That the FBI conducted illegal electronic surveillances of King.

RESPONSE: This is not true. All electronic surveillances of King were legal.

(3) ALLEGATION: The FBI mailed an anonymous tape and letter to King. According to interpretation by various individuals in the media and the Senate Intelligence Committee, contents of this letter suggested King commit suicide.

RESPONSE: There is no record in the official FBI files to verify that any mailing of anonymous letter or tape recording to King was an official FBI action or with FBI approval. As to the suggestion that the letter sent to King urged his suicide, we can find no basis for any conclusion that the anonymous letter urged King's suicide and we do not know what the letter urged. All we do know is that the draft, or original of what might have been the letter was found in papers left at the FBI by a former Bureau officer.

(4) ALLEGATION: The FBI played tapes of monitored King conversations to persons outside the FBI.

RESPONSE: There is nothing in the files of the FBI to substantiate such an allegation.

(5) ALLEGATION: Information developed during our investigation of King was disseminated outside the Executive Branch of Government.

RESPONSE: This is true. Although our primary dissemination regarding King was made within the Executive Branch, there were some limited dissemination* to other U.S. Government elements such as Congressmen. In several instances, on a highly selective basis, dissemination was made outside the Federal Government to leaders in religious, academic and news media fields.

(6) ALLEGATION: The FBI conducted a campaign to discredit and neutralize King.

RESPONSE: The FBI during its investigation of King initiated actions, including several under our Counterintelligence Programs, to neutralize and discredit King. There was no statutory basis for such actions. As to the possible motive for the activity, because of reasons of privacy and delicacy, possible motive is not proper subject for public discussion.

(7) ALLEGATION: That the FBI was in some way involved in the assassination of King.

RESPONSE: False. There is no evidence to support such an allegation.

---

*Dissemination did *not* include playing of any tapes.

CODE   **TELETYPE**   **URGENT**

TO SACS KANSAS CITY   JUNE 30, 1976
        LOS ANGELES
        MEMPHIS
        SAN FRANCISCO

DIRECTOR FBI (100-106670)
    MARTIN LUTHER KING, JR.
    FOR INFORMATION OF KANSAS CITY, LOS ANGELES AND
SAN FRANCISCO, THE ATTORNEY GENERAL HAS ORDERED A
REVIEW OF THE FBI'S INVESTIGATION OF MARTIN LUTHER
KING. ASSIGNED TO CONDUCT THIS REVIEW IS A TASK
FORCE WORKING UNDER DIRECTION OF THE OFFICE OF PRO-
FESSIONAL RESPONSIBILITY (OPR) OF THE DEPARTMENT OF
JUSTICE. THE ATTORNEY GENERAL HAS INDICATED THE RE-
VIEW IS TO RESOLVE THE FOLLOWING FOUR QUESTIONS.
    (1.) WAS THE FBI INVESTIGATION OF KING'S ASSASSINA-
TION THOROUGH AND HONEST?
    (2.) IS THERE ANY EVIDENCE THE FBI WAS INVOLVED IN
THE ASSASSINATION?
    (3.) IS THERE ANY NEW EVIDENCE WHICH HAS COME TO
THE ATTENTION OF THE DEPARTMENT CONCERNING THE
ASSASSINATION?
    (4.) DOES THE RELATIONSHIP BETWEEN THE BUREAU AND
KING CALL FOR CRIMINAL PROSECUTIONS, DISCIPLINARY
PROCEEDINGS OR OTHER APPROPRIATE ACTION?
    THIS REVIEW IS A CONTINUATION OF A "PARTIAL RE-
VIEW" RECENTLY CONDUCTED BY THE CIVIL RIGHTS DIVI-
SION OF THE DEPARTMENT UNDER DIRECTION OF ASSISTANT
ATTORNEY GENERAL J. STANLEY POTTINGER. AFTER THE
TASK FORCE COMPLETES STUDY OF ASSASSINATION FILES IN
SELECTED FIELD OFFICES, IT WILL CONDUCT EXAMINATION
OF OUR INTELLIGENCE INVESTIGATION OF KING AND ANY
SECURITY FILES RELATING TO BASIS FOR THE INVESTIGA-
TION. ALL PERSONNEL ON THE TASK FORCE ARE AUTHOR-
IZED TOTAL ACCESS TO PERTINENT FILES AT FBIHQ AND IN
THE FIELD. THIS WILL INCLUDE COVER PAGES OF COMMUNI-
CATIONS CONTAINING IDENTITIES OF SOME FBI SOURCES, IN-
FORMANTS WHO WERE NOT AFFORDED SYMBOL NUMBERS
AT THAT TIME AND INDIVIDUALS WHO EXPRESSED OR IM-

PLIED CONFIDENTIALITY. INFORMANT FILES ARE NOT TO BE
MADE AVAILABLE TO THE TASK FORCE WITHOUT PRIOR
FBIHQ AUTHORITY.

THE OPR REVIEW BEGAN AT FBIQH ON MAY 10, 1976, WITH
REVIEW OF ASSASSINATION FILES OF FBIHQ AND WASHING-
TON FIELD OFFICE.

DURING THE PERIOD JUNE 14–24, 1976, THE TASK FORCE RE-
VIEWED KING ASSASSINATION AND SECURITY FILES IN THE
MILWAUKEE AND MEMPHIS OFFICES.

TO CONTINUE ITS REVIEW, MEMBERS OF THE TASK FORCE
IDENTIFIED AS JAMES KIECKHEFER, WILLIAM WHITE AND JO-
SEPH GROSS TENTATIVELY PLAN THE FOLLOWING TRAVEL:
DEPART WASHINGTON, D.C., JULY 6, 1976, FOR KANSAS CITY,
REMAINING THERE JULY 7–8, 1976; DEPART KANSAS CITY
JULY 8, 1976, TO ARRIVE AT SAN FRANCISCO OFFICE ON THE
MORNING OF JULY 9, 1976; PROBABLY DEPART SAN FRAN-
CISCO JULY 11, 1976, TO ARRIVE AT LOS ANGELES OFFICE ON
THE MORNING OF JULY 12, 1976, FOR AN APPROXIMATE FIVE
DAY PERIOD BEFORE RETURNING TO WASHINGTON, D.C.

THE TASK FORCE HAS INDICATED THAT TRAVEL TO KAN-
SAS CITY IS BASED ON LOCATION OF PRISON FROM WHICH
JAMES EARL RAY ESCAPED. IN ADDITION TO KING-RELATED
FILES TASK FORCE DESIRES TO REVIEW KANSAS CITY 157-
472, WHICH INVOLVES AN ALLEGATION THAT A KLAN ORGA-
NIZATION OFFERS TO KILL KING.

TRAVEL TO SAN FRANCISCO AND LOS ANGELES IS BASED
ON THE AMOUNT OF TIME KING IS KNOWN TO HAVE SPENT
ON THE WEST COAST, ACCORDING TO TASK FORCE PERSON-
NEL. IN ADDITION TO KING-RELATED FILES, TASK FORCE DE-
SIRES TO REVIEW LOS ANGELES 157-869, REGARDING A PLOT
TO ASSASSINATE KING AND LOS ANGELES 157-651, WHICH
CONCERNS A KLAN THREAT ON THE LIFE OF KING. ALSO OF
INTEREST IS LOS ANGELES FILE 100-24345, SECTION C, CAP-
TIONED "COMMUNIST PARTY, USA—NEGRO QUESTION," CON-
CERNING ELECTRONIC SURVEILLANCE OF KING. IN SAN
FRANCISCO, OF PARTICULAR INTEREST IS 100-51914, CAP-
TIONED "COMMUNIST PARTY, USA—NEGRO QUESTION,"
WHICH PERTAINS TO THE ELECTRONIC SURVEILLANCE OF
KING IN HAWAII AND SACRAMENTO.

SACS, KANSAS CITY, SAN FRANCISCO AND LOS ANGELES
ASSIGN COORDINATOR TO HANDLE LIAISON WITH TASK

FORCE PERSONNEL AND PROVIDE OFFICE SPACE IN WHICH
TO CONDUCT REVIEW. CONFIRM ARRIVAL AND DEPARTURE
OF TASK FORCE PERSONNEL AND KEEP FBIHQ ADVISED OF
SIGNIFICANT DEVELOPMENTS.

FOR INFORMATION OF MEMPHIS, TASK FORCE LEADER
FRED G. FOLSOM AND JAMES WALKER PLAN TO RETURN TO
MEMPHIS ON JULY 6, 1976. THEIR PLANS ARE TO REVIEW EVI-
DENCE IN THE ASSASSINATION CASE AND POSSIBLY CON-
DUCT INTERVIEWS WHICH MAY INCLUDE BOB JENSEN,
FORMER SAC OF THE MEMPHIS OFFICE, TWO FORMER ASSIS-
TANT UNITED STATES ATTORNEYS AND JAMES EARL RAY.
THERE IS NO INDICATION AT THIS TIME FBI EMPLOYEES ARE
TO BE INTERVIEWED. MEMPHIS CONFIRM ARRIVAL AND DE-
PARTURE OF TASK FORCE PERSONNEL AND KEEP FBIHQ AD-
VISED OF ALL SIGNIFICANT DEVELOPMENTS.

[Section 99]

CODE ˋ TELETYPE NITEL

JULY 29, 1976

TO: SACS ATLANTA
BIRMINGHAM
CHARLOTTE
CHICAGO
NEW ORLEANS
NEW YORK
SPRINGFIELD
ST. LOUIS

FROM: DIRECTOR, FBI (100-106670)

MARTIN LUTHER KING, JR.

REBUTEL TO ALL OFFICES DATED JULY 28, 1976, WHICH
SET FORTH BACKGROUND INFORMATION CONCERNING RE-
VIEW OF OUR MARTIN LUTHER KING, JR., INVESTIGATIONS
BY A TASK FORCE OF THE OFFICE OF PROFESSIONAL RESPON-
SIBILITY (OPR), DEPARTMENT OF JUSTICE.

PURPOSE OF THIS TELETYPE IS TO ALERT RECIPIENTS RE-

GARDING PLANS OF OPR TASK FORCE PERSONNEL TO VISIT
THEIR OFFICES TO CONTINUE REVIEW OF OUR KING
INVESTIGATIONS.

DURING AUGUST 1976, TASK FORCE PERSONNEL FRED FOL-
SOM, LEADER; JAMES WALKER; JOSEPH GROSS, JAMES KIECK-
HEFER AND WILLIAM WHITE WILL ARRIVE AT THE
FOLLOWING OFFICES ON DATES INDICATED: ATLANTA AU-
GUST 2–3, 1976; BIRMINGHAM AUGUST 4–5, 1976; AND NEW
ORLEANS AUGUST 5–6, 1976. PRIOR TO JOINING THE GROUP
IN ATLANTA, WALKER WILL ARRIVE AT THE CHARLOTTE OF-
FICE ON THE MORNING OF JULY 30, 1976. WITH EXCEPTION
OF ATLANTA THE TASK FORCE DESIRES TO REVIEW KING AS-
SASSINATION FILES (MURKIN), THE INTELLIGENCE INVESTI-
GATION OF KING AND ALL KING-RELATED SECURITY FILES.
IN ATLANTA THE TASK FORCE IS ONLY INTERESTED IN RE-
VIEWING MURKIN FILES AND PLANS A SECOND TRIP TO AT-
LANTA AT A LATER DATE TO REVIEW ALL SECURITY FILES.

DURING THE WEEK OF AUGUST 16–20, 1976, TRAVEL IS
PLANNED TO CHICAGO, ST. LOUIS AND SPRINGFIELD, AL-
THOUGH DURATION OF TIME IN EACH OFFICE IS UNKNOWN
AT PRESENT. ALL KING-RELATED FILES ARE TO BE RE-
VIEWED IN ST. LOUIS AND SPRINGFIELD. IN CHICAGO THE
TASK FORCE IS INTERESTED INITIALLY IN REVIEWING ONLY
THE MURKIN FILE AND PLANS A LATER VISIT TO REVIEW
THE KING INTELLIGENCE INVESTIGATION AND RELATED SE-
CURITY FILES. ADDITIONAL DETAILS REGARDING TRAVEL OF
THE TASK FORCE DURING THE PERIOD AUGUST 16–20, 1976,
WILL BE PROVIDED. NO SPECIFIC DATES FOR TRAVEL TO
NEW YORK HAVE BEEN SET OTHER THAN IT WILL BE AFTER
AUGUST 20, 1976.

IT IS NOTED THAT ALL PERSONNEL ON THE TASK FORCE
ARE AUTHORIZED TOTAL ACCESS TO PERTINENT FILES AND
SUBFILES AT FBIHQ AND IN THE FIELD REGARDING INVESTI-
GATION OF KING, HIS FAMILY MEMBERS AND ASSOCIATES.
THIS WILL INCLUDE COVER PAGES OF COMMUNICATIONS
CONTAINING IDENTITIES OF SOME FBI SOURCES AND INFOR-
MANTS WHO WERE NOT AFFORDED SYMBOL NUMBERS AT
THAT TIME AND INDIVIDUALS WHO EXPRESSED OR IMPLIED
CONFIDENTIALITY. INFORMANT FILES ARE NOT TO BE MADE
AVAILABLE WITHOUT PRIOR FBIHQ AUTHORITY.

BECAUSE OF SENSITIVITY INVOLVING OUR INVESTIGATION

OF STANLEY DAVID LEVISON, IT HAS BEEN RECOMMENDED
TO THE DEPARTMENT THAT HIS FILE AT FBIHQ AND IN THE
FIELD BE RESTRICTED TO REVIEW BY FOLSOM ONLY. THE
DEPARTMENT HAS NOT RENDERED A DECISION ON THIS REC-
OMMENDATION. THEREFORE, UNTIL FURTHER NOTICE, RECIPI-
ENTS ARE TO DENY ALL TASK FORCE PERSONNEL ACCESS
TO LEVISON'S FILE.

RECIPIENTS ASSIGN COORDINATOR TO HANDLE LIAISON
WITH TASK FORCE PERSONNEL AND PROVIDE OFFICE SPACE
IN WHICH TO CONDUCT REVIEW. CONFIRM THEIR ARRIVAL
AND DEPARTURE BY TELETYPE AND KEEP FBIHQ ADVISED
OF SIGNIFICANT DEVELOPMENTS.

NOTE:

The Attorney General has ordered a review of our King investigations. It is to be conducted by a Task Force of OPR and is a continuation of a previous review by the Civil Rights Division of the
Department.

Recipients have been telephonically furnished contents of teletype.
Task Force personnel have been advised addresses of offices and appro-
priate FBI personnel to contact. Recipients have been instructed to refer
any questions concerning the review to Deputy Assistant Director J.O.
Ingram, who is coordinating the review for the Intelligence Division of
SA J.T. Aldhizer.

Folsom denied our request to restrict review of Levison file to himself
only. By letter dated 7/29/76, we recommended to Assistant Attorney
General Pottinger, Civil Rights Division, that access to Levison's file be
restricted and that the Attorney General support our position in writing.

[Section 100]

UNITED STATES GOVERNMENT
Memorandum

TO: Mr. Jenkins   DATE: 8/3/76

FROM: A J. Decker

SUBJECT: RELEASE OF DOCUMENTS CONCERNING
         MARTIN LUTHER KING TO THE KING ESTATE

... DETAILS: You will recall the Attorney General has recently agreed
to release to representatives of the Martin Luther King estate certain
information from FBI files (that which has previously been furnished
to the Church Committee) pertaining to Martin Luther King. This is
not being treated as a Freedom of Information—Privacy Acts (FOIPA)
matter; however, representatives from our Section recently participated
in a discussion with Department of Justice officials along with representatives from Legal Counsel Division and Intelligence Division regarding
the establishing of guidelines for processing file material. During this
discussion the question was raised concerning the impact the release of
material to the King estate would have upon other requesters seeking
the Martin Luther King file. No conclusions were reached concerning
this issues at this discussion, since the question was raised only for the
purpose of insuring the Department was aware of all ramifications involved in the Attorney General's decision to release material to the
King estate. We advised the Department that we had in fact received
requests for the King file under FOIA from third parties, but that we
declined disclosure on the basis of the Privacy exemption of FOIA.

On July 27, 1976, Steven Blackhurst, Office of Professional Responsibility, Department of Justice, contacted SA Thomas H. Bresson concerning captioned matter. Blackhurst advised he had been recently in
contact with representatives of the King estate and the above subject
matter was discussed with them. Blackhurst advised they stated it was
their desire that the FBI resist disclosure of the King file to third parties.
SA Bresson advised Blackhurst that we have considered the application
of the Privacy exemption to FOIA records as one of the most troublesome aspects in implementing the FOIA, and pointed to the fact the
Bureau has taken in the past a very strict interpretation in favor of

protecting third persons' privacy. He was advised, however, that stand on privacy has been overruled by the Deputy Attorney General on appeal in some instances and the Privacy issues, particularly with regard to deceased parties, is not well settled. He was advised that our policy would be to continue to handle all requests for the King file by third parties in accordance with established FOIPA procedures.

Mr. Blackhurst requested that his office be advised if the Bureau decides in the future to release the documents concerning Dr. King that are now under consideration for release to the King estate to third parties under FOIA.

[Section 101]

October 28, 1976

BERNARD S. LEE v. CLARENCE M. KELLEY
ET AL. (U.S.D.C., D.C.) CIVIL ACTION
NO. 76-1185

Unless otherwise noted, all information herein is unclassified.

INTRODUCTION

The original complaint in this matter alleges that plaintiff and a number of other persons, in the spring of 1963, met in a private room rented by the late Dr. Martin Luther King, Jr., in the Willard Hotel, Washington, D.C., for the purpose of assembling to petition their Government for redress of the civil rights of minorities. It further alleges this session was bugged and tape recorded by the defendants, or some of them, and that a copy of said tape was mailed anonymously to Mrs. Martin Luther King, Jr., about November 1, 1964, thereby disclosing the contents of this tape recording.

FILE REVIEW

A review of logical files of this Bureau, including records of our Washington Field Office and Atlanta Field Office, reveals no information concerning an alleged bugging of the Willard Hotel, in the spring of 1963, as alleged in plaintiff's complaint. Federal Bureau of Investigation Headquarters (FBIHQ) files, as well as those of the New York and Atlanta Field Offices, indicated that the Southern Christian Leadership Conference (SCLC) itself was never the subject of microphone surveillance coverage at any time. Logical records at FBIHQ and the New York and Atlanta Field Offices fail to indicate plaintiff Bernard S. Lee was ever the subject of an active FBI investigation or that he was ever the primary subject of either telephone or microphone surveillance coverage.

ALLEGED MAILING OF TAPE RECORDING TO MRS. KING

(1) File Review

Exhaustive reviews of logical FBIHQ files in connection with this suit and prior inquiries concerning the King investigation by the Senate Select Committee to Study Governmental Operations With Respect to Intelligence Activities (SSC) have developed no hard evidence to indicate a copy of a tape recording of the events at the Willard Hotel was mailed to Mrs. King as alleged in the plaintiff's complaint.

(2) Recollections of SA Lish Whitson Regarding a Package He Mailed

During interviews by SSC staff member Michael Epstein, retired FBI Special Agent (SA) Lish Whitson furnished the information reflected in Exhibit B, attached.

(3) Recollections of SA . . . Concerning Preparation of a Package by Former Assistant Director William C. Sullivan

SA . . . recalled an incident in which he furnished an address for King's home in Atlanta, to then Assistant Director William C. Sullivan. See attached Exhibit B-1.

(4) Items Discovered in Office of Former Assistant Director Sullivan

At a time subsequent to the departure from the FBI by former Assistant Director Sullivan, an inventory was made of materials which remained in his office. Among other items discovered was an original of an undated typewritten letter addressed to "King." A memorandum concerning that letter and other materials found in Mr. Sullivan's office is attached as Exhibit B-2. It is noted that the tapes referred to in this Exhibit were reviewed by SA W.D. Campbell and contained no reference to King, Lee or the SCLC. The memorandum makes reference to three tape recordings found in Mr. Sullivan's cabinet. When a review was made of those tapes on January 27, 1975, a log was made which contained a synopsis of the items on the tapes and that log reflects no reference to Martin Luther King, Jr., the SCLC or Bernard S. Lee.

The FBI attempted in November 1975, to locate fingerprints of Sullivan on the letter to "King" with negative results. The FBI Laboratory compared the type on the letter with known specimens of typewriters at the Bureau, available to Sullivan, with negative results. It is noted this letter is an original and neither it nor any copies of it ever formed a part of an official FBI file. The results of the above two examinations are contained in Exhibit B-3, attached.

DISSEMINATION OF INFORMATION CONCERNING KING AND PLAINTIFF'S KNOWLEDGE OF THE FBI'S INTERCEPTION OF PLAINTIFF'S COMMUNICATION

Paragraph 5 in plaintiff's original complaint alleges plaintiff's recent awareness of the existence of a tape and alleges that the tape has been exposed to individuals outside of the Executive Branch of the Government. A review of investigative files relating to King has produced no positive evidence which would indicate that a tape of the events at the Willard Hotel has ever been played to anyone or heard by anyone outside the FBI, with the exception of J. Stanley Pottinger, Assistant Attorney General, Civil Rights Division, Department of Justice. Mr. Pottinger, on authority of the Attorney General, listened to one tape from the Willard Hotel electronic surveillance of King. This tape and a number of transcripts were reviewed by Mr. Pottinger on December 19, 1975.

[BUREAU DELETION]

AUTHORITY FOR INTERCEPTION OF COMMUNICATIONS

Paragraph 6 of the complaint by Lee alleges that the defendants caused oral communications of Lee and his conferrers to be surreptitiously intercepted and recorded by a hidden electronic listening device without warrant or other authorization.

The following is set forth regarding electronic surveillance coverage afforded Martin Luther King, Jr., and the SCLC (noting as set forth above, Lee was never the subject of active investigations or the primary target of electronic surveillance of any type): In 1963 Bureau investigations of Martin Luther King, Jr., and the SCLC established a close association between King and Stanley David Levison, a concealed member of the Communist Party, U.S.A. (CPUSA), and Clarence Benjamin Jones, an attorney with CPUSA connections. Prior to October 1963, the Attorney General had approved telephone or microphone surveillance in New York City covering Levison, Jones and the Ghandi [sic] Society for Human Rights, an organization with which Jones served as General Counsel, which was formed to lend support to King. (Secret)

By letter dated October 18, 1963, to the Attorney General, the FBI requested authority to place technical (telephone) surveillance on the headquarters of the SCLC, 330 Auburn Avenue, Northeast, Atlanta, Georgia, or any future address to which it might move. The Attorney General approved this coverage on the SCLC office in Atlanta on October 21, 1963. A copy of this request with the Attorney General's approval indicated thereon is attached as Exhibit C.

In order to intensify coverage of King, the FBI by letter to the Attorney General dated October 7, 1963, requested authority to place a technical or telephone surveillance on King at his then current residence or any future address to which he might move. In the same letter it was requested that authority be given to place a technical surveillance at the SCLC office, 312 West 125th Street, New York City, or at any other address to which it might move.

Attorney General Robert F. Kennedy approved the above requests for technical surveillance on King at the SCLC office in New York City on October 10, 1963. See Exhibit D attached.

ELECTRONIC COVERAGE OF THE SCLC

On October 24, 1963, a technical or telephone surveillance was installed on the SCLC office in New York City. This installation was terminated January 24, 1964, because the coverage developed no information of value and because the SCLC in New York City had no director. Technical surveillance of SCLC in New York City was reinstituted July 13, 1964, at Room 1202, 15 East 40th Street. This was the address of the Ghandi [sic] Society for Human Rights and SCLC was assigned room 1202 of this address. This installation terminated July 31, 1964, when the SCLC moved to a new address. The New York Office felt continued technical surveillance would be unproductive and in August 1964, recommended no continued coverage of the SCLC.

Technical surveillance of the SCLC office of 330 Auburn Avenue, Northeast, Atlanta, Georgia, was installed on November 8, 1963. It was discontinued June 21, 1966, on instructions of Attorney General Nicholas deB. Katzenbach, who on the memorandum noted, ''I think this coverage should be discontinued particularly in light of possible charges of a criminal nature against Hosea Williams and possibly others.'' (Car theft case)

A review of logical files and indices at FBIHQ revealed that no microphone surveillance of the SCLC occurred.

ELECTRONIC COVERAGE OF KING

(1) Claridge Hotel. Atlantic City, New Jersey

Telephone surveillance was in effect against Martin Luther King, Jr., at the Claridge Hotel, Atlantic City, New Jersey, during August 22–27, 1964. Prior to King's arrival in Atlantic City, coverage was installed in Rooms 1902 and 1923 since these two rooms had been set aside for use by King. Upon arrival, King checked into Room 1923 and his associate, Lee, into Room 1902.

Although Lee was not intended to be the actual target of the telephonic surveillance, a card to this effect was prepared to FBIHQ because of his occupancy of Room 1902. This card is filed in the National Security Electronic Surveillance file which is a listing of individuals who have been subjects of electronic surveillance by the FBI. No separate authority for this coverage in Room 1902 on Lee was obtained. Authority utilized was that obtained from the Attorney General to cover King's residence and any residence to which he might move.

In 1975, following adverse publicity, our Inspection Division initiated a review of FBI actions and coverage at the Democratic National Convention, held during August 1964, in Atlantic City. During this review it was determined that the only electronic surveillance at Atlantic City involved telephone surveillance on King at the Claridge Hotel and a microphone surveillance on King at the joint headquarters of the Student Nonviolent Coordinating Committee and the Congress of Racial Equality. All telephone surveillance logs maintained in the Newark Office on coverage of King were forwarded to FBIHQ for review by the Inspection Division.

These 78 pages of overhears were recently reviewed and copies of those pages containing overhears of Bernard S. Lee, F.L., and other variations of Lee's name are attached as Exhibit E.

The only known dissemination of information obtained from above electronic surveillance was through memoranda prepared by C.D. DeLoach to Walter Jenkins, aide to President Johnson. These memoranda were reviewed and the only information disseminated concerning Lee is found on page 3 of DeLoach memorandum dated August 25, 1964, (attached as Exhibit E-1.)

In response to FBIHQ inquiry in captioned lawsuits, the Newark Office of the FBI submitted teletype dated August 10, 1976, explaining coverage of King in Atlantic City, and noting Lee overhears. A copy of this teletype is attached as Exhibit E-2.

(2) Microphone Coverage of King

The FBI conducted microphone coverage on Martin Luther King, Jr., at the following locations and for the indicated periods of time set forth below:

DATES OF SURVEILLANCE	LOCATION
*January 5–7, 1964	Willard Hotel, Washington, D.C.
January 27, 1964	Shroeder Hotel, Milwaukee, Wisconsin
February 18–20, 1964	Hilton Hawaiian Village, Honolulu, Hawaii
February 20–21, 1964	Ambassador Hotel, Los Angeles, California
February 22–24, 1964	Hyatt House Motel, Los Angeles, California
*March 19–20, 1964	Statler Hotel, Detroit, Michigan
April 23–24, 1964	Senator Hotel, Sacramento, California
July 7–9, 1964	Hyatt House Motel, Los Angeles, California
September 28, 1964	Manager Hotel, Savannah, Georgia
October 2, 1964	
*January 8–11, 1965	Park Sheraton Hotel, New York City
January 28–31, 1965	Americana Hotel, New York City
March 29–31, 1965	Park Sheraton Hotel, New York City
May 12–13, 1965	Sheraton Atlantic Hotel, New York City
October 14–15, 1965	Astor Hotel, New York City
October 28–30, 1965	New York Hilton Hotel, New York City
November 29–30, 1965	Americana Hotel, New York City
*January 22, 1966	Americana Hotel, New York City

Actual overhears of Lee occurred on King microphone surveillances at the following locations which have been designated above by an asterisk:

(a) Willard Hotel, Washington, D.C.

Microphone surveillance of King was effected at the Willard Hotel, Washington, D.C., during January 5–7, 1964. See Exhibit A for authorization of surveillance.

Transcript of this microphone surveillance was reviewed for overhears of Lee. Documents attached in Exhibit F represent only instances wherein Lee was definitely identified. It is noted that throughout the transcripts there are many references to conversations involving unidentified males, which could possibly be Lee. However, there appears no feasible way to determine if any additional overhears of Lee were obtained.

With respect to dissemination of information obtained from the microphone surveillance at the Willard Hotel, Sullivan to Belmont memorandum January 13, 1964, captioned, "Communist Party, U.S.A.—Negro Question, Communist Influence in Racial Matters, Internal Security—Communist," recommended that a memorandum containing surveillance results be furnished to the Attorney General and

Mr. Jenkins. Mr. Hoover noted that a copy need not be given the Attorney General but approved dissemination to Jenkins. This memorandum contains a notation, "Handled January 14, 1964—with Jenkins and the President," and initialed by DeLoach. (See Exhibit F-1) It is noted that the Willard was disseminated to the Department of Justice. However, information disseminated contained no reference to Lee.

It is noted that the March 1964, memorandum contained no overhears involving Lee directly. However, the initial paragraph identified Lee as an official of the Southern Christian Leadership Conference, who checked into the Willard Hotel on the evening of January 5, 1964.

(b) Statler Hotel, Detroit, Michigan

This surveillance was conducted March 19–20, 1964, in Rooms 1270 and 1272 of the Statler Hotel, Detroit, Michigan. Authorization is shown in attached Exhibit G.

A letter apparently forwarded to former Assistant Director W.C. Sullivan dated April 1, 1964, from Jack Callaghan of the Detroit Office, enclosed the original information secured as a result of this surveillance. Transcripts of this coverage were reviewed and pages which contain overhears of Lee, who accompanied King during his Detroit visit, appear in Exhibit G-1.

With respect to dissemination of information obtained from coverage in Detroit, the attached Baumgardner to Sullivan memorandum dated April 13, 1964, enclosed memorandum containing results of the surveillance for information of the Director. The memorandum of April 13, 1964, noted that information concerning King . . . and that no dissemination of that type information was necessary. However, since the Detroit coverage gathered information indicating King was to go on a hunger strike, information to that effect was furnished Mr. Jenkins and Assistant Attorney General Burke Marshall, Civil Rights Division. There was no indication that overhears of Lee were disseminated. Copies of these documents regarding dissemination are attached as Exhibit g-2.

(c) Park Sheraton Hotel, New York City

This coverage was in effect against King during January 8–11, 1965, at the Park Sheraton Hotel, New York City, in Rooms 2541 and 2543. Andrew Young and Bernard Lee occupied Room 2541. See Exhibit H for authorization.

No tapes or transcripts reporting results of this surveillance were provided FBIHQ. However, New York reported results in two teletypes dated January 9, 1965, and January 10, 1965, both captioned, "Martin Luther King, Jr." At FBIHQ this information was incorporated into

Baumgardner's memorandum to Sullivan dated January 10, 1965. In this memorandum, it was indicated that dissemination of information from this microphone coverage was not contemplated. Therefore, the only dissemination regarding results of this coverage was made inside the FBI. Copies of these communications are attached as Exhibit H-1.

(d) Americana Hotel, New York City

This coverage against King was instituted on January 22, 1966, at the Americana Hotel, New York City, as King and his party had reserved Rooms 3435, 3436 and 3437. Approval for this installation was granted by W.C. Sullivan, but Associate Director Clyde Tolson disapproved and noted on Sullivan's memorandum to remove the surveillance at once. (See Exhibit I) However, file shows three memoranda which contain results of the coverage. Effort to locate communications transmitting these memoranda to FBIHQ was negative. Only one of these three memoranda contained overhears on Lee. Copies of the Sullivan memorandum and the memoranda containing Lee overhears are attached as Exhibit I-1.

There is no known dissemination outside the FBI of information contained in the results of this surveillance, except during 1968 when data regarding King was compiled at the request of President Johnson.

It is noted that authorizations for microphone surveillance were not signed by the Attorney General, but were approved by certain FBi officials acting on authority delegated to them by the Attorney General. With respect to microphone surveillance of King, Attorney General Katzenbach was advised, after the fact, of microphone surveillances initiated on May 12, 1965, October 14, 1965, and November 29, 1965. Copies of memoranda reflecting these three notifications are attached as Exhibit J.

It should also be noted that microphone surveillance was authorized against King at the Sheraton Park Hotel March 29–31, 1965. Lee was to accompany King on this trip. However, neither King nor Lee occupied these rooms during this period, having registered at a different location in New York City.

In 1968, President Lyndon B. Johnson requested all information concerning King in possession of the FBI. In response, copies of all FBI communications previously furnished the White House were consolidated into six volumes entitled ''Communications Concerning Martin Luther King, Jr.'' (classified Top Secret). These documents are being reviewed to discover any additional information regarding Lee overhears which may have been disseminated. In addition our search of logical Bureau files in an attempt to retrieve additional overhears of Lee and dissemination of same is continuing.

[Section 102]

UNITED STATES GOVERNMENT
Memorandum

TO: Mr. Gallagher   DATE: 1/19/77

FROM: J. S. Peelman

REPORT OF THE DEPARTMENT OF
JUSTICE TASK FORCE TO REVIEW
THE FBI—MARTIN LUTHER KING, JR.
SECURITY AND ASSASSINATION
INVESTIGATIONS

PURPOSE: To advise of contents and observations concerning captioned report, and to furnish our observations to the Attorney General (AG) in attached letter.

SYNOPSIS: Department of Justice Task Force, Office of Professional Responsibility (OPR) has furnished a copy of its report of review of the FBI's investigation of Dr. Martin Luther King, Jr. Task Force reported the following re *"The Assassination Investigation"*: It is satisfied the FBI did a credible job in attempting to identify any conspiracy; James Earl Ray judicially confessed that he intended to and did kill Dr. King; the investigation was thoroughly, honestly and successfully conducted; the evidence pointing to guilt of Ray was conclusive; found no evidence of any complicity on part of Memphis Police Department or FBI; the sum of all evidence of Ray's guilt points to him so exclusively that it makes the point no one else involved; it unearthed some new data which answers some persistent questions the FBI did not seek; but FBI concentrated on principal in case and found no dishonesty in this; by "hindsight" task force believes Ray's brothers could have been interrogated further; discussed "Bureau disdain for Department supervision;" and it found no new evidence which calls for action by state or Federal authorities. Task Force makes "Recommendations—As to the

Murder Investigation,'' and our observations concerning these recommendations and report set forth in attached letter to AG.

With respect to ''The Security Investigation'' of King, the OPR Task Force was to determine if the relationship between the FBI and King called for criminal prosecution or disciplinary action against Bureau personnel and if the FBI was involved in King's assassination. Task Force reviewed security files of King, the SCLC and our files relating to communist influence in the Civil Rights movement. The Task Force concluded that opening of King Investigation in 1962 was justified, but its continuance was unwarranted since there was no evidence that King was a communist or affiliated with the CPUSA. Report states that the dispute between King and Mr. Hoover was a major factor in the Bureau's determination to discredit King and documents ''an extensive program within the FBI'' to discredit him. Report discloses surreptitious entries against Levison, . . . In its critical evaluation the Task Force believed investigation of King should have terminated when Levison disassociated himself from the CPUSA in 1963 and our discrediting actions were unwarranted and very probably in violation of Civil Rights Statutes. Report states the AG and Department of Justice failed in supervision of FBI intersecurity activities.

Briefly, Task Force recommendations as to the security investigation are as follows: (1) no criminal prosecution of Bureau personnel because five-year Statute of Limitations has expired; (2) no disciplinary action against personnel in active Bureau service: (3) tapes and transcripts of microphone surveillance in King case be sealed, sent to Archives and that Congress authorize and direct destruction of that material including reports derived thereof; (4) endorsed intradepartmental supervision of FBI by Department of Justice (OPR) and legislative oversight by the Senate Select Committee on Intelligence; (5) that the unauthorized malicious dissemination of investigative data from FBI files be made a felony rather than the presently described misdemeanor; (6) that the FBI have no authority to engage in COINTELPRO-type activities.

Our observations concerning the OPR report on the security investigation of King are set forth in attached letter to the AG.

Per request of OPR, we have been assisting Task Force in its preparation of a report it intends to make public which is protective of privacy rights, sensitive sources and classification concerns.

OPR instructed original version of the Task Force's report was to be classified ''Top Secret'' and requested Bureau-designated individuals to assist Task Force in classifying the original report and in preparing a publicly releasable report. Document Classification Officer (Security

Officer) of FBI was designated to assist Task Force representatives in classification matters and on 1/17/77, the report, Appendix A and Appendix B were classified on a paragraph-by-paragraph basis. Document Classification Officer (DCO) on 1/18/77 assisted Task Force in preparation of sanitized version invoking where possible approved classification standards. In spite of paraphrasing, sanitized report could be detrimental to this Bureau's counterintelligence interest in that sources and methods may, through logical speculation, be identified.

All information in this memorandum is unclassified unless otherwise indicated.

RECOMMENDATION: Attached for approval is a letter to the AG setting forth our observations concerning this Task Force report.

DETAILS:

BACKGROUND: In 1975, the United States Senate and the United States House of Representatives Select Committees on Intelligence Activities conducted inquiries and held public hearings concerning the FBI. Following disclosures made during these hearings, the AG directed, in November 1975, the Civil Rights and the Criminal Divisions of the United States Department of Justice to review the files relating to Dr. Martin Luther King, Jr., and make a recommendation as to whether the assassination case should be reopened.

In April 1976, the AG announced that, based on the preliminary review by the Civil Rights Division, the tentative conclusions were: (1) there was no basis to believe that the FBI in any way caused the death of Dr. King; (2) no evidence was discovered that the FBI investigation of the assassination of Dr. King was not thorough and honest; (3) instances were found indicating that the FBI undertook a systematic program of harassment of Dr. King in order to discredit him and harm both him and the movement he led.

The AG then ordered that the OPR of the Department complete this review, and that answers to the following questions be furnished to the AG and to FBI Director Clarence M. Kelley: (1) whether the FBI investigation of Dr. King's assassination was thorough and honest; (2) whether there is any evidence that the FBI was involved in the assassination of Dr. King; (3) whether, in light of the first two matters, there is any new evidence which has come to the attention of the Department concerning the assassination of Dr. King; and (4) whether the nature of the relationship between the Bureau and Dr. King calls for criminal prosecutions, disciplinary proceedings, or other appropriate actions.

Since May 1976, a Task Force of Departmental Attorneys under the OPR has been reviewing our investigative results, both at FBIHQ and in the field, of both the assassination investigation (civil rights investigation) and our security investigation of Dr. King.

REPORT OF DEPARTMENT OF JUSTICE TASK FORCE—OPR:

By memorandum 1/12/77, Michael E. Shaheen, Jr., Counsel, OPR, United States Department of Justice, furnished to the Director of the FBI a "Report of the Department of Justice Task Force to Review the FBI—Martin Luther King, Jr., Security and Assassination Investigations." Mr. Shaheen also requested to know the names of those Bureau employees the Director intended to designate to classify these materials and to assist the Task Force in preparing a publicly releasable report that is protective of privacy rights, sensitive sources and methods and classification concerns. (Response made to Mr. Shaheen in this regard by letter 1/17/77.)

This report consists of 149 pages plus the appendices. After the "Introduction" this reports consists of "The Assassination Investigation," "The Security Investigation," "Recommendations," and the "Appendices," which consists of "Documents Cited in Report," "Interview Memoranda," and "Notes from FBI Files and Records from Other Sources." The Task Force advises this report is based upon review of FBI files (at FBIHQ and in the field), witness interviews (as conducted by the Task Force) public source material including newspaper accounts and books, review of the AG's file, files of other Government agencies and the Memphis Police Department as well as on-the-spot inspection of the crime scene by the Task Force and a review of the local court records (where James Earl Ray was prosecuted).

THE ASSASSINATION INVESTIGATION:
Dr. Martin Luther King, Jr., was assassinated on 4/4/68, in Memphis, Tennessee. The FBI, based upon the request of the United States Department of Justice, instituted an immediate civil rights investigation into this assassination. Based upon our extensive investigation, James Earl Ray was identified as the assassin and subsequently pled guilty to this murder in State Court in Tennessee. He presently is in local confinement.

The Task Force report states that "based on our review of the files, the task force is satisfied that the FBI did a credible and thorough job in attempting to identify any possible conspiracy or persons who could have been involved in the murder," (Page 63). The Task Force states it hoped to have an opportunity to go over the facts with James Earl Ray, (Pages 85 and 86). (It is noted Ray never consented to an FBI interview.) Ray agreed with the advice of his attorney and did not consent to an interview by the Task Force (Page 86). In reviewing the local guilty plea of Ray the Task Force states, "Thus, Ray has judicially confessed that he intended to and did kill Dr. King," (Page 87).

The Task Force addresses the claim of Ray to author William Bradford Huie that he "drove 'Raoul' away from the crime scene after the murder wholly unaware of the killing of Dr. King. In this version 'Raoul,' or 'Roual,' is the mysterious killer who Ray thought to be an international gun-runner," (Page 88). (Our investigation never identified the existence of "Raoul" or "Roual.") The Task Force also examined the allegation that Ray was "set up as a 'patsy' for 'Raoul.'" The Task Force states "The task force views the exculpatory content of these varying and patently self-serving tales to be unbelievable. The varying details are materially self-refuting. Ray first admits full guilt," (Pages 88 and 89). The Task Force also states "We conclude on the basis of the evidence examined that there was no such conspiracy," (Page 90).

In examining Ray's "Sources of Funds" the Task Force states "Therefore, the Bureau was particularly interested in determining his sources of income," (Page 98). In discussing the "Critical Evaluation of the Assassination Investigation," the Task Force states "First, the task force has concluded that the investigation by the FBI to ascertain and capture the murderer of Dr. Martin Luther King, Jr., was thoroughly, honestly and successfully conducted," (Pages 106 and 107). "Second, the task force views the evidence pointing to the guilt of James Earl Ray as the man who purchased the murder gun and who fired the fatal shot to be conclusive," (Page 108). "Third, we found that conspiracy leads (aliunde Ray's versions) had been conscientiously run down by the FBI even though they had no possible relation to Ray's stories or to the known facts. The results were negative. We found no evidence of any complicity on the part of the Memphis Police Department or the FBI;" (Pages 108 and 109). "But the sum of all of the evidence of Ray's guilt points to him so exclusively that it most effectively makes the point that no one else was involved," (Page 109). "Fourth, it is true that the task force unearthed some new data—data which answers some persistent questions and which the FBI did not seek. But the Bureau concentrated on the principal in the case and much was not considered important to his discovery and apprehension. We find no dishonesty in this," (Page 109). "By hindsight the task force believes Jerry and John Ray (Ray's brothers) could have been effectively interrogated further to learn their knowledge, if any, of James

Earl Ray's plans, his finances and whether they helped him after King's death,'' (Page 110).

In discussing the "Bureau's disdain for Department supervision," the report states that "the FBI 'Legat' in London was instructed not to take orders from Vinson (HQ 44-38861-4507)," (Assistant Attorney General Fred Vinson) (Page 110). Although this citation is incorrect as pointed out to the task force on 1/17/77, it is noted in this regard that the Legat in London had liaison with the London authorities regarding Ray's extradition to the United States, and it was then and still is established policy in civil rights cases for the Department to make any requests to FBIHQ.

Also on Page 143, the task force states, "The task force does not fault the technical competence of the investigation conducted into the death of Dr. King.'' We found no new evidence which calls for action by state or Federal authorities. Our concern has developed over administrative detection tactics.

TASK FORCE RECOMMENDATIONS AS TO THE MURDER IN-VESTIGATION AND OUR OBSERVATIONS: In the attached letter to the AG our observations are set forth concerning the Task Force recommendations and the report. Therefore, the Task Force recommendations as to the murder investigation are not summarized in this memorandum.

SECURITY INVESTIGATION: As stated above, the OPR Task Force was specifically requested by the AG to determine if the relationship between the FBI and King called for criminal prosecutions, disciplinary proceedings, or other appropriate action. In addition, examination of King and related security files was to determine if the FBI was in any way involved in the assassination of King.

In its review the primary security files of interest to the Task Force, in addition to the King security file, were as follows: Communist Infiltration of the Southern Christian Leadership Conference (SCLC); Communist Influence in Racial Matters; Communist Party USA (CPUSA)—Negro Question and Stanley David Levison.

In its final report, the Task Force devotes pages 112–139 to a discussion of our King security investigation, utilizing subheadings entitled, "FBI Surveillance and Harassment of Dr. King," and "Critical Evaluation of the Security Investigation." The Task Force issues six recommendations as to the security investigation of King.

In its report, the Task Force traces the FBI's relationship with King to include initiation of investigation in 1962, which was based on his association with Levison, and Communist Influence in the Civil Rights movement, the degree of which was debated in internal memoranda between Mr. Hoover and the Domestic Intelligence Division. The Task Force concluded opening King's investigation in 1962 was justified, (Page 122); that its continuation was unwarranted, (Page 123); the Bureau to date has no evidence whatsoever that King was ever a Communist or affiliated with CPUSA, (Page 123); and that, the SCLC, under King, was anything other than a legitimate organization devoted to the Civil Rights movement, (Page 124). Further, the Task Force reported that Bureau files examined lacked any information that Levison's advice was dictated by the CPUSA or contrary to the interests of the United States (Page 124).

The Task Force discussed the public dispute between King and Mr. Hoover, concluding that this persistent controversy was a major factor in the Bureau's determination to discredit King and ultimately destroy his leadership role in the Civil Rights movement, (Page 126).

With respect to electronic surveillance of King, the Task Force report alludes to findings of the Senate Select Committee on Intelligence (SSC), which compiled a list of telephone and microphone surveillances against King. The OPR report names five additional installations not previously reported by the SSC since, according to OPR, they appeared to have been unproductive either because King did not reside at the hotel as planned or that the recordings made did not pick up any significant information, (Pages 126–127). The Task Force reviewed selected portions of transcripts of electronic surveillances of King and reviewed several tapes to check accuracy of transcripts with the original tapes. The Task Force concluded the transcripts were basically accurate, although some material was not put on the transcripts because that portion of the recording was garbled or unclear or it was considered unimportant, (Page 130).

The Attorney General   January 21, 1977

Director, FBI

REPORT OF THE DEPARTMENT OF JUSTICE TASK FORCE TO
REVIEW THE FBI—MARTIN LUTHER KING, JR., SECURITY
AND ASSASSINATION INVESTIGATIONS

All information contained in this letter is unclassified unless otherwise indicated.

By my memorandum dated January 17, 1977, I confirmed to Mr.
Michael E. Shaheen, Jr., Counsel, Office of Professional Responsibility,
the receipt of captioned report and its appendices.

On January 17, 1977, a conference was held with Mr. Shaheen, Task
Force Leader Fred G. Folsom, Jr., and members of his Task Force and
Inspector, Deputy Assistant Director James O. Ingram; Section Chief
Joseph G. Deegan and James S. Peelman; and members of their respective staffs in the General Investigative Division and representatives of
our Intelligence Division; and our Records Management Division (Document Classification Officer and Privacy Act Representatives).

Mr. Shaheen advised that corrections of patent errors in the report
could be made during this conference and any additional observations
could be submitted to the Department in writing.

In addition to the errors noted, the following observations are being
set forth concerning this Task Force report for your consideration and
evaluation:

The Assassination Investigation

On page 101 the Task Force states that, "The Bureau apparently
discounted the significance of any contact between Ray and his family
. . . the Bureau should have pursued this line of investigation more
thoroughly." On page 105 the Task Force states, "Thus, at least one
family member, Jerry, had lied to the FBI and had become subject to
federal criminal charges for aiding a fugitive. He was never confronted
with these facts by the Bureau." On page 106 the Task Force states
that, "We concluded that the FBI abandoned a significant opportunity to
obtain answers from family members concerning some of the important
questions about James Earl Ray which still remain."

On page 109, the Task Force states, "Fourth, it is true that the Task
Force unearthed some new data—data which answers some persistent
questions and which the FBI did not seek. But the Bureau concentrated

on the principal in the case and much was not considered important to his discovery and apprehension: we find no dishonesty in this." "By hindsight the Task Force believes Jerry and John Ray (Ray's brothers) could have been effectively interrogated further to learn their knowledge, if any, of James Earl Ray's plans, his finances and whether they helped him after King's death" (page 110).

Our observations concerning the above statements by the Task Force are that family members were interviewed by the FBI approximately 50 times from April to June of 1968. Additionally, toll records were reviewed and contacts identified in the case of Carol Pepper, (Ray's sister), and the Grapevine Tavern, owned by Pepper and run by John Larry Ray. Bank records were also checked regarding Carol Pepper, John Larry Ray and Jerry Ryans (Ray's father). Neighborhood sources had also been developed and credit records were checked. These family members were interviewed for any information concerning Ray's background and location.

Jerry Ray was interviewed, for example, at least 10 times between April 19, 1968, and May 1, 1968. He was interviewed for all background concerning the Ray family, his contact with Ray and his source of money, was confronted about certain false information he had furnished, and was advised of the provisions of the Harboring Statute.

John Ray was interviewed, for example, at least four times between April 22, 1968, and May 4, 1968, for background information, whereabouts of Ray and his source of money, and was advised of the provisions of the Harboring Statute.

While Ray was a fugitive the FBI requested the Department by memorandum dated May 3, 1968, to approve a technical surveillance at the residence of Pepper and Grapevine Tavern. The Department took no action on this request and the FBI withdrew this request by memorandum dated June 11, 1968, after Ray was apprehended.

The Task Force itself notes our previous investigation concerning Ray's family on page 59 wherein it states, "In connection with this search, Ray's family was identified, located, physically surveilled and periodically interviewed for information."

Our observations concerning our extensive previous investigation concerning Ray's family were brought to the attention of Mr. Shaheen and the Task Force on January 17, 1977, for their consideration and evaluation. It is further noted that all of our investigative results, including those involving Ray's family, were promptly furnished to the Civil Rights Division for its consideration as to whether any additional Federal action was warranted.

On page 110 of this report the Task Force states, "Finally, the Task Force observed instances of FBI Headquarters' reluctance to provide the Civil Rights Division and the Attorney General with timely reports on the course of the murder investigation. For example, early in the investigation in a reaction to a press report of Attorney General Clark's expectation of making a progress report to the nation, FBI Director Hoover wrote: 'We are not going to make any progress reports.' "

In its "Recommendations"—"As To The Murder Investigation" the Task Force states:

(1) "The progress of such sensitive cases as the King murder investigation and the development of legally sufficient evidence to sustain prosecution are properly the ultimate responsibility of the Division of the Department having supervision of the kind of criminal prosecution involved. The Division head should delineate what progress reports he wishes. The Bureau should not be permitted to manipulate its submission of reports to serve its purposes, such as the protection of its public relation efforts, or the prevention of the responsible Division of the Department from causing the Bureau to pursue a line of inquiry which the Bureau does not approve. The Attorney General and his assistants are the officers most accountable to the electorate and they, not the police agency, must maintain effective supervision" (page 143).

Observations were made to Mr. Shaheen and the Task Force on January 17, 1977, for their consideration and evaluation, that timely reports were submitted to the Department even though they may have not been labeled "progress reports." It is further noted, as an example, that between April 5, 1968, and April 17, 1968, (the date the complaint was filed in Birmingham, Alabama, discussed hereafter) at least nine memoranda were furnished by the Director of the FBI to the Department concerning the developments of this investigation. Additional pertinent memoranda, of course, continued thereafter on a timely basis. Our Field Offices also submitted timely reports which were furnished to the Department and the following are several examples: A Memphis report dated April 17, 1968, consisting of 185 pages was furnished to the Civil Rights Division (CRD) on May 6, 1968, an Atlanta report dated April 18, 1968, consisting of 120 pages was furnished to the CRD on May 6, 1968; a Birmingham report dated April 17, 1968, consisting of 176 pages was furnished to the CRD on May 6, 1968. Additional reports from our Field Offices continued to be furnished to the Department on a timely basis. It is further noted that it appears "progress reports" to the nation would have been inadvisable and the Task Force in effect answers this issue on page 106 where it cites Departmental rules against disclosure or raw investigative files. The FBI was investigating a criminal matter and reports were submitted on a timely basis to the Department for its consideration as to whether any Federal action was warranted. The Department could have issued its own "progress reports" based upon the timely reports submitted by the FBI.

In its "recommendations" on page 144, the Task Force states:

(2) "As a corollary of our espousal of tighter Department authority over the FBI, we recommend that the Bureau's public relations activities and press relations be controlled by the Attorney General's Office of Public Information. Clear directives to prevent the development of personality cults around particular Bureau Directors and officials should be drawn. Bureau press releases should be cleared through the Office of Public Information."

It is noted that in the assassination investigation the Director instructed that "no comment" be made during this investigation. When it was necessary to make a major press release in the assassination investigation, it was made with the approval of the Attorney General and was made jointly with the Attorney General.

Departmental Order #24-60 issued September 8, 1933, and periodically restated, instructs that "All publicity whether relating to cases pending or to administrative, business or policy, must be authorized and given to the press through the Office of the Attorney General." The implementation of these instructions is carried out through the Public Information Office of the Department of Justice. Continuous liaison is maintained with the Public Information Office by the External Affairs Division of the FBI and there have been no problems with this arrangement. All press releases, issued by FBI Headquarters, are cleared through the Department's Office of Public Information, as provided for under Departmental Orders.

On page 110, the Task Force states, "The Bureau's preparation and filing of the criminal complaint against 'Galt' on April 17, 1968, before a U.S. Commissioner at Birmingham without first clearing with the Department, and the after-the-fact submission to the Attorney General of a draft press release about the complaint are illustrative of the Bureau's disdain for Department supervision (HQ 44-38861-1555, 1565)."

Also in its "recommendations," the Task Force states on page 144:

(3) "The Task Force recommends that no criminal action in sensitive cases should be instituted by the FBI without Department approval which would include, in appropriate cases, the approval of the United States Attorneys Offices."

Observations were made to the Task Force on January 17, 1977, that the FBI file on civil rights assassination investigation (serial 44-38861-1555) reflects [that] the Attorney General authorized the filing of the complaint, and serial 44-38861-2323 reflects the United States Attorney's Office, Birmingham, authorized the filing of the complaint. Mr. Folsom stated the Task Force would take this under review. It is further noted that although the name of the Special Agent(s) of the FBI who contacted the Department is not set forth, serial 44-38861-1555 (a FBI memorandum) reports that on April 16, 1968, the Attorney General authorized the filing of a complaint charging Eric Starvo Galt (an alias for Ray) with violation of Title 18, U.S. Code, Section 241 (Civil Rights Conspiracy Statute). Serial 44-38861-2323, (a Birmingham FBI report) reports that on April 17, 1968, the facts of this matter were discussed by the FBI with Assistant United States Attorney R. Macey Taylor, Birmingham, Alabama, who authorized the filing of a complaint charging Eric Starvo Galt for violation of Title 18, U. S. Code, Section 241. Serial 44-038861-2323 further reports that a complaint was thereafter filed before United States Commissioner Mildred F. Sprague, Birmingham, on April 17, 1968. It is further noted that in 1968 and up to and including the present time, it was Departmental policy in civil rights matters to obtain authorization for the Department prior to instituting "criminal action" (instituting Federal process such as filing a complaint or seeking an indictment, etc.). Also it was the policy of the FBI in 1968 and up to and including the present time to obtain the authorization of the Department and/or the appropriate U.S. Attorney's Office prior to the institution of any Federal process.

The last "recommendation" concerning the assassination investigation on pages 144–145 states:

(4) "It was observed that almost no blacks were in the FBI Special Agent's corps in the 1960's and none in the Bureau's hierarchy. This undoubtedly had the effect of limiting not only the outlook and understanding of the problems of race relations, but also must have hindered the ability of investigators to communicate fully with blacks during the murder investigation. By way of illustration had there been black Agents in the Memphis field office participating fully in the investigation of Dr. King's murder, it is unlikely that the interviews with at least three black members of the Memphis Police and Fire Department would have been overlooked. It is also very probable that black citizen 'led' input would have been greater." This appears to be more of an opinion or observation rather than a "recommendation."

This recommendation makes reference to three black members of the

Memphis Police and Fire Department whose removal from assignment at a fire station, a surveillance lookout for the motel where Dr. King was staying, was reported as a basis for the House Select Committee to investigate the assassination of Dr. King (pages 26 and 33). This Task Force report examines the basis for the removal of the black detective concerning a reported threat on his life and also states on page 37 that, "Our investigation has not disclosed any evidence that the detail of Walace and Newsum (the two black firemen) was in any way connected with the assassination of Dr. King." It is further noted that based upon a request of the Civil Rights Division in September of 1968, we conducted certain investigation[s] concerning the information regarding the removal of this detective and firemen. Although we did not interview these three individuals, we did furnish results of our investigation regarding their removal to the Civil Rights Division by memorandum dated November 21, 1968, and no additional investigation was requested.

The Security Investigation

The following observations concerning the section of OPR's report which deals with the FBI's security investigation of King were brought to the attention of Department representatives at the above-mentioned meeting on January 17, 1977, at FBIHQ.

General Observations

(1) In a number of instances the Task Force report refers to "The Deegan File," a cabinet which contained sensitive documents and tapes in the King security investigation. The Bureau uses no such terminology to describe this material. Documents and tapes in this cabinet are properly charged out of official Bureau files and are merely stored in a cabinet located in the office of Mr. Deegan, Chief of the Domestic Security Section, General Investigative Division.

(2) The Task Force report fails to show that the personal life and character of King were significant in making an intelligence assessment of King. This factor stressed by SA ... during interview by OPR is also omitted in the recorded interview which is contained in Appendix B.

(3) The OPR report makes no recognition of the "tenor of the times" during which King was investigated. Those were the years of considerable racial strife throughout the nation, when subversive and other disruptive elements were attempting to capitalize for their own advantage on the social awakening in our country and on the civil rights issue.

Specific Observations

(1) Page 127—Concerns installation by the New York Field Office on January 21–24, 1966, of a microphone surveillance against King at

the Americana Hotel. It should be noted the documentation for this information is in FBIHQ file 100-106670-2224X rather than 2224 as indicated in the OPR report. The Task Force report states that Assistant to the Director DeLoach ordered the microphone removed at once and advised the Director that "no one here" approved the coverage. A review of this serial indicates these instructions were written by Mr. Tolson and not DeLoach. The OPR report indicates Mr. Sullivan author- ized this coverage, but a review of the serial fails to indicate clearly who actually made the authorization. On page 128 the report implies that coverage continued after the microphone was removed. There is no such indication in the Bureau files as to the amount of time that lapsed following instructions to remove the surveillance to when actu- ally removed. Therefore, there is no way to determine if surveillance continued in violation of instructions.

(2) Pages 138–139—In a discussion of Bureau policy concerning surreptitious entries, the Task Force noted that "such approval was granted with respect to Mr. Levison and Dr. King" (page 139). This implies that the Bureau conducted surreptitious entries against King. There were no surreptitious entries as such conducted against King. In installing some microphone surveillance against King, however, trespass was necessary.

[(3): Bureau Deletion]

(4) Page 146—The report identifies four Bureau officials who ordered and directed counterintelligence activity and "illicit" dissemination of investigative data to discredit King. It was pointed out to Department officials that identification of present or former Bureau officials respon- sible for actions against King could jeopardize their personal safety.

The below additional observation, not made during the conference on January 17, 1977, are submitted for consideration of the Department:

(1) Page 112—The report indicates that Mr. Alex Rosen, Assistant Director of the General Investigative Division, advised Mr. Hoover of information concerning King, as reported in a memorandum from Scat- terday to Rosen dated May 22, 1961. A review of this document reveals that Rosen's initials are not on it [nor] is there any indication Rosen was aware of the memorandum. Therefore, there is no indication that Mr. Rosen advised the Director of such information, although it is acknowledged that Mr. Hoover was made aware of the information.

(2) Pages 120 and 124—In these two instances the OPR report indi- cates that investigation of King and SCLC was predicated on belief they were under influence of the Communist Party, United States of

America (CPUSA). It should be noted that King and SCLC were investigated for communist influence and not just influence of the CPUSA.

(3) Page 126—The report refers to informant symbol numbers assigned to microphone surveillances of King. The Department should note that informant symbol numbers are used internally to control and administer informant operation and are not disseminated outside of the FBI.

(4) Page 126—The report states that the persistent controversy between King and Mr. Hoover was a major factor in the Bureau's determination to discredit King and ultimately destroy his leadership role in the civil rights movement. The report fails to acknowledge that the primary factor in investigating King was the national interest and not the Hoover-King controversy.

(5) Page 134—With respect to a recommended counterintelligence proposal by the Atlanta Office, the report states the Task Force was unable to determine whether such actions were undertaken since they were neither approved nor disapproved by the Director. It should be noted that the Bureau communication acknowledging receipt of the proposal from Atlanta further instructed that Atlanta would be advised if such a counterintelligence tactic was to be utilized in the future. This additional information is omitted from the OPR report and there is nothing in the files to reveal any approval of the tactic.

(6): [Bureau Deletion]

(7) The OPR report fails to recognize one other important factor in the Bureau's recognition of King as a security risk. This concerns the fact that King was warned at the highest levels of Government (President and Attorney General) that he should discontinue his association with communists to prevent harm to his movement. His continued association with communists indicated King chose to ignore this responsible advice.

While this Bureau's Document Classification Officer (Security Officer) has carefully reviewed and classified on a paragraph-by-paragraph basis the Task Force's "Top Secret" report, he has noted the information in this report is extremely sensitive and if compromised could cause exceptionally grave damage to the national security. Additionally, while the Document Classification Officer has invoked what in his opinion are all available standards relating to areas of classification, in assisting the Task Force in preparing [a] sanitized version of the report, nonetheless because of previously-released information there is concern through logical speculation and processes of elimination that disclosure of the sanitized report could jeopardize this Bureau's sources and methods of intelligence.

[Section 104]

UNITED STATES GOVERNMENT
Memorandum

TO: Mr. Moore   DATE: 4/25/77

FROM: S.S. Mignosa

BERNARD S. LEE
VERSUS
CLARENCE M. KELLEY
ET AL;
(U.S.D.C., D.C.)
CIVIL ACTION NUMBER 76-1185
BUFILE 62-117194

SOUTHERN CHRISTIAN LEADERSHIP
CONFERENCE (SCLC)
VERSUS
CLARENCE M. KELLEY
ET AL;
(U.S.D.C., D.C.)
CIVIL ACTION NUMBER 76-1186
BUFILE 62-117193

PURPOSE: To furnish an inventory of sensitive material pertaining to Martin Luther King, Jr., which material is maintained in a locked file cabinet in Room 4092, JEH, and to recommend the Document Classification Review Unit, Records Management Division (RMD), review this material for classification purposes; thereafter, the Records Systems Section, Records Branch, RMD, furnish this material to the National Archives.

SYNOPSIS: The SCLC complaint was filed 6/25/76, and seeks $5 million from present and former Bureau officials. The Bernard S. Lee complaint, which was also filed 6/25/76, seeks $1 million from the same defendants. Both suits seek to compel the FBI to furnish the courts with all tape recordings, transcripts, and memoranda resulting from tapes of plaintiffs' conversations. An amended complaint was filed on 9/29/76, in both civil actions to address certain issues listed in the defendant's motion to dismiss. On 1/31/77, U.S. District Court Judge ordered that the motions to dismiss the amended complaints in both civil actions be granted because the Statute of Limitations had run [out]. However, the judge ordered that results of microphonic and telephonic surveillances of King and the SCLC be turned over to the National Archives within 90 days of the date of the dismissal order. The dismissal order is due to expire 4/30/77, but the Department of Justice has asked the court for an extension of 90 days.

RECOMMENDATIONS: That the Document Classification Review Unit review the material mentioned herein (designated by*) for classification.

That the Records Systems Section furnish this material to the National Archives.

DETAILS: The SCLC complaint was filed on 6/25/76, and seeks $5 million from Mr. Kelley; Mr. DeLoach; Mr. William C. Sullivan; Mr. John P. Mohr, executor of the state of Clyde A. Tolson, deceased; and 10 unknown FBI Agents.

The Bernard S. Lee complaint, which was also filed on 6/25/76, seeks $1 million from the same named defendants and from 2 unknown FBI Agents. Both suits seek to compel the FBI to furnish the courts with all tape recordings, transcripts, and memos resulting from tapes from plaintiffs' conversations.

Amended complaint was filed on 9/29/76 in both civil actions to address certain issues raised in the defendants' motions to dismiss, filed 9/27/76.

On 1/31/76, U.S. District Judge John Lewis Smity, Jr., ordered that the motions by Federal defendants to dismiss the amended complaints in both civil actions be granted because the Statute of Limitations had run [out]. He further ordered that within 90 days all known copies of the recorded tapes and transcripts thereof, resulting from the FBI's microphonic surveillance, between 1963 and 1968, of the plaintiff organization's former President, Martin Luther King, Jr., and all known copies of the tapes, transcripts and logs resulting from the FBI's telephone wiretapping, between 1963 and 1968, of the plaintiff organization offices in Atlanta, Georgia, and New York, New York, the home of Martin Luther King, Jr., and places of public accommodation occupied by Martin Luther King, Jr., be assembled to FBIHQ. He also ordered that an inventory of the tapes and documents be delivered to him and the tapes and documents themselves be delivered to the custody of the National Archives and Records Service.

The dismissal order is due to expire 4/30/77, but due to the volume of material to be reviewed in this matter, the Department of Justice has asked the court for an extension of 90 days.

The following is a list of sensitive materials pertaining to Martin Luther King, Jr., maintained in a locked file cabinet in Room 4092, JEH. Only those serials marked by * are to be reviewed and turned over to National Archives:

Drawer 1

*1. 1/27/75 Workpaper on Review of W. C. Sullivan materials (original removed per Deegan memo to Mr. Wannall, 12/12/75, "Martin Luther King, Jr.").

*2. Six-volume film entitled "Communications Concerning Martin Luther King, Jr." "TOP SECRET."

3. Request to Place a Technical Surveillance on King's Residence and on the SCLC Office, Evans to Belmont memo dated 10/10/63 (100-106670-24).

4. Memo from Burke Marshall to Mr. Hoover re Hunter Pitts O'Dell dated 9/30/63 (100-358916-272).

5. Memo, Evans to Belmont, dated 7/25/63, Jones-approved, King-denied. Memo to Attorney General, 7/23/63 (100-106670-171).

6. Evans to Belmont memo re Martin Luther King, Jr., and Communist Influence in Racial Matters dated 10/21/63. Memo to Attorney General, 10/18/63 (Tech approved 10/21/63, on SCLC) (100-106670-259).

7. Request to continue technical surveillance an additional six months, 10/27/65 (100-442529-1553).

8. Information re discontinuance of surveillance at Americana Hotel, New York City, 11/30/65, dated 12/1/65 (100-106670-2183).

9. Attorney General to Mr. Hoover, 12/10/65—"advises caution be taken in terms of non-FBI people involved in installation of techs" (100-106670-2184).

*10. Memo dated 12/21/64 furnished to interested officials of the Government and containing additional information relating to the personal conduct of Martin Luther King, Jr. (100-442529-555).

11. Memo from Sullivan to Belmont, 11/27/64, re addition of information to "communism and the Negro Movement—A Current Analysis" (100-442529-505).

12. Memorandum from Baumgardner to Sullivan recommending that National Science Foundation (NSF) be furnished information concerning Communist influence exerted on SCLC and King, dated 12/17/64.

13. Memorandum from Sullivan to Belmont, 12/21/64, re additional information received re King's conduct at Memphis and Oslo, Norway (100-442529-555).

14. Letter from Hoover to Haworth of NSF dated 12/21/64, furnishing him with an additional memo re Martin Luther King's personal conduct (100-442529-555).

15. Letter from Hoover to Carl T. Rowan dated 12/21/64, furnishing him with a copy of a study entitled, "Communism and the Negro Movement—A Current Analysis" (100-442529-539).

16. Letter from Hoover to Haworth, NSF, 12/18/64, furnishing him with a copy of "Communism and the Negro Movement—A Current Analysis" (100-442529-538).

17. Hoover to Attorney General furnishing him with a copy of "Communist Influence in Racial Matters—A Current Analysis," dated 4/10/67 (100-442529-2139).

18. Hoover to Attorney General furnishing him with a copy of "Martin Luther King, Jr.,—A Current Analysis," dated 3/14/68 (100-106670-3230).

19. Memo to the Attorney General dated 6/22/66; Technical Surveillance on SCLC was discontinued 6/21/66 (100-44252901876).

20. Two clippings of newspaper articles by Carl T. Rowan, 6/15/69, *The Sunday Star,* and 6/20/69, *The Evening Star.*

*21. Possibility of Effecting a Technical Surveillance on Clarence Benjamin Jones and Martin Luther King, Jr., Evans to Belmont memorandum, 7/16/63 (100-3-116-41).

*22. Memorandum, Baumgardner to Sullivan, 4/13/64, captioned, "Communist Party—USA, Negro Question Communist Influence in Racial Matters, Internal Security—Communist."

Drawer 2

*1. Elaboration data regarding white paper (release pages 57–61).

2. Miscellaneous Pertinent Serials:

    *a. 100-442529-126, with enclosures—turn over enclosures because transcript material

*b. 100-106670-517.
*c. 100-106670-520.
*d. 100-106670-523.
*e. 100-106670-529.
*f. 100-3-116-1112.

(There are 4 copies of each of the above-listed serials contained in 4 separate, but identical packages.)
3. Las Vegas 4/27/64—Pertinent Serials.
    a. 100-106670-414, with enclosures.
    b. 100-106670-NR-LV airtel, 5/25/64, captioned, "Communist Party, USA, Negro Question, Communist Influence in Racial Matters, Martin Luther King" (original in 100-3-116-1495).
    c. original of above 100-3-116-1495.
    d. 100-3-116-1512, with enclosures.
    *e. 100-106670-3559, with enclosures.

Delete pages 10–12 (material under heading *"King Personal Conduct"*).

*4. New York City, 1/21-23/66—Pertinent Serials 100-106670-2224X—Transcript.
*5. Ticklers—Detroit, Michigan, 3/19–20/64, Statler Hotel, Detroit, Michigan.
*6. Ticklers—Washington, D. C., 1/5–7/64, Willard Hotel, Washington, D.C.
*7. Ticklers—Miscellaneous (portions have tech data).
*8. Ticklers—New York City, 10/14–15/65, Astor Hotel, New York City.
9. Ticklers—Los Angeles, California, 7/8–9/64, Hyatt House Hotel, los Angeles, California.
10. Ticklers, New York City, 10/28–30/65, New York Hilton Hotel, New York City.
11. Pertinent Serials—Los Angeles, 7/8–9/64.
*Baumgardner to Sullivan memo, 7/15/64, 100-106670-NR
    100-3-116-1866,
    100-3-116-1865, with enclosures
*Baumgardner to Sullivan memo, 7/17/64, 100-106670-NR (original in 100-3-116-1866)
*Letter to Honorable Walter W. Jenkins, 7/17/64, 100-106670-NR (original in 100-3-116-1866)

*100-3-116-1866
  100-3-116-1866
  100-3-116-1939, with enclosures
    (4 copies of above).
12. Pertinent serials—Detroit 3/19–20/64.
*Baumgardner to Sullivan memo, 4/13/64, 100-106670, with enclosure
  NR (original in 100-3-116-1197)
*100-3-116-1197, with enclosure
*100-3-116-1456
    (4 copies of above).
13. Pertinent serials, Los Angeles, 2/20–21, 23, 24/64.
*100-3-116-1051, with enclosure
*100-3-116-1952, with enclosure
    (4 copies of above).
*14. Pertinent serials, Sacramento, 4/23–24/64, 100-3-11601339, with
  enclosure (4 copies of above).
15. Pertinent serials, Honolulu, 2/18–20/64
100-3-116-1049
*100-3-116-1978
*100-3-116-1050
100-106670-NR (original in 100-3-116-1953)
Baumgardner to Sullivan memo, 3/4/64, with enclosure
*100-3-116-1053
100-3-116-1143
(4 copies of above).
16. Pertinent serials, Washington, D. C., 1/5–6/64
*100-3-116-761 (enclosure)
*100-106670-NR (original in 100-3-116-761)
Sullivan to Belmont memo, 1/13/64
*100-3-116-761
100-3-116-762
(4 copies of above).
17. Pertinent serials, New York City, 10/14–15/65
*100-106670-1976
100-106670-1975 and 1980
*100-106670-2031
(4 copies of above).
18. Folder "Honolulu Trip" (containing ticklers)
*AT airtel, 12/24/63, captioned "Communist Party, USA, Negro Ques-
  tion, Communist Influence in Racial Matters, IS-C "
AT letter, 1/2/64, captioned "

LA airtel, 1/3/64, captioned "
*AT letter, 1/8/64, captioned "
*AT letter, 1/14/64 captioned "
*AT letter, 1/15/64 captioned "
*AT letter, 1/15/64 captioned "
LA airtel, 1/17/64 captioned "
LA airtel 1/21/64 captioned "
Honolulu letter 1/22/64 captioned "
White paper captioned "
Buairtel 1/29/64 captioned "
Baumgardner to Sullivan memo, 1/28/64 captioned "
Bulet, 1/31/64 captioned "
Discussion Data . . . between SF Supervisor and Seat of Government
    personnel captioned "
Baumgardner to Sullivan memo, 2/4/64 captioned "
Buairtel to Honolulu, 2/5/64 captioned "
Buairtel to AT, 2/5/64 captioned "
*AT airtel, 2/3/64, captioned, "Communist Party, USA, Negro Question,
    Communist Influence in Racial Matters, IS-C, Martin Luther King,
    Jr.
Buairtel, 2/7/64, captioned, "Communist Party, USA, Negro Question,
    Communist Influence in Racial Matters, IS-C"
AT airtel, 2/5/64, captioned, "Communist Party, USA, Negro Question,
    Communist Influence in Racial Matters, IS-C, Martin Luther King,
    Jr."
LA airtel with enclosure, 2/5/64, captioned "Communist Party, USA,
    Negro Question, Communist Influence in Racial Matters, IS-C"
LA airtel, 2/7/64, captioned "
AT teletype, 2/8/64 captioned "
AT airtel, 2/10/64 captioned "
HO let, 2/10/64 captioned "
SF airtel, 2/11/64 captioned "
*AT radiogram, 2/13/64, captioned "Communist Party, USA, Negro
    Question, Communist Influence in Racial Matters, IS-C, Martin Lu-
    ther King, Jr."
SF radiogram, 2/13/64, captioned "
HO radiogram, 2/13/64, captioned "
BA teletype, 2/14/64 captioned, "Communist Party, USA, Negro Ques-
    tion, Communist Influence in Racial Matters, IS-C"
LA airtel, 2/14/64, captioned "
AT radiogram, 2/14/64, captioned "Communist Party, USA, Negro

Question, Communist Influence in Racial Matters, IS-C, Martin Luther King, Jr.''

AT radiogram, 2/16/64, captioned ''Communist Party, USA, Negro Question, Communist Influence in Racial Matters, IS-C''

HO radiogram, 2/17/64, captioned "

LA airtel, 2/17/64 captioned "

HO radiogram, 2/17/64, captioned ''Communist Party, USA, Negro Question, Communist Influence in Racial Matters, IS-C, Martin Luther King, Jr.''

HO radiogram, 2/18/64 captioned "

LA radiogram, 2/19/64, captioned ''Communist Party, USA, Negro Question, Communist Influence in Racial Matters, IS-C''

HO radiogram, 2/19/64, captioned ''Communist Party, USA, Negro Question, Communist Influence in Racial Matters, IS-C, Martin Luther King, Jr.''

BA airtel, 2/18/64, captioned, ''Communist Party, USA, Negro Question, Communist Influence in Racial Matters, IS-C.''

AT radiogram, 2/19/64, captioned "

LA radiogram, 2/19/64, captioned "

*HO radiogram, 2/19/64, captioned ''Communist Party, USA, Negro Question, Communist Influence in Racial Matters, IS-C'' and ''Martin Luther King, Jr.''

*J. A. Sizoo to Sullivan memo, 2/20/64, captioned ''Communist Party, USA, Negro Question, Communist Influence in Racial Matters, IS-C''

2/20/64 captioned "

*AT radiogram, 2/20/64, captioned "

HO radiogram, 2/20/64, captioned "

*AT teletype 2/21/64, captioned "

AT radiogram, 2/20/64 captioned "

HO radiogram, 2/23/64, captioned "

*AT radiogram, 2/24/64, captioned "

*Sullivan to Belmont memo, 2/22/64 captioned ''Martin Luther King, Jr. IS-C''

LA teletype, 2/25/64 captioned, ''Communist Party, USA, Negro Question, Communist Influence in Racial Matters, IS-C''

LA let, 2/24/64 captioned "

LA let, 2/24/64 captioned "

LA let, 2/24/64 captioned "

LA let, 2/24/64 captioned "

LA let, 2/25/64 captioned "

SF airtel, 2/25/64 captioned "

SF airtel 2/25/64 captioned "

LA let, 2/26/64 captioned "

LA let, 2/26/64 captioned "

*LA let, 2/27/64 captioned "

*SF airtel, 2/27/64 captioned " with enclosures

*SF airtel, 2/28/64, with enclosures, captioned "

SF airtel, 2/28/64, with enclosures, captioned "

BA airtel, 3/2/64 captioned "

LA let, 3/5/64 captioned "

HO let, 2/28/64 captioned "

*Baumgardner to Sullivan memo, with enclosures, 3/4/64

Baumgardner to Sullivan memo, 3/18/64 captioned "

HO let, 2/21/64 . . .

SF let, 3/25/64 . . .

Personal letter to W.C. Sullivan from . . .

Bulet to LA, 3/12/64

LA let, 4/6/64

La Let, 4/13/64 "

*Atlanta airtel, 3/10/64 captioned, "Communist Party, USA, Negro Question, Communist Influence in Racial Matters, IS-C" and "Martin Luther King, Jr."

*Buairtel, 3/13/64 captioned "Communist Party, USA, Negro Question, Communist Influence in Racial Matters, IS-C

LA airtel, 3/18/64 captioned "

*AT airtel, 3/19/64 captioned "

0-1, 4/1/64

0-1, 4/3/64

LA airtel, 4/10/64, captioned "

Buairtel, 4/15/64 captioned "

*LA airtel, 4/16/64 captioned "

LA airtel, 4/20/64 captioned "

LA airtel, 7/22/64 captioned "

Envelope containing photographs of: [names deleted by Bureau]

Buairtel, 2/7/64 captioned "

SF airtel, 2/10/64 captioned "

Buairtel, 2/12/64 captioned "

Buairtel, 2/17/64 captioned "

Butel, 2/17/64 captioned "

Baumgardner to Sullivan memo, 2/26/64 captioned "

Sullivan to Belmont memo, 3/5/64 captioned "

19. Folder "4/24/64, West Coast Trip, including Las Vegas," (contains tickler copies of the following):

*AT airtel, 3/23/64 captioned, Communist Party, USA, Negro Question, Communist Influence in Racial Matters" and Martin Luther King, Jr.
*AT airtel, 4/6/64 captioned "Communist Party, USA, Negro Question, Communist Influence in Racial Matters, IS-C"
SF airtel, 4/23/64 captioned "
LA airtel, 4/23/64 captioned "
SF teletype, 4/23/64 captioned, " and "Martin Luther King, Jr."
*SF teletype, 4/24/64 captioned "
*LA teletype, 4/24/64 captioned "
*LA teletype, 4/24/64 captioned "
SF radiogram, 4/24/64 captioned " and "Martin Luther King, Jr."
*SF radiogram, 4/24/64 captioned " and "Martin Luther King, Jr."
*AT airtel, 3/23/64 captioned " and "Martin Luther King, Jr."
*AT airtel, 4/6/64 captioned " and "Martin Luther King, Jr."
SF airtel, 4/9/64 captioned "
*AT airtel, 4/17/64 captioned "
AT teletype, 4/20/64 captioned "
*AT radiogram, 4/23/64 captioned "
LA teletype, 4/24/64 captioned "
LA teletype, 4/26/64 captioned "
*LA teletype, 4/27/64 captioned "
*LA radiogram, 4/26/64 captioned "
LV teletype, 4/27/64 captioned " and "Martin Luther King, Jr."
SF airtel, 5/6/64 captioned "
Bulet, 5/18/64 captioned "
LV teletype, 4/27/64 captioned " and "Martin Luther King, Jr."
Baumgardner to Sullivan memo, with enclosures, 5/25/64
LV airtel, 5/25/64 captioned " and "Martin Luther King, Jr."
Work paper, 6/13/64 captioned "
Memo, Baumgardner to Sullivan with enclosures, 6/11/64
*LA airtel, 4/27/64 captioned "
0-1, 6/15/64
LA let, 6/19/64 captioned "
*Brennan to Sullivan memo, captioned " and "Martin Luther King, Jr.," 4/27/64
Sullivan to Belmont memo, 4/23/64 captioned "
Sullivan to Belmont memo, 4/23/64 captioned " and "Martin Luther King, Jr."

Sullivan to Belmont memo, 4/23/64 captioned "
Sullivan to Belmont memo, 4/23/64 captioned "
Sullivan to Belmont memo, 4/23/64 captioned " and "Martin Luther King, Jr."
Sullivan to Belmont memo, 4/23/64 captioned "
*Baumgardner to Sullivan memo, 4/24/64 captioned "
JA Sizoo to Sullivan memo, 4/25/64 captioned " and Martin Luther King, Jr."
*20. Box marked "Washington, D.C., 1/5–6/64 Reference 100-442529-829—"Hand Delivered" containing 15-5" reels bearing the same notation as appears on the outside of the box with one exception, the reels are marked, "1 of 15" etc. and carry additional date of 11/19/64. In addition, this box contains (one) 7" reel bearing file #100-3-116-1523 and notation "Reference Atlanta letter, 6/8/64, 100-3-116-1523 from . . . conversation between Mr. and Mrs. M.L. King, 5/31/64. No transcript.

Drawer 3

1. Enveloped marked "Photographs of Principals at Los Angeles with 2 rolls of Motion Picture Film."
*2. Envelope marked "New York City 10/28–30/65 Original Transcript"—serial 100-106670-2092.
*3. Envelope marked "Los Angeles, 2/20–21, 23–24/64, original transcript"—serial 100-3-116-1049.
*4. Envelope marked "Washington, D.C., 1/5–6/64 original transcript"—serial 100-106670-1024.
*5. Envelope marked "Sacramento 4/23–24/64 original transcript."
*6. Envelope marked "New York City, 10/14–16/65 original transcript (long and short version)" —serial 100-106670-1990.
*7. Envelope marked "WFO Original Notes" (contains hand written notes of overhears).
*8. Envelope marked "Washington, D.C., 1/5–6/64, Original Notes of WFO Transcript."
*9. Envelope marked "Los Angeles, 7/8–9/64 Original Transcript"—serial 100-106670-1024.
*10. Box containing 3 5-inch and 18 7-inch reels—marked "Los Angeles 2/20–21, 23–24/64—Reference 100-3-116-1112, 3/26/64, Registry #928677" (all tapes have same notation as that on box).
*11. Box marked 1. "Detroit 3/19–20/64, reference 100-442529-530, registry information attached. 8 7-inch reels";

2. "New York City 10/14–15/65, reference 100-106670-1990 6 7-inch reels";

3. "New York City 1/28–30/65, reference 100-106670-2092, from New York Office, 11/4/65 by R/S to Sizoo. Initialed for file by . . . 3 7-inch reels" (box contains 17 reels as above).

Drawer 4

*1. Copy of Transcript—Washington, D. C. 1/5–6/64 (3 copies of above).

*2. Copy of Transcripts—Honolulu 2/18–20/64; Los Angeles 2/20–21, 23–24/64; Detroit 3/19–20/64; Sacramento 4/23/64; Los Angeles 7/8–9/64; New York City 10/14–15/65; and New York City 10/28–30/65.

(3 copies of above).

*3. Box marked 1. "Sacramento 4/23–24/64, reference 100-3-116-1339";

2. "Honolulu 2/18–20/64, Reference 100-3-116-1112, Registry #928677, 2/26/64 from Los Angeles to Washington, D.C., 2 5-inch and 7 7-inch reels";

3. "Los Angeles 7/8–9/64, Reference 100-3-116-1741, Registry #928432 from Los Angeles 7/15/64 5 5-inch reels" (box contains 19 reels of tape which have corresponding marking to those on outside of box);

*4. Box marked "Contents, # Reels, Duplicate tapes 2 7-inch, 2 5-inch composite tapes 3 7-inch, 2 5-inch; Atlanta tape 1 7-inch" (box contains 10 reels of tape which have corresponding markings to those on outside of box.).

1980

1980

March 25, 1980
Letter: David G. Flanders, Chief, FOIA, to the Honorable Gerry E.
Studds

[Section 104]

March 25, 1980

Honorable Gerry E. Studds
House of Representatives
Washington, D.C. 20515

Dear Congressman Studds:
This is in reference to your recent request for comment regarding
your constituents' inquiries which were forwarded to us by your note
dated March 6, 1980. Copies of this correspondence and enclosures are
provided for your convenience.

In response to the question of why records pertaining to Dr. Martin
Luther King were placed under seal, I would refer you to two civil
actions filed in the United States District Court for the District of Columbia. These suits, *Bernard S. Lee vs. Clarence M. Kelley, et al.,* Civil
Action Number 76-1185, and *Southern Christian Leadership Conference vs. Clarence M. Kelley, et al.,* Number 76-1186, were brought
against members of the Federal Bureau of Investigation (FBI) for alleged wiretapping in violation of rights guaranteed by the Constitution
of the United States. Both plaintiffs were seeking money damages and
requested that all records of the monitored conversations be destroyed
or impounded.

On January 31, 1977, the court ordered that "all known copies of
the recorded tapes, and transcripts thereof, resulting from the FBI's
microphonic surveillance, between 1963 and 1968, of the plaintiff's
former president, Martin Luther King, Jr; and all known copies of the

tapes, transcripts and logs resulting from the FBI's telephonic wiretapping between 1963 and 1968, of the plaintiff's offices in Atlanta, Georgia, and New York, New York, the home of Martin Luther King, Jr., and places of public accommodation occupied by Martin Luther King, Jr., be turned over to the custody of the National Archives and Records Service to be maintained under seal for 50 years.

Other records pertaining to Dr. King and the Southern Christian Leadership Conference, located at FBI Headquarters, Washington, D.C., are presently being processed for release under the provisions of the Freedom of Information Act. These records, when processed, will be available to any requester upon payment of duplication fees at the rate of 10 cents per page. It is anticipated that this material will be ready for release in approximately three months.

I hope that this information will be responsible to your constituents' inquiries.

Sincerely yours,

David G. Flanders, Chief
Freedom of Information—
Privacy Acts Branch
Records Management Division

Index